BOOKS BY CHARLES A. MADISON

YIDDISH LITERATURE
Its Scope and Major Writers
BOOK PUBLISHING IN AMERICA
THE OWL AMONG COLOPHONS
LEADERS AND LIBERALS IN
20TH CENTURY AMERICA
AMERICAN LABOR LEADERS
CRITICS AND CRUSADERS

Frederick Ungar Publishing Co.

New York

YIDDISH
LITERATURE

Its Scope and Major Writers

CHARLES A. MADISON

To
the Yiddish writers
who made this book
possible

PREFACE

YIDDISH LITERATURE has had a phenomenal development during the past century. For hundreds of years Yiddish was the common speech of millions of Jews, most of them concentrated in Eastern Europe, but its literature was largely limited to homiletic and fictional compilations addressed to women. Up to the end of the 19th century both pious and enlightened Jews disdained this "jargon" for literary or scholarly purposes. It was only after Mendele Mokher Sforim, Sholom Aleichem, and I. L. Peretz had demonstrated the artistic potential of the language—and after the mass of Jews had simultaneously obtained both the sophistication and the leisure to read secular writings—that Yiddish gained general acceptance and became the preferred medium of numerous young writers. For a half century thereafter Yiddish belles lettres flourished with a richness unequalled by any of the minor national literatures.

The tragic events of the 1940's—Nazi crematoria and the suppression of Yiddish under Stalin—have extirpated or stifled the main body of Yiddish readers as well as many writers. Since then the nearly three million Jews now in the Soviet Union are being forcefully weaned from their mother tongue. Moreover, most Jews throughout the diaspora are voluntarily, and understandably, discarding Yiddish for the language of their adopted land. Even in the United States, where its nearly six million Jews form the largest Jewish center in the world, and where Yiddish flourished less than a generation ago, most of the younger writers now employ English as their means of literary expression. Currently Yiddish appears to thrive mostly in Israel, where it was disdained or ignored until around 1950, and it is perhaps there that the future of Yiddish literature may lie.

In this book, while making no pretense of providing a comprehensive history of this literature, I have sought to indicate the development of Yiddish from its Germanic origins to its present linguistic maturity, and to discuss the work of a number of major writers, as well as that of many of lesser significance during the past century, in order to suggest the scope, opulence, and specific character of this literature. Thus I have dealt with its emergence and efflorescence in Czarist Russia, its establishment and range in the United States, its encouragement and suppression in the Soviet Union, and its expanding activity in Israel. Individual treatment is given to the fourteen writers who are historically and artistically of prime importance, and five chapters deal interstitially with other writers who have contributed to the particular prominence and predilection of Yiddish literature. The limits of space and lesser general interest have necessitated only incidental mention of the considerable body of literary criticism (see source bibliography) and the slighting of works of numerous scholars and publicists.

Because only a relatively small part of the literature is available in English translation—a listing is given in a bibliography—and because even that part is not known to many readers, I have outlined much of the content of major novels, plays, and poems by authors who are discussed in detail. Writing as a critic as well as historian, I have praised or deprecated individual works in the light of my own evaluation, and I only hope that my presumed prejudices have not impaired my critical judgment. Again, since it was not feasible to include all writers, I am keenly sensible of my personal bias in the selection of authors and trust I have made no glaring error of choice.

Owing to the lack of standardization in the spelling of Yiddish names and titles in English, I have followed American usage with such names as Sholom Aleichem, but have employed approximate phonetic spelling otherwise. The titles of periodicals are followed by their English meaning in parentheses; most of the titles of books are rendered only in English, since the Yiddish would have little meaning to most readers. The quotations in the text are in my own translation; those in verse are rendered in prose to give the literal sense of their content. The source bibliography includes most of the books and articles I have read in the course of my research; in the text itself are listed the titles and dates of publication of the works of each author treated at some length. Special mention must be made of Zalmen Reisen's *Lexicon of Yiddish Literature* and the six completed volumes of the new and enlarged edition published by the Congress for Jewish Culture, which I have found indispensable. A list of Yiddish books in English translation is included for the convenience of interested readers; in the text an asterisk follows the titles actually discussed.

It is a pleasure to express my gratitude to Dinah Abramovitz, librarian of YIVO (the Yiddish Scientific Institute), where I spent months of fruitful research; to Abraham Berger, librarian of the Jewish Division of the New York Public Library, where I was an almost daily visitor during a period of two years; to Messrs. Berger, B. Z. Goldberg, Yudel Mark, and J. Birnbaum; to a Yiddish poet and critic who prefers not to be named; and to Lucy S. Dawidowicz, all of whom have read critically one or more chapters; and finally to my wife, Edith H. Madison, who read the entire manuscript with painstaking care and helped me avoid numerous inelegancies of style and diction.

C. A. M.

CONTENTS

CHAPTER ONE

JUDEO-GERMAN
TO MODERN YIDDISH

THE JEWS became a bilingual people long before their dispersion in the first century A.D. Hebrew was their "holy tongue"
for religious study and prayer, as it has been ever since; but
the daily discourse of the educated was often carried on first
in Greek and later in Latin, and the speech of the rural folk
was mostly Aramaic. Outside of Judea, the Septuagint replaced
the Hebrew Old Testament in Jewish communities whose
members no longer knew the language of their fathers. Jewish
historians like Philo and Josephus wrote in Greek and Latin,
respectively, even as centuries later Maimonides wrote in
Arabic and other Jewish scholars employed the language of
the country in which they lived.

Even before the dispersion from Palestine in A.D. 70, Jews
were to be found in all civilized communities. A number of
them followed the Roman legions into northern Europe.
Wherever they settled they readily mingled with their neighbors but continued to observe their religion and rabbinical
precepts. Nearly all of them knew enough Hebrew for prayer
and study, but they also spoke Latin and the local dialect.
In fact, until modern times they were, as a group, more highly
educated than their European neighbors; throughout the cen-

turies and under the greatest difficulties they adhered to a system of continuous Hebrew study. "This system of continued education," Cecil Roth stated, "conferred on the Jews everywhere a fundamental unity. No matter where they lived or what language they spoke, the pattern of their lives was in essentials the same." This cultural accord more than once saved them from extinction during periods of severe persecution.

In their use of the local language, whether Spanish or French, Italian or German, they tended to include Hebrew words and idioms when addressing one another. In personal or business correspondence they transliterated the language they employed into Hebrew characters, and that also stimulated the addition of Hebrew terms. As a result their speech gradually differed more and more from that of their non-Jewish neighbors. Max Weinreich also pointed out that they used local speech selectively: "The Jews never took over the whole stock of the coterritorial non-Jewish language (or languages) indiscriminately; they did take over only certain segments which have to be defined socially or territorially, or both."

Jews apparently came with the Romans into the settlements along the Rhine. It is recorded that in 321 Constantine denied them certain privileges. For the next 500 years little is known about their status or activities, since few records of the period are available. In the 10th century there is evidence that they engaged in commerce, viticulture, and finance. They spoke Middle-High German with a mild admixture of Hebrew. A number carried on trade with Jewish merchants in distant countries and some became quite prosperous. Their settlements were relatively small, seldom exceeding several hundred. In some towns they developed *yeshivas* (seats of higher learning), usually headed by a scholar of note. Rashi (Reb Shlomo ben Isaac, 1040–1105), for instance, went to study in the yeshiva at Mainz in his youth and therefore knew the language of that locality in addition to his native Provençal.

The Crusades, beginning in 1095, played havoc with these Jewish communities, then consisting of only around 15,000 souls. Inspired by bigots and fanatics and tempted by acquisition through pillage, Crusaders fell upon these hapless Jews with club and sword—killing, maiming, robbing, raping. In some towns these "nonbelievers" were offered a choice of the Cross or expulsion. Migration from town to town, from principality to principality, saved the remnant from extinction. During the next few centuries, deprived of their early rights and privileges and forced to limit their activities to money-lending and petty trade, Jews were again and again compelled to flee from their homes to save their lives. Moving mostly eastward, they presumably mingled with Jews driven westward by Muscovite oppressors. As a result of these frequent hegiras the language of the Jews in Central Europe gradually changed from Middle-High German into a distinctly different dialect, based on the original tongue but modified in locution and idiom.

In the 12th century anti-Semitism continued to spread. Benjamin of Tudela was still able to travel (1160–1173) as far as China, and became the first European to describe the Assassins in Syria and the commerce in India and China. Yet a prominent Jewish minnesinger like Süsskind von Trimberg, who had for a time been a popular performer among Germanic nobility, was stopped from appearing before Christians. In a poem, "Why Should I Wander Sadly," he exclaimed:

> Be silent, then my lyre/ We sing 'fore Lords in vain,/ I'll leave the minstrel's choir,/ And roam a Jew again.

He and others like him, entertaining Jewish gatherings, no doubt added piquant Hebrew expressions for the greater enjoyment of their audiences. For then and later Jews indulged in such pleasures on certain occasions, particularly during periods of relative quiescence. With Hebrew reserved for prayer and study, and no longer well known to most women and a good many men, the language current in daily intercourse in and out of their homes gradually became molded into a primitive form of Yiddish.

Sporadic expulsions and massacres, resulting from superstitious accusations that Jews had brought on the Black Death

3

Plague of 1348, initiated another series of migrations from duchy to duchy, from one town to another, southward to North Italy and eastward to Bohemia and other Slavic lands. To these wanderers were added the Jews driven out of England in 1290 and out of France in 1306 and 1394. Forbidden to own land, excluded from guilds, in a number of places confined to ghettos, treated as pawns and sources of ransom by kings, nobles, and bishops, Jews asserted their will to survive by intensifying their devotion to Jehovah and keeping themselves alive in any way they could—mostly by meekness—and, in extremity, dying by martyrdom. The greater the wall between themselves and their Gentile neighbors, the more their speech differed from the original German.

What saved the Jews from total extinction during these turbulent centuries was the sporadic nature of their persecution. Driven out of one town or duchy, they usually found shelter with some noble or bishop who hoped to gain financially from their presence. Thus in a number of places, for a decade or a generation, Jewish communities obtained local protection and achieved relative stability. Once settled, these Jews required reading matter and entertainment, and scribes and minstrels soon adapted topical romances as well as Hebrew lore to the wishes of their audiences, predominantly female. These verses and tales, composed in current Yiddish, formed many an evening's enjoyment. The wealthier and more educated women engaged scribes to copy currently popular romances and religious adaptations for their personal edification.

Among the better-known stories widely read during the medieval period were those concerning King Arthur's Round Table as well as those about Dietrich von Bern and Hildebrandt. In their Yiddish versions references to Christian rites were omitted, and accounts of battles and tournaments worded in terms of Jewish piety. Equally popular were quasi-religious works adapted from Old Testament and Talmudic sources. *The Samuel Book*, composed in the 14th century and probably the oldest Yiddish poem, dealt with King David in the form of a medieval romance. *The King Book*, appearing later, was modeled after the earlier work. In addition there were songs and stories dealing with Queen Esther, usually recited on Purim evening, and other Jewish heroes and heroines. Sabbath verses and extemporaneous compositions sung by the *badkhen*, or minstrel, at marriages and other family and religious celebrations added to the Yiddish literature of these centuries.

The most renowned of the popular romances in Yiddish, *The Bovo Book*, was written by Elia Levita for the entertainment of "all pious women." Born near Nuremberg about 1469, Levita became a successful teacher, scholar, and poet. He settled in northern Italy, where he composed *The Bovo Book* in 1507 (first printed in 1541) and *Paris and Vienna* in 1514. Both of these works combined the chivalry of the medieval romance with the Italian ottava rima style. In 1514 he was engaged by Cardinal Egidio de Viterbo as a Hebrew teacher and remained with him for 13 years. Levita's Hebrew grammar, composed during this period, made him the teacher of Hebrew to Christians of his day.

The Bovo Book was adapted from a late Italian version of the Bevis of Hampton romance and written in current Yiddish. A highly fanciful story, it was made acceptable to pious Jewish readers by use of Jewish expressions and connotations. In one place, for instance, Bevis's wife is worried because her twin sons have not yet been circumcised; the narrative ends with the pious hope that the Messiah would soon bring all Jews to Jerusalem. The romance has retained its popularity to modern times and was frequently reprinted. *Paris and Vienna*, based on a Provençal 14th century romance, was a better-written story but somehow failed to achieve similar popularity, perhaps because its characters remained Christian.

Anti-Jewish prejudice in Western Europe did not slacken during the Renaissance period. In Poland, however, and other parts of Eastern Europe, the nobility and governments had become hospitable to Jews in their need of a middle class to serve as intermediaries between nobles and peasantry and to establish trade relations with countries to the west. In time

Jewish settlements dotted Slavic lands. In 1551 King Sigis-
mund Augustus of Poland gave the Jews in his land a charter
entitling them to conduct their internal affairs outside of the
jurisdiction of civil law courts, thus establishing the rabbinical
Kahal as the legal authority responsible only to the king; it
continued to function until 1821. Normally these Jews would
in time have adopted the Slavic language, even as their ancestors had embraced Middle-High German. Culturally superior to their new neighbors, however, and relatively secluded
from them, they merely added a number of Slavic terms to
their Yiddish speech. Once firmly established, they organized
yeshivas which soon attained a high level of scholarship and
attracted students from other parts of Europe.

Pious Jews tended to pore over a religious tome when not
engaged in making a living. They esteemed study for its own
sake so highly that not a few left to their wives the responsibility of the family's livelihood while they spent most waking
hours in the synagogue. Even the uneducated Jew, who had
only a bare reading knowledge of Hebrew, devoted his leisure,
usually on the Sabbath, to perusal of the Psalms or a work of
simple religious lore.

The situation was quite different for the Jewish woman.
Custom curbed her educational opportunities, absolved her
from most of the religious ritual incumbent upon the Jewish
male, and greatly circumscribed her social activities. Housekeeper and nurse, often the family provider as well, she
counted for little and her place in the synagogue was confined
to a curtained balcony. Like most women of the time, those of
the Jewish communities grew up in deep piety and remained
steeped in superstition. In prayers prepared for them in Yiddish they addressed themselves personally to Jehovah, the
patriarchs, and the saints of both sexes in behalf of their family
welfare. They called especially on the saintly women of the
Old Testament to intercede for them in times of illness, severe
childbirth, or similar trials. They also resorted to various
superstitious remedies and nostrums, many of which are
among the relatively few Yiddish records which have survived
to our day.

The more educated and affluent women were keenly inter-ested in the lay romances written in the only language they knew. But if their fancies fed upon the profane stories on a weekday evening, many gave their Sabbath afternoons to *The Samuel Book* or similar pious work. Later, when rabbin-ical criticism of lay literature stimulated Yiddish versions of religious lore, Jewish women read or listened to them with devoted attention.

One of the first of these religious adaptations was a trans-lation of the Psalms in 1490. Other such works appeared during the 16th century, among them an adaptation of Song of Songs. More popular was *The Maaseh Book*, a collection of Talmudic and medieval tales after the manner of *Gesta Romanorum*. Of its 250 allegories and anecdotes, 157 are of Talmudic origin, 25 have their setting in Regensburg, a number deal with incidents concerning the city of Worms, and the re-mainder are of various origin. This work served to give the Jewish folk tale a spiritual and pious character, thus making it palatable to religious leaders as well as attractive to its many women readers and listeners (more women were eager to listen because they did not know how to read). Its two dominant motifs—fear of an inimical environment and belief in magic —were in keeping with the prevailing superstition.

The most influential and widely read book in Yiddish up to the end of the 19th century was the Pentateuch adaptation known as *Tzena Urena*, from the Canticles phrase on the title page: "Go forth and behold, o ye daughters of Zion." Previous sporadic and partial versions were literal, dry, and dull. Jacob ben Isaak Ashkenazi (1550–1628) paraphrased rather than translated the Books of Moses, omitting routine parts and adding illustrative homilies for the greater appreciation of his readers. The first known edition appeared in 1618, its lyrical emotionalism and didactic piety quickly taken to heart by every Jewish woman able to read or absorb its contents orally. For nearly three centuries it was the most cherished book in the Jewish home. Two other translations of the Old Testament were printed in Amsterdam in the latter half of the 17th cen-tury with rabbinical approval, but failed to attain wide readership. Other homiletic works in Yiddish appearing during that period were *Brantspiel* (1602), and *The Good Heart* (1620). The first, by M. H. Altschuler, was written specifically for women and discusses problems of interest to them, such as family life and female modesty and hygiene, in a didactic and pious manner. The second, prepared by Isaak ben Eliakum, is preachy and dogmatic; dealing with habits of behavior, education, and strict piety, it achieved its widest popularity in the 18th century following the greater rigor advocated by orthodox rabbis in the wake of Shabbati Zevi. Both volumes, incidentally, were praised by Glückel of Hameln.

Her *Memoirs* was a work of striking merit, written in vigorous and vibrant Yiddish. Glückel was born in 1645, the daughter of one of the elders of the Hamburg community. She married Khaim of Hameln and settled there. When he died in 1689, he left her the widowed mother of 12 children. She began to write her *Memoirs* in 1691, but put the writing aside when she was remarried to Cerf Levi in 1700. Twelve years later, again widowed, she resumed her writing and completed the work in 1719. Her reminiscences make clear how strong an influence the various books of preaching and criticism had upon the women of her time. They also reveal her epic outlook on life, her lively imagination, and her love of learning. She was a successful business woman, selling jewels on credit, and her various transactions make informative reading. Her aim in writing the book was to teach her children how to live wisely and well, and her incidental stories were intended to entertain as much as to moralize. Indeed, she has provided an invaluable and highly readable description of Jewish life of that period.

That Yiddish had become widespread as the language of the Jews may be gleaned from the business and personal correspondence that has come down to us. One of the earliest extant letters in Yiddish was written in Ratisbon in 1478 to a widow named Pelain, who was imprisoned on the charge of having profaned a consecrated wafer. Nearly a century later (1567) Rachel, wife of Rabbi Eliezer Sussman Ashkenazi of

Jerusalem, wrote a Yiddish letter to her son Moses in Cairo. In 1588 a merchant of Cracow wrote to his son in Prague about his eagerness to escape the current plague and to make clear his concern for the youth's welfare. At the outbreak of the Thirty Years War (1619), the courier of a Jewish private postman in Prague was intercepted by Austrian soldiers while on his way to Vienna, and the 54 letters in his pouch were confiscated and stored away. At the turn of the 20th century the packet was accidentally discovered and the letters made public. Of interest is that most of them were written in Yiddish, and that even those who knew Hebrew preferred the homely Yiddish as the more "fluent language."

The early years of the 17th century were relatively quiescent for European Jews. Despite the endemic intolerance and oppression which continued to curb their activities and opportunities, they managed to thrive both materially and culturally. Their printing presses in Italy and Holland, as well as in Bohemia and Poland, produced a number of volumes in Hebrew and Yiddish. Didactic works in the latter language dominated the output, which also included reprints of romances, folk tales, translations and adaptations of current European fiction, and other items of interest primarily to women. In the course of time Yiddish was further modified in syntax, morphology, and vocabulary, simultaneously accommodating itself to and influencing the speech of the people.

The decade beginning in 1648 was cruelly calamitous for the Jews of Poland and the Ukraine. About half of the more than 500,000 Jews living in that region were massacred and pillaged by rebelling kossaks led by Bogdan Khmelnitski. Nearly 700 Jewish settlements were destroyed, together with their cultural and religious institutions. In Nemerov alone, around 10,000 Jews chose martyrdom rather than embrace Christianity. The surviving remnant fled westward, and many were warmly received by their more fortunate fellow Jews. Once the kossak hordes were subdued, Jewish settlements were quickly re-established, and life for the survivors resumed its usual course. In the process of intermingling, however, Yiddish speech underwent further development.

The traumatic massacres, endangering the very survival of the Jews in Eastern Europe, intensified their yearning for final salvation by God's Messiah. "When a people is plunged in deep despair," Shmarya Levin truly stated, "when there seems to be no hope of normal rescue, there is born a belief in miracles." Strong wishfulness breeds self-deceit. When Shabbati Zevi "revealed" himself as the anointed Messiah, tens of thousands of hapless Jews, desperate and yearning for relief, hailed him as their deliverer and prepared to follow him to Palestine. His failure in Turkey and his apostasy did not at once disillusion his followers, as they believed their redeemer was undergoing torment before final triumph. For nearly a century thereafter groups of deluded Jews continued to look for a Messiah. Steeped in spiritual bewilderment and moral chaos, a few gradually yielded to perversions that made the last of the quasi-messiahs, Jacob Frank, repudiate the Talmud, indulge in orgies, and finally convert to Christianity.

Orthodox rabbis fought these heretical manifestations with all their pietistic powers. "Rabbinism," according to Jacob Raisen, "became synonymous with rigorism, the coercion of untold customs became unbearable, and the spirit of Judaism was lost in a heap of innumerable obligations." Fanatic rigor on one hand and extortionate taxes on the other made life almost intolerable for the Jews of Eastern Europe.

Relief came to many in the form of Hasidism, founded by Israel ben Eliezer (1700–1760), known as Baal Shem Tov (Master of the Divine Name) or Besht by contraction. Israel was orphaned early and grew up in penury and solitude. Not a particularly bright pupil, he later served as an assistant to a teacher and as a sexton. He behaved as a simple commonplace man until he "revealed" himself as a healer of the sick and comforter of the disconsolate. Soon known as the "wonder rabbi," he attracted people from near and far who came to him to be blessed. Various myths began to accrue around his name, and his miraculous powers were broadcast enthusiastically by his growing number of zealous followers.

In contrast to the rigorous discipline enforced by orthodox rabbis, Besht preached an emotionally mystical communion with God. He wrote no books, but orally maintained that it was not enough to obey God's commandments: It was necessary to feel Him with all of one's senses; God was present everywhere and in everything; the mind was limited, but the heart, like an ocean, was boundless. He urged prayer with joy, with enthusiasm, leading to indulgence in spiritual ecstasy. He insisted that God loved those devoted to Him with all their hearts; that to love ecstatically was more acceptable to Him than strict adherence to rabbinic ritual. His emphasis on feeling as superior to knowledge was particularly appealing to the mass of poor and little-educated Jews. The common subsequent saying, "The rabbi advised making merry," helped them to sublimate their poverty and misery in exultant elation.

The Master enhanced the status of Yiddish by using it in all his discourses. One of his outstanding successors, Rabbi Levi Isaak of Berditchev (1740–1809), was renowned for his Yiddish prayers in behalf of the people. A fine scholar, he found goodness in everyone and was devoted to the welfare of the poor. His protective attitude is commemorated in song and story. Rabbi Nahman of Bratzlav (1772–1810), a great-grandson of the Master, was one of the most original as well as imaginative Hasidic leaders. Mystical from early childhood, imbued with love of nature and an excited fantasy, he tortured his body to achieve greater spirituality. In 1798 he traveled to Palestine in the face of untold hardship. On his return he became critical of his fellow rabbis, and they made life miserable for him. His self-confidence unshaken, he moved to Bratzlav and lived there until his death from tuberculosis. Like other Hasidic rabbis, he employed Yiddish in his preaching and advised his followers to pray in Yiddish in order to express themselves more freely and fully than they could in Hebrew. No writer, he was fortunate in having a devoted disciple in Nathan Sternberg, to whom he dictated his volume of *Narrative Tales,* and who edited it for posthumous publication. These stories, told in a clear idiomatic Yiddish, combine symbolic fantasy and lyricism with fine literary quality. Each tale is permeated with a fiery yearning for the eternal, with a poetic imagination that sublimated superstition and egocentricity into highly fabulous stories. A typical passage is the following from the beautifully told "Seven Beggars": "There is a mountain, and on the mountain stands a stone, and out of the stone runs a spring; and everything has a heart and the heart of the world has a figure—*the nail of the foot of the heart is heartier than everyone's heart.*"

The spontaneity of Yiddish prayers by Hasidic rabbis and the imaginativeness of their emotional outpouring gave the common speech of the Jews a range and richness it had hitherto lacked. Peretz stated in a letter: "Two elements played the greatest role in the development of the Yiddish language —the Jewish woman and Hasidism." Samuel Niger (Charney, 1883–1955), a leading Yiddish critic, wrote of the Hasidic movement: "It aroused and awakened all the powers of creative being. It alerted our senses, fructified and winged our fantasy." In fact it enriched Yiddish literature with hundreds of stories, parables, adages, and anecdotes by and about Hasidic rabbis; many of these narratives were tales of wonder and make-believe that simultaneously served to liberate the individual from rigid dogma and enhance his worthiness as a human being. Its folklore, having its source in the people, served to enlarge the scope of Yiddish literature and to refine it linguistically.

During these turbulent centuries oral myth and tradition flowed in rich sluices through the cultural channels of Jewish life. The speech of women was enriched with pungent and picturesque proverbs, and the epigrams and witticisms of Talmudic students were not long in passing into the mainstream of the language. Songs of childhood and love were heard everywhere, as were ditties and ballads of the apprentice and the maid servant. Lay preachers, traveling from synagogue to synagogue, were highly adept in rhetorical inventiveness, and strove to make their moralizing at once palatable and effective by means of striking metaphor and homely parable. All this verbal treasure, refined and enhanced in the process of repetition, did much to make Yiddish serviceable as the linguistic medium of a harried but life-loving people. A good part of this recorded material was collected by Rabbi David Oppenheimer of Bohemia with the aid of his uncle Samuel Oppenheimer, banker to the Austrian government, and is now deposited in the library of Oxford University.

Intellectual liberty was the battle cry of the rationalists in the latter half of the 18th century. The ideas of the Encyclopaedists, of Voltaire and Rousseau, were not long in influencing the growing number of German intellectuals. One early exponent of these advanced ideas east of the Rhine was Jewish thinker Moses Mendelssohn (1729–1786). Acutely aware of the vast gulf between the medieval dogmatism of his fellow Jews and the intellectual insurgence of the educated and alert Europeans, he sought to break the religious gyves which encumbered his brethren and lead them into the light of current rationalism. With Luther's example before him, he decided that a German translation of the Old Testament would serve not merely to eliminate what he believed to be the intriguing but corruptive casuistry of the Talmud, but also help the Jews to learn pure German speech. In 1773 he published the Pentateuch, together with commentaries, which he considered "the first step toward enlightenment." Not long after appeared the remainder of the translation, prepared with the help of talented assistants. The work was truly epochal. Orthodox rabbis fought it bitterly, burning it symbolically in a number of towns, but they failed to weaken its radical influence upon the majority of German Jews.

Until the latter decades of the 18th century, Yiddish was the common speech of Jews in German lands. Mendelssohn himself corresponded with his betrothed and his father in that tongue. Yet his agitation and the increasing wealth and consequent social ambitions of some enterprising Jews combined to denigrate the use of Yiddish. The Seven Years' War ending in 1763 had enriched a number of Jews engaged in financing and supplying the armies of Frederick the Great. Eager to

enjoy their new affluence and soon aware of their social backwardness, they became anxious to find release from the numerous restrictions placed upon them as Jews. By means of
generous contributions and secret bribes, a number of them
managed to obtain permission to reside in Berlin and other
cities hitherto forbidden to them. To gain acceptance by their
Christian neighbors they began to emulate them in dress and
comportment as well as speech. Unaware of the linguistic
process by which Yiddish became a separate language, they
and their rationalistic spokesmen began to disdain it as a crippled and corrupt German jargon. Mendelssohn and his followers led the attack. Although he himself continued to cherish
Judaism as a religion and merely desired to remove the superstitious dogmas encrusted upon it through the ages, the sagacious hunchback philosopher unwittingly became instrumental
in leading the German Jews into the maw of assimilation.
"What will the Gentiles say?" motivated a self-hatred in many
of his disciples which made them ready to deny their Jewishness in the hope of finding favor with non-Jews. As Theodor
Lessing has stated: "Moses Mendelssohn made more or less a
clean sweep of the historic Jewish past in order (as Heinrich
Heine was later to phrase it) to obtain for the Jews a valid
ticket for entering European civilization." Many indeed sought
acceptance by means of apostasy.

Before long Yiddish became an object of ridicule and abom-
ination among "enlightened" German Jews, to whom it seemed
a humiliating reminder of the yellow badge forced upon their
forefathers. It continued to be spoken by the less educated for
another generation or two, and a few reformers continued to
use it in their efforts at education, but Yiddish as a language
ceased to be employed in Germany by the middle of the 19th
century.

It is noteworthy, however, that the first Yiddish works in
modern times were written by German Jews. Dr. M. Markuze
left Prussia for Poland in order to practice medicine among
the poor Jews of the town in which he settled. His book on
medical treatment was written in Yiddish because he wished

to help the thousands of Yiddish-speaking Jews who had no ready access to a doctor. Influenced by Moliere's *Tartuffe*, I. A. Eichel, a student of Kant, wrote *Reb Hennoch* (1793), a refinement on the Purim play in which Hasidic characters appear as hypocritical and lecherous and the enlightened protagonists as forthright and honest. Three years later Aaron Wolfsohn, friend of Mendelssohn and bitter opponent of both the Talmud and Yiddish, wrote *Frivolity and Religiosity* in an effort to drive out the usual Purim play, which he considered shameful. In both comedies the characters are drawn fairly realistically, with the older pious types speaking Yiddish and those representing the rationalists using German. Thereafter no Yiddish work of any consequence emerged from the pen of a German Jew.

The urge to enlightenment, destructive of the orthodoxy of the German Jews, spread eastward. Brought back by merchants who had gone to Koenigsberg and other German cities on business, it at first appeared only sporadically and feebly in Poland and the Ukraine; most of these heralds of rational ideas transmitted them without clarity or conviction, and the antagonism of pious leaders sufficed to quash them before they could do any damage. In Galicia, however, bordering on Germany, the message of religious enlightenment found fertile ground. Brody, then a center of international commerce, was visited by traders from the west as well as the east, and in mingling most men could not help being affected by the intellectual agitation; a number of these businessmen were also men of learning who appreciated the value of rational ideas. Even more important were the young men of intellectual curiosity who became zealous reformers.

A leading Galician reformer, Mendel Leffin, was actually born in Sanatov, Podolia, in 1749. The accidental perusal of a book of mathematics aroused his interest in secular study. He went to Berlin, learned German and French, and came into close contact with the Mendelssohn circle. In Brody, where he subsequently made his home, he associated with local scholars as enlightened as himself in addition to numerous commercial visitors. Assisted by a liberal Polish nobleman favorably impressed by his mathematical erudition, Leffin was able to publish Hebrew tracts on education and natural science. He soon realized, however, that the mass of Jews whom he wished to reach knew little Hebrew, and decided to approach them in Yiddish. His translation of the Proverbs and Ecclesiastes, in the living speech of his fellow Jews rather than the stereotyped Judeo-German of *Tzena-Urena,* was criticized by some fellow intellectuals as a profanation of the holy tongue, and warmly defended by others. His own position was that all languages were at first crude and cramped but in time became the polished medium of scholarly and creative writers. Of one of his critics, N. Khrokhmal (1785–1840), a prominent Hebrew scholar, he stated: "He isolated his wisdom from his poor brothers who sit in the dark." Later his *The First Hasid* and other writings in Yiddish were read in manuscript by many of his admirers.

Brody was the home as well as host of a number of intellectuals (*maskilim*), most of whom cherished Hebrew and disdained Yiddish. Of those who followed in Leffin's footsteps, Joseph Perl (1779–1839) and Y. Bick (1770–1831) were most prominent. The first, forced by his parents to study for the rabbinate, learned German secretly and later became highly educated and a strong antagonist to Hasidism. Bick alienated many reformers by his insistence on the need to value old Jewish traditions. After 1824 he even defended Hasidism, accusing his critics of preaching enlightenment and practicing authoritarianism.

The *Haskolah* (enlightenment) movement in Russia began to assert itself early in the 19th century. At first it made little headway through the almost impenetrable brushwood of medieval orthodoxy and rabbinical opposition. For centuries the Jewish towns of Poland and Podolia had functioned autonomously, but at the will and with the permission of an indifferent and inimical government. *Kahal,* the institution governing these communities, collected taxes and controlled the social and religious life of their pious inhabitants. Conditions began to worsen in the late 18th century, when government oppression deprived many Jews of their habitual occupations as innkeepers and liquor dealers and forced them to crowd into small towns already filled with Jews unable to earn their living.

For generations the town rabbi was spiritual leader of his congregation. In the 18th century the increasingly popular Hasidic rabbi sought to arrogate to himself the authority of the local rabbi. The struggle for control was at times severe and distressing. Rabbi Elijah ben Solomon (1720–1797), known as the Vilna Gaon, was an uncompromising fundamentalist and the sharpest critic of Hasidism. Extremely erudite, highly intellectual, personally ascetic and retiring, he insisted on exact knowledge of the Talmud, to the extent of making it consonant with scientific data. In his view Hasidism was vitiated by superstition and spuriousness. His fame was great enough to keep Hasidism from taking root in Lithuania, but in Poland and the Ukraine the power of the Master of the Divine Name and his successors overcame all opposition until almost the end of the 19th century.

In the early years of enlightenment, the orthodox and the Hasidim were attacked with equal severity. The *maskilim* sought to liberate the mass of Jews from the dogmatism and superstition which kept them within the confines of medievalism. First to sound the cry of reform was I. B. Levinsohn (1788–1860), known as "the Mendelssohn of the Russian Jews." A child prodigy, he became a noted Hebrew scholar. Illness sent him to Brody, where he associated with the leading intellectuals; on his return to Russia he became a teacher and reformer. His first important Hebrew work, *Study in Israel,* aimed "to improve the upbringing and education of the Jewish youth." His *The House of Judah* had a similar purport. Both tracts were favorably received by his few enlightened readers and went far to develop the *Haskolah* movement in Russia. Although he opposed Yiddish and considered it "a mixture of degenerate words," he wrote *The Heedless World* in

1 7

that tongue in order to reach a wider audience than had his Hebrew volumes. His thesis, common among subsequent Yiddish writers, was that "the poor man is always the scapegoat," and he blamed the wealthy and religious leaders for the evils found in the Jewish community—particularly those which oppressed and exploited the poor and kept them in ignorance. The work, ironically, remained in manuscript until 1888, when it was published in Sholom Aleichem's *Yiddish Folk Bibliotek*, but its influence among intellectuals, who read it in manuscript, leavened the reform movement. It is interesting that he urged his fellow reformers to be more tolerant and not expect the ignorant Jews readily to embrace their teachings. Like so many early reformers, he believed that the Czarist government sought to be helpful and advocated loyalty to and dependence upon it. He also favored study of Russian as a means to better citizenship. In *The Heedless World*, for instance, he depicted Nicholas I in a favorable light. For years he lived in poverty, loneliness, and ill-health, with financial aid now and then ameliorating his distress.

The *maskilim* in Russia came up against much greater difficulties than had their predecessors in Germany. The Jews in small towns, who comprised the vast majority, were still steeped in other-worldly aspirations. Fear of Satan as the archenemy and belief that wholehearted faith was the touchstone to spiritual salvation in time made reason subservient to taboos and dogmatic ritual. Traumatic persecution and dire poverty made many yield readily to the comforting release of emotional excitement generated by Hasidic ecstasy. Even the orthodox opponents of Hasidism were deeply pious and moralistic; although they encouraged learning, they limited it to holy writ, so their accrued intellectual strenuousness was expressed in scholastic commentaries on the Torah and the Talmud.

By the middle of the 19th century the force of circumstances burst open the gates of their spiritual ghettos. A number of Jews began taking an active part in the development of the Russian economy, ultimately to their considerable enrichment. Simultaneously a much larger number, suffering from grinding poverty in their native towns, started to drift into cities in search of employment. Their reorientation tended to break the boundaries of their medieval isolation. Moreover, by a process of osmosis, even those who remained in small towns could not help hearing the siren voices of modern enlightenment.

A new and strange external world began to lure the more venturesome of the restless yeshiva students. The wonders of science, the logic of rational thought, and the delights of secular literature captivated many of them and engendered an eagerness to share their new and enriched life with the Jewish community as a whole. Soon they promoted the blessings of enlightenment with the enthusiasm and intolerance of impassioned converts. The result of their efforts was streaked with tragedy: clashing conflicts between fathers and sons, rabbis and reformers, faith and fact. It took nearly a century for the fundamentalism of the ghetto to yield reluctantly to the social and educational innovations advocated by the reformers. By that time, however, the cataclysm of war, revolution, massacres, and Nazi genocide gave a deathblow not merely to medievally oriented orthodoxy but to Jewish life itself.

Levinsohn's advocacy of reform began to take effect after 1830. Newly emancipated intellectuals strove zealously to impregnate their fellow Jews with the progressive ideas of Western Europe. Their Hebrew and Yiddish writings, mostly in manuscript, circulated more or less secretly in every yeshiva and house of study, and many a youth was enticed into tasting the knowledge of the Gentiles. A number soon rebelled against a life of sacerdotal cogitation and fled to the cities of Europe for their education.

So radical a transition of necessity releases a tremendous amount of intellectual energy. The religious cultivation of millennia, the social vitality of a compact people, the spiritual vicissitudes of a persecuted minority, the latent art of an ancient and isolated folk group—these elements, energized by the sudden slackening of traditional inhibitions, became the surging substance of a Jewish renascence during the second half of the 19th century. In this cultural effervescence, emergence of a modern Yiddish literature became manifest. With religious barriers broken, spiritual release quivering in the heart, and discovery of a new world a secret bursting with its own importance, the impulse to express one's ideas and ideals became irresistible. Scores of young men, heirs to a fabulously rich lore, who would in generations past have dedicated their talents to explication of a portion of the Talmud, now devoted themselves to works aiming to liberate and liberalize their hoped-for readers. Among them were of course some who wrote not merely to educate but to entertain. At first they deemed it honorific to write in Hebrew, and a few fortunate ones had their work printed in the two or three available Hebrew periodicals; later, as they discovered that they could best express their thoughts in Yiddish and would thereby reach most readers, they turned more and more to their mother tongue. Much of their work was amateurish and of little literary merit, but here and there emerged a writer of ability.

Israel Aksenfeld (1787–1866) was born in Nemirov of extremely pious parents and raised as a Hasid. Yet he managed to learn foreign languages and traveled to Germany on business during the Napoleonic Wars, where he discovered a "new world" and embraced enlightenment. In 1824 he settled in Odessa, in time became a notary and lawyer, and made his home a center of intellectual reformers. He was a prolific writer, imbued at once with an urge to reform and a sense of literary quality. Unlike Levinsohn, he wanted to reach the ordinary Jew and therefore wrote only in Yiddish, the first to do so. "To write in a language understandable to the common people; to bring out comic yet didactic events of real life; to attract the reader with fiction, such as will reveal truth, but in the form of an interesting story—this difficult task I undertook."

His best-known work, *The First Jewish Recruit in Russia* (1835), deals with the *recrutchina* decree issued by Nicholas I in 1827. The order to draft Jewish children for army service of 25 years duration naturally caused deep distress among

Jews, and resulted in numerous inequities upon the poor and humble. In this play, the town's leading Jews arrange to provide the needed recruit and at the same time rid themselves of a youth lacking in piety by assuring him that the girl he loved had asked for his enlistment. When she learns of this machination she dies of anguish and her mother thereupon becomes insane. The characters are relatively individualized, but with an overlay of caricature. They are depicted as Aksenfeld knew them: realistically, concretely, humorously, in the main didactically, in simple, earthy Yiddish. He believed, like Levinsohn, that recruitment of Jews into the army would serve their interest as citizens and therefore did not criticize the decree itself. The second of his well-known works, *The Jeweled Head Kerchief*, tells about a young man eating on a fast day, greatly abused and vilified by the pious, and dragged to a Hasidic rabbi who fines him a sum of money for his avarice. Here Aksenfeld is very critical of dogmatic piety and hypocritical town leaders.

Since only two Jewish printing shops were permitted in Russia up to 1862, both of them inimical to reformers, and since censorship made publication abroad practically impossible, Aksenfeld's works remained in manuscript. With censorship eased somewhat in 1862, he managed to print both plays in Leipsig. Two years later, having decided to migrate to Paris, where his sons had established themselves, he offered his manuscripts to Jewish reformers in Odessa for 400 rubles, but the transfer did not materialize. A year after his death in 1866 his *Man and Wife: Sister and Brother*, a work which stressed the evil effects of Hasidism on Jewish life, was published in Odessa. Most of his remaining manuscripts were lost, but not before they had been read by enough persons to exert their influence on the reform movement.

Shlomo Ettinger (1800–1856) was perhaps the most talented of the early intellectual reformers. He was born in Warsaw and lived in Zamoscz, then a center of cultural activity. Supported by his wife, he went to Lemberg in Galicia to study medicine, but on his return had to practice without official approval owing to quondam restrictions. While still in Lemberg he had read *Tartuffe, Robinson Crusoe,* and other works of literature, and was later stimulated to write numerous fables, verses, and *Serkele,* a comedy with a skillfully developed plot. The intent of his critical exposure in this play is obvious but not obtrusive. As in the comedies by Eichel and Wolfsohn, the hero speaks in a Germanic Yiddish because he came from Prague, while the pious hypocrites use a localized Yiddish. The student hero, being emancipated, is accused of a theft committed by the Tartuffish Gavriel. After much ado, all ends well, with the innocent rewarded and the guilty punished. Of particular interest is the natural and vivid dialogue. Ettinger took pains to improve the language and employed a number of neologisms rather than the current Germanized expressions. Among his other works are *The World Fooled,* which also contrasts hypocrites and scoundrels with honest and simple folk, and an adaptation of *Robinson Crusoe.* Most notable is *Rags,* in which various pieces of cloth boast of their origin and bemoan their sad end—only to be told by the drayman that they are worthless. Having no means to get his compositions printed, he circulated them in manuscript. An original, corrected edition of *Serkele* and other of his writings was prepared by Max Weinreich and published in Warsaw in 1925.

A. B. Gottlober (1811–1899) received a traditionally pious education and was married at the age of 15. When the recruiting law was promulgated in 1827, Gottlober, fearing induction, went to Lemberg, where he came in contact with emancipated intellectuals and began his secular education. On his return to Russia his lack of piety resulted in divorce and years of hapless wandering in search of employment. For a time he sojourned with Levinsohn, gave private lessons where he could find pupils, and taught at the Zhitomir rabbinical school. While there he met Sholom Abramovitch (Mendele). When the government closed the school, Gottlober resumed his travels and experienced dire poverty in his old age until his children began to provide for him.

Unlike Aksenfeld, Gottlober considered Yiddish a "shameful" dialect which gave the Jews the character of "Gypsies, an uneducated people." In his advocacy of Hebrew he stated: "I have known for a long time that we will only be able to help our people and to heal its wounds if we will speak to it in its own language. Only then will it be ready to discard *its degenerate jargon.*" Yet he was enough under the influence of Leffin and others to write verses in Yiddish, explaining: "I was moved to speak to the people in their own tongue." A number of his Yiddish poems, circulating in manuscript and readily memorized, achieved wide popularity. "Poor Israel" was sung in many homes. The satire, "Song of the Sabbath Pudding," an adaptation of Schiller's "Song of the Bell," exposed Jewish failings. *The Veil* or "Two Weddings in One Night," a comedy based on a Kotzebue farce, later influenced Goldfaden's similar work, *The Two Kuni-Lemels* (Simpletons). *The Gilgul* (Metamorphosis) is a sharply satiric tale, in a sense foreshadowing Mendele's *Little People,* in which a dead soul tells how in life it was both pious and respected, though at the same time a usurer and exploiter of the poor. These and other works have given Gottlober an honorable part in the development of Yiddish literature.

I. M. Dick (1807?–1893) was the first highly popular writer of Yiddish fiction. His stories were not only published as soon as written but also widely read by men and women alike. A fine student with a keen sense of wit, he grew to maturity as a Hebrew scholar and began giving private lessons in his native Wilno. Secretly, however, he had studied German with a friendly priest and readily joined the movement for religious reform. Eager to bring the fruits of enlightenment to his readers, he was too broadminded and too much the storyteller to seek reforms by means of open criticism and preachment. Desirous of reaching the largest audience, he wrote in Yiddish; when questioned, he explained that to demolish an old building one must use a heavy pick axe and not a golden needle. Not to repel the pious, he kept to the style of the old moralizing tomes. He was not sensitive to the linguistic values of Yiddish and employed it conventionally to convey his fictionalized moralities, yet he was too much the writer not to make the best use of his literary means of expression. In time he relinquished his earthy vocabulary for a Germanized Yiddish then favored by some reformers.

Dick was a genuine storyteller, and his narratives were lively and humorous. The homilies and advice coating his novelettes—urging his readers to respect manual labor, live cleanly, abandon early marriages, and cherish women—did not impair the merit of his tales. His plots seethed with intrigue and villainy, but in the end righteousness always triumphed. *The Tumult* and *Khaitzikel Alone* are typical. The first was based on a rumor in 1835 that Jewish girls under 16 and Jewish boys under 18 would not be allowed to marry. Since the custom of early marriages was common, parents became panicky and hastily married their young children with little regard to congeniality or desirability. How this took place in one town forms the content of the story, told with mild satire and bold humor. In the preface to *Khaitzikel Alone,* addressed as always, to "Dear lady readers," he stated that it was "a beautiful and true story that occurred in the town of Elum (Wilno) about 25 years before. From it may be learned how parents should bring up their children." He told how the wife of an enriched man insisted on aping her betters; she pampered her son, employed private teachers who flattered rather than taught, and permitted him to grow up spoiled and boorish.

Jewish printing in Russia was first permitted in 1783 by Katherine II. After 1815 Alexander I severely restricted it, but in 1836 Jewish presses were allowed in Wilno and Zhitomir under strict censorship. In Wilno printing was done by Baruch Romm, who started in 1799, and the plant remained in the family control until World War II. Until late in the 19th century it was a stronghold of orthodoxy and usually rejected works by reformers. Dick, however, became its most popular author, approximately 100,000 copies of his booklets having been sold prior to 1861. Four years later he contracted with the firm to deliver a novelette a week, 48 pages long, for which he received six rubles. This he did for some years thereafter, completing about 400 stories in all. An edition of between 4000 and 6000 copies of each new work appeared nearly every fortnight, and book peddlers disposed of them in the marketplaces on Fridays. Housewives, buying their groceries for the Sabbath, usually included a copy of the latest story among their purchases. H. B. Sternshnider, a contemporary resident of Wilno, wrote: "There isn't a man or woman, old or young, or boy or girl, who had not read the stories of I. M. Dick with much enjoyment."

Dick's writings lost much of their appeal in his later years, when Shomer (N. M. Shaikevitch, 1849–1905) began to write his more exciting, if less meritorious, fiction, and the more educated readers turned to the works of Mendele and his literary contemporaries. As a result, Dick suffered neglect and poverty in his old age. Historically, however, he has a secure niche among early Yiddish writers. Niger has described his achievement as a storyteller:

> Dick was, in short, devoted to the spirit and program of the reform period, and the main purport of his writing was to teach and criticize and explain—as it was then understood. But deep in his heart he enjoyed telling stories . . . and sometimes forgot that he was a reformer and told a story for its own sake, and included witticisms for themselves, and if not portraits of typical persons, certainly successful caricatures.

His stories, indeed, were read with profit by neophyte writers, and his influence is evident in Mendele's early fiction.

Restrictions forced upon the Jews during the reign of Nicholas I made their existence onerous and haphazard. Crowded and confined within a circumscribed Pale, the majority was endemically impoverished. Yet they were at least obliquely affected by economic and social developments. Wars, new inventions, and other current phenomena exerted a modicum of influence even on backward villages. As more and more Jews found their way to the larger cities, a number of them illegally, their curiosity as to what was happening in the world made evident the need of a periodical that would provide news of current events. Most Jews were not yet able to read Russian and had only a scant knowledge of Hebrew, but the government at first refused permission to any journal specifically for Jewish readers.

The first breakthrough came in 1857, when the government allowed importation from Germany of the Hebrew *Hamagid*, a periodical found harmless by the censors. Some time later consent was obtained for the publication of *Razsvet* (Dawn), a Jewish weekly in Russian. Edited by intellectuals who disdained Yiddish as a language, the magazine staunchly urged study of Russian as a means of good citizenship. Ossip Rabinovitch, one of the enlightenment leaders, called for an end to the cringing and scraping of Jews before their Russian fellow citizens. In the same article he castigated the Jews for continuing to adhere to "the crippling Jargon, which sounds so ugly, is so incorrect and poor, and is unable to express a single lofty thought. . . . We must therefore discard the rags which we had inherited from the dark middle ages."

These Russophile reformers maintained their agitation for another two decades—until the pogroms of 1881 convinced most of them of the folly of their position. When strict censorship and inadequate readership caused the demise of *Razsvet* in 1861, it was soon replaced by *Sion*, which was limited to innocuous discussions of Jewish literature and history. Later *Razsvet* was revived and continued for a number of years.

Other reformers became ardent Hebraists and strove to spread knowledge of the holy tongue among Jewish children. A common slogan of this group, enunciated by the poet I. L. Gordon, was: "Be a Jew in your tent and a man abroad, a brother to your countrymen and a servant to your king." Outstanding among the Hebraists was Alexander Tzederboim who, for all his insistence on social reform, was primarily an intrepid and vain journalist. After much persistent effort, he in 1859 received permission to publish the Hebrew *Hamelitz* in Odessa as a means of inculcating piety and patriotism into the minds of his readers. After four years of endeavor he had less than

1000 subscribers, a number of whom, however, circulated their copies to many of their townsmen. All the while, of course, a few intellectuals maintained that reforms could be achieved only through the medium of Yiddish, the speech of most Jews.

As far back as 1686 an Amsterdam publisher had brought out the first Yiddish periodical, *Die Kuranten,* which appeared on Tuesdays and Fridays for a little over a year and contained news of Jewish interest from various parts of the world. The next Yiddish journal, *Der Beobachter an der Weichsel* (The Observer on the Vistula), appeared in Warsaw in 1823 and stopped with the 44th issue. In 1861 Mendele and his friend Joshua Lipschitz, who subsequently published a Yiddish-Russian dictionary, influenced Tzederboim to request government permission for a Yiddish supplement to *Hamelitz.* Lipschitz at that time favored the use of Yiddish even more than did Mendele, insisting that its opponents were wrong in calling it decadent. "Decadent," he pointed out, "may be called that which used to be better but became spoiled. But how can one claim that other languages were any better at their beginning? They too emerged, as our language, from other languages, so why are they not considered decadent?" When consent was obtained after much intercession and repeated appeals, and despite the strong opposition of Russophile reformers, Tzederboim called the Yiddish section *Kol Mvasser* (Voice of the Messenger).

Established as a means of advocating patriotism, education, and religious reform, *Kol Mvasser* soon began to serialize such works of fiction as Mendele's *Little Person* (1864) and Yoel Linetsky's *The Polish Youth* (1867), both having a didactic intent but written with literary flair. These and other works gave an appeal to the Yiddish supplement which the Hebrew *Hamelitz* lacked. Although its circulation was relatively small and some towns had only one subscriber, each issue was read and heard by most of the purchaser's friends and acquaintances. As one writer pointed out, "People who could not read any other language read *Kol Mvasser* with a real hunger, opening mouth and ears, and enjoying everything they read."

In 1869 *Kol Mvasser* became independent, but ceased publication in 1872. During the decade of its existence it was tremendously influential in the encouragement of Yiddish writing and in standardizing spelling, grammar, and vocabulary. It was both educational and literary in content, with its articles on popular science and general knowledge serving as adult education lessons to many of its readers.

Yiddish periodicals appeared in Galicia and the United States in the early 1870's, but were of minor importance and did not last long. In 1881 Tzederboim managed to bring out *Yiddish Folksblatt,* which had a Zionist impetus and favored Hebrew, but also published the early work of Sholom Aleichem, M. Spector, S. Frug, and others who later became prominent Yiddish writers. It ceased publication in 1890. Later *Der Yud* (The Jew, 1899), first a monthly and soon a weekly, and *Der Freint* (The Friend, 1903), the first Yiddish daily in Russia, printed the cream of Yiddish writing at the turn of the century.

Yiddish books and periodicals served well the efforts of social and religious reformers. To them must be added the *badkhen* (bardic minstrel), among whom Eliakum Zunser (1840–1913) * was the most prominent, and the Yiddish actor. The tradition of Purim players and bards was of course of ancient origin. In the middle of the 19th century, when Brody became a center for international business, merchants who came from various neighboring countries looked nightly for entertainment. Berl Margolius (Broder) and Wolf Ehrenkranz (Velvel Zbaraver), Yiddish folk singers with an inclination to comedy, amused these merchants with witty songs and impersonations. They also served at weddings, feasts, and special occasions. Later, having developed a form of entertainment under the name of Broder Singers, they began early efforts at theatrical performances. During the Russo-Turkish War, when a number of merchants congregated in Rumania as suppliers of war materiel, the singing and acting of these Broder Singers

* See Bibliography of English translations.

assumed professional status, and their need of dramatic material became urgent.

To their good fortune they were able to attract Abraham Goldfaden (1840–1908) to their ranks. He had been a student at the Zhitomir rabbinical school and had taken a leading part in the school production of *Serkele;* he had also written Hebrew verse. When he failed in business and as publisher of a periodical, he turned to the Broder Singers as a means of gaining a livelihood. At first he directed performances in the style of *comeddia dell'arte.* When he managed to obtain more actors, including women, he soon took them on a tour of cities in Eastern Europe. To vary the repertoire, he began to compose operettas, writing the text and music and staging them as well. His success was widespread. In 1879 the troupe toured various cities of Russia with such popular operettas as *Shmendrik* and *The Two Kuni-Lemels.*

These and other plays, while of little artistic worth, were satirical in content and made good-natured fun of Jewish foibles and prejudices. When Peretz later criticized Goldfaden for abusing his talents by limiting himself to trashy farces, the latter commented: "Without these pieces there wouldn't be any Yiddish theater today. And I don't know which is worse: to have nothing or to have something that can be improved and completed. I have trod the way. Let others come and create better things." When the Russian government banned the performance of Yiddish plays in 1883, Goldfaden and his group of actors traveled to other parts of Europe and to New York. By that time many Jews had tasted the pleasures of the theater and preferred it to the synagogue service. The Yiddish stage soon flourished in other parts of Europe, and particularly in the United States.

Another contributor to Yiddish literature, on a low level and much maligned, was the highly popular Shomer (N. M. Shaikevitch). Having received a traditional education in Hebrew, he emerged as a typical intellectual, interested in writing and behaving like a ne'er-do-well in business. He married early and lived with his growing family in the home of his father-in-law. He read intensively of current fiction, particularly the novels of Eugene Sue and Paul de Kock. When he was 27 he left home for Wilno with a Hebrew manuscript he had written. Told by the editor that he preferred Yiddish stories, Shomer obliged. When more were requested, he wrote so speedily that the editor had to cry halt. For a time he taught to make ends meet. Then he began to write longer works of fiction, and was prolific enough to produce six or more a year.

His motto was to give his readers "a highly interesting novel, a genuine slice of life." Typical of his stories was *Roshkele Kossack*, described on the title page as "a characteristic story of Jewish life which can well serve as a mirror to evil women." Actually he was highly romantic, and his moralizing was but a patch upon trashy but titillating stories. His plots were involved and mechanical, his style pompous and bombastic, his Yiddish Germanized and stilted. Yet the action had sufficient verve and the stories enough intrigue and suspense to hold many readers enthralled.

For about a decade, Shomer's popularity exceeded Dick's of a generation earlier. He was read not only by the proverbial servant maid and apprentice but by many mothers and daughters of intellectuals and by thousands of men who formerly would have bent over a religious tome. It was only in the late 1880's, when Sholom Aleichem's harsh and denigrating attack upon him and his peers in *Shomer on Trial* appeared, that the vogue of this popular fiction declined somewhat. Sholom Aleichem and other intellectuals did not realize that Shomer had attracted thousands of readers who previously had never looked into a Yiddish book. By cultivating their taste for fiction, he in fact prepared them for writers who were readying the effervescence of modern Yiddish literature.

A major obstacle to the development and general acceptance of Yiddish fell away after 1881, when the pogroms of that year slackened the antagonism of many aggressive reformers. In the 1860's, when the serfs were freed and various political restrictions relaxed, and economic enterprise brought wealth to a number of energetic Jews, it was easy for these reformers to believe that the Jews needed only to discard their medieval orthodoxy to achieve the rights of full citizenship. In their zeal they attacked dogmatic piety and Hasidism as obscurantic and pernicious. Some of them verged on abandoning their Jewish identity, and not a few ended in apostasy; others, accepting I. L. Gordon's slogan, became Hebraists at home and Russians when away from it. Their contempt for Yiddish was part of their self-hatred, and therefore the more violent.

After 1881, when it became evident that the Russian government had instigated the peasantry against the Jews and was responsible for the pogroms, these reformers were forced to admit that their advocacy of Russification was a delusion. Their frustration led them to listen sympathetically to the few who had long been preaching Jewish nationalism and Zionism. Joseph Raisin stated: "They sobered down from orgies of assimilation, and the worshippers abandoned their idol. Those who had almost forgotten that they were of the camp of Israel began to return to its tents."

Many who had considered themselves Russians of the Mosaic faith began to realize that they were in fact members of an ancient people with a proud if tragic history and a determination to survive and flourish. They soon discovered fresh and attractive values in the old Jewish ways and traditions. Emulating Russian radicals of the 1880's, they went to the people. The chief beneficiary of this altered attitude was Yiddish. Simon Dubnow, the eminent Jewish historian, reminiscing about 1881, when a new Yiddish periodical was about to be started, described how Yiddish was then regarded:

All of us, young and old, at that time looked down our noses upon "Jargon" as a literary medium; that is, we, the educated, were creating a literature in the language of our native land, Russia, which must become our future language, and in part also in Hebrew—the language of our past; but the poor uneducated masses must also be given a medium with which to educate themselves and to rise to our level, and it was necessary to create a temporary literature in their speech, "Jargon," until they learned to read Russian.

Eight years later D. Brant, a contributor to Sholom Aleichem's *Yiddish Folk Bibliotek*, indicated a more benign acceptance of Yiddish:

How long ago was it that we sought in every possible way, while walking in the street or sitting in a train or house, to hide our Jewish identity? Now we have discarded this false shame. We are not even ashamed to speak "Jargon," *because it is the speech of the people.* Moreover, our best writers in Russian and Hebrew have recently begun to write in "Jargon" in order to get nearer to the people, in order to be understood by them and be of use to them.

CHAPTER TWO

MENDELE MOKHER SFORIM

Foremost Yiddish Satirist

THE SOCIAL CATACLYSM of the 20th century in Eastern Europe has completely destroyed the ghetto life of the Jews in that part of the world. The compact Jewish towns, remaining an image of composite beauty and squalor in the minds of those who grew up in them, have been forever relegated to the historic past. Only in the vividly searing pages of Yiddish literature may one read about them as they were—physically idyllic and depressing, spiritually sincere and stultifying.

These *Shtetls*, inhabited almost wholly by pauperized Jews and largely self-governing, were both ugly and unsanitary. Their few streets lay sprawling and unpaved, lined with dwellings more like hovels than habitable houses. Spring thaws, aided by rain, covered these thoroughfares with soft, deep mud; in the hot summer days this mud, dried to a powder, parched the throats of passersby. The one marketplace, an open, unattractive square bordered on each side by paltry stores and stalls, was regularly crowded by wagons of produce from nearby farms and scores of Jews seeking timidly or harriedly to earn a few pennies as traders. Verdant nature was almost wholly absent from these dilapidated settlements, although it luxuriated in adjacent fields and forests.

Outwardly these Jews appeared untidy, ragged, and quaint. The vast majority lived in grim want, eking out a bare subsistence by working for or trading with one another and with the surrounding peasantry. Life was accepted as an ordeal, work as a necessary sop to their attenuated stomachs, often alleviated by religious fasts. But if their external existence was bleak and burdensome, their spiritual activity was gratified daily by unquestioned faith in the rectitude of Jehovah. Religious piety was to them the essence of human aspiration. They punctiliously observed Judaic rites and obligations and took comfort in the hope that their sublime and almighty God would be mindful of their prayers and supplications. Their synagogue, usually the largest structure in town, though without the architectural splendor and decoration of Christian churches, was their house of prayer and study, social center, and religious anchor. Those few who were relatively secure financially or whose wives attended to their material needs—and of the latter there were a good many—sat most of the day and evening immersed in Talmudic study and speculation.

Their knowledge of the outside world was circumscribed and naively inaccurate; their general outlook and behavior were still governed by the customs and habits of thought acquired from medieval forefathers or prescribed by Hasidic rabbis. They were indeed "dreamers of the ghetto," their fusty fancies often absorbing brains worthy of philosophers.

As was to be expected in any assemblage of men, a few in each town were outwardly pious and scholarly and yet aggressive and hypocritical enough to arrogate to themselves civic powers, enjoy self-granted perquisites, and batten upon the tax-ridden poor. These city fathers, posing as philanthropists, took callous advantage of their association with bribed Russian officials and became cankers aggravating the misery of their exploited townsmen.

Participants in the *Haskolah* movement, having freed themselves from the constraint of the yeshiva and having acquired a lay education, recoiled from what appeared to be the corroding fanaticism and hypocrisy rampant within the Jewish community. In their efforts to extirpate the superstitious accretions and social inequities from their midst they concentrated their attacks on the civic and spiritual leaders, whom they considered the chief culprits. After the death of Nicholas I, when the government of Alexander II seemed to relax some of the restrictions against Jews, these reformers intensified their endeavors to liberate the people from their medieval backwardness. Dr. I. Eliashev, the noted critic, has stated that they "stopped at nothing in order to uncover everything that was sick, weak, rotten, and dead." The rabbis and the pious leaders fought back with all the powers at their command, but conditions were against them and their control of the people gradually weakened and withered.

Among the effective reformers were those who wrote in Yiddish in their eagerness to reach directly the people they sought to emancipate. The popularity of Dick's didactic stories prepared many for the writings of reformers whose work possessed greater literary merit. One of the first to gain a wide audience for Yiddish verse was Mikhel Gordon (1823–1890), born in Wilno. He wrote poems critical of dogmatic piety and superstition. In the 1850's they were circulated widely in manuscript, memorized by many, and sung with tunes composed by Gordon. In *The Beard and Other Songs*, published in 1868, and in other of his poems he urged Jews to throw away their pride in being "the chosen people" and take up worldly education. His "Arise, My People" was particularly effective in this endeavor.

His younger brother-in-law, I.L. Gordon (1829–1892) was an even better poet. Although he wrote primarily in Hebrew, his verse was surcharged with the zeal of reform. A government rabbi, he was active in civic affairs, critical of the use of Yiddish, and favored Russification. Writing to Sholom Aleichem, he expressed surprise that one who knew Russian and

Hebrew as well as he should resort to Yiddish as his literary medium, which "one can tolerate as a necessary evil, as a means of expressing the best ideas to our ignorant masses, but on no account must one encourage its development and efflorescence." Yet his Yiddish poems, published in 1886, while highly didactic, graced the language he disdained.

To these poets must be added Goldfaden and Zunser, both previously mentioned, and Mark Warshavsky (1848–1907). The operettas by Goldfaden featured songs which were widely sung, and the songs of the latter two had a folk quality that made them highly popular. Warshavsky's emergence as a lyricist is of particular interest. A practicing lawyer in Kiev, he was of a jolly disposition, with a penchant for improvising songs that delighted his friends and made up many an evening's entertainment. Sholom Aleichem, then living in Kiev, heard him perform one evening, and, perceiving their authentic folk quality, persuaded him to write down the songs together with the music he had composed for them. A volume of them was published in 1900 and achieved immediate popularity. Sholom Aleichem and he toured a number of cities, one reading his stories and the other singing his songs to large appreciative audiences.

Simon Frug (1860–1916) was a poet of a higher order. He began to write in Russian, was favorably received by critics, and published three volumes, much of the material concerning his Jewish youth. His pure lyrical tone was regarded highly by both liberal Russians and emancipated Jews. Like so many other reformers, however, he discarded his Russophilism in the 1880's and began to write in Yiddish, giving voice to current Jewish woes. He sang wistfully of the Jewish child brought up in the dank ghetto, ignorant of the bright and beautiful life away from it. Zionism also fired his imagination and he wrote impassioned lyrics about life on Zion's soil and the pioneering spirit of the kibbutz.

Yoel Linetsky (1839–1915) was one of the prominent Yiddish writers in the second half of the 19th century. The precocious son of an ultra-pious rabbi, he was forced in his early

youth to bathe in cold water several times daily to keep his
body pure. Suspected of heretical thoughts as he entered his
teens, he was married in the hope that this would keep him
from temptation. By this time, however, the worldly virus was
deep in his thoughts and, as an antidote to his heresy, his
father compelled him to divorce his child-wife and marry a
deaf moron. Thereupon young Linetsky ran away to Odessa,
where he earned his bread by giving private lessons and used
his free time to study. While on his way to Breslau for further
schooling, he was caught at the border and returned to his
father's home. Soon he escaped again, this time to Zhitomir,
where he continued his studies and married a girl of his choice.
In 1863 he went to Kiev, where he had difficulty earning a
bare living. In the meantime he had written a good deal of
Hebrew and Yiddish verse and began to publish it in 1865.
In 1867 he sent part of *The Polish Youth* to Tzederboim, and
the first installment in *Kol Mvasser* was read with great interest; by the time the novel was completed Linetsky's prominence was assured. It did not bring him any money, however;
nor did his subsequent work, including translations, allay his
poverty. He became increasingly bitter and pessimistic.

The Polish Youth, largely autobiographical, was the work of
a man of talent who had been spiritually crippled by his
fanatical father. It was written with little attention to diction,
in a loose and episodic style, peppered with Russian words and
phrases and punctuated with asides and unrelated reflections.
Yet it had vigor, wit, passion, and vivid descriptions. Its condemnation of Hasidic excrescences was so extreme as to make
the sect seem grotesque and degenerate. The satiric depiction
of the rabbi's court highly exaggerated the hypocrisy often
characterizing the real thing. Every aspect of Hasidic life was
described with acidulous mockery, and the rascality of some
of the leaders matched the villainy of melodrama. The net
effect of the book, however, was wholesome. Its readers readily perceived Linetsky's aim to save Jewish youths from the
superstition and suffering he himself had experienced. It was
easy for many to identify themselves with one or another of

the victimized characters, and they relished the final discomfiture of the hypocrites and evildoers. Even Hasidim, who denounced the book publicly, read it privately with great interest. Its popularity continued for a generation, and in 1895 Linetsky brought out a revised edition to rectify some of the alterations made by Tzederboim in the original manuscript, so "that it was difficult to separate the good from the bad." In effect he greatly modified his caustic attitude toward Hasidism and sought to find something worthy even in those he censured. His altered tone was noticeable earlier in "The Worm in Horseradish," which appeared in *Yiddish Folk Bibliotek* in 1888, a work considered a sequel to the novel which brought out the admirable aspects of Hasidism as well as the filth and poverty pressing upon Jewish life.

Two other writers achieved a modest but solid position in the Yiddish literature of the period: Jacob Dinesohn (1856–1919) and Mordecai Spector (1858–1925). The first, a protégé of Mikhel Gordon and Dick, attained early prominence with the publication of *The Dark Young Man* (1877), a sweetly sentimental story of thwarted love. It seemed to be just what the increasingly large number of feminine readers wanted, and it made them as happy to shed tears over the unkind fate of the lovers as had been the readers of Goethe's *Werther* a century earlier. Of interest is the fact that its popularity indicated how far Jewish women had departed from pious reading of *Tzena-Urena* and even from Dick's stories. Dinesohn's later work, written after he had become intimately associated with Peretz, was less sentimental, more concerned with the proper upbringing of children, and gently moralistic.

Spector was more than the realist, observer, and historian. *A Novel Without a Name, Paupers, Reb Treitel,* and especially *The Jewish Peasant* are stories based on actual events which discuss problems of current interest. He described the daily life of his characters with detailed accuracy that made his books of folkloric value to later writers. Like Dinesohn, he did much to encourage literary neophytes and to further the development of Yiddish literature. His *Hoizfreint* (House Friend), appearing in Warsaw in 1888, was a miscellany that included the first fruit of promising writers. Somewhat later he joined Peretz in the publication of *Yom Tov Bletter* (Holiday Leaves), an occasional collection of literary interest.

The foregoing writers expressed but feebly the cultural forces released by the *Haskolah* movement, their didactic zeal exceeding their creative efforts. The time demanded a writer of extraordinary capacities: an artist able to lift the stigma denigrating Yiddish and establish it as a literary language; a chronicler with the trenchancy of a keen satirist and the empathic insight of the seer; a reformer intimately familiar with the weaknesses of the ghetto environment but fully aware of the futility of sterile invective. Fortunately for Yiddish literature the "moment," with Taine-like fortuity, brought forth such a writer in Sholem Abramovitch. With his youth and spirit firmly rooted in traditional Judaism, his artistic intellect assimilating the culture of modern Europe, his heart wholly devoted to the betterment of his people, and, above all, an increasingly refined capacity for literary expression, Mendele was indeed the very person measuring up to the needed task.

Sholem Jacob Abramovitch (originally Broido) became the "grandfather" of modern Yiddish literature by virtue of being a descendant of the prophets of Israel and a son of the Lithuanian Pale. The year of his birth is not definitely known, but most historians now assume it was around 1836. A precocious youth, memorizing much of the Old Testament by the time he was nine years old, quick of wit and a ready mimic, he was well known among his townsmen of Kapulye, in the province of Minsk. As a student of the Talmud in his early teens he showed exceptional promise. During these happy years he absorbed the memorable stories and impressions which were the heritage of every open-eared youth who spent much of his time in the synagogue—material which he later used in his books. When he was 14 the death of his father, one of the popular men of the town, left his family impoverished and caused Sholem to leave home for the houses of study of nearby towns. Like most Talmudic students, he "ate days" and slept on the bench on which he studied. Life was hard for him and often depressing. When his mother married a miller, Sholem went to live with her. In the serenity of the countryside, near a deep forest and a meandering river, alive with all species of birds and animals, Sholem's response to nature began to express itself in Hebrew verse.

He was too much the child of his ghetto environment to remain long in the solitude and isolation of his stepfather's mill. Returning to Kapulye, he was lured by an elderly vagabond-beggar, Abraham the Lame, into accompanying him to the Ukraine, where he would be assured of a good teaching position. With them on the rickety wagon was the youth's aunt in search of her vanished husband. Once out of town, Abraham became an alms collector for his presumably indigent passengers. He also sought to marry off Sholem to earn a brokerage fee, but Sholem refused to be intimidated. A providential meeting with a young relative in Kamenetz enabled him to free himself from the mendicant's entrapment. The ordeal was not, however, without its compensations. His experiences and observations while mingling with other vagabond-beggars and during visits to houses of study deeply impressed themselves on his imagination and served him well as material for later writings.

In Kamenetz he resumed his Talmudic studies. Already infected with the virus of worldly knowledge, he fortunately made the acquaintance of A.B. Gottlober, to whom he showed his literary efforts. The older writer encouraged him and arranged for his daughter to teach Sholem the elements of Russian, German, and arithmetic. His Talmudic virtuosity became apparent to a good many in the synagogue and led to his marriage to the daughter of one its respected members. The girl was dull-witted, however, and after three years of incompatibility he obtained a divorce. In the interim he had passed the examination for teachers in government-sponsored schools and was given a position in one of the city's Jewish schools.

One day he received a letter from an older brother complaining about his hardships as a teacher in a village *kheder* (elementary school). In reply Sholem became so engrossed in expounding the art of pedagogy that the letter became a trenchant essay on the principles of modern education. He extracted the more personal part and left the original on his table. One of his friends read it and forwarded it to Gottlober, who had moved to another city. The latter sent it with his recommendation to the editor of *Hamagid,* newly established in Germany. The published essay created a furor among intellectual reformers interested in pedagogy; it was not only written in a clear and simple Hebrew but presented the methods of successful teaching with constructive and persuasive logic. Overnight the 21-year-old Sholem attained the respect of his learned elders.

A year later, in 1858, bored with the monotony of life in Kamenetz, he moved to Berditchev, then a commercial and intellectual center. The city itself he found filthy and drab, but its rustic environment greatly pleased him. He married Pessie Levin, with whom he lived to the end of his life, and his wealthy father-in-law supported him while he devoted himself to writing and communal affairs. He continued to study the philosophy of pedagogy and urged teachers to learn the workings of young minds, discover inborn abilities, respect their pupils, and cultivate patience and sympathy. He was critical of reformers who disregarded the basic causes of Jewish backwardness and who, in condemning orthodoxy and dogma, were actually undermining the essence of religion along with its encrusted ritual.

More than once he attempted to write didactic fiction, and actually published the first version of *Parents and Children,* a complicated social satire. He realized, however, that the current Hebrew was too unwieldy as a fictional medium; moreover, if he was to reach the mass of Jews he would have to write in the language they knew. In a happy moment he decided to reserve Hebrew for loftier purposes and write in Yiddish that which he intended for popular reading. Later he wrote:

> As I observed the life of my people, I wanted to give them stories of Jewish life in the holy tongue. Most of them, however, did not know the language; they spoke Yiddish. And what did a writer gain from his thought and labor if they were of little use to his people? This question—for whom do I labor?—gave me no peace and deeply disturbed me; for the Yiddish of my day was an empty vessel, containing nothing good or beautiful—only mockery, foolishness, and chatter, the work of stultifiers, who did not speak sensibly and had no reputation. And the women and the uneducated men read this stuff without understanding. And others, though not knowing any other language, were ashamed to read Yiddish because it might reveal their backwardness. . . . Our writers, who knew languages, but who concentrated on Hebrew and made no contact with the people, looked at Yiddish with disdain and great mockery. And if one out of ten sometimes remembered the "cursed" language and wrote something in it, he hid it under seven locks, under his holy prayer shawl, in order not to reveal his shame and besmirch his reputation. Great was my hesitation when I realized that if I made use of this "unworthy" dialect I would cover my reputation with shame. I listened to the discouragement of my admirers, the lovers of Hebrew, who insisted that I would attenuate my name and honor among Jews by giving my strength to this strange speech. But my love of the practical conquered my empty vanity and I resolved: come what may, I will take pity on Yiddish, the rejected daughter, and work for the people.

In 1862 he and his friend Lipschitz, as already mentioned, persuaded Tzederboim to issue *Kol Mvasser* as a supplement to the Hebrew *Hamelitz*. He maintained that "a literature which does not concern itself with the people and their needs and is not influenced by them—cannot have any effect on them. The people will have nothing to do with it, and that makes it superfluous." Unlike other reformers, he had no prejudice against Yiddish, and when he began to write in it he not only avoided the current Germanized and careless usage but sought to give it the idiomatic firmness of a literary language.

To encourage Tzederboim in the continuance of *Kol Mvasser*, Sholem sent him his first Yiddish story, *Dos Kleyn Mentchele* (The Hypocrite), literally Little Person, a work of 30-odd pages. It was serialized in 1864. Still hesitant to arouse the wrath of the Hebraists, he did not wish to use his own name and hit upon the pseudonym of Senderel the Bookseller, whom he described as a hawker of religious writings from town to town. Tzederboim, fearing that readers might ascribe the satire to him—Senderel being a variant of Alexander—changed the name to Mendele. Although little more than a bare narrative in its first edition, the satiric impact of the little book was devastating. As in his later books, Mendele depicted Jewish life with intimate knowledge and insight. He did not hesitate to call evils by their right names, believing that sores healed best when exposed to fresh air. As he wrote to Sholom Aleichem in 1890: "A prick hurts, but then the wound heals sooner."

The "little man" in the story grew up an orphan, beaten and abused by everyone both as a pupil and as an apprentice. In time he discovered that the community leaders were *little people*, hypocrites who exploited their townsmen to their own advantage while posing as benefactors. As he had heard one of them remark: "If you have money—you have the world, but to have money one must be a little man." Practicing this philosophy when he grew up, he robbed and cheated while posing as a do-gooder, until he became rich. In his old age, however, he felt conscious-stricken and decided to leave his wealth for the education of the poor. His will, which comprises most of the story, exposes the evil ways of the rich, the callous parasites who battened upon their indigent townsmen, and his confession ends with the injunction: "Let the whole world know that wealth does not make one happy, that happiness comes from a good heart and good deeds."

Mendele's next work, *The Magic Ring*, appeared in 1865.

This was also a very short work, 42 pages, but its satire was again expressed without circumlocution. The title page read: "*The Magic Ring*, with which each person could achieve whatever his heart wished and desired and could through it make himself useful to the world." As strongly didactic as his first effort, the story makes clear that this magic ring is synonymous with wisdom and may be gained by means of education. "With wisdom," he declared, "a person can achieve anything he wished."

Still more the reformer than the artist, he insisted that the lot of his fellow Jews must be improved without depriving them of their spiritual heritage. To those intellectuals who lacked this sensitivity and argued for radical transformation of Jewish life regardless of the consequences, he said in 1865:

> If you really want to improve the conditions of your people, you must discard your moralizing accusations of their primitiveness and superstitions and ask the government to give us equal rights and open up the needed means of subsistence. But ask without conditions and do not attach the question of education to them.

Three years later, commenting on a published attack on Jewish religion, he wrote: "Be careful not to disturb the Talmud, because Jews breathe with it; it is the soul of their belief. They had endangered their life for it, died as martyrs on the auto-de-fé." In this attitude he was 20 years ahead of most of his fellow reformers.

In 1869 he published the original versions of *Fishke the Lame* * and *The Meat Tax*. The first was a sketchy tale of the Jewish poor, the second a play dealing with exploitation of the poor by well-to-do community leaders, with the telling subtitle: "The Gang of Do-Gooders." It was a personal castigation of the Berditchev city fathers and caused some of them great material harm. They retaliated by making life intolerable for Mendele, and in 1871 he left for Zhitomir, where he entered the rabbinical school. Communal leaders continued to be hos-

---

* All titles followed by an asterisk have English translations and are listed in Bibliography.

tile and prevented him from obtaining a rabbinical post upon graduation. Up to that time he was assisted financially by his sympathetic father-in-law; when the latter became impoverished, Mendele had to live in precarious penury, as income from his writings was negligible and his work as translator yielded him little.

While in Zhitomir he wrote *The Kliatche* * (Dobbin) or "Compassion for the Living" in 1873, and *The Travels and Adventures of Benjamin III* * five years later. Both were very favorably received, but his income remained minimal. Later he confided to his friend Dubnow: "My expenses were large, having a family of seven. My income from books did not even suffice for house rent. . . . It came to a point where I wasn't sure of the next day." Fortunately, Baron Horace Ginsburg, who had known him in Kamenetz and admired his work, came to his financial assistance with a monthly stipend until 1881, when Mendele was engaged as the principal of a Jewish school in Odessa. There he remained to the end of his life, assured of a steady, if limited, income.

From 1878 to 1883 his pen was idle. Only in 1884, when he was honored on his 25 years as a writer, did he publish a Yiddish adaptation of Leon Pinsker's *Autoemancipation,* and *The Draft,* a middling drama depicting the evils connected with enforced army service—with the rich as villains, and the moralizing showing through the dramatic veneer. In the preface he suggested the reason for his long silence:

> The sorrows of recent years [culminating in the massacres of 1881] have petrified my heart, so that my tongue could not speak nor my hand write a single line. It was a silence which, if it grips a person in anguish, costs more in life and health than the shedding of bloody tears. And if it persists for a time without relief, it endangers one's very existence. . . .

He also had more personal reasons for reticence. First his daughter Rachel, of whom he was very fond, died at the age of 18. Then his only son Michael was arrested on political charges and exiled to Siberia. There he lived with a Russian girl but did not marry her, as he could not do so without first accepting Christianity. Later he was compelled to apostatize in order to enter his children in the local school—an event which deeply aggravated Mendele's Jewish consciousness. To a friend he confided late in 1881: "I feel a rent in my heart that will never heal." Later he wrote to Sholom Aleichem: "There are times when melancholy overwhelms me and I sit alone, pensive, worried, isolated, and silent." Nor was his new position without serious drawbacks. To the same friend he stated:

> The work absorbs my entire time, leaving me not a free minute for anything but my cursed position. In my old age I've become a kind of "dobbin." . . . To be a dobbin with a sensitive soul and human nature—ah, that is a hellish pain. A hundred times more fortunate is he who has the appearance of a human being and the nature of a dobbin. . . . Ah, my dear friend, my strength ebbs in the increasing struggle for existence! The world of my ideals is slowly sinking in a fog, and reality is dark and sad.

Once the personal pain subsided, however, he managed to throw off his depression and find leisure for his writing. "A fresh flow of warm feeling" enabled him to begin rewriting *Fishke the Lame, The Dobbin*, and *The Magic Ring*—purifying the style, softening the didactic approach, enlarging the thematic motivation, and greatly expanding the treatment. The *Ring*, for instance, was extended from its original 42 pages to 400. His critical acuteness was at its maturest intensity. "The greatest art," he declared, "lies in that which one does *not* say." To Joseph Klausner he wrote:

> To be a writer one must first be a *murderer*. The writer thinks he has composed some beautiful things; only they are not pertinent to the main theme. Yet he feels sorry. Oh, it's a shame to erase it: it is so beautiful! And I tell him: "Have no pity!" One must be obdurate and erase! *Erase without pity* all the pretty phrases and expressions and descriptions which are not needed for the work. . . . Only such obduracy make the writer worthy of the name.

Mendele practiced what he preached with merciless zeal.

He also translated his Yiddish writings into Hebrew, which

he continued to prize highly, simultaneously reworking the content to suit the new medium. In the process he so improved the diction and style of the current Hebrew that younger writers in that language used him as a model. It seemed that in polishing and purifying his Yiddish he had also learned how to employ the Hebrew of the prophets with greater freedom and pliability. In 1900 a Hebrew edition of his major writings came from the press. Yet he continued to cherish Yiddish, and in 1904 wrote critically to Sholom Aleichem: "In God's name do not call the Yiddish language 'Jargon'; you hear, 'Jargon' is shameful. I hate 'Jargon'! Do you understand?"

His last major work, the autobiographical and beautifully written *Shlome Reb Khaim's*, appeared in 1899. Yet he continued to use his trenchant pen to the end of his life, and his stories and articles graced the pages of various periodicals. Each occurrence of significance to the Jewish people, whether joyous or sorrowful, found him ready to share or solace. In 1903 the Kishinev pogrom deeply depressed him. "I am constantly angry," he wrote to Dubnow. "My spirit is agitated, and I often lament quietly over the tragedy of my people." Four years later, while in Switzerland, he was asked to contribute to the socialist *Folkzeitung*. He regretfully refused because the 1905 massacres had so distressed him that he could no longer write with mere intimation and innuendo, and knew that his forthright expression would send him to exile in Siberia.

> If I should now write, my heart would flare and my blood would boil. . . . I must not do this, as I cannot remain an emigrant and I am too old for exile. . . . I, an old man, have in the days of the pogrom in Odessa hid in the janitor's pigsty. Like a pig I lay hidden! Instead of taking hold of an axe and splitting their heads —I crawled away and hid for days—like a pig! I cannot write about that! If I should sit down to write I would not be able to keep from writing something that would become my "act of accusation" to send me to exile.

When, at about that time, he was invited to visit the United States, of which he had a low opinion owing to the pirating of his books by irresponsible publishers in New York, he retorted: "What have I to do with the rich, with dollars? I must return to Russia, to my home, to my poor. I still have much to do."

The celebration of his (approximately) 75th birthday in 1909 was a folk holiday wherever Yiddish was being read. In city after city he was warmly honored. What pleased him most was the homage paid him by Jewish baggage porters at railroad stations. The chief celebration occurred in Odessa, where he was greeted by the leading Jewish writers and intellectuals, among them Bialik and Frug. He responded:

> Our sages have said that a Jew has two souls, a weekday one and a holy one. Our Hebrew language is the holy one, a holy and pure language, in which the world is seen as in a mirror, and which is as old as the world and whose spring will never run dry. The other language is the weekday one, of pain and suffering, as sad as the Jewish soul is during the week. And these two souls, these two languages, which I have to thank for your presence today, I would not want to exchange for another language.

On this occasion his fellow writers presented him with this "word bouquet."

> You are the first to have concentrated in both Yiddish and Hebrew the total creative power of the Jews in past generations —and made both new languages; and you are the first to give us in both languages the artistic story and narrative with the accent which has become the Mendele stamp. No writer today is free from your influence, none who did not attend your school.

During his final three years, after a life of physical vigor, he suffered from eczema and subsequently from general debility. A mild stroke temporarily paralyzed his left side. The war beginning in 1914 saddened him grievously. To Bialik he remarked in 1916: "The sickness of the soul is much worse than the sickness of the body." A year later he died.

Mendele took life earnestly, and nothing in his purview left him unaffected. A pious Jew—he remained religious to the end of his life—and an intellectual reformer, he felt impelled to right wrongs as he saw them. Because he came on the verge of social transition from medieval orthodoxy to an acquiescence in modern rationalism—when encrusted superstitions and obsolescent dogmas cried for exposure and removal—he was all the more eager to hasten the transformation for the greater good of the people. With his double-edged sword of satire and stricture he struck at social stagnancy and the evils it engendered.

Like other Jewish intellectuals of his generation he knew only too well the deplorable conditions which kept the mass of Jews in misery and wretchedness; but he also had what many of his fellow reformers lacked—the abundant good sense to know that "no dance comes before the feast." While others assumed that education and assimilation were the panacea for all social ills, Mendele concentrated on economic amelioration. One of his prominent characters exclaimed: "With what right would you deprive one from eating, breathing, until he has learned some trick? Each being at its birth is first of all a living thing, provided by nature with all the senses and with a complete body primarily to get for itself the necessities of life." Much as he appreciated the benefits of education, devoting much time and thought to its improvement, he maintained that once the Jews were relieved of their enervating and degrading poverty they would relish reforms as a matter of course. He therefore dedicated himself to the exposure and elimination of endemic indigence among his fellow Jews.

The satirist is intrinsically a moralist. In Mendele's early writings the didactic intent dominated, at times protruding itself with insistent obviousness. Art for its own sake was never completely absent from his stories—a temptation he could not wholly repress—but more important to him was the need of reform. Weker, the intellectual in *The Meat Tax*, exclaimed: "At a time when our people, our poor people, suffer in Babylon, break the strings of the Jewish violin. Jews were not born to sing, to play . . . graver matters must occupy their minds." In his later work, however, aware that reforms were taking effect, his didactic tone lessened markedly until it was wholly absent in *Shlome Reb Khaim's*, giving way to the artist luxuriating in truth and beauty.

The Meat Tax was his most effective call for social awakening among Russian Jews. Weker was the first social propagandist in Yiddish literature. With the voice of Mendele, through the mouth of Weker, sanctimonious city fathers who thrived upon the high tax levied upon kosher meat were savagely excoriated—exposed in all their greed and hypocrisy, in all their smug selfishness. Speaking through Weker, he called upon the people to join him in the attack:

> No, my patience is at an end. I can endure it no longer! Cursed be he who sees such evils and is silent! Cursed be the coward who fears to speak the truth! Cursed be he who stops his ears not to hear the cries and sighs of the unfortunate, of the insulted and the needy; cursed, execrated be all who sell their conscience, all who are able to help with a word, with the pen, and yet stand aloof for fear of a slight hurt.

So forceful was this exposure of a common and grievous evil that it went far to indict its perpetrators and bring relief to those it victimized. Like *Uncle Tom's Cabin*, the play became a battle cry and an effective weapon in the hands of reformers.

Even as *The Meat Tax* awakened the social consciousness of the Russian Jews, *The Dobbin* stirred their national spirit. Mendele wrote it at white heat, completing the first draft in three weeks. He intended it, according to Dinesohn, "especially for the intelligent public, for the educated, who could understand his meaning and perceive his intent and connotation." In this allegory the Jews are shown as a composite whole, face to face with the outside world. He presents them as a scurvy horse who was once a prince but had become bewitched as a dobbin. The poor beast talks to the deranged Isroel, his current master, with an understanding and pathos that make one aware of the contrast between the princely soul and the emaciated brute, of the true nature of his wretched status.

Here Mendele satirizes, ridicules, moralizes, philosophizes.

In the monologues which make up most of the book he criticizes the condition of Jewish life; he scorns stupidity, excoriates hypocrisy, and condemns greed, war, and brutality. Throughout he mingles fantasy with fact. He has Isroel say: "People know, never fear, that riches are rubbish; here today, gone tomorrow. But the man of culture, of learning—why, he is the very symbol of gold." The dobbin, however, takes no comfort in philosophy, moralizing, or fatuous sympathy. "I do not want to hear of pity, of usefulness; I am like other living beings—like them I have the right to live."

Thus far the reformer had predominated in Mendele. He coated his propaganda with a palatable narrative to make it more acceptable. In the 1880's, however, with reforms taking root and his own artistic development reaching maturity, his interest in the esthetics of writing became paramount. Not that he favored art for art's sake. In a letter to Sholom Aleichem toward the end of the decade he declared: "I demand that besides being beautiful a portrait should also have life, mind, and spirit, as that of a living person; in addition to fine rhetoric a description ought also to contain real thought."

The Draft was a transitional work, with his art and moralizing quite well balanced. The theme stresses the evil of a system in which young men are torn from their wives and betrothed, from their homes and studies, and sent to some distant part of Russia to suffer the strict regimen of army life. Character portrayal is not neglected, however. Although the protagonist lacks the vivid forcefulness of artistic insight, the minor characters are skillfully drawn and move with verve and vitality. The polish and sparkle of his prose are also notable, giving evidence of a style at once rugged and refined.

The final version of *The Magic Ring*, written in 1888 for Sholom Aleichem's *Yiddish Folk Bibliotek*, emerged as a work of high literary achievement. To Sholom Aleichem he wrote:

Under the name of one of my old brief works of a few pages I have begun to write for you a *completely* new book in which I shall present Jewish life and the important problems confronting us. I wish to delineate sharply the Jewish position and show how it may be improved. . . . *The Magic Ring* is not a mere story, the kind others are now writing. It is not a doll to play with, but a living creation with blood, a soul, human feelings, and human face.

Containing little moralizing, the book describes Jewish life of that time with a breadth of view and sympathetic insight unsurpassed by any other Yiddish writer. Almost every type of Jew sits for his portrait, and Mendele draws them with Rembrandtian ruggedness and power. In his preface he stated: "To influence a people one has to be bone of their bone, flesh of their flesh; one has to have suffered their sorrows and felt their pain." Having experienced all this with the sensitiveness of the true artist, he succeeded in exerting an influence greater than any of his contemporaries. More than in his other writings, this one excelled in the description of nature, the delineation of mass psychology, and the delicate harmony of content and form.

In the preface to *Shlome Reb Khaim's*, the unfinished memoir of his youth which was his final major work, Mendele expressed his mature view of his people:

> The life of the Jewish people may appear ugly externally, but it is beautiful inwardly. A strong spirit possesses them, a heavenly spirit which always blows like a wind and lifts the waves in order to wash away the filth and foulness. The thunder and lightning, the pogroms and storms, that befell them, served to cleanse them and give them new strength. The Jewish people are like the old Greek philosopher Diogenes, their heads high in the sky, fully conscious of God's greatness, and themselves living among the nations of the world, as he in his barrel, crowded in narrow quarters. Under the piles of dirt in *kheders,* yeshivas, and synagogues glows the flame of the Torah and spreads light and warmth to all mankind. All our children, poor and rich, short and tall, study and know its content.

The book depicts the beautiful phase of ghetto life: the expansive religious spirit of otherwise wretched beings. His parents and townsmen are drawn with unforgettable charm.

It was as if he had said to himself: "In my young manhood, when it was necessary, I gave all that was in me in the effort to improve the lot of my people. Now, when I am old and without the vigor of youth, and when I am no longer needed in the front ranks of reform, I shall allow myself the leisure to write for my own pleasure." This indulgence, permitting him to reminisce at length, gave the book historic value in addition to artistic superiority. Its descriptions of synagogue life, Jewish trades and occupations, clothing and home furnishing, the Sabbath and holiday spirit, celebrations and woes, and other aspects of the Jewish milieu in the early decades of the 19th century are presented with the ethnic accuracy of the social historian and the sympathetic insight of the novelist.

Mendele's satire and mordant humor, his moralizing and his art, are most characteristically evident in *Fishke the Lame* and *The Travels and Adventures of Benjamin III*. Like most of his books, the final version of *Fishke* is not technically a novel. Dichotomous in structure and heterogeneous in development, it is rather what the subtitle connotes. "A Story of the Jewish Poor." It is also a veritable epic of the Jewish vagabond-beggars who crowded local poorhouses and depended upon alms for their existence. Having personally experienced life in their midst during his impressionable youth, he later wrote: "All my life I hated the Jewish beggar-bag; that is why I described it so critically." In the preface to Fishke he stated: "I always have to deal with the poor, the paupers, the unfortunates. . . . I dream only of beggars. Before my eyes there always hovers a beggar-bag—the huge, old Jewish bag. . . . No matter what I wish to say or write, I can't help thinking of the beggar-bag." Some time later he explained that "when Sholom Aleichem writes something comical he laughs at it with all his heart. And I—my heart aches on such occasions. When one tells a witticism, others laugh, not the wit. And I— I weep, I do not laugh. I did not write *Fishke the Lame* as something to laugh at."

Mendele's intuitive empathy gave him a profound insight

into the complex character of the average Jew. He knew that endemic poverty and constant precariousness were more potent in subjecting him to his medieval stagnancy than the combination of all other social and religious factors; that continued economic want at once stimulated his senses and made him slothful. One of his characters thus philosophizes about his indigence:

> Want rouses me from my bed, want keeps me on my feet, want compels me to ride my horse, and want beats me in the neck and moves me from place to place. . . . Only the first move is difficult for the Jew. Once started, he glides as if greased; he crawls even where it is not necessary, where he is not wanted; he even climbs straight walls. . . . A Jew lives on the go. Want compels him to run, to bustle to act, to work; let this want be slackened the least bit and he becomes passive and inert.

Anxious to have these indigent Jews see their wretched existence as he saw it, and recoil from their social and religious excrescences as he did, he described their poverty satirically, even harshly. He attacked the poorhouse in particular because it had become one of the venerable institutions of the Jewish town, a sop to the social conscience of the benevolent. To men, women, and children inured to crowding the streets and public places with hands outstretched, the poorhouse was a shelter as well as a social center. In the middle decades of the 19th century, when poverty was particularly acute, hordes traveled from town to town in regular circuits, as he himself had unwittingly done with Abraham the Lame, and not a few resorted to thievery and vandalism. In *Fishke* he depicts penetratingly the state of beggary as he found it in the synagogue court, the public bathhouse, the poorhouse, and on the outskirts of each settlement. The following description of a poorhouse is a random example:

> When I only think of it, my skin begins to itch and I must scratch myself. It looked like a very ancient inn: now a shanty with crooked, sagging walls, and with a roof like a battered felt hat, cocked in front and almost reaching the ground in the rear. One

could easily see that this poorhouse was about to tumble down, that it was ready to crumble into a heap of refuse; but the towns-people have driven this intent away, and have forcibly gained its consent to be propped up by branches and a post or two, and thus to remain standing for years on end.

Through an imaginary gate one enters into a large anteroom. The crevices in the walls and the fallen plaster permit the light of day to enter. The earthen floor has numerous pits, some filled with garbage slop and sending forth a deadly odor, others with rainwater which trickles through the thinned, sievelike thatch. Rotten, foot-trodden straw is scattered everywhere, mixed with all kinds of junk: torn beggar-bags, discarded straw leggings, decayed shoetops, old soles and wornout heels with rusty nails, earthen scraps, broken wheel bands, wheel spokes, hair, bones, broom straws, and the like. This rubbish emits a composite odor that staggers the newcomer. To the left of the hallway a filthy door opens unwelcomely on rasping hinges into the main room. The small, narrow windows are paned partly with glass and partly with greased paper, and some are stuffed only with rags; all are very dirty, with moldy corners, and covered with aged, yellow-green and crazily sparking colors that stab the eye as a scratch on glass grates on one's ear. About the plaster-cracked walls, near a large brick stove, are long, narrow benches, and over them are hooks of various sizes. From the grimy ceiling several ropes support long, narrow poles. The hooks and poles are covered with coats, skirts, and numerous other garments, as well as beggar-bags belonging to those who came here on foot or in wagon loads, and who remain together in this room, young and old, husbands and wives.

The effect of these descriptions on his readers, many of whom supported such and similar eleemosynary institutions, was enormous, as they suddenly perceived their presumed philanthropy in all its repelling ugliness. They felt impelled to remove the social scabs and heal the sores that disfigured the civic organism of which they were a part.

Fishke's canvas is large, the portraits in it are lifesize and animated. Of special significance is Mendele's verbal skill in depicting the love that united two cripples, Fishke and Anna. The grim realistic background heightens their almost idyllic affection. Ordinarily it would be rather questionable that an abject drudge like Fishke, whose appearance is repulsive, whose esthetic sense is nil, whose thoughts are fragmentary and incoherent, and who married a blind beggar girl because her misfortune would bring them more than average alms, could be capable of pure and ardent love; the like doubt pertained to the sloppy, ragged, homely, meek, hunchbacked Anna. The mere expression of love on the part of these two vagrants was risking the cliché of vapid sentimentality. Yet their affection is developed into a passion pure and potent, found only in romantic poetry. Their relationship is depicted with such masterly simplicity and profound naturalness that we become aware not of their ungainly exteriors but of the genuineness of their feeling and devotion. Their excessive suffering in consequence of their clandestine meetings cannot but intensify our sympathy with their unhappiness. The following passage, Fishke's unaffected reply to those who make mock of his love for Anna, reveals Mendele's art:

Why should I deny it? I first began to love her out of great pity, later for herself. Something drew me to her: I gained life from sometimes sitting and chatting with her. . . . What? nothing. Just so. Either chat or be silent and gaze at one another. A goodness lay over her face. Her looking at me was like that of a devoted sister upon an unfortunate brother at a time when he feels ill, very ill; and taking my sorrows to herself, tears would appear in her eyes. Then I felt as if a warm balsam was flowing through my body. I thought—I don't know myself what. Something glowed within me, petted my soul: "Fishke, you are no longer alone in this great world, no longer as lonely as a cliff," and hot sudden tears wetted my eyes. . . .

Mendele also wrote some excellent natural description in *Fishke*. Even in *The Dobbin* his love of the outdoor world had cried for expression: "Something impels my soul, a yearning, a desire—to stroll is my whole life. In the field, in the forest, I am not at all what I am in the city. I feel free, released from the yoke. . . . I imbibe joy, I swoon with pleasure at the work of Him above, and I yield with all my senses and become immersed in God's beautiful world." The intent reformer tried to repress this love of the outdoors, but the poet in him refused to be silenced. Later he yielded more and more to this "evil" impulse, and in *Fishke* he enjoyed doing so. "The evil one brings to my nose the pleasant odors of fresh hay, plants, and vegetables, smells that fill my being. He has song birds sing tunes that tickle my soul. He makes a warm breeze play on my face, shake my earlocks, and whisper in my ears: Look, enjoy yourself like a human being, you foolish Jew!" And Mendele did—and told what he saw and how he felt. This often verged on lyric poetry.

In naming his book *The Travels and Adventures of Benjamin III*, Mendele was humorously associating his mock-hero with Benjamin of Tudela, the noted traveler in the 12th century, and with the Moldavian Benjamin who had visited Asia and Africa in the 1840's. The satire, according to Mark Wiener, was written as a caustic criticism of "the crippling degeneracy of the relation of the Jews to reality, of their estrangement from the world, of their stupid isolation from their surroundings." The work abounds in irrepressible humor, for Mendele was, at the time he wrote it, at the height of his powers and able to accomplish his critical intent with laughter rather than moralizing.

The Zionist idea in the late 1870's was a nebulous and mystic longing of the orthodox Jews, who regularly prayed for return to the Jerusalem of David and Solomon. They firmly believed in the eventual advent of the Messiah, who would blow on the ram's horn, gather the children of Israel from the four corners of the earth, and bring them into the land of their forefathers —where every man will sit under his fig tree and milk and honey will flow in streams. Underfed scholiasts, steeped in Hebrew lore, disputed among themselves as to the exact location of the Ten Lost Tribes, the "red Jews" whose powerful kingdom lay behind the mythical Symbatyon River and only waited for the signal to overpower the Turks and wrest Palestine from them.

Mendele was painfully aware that these reveries and seductive fantasies were an unconscious effort to ward off deep despair; in the struggle to survive in the midst of deplorable poverty, a lack of sophistication became a saving factor. One of his characters, when asked how he earned his living, replies artlessly:

> His Name be praised, I have as you see a present from His beloved Name, an instrument—a voice to sing; so I am often engaged as cantor in the synagogue. I am one of the best *mohels* [ritual circumciser] and matzoh-makers in the world; I am also a marriage broker—sometimes successfully; I have, between us and the lamppost, a blind still which yields me a little something; nor is a goat lacking to me, which, without an evil eye, gives some milk; and not far from here I have a well-to-do relative who helps me out when in need. But besides all these things, I assure you that the Lord is a Father and the Jews are very compassionate, and there is no need to complain.

Mendele knew that in such dire circumstances men must have deep faith to persist, that they cherished the idea of the Messiah as a veritable godsend. He wished, however, to eliminate this form of escape and make them face the world realistically and seek economic equality with other peoples. To this end he sought to expose the folly of foolish revery. His Benjamin is depicted as an extreme yet not uncommon representative of the synagogue habitués: a man steeped in lore learning with his mind enmeshed in its myths and legends, among them the existence of the "red Jews." His fantasy in time becomes surcharged with a desire to reach these lost tribes and give them the signal for the salvation of the Jews in the Diaspora. He is described as a young married man who lives in an unending daydream, possessed of an irresistible desire to perform great deeds, to achieve the liberation of Israel. Unlike his great prototype Don Quixote, however, he is merely a parody of a hero: timid, cowardly, gullible, and grotesque. He further differs from the Spanish knight, who was completely unlike his neighbors, in being merely a more extreme representative of the synagogue Talmudists.

Benjamin's plans for the pilgrimage having come to a head, he makes several trips to a nearby forest to experiment with the unknown. The sight of a woodcutter in the distance makes him almost faint from fear, but he bravely persists in his quest. For his companion he chooses Sanderel "the woman," an ignorant, meek, foolish man who earned his sobriquet by attending to the household chores while his wife earned their pitiable living, a man with no will of his own who always agreed with what people told him.

Escaping one day from their wives, the two set out on their perilous mission, taking with them their prayer shawls and philacteries—and a beggar-bag. Never having been away from their native town, they find everything wondrous strange and deeply fearful. Benjamin interprets things to be as foretold in the books he has read. The first village he comes to seems to him bordering the end of the earth, and the nearby river he takes for a raging ocean. He does not hesitate to disclose his mission to the Jews he meets, and some believe him inspired. After various incidents during their brief peregrination (of a petty nature but magnified by Benjamin into hair-raising escapades), the two adventurers are ingloriously returned home.

Benjamin is a work of gentle satire. It ridicules the Jews of the medievally oriented towns for their persistent dreams of salvation by a mythical Messiah. Written in a style at once exact and luminous, the narrative is charged with a hilarious humor that mocks to scorn the myths it exposes. The reader finds in it, in the words of Niger, "not an ordinary view of life but a slice of life seen in the crooked mirror of caricature." The symbolic significance of the two characters—Benjamin as a parody on the Talmudic daydreamer and Sanderel as a satire on the meekness of the mass of Jews—emerge conspicuously and effectively. Jews laughed merrily at the grotesque behavior of Benjamin and Sanderel, but also perceived the large element of truth in their exaggerated reveries and credulities.

Mendele the Bookseller was the first Yiddish writer to give the speech of "the servant girl and tailor apprentice" the prestige of a literary language. Out of the crude and conventionalized dialect he created verbal nuances of expression its detractors had insisted it could never have. His artistic intuition directed him unerringly in making the idiomatic speech of the masses the basis of a diction capable of voicing the subtlest feelings and thoughts. His phraseology was so expansive and exact, especially in his revisions and later writings, that even critics of Yiddish had to admire its freshness and freedom. So rapidly, however, has the language advanced in the work of the writers who came after him that many contemporary readers require a glossary to get the full meaning of the obsolescent terms in his books.

Generally acknowledged as the foremost Yiddish satirist, he has given Yiddish readers a full and unforgettable depiction of orthodox Jewish life. Khaim Zhitlovsky, the astute publicist, pointed out: "Mendele's talent was forged at a time when *Kahal* [communal self-rule] still governed Jewish minds, when the masses were stuck in swamps of ignorance, inhuman poverty, neglect, absolute estrangement from the outside world without a basis for a decent living." *Kahal* was an integral part of his own life, and he portrayed it accurately and critically, yet with a sympathy that penetrated the heart of the reader.

Highly admired as the classic "grandfather" of modern Yiddish literature, Mendele became a literary tradition long before he reached old age. His fictional technique, more that of the moralist than of the novelist and flawed with some of the characteristics and mannerisms of timeworn convention, appears antiquated and obsolescent to the modern reader. By the time he died intellectual Jews, stimulated by his efforts, had attained an esthetic sophistication far exceeding his own. Consequently, his stories and satire, while of classic merit and great historic interest, have become rather remote in theme and treatment. His memory is honored, but he is seldom read.

CHAPTER THREE

SHOLOM ALEICHEM

A Humorist of Veritable Greatness

"SHOLOM ALEICHEM" (peace be unto you) is a common expression of greeting among Hebrew or Yiddish speaking Jews. In the 20th century the phrase has also become synonymous with the pen name of Sholom Rabinovitch, the most beloved Yiddish author. The mere mention of this pseudonym exudes a delight quite excluding any other connotation.

Until recent years Sholom Aleichem's writings were little known to non-Yiddish readers. A genuine humorist, his style is intrinsically idiomatic and his subject-matter intimately and exotically Jewish, so that much of the allusion and gaiety of his stories inevitably evaporates in translation. In Eastern Europe some of his works have appeared in several languages, and more recently a good part of his writing has become available in English; although even the most successful translation has failed to overcome completely the barriers of complex idioms and an eccentric milieu, enough of his ebullient humor has percolated through to reveal his greatness as a writer.

Sholom Rabinovitch—his early years are depicted in *From the Fair* (1916; *The Great Fair,* * in English, 1955) was born in March, 1859, in Pereyaslev, a town in the Poltava province. His father was "a tall man, with a forever-worried face, a broad-wrinkled forehead, a sparse finely formed beard. He was pious and sagacious, knew Hebrew, played chess, was a connoisseur of pearls and diamonds, and was considered the richest man in town." His mother, a frail little woman, was of the tribe of Amazons; she was "a fast worker and managed the general store." The family lived in Voronkov, a nearby village, during Sholom's childhood, and there he gained his first impressions of what later became the basis for much of his writing. Voronkov he later described as "very small" but with material for "many beautiful stories and legends."

From early youth an avid lover of tales, he was readily influenced by Shmielek, his story-concocting playmate, whom he paid with delicacies for yarns invented in the process of narration. Typical was the story of the Voronkov treasure, presumably hidden by the cruel kossak Bogdan Khmelnitski.

> Don't you know Khmelnitski? What a child you are! Khmelnitski was a bad man, a regular Haman even before Khmelnitski's time [a Yiddish saying exploited for its humor]; even a babe knows that! This Khmelnitski, this evil one, this Haman, had robbed the rich Poles and Jews of billions of rubles and brought them all to us, to Voronkov. Here he buried the treasure one night on the other side of the cemetery by the light of the moon, hid it so that no man should ever find it.

Sholom early developed a talent "to copy, to imitate, to mimic. . . . To grasp the ridiculous in everything and everyone: that was almost a disease with me." His mimicry amused bystanders and embarrassed his parents. Quick of mind and motion, charged with juvenile wit, blessed with a vivid imagination and a retentive memory, he soon knew the life of the townspeople to the minutest detail.

This blissful period of his childhood ended when his father became financially distressed owing to a partner's dishonesty. On the verge of bankruptcy, he moved the family back to Pereyaslev to operate an inn. Too young to be shaken by economic vicissitude, Sholom welcomed the change, which to him meant the conquest of a new world.

At the age of 12 he began to read current Hebrew writings.

After perusal of Abraham Mapu's *Love of Zion,* he concocted a similar story and called it *The Daughters of Zion.* A little later, having read a Hebrew translation of *Robinson Crusoe,* he composed an account of a Jewish Crusoe. He was also beginning to feel the charm of feminine pulchritude, and a juvenile passion agitated him before he was 14.

The death of his frail mother and his father's remarriage to a shrewish woman from Berditchev, whose complaints and numerous curses he soon listed alphabetically with great relish, extending them to several pages, hastened his maturity. His father, pleased with his literary efforts, sent him to a government school, where he studied Russian and secular subjects. His curiosity was unappeasable, and he scrutinized and analyzed whatever he saw. He observed the numerous cantors and musicians who patronized his father's hostelry—attending their rehearsals, eavesdropping upon their talk and confidences. Later they furnished the themes of *Yosele Solovey* and *Stempenu,* two of his early novels.

Two years after his first infatuation he became enamored of the attractive daughter of a cantor, courting her with artless persistence. When he believed himself on the verge of success, the girl suddenly eloped with a Russian youth. The shame and shock aggravated a coincidental illness. When he finally recovered, he found himself a mature man.

At the age of 17 he obtained employment as a teacher in a nearby village, but a semester in the school yielded only aggravation and discontent. Soon, however, chance brought him a tutorship to the daughter of a wealthy provincial Jew. With this family he remained three years, a period of enjoyable self-advancement and personal gratification. His employer managed to free him from military service. Somewhat later, when the father discovered a growing affection between tutor and pupil, Sholom was abruptly dismissed. A brief sojourn in Kiev ended in the loss of his savings and forced deportation to his native Pereyaslev.

Several months later he became a government rabbi in Lubni, a nearby town, a position he kept until 1883. Having continued to write Hebrew prose while tutoring, he published his first piece in 1879 and several other sketches not long after. When he learned of the existence of Tzederboim's *Yiddish Folksblatt,* he decided to submit some recent compositions in Yiddish; in 1883 this was still an act of daring on the part of an intellectual and a rabbi. Yet the urge to write in the language he knew best, and employed by his much-admired Mendele, was irresistible. He remembered how his father, surrounded by friends, had read a Yiddish story which made everyone laugh to tears, and he resolved to write similar humor for Yiddish readers. He rejected such criticism as that of the highly esteemed poet, I. L. Gordon, who as late as 1888 chastised him for favoring Yiddish: "It is a badge of shame of the driven wanderer, and I have always considered it as the duty of every educated Jew to see to it that the dialect should gradually disappear from our midst."

He was greatly encouraged when Tzederboim published his stories. To please his father and father-in-law, both of whom preferred that he write in Hebrew, he employed the pseudonym of Sholom Aleichem. S. Dubnow's praise of "The Pocketknife" elated him, Dubnow then being the forthright and highly regarded "Criticus." "Who knows?" he stated later. "If he had been critical, I might never have tried to write again." This story was indeed a special event in the rise of Yiddish literature. The feelings and reactions of a Jewish boy to his cherished possession was described with a simplicity of diction and humorous pathos never before seen in that commonly contemned "Jargon."

Somewhat earlier the father of his former pupil, realizing his daughter's persistent love for Sholom, had acquiesced in their marriage. Sholom engaged in business to make a living, but the urge to write remained irrepressible. In one letter he stated somewhat later: "Solomon Rabinovitch is for four hours a day a wheeler-dealer ·on the bourse, almost an ace, praised be His Name. But from about five in the afternoon until three or four in the morning I am Sholom Aleichem." He wrote a good deal, much of it satirical and moralistic. Yet he lacked the didactic impulse of most of his contemporaries, finding it more natural to be humorous. Later, still criticized for treating serious subjects lightly, he commented: "What shall I do when laughing is a kind of sickness with me since childhood?" To his friend Y. H. Ravnitsky he explained in 1886 that his forte was both to mock and amuse, but to mock lovingly, sympathetically.

His father-in-law's death in 1885 made him a man of wealth. He continued his activity on the Kiev bourse, but paid more attention to literary matters. He had started a correspondence, largely onesided, with Mendele, whom he greatly admired and addressed as "grandfather." In 1884, on Mendele's 25th anniversary as a writer, he informed the older man that he was "an admirer who works in the same field that you have plowed, and follows largely and deliberately in your traces, which you have left so sharply in the field of our Jargonic literature." In addition to doing much writing, completing *Sender Blank* and numerous shorter pieces of fiction, he was deeply interested in the work and condition of other Yiddish writers.

The popularity of Shomer and his imitators, whose lurid fiction Sholom Aleichem considered hurtful to the literary taste of their naive and uneducated readers, compelled him to condemn them in *Shomer on Trial* (1888). He was particularly critical of their emphasis on sensational and spurious plots and urged instead "portrayals familiar to us, of which we have an idea, which probably can happen in real life . . . not like Shomer's, which become fantastic, so that a poor teacher becomes a lord, a chimney sweep becomes a count, the dead come to life and the living die . . . diamonds worth millions lie in the sweepings." Most of all he wished to encourage better Yiddish writers by publishing their work at generous fees and thereby furthering the development of Yiddish literature.

In 1888 he arranged to publish his *Yiddish Folk Bibliotek*, an anthology of specimens from the best writers. He paid relatively high fees for contributions, among them Mendele's revised *The Magic Ring* and I. L. Peretz's "Monish." His own *Stempenu* * was included, a sentimentally appealing story of Jewish musicians, treating sympathetically and with soft humor the haphazard and hard life of a fine violinist. In the same year his novel *Sender Blank*, a satirical portrayal of Jewish newly rich characterized by cultural emptiness and bourgeois greed, was serialized in *Yiddish Folksblatt*. A second volume of his anthology appeared in 1889 with a similar cast of contributors. It also included his novel, *Yosele Solovey*, which represented another phase of artistry within the Jewish milieu—singers who sweetened the synagogue services. Its rich humorous prose underlined the pathos of their often thwarted lives.

In 1890 the Kiev bourse relieved Sholom Aleichem of his wealth. In consequence of his bankruptcy he had to flee abroad to avoid imprisonment. To Dubnow he wrote: "Your broken friend . . . slipped and lost himself, lost to the world of gold and paper." When his affairs were settled through the aid of his mother-in-law, he returned to Russia and resided for a time in Odessa, where he sought to earn his living as a stock and insurance broker. While thus occupied he observed the numerous ne'er-do-wells who, much like himself, were building dream castles and going hungry. In 1892 he wrote "London!"—the first of the remarkable exchange of letters between Menachem Mendel, the luckless but irrepressible speculator, and his wife Shayne Shayndel, the earthy, commonsensical villager who considered the city a cesspool of iniquity.

In 1893 Sholom Aleichem returned to Kiev, where he began anew to seek his livelihood on the stock exchange. He remained primarily a writer, however, and by 1903 permanently forsook the marketplace. Writing became his whole life, and he worked at it with enthusiasm and great care. He wrote fast, but rewrote again and again, and so complete was his concentrated effort that he sometimes bit his nails until his fingers bled.

He soon became the central figure in the Jewish literary

group of Kiev. Forced to depend upon his writing as a source of income, he fared badly materially, but his stories were highly popular and he was hailed everywhere as a folk hero and drawn into various Jewish affairs. Among other things, in 1903 he helped Maxim Gorki edit a Russian anthology of Yiddish writings—which the censor kept from publication. Young authors found him a generous friend and adviser. With them in mind, but no doubt thinking of himself as a conspicuous example, he complained that "not one of our writers earns his living from his pen." While avoiding dependence on the wealthy Jews of Kiev, he hoped in vain for a maecenas to relieve his poverty. When sick and in need, he wrote caustically about unethical publishers and the indifferent rich.

The massacres of 1905—he and his family had to hide to escape the Kiev *hooligans*—drove him from Russia. He sojourned in Switzerland, and visited London and New York. While in the United States he was urged to talk at meetings about the pogroms to accelerate collection of funds for victims, but he refused. "I read only my work . . . and the audience laughed heartily, lost a tear incidentally, and that was most important." On his return to Europe he gave similar readings in a number of the larger cities. While in Baronovici he became very ill, and doctors urged him to go to Nervi, Italy, to recuperate. Feeling downcast and without funds, he wrote to his friend M. Spector: "You can well imagine how I feel. At a time when there, in my beloved home, Jews are enjoying my holiday [his 25th anniversary as a writer was widely celebrated], I am here alone, sick, isolated, woebegone, and I weep. . . ." His frustrated dealings with grasping publishers and callous theatrical managers only added to his discouragement. Writing to I. Zevin of the New York *Tageblatt*, he deplored the vulgarity of the men who controlled the Yiddish theater: "At the moment I feel that the bargaining [over one of his plays] is like that concerning an ox. They want to buy an ox most cheaply, and they see to it that not only the meat, but the fat of the ox, and even the pelt alone, should be worth the price." His devoted friends finally arranged to repurchase the copyrights of his books, and issued a collected edition with himself as beneficiary.

From 1908 until 1914 he lived in Italy as often as he could in order to take advantage of the salubrious climate. He kept writing all the time, even when unable to leave his bed, and his warm and hearty humor was not in the least tinctured with the worries and suffering pressing upon him. Soon after the outbreak of World War I he managed to migrate to New York. The sudden death of his oldest son, and news of the dreadful fate of many Jews in the eastern war zones, proved too great a strain upon his delicate constitution, and on May 13, 1916, his heart gave way. To the last day of his life he continued to write *From the Fair*, reminiscences of his childhood, for serialization in a newspaper—a work that added to his total achievement.

Sholom Aleichem's writings are, to a greater degree than those of most authors, the literary expression of his personal experiences. However he may have dilated, enhanced, or elaborated his sense-data, he seldom let his imagination feed upon itself. All of his stories tell of some one, or of some phase, of the Jews he had observed and knew intimately; in every one of his characters he put something of himself or his own experience.

He drew his material from both the stagnant small town and the bustling city, although the former was the recipient of his warmer sympathy. The medieval religious outlook on life of the villagers, their usually meek and submissive deportment, and their pathetically meager existence appealed to him with greater immediacy than the precarious bustle and bluster of their urbanized brethren. Contemplating these various types of Jews (and they absorbed his waking thoughts), he could not but laugh at their foibles and flutter, but deep in his laughter lay the essence of his sympathetic sensibility.

The Jews he described were much the same as those depicted by Mendele—with this difference: they were already in the process of acclimating themselves to the hostilely strange ways of modern life. Most of them continued to feel the steely grip of poverty. This indigence, made acute by forced re-orientation coupled with further governmental restrictions, tended to quicken their conceits and lull their reason in the frantic hope of miraculous gain. Even those who remained in their native towns and clung to their orthodoxy were in some way affected by the invasion of contemporary inventions and technology. Sholom Aleichem saw them in this state of flux, and his stories reflected his humoristic view of their plight. How his conception of them differed from that of Mendele is evident in the very names of their composite towns. The older writer's Kabtzansk, literally Poorville, satirically connotes the dire economic condition of its inhabitants. Kaserilevke, the home of Sholom Aleichem's typical characters, has a similar significance, but with a disparity of nuance explained in the following passage:

> The Jewish poor have many names. They have been called the needy, the impecunious, the indigent, the impoverished, beggars, mendicants, and dependents. Each name is uttered in pity or contempt. But they have another name: the Kaserilek. This name is pronounced in a wholly different tone. One says, for instance, "My, but I'm a Kaserilek!" A Kaserilek is not merely a starveling, a luckless fellow; he is, if you please, a poor man not downcast by his poverty. On the contrary, he makes a joke of it!

His Kaserilevke is situated in an obscure corner of the world, "orphaned, dreamy, hypnotized, interested only in itself." Nothing worldly matters at first to its inhabitants except as it concerns their immediate needs, although their curiosity is, from their peculiar point of view, as wide as the universe. They are insignificant yet conceited, poor yet jolly, naive yet charged with mother-wit. When one is asked how he earns his living, his reply is similar to that of Mendele's Jew, but more laconic: "How we earn our living? Just as you see, ha, ha! One lives. . . ." A few sketches of these Kaserilevkites will indicate how truly and vividly they are drawn:

> Moishe was—but I cannot tell you what he was. He was a Jew. Whence his income was difficult to discover. He lived like many

other thousands, tens of thousands of Jews in Kaserilevke: he kept himself near the local squire; that is, not near the squire himself but near the administrators of his estate, and not so much near these stewards as near the Jews who dealt with them. . . . But whether this brought him any income is a matter of speculation for the idle, as Moishe disliked to boast of his luck or bewail his misfortunes. He always appeared happy, with cheeks always red; one mustache was somewhat larger than the other, with his hat inclined to one side, and with his eyes always smiling and friendly. He was always in a hurry, and always, at any time, ready to walk ten miles to help friend and stranger alike.

Yoshe Heshel is an even finer specimen:

He is one of those Jews who are always in a hurry, ever on the go; who are always head over heels in business: a business consisting of only wind. Such as he live on wind. He conceives the world as a fair, to which one came sniffing, sniffing for some bargain. Void of any well-defined project, he would come to a county fair ready to price everything in sight, to buy and sell from hand to hand, regardless of profit or loss. A ruble more or less was inconsequential, so long as the transaction was honest. At the end of such a fair his enterprise left him penniless but undismayed. He only stroked his beard and said to himself, "Now that I have, praised be His Name, concluded the business of the fair, I must run somewhere to get a loan for traveling expenses."

Incapable of earning a living, Yoshel Heshel must depend upon his wife and grown daughter to provide the necessities of life by sewing shirts. But they seldom have sufficient work.

What do they do when there is no work? They suffer hunger; that is, they go to bed on an empty stomach and, with God's help, rise on the morrow to continue the fast. You may be certain no man will ever know this. Yoshe Heshel is not one to tell tales, to bewail his lot, to ask for help. . . . He would rather die! Yes, die! In short, Yoshe Heshel is one of the proud poor who suffer hunger on the quiet, without ceremony, without trumpetry. Not even the charitable know of his plight. It is fortunate that Yoshe Heshel is a Jew, and a very pious, honest Jew, who believes in God, who serves God, who loves God ardently, who loves God's spirit as a lover his bride. . . . Usually shy, dispirited, a worm for everyone to tread upon, he changes into a cheeky fellow once in the synagogue. There, in the house of God, he does not believe in richés, in aristocracy; he reduces everything to mere dust; he is convinced that all are equal before God. . . .

Although a pathetic character, Yoshe Heshel emerges as an object of mirth because Sholom Aleichem stressed not his adversity but his pliant acquiescence in it; not his hunger but his meek submission to the cudgels of fate. Yet the laughter he arouses is charged with sympathy and esteem.

Sholom Aleichem's humor plumbs the depths of sentiment in "An Easy Fast," a sketch reminiscent of Peretz's "The Messenger." Here human life is shown yielding to the perseverance of poverty, a theme usually treated with pathos. Sholom Aleichem, however, divests it of all sentimentality. Khaim Khaikin is an elderly man no longer able to work and without means. The thought that he is wholly dependent on the meager earnings of his children grieves him terribly; he dislikes being a burden on anyone, even his own children. His heart feels cramped when he is forced to eat in their presence, acutely aware that every morsel he takes deprives them of that much food. To avoid this excruciating feeling he resorts to fasts. When there is no religious justification for abstaining from food he tries to avoid his solicitous children by lingering in the synagogue or taking a stroll at mealtimes. When they compel him to eat with them he secretly distributes his portion to the younger children. At the approach of a religious fast he feels more at ease; none dare ask him to eat on such a day! If possible, he prepares for the fast by abstaining from food on the previous day in order "to make it easier." On the day before the fast of the Ninth of Ab, commemorating the destruction of the Temple in Jerusalem, Khaim comes to the synagogue, sits down leisurely on an overturned bench, as was the custom on that occasion, and begins to read a religious book. Drowsiness gradually possesses him; hallucination soon follows.

And Khaim Khaikin keeps his eyes shut, and he finds himself in a queer world, a new world, one which he has never, never yet seen. Angels hover before him. In observing them he recognizes his own children, all of them, grown-up and babes. He wants to tell them something, but he cannot speak. . . . He wishes to apologize to them, to explain why he is not guilty. . . . Not he! . . . How can he, Khaim, be blamed because so many Jews have collected together in so small a place to crowd, oppress, and devour one another? How is he to blame if men force human beings to sweat, to bleed? How is he to blame if people have not yet reached the stage where one man would not exploit his fellow man as he would a horse, and where a horse too is to be pitied, being a creation of God, a living thing? . . . And Khaim Khaikin keeps his eyes shut and sees everything, the whole world, all worlds; and everything is clear and light, winding like smoke; and he feels that something is leaving his body, from within, from the heart, and rises, rises straight up, separating from his corporeal self; and he feels himself light, very, very light; and he emits a deep sigh, a very prolonged sigh. He feels relieved; then —nothing, absolutely nothing.

Here is another phase of Kaserilevke. Mordekhai Nosen, the wealthiest Jew in town by its own miniscule standards, is not at all like his indigent neighbors. In depicting him, Sholom Aleichem's sympathy grew cooler and his humor became less genial.

Mordekhai Nosen is a tall man with long hands, thin and withered. His face, as square as that of a Chinaman because of protruding cheekbones, is covered with a sparse beard. He appears as if he is harboring some secret: his lips are always shut, his mouth slightly to one side; his mien is always serious, his forehead full of wrinkles; he never speaks loudly, never an extra word. But he becomes a changed man when in the presence of town officials. The wrinkles disappear, his face brightens, his lips unlock, his mouth straightens; he begins to talk: a truly different Mordekhai Nosen. Do you know why he acts so humbly before these officials? Solely for the love of eminence, out of pure vanity; only for the words, "Why, Reb Mordekhai Nosen, who is so esteemed by the officials as you?" uttered by a fellow Jew in need of some favor. Indeed for the word "esteemed" he would suffer all humiliation and expense! A peculiar man is Mordekhai Nosen.

Some of the wealthier Jews were in the habit of providing an annual feast for their townsmen. As was natural, the poorer the Jew the less was made of him on these occasions. "Hannuka Pancakes" describes such an event. Several tables are placed in the rear of the house for the poor, whom the family factotum treats with rude arrogance. Desiring the meal yet deeply humiliated, they devour the pancakes in haste and abasement. On the way home they let their fantasy have free play, and their humbleness is for the moment forgotten. The falling snow gives their fancy a new turn:

> How would it, for instance, incommode the Lord Almighty, if these snowflakes should suddenly turn into diamonds and saphires? We would then bend down, fill our pockets with handfuls, come home, and say to our wives: "Here, Esther, do with them as you please. If you wish, turn them into money; if you wish, into jewelry for yourself; if you wish, into both; only leave me alone." We would then not need to depend upon the Steiners and their pancakes; as we say in our prayers, "Deliver me not into the hands of man!"

Kaserilevke did not, of course, contain only poverty and its distressful consequences. Various idyllic aspects quickened its somber life. First there was the Sabbath, on which even the most wretched Jew became a self-respecting, leisurely human being, forgetful of weekday cares and anxieties. The serene atmosphere, ease of mind, and inner peace that pervaded the Jewish community on a Sabbath afternoon was one of its undeniable charms. At intervals there were long and joyous holidays, bringing in their wake exhilaration and pleasure. And if Sholom Aleichem was able to extract humor from the dross of life, he was truly exuberant when depicting its more cheerful occasions. Without the need of diverting pathos and pain, his humor assumed a carefree and natural mirthfulness.

The life of the small Kaserilevke boy provided him with

another source of gay humor. Sholom Aleichem's several volumes of stories about him added a most attractive element to Yiddish literature. His boys love life: unlike the little Jews of other authors, they are irrepressible, mischief-loving urchins. S. Niger said of them:

> What a blessing was the healthy, naive humor of the child to the Jewish reader! No other writer was able to gather the scattered seeds of childish humor from among the Jews and plant them with so much art in his children portraits. In this achievement Sholom Aleichem is even more alone than in his creation of Tevieh, certain aspects of whom are found in other writers.

These children play games, run, jump, fall, get hurt, and do not mind it. They play pranks, are punished, and soon invent new ones, as is the way of normal boys. Every holiday, every season of the year, finds them eager to extract the most from the immediate moment. It is as if they have some intuitive foreboding of the cares and anxieties awaiting them in the years ahead, and are the more eager for mischief and fun while still children. Even in the midst of sorrow, when the faces of their elders are long and knit, they are most impressed by the, to them, amusing aspects. In story after story the principal theme concerns the boy anxious to act the child in opposition to parents, rabbis, and customs forcing him to behave like a little adult.

"The Pocket Knife," "The Violin," "The Watch," "The Flag," and similar stories concern boys prevented by poverty from owning these treasures, or by their fathers from using them. To possess a knife, for instance, was considered unbecoming to a Jewish boy studying Hebrew lore. Yet every one of them secretly longed for one and usually managed to acquire something with a sharp edge. In "The Pocket Knife" the father finds his young son toying with a knife and exclaims: "A knife? What a child! What a lad! Can you not be with a book? A youth of eight years! I'll show you knives, you hoodlum! Knives all of a sudden! . . . The only plaything for a Jewish boy from his fifth birthday is a book; and not a children's story, but a religious tome!" Not that a Jewish father does not love his children enough—he loves them only too zealously; his strictures come from his concern for their future well-being. In this story the boy becomes seriously ill. When passing a crisis he hears his anxious father talking in so soothing a tone that he thinks: "If I were not ashamed, I should like to give him a hug and kiss, but hee, hee, hee, how can one kiss a father?" The ghetto child seldom kissed his father, even as the child in the Puritan family seldom kissed his.

Although Sholom Aleichem has written at length about boys, he hardly touched upon the Jewish girl. In this neglect may be seen how dependent he was on his sense-data. It was easy for him to write about boys because he only had to dip into his memory to do so. In his childhood, however, girls were a breed apart, and he was hardly aware of them until adolescence. Then his own emotional experience provided him with the lovely heroine for "Song of Songs." In this story he waxes truly poetical. Refreshing in theme, pure and biblical in style, it comes like the waft of a rose out of the Kaserilevke stench.

When Jews began to migrate into cities in the latter decades of the 19th century, some legally but mostly illegally, they made up a bizarre group. Without means, unskilled in any trade, unsophisticated, they became the hapless pawns of chance. In the desperate attempt to survive they took up any work that came their way. The Moishes and Yoshe Heshels, once in the city slums, became agents, brokers, salesmen, tradesmen; the less educated took up tailoring and other manual crafts. Few earned enough to keep body and soul together. The precariousness of their existence, more intensive than in their native towns, fired their fantasies and caused some of them to visualize substantial incomes, to conjure up suddenly acquired wealth. Undaunted by unfavorable conditions— there were too many after too little—these *luftmenschen* began to depend upon chance and pay homage to luck. In the process they landed in the realm of the grotesque, where the lottery appeared a solid and certain investment. It seemed so wonderful to win a fortune at a stroke! For a time Sholom Aleichem was one of them, though at an artistic remove, and observed them closely and compassionately.

Economic dreariness and failure were not their only besetting plight; government hostility aggravated their uncertain existence. Few Jews acquired the status of urban citizenship. Restriction after restriction was promulgated for the purpose of harrying the Jews undergoing social mutation. Efforts to avoid such unfair regulations as the draft, highly limited citizenship rights, the percentage norm in schools, and other handicaps resulted in many comic as well as cruel situations. Sholom Aleichem described these in a number of excellent stories and monologues. Two narratives, dealing with the same theme, illustrate the range, subtlety, and wholesomeness of his humor.

"The Lottery Winner" depicts the cleaving of the new generation from the old, and the aggravated results of educational restrictions. Benjamin, the son of a pious beadle, is a precocious child and the pet of the synagogue community. His poor father is justly proud of him and expects him to become "a light in Israel." When Benjamin learns in early adolescence of the world outside the synagogue, he conceives a great longing for a university education. Knowing his father's inimical attitude toward secular study, he secretly leaves home for the city. After much privation and intensive preparation he receives a high rating in the entrance examination—only to be excluded because of the percentage norm for Jews. In despair, he apostatizes and is at once welcomed by the university authorities. When news of Benjamin's recreancy reaches his father, the entire town is already agog at the unpardonable act. The shock to the pious beadle is severe. Shame and anguish paralyze his tongue and drive him from the sight of his synagogue cronies. In accord with Jewish custom he and his family consider Benjamin dead and sit down for the week of mourning. One of the bereaved man's friends comes to comfort him, but all his attempts are in vain.

> The visitor wishes to say something, but knows not what. After several efforts at vocalization speech finally comes; once started, he knows not how to stop, how to extricate himself without pain to the bereaved. . . . "Te," he addresses the beadle with the first words that come to mind, "everything is for the best. It is only, as we say, a trial of the Lord, because everything, you understand, come from Him. Nothing may be done without His permission; a human being does not move his little finger here below before he is commanded to do so from above. . . . He is, what's the use of talking, a real Master. Oi, a Master! And He is being obeyed and very much obeyed, oi, oi, oi. . . . Therefore, you understand, everything is as it should be. The evidence for this comes from the fact that if things should have been different, they would have been so: for who can compel Him to have them thus and not otherwise? And if He should desire things to be different, could one have them otherwise? No! Then let things better be different, that is, let them better be thus and not otherwise. . . .

As in "An Easy Fast," the situation is truly pathetic. What can be more calamitous to a pious Jew than the apostasy of a beloved and only son? Yet so unalloyed and adroit is Sholom Aleichem's art that the reader's attention is focused not on the grief of the father but on the manner in which he accepts and absorbs his sorrow. Had the beadle, for instance, been of Learian mold, the result would no doubt have been tragic; being a Kaserilevkite—a pious, reflective, submissive Jew, accepting his faith in God without question—he emerges as an object of pathetic humor.

Restrictive education is treated comically in "Gymnasium," a popular monologue. The father in this story is a successful urbanized Jew. He is secure enough materially to think of things other than economic, and his aims are those that come with prosperity. His wife, as might be expected, is a social climber and wants her son to have a formal education: "he should at least be a doctor or lawyer." But the percentage clause—one Jewish student to ten Russian students—frustrates all their efforts, and the greater the endeavor the more futile the result. In the following early passage the father recounts his interview with the principal of a gymnasium:

"What may be your wish?" he inquires, and asks me to be seated. So I say quietly into his ear: "Gracious sir," say I, "we," say I, "are not rich people; we have," say I, "a small establishment, and an extraordinary good son, who," say I, "wants to study, and I also want him to, but my wife especially desires it. . . ." But again he asks: "What is your wish?" So I move closer to him and repeat: "Dear sir," say I, "we," say I, "are not rich people, we have a small establishment, and an extraordinary good son, who," say I, "wants to study, and I also want him to, but my wife *especially* desires it. . . ." And I stress the "especially" he should understand me. But he, having the mind of a peasant, does not apprehend and now asks in anger, "What do you want?" So I slowly put my hand in my pocket, and slowly take it out, and tell him slowly: "Understand me, gracious sir, . . ." and I put my hand in his and squeeze it. . . . In short, it's done! He immediately grasps my meaning, takes out a little notebook, asks me my name, the name of my son, and in what class I should like to have him enter. At this I thought: "That's the way to talk!"

Here the circumstances are the reverse of those in "The Lottery Winner." The father does not experience true sorrow; he is only inconvenienced, at most frustrated. Though ostensibly veneered with urban sophistication, he very soon reveals his Kaserilevke origin. Speaking in the Russianized Yiddish of the city Jew, he arouses droll, contagious laughter with every phrase—Sholom Aleichem's sympathy with him being overshadowed by sheer amusement.

The wealthier Jews in the cities yield readily to the pleasures and frivolities of the newly rich: family discord, social jealousies, and gossip along with summer vacations, excursions to famous doctors, and similar luxuries. Sholom Aleichem perceived them as former Kaserilevkites divested of their piety, modesty, and geniality, and depicted them accordingly. "Summer Life" describes such a group on vacation. Written in letters between those in the resort and those in the city, it delineates their insincerities, pettiness, jealousies, and vanities with an irony bordering on caricature. His heart seemed to cool when dealing with bourgeois characters, and he observed them with his mocking eye only.

The revolutionary and Zionistic movements, with their di-divergent factions, were in the 1900's finding earnest and enthusiastic disciples among emancipated Jewish youth. Disintegrating conditions over the country, then being defeated in war and verging on revolution, aggravated by the 1903–1905 pogroms and the intensified oppression that followed, deeply affected these idealistic and zealous young men and women, as intense in their radicalism as was their fathers' faith in Jehovah. Sholom Aleichem recorded this social turbulence with his usual sensitivity and humor. In *The Deluge* the father is so engrossed in business that he tends to neglect his family. With the mother old-fashioned and indulgent, the children become the prey of their agitated environment. The elder son and daughter, entering maturity just prior to the upsurge of radicalism and tempted by their father's sudden wealth, yield to luxurious debauchery. The younger children, caught in the whirl of unrest, become fanatic revolutionists and Zionists. The brunt of this discord and disparity is borne by the parents. Although the theme has a serious content, Sholom Aleichem treated it with the obliqueness of his gentle mirth.

The pogroms beginning in 1903 made life in Russia more difficult and dreary than ever before for its millions of Jews. They began a mass migration to the United States, South Africa, Argentina, and other countries where they could gain ready entrance. With little or no means, and almost no knowledge of the world outside of their native towns, they set forth armed only with faith in God and the urgency to escape. Wandering westward through Austria and Germany, they met with innumerable obstacles and inconveniences, but their strong impetus to survive and settle drove them irresistibly to their destination. Sholom Aleichem was among them, both as victim and observer, sharing their experiences; nothing eluded his keen senses and deep sympathy.

Motel: Toward America * is a veritable epic of Jewish life during the first decade of this century. Beginning with a description of the small town in which modern thought and inventions were getting a timorous welcome, Sholom Aleichem takes his characters through western Russia, across the border to Austria and Germany, through Belgium, into London, and finally to the ocean liner on its way to New York. He depicts this hegira of hapless and harried Jews, starting in the face of governmental restrictions, striking the protruding reefs of the border, surging past crest and trough across central Europe, riding the turbulent Atlantic, and landing on tear-drenched Ellis Island. In *Motel: In America* and *New Kaserilevke* Sholom Aleichem followed these immigrants to New York and described their efforts to establish themselves in a new and strange environment. With his quick eye and sharp ear he was aware of their every move, sensitive to their every mood; in writing about them he gave artistic form, embellished by sympathetic humor, to comic incidents and oblique behavior.

Successful as he was in creation of character, Sholom Aleichem was too much the humorist to write first-rate fiction. At the outset of his career, eager to wean the naive Jewish reader from the lurid Shomer romances, he wrote *Sender Blank, Stempenu,* and *Yosele Solovey,* authentic stories of Jewish life. To make them palatable he infused the action with elements of human interest. Yet the love displayed by his characters was the reticent and repressed emotion of the traditional Jew. In *Stempenu,* for instance, Rachel, though unhappy in her marriage, buries her love for the musician deep within her and resists strong temptation. As if apologetic of this, Sholom Aleichem, in the opening of one of the chapters, explains the absence of intrigue and passion:

The reader must think to himself that he is being served a dull supper, he having been brought up on those "highly interesting" romances in which occur hangings and drownings, poisonings and shootings, or in which a rabbi becomes a count and a servant girl changes into a princess. . . . What shall I do, since we have no counts and princesses? We have only ordinary Jews, ordinary wives and daughters, and ordinary musicians.

Authentic and wholesome as was the life he depicted, it nevertheless lacked the depth and sustained insight of great fiction. This was equally true of his later novels—*The Deluge*, *Wandering Stars*, and *The Bloody Jest*, written as newspaper serials under trying circumstances. *The Wandering Star**, for example, describes the conditions obtaining at the birth of the Yiddish theater in Eastern Europe and in America. The atmosphere is presented realistically and humorously, but the injection of sentimental romance deprives the protagonists of artistic vitality. It was as if something of Shomer had infiltrated the action. His several plays likewise have the stamp of his warm humor, yet fail to measure up to his major works.

Although Sholom Aleichem's humor stresses the peculiarities and incongruities of a people undergoing radical transformation and oppressed by a hostile government and inimical social forces, he has achieved his best work in the creation of character. He has given Yiddish literature a number of fictional beings more real to his readers than the people around them; creations that grow, mature, and rise to imaginative heights. The following four major individuals embody his supreme artistic achievement.

When a well-known Jew became endeared to his townsmen, his name underwent expansion. Reb Yosef, the old rabbi of Kaserilevke, early came to be called Reb Yosefel. Not a soul in the town but adores the venerable man when he enters the pages of Sholom Aleichem's writings. He is indeed an idealized sage. The hero of numerous stories, he is portrayed as a revered octogenarian, blessed with good sense and actuated by the deepest altruism. Afflicted with loneliness, indigence, and illness, he retains his implicit faith in the goodness and rectitude of Jehovah. Considering himself but a speck in the ever-to-be-praised world of God, he is always modest and humble. With the phrase, "Vanity of vanities, all is vanity," he has succeeded in allaying his misery.

> He has reached the conviction that all the suffering and wretchedness with which the Lord visits him come from one of two ways: either it is a trial, a visitation from His beloved Name, a castigation while in this sinful, foolish world, or he really deserves the punishment; if not for his own sins, it is surely for those of his poor sinning brothers, the children of Israel, who are responsible for one another, and are due to suffer for each other. This is the conclusion Reb Yosefel arrived at, and he never complained even for a moment. He discarded this world with its vain pleasures, dismissed it with the smile of a philosopher.

Reb Yosefel was delineated as a noble leader of a medievally oriented Jewry—the rabbi who was disappearing together with the static culture he fostered. He was still the old patriarch, concerned for his flock not merely because they were his parishioners but also because they were human beings. Honest and sincere in all things, loving all living creatures, keeping soul and body in their respective places with rigorous piety, he succeeded in inspiring his fellow Jews with the reverence, awe, and poetry which went far to nullify the unsavory effects of their superstitious and blighting beliefs. Endowed by his Creator with the composite Jewish virtues, he was dedicated to the service of his people. And he found much to do! He went about Kaserilevke soothing the sore at heart, advising the perplexed, chastising the selfish, and collecting alms for the needy. In the process he talked, moved, and thought with unforgettable reality. The following two incidents are characteristic.

Reb Yosefel undertook to provide his beloved town with all essential improvements; not through his own means, of course, since he was always penniless, but by soliciting contributions from the charitably inclined. When the need for an old folks home became urgent, he proceeded as usual to seek funds

from those in a position to give. When a wealthy merchant
came to town, Reb Yosefel at once went to see him about a
contribution. Arriving at the inn, he was told the guest was
not to be disturbed. Nevertheless he tapped at the man's door
to announce his approach and entered the room. The wealthy
stranger was so angered by this brazen mendicity and unwel-
come familiarity of the quaint intruder that he lost his temper
and gave the old man a cuff on the ear. The octogenarian only
felt his face for blood and said mildly: "Well, so be it; this you
gave *me*, so to say. What now, my good man, will you give for
the decrepit sick, I mean for the old folks home?" When the
rabbi left the short-tempered merchant, one side of his face
was redder and shinier than the other, but he was in possession of a large enough contribution to begin building his pet
project.

At another time he headed a delegation sent to a nearby
city to collect money for the sufferers of a recent fire in Kaserilevke. While canvassing some of the wealthier Jews, he and
his fellow townsmen were arrested for entering the city without passports. Through the intercession of one of the influential Jews they were soon released. Before letting them go the
officer in charge, amused by the quaintness of these terrified
rustics, asked who was the "chief rabbi" among them. The
question put fear into their timorous hearts; their imagination
at once assumed some dire punishment. Only the old rabbi
was undaunted.

"It is I," Reb Yosefel spoke up in a peculiar tone, and stepped
forth courageously, as if ready to take the entire condemnation
upon his own head, as if willing to sacrifice himself for his
fellow Jews at a moment's notice. Handsome, very handsome
was the octogenarian graybeard at that instant. A youthful fire
was lit in his aged eyes; but his hands trembled and his shoulders
shook. He waited for what was to be said to him, ready for everything, for the worst that evil people might be moved to do.
Whom should this octogenarian fear? He placed one hand on the
small of his back and looked at his inquisitor with such boldness
and self-esteem that the death-fearing Kaserilevkites saw their
rabbi in a new light.

"I can bet you any amount that no one in the whole world is so satisfied with the warm, sunny spring as I, Motel, the son of Payse the cantor, and the neighbor's calf, who is called Meny (it is I, Motel, who have named her so)." These child-like words open the first book bearing his name and bring the eight-year-old boy into being. Chief of Sholom Aleichem's boy creations, he is molded pretty much in the image of his own childhood. Motel represents the transitional generation in its youthful state: inheritor of Kaserilevke culture and destined exemplar of the urbanized Jew.

Motel and Meny come out on this first day of spring, and both enjoy it immensely. After describing his own pleasure, Motel continues:

> Meny, the neighbor's calf, first dug her black, wet chin into the dung, then kicked three times with her front hoof, lifted her tail, jumped on all fours, and issued a dull meh. The meh was so comical that it made me laugh, and I imitated exactly the same meh with the same intonation. This must have pleased Meny, for she soon repeated the same movements with the same jump and cry. I, naturally, imitated her to the minutest detail. Thus several times: I gave a jump and so the calf; the calf gave a meh, and I a meh.

This interpretative attitude in Motel is also shown toward his elders. Every word, every act, appears comical to him if it does not coincide with his preconceived idea of it. When his father becomes very ill and his mother is forced to sell the furniture piece by piece to pay the doctor and buy medicines, he thinks it amusing that she should conceal the truth from his father. It appears to him a violation of ethics for a mother to lie and a father to be fooled. But if concealing the truth is to him a laughable matter, the manner in which it is done is even more so. He thus describes it: " 'What's the matter?' father asks from the sickroom. 'Nothing,' mother answers him as she wipes her eyes, and her lower lip and jaw tremble so that it is impossible not to burst into laughter."

His childish mind is amused because it is still unable to perceive the reason for his mother's equivocation; he feels superior to his father, who is fooled, while he is not. Unaware that his father is dying or of its effect on the family, he is excited by the depletion of his home's contents. It is only when his father is actually dead and the wailing of his mother brings him from his play into the house that the concrete manifestation of pain and grief produce in him similar emotions.

My mother continues to weep and faint in turn while in the arms of my brother Elihu. And my brother Elihu, who does not cease crying himself, continues to reproach her: "Today is a holiday, mother, today is Pentecost, mother! Mother, it is forbidden to cry, mother!" And at once everything becomes clear. And I feel a cramp in my heart and a tug at my soul, and I want to cry, and I don't know what for. . . . And I pity my mother. . . . And I go up to her from behind, and tell her in the manner of my brother, as tears roll from my eyes, "Today is a holiday, mother, today is Pentecost, mother! Mother it is forbidden to cry, mother!"

Sorrow has loosened his mother's tear ducts. In his innocence he says: "Crying is as natural with her, for example, as eating or praying is with you. I don't understand how a person can have so many tears." But he develops rapidly and soon perceives the truth. "When Elihu began to scold her for her continuous crying, she told him, "What a foolish child you are! Do I force my tears? Tears come. . . ." And in what follows Motel discerns her state of mind with greater empathy than his older brother.

An instance of Sholom Aleichem's art in showing how a child's mind reacts to a tragic event is his telling how Motel learns the meaning of a pogrom from one of his older companions:

"You don't know what a pogrom is? What a ninny you are! A pogrom is something that occurs everywhere. It begins almost out of nothing, but once it starts it continues for three days."
"What is it, then?" I ask. "A fair?"
"What fair? A nice fair! Windows are broken, furniture is broken! Pillows are torn! Feathers float down like snow."
"What for?"

"What do you mean what for? A pogrom is not against homes alone. A pogrom is also against stores. Stores are broken into, and their goods are thrown into the street, carried away, soaked with gasoline and burned."

"Go on!"

"What do you mean? Do you think I only imagine it? Later, as the robbing ends, they go through homes with axes, with irons and clubs, with the police in the rear. They sing and whistle and shout, 'Come on, fellows, kill the Jews!' And they beat and stab and kill. . . ."

"Whom?"

"What do you mean whom? Jews!"

"What for?"

"Some what for! It's a pogrom!"

"And if it's a pogrom, so what?"

"Go on, you're a calf. I don't want to talk to you about it."

Motel grows and develops with every related incident. If he seems too knowledgeable for his age, it is because, as a product of Kaserilevke, he too soon becomes a little adult. He reveals his inmost thoughts in a manner that stamps them indelibly upon the reader's mind. His impressions are charged with sensitiveness and humor. He describes everything and everybody as his senses perceive and his imagination interprets. Each narrative adds to the wholesomeness, simplicity, and fineness of the boy's spirit. Impressionable and pliant, he adjusts himself to every situation without a jolt or jar. His heart throbs with warm sympathy; his love of living things is quick and strong; his intuitive mind in time perceives the more delicate nuances of life. He is in truth a child philosopher, always eager to probe into the why of everything, and underlying his entire being is a rich vein of humor, gentle and refined.

In the preface to the second edition of *Menachem Mendel*, Sholom Aleichem declared:

Menachem Mendel is no hero out of a novel, and especially no mere imaginary figure. He is a typical Jew with whom the author is intimately acquainted. Meeting in 1892 on the Odessa minor bourse, we went through, hand in hand, all the seven compartments of Gehenna. We speculated on the Yehupets [Kiev] stock exchange, "traveled" to Petersburg and Warsaw, withstood many crises, drifted from one enterprise to another, finding—oh, woe—not much in any, and were compelled to do in the end what most Jews do—immigrate to America.

Menachem Mendel is much more to the reader than these bare facts indicate: he is a citified Yoshe Heshel become the supreme *luftmensch,* a grotesque product of the 2000-year struggle of the Jews to survive under adverse and at times almost impossible conditions. Business, speculation, get-rich-quick schemes have become to him not merely a means of earning a livelihood but a passionate and irresistible end. He is fascinated not by wealth itself but by the idea of acquiring it suddenly and fortuitously. His repeated failures do not for a moment keep him from plunging into the first quixotic scheme that comes his way. In his excitement he often borders on paranoia; Dr. Eliashev, the first important Yiddish critic, interpreted him as "the Jewish insanity streak in the person of an insignificant Jewish businessman."

Menachem Mendel is married and the father of three children when he goes to Odessa to claim the remainder of his wife's dowry from a broker's office. For the first time in a bustling city, his fantasy begins to seethe with dreams of sudden riches. The bourse atmosphere obsesses him. The hearsay knowledge that a few speculators have amassed fortunes fires his fancy with the grandeur of doing likewise. He feels jubilantly optimistic and writes to his wife Shayne Shayndel that she will soon have a wealthy husband. Again to quote Eliashev:

Thousands of plans, projects and deals fly about in his mind like spirits and demons. If he stops to think for a moment, it is a sign that to the thousands of schemes in his head is added a new and larger one. Menachem Mendel is in a constant fever. Each impression suggests ten possibilities; for he lives in a dream world, so that butter and leather, wheat and needles are all the same to him.

Having lost his capital, Menachem Mendel wishes he were dead. But only for a little while. When he receives the money his wife sends so that he can return home, he goes instead to Yehupets (Kiev). There he embarks on other wild-goose ventures, becomes enmeshed in the financial maze of the stock exchange, and suffers the repeated agonies of chronic failure.

Shayne Shayndel is of an earthy mold. A typical Kaserilev-kite, encouraged by a mother who expresses her practical sense in common but apt aphorisms, she keeps urging her husband to drop his harebrained schemes, let the evil city burn to the ground, and return home to her and their children. "I don't understand, even if you behead me, what kind of stuff it is that one cannot see it! Is it a cat in a bag? . . . Listen to me, Mendel, I don't like it. I was never used to such airy dealings." And she adds that mother's comment on his enterprise is that "from air one catches cold." To another of his grandiose dreams she replies: "You can say what you will, but until I see with my own eyes I won't believe you; not because I think you're a liar, but because all that those fine Yehupets people tell you, you consider holy writ." When luck temporarily favors him and he is the ecstatic possessor of several hundred rubles, she tells him:

> What? You are jubilant, excited? "Stocks," "Transports," "Portfolios," indeed! You beguile yourself with the idea that one can become rich in the time it takes to say "Hear, O, Israel!" "A delusion," mother says, "is worse than a disease." Stupid! Why talk of fortunes, lucky breaks, stocks, dividends? Nonsense! They are all worth an egg-shell! One does not get rich empty handed.

Reproach can no longer discourage Menachem Mendel. He is so immersed in the exchange gossip and rumor that common sense has ceased to affect him. The thought that Brodsky, a prominent Jewish millionaire in Kiev, is a member of the stock exchange is unimpeachable evidence to his frenetic mind of the lucrativeness of speculation. In a postscript to one of his letters he adds:

You must think, dearest wife, that I am the only one dealing in stocks. Brodsky also trades with them. The difference between us is: when I wish to place an order I must first figure out how much I can stomach; when Brodsky begins to buy, he orders 1000 shares, 5000 shares, 10,000 shares. Brodsky is no joke! When he rides through in his carriage, Kreschatik [Kiev's principal street] trembles, and all the Jews doff their hats, and I among them. It would be fine if I should some day become a Brodsky. With the help of God, little stupid. . . .

Bad news from Petersburg again wipes him out. Dazed, he cannot understand how and why it happened. Soon, however, his optimism surges forth and he is again the schemer. "Luckily," he tells his wife, "I have betimes thought of undertaking another means of livelihood, a respectable livelihood." He becomes an agent. "One need only be able to lie," he asserts, "and be insolent into the bargain, and one is already fit to be an agent." Able to do neither, he fails miserably. Subsequently he deals in sugar, real estate, forests, and oil; he even tries to be a marriage broker and to become a writer. "I now have a new occupation, a completely new one, somewhat nicer and easier. I've become a writer. I write. You will no doubt ask how I come to writing? It's from Heaven." In reply his wife quotes her mother: "A sick one will get well, a drunkard will become sober, a dark one will become light, but a fool remains a fool."

Menachem Mendel is essentially a comic character. A dreamer, mentally agile, earnestly eager, he is at the same time childishly naive and helpless in a world of hard and shrewd traders. He is at the mercy of an overexcited fantasy which leads him into absurd behavior. For Reb Yosefel and Tevieh religious faith was the mainspring of their existence; Menachem Mendel has no such solid anchor and is buffeted by the whims of chance. Consequently his every impulsive act and move, stimulated primarily by desperate hope of fortuitous gain, appears exaggerated and ludicrous, since inevitably each one fails. In describing his gullible enthusiasm over matters doomed to disappoint him, Sholom Aleichem makes clear that this behavior is not so much the result of a diseased imagination as of an inimical environment. Trained, as so many of his kind, in neither a trade nor a profession, without worldly sophistication, with his opportunities for earning a living greatly restricted by a hostile government, yet with a mind steeped in Hebrew lore and medieval ways, Menachem Mendel is depicted as more a victim of unfavorable circumstances than of his own inadequacy. No man is in full control of his intellect when in the grip of chronic starvation. Menachem Mendel's effort to free himself from penury, stimulated by his *luftmensch* upbringing, forces him to trust in luck and in his naive ingenuity until he becomes addicted to speculation. His implicit faith in his unrealistic and ridiculous schemes merely emphasizes the pathos of his misfortune. Because his conceit combined with gullibility make his behavior extreme and ludicrous, he appears an object of laughter; but the laugh takes not the form of ridicule but of compassion. One feels that he has not really deserved his repeated failure and despair.

Every major writer secretes his inmost self into at least one of his works. Sholom Aleichem was no exception. Although he has stamped his personality and art upon most of his writings, the stories of *Tevieh the Dairyman* * best display his greatness. In this rustic, traditionally religious Jew he has embodied his highest humor, his truest philosophy of life; during the score of years in which he concerned himself with the character, he concentrated his utmost affection, warmest sympathy, and deepest spiritual probings upon this unfortunate milkman.

Tevieh differs conspicuously from Menachem Mendel in both attitude and behavior. Indeed, these two characters represent the polarization of nearly all of Sholom Aleichem's creations: one verging on the pathological and the other being spiritually centripetal. Tevieh is a typical, if artistically heightened, product of orthodox Jewry: he adheres unquestionably to his faith in Jehovah, accepts the buffeting of fate as God's will, procures his bread with the proverbial sweat of his brow, and considers the idea of wealth a satanic temptation. Menachem Mendel is a Kaserilevkite in the process of urbanization, tossed about on the stormy waves of economic precariousness, with his fantasy rising rocket-like on imaginary gain and sinking to despair at the impact with hard reality.

The two are clearly contrasted in the only story in which both appear. Tevieh, a poor dairyman with several marriageable daughters, while in Yehupets on business is for once tempted by the sight of many valuables in store windows and thinks to himself:

> Dear God, if I owned even a tenth part of what this is worth—what would I then ask of God, and who would be like me? First I would marry off my eldest daughter, give her a dowry of 500 rubles in addition to wedding presents, clothing, and expenses; I would sell my horse and wagon, move to the city, buy a seat on the east wall of the synagogue, buy my wife, long may she live, some pearls, and hand out charity like the most generous of men.

Just then he sees Menachem Mendel, a distant relative, and before he realizes it is persuaded to invest his hard-earned savings—100 rubles in all—in a get-rich-quick stock. Inevitably his speculation results in complete loss and he feels robbed. Yet so innate is his understanding of human nature that he perceives the motive as readily as the result. Seeing Menachem Mendel's misery, he does not blame him for losing the money; aware that if he had not yielded to temptation he would still have his 100 rubles, he even comforts his tempter by telling him: "Money, brother, one must work for." Thus, while he reacts philosophically with an irony that saves him from grief, Menachem Mendel, having neither objectivity nor a true sense of values, becomes disconsolate—only to upsurge emotionally at the thought of a new scheme.

Tevieh enters these stories as a common drayman, working hard and suffering dire poverty. A lucky chance, causing him to bring two wealthy women who had lost their way in the woods to their grateful relatives, yields him a cow and enough cash gifts to enable him to set himself up as a dairyman. Life becomes easier for himself and his family, but he remains troubled about his dowryless daughters. Although he considers them attractive and accomplished, he knows that this means little without a marriage portion. He soon learns, much to his sorrow, that his daughters have minds of their own, and that in a world in social transition the lack of a dowry is the least of their disadvantages.

One day he is told that a wealthy butcher in the town wants to marry his eldest daughter. At first he recoils from the idea that his beautiful Tzaytel should become the wife of this coarse and commonplace widower, but he gradually acquiesces in the thought, knowing that the marriage would bring the girl material well-being. Tzaytel, however, has her own plans. She is already in love with a poor tailor of her own age and pleads with her father to grant his consent. Tevieh has no will to stop her from marrying the man of her choice and is sad to see her continue her indigent existence.

Hodel, his second daughter, decides to marry a zealous revolutionist. Tevieh is perplexed, finding it difficult to accept the idea that a young girl should become the betrothed of a strange youth without the consent and blessings of her parents. Confronted by this situation, however, he has not the heart to stop her from meeting with the brazen youth. In the end he consoles himself with the thought that she might have done worse, and gives his consent. Soon after, the young man is arrested and exiled to Siberia, and Hodel decides to accompany him to his desolate destination. No words of Tevieh can dissuade her. Again he accepts the infliction of fate, and although his heart almost breaks at the idea of her departure, he provides for her as best he can for the long and difficult trek. At the railroad station, very depressed, he relates, "I alone keep myself as cool as steel and iron; that is, as the saying goes, inwardly I seethe like a samovar, but to reveal my feelings—feh, Tevieh is no woman. . . ."

Tevieh next experiences the most agonizing adversity possible to an orthodox Jewish father. Eva, his third daughter, becomes enamored of a young Russian and accepts Christian-

ity in order to marry him. This time he balks: the blow has
struck at the very basis of his fundamental faith; unable to
prevent it, he cannot submit to it. While the beadle in "The
Lottery Winner" is stunned by the calamity, Tevieh steels
himself against reconciliation. One need only recall the scene
in the forest where Eva runs after him to beg his forgiveness,
and how he forces himself against his natural inclination "to
jump off the wagon and embrace her," to realize the depth of
his grief. Even when Eva seizes hold of the horse and exclaims, "Father, I shall die if you move. I beg you hear me
first," he holds fast. " 'So,' I think," he tells himself, " 'Father
dear,' eh; you want to take me by force? No, my soul! If so,
then you don't know your father! . . . and I began to beat
the horse as hard as I could. . . . Tevieh is no woman,
Tevieh knows how to deal with Satan. . . ." He flees from her
as from an evil spirit; and while his wound remains as wide as
his heart, he simply cannot put God to shame!

This is not the end of his affliction. Shprintze, his fourth
daughter, falls in love with a fickle youth, the son of a wealthy
and haughty widow. On learning of the affair, which she
scorns as beneath her station, the mother sends her son away
to a distant city. The simple and trusting girl, deprived of her
lover and already with child, drowns herself. Tevieh's grief is
aggravated by the cruel arrogance of the youth's vulgar uncle.
After this abuse, making mock of his self-respect, Tevieh says:
"I approached my horse and wagon, put my face into it and
—you won't laugh at me?—I cried and cried and cried. . . ."
What depressed him most was the callous coarseness of these
rich. "With God," said he, "I'll manage to get along—what
troubles me are people, why people should be so bad when
they could be good."

His next daughter, Golde, is as beautiful as her older sisters
and has no difficulty in attracting suitors. But her mind dwells
on her aged and unhappy father. Wishing to ease his remaining years, she marries a rich but vulgar businessman. At first
Tevieh rejoices: at least one daughter is well married. But
when he visits her one day and notes the unbreachable gap

between his sensitive daughter and her coarse husband, her sacrifice becomes painfully obvious.

Tevieh's Job-like fate is climaxed by a government regulation driving him out of his village home, so that he has to seek a new abode in his old age. Still the homely philosopher, he addresses himself to his Maker:

> Ach, Creator of the world, dear God, why do you have to bother with such as Tevieh? Why don't you sometimes play a trick on, for instance, a Brodsky or a Rothschild? Why don't you teach them the chapter, "Get thee out of the country"? It would, it seems to me, suit them much better. . . . Let them also see that we have a mighty God!

Normally the events in Tevieh's life would hardly be a fit subject for the humorist. Yet the monologues of this unfortunate Jew, ostensibly related to their author, make one laugh much and often. In episode after episode Tevieh's character grows in stature. Yet he does not tower as a modern Job, or a tragic Lear cruelly treated not so much by his daughters as by harsh circumstances. The reason is that we are not for a moment permitted to forget his Kaserilevke origin; it affects his character like an oblique shaft of light in a dark room. In the midst of distress he manifests a pious fatalism, a wholesome artlessness, a habit of aptly misquoting and mistranslating Hebrew passages, a suppleness of spirit—elements woven into the fabric of his being with consummate skill. In combination they turn tragedy into mellow mirth. The highest humor results from the manner in which he meets and acquiesces in the buffeting of his fate. As he relates his misery, with a naive philosophical acceptance that reveals his inward distress, one laughs the more heartily to repress rising sympathy. For his woes are not only personal but also Jewish, and that gives them a ready universality. Thus, after the pathetic scene in the forest with his apostatized daughter, he tries to find solace in the fatalistic thought: "A man's a fool! A wise man must not set his heart upon his misery, and must understand that life is as it should be, because if it was to have been different it wouldn't be as it is." One smiles at this pious determinism as a form of idiosyncrasy and conveniently smothers the welling sympathetic sorrow.

Tevieh would, of course, have been disconsolate without his ability to accept his agony with a philosophical smile, and the conscious belief that it came to him as a trial of the Lord. If his mind tended to reflect, his heart was warm and expansive. He was naturally altruistic. Aware of the pettiness of life, he also knew of what depth of sorrow the heart was capable, the insignificance of everything else compared with that sorrow, and of the need to alleviate it as much as humanly possible. Hence his all-embracing sympathy, the more admirable because of his narrowly pious upbringing. For the good of others he was ready to rise above his innate prejudices, restrain selfish impulses, and yield whatever authority was still his. To arrive at such true humility and wisdom one must first reduce everything to fundamentals, strip all values to their essentials, expose all pomp and vanity to their relative futility. This perspicacious insight brought Tevieh a measure of relief when mere reflection was ineffectual. The reader, while laughing heartily at his foibles and fatalism, loves him for his mitigating altruism.

Humor, the noblest form of laughter, generates genial enjoyment combined with congenial sympathy. Humor sees the incongruities of life and seeks to lessen the poignancy arising from them. It essays to soften with mirth the unavoidable harshness of existence, to span with a smile the abyss that sometimes separates man from man. A humorist perceives human weaknesses with greater insight than the satirist, but seldom forgets that he too is not free from them. Unlike the satirist, he is never overwhelmed by human meanness or stupidity. To him the world is a puny microcosm, not to be scolded or scorned, but countenanced and smiled at. His precept is: smile while you may; sorrow may stop it soon enough.

Sholom Aleichem's generation of Jews was fertile with elements of humor. It was in the inevitable process of transition;

harsh circumstances were relegating its medieval form of life to the irrevocable past, forcing each one to adapt himself to modern ways as best he could. Naive, quite gullible, wholly unprepared, these Jews were bewildered by the maze of urban modernity, confounded by their inability to tell the real from the apparent; necessity gave them no reprieve, compelling them to seek the means of subsistence hastily and haphazardly. For a time some of them unavoidably committed fantastic and ridiculous acts. To the casual observer, unaware of the genuine pathos motivating it, their behavior seemed highly comical. Sholom Aleichem knew this generation as well as Mendele knew his. Addressing himself to the reader in one of his stories, he said:

> I come, my dear friend, from Kaserilevke. There I was born, there I was brought up; there I was educated and there I was married. Afterward I sailed forth in my little bark on the great, wide, and powerful ocean called life, where waves cover the housetops. And although one is always being tossed and rocked on the raging surface, I have not for a moment forgotten my dear beloved home, Kaserilevke, long may it exist, nor my dear beloved brothers, the Kaserilevke Jews, may they thrive and increase. Whenever I hear of some misfortune, of a calamity, of a disaster, I think at once: what is going on *there*, in my native home.

He perceived the oblique direction of their transitional behavior and exposed the pathos of their altered status with compensating humor. In 1911 he stated in a letter: "I tell you it is an ugly and mean world and only to spite it one mustn't weep! If you want to know, that is the real source, the true cause of my constant good spirits, of my, as it is called, 'humor.' Not to cry out of spite! Only to laugh out of spite, *only to laugh!*"

He may truly be termed Kaserilevke's supreme achievement. His self was blended so successfully with the spirit of his people that in one sense his writings do not bear so much the stamp of individual authorship as that of genuine folklore, poetically interpreted. Had he lived in an earlier century, his stories would no doubt have circulated anonymously. As it was, his work became the literary expression of his generation to a greater degree than that of any other Yiddish writer. He had little of the self-consciousness of the modern artist, although he was too much Mendele's "grandson" not to rewrite and polish his stories many times. His senses seldom allowed him leisure for reflection; they crowded his consciousness with impressions and stimulated his imagination to incessant activity. The merest perception, the most casual observation, tended to excite his irrepressible humor.

As he was ever with and of the Jews of his time, he unwittingly became their literary chronicler, recording their deeds and aspirations, their misfortunes and tribulations, with the accuracy and sympathy of the intuitive writer. How truly the artist he was is evidenced in the following incident. While still a young man he visited his friend and mentor Mendele to have him read critically his latest story. "What is your purpose in writing it?" asked the older man. The query nonplussed him for the moment. Recalling it later, he said: "I confess that this was to me a new America discovered. It was then five years that I was writing, have written, praised be His name, so many things, and not once had I asked myself, 'What is my purpose?' What purpose can a writer have? A writer desires to write, for if he would not desire to write he would not be a writer. . . ."

Although he wrote primarily out of his own experiences, he made himself the artistic voice of his people. Little of his ego came to the surface. His literary self was chameleon-like in its happy blending with the characters he portrayed. His ear for authentic speech was unerring. His Jews talk naturally, with their own idiosyncrasies and peculiar idioms. Thus, most of his work is in the form of monologues or letters. His characters, at once unique and typical, are authentic representatives of the Ukrainian Jews at the turn of the century. They recalled a recent past imbued with nostalgic memories in the minds of many of his readers, and "something of Sholom Aleichem" became essential at Jewish gatherings and concerts.

For all the folkloric effect of his writings, he was ever the conscious and painstaking artist. Poverty and the conditions of newspaper serialization—the chief medium of publication in Yiddish—forced him to write regardless of his health or state of mind. Yet he never considered a work finished until he had revised and improved it to his heart's content. To a friend he wrote:

> A kind of Mephistopheles sits within me, and he laughs, mocks, pokes fun at my writings. Every time I write something and read it with enthusiasm, as is usual with an author, he only whistles through his lips and his eyes smile. If I could catch him I would choke him! It sometimes happens that he listens to me quite seriously and nods his head. This makes me think that he approves, and I send it to the printer—when he explodes with laughter—this Mephistopheles, may he burn!

Yet the urge to gain approval of his inner critic never slackened. Writing to the editor of *The Friend* to apologize for the delay in sending him the manuscript of *The Treasure* for serialization, he said: "Before I let anything out of my hands I must cut it apart at least five times, and then I must polish it, sharpen it—a misfortune! From a four-act comedy it was transformed into a one-act tragic-comedy with a prologue—sharply reducing the number of lines—isn't this insane?" And to the very end of his life he continued to choose his words and phrases as if he were matching pearls.

CHAPTER FOUR

ISAAK LAYBUSH PERETZ

The Father of Modern Yiddish Literature

THERE ARE evidences that Peretz's family was one of the
Sephardic group of Spanish Jews who settled in Poland not
long after their expulsion in 1492. His immediate ancestors
were anti-Hasidic, and a number of them were scholars and
businessmen of high repute. Although his parents were not as
wealthy as their predecessors, they adhered to the family's
charitable tradition.

Isaak Laybush, born in Zamoscz in 1852, received the usual
training in Hebrew lore. Bright and thoughtful, he in his
early teens exhibited feats of learning that gained him the
plaudits reserved for a prodigy. Even at this time he was
speculating about the meaning and end of life, digging to the
depths of his being with the sharp nails of doubt. Wherever
men congregated, he listened and pondered. At the time he
appeared, as he remembered, with "little thin hands, and feet
—like sticks; a large head and a wrinkled forehead; beneath
—large, searching, groping, painfully questioning eyes."

At the age of 15 a happy chance gave him access to a relatively large private library owned by one of the town's few
intellectuals. There for the first time he saw books in languages other than Hebrew. He already had a smattering of
Polish and Russian, and with the aid of translations and

grammars soon acquired a reading knowledge of German and French. One can imagine with what avidity he read book after book—indiscriminately, enthusiastically, obliviously. Maimonides and Spinoza he had read in Hebrew; now he perused the work of non-Jewish philosophers, mostly German, and various works of science, so that his biblical concept of the world was dislodged by a view more consonant with modern thought. Fiction and poetry he read eagerly and uncritically, enjoying alike Dickens, Dumas, Sue, Shakespeare, Heine, and later poets and novelists. For months on end he lived in this new world, fascinating and unfamiliar. Like other naturally inclined writers, he was soon composing verses in Hebrew, Polish, and even Yiddish, much encouraged by an uncle whom he admired.

When Peretz was 18 he became engaged to the daughter of G. J. Lichtenfeld, an intellectual and mathematician. As was the custom at the time, the engaged couple did not meet until the day of their wedding, but that did not concern young Peretz in his eagerness to associate himself with a father-in-law of known enlightenment. Similarly, Lichtenfeld approved of the match when told by Peretz's uncle about his nephew's literary aspirations: "He writes and discards, writes and tears up, writes and burns up." After their marriage in 1870 the young couple found themselves unsuited to each other. The girl, having had a secular education, considered herself culturally superior to her self-taught husband, and thought little of his literary endeavors. At her urging he studied bookkeeping and tried to earn a living at various business ventures—only to fail in each one. Divorce followed after five years of uncongeniality, and Peretz assumed the care of their son Lucian. He then went to Warsaw to study law, and in time developed a fair practice in Zamoscz. In 1878 he remarried, this time happily.

Peretz began to write in Yiddish during adolescence, but destroyed most of it. His Hebrew poems were published in the early 1870's and were well received. Increase in the number of clients and his civic activities kept him from writing for nearly a decade, and not until 1887 did he again publish some Hebrew poems. The next year an envious competitor denounced him to the government as a socialist, and he lost the right to practice law. When he appealed for reinstatement to the minister of justice in St. Petersburg, the latter dismissed him with the curt statement: "That's nothing; one fewer Jewish lawyer in Russia."

In financial need, Peretz turned to writing. Embittered by social and personal harassment, he decided against writing in Polish. Yiddish continued to appeal to him. As early as 1886 he said: "In that language are hidden the weeping of our parents, the outcries of many generations, the poison and the bitterness of history. It contains the dearest diamonds—Jewish tears which became hardened before they had dried."

Learning that the Kiev maecenas Sholom Rabinovitch was planning to publish his *Yiddish Folk Bibliotek* and paid well for contributions, Peretz sent him "Monish" and several prose sketches. In an accompanying letter he explained that he had hitherto burned everything written in Jargon, and that he wrote only for his own pleasure. "If I think of the reader at all, I think of him as one of a higher level of society, one who reads and has studied in a living language." A little later he confessed that, having read very little of Yiddish writing, he had confused Mendele with Sholom Aleichem. "I am ashamed to say it, but in our town there is not one book in Jargon, and I am in no condition to buy any at present. . . . I heartily permit you to revise my work and the expressions which are not intelligible to Russian and Lithuanian Jews. But please be careful with the meter." He proposed that the two of them, "to enrich the language," publish a book on psychology based on Wilhelm Wundt's work and studies in Jewish history, especially for women readers—but nothing came of that.

When "Monish" appeared in print, Peretz was greatly annoyed about Sholom Aleichem's several emendations; referring to the generous fee of 150 rubles, he stated: "None of your honey, and none of your sting." Although he also contributed to the second volume of *Yiddish Folk Bibliotek*, he and Sholom Aleichem did not become friends. The latter, the realist, failed to appreciate Peretz's symbolic mysticism, and Sholom Aleichem's humor was too close to the marketplace to meet the poet's high literary notions. Several subsequent incidents served further to keep them apart. It was only years later, when Sholom Aleichem read Peretz's *Intimate Folk Tales*, that he wrote to him: "I approached the mirror and slapped myself twice for not knowing up to now how to appreciate your worth!" This gesture brought about a happy reconciliation.

With Mendele, Peretz was also quite aloof, and later credited him only as being "the first": "He was the first who showed love and respect for his artistic instrument—the Yiddish word—and kept it pure . . . and was therefore the first to create a Yiddish style."

In 1890, without employment and in want, Peretz eagerly accepted the offer of Jan Bloch, the Warsaw philanthropist, to study the life of the Jews in the small Polish towns. He and Dinesohn, with whom he soon became intimate, visited community after community, gathering statistical data and observing cultural customs. His report, later issued as *Travel Pictures*, was an illuminating delineation of the life led by the mass of Polish Jews. Dr. Eliashev said that "he wrote about the towns he visited with the objectivity of the investigator. He found everything in a state of degeneracy—impoverished, listless, dead." Late in 1890, back in Warsaw, Peretz was engaged as bookkeeper by the *Gmineh*, the Jewish Civic Center, at a meager salary—540 rubles a year, gradually increased to 2400—and kept the job to the end of his life in 1915.

Peretz in 1890 was in the prime of life. Of medium height, with broad shoulders and a large head, he impressed all who met him with the extraordinary brilliance of his dark eyes. His bearing was aristocratic, proud, without the least semblance of the ghetto Jew. He was energetic of movement and unstable of mood. Devoted and friendly, he soon attracted neophyte writers, awed youths who came to him as truth seekers and drew comfort and encouragement from this high-minded mentor. His home became the cynosure of the young as well as of older writers. Niger wrote: "This house, Tzigliana No. 1, became a center for Jewish radical thought. There the foundation was laid for Yiddish literature not as a means, but as an end in itself. Out of that house came forth the thought of Yiddish, the poetic rebirth of Hasidism, the love of the folksong and the folktale."

He was ever concerned for the welfare of the mass of Jews, and often castigated wealthier Jews for being less civic-minded than he thought they should be. At the outbreak of World War I he suffered deeply when many Jews were driven out of their homes, and helped as many as he could with food and shelter. Yet he was for the most part subject to the loneliness of the lofty, with the gentle Dinesohn being his only intimate companion.

So extraordinary was his eminence among fellow Jews toward the end of his life that his funeral attracted the largest crowd in the history of Warsaw. Yet so antagonistic were the Poles toward the Jews in 1915 that not a word of his death appeared in the Polish press.

Peretz's intense Jewishness was as evident in his civic work as in his writing. He loved his people with the passion of the inspired leader, and with the zeal of the prophet he sought to exalt them body and soul. As all intellectual reformers of the time, he wanted to free them from their superstitious beliefs, abject meekness, and enervated passivity. Proud Jew that he was, he resented the bartering of self-respect for a bit of bread. Believing also that "the old rabbinic bat had spread its wings over the confused populace," he attacked the orthodox religious leaders as enemies of progress.

He wanted the Jews to become self-sufficing and self-respecting human beings, and appealed to his fellow intellectuals to help make them so. In 1891 he published two issues of his *Yiddish Bibliotek* as a means to that end. In the preface to the first volume he wrote:

Our program is education. We want to educate the people: to turn fools into wise men; to make intelligent persons out of fanatics; out of idlers and *luftmenschen*—workingmen, useful, honest people who work for themselves and thereby benefit society. . . . We say simply: We Jews are as human as all human beings! We have virtues, we have faults. We are neither demigods nor demons, only human. And human beings should educate themselves, become wiser, better, finer with every passing day.

His cry was not a voice in the wilderness. Reformers of the previous decades had been badly shaken by the pogroms of 1881 and the intensified anti-Semitism in the years thereafter. Only a few continued to disdain Yiddish as a corrupt dialect and to maintain that Jews must use the language of the land in which they lived. A good many had turned Zionist and argued for a national revival of Hebrew. More and more, however, realized that they must go direct to the people, speak to them in the one language they knew, and help them to acquire the culture and status of modern Europeans. Peretz, one of their leaders, said that "whoever wants to know the people, and teach them, must know how to speak and write in Yiddish." Yet even he was too much the sensitive artist to employ that tongue in its current crudity. In 1888 he had explained to Sholom Aleichem his position in connection with his use of a literary Yiddish:

As we shall express new ideas, we must give them new forms, new expressions, since the old garment doesn't fit the new one; the expressions will at first appear strange, but in the end they will penetrate the reader's mind and enrich his intellect. For that reason I have made no effort to limit my thoughts and to curb them to the common speech. On the contrary, I have resorted not to his speech but to the language that best expresses the riches most strongly, so that the uneducated reader might educate himself.

Eager to purify and enrich the Yiddish language, he castigated assimilationists who continued to advocate its replacement by Russian or Polish. When Jewish writers and intellectuals, at a meeting in his honor in St. Petersburg, spoke only in Russian, he jumped up and exclaimed: "I cannot, I will not. . . . You insult me with your Russian speeches. It is an insult that you should speak to me in a foreign tongue! It is an insult to the people!" The outburst nullified his mission to raise funds for a Yiddish theater, but he did not regret it.

To those who urged Hebrew as the national language he was more conciliatory. "Jargon makes no pretense to replace the mother's position in a Jewish home; that position belongs and must belong to Hebrew; . . . Jargon is only a nurse who wishes to teach how to walk, sit, speak." Later, however, he made Yiddish the equal of Hebrew. In 1894 he wrote:

> It is about time for the *intelligentzia* to relegate to the old archives the questions, Is Yiddish a language? Can there be a language without a grammar? Can a patchwork of different languages and of different periods be called a language? This is merely the old obfuscating cavil which will always be pecked at by the barren hens of our literature; the true *intelligentzia* must realize that Yiddish is a fact that came not of our volition and will not disappear over night at our desire . . . that a language is whatever means people use to communicate with one another, that four million beings who speak and understand only Yiddish are also people, and that whoever wishes to educate them must accept their language as the means.

At the same time he addressed himself to Yiddish writers to urge linguistic improvement: "We want to pull up the weeds by the roots, to cut down the briars, to burn the tares, to sow the pure grain of human ideas, human feelings, and knowledge."

His influence on Jewish intellectuals in Poland as well as on aspiring young Yiddish writers everywhere was enormous. Up to the end of his life he remained their inspiring leader. His views and opinions were eagerly solicited, and he imparted them generously and forthrightly on the platform and in his considerable journalistic writings, both in Yiddish and in Hebrew. He discussed every topic of current interest with cogent effectiveness. With poignant satire and cutting irony he fought the anti-Semitic eruptions of the time, making mock in particular of Polish diatribes, exposing their deceitful pretensions, and encouraging Jews to insist on their ancient and just rights. He readily entered into polemics with Polish publicists who connived at the injustices done to his people, and demolished their claims with pertinently trenchant arguments.

With equal forcefulness and on a larger scale, Peretz fought the shams, fanaticism, and intolerance within the Jewish community. Like Mendele and Sholom Aleichem, he described the life of the Polish Jews as he found it at the time: the old order crumbling at the edges and the new one struggling to emerge. He wrote about the prevailing poverty, the lack of work opportunities; how hunger caused some to resort to fantastic ways of gaining a few pennies. The following excerpt indicates how one Jew reacted to his precarious way of life:

Money, praised be His Name, I have none! Neither I nor the Jews around here! Except perhaps the reformed Jews in the large cities. . . . We have no money! A trade I have none—neither did my grandfather! Nevertheless, at the will of His Blessed Name, I live; and for over fifty years at that! And—when it is necessary to marry off a child, one does it without means as well. . . .

Closer questioning elicited the information that this Jew was simultaneously a justice of the peace, an agent, a trader, a marriage broker, and a messenger. From all these occupations he eked out a bare existence, yet he was considered by the less fortunate as well-to-do.

Most of these Jews were Hasidim whose appearance matched their medievally oriented minds. Their clothes were of a peculiar pattern—obliquely similar to the garments worn by feudal Poles; their beards were untouched by steel or comb; their ear curls sometimes reached below their chins. Extremely pious, they considered spiritual concentration more important than providing for their families, so that many depended upon their wives to attend to material needs. Since to enter Paradise was their dearest goal, they fought desperately against the "godless" western ideas undermining the piety of their children.

Thus Peretz found them in the 1890's. Their economic plight aroused his sympathy, but their religious fanaticism made him caustic. His satire was directed especially at the town rabbi, presumed shepherd of his people, keeper of His holy laws. He depicted him as a mere caricature of his predecessors, the patriarchs who guided and comforted their charges, with his interest limited to ritual questions and narrow interpretation of obsolescent laws. He was equally critical of the Hasidic rabbis, whose pretense to miraculous powers he considered pseudo-religious charlatanry. In numerous articles and sketches Peretz sought to nullify their influence upon the mass of Jews.

He was also condemnatory of urbanized Jews who were flagrantly overreaching themselves in their endeavor to attain social status. With sarcastic acerbity he exposed their myopic behavior and the pathetic futility of their assimilationist striving. He disdained their shedding the good with the bad of their Jewish inheritance: their loss of racial dignity, fawning and cringing in the presence of gentiles, posing as "Poles of the Mosaic faith." His aim was to bring harmony within the fold of Israel: to waken in his fellow Jews pride of self and of their people, to bring understanding and sympathy among the several classes of Jews, and to lead all of them to a higher level of culture.

An instance of his position was his manner of handling the question of circumcision, much debated at the time. Regarding the rite as an ancient custom, he pointed out to the pious Jews how dangerous it was to base religion on a sacrificial act. Aware, however, of the futility of reasoning with entrenched orthodoxy, and eager to unite both groups in the face of external oppression, he cautioned the opponents of circumcision to keep distinct the ends and the means:

> Pious Jews are a suppressing majority. To the pious Jew everything is holy. The pettiest law recorded in Hebrew lore, the most insignificant and foolish custom—the entire Diasporal rope that

winds from generation to generation around his neck and throt-
tles and almost chokes him out of his breath—he regards as holy!
Yet one must confess—tragic as it may be and strange as it may
sound—that this shortening of breath, this opiating of the Jewish
life-pulse, have greatly helped the Jews to withstand and to
endure the coal-black and blood-red times of the Inquisition, the
massacres, and the like periods of woe that no other nation could
survive. . . . Therefore, as the large majority of the Jews consider circumcision as an exclusive act of adherence to the Jewish
people, it is necessary for each free-thinking Jew, as a Jew, to
submit in order not to be torn from the tribe. . . . On the other
hand, as a free thinker he has the right, and in more propitious
times the duty, to fight for such a conviction with all the power
of the explicit word.

In his journalistic writings Peretz was the serious and spirited social reformer. As a polemicist he exposed wrongs within
the Jewish community and defended it from its overt and
covert enemies. In this phase of his writing he was the inspired truth-seeker, hater of sham, contemner of servility,
enemy of dead tradition, advocate of the living ideal, and the
eloquent and effective Jewish leader.

Peretz was a publicist of necessity but an artist by inclination. Were he not living at a time when modern industry and
liberated rationalism were bringing havoc and harassment to
the Jews of Eastern Europe, so that their vicissitude became
his vicissitude and their plight his plight, his writing might
have assumed a gemlike wholeness instead of being spar-
klingly fragmentary. Consciously avoiding the seclusion of the
ivory tower, however, he devoted his charged feelings to his
didactic and polemical efforts. He also sought to achieve his
purpose by fictional means, and provided a symbolic moral in
a number of his stories.

In one sketch a garrulous furrier philosophizes about the
shtreimel—the fur hat traditionally worn by many rabbis and
Hasidim. He argues sarcastically, and brings up a number of
pertinent incidents, to demonstrate that people respect the

shtreimel rather than those wearing it—reminding one of
Thackeray's famous cartoon of Louis XIV. In another tale a
vacillating rabbi of Chelm is caricatured as a little innocuous
"man satisfied with his mite and without a temper." When a
certain Yekel is beaten several times by a drunken churl who
serves the Jews on the Sabbath, he complains to the rabbi
and is each time pacified by word rather than deed. When
Yekel is beaten in the synagogue yard, the rabbi becomes
alarmed, fearing a threat to the entire congregation. Calling
a meeting of his parishioners, he explains the situation and
concludes: "If I have any voice in the congregation, and if
my advice were honestly to be requested, I should say the
following: Yekel should first of all, even tomorrow at dawn,
leave town with the help of God. . . . And in order to save
the congregation from further danger the peasant should receive an increase in pay." And Peretz the moralist cannot
refrain from adding: "You laugh? And yet somewhat of the
spirit of the Chelm rabbi is to be found in everyone of us."

Peretz championed the rights of the Jewish woman. Her
lowly position in Jewish life—ignored as a girl and merely
tolerated as wife and mother—seemed to him a barbaric condition not to be endured. In poem and story he wrote caustically of her role as sole provider, her forced meekness, and
her work in the sweatshop. He was particularly incensed at
the practice of keeping girls in poor homes without schooling,
and of giving those in wealthier urban homes a completely
non-Jewish education. He relates that in "a school for Jewish
girls in a large Jewish city . . . whose mothers wear the prescribed wig and whose fathers dress in satin caftans and fur
hats," a teacher asked who knew Yiddish or the Hebrew
alphabet. "All were quiet." This situation is treated in "The
Outcast." A girl is given lessons in foreign languages but not
in either Hebrew or Yiddish. Ignored by her father and indulged by her mother, she gives her time to reading romances
and dreaming of adventure. One day she is attracted to a
Polish youth, elopes with him, and is converted. Her action

drives her pious parents to a premature death. Years later she meets her brother and her mood is repentent yet accusatory:

> You Jews are guilty! What did I know of your bloody struggle with them? You knew it; you were taught in *kheder*. My books did not mention a word of it. . . . I did not betray you—I did not *know* you! I knew nothing of your sorrow, I was never told a word of it. . . . Your secrets were never disclosed to me. . . . Why did you not tell me of *your* love—of the love that feeds upon blood? Why did you not show me *your* beauty, your eternal blood-stained beauty? Beauty, love, spirit—you kept to yourselves, for men only. . . . You cast *us* out!

These words are Peretz's, giving voice to his indignation. The dangerous disparity between the pious gabardined youth and the sentimental Polonized girl worried him. At the end of the story he added this italicized coda: *"Let her be judged by Him who is over nations and their complex bloody struggles."*

The Jewish girl who remained within the fold sometimes found life a succession of sorrows. Usually married to a youth whose chief virtue was knowledge of Hebrew lore, she had her hair shaved off on the day of her wedding and was thereafter expected to assume the confining practices of the pious Jewess. "In the Postchaise" tells her story from the point of view of a neighbor, an intelligent Pole:

> For hours together she would stand by the window, hands on her breast, and gaze sadly at us or at the stars with tear-stained eyes. We saw that she was always alone—your men never seem to have any time—always sad and wistful. Her sorrow was imprinted on her pale face. . . . She wanted to live, to love and be loved. . . . No, you can say what you will, this injustice often happens among you: you sell your daughters. . . . It is true, in time they become accustomed to this life, in time they forget. . . . They are pious, they are good and patient. . . . But who can count the bitter tears that fall upon their grieved faces before their eyes run dry? Who can calculate their heart pangs before they become reconciled to a living death?

Again it is Peretz speaking, overstating the truth perhaps, his anger heightened by compassion.

Years of poverty and drudgery, of worry and grief, slowly transform the young married Jewess into a servile and subservient wife. Harsh as is the lot of her husband, hers is worse: she must bear his mastery in addition to providing for their home, for the pious Jew must study to prepare his soul for Paradise. This aspect of Jewish life is described ironically in such stories as "In the Basement," "The Anger of a Jewish Woman," and "Mendel Breines." The first is an idyllic tale of a newlywed couple who love each other shyly yet ardently in the midst of poverty and squalor. Occupying one corner of a basement, with the other corners taken up by families as poor as themselves, they have no privacy. The wife is especially perturbed by an old hag who cannot understand how any woman can keep from berating her husband. Since her husband, a teacher has only three pupils, the cloud of poverty darkens her life. To eke out their existence, she begins to sell onions. However much she loves her husband, she cannot drive from her mind the wizened face of the hag who no doubt was once a tender and devoted bride.

In "The Anger of a Jewish Woman" the husband's arrogance, his indifference to the needs of the family, and his wife's inability to earn enough for their needs, brings their existence to a pathetic pass. Angered by his seeming disinterest at a time when they are with a sick child and without food, she interrupts his study to urge him to do something about their plight. Her brazenness shocks him:

Listen thou woman. . . . Doest thou know how grievously one sins by interrupting someone at study? Not to permit your husband to study, ha?! And who provides for the bird? Always disturbing the Lord, always temptation, always *this* world. Foolish woman—shrew! Not to permit a husband to study deserves Gehenna!

Only the piteous cry of her feverish child thwarts her desperate attempt to hang herself.

The wife is an adequate provider in "Mendel Breines," only she works herself to the bone in pampering her stupid husband. Although he appreciates her care, he selfishly accepts her coddling without question and is very much surprised when she dies from sheer exhaustion.

In these tales Peretz depicts the life of the orthodox Jews vividly and realistically, yet their traits, customs, and attitudes are seen from the point of view of the social reformer. Like Mendele, he speaks out vociferously against the blemishes and inadequacies he finds within the Jewish community; as a consequence he expresses himself artistically in a minor key.

Poverty being so egregiously prevalent among the Jews of his time, Peretz, like other Jewish writers, could not but deal with it at some length. And like them he stressed the Jews' ability to survive as a result of their spiritual faith and personal perseverance. Two of his best-known stories—"The Messenger" and "Bontche Silent"—are at once noteworthy and typically Peretzian. The first describes the death of an old messenger. On his way to a neighboring town in the thick of a winter storm to deliver a valuable packet, he feels a pain in his left side and his inadequately clothed body is half-frozen. Yet he trudges on, intent on reaching his destination and delivering his parcel. Gusts of wind draw tears from his aching eyes, swirls of snow impede his steps, but he persists and promises to buy himself a pair of spectacles with his first savings.

Incidents from his past life flit through his consciousness like little sprites. As a child he was drafted into the army of Nicholas I, and for 35 years remained in the depths of arctic Russia—25 of them with gun in hand. All these years, although he had hardly met a Jew and had to undergo the regimen of the army, he had clung resolutely to memories of his early youth. When at last he returned to his native town he began to practice the piety he remembered. He married and worked as a night watchman. Dire poverty turned his wife into a shrew, and she made life miserable for him. Yet she cared for him in her way, and when there was no food in the house she worried more for his sake than for hers. After years of struggle she died of malnutrition. Their four children drifted away, and he remained alone, working as a messenger and reading Psalms when free. He never complained, never grumbled.

"Meantime the frost increases. His beard and mustache are iced. Still his body is not uncomfortable and his head feels quite warm, with drops of sweat on his brow. Only his feet become more and more cold." He would like to rest a bit, only he is ashamed: it is the first time in his life that he is finding it difficult to walk a distance of ten miles at a stretch. His feet grow heavier and colder with every step. "Arguing contrariwise, he thinks to himself: What if I do rest? A minute, half a minute! Perhaps I should. Let me but try! My feet have been obeying me for so long, I shall obey them also this once!" He sits down. Pains come shooting to his head and heart, and at the thought of sickness he fears most for the valuable packet. Dusk approaches. He commands himself to rise, and in the hallucination which comes over him believes himself to have risen. His mind wanders, and he sees himself at home, with all his children visiting at once. Their embraces are too vehement.

"Easy there, children! Easy, do not press me so hard! I am no longer a young man; I am over seventy! . . . Easy, you're choking me, easy, children . . . old bones! Easy, I have money in my bosom! I am, praised be the Lord, trusted with money! . . . Enough, children, enough. . . ." And it was enough. . . . With his hand in his bosom pocket he remained stark. . . .

Here Peretz is primarily the artist. In its eleven pages this story gives us an unforgettable portrayal of a sturdy septuagenarian of simple and deep piety. The narrative is restrained, humorous, and persuasive, progressing with the sure strides of subtle art. In his death the docile, honest, and tenacious old man comes alive in the reader's imagination.

"Bontche Silent" * presents another aspect of the same type of Jew. On earth the meek and uncomplaining porter was a human zero, and his death was entirely unnoticed. "Bontche lived in silence, and silently he died; he passed through *our* world like a shadow. . . . A shadow! His image was impressed on no one's mind, in no man's heart; he left not an imprint!" In the seven heavens, however, his death caused a sensation. "Young angels with brilliant eyes, golden wire-wrought wings and silver slippers flew rejoicing toward Bontche! The flutter of wings, the patter of slippers, and the happy laughter from the young, fresh, rosy mouths filled the heavens and reached to the Blessed Seat, and God Himself knew of Bontche's arrival."

Timid Bontche is overawed by this reception, thinking it a fantastic dream. "And his fear increases when he sees the diamond and alabaster floor of the Hall of Judgment! 'And my feet stand on such a floor! . . . Who knows what rich man, what rabbi, what saint they have in mind—when he comes, I'll get it, all right!' " He does not realize that the Angel for the Defense has begun to tell the story of his life. Only as he recognizes incidents from his own wretched exist-ence does he become persuaded that it is about him after all. The Angel relates how Bontche was tormented by a shrewish stepmother; how, in a winter night, he was driven from home by a drunken father; how he hungered and suffered and over-worked; how he saved a rich man from certain death and was rewarded with work and a bride who was already with child; how he was betrayed by his wife, mistreated by *her* son, and later mortally wounded by his "benevolent" employer; and how under all these conditions he remained silent!

He was silent even in the hospital, where one may cry out! He was silent even when the doctor would not approach his bed without a fee, and when the nurse would not change his sheet without pay! He was silent when dying, and silently he emitted his last breath. . . . Not a word against God, not a word against man! Dixi!

The Angel for the Prosecution makes several attempts to speak, then says: "Gentlemen! He was silent. I too will be silent!"

The Lord then speaks softly to Bontche, calls him "my dear Bontche," and tells him he may have whatever he desires, for he is worthy of what is most precious. When assured of this several times, Bontche, whose heart weeps from joy, says smilingly: "If this be so, I would like every morning a hot bun with fresh butter." Peretz concluded: "The Judge and the Angels lowered their heads in shame. The Prosecutor laughed."

Ostensibly the old messenger and Bontche are similar conceptions. Both are simple subservient creatures, ill abused, depicted with like sympathy. In the first story, however, the emphasis is on portrayal of character—the intuitive expression of the quintessence of a docile human soul. Bontche, on the other hand, becomes a springboard for social satire and religious irony. The meek porter's life is made a protest against man's abuse of man, an oppressed man's cry for human justice. There is something Christlike about Bontche. His abject suffering is dramatized to make him crushed, blood-stained, and forgiving. Yet Peretz also makes mock of his meekness, intimating that, in order to be heard, it is sometimes necessary to shout—especially on earth. As the Lord tells Bontche: "You yourself perhaps did not know that you could cry, and that your cry could have caused the wall of Jericho to tumble and collapse. You yourself did not know of your latent power. . . ."

Bontche's fatalistic attitude irritated Peretz because it symbolized the pious Jew's complete credence in life after death, his belief that suffering on earth would be compensated by pleasures in Paradise. Peretz knew only too well that the resulting meekness and self-abnegation were suicidal in an unconscionable world, especially as the faith that had kept the Jews alive for centuries was losing its hold upon them. Yet he loved the poor porter and the old messenger and sympathized with their naive piety, artless minds, and simple wholesomeness, and his portrayal made them memorable additions to Yiddish literature.

Peretz was no Hasid. "Inwardly I was and remained a Jew, with a Jewish, more or less clear biblical outlook on the world." He became a publicist out of love for his people, but was always essentially a poet and romanticist. "To current facts," he stated, "even in private life, I react weakly or not at all. Facts for the most part are trivial: motives—mixed and confused, colors—gray, tones—loud, lines—heavy. . . . In recollection they become refined and purified." Disdaining the ordinary, the commonplace, the little people all about him, he yearned for the heroic, the noble, the spiritually exalted. Critical as he was of dogmatic piety and dry legalism, which in combination were burdening the Jewish community with a pernicious lethargy, he was among the first to delve into the spiritual sources of Jewish life. In time he discovered in Jewish folklore and the ideals of Hasidism the warm spring of emotional Judaism.

If you have no God, you look for idols, and these give no *Torah*. Our road is back, back to our past, back to the Bible. Speaking for myself, what we have to do is to find in Jewish life what has been created by and belongs to the people, what the people relate about themselves—the Hasidim and the rest. The Yiddish writer has to take all this rich material and work it up in his own spirit. That is Yiddish literature.

The Jewish spirit, product of centuries of external oppression and religious concentration, combines in its full manifestation both pathology and profundity, grotesqueness and greatness. In depicting what he termed "the bloody beauty of our Diaspora existence" in his Hasidic and folkloric stories, Peretz extracted its inward essence and ignored its external excrescences. He was fascinated by the poetic personalities and romantic exuberance of the founders of Hasidism—their ecstatic love of God, mystic communion with Jehovah, lowly humaneness, and ethical righteousness. Without accepting their ideology and conceits, he gave artistic expression to their ideals, which had become part of Jewish folklore. The more he familiarized himself with the rich legends and reveries associated with these wonder-working rabbis, the more he perceived the distilled beauty of these folk tales—"the magic and the truth of art itself." In retelling them in his inimitable style he gave Yiddish literature a new song of songs of the Jewish spirit.

For all his rational European veneer, Peretz was deeply drawn to the beatitude of exalted revery, the splendor of the soul communing with the Godhead. Even in his mature years, in the presence of intimate friends, he would sometimes hum a Hasidic tune without words which repeated itself endlessly. To him song was not mere musical expression but symbolic of the loftiness of life. One of his rabbis thus explains its significance:

> There is a song that depends upon words: such a song is of very low degree. . . . There is one of a higher degree: a song that sings of itself, altogether without words—only music! But even this song requires sound . . . and lips through which to pass! And lips are matter! And a voice, though of delicate matter, is matter still! . . . The true song sings of itself and without sound. . . . It sings from within, from the heart, from one's very being! . . .

Peretz's own generation was very far from such true song. Of a proud, aristocratic nature, he suffered to see how shriveled and shrunken the spiritual life of the urbanized Jew had become. To imbue him with a pride in his Jewish origin, he turned to the great Hasidic rabbis and the sources of Jewish folklore for his literary material—sources woven with the golden threads of myth and legend. He stressed the rabbis' mystic love of sheer song, their belief that all of life was one song:

> For each man is a musical instrument, and the life of man is a song, whether a joyous or a sad song, and when he completes his song it flies out of his body, and this song—that is, his soul—joins anew the great chorus before His Blessed Seat. . . . And woe to the man who lives without his song; he lives without a soul, and his life is a screech and a sigh—it is no life.

To awaken this song within the soul of the modern Jew, Peretz eulogized the spiritual quality of Hasidism. "Between Two Mountains" contrasts the essential difference between the poeticized Hasid and the orthodox ritualist. The latter regards religion as a relationship between God and man. He prays alone and in silence even in the synagogue. His attitude is matter-of-fact: he believes that by faithfully performing his religious obligations he will gain Paradise. Not so the Hasid, to whom religion is an exciting, joyous experience. He envisages God not as a stern Jehovah but as a loving Father. In the synagogue he prays as a child amidst the children of the Almighty; he prays aloud, as to a father, waxing enthusiastic and forgetting his worldly self in spiritual ecstacy. In this story the ritualist rabbi is the older of the two, very learned, stern, cold, rigorous, zealous, and proud; the Hasid, equally learned, once a pupil of the other, is mild, warm, soft, sympathetic, and forgiving. Having left his former teacher because his soul could find no breathing space in ritualism, he now tells him:

> Your teaching, rabbi, is overfine! Without compassion, without pity! Therefore it is without joy, without free breath . . . like cast iron; iron laws, copper statues . . . and very abstruse, fit only for scholars, for the few. . . . Tell me, rabbi, what have you for the people—for the woodcutter, the butcher, the laborer, the ordinary Jew? . . . Especially for the sinful Jew? . . . To speak plainly, your teaching is hard, hard and dry, because it is only the body and not the soul of the Torah!

He then shows the older rabbi the results of his Hasidic teaching. The day being Pentecost, he takes him to the porch and asks him to look on the green bordering the town. There groups of his followers bask in the sun; poor and rich alike are rejoicing in the lap of God's meadow.

> All groups are gazing with wonderfully eager eyes at the rabbi on the porch. . . . The thirsty eyes suck the light upon the rabbi's face; and the more light they suck the louder they sing . . . louder and louder . . . more lustily and holier. . . . And each group sings its own song, and songs and voices intermingle in the air, and only *one* song reaches the rabbi's porch, *one* tune . . . as if all are singing only one song. And everything is sing-

ing: the sky, the lost souls, the earth beneath, and the soul of the world, everything is singing!

"It is time for afternoon prayers!" just then exclaims the ritualist, and the charm of the scene vanishes.

Peretz was of course more interested in effect than in fact. He exaggerated the rapture of one and the rigor of the other to make the point more eloquently. For he is here presenting not so much the differing philosophies of two rabbis as he is his conception of them, imbuing Hasidism with romantic glamor because of its innate emotional appeal.

The rich folklore he uncovered—tales, legends, anecdotes— concerns largely wonder-working rabbis and secret saints who were endowed with supernatural powers which they often employed to right wrongs and reward the just. Pious Jews, Hasidim in particular, depend upon this intercession and ask for it in time of affliction or personal sorrow; the miraculous manner in which these requests are granted forms the basis of a number of his stories. In all of them man is judged not by his appearance but by his acts, and not so much by results as by intentions. Each folktale is told with great skill and verbal beauty. In each Peretz probes the deep recesses of human frailty, human goodness, and human greatness. Whether they treat of Hasidic miracles, incidents relating to humble yet lovable men and women, or flights of poetic nobility and folk fantasy, each adds to the quality and scope of his artistic achievement.

"Berl the Tailor" is a typical Hasidic tale. This poor worker gets mad at God and refuses to serve Him. The all-knowing Rabbi Levi Isaak learns of Berl's rebellion from his communion with Heaven. Before Yom Kippur he sends for Berl and the latter tells him, tailorlike, that he is angry with God because He does not provide him with an adequate living. The rabbi agrees with the justice of the complaint, obtains Berl's readiness to forgive God, and God in turn forgives Berl.

"At the Head of the Dying" tells of a pious usurer who dies and is taken by the Black Angel, while a less pious Jew who was always helpful to others is taken to Heaven when he dies.

At Heaven's gate, however, the latter asks the Angel leading him: "And what will I do there, Angel? There where none needs my soul, my heart, nor my sympathetic tear, nor my word of comfort, nor my hand to lift one from the pit?" As the Angel offers him no satisfactory answer, the soul decides to go with the Black Angel to the abode of the sinners.

In "Seven Good Years" the Prophet Elijah tells a very poor but pious man that he can have seven years of riches now or toward the end of his life. The man consults his wife and agrees to have it now. Immediately he becomes a man of wealth. When the seven years pass, Elijah comes for an accounting. He is told that, as the steward of the gold in his possession, the man spent much on charity but took for himself only the tuition fees for his sons. Heaven then decrees that the good man may continue to keep the money.

"The Baal Shem Arranges a Match" concerns a pious Jew who is rich but childless. Supplicating Besht for his wife's fertility, he is told that he could have a child but would lose his wealth. He agrees, and the rabbi's promise is realized. Years later, reduced to beggary, the Master of the Divine Name advises him to go from town to town until he comes to one where the rabbi's name is unknown. In a town in Germany he meets a Jew who has never heard of the founder of Hasidism, but invites him for the Sabbath. It happens that this German Jew had gained his prosperity from the lumber his impoverished guest had lost in a storm years previously. In their conversation the host confides that his daughter swoons when introduced to a prospective groom, and the guest urges him to visit the miracle-making Besht. As the two of them and the troubled girl reach the rabbi's court, they are met by the son of the poor man; the girl is at once attracted to him. The rabbi then explains how he had prearranged these events, and marriage ensues.

"Yokhanan the Watercarrier" tells of the superiority of the pious over the learned. The protagonist is one of the 36 secret saints who, legend has it, keep the world from destruction.

He is poor, unlearned, and supplies the synagogue scholars with water—a task he volunteers willingly out of his respect for learning. He himself reads the Psalms when free.

> There are some scholars from whose study a fresh odor arises, as of new-baked bread: that is a simple student, innocent of heart; and there are some of higher degree from whom a perfume comes as of new apples; and still others who remind one of the flowers of the field, and the highest are like precious spices.

Yokhanan loves all except one from whom he smells the black pitch of Cabala, and deliberately avoids him. The rabbi in the synagogue notices this and soon forces Yokhanan to confess his reason for doing so. One night the rabbi is visited in a dream by his long-departed father and urged "to put out the fire." On awaking he notices flames surrounding the hut occupied by the Cabala scholar. Yokhanan is already at the rabbi's door, axe in hand. Together they approach the hut and find it filled with evil spirits celebrating the scholar's wedding with Lilith. Yokhanan splits her head, the scholar is carried off by the evil spirits, and the flames die down.

In another story Reb Yehiel, a generous philanthropist, comes home one day and finds a Jew about to hide under his coat two silver candlesticks. Assuming rightly that the poor man had come for a loan for Passover or to marry off a daughter, and was tempted to steal, he acts as if unaware of the misdeed and takes the candlesticks from the man's bosom as if to evaluate them as a basis for a loan. "I'll tell you what," he says to the shaken and confused man. "I'll simply lend you 35—all right, all right, I'll make it 40 rubles. . . . And when the time comes you'll pay me back."

"At the Risk of One's Life" is set in ancient Palestine. A pious and highly learned head of a Safed yeshiva is approached by a youth who is anxious to study, but had been cursed with forgetfulness by the head of the Jerusalem yeshiva because the youth's sophistry and arrogance had put an honest scholar to shame. He interests the wise rabbi and is permitted to join the other students despite his locked memory. Handsome and winsome even in his torn garments, which he refuses to cast off in his earnest effort at expiation, he soon attracts the rabbi's beautiful daughter. Although the rabbi has long sought a husband for her and has rejected many fine youths who wished to marry her, he finds himself favoring the unfortunate student. One day, understanding the speech of animals, he overhears one serpent telling another that he was sent to poison the student, as it was fated, on the eighth day after the wedding. The rabbi is upset to think that his daughter should be widowed so soon after her marriage, but she accepts her fate and seeks to give her life to save her lover's. On the appointed day she puts on his garment, enters the garden, and is bitten. Her soul rises upward, but the error is quickly discovered. Her soul is immediately returned to her body and her husband permitted to live.

The bare bones of these stories impart not a whit of the poetic flavor and verbal beauty with which Peretz has fleshed them. These and other narratives of similar content possess a literary quality and imaginative depth found only in distinguished fiction. What heightens their worth to the Yiddish reader is the felicity with which Peretz treats the spiritual essence of Hasidism and Jewish folklore. The following two stories illustrate these qualities even more emphatically.

"If Not Higher" tells of a Hasidic rabbi who, during the week before the Holy Days, disappears for a time every morning. His followers think:

> Where could he be? Presumably in Heaven! Little business does a rabbi have to attend to before God during these fearful days? Jews, without an evil eye, are in need of work, of peace, of health, of desirable marriages, of goodness and piety, and their sins are many. And Satan with his thousand eyes sees from one end of the world to the other. And he sees and accuses and prosecutes. . . . And who should help them if not the rabbi?

A Lithuanian Jew, a non-Hasid, who has recently settled in the town, mocks at the idea of the rabbi visiting Heaven.

Even Moses, he argues, could not enter Heaven. Being a stubborn *Litvak,* he resolves to ascertain where the rabbi does go—perhaps with the idea of exposing him. One night he hides himself under the rabbi's bed. Early the next morning he sees to his astonishment that the rabbi dons coarse peasant garments and leaves the house very quietly, taking an axe with him. Following him at a distance, curious and excited, the *Litvak* sees the rabbi walk quickly to a nearby wood, chop down a tree, split it into firewood, tie it into a bundle, and carry it to a shack housing a sick widow. There, posing as a peasant woodcutter, the rabbi assures the poor woman that he is in no hurry for payment, and even starts the fire in order to keep her from leaving her sickbed. "The Lithuanian saw all that and became a Hasid. In aftertimes, when a Hasid would tell how the rabbi rises mornings during the week before Rosh Hashonah and flies to Heaven, the Lithuanian no longer laughed but admitted quietly, 'If not even higher!' "

"Three Gifts" * is the story of an ordinary Jew, some centuries back, whose sins and virtues were so equally proportioned that when he died his soul could be adjudged neither Paradise nor Gehenna. A merciful angel advised the luckless soul to return to earth and obtain three gifts with which to please the saints in Heaven—gifts revealing evidences of exceptionally fine deeds—and the saints would surely gain it entrance into Paradise.

For many years the soul hovered about the earth and met nothing of use to it. One day it came upon an unusual scene: robbers were in the process of plundering a rich Jew. One of them held a knife to his heart, ready to pierce it at the first move. But the Jew seemed quite peaceful, murmuring to himself, "The Lord hath given, the Lord hath taken, praised be the Lord." Suddenly he saw that one of the robbers was taking a small bag from a secret drawer. Forgetting all caution he cried out to leave it alone—when the knife pierced his heart and he fell dead. On opening the bag, expecting precious jewels, the robbers found only a bit of earth—earth from the

Holy Land which the Jew was saving for his burial. A blood-stained grain was at once accepted as the first gift.

Again many years passed without an unusual event. The soul thought:

> The world came as a living spring out of God's fount and flows and flows on with time. And the more it flows the more earth and dust it gathers into itself; it becomes more drab and less clean; fewer gifts can one find in it for Heaven. . . . The people appear smaller; driblets their virtues, dust their sins, good deeds not to be seen with the naked eye. . . .

Just then it heard a fanfare of trumpets. In a medieval city in Germany the beautiful daughter of a rabbi, having summarily been found guilty of witchcraft, was sentenced to be tied by the hair to the tail of a horse and dragged the length of the city at full speed. The girl accepted her fate bravely but asked for several pins with which to fasten her skirt to her bare legs in order not to expose her modesty. A blood-stained pin was accepted as a second gift.

Once more seasons and years followed in dreary succession. Again the soul was saddened by the mediocrity of man. Then it was attracted by sounds of a drum coming from a prison court, where a gantlet had been formed by two rows of soldiers in order to flog a Jew for some minor offense as he ran past them. The victim was half-naked but with a skullcap on his head. He began to hurry past the excited soldiers, accepting their blows without flinching. "And long whips swished in the air like evil spirits and wound about the body like snakes. And the blood spurted from the wasted body, and did not cease to spurt." One whip was swung too high and swished the cap from the Jew's head. Becoming aware of it after he had taken several steps, he turned back amid the blows of the whips to pick it up so as not to commit the sin of bareheadedness. The blood-stained cap made up the third and final gift.

The story is told with simple and poignant grandeur. With consummate art Peretz depicts the human qualities he cherishes: self-sacrifice for an ideal, the spirit mastering the flesh, self-esteem ennobled by death. About each of the three victims he sings a song most beautifully. The biblical ardor of the narrative is achieved with an unusual economy of diction. Each phrase possesses high suggestiveness; the very dots impregnate the events with the poignancy of what remained untold.

Peretz was most of all a poet: a lover of verbal beauty, a singer of the mystical and the loftiness in man. His first Yiddish poem, "Monish," gave the incipient literature a ballad whose beauty of thought and rhythm compared favorably with the best in current poetry in other languages. Monish was a most precocious youth, beautiful of body and incisive of mind—so pious and erudite as to endanger Satan's dominion. Fearful of his hold on mankind, the Evil One sends Lilith to lure the dangerous youth into sin. Her song and her pulchritude—symbolizing modern rationalism—are irresistible. Yielding to the advice of his Bad Angel rather than that of his Good Angel, Monish becomes Lilith's slave and victim. The poem was the first romantic ballad in Yiddish, wittily satirical, socially critical, with a mellifluent rhythm reminiscent of Heine but new to Yiddish verse.

He wrote numerous lyrics expressing his sympathy for the poor, indignation at injustice, and predilection to romance. His verse was wrought skillfully, possessed striking imagery, and was imbued with a rugged, if lofty, spirituality. Influenced early by Heine, he later regretted having emulated his "self-hatred." Peretz came to feel that satire in verse did not become the Yiddish poet. To Yehoash he wrote in 1907: "Let's be prophets, leaders, not clowns." This he assayed in his dramatic verse. *In Polish oif der Kayt* (Expiation) treats man's subjection to the world about him in lilting lines and inspired imagery. *Night in the Old Marketplace* is a tragedy of life and death, a work of philosophic fantasy symbolizing human striving and an innate yearning for salvation. Max Reinhardt, the famous German theatrical director, considered staging it and called it "a rare specimen of a universalist-symbolic play."

Peretz's greatest work is undoubtedly *The Golden Chain,*
a poetic drama of romantic imagination and philosophic profundity. More than any of his other writings it expresses his
idealistic insight into Jewish spirituality. A rabbinic family is
presented dramatically unto the fourth generation, with each
forming a distinct stage in the Hasidic movement. Its ecstatic
apotheosis appears in the person of Reb Shlome; his son Pinkhos upholds its rigid fanaticism; the grandson Moshe em-
bodies its spiritual diminuendo; and its pathetic disintegration
is manifested in Leah, Moshe's daughter. The continuity of
the golden chain, broken by Moshe's inner weakness, is duti-
fully taken up by his son Jonathan. Miriam, Moshe's wife, is
wistfully prophetic, and comments on the fate of the family
with the finality of a Greek chorus.

Reb Shlome lived in the early years of the 19th century,
his world not yet assailed by the cold knowledge of secular
science. Intensely pious, he is governed by his emotions rather
than his intellect, believing that God's grace lies in the heart
and not in the mind. A very proud Jew, the conscientious
shepherd of his flock, he feels responsible for the behavior of
the least of its members. A fervid idealist, he seeks to enhance
and ennoble the whole world with his visionary ideals. From
his high eminence, however, he perceives only the puniness
and prosiness of its swarm of pygmies: dwarfed and frozen
little souls selfishly begging for petty favors "while a whole
world hovers between life and death."

As the ambassador of man to Heaven, he deplores his need
to represent mean and puny beings, without ideals, dejected
and woeful. Gradually he persuades himself that the world
exists to no good purpose—that on its ruins a more ideal world
might be built—and resolves to exert his supernatural powers
to this effect.

When the drama opens, he refuses to declare the Sabbath
at an end, though the stars have become visible, knowing that
it can cease only with his evening prayers. He is an inspiring
man: tall, gray, pale, with an unusually high forehead and
large open eyes. A childlike smile wreathes his sorrow-

shriveled face, and he is clothed in white except for a pointed black skullcap. His attitude deeply disturbs his congregation —everyone feels the dreadful weight of his resolution. Yet he remains adamant. With the fervor of an impassioned prophet he declares that the world must be freed from pain and fear.

> The Sabbath shall continue—the Sabbath! Forcibly I will detain the Sabbath! . . . The world must be freed! . . . Let the Sabbath continue! The Sabbath! No plowing, no sowing, no building, no repairing, no trading, no traveling. . . . Let the world be destroyed! And we—we Sabbatic, we holy-spirited, we soul-purified Jews shall pass over the debris . . . to Him, to Him! Singing and dancing we shall go to Him! . . . And we do not ask and we do not beg—towering proud Jews are we! We shall tell Him: "We could wait no longer!"

His congregation of Jews are too foggy-minded to perceive his ecstatic vision. More earthly matters occupy them. They are concerned with their fleshpots; they are not interested in what lies beyond the pinnacles of Pisgah! They want the Sabbath to end so that they might begin to trade and travel; they need bread, not visions. So they turn to Shlome's son Pinkhos. He strikes them as better-fitted to represent them before God; he at least does not soar out of their myopic sight! They persuade him to usurp his father's rabbinate and declare the Sabbath at an end. When Reb Shlome learns of the betrayal of his "black son" he collapses and rises no more.

Members of the congregation soon learn to their sorrow that in opposing his father's ideals Reb Pinkhos has not lowered himself to their sordid level. He personifies the unswerving zealot—the fanatical aspect of Hasidism. He holds in contempt the sympathetic humaneness and ecstatic idealism of his father. Strict of manner and without pliancy, he banishes from his sight whatever is bright and sparkling. Even his vestments are black. In his zeal to gain Paradise he accepts with fatalistic rigidity the religious obligations and traditions of Hasidic ritual. As Miriam prophesies, his zealotry causes the house to be darkened by clouds from the West. Unlike his father in seeing not the sinner but sin, he is without mercy.

Stronger-willed than the visionary Shlome, he almost destroys the world he seeks to save in fighting what he considers the battle of the Lord, he expels rabbis from their offices, brings the rich to beggary, and foments discord within and among congregations. Addressing some followers who ask for his blessing, he exclaims: "Farewell, your words are in vain; with fear you came, in fear go your way. . . . Virtuous must all be! 'I chasten the world—like silver—with fire!' says the Lord. 'Winds have I sent to gather all her ends—and cast out all sin. . . . And sinners, like thorns, must be plucked!'" His reign of repression disturbs the very foundations of religion; his blind fanaticism drives many youths away from the fold.

Reb Pinkhos bent those nearest to him to his fanatic will. Reb Moshe, his son and successor, is especially victimized. Naturally of a mild mien, he grows up a timid and weak-willed man. His grandfather he had adored; his father he feared. Well-intentioned, eager to follow in the path of the noble Shlome, he has been too cowed by his father to assert himself—thus representing the generation whose offspring initiated the crusade for enlightenment. When he inherits his office he tries his utmost to be worthy of his trust, but the task is tremendous, the time very trying, and he lacks confidence in his own powers. "They took a feeble man," he confesses, "and placed in his hands the key to profits, rain and snow— I can't bear it. They took a feeble man: 'Conduct a world, talk to the world. . . .'" He does his best—and has a vision:

An eagle am I: broad, white, strong wings have I . . . and about me are the "young." And I lead them into blue space, up, up, higher and higher! I spread my wings over my eaglets. Now and then I look about me to see that none falls, that none tarries, and I strengthen the weak with a glance, and lift the falling with a call. And we fly . . . far, far over the earth, over the world; and I call and my voice echoes across the seas, over mountains and meadows, over fields and forests, towns and cities . . . the voice echoes, the voice of the leader, of the true giant. . . . Suddenly—"Swindler!" I hear myself called. . . . Who knows? Perhaps it is Leah, perhaps something in my own heart. . . .

Leah, his daughter, speaks out rebelliously, representing the generation that broke the gyves with which Reb Pinkhos sought to shackle them. Unlike the others in the household, she refuses to be intimidated by her grandfather's strictures. Her love for Doctor Bergman—the giver of light—amplifies her strength; from him she learns the significance of science When her mother tells her that all must yield to Reb Pinkhos's will, Leah exclaims: "Not all! People without will . . . wrapped in shadow, enveloped in mist, stark with pain and fear. . . ." She also tells her ailing mother: "You shall not be a sacrifice on their altar! You shall not die without succor as *he* did. . . ."—"he" referring to Reb Shlome, who had died for want of medical aid. In the ensuing conflict she forsakes her parents to go with Bergman.

Years pass. The union of Leah with Bergman brings forth a child born blind: with eyes open but without sight. Humbly Leah comes to her mild father for help, hoping that what medical science cannot accomplish, a miracle may. She confesses that the light which had attracted her is cold. "Snow is clear—and snow is cold, snow is death!" She has given up science as a rope that choked and returned to God. "There can be no chaos. If there is a world, then there must be one who governs the world—there must be an eye that oversees us; a heart beats in us—the world must therefore have a heart. . . ." She begs her father and her brother to pray for her and her child.

Reb Moshe, the kind soul and devoted father, does so in a most sacred manner, invoking the long line of rabbinic ancestors to his aid. His effort is in vain. He has tempted God, and God will not be tempted. Having proved to be too frail a link in the golden chain, his son Jonathan succeeds him as rabbi.

Jonathan possesses some of the characteristics of both Shlome and Pinkhos, and he sees in Bergman a messenger of Satan. "A magician is he! . . . He denies Heaven—there are only stars, kind of planets . . . and no miracles—and no prayer helps—only law." He warns his sister of his own vision:

I was in Heaven. . . . Lightsome sweet doves flew round and
round me, touching my clothes, my cheeks as they flew, and they
caressed and kissed my neck . . . and they flew before me and
looked into my eyes and murmured into my ears: "Believe . . .
believe . . . believe. . . ." I hear footsteps, two appear . . .
he and she . . . he—a man of stone with the sheen of razors in
his eyes; she—with knife in hand. . . . (To Leah, very much
agitated) "How comes the knife to you?" He tells you, 'cut,' and
you obey! You circle the knife about, it lightens—a fiery wheel.
. . . And the doves, those that come upon the knife, fall . . .
fall stabbed. . . . They die bleeding, and bleeding they mur-
mur: "Believe . . . believe . . . believe. . . ."

In the final scene Jonathan, fervid in his faith and endowed
with Shlome's imaginative vision, attempts to forge the golden
chain anew.

Jonathan and Leah symbolize the two chief factions of
Peretz's generation: one accepting the ancestral faith, obviously impaired, with anxious resolve; the other discarding it
impulsively but uneasily for the rationalism of science. To
Peretz the living truth was composed of both science and
spirit, and of the two spirit was the more vital, for the spirit
in man will not be denied. The laws of science have little
power to succor man in emotional crisis, yet for modern man
to ignore science could lead only to spiritual vacuity. These
self-evident truths he stressed with poetic vigor and imaginative insight.

In *The Golden Chain* he presents with crystal clarity the
essential nature of Hasidism: its ecstasy, idealism, fanaticism
decadence, and belated poetic revival. The action is expressed
in exquisite poetry. With Goethian grandeur he creates a
realm with a phrase and probes the human spirit with a word.
With symbolic subtlety and artistic intuitiveness he delves
into the depths of Judaism. And in the process the main characters perch lifesize on the fiery wings of dramatic creation.

Peretz was not so much a writer who happened to have
been born a Jew as a Jew with the ability and urge to depict
Jewish life profoundly and artistically. "To be Jewish," he

declared, "is our only way to be human. . . . To find the essence of Jewishness in all places, all times, in all parts of the scattered and dispersed world-folk; to find the soul of all this and to see it lit with the prophetic dream of a human future —that is the task of the Jewish artist." Fully aware of the circumstances in which his people found themselves, of their particular qualities and failings, and of their spiritual status, he could not but assume the role of provocative polemicist and direct them toward social and religious insurgence. This part of his writing is always ethical, though not as obtrusively as Mendele's.

In his literary work he was a great experimenter. In prose and verse he essayed every form, rhythm, and style suited to his purpose. He was indeed more the inspired artist than any of his contemporaries—always writing with high seriousness; realizing from the first that he was one of the founders of a new literature, and in large part responsible for its character and growth. He therefore deliberately sowed the seeds of literary art. Endowed with the gift of versatility, he wrote in various genres. His innate delight in experimentation was stimulated by the new literary currents then prevailing among Western writers. He wrote in turn as a naturalist, a realist, a romanticist, a symbolist, and an impressionist, in each form creating an artistic pattern for younger Yiddish writers. He never lost his youthful suppleness, and continued to experiment and to encourage new writers to the end of his life.

Yet he did not create a literary school and left no direct descendants. Pinski, Yehoash, Reisen, Nomberg, Asch, Hirschbein, and many others were privileged to be his friends and pupils, but none attempted to emulate him. In his enormous correspondence with literary neophytes—carried on with Dinesohn's invaluable stimulation and aid—he set them a high standard and goaded them to greater efforts by means of criticism, admonition, and approval. An enemy of verbosity, he often urged them to compress sentences into words and paragraphs into two sentences; to be extremely careful of their diction, choosing the one correct word out of the ten that come to mind; to write about things they knew best and express themselves simply and beautifully. Despite this activity, he founded no school chiefly because his style was inimitable. None writing in Yiddish, with the possible exception of Yehoash, Opatoshu, and Bergelson, could approach him in stylistic excellence.

Although an ethicist in his thinking, in the expression of his subject-matter he was the genuine esthete. Once a theme ripened in his mind, he concentrated not so much on its content as on its form. His insistence on the exact word, the most effective image and phrasing, exercised with Flaubertian painstaking, gave his style a laconic pithiness. His frequent dots, indicating ellipses, so characteristic of his writing, often convey more than explicit statements. Although he was fully conscious of his great talent, and sometimes gave the impression of being conceited, he could never bring himself to regard his writings as finished products. *The Golden Chain,* for instance, was rewritten five times, and other works were revised again and again. In consequence he often achieved verbal brilliance along with genuine spontaneity of expression. For his ear was as sensitized as a fine photographic plate, and he heard and remembered the essence of folk speech. In all his stories, particularly the Hasidic and folk tales, he gave artistic form to the living language of the Polish Jews.

Because Peretz's style is dynamic in character, his dots assume the significance of unuttered gestures: the shrugs and eye movements of a person speaking, so subtly charged with overtones by the preceding words that the reader's imagination supplies the suggested nuances of meaning with the pleasure of a collaborator. Like the work of all thoughtful writers, his also possesses a three-dimensional connotation: his intent, while intelligible to the simple reader on a superficial level, sometimes eludes complete comprehension by even the sophisticated critic.

The dynamism of his style gives the breath of life to his characters. "For Peretz," A. A. Roback stated, "a character is always *in movement*. It keeps becoming a *personality*." Be they rabbi or lout, leading citizen or outcast, worker or idler, rich or poor—all are depicted with insight and sympathy. Even in that part of his work in which he is as much the reformer as the artist he rarely permitted the moral to obscure the motivation. In the wide range of his characters we come to know intuitively the spiritual idealism of the Jews of his generation as well as their material woes and individual faults and frailties. Coming from the crowded and confining ghettos, they appear to us as human beings groveling for bread and yet aspiring to God, seeking the truths of science while clinging to the truths whose surface has become tarnished, but whose spiritual soundness is everlasting.

CHAPTER FIVE

YIDDISH
COMES TO AMERICA

THERE IS NO definite knowledge of when the first Yiddish-speaking Jews came to the American continent. Since Haym Solomon, who helped finance the American Revolution, was a Polish Jew, he no doubt knew Yiddish. The abortive German uprising in 1848 initiated a considerable migration of Jews to this country, and some of them presumably still spoke Yiddish. About that time a few adventurous youths escaping from military service in the Russian army also found their way to the United States, followed by an even larger number driven out by hunger and oppressive laws in the middle decades of the 19th century.

It was in the 1880's, however, that immigrants from Eastern Europe began to reach the United States in considerable numbers. The pogroms in Russia and dire economic conditions in Rumania, Galicia, and adjacent areas caused nearly 400,000 Jews to enter this country during that decade. Somewhat later the arbitrary expulsion of Jews from Moscow and other Russian cities brought another quarter of a million Jews to both American continents as well as to South Africa.

Most of these Jewish immigrants settled in the tenements of New York's East Side. Many were still steeped in the medieval piety of their forefathers, naively limited in their perception of the world, without a specific trade or profession, and without knowledge of English, uprooted and penniless. To their good fortune—or misfortune—many of the German Jews, having preceded them by some 30 years, had become owners of clothing factories and were in need of workers to supply the increasingly wide demand for ready-made garments. They opened their sweatshops to these newcomers, thereby helping their coreligionists as well as increasing their profits.

It was not easy for these immigrants to adjust to their new and economically onerous life, but with characteristic Jewish persistence they proceeded to satisfy religious and cultural needs as best they could. They established synagogues in rooms over stores and saloons, formed associations based on the towns or areas of their origin, and attended night school and listened to lectures. Like the Israelites out of Egypt, they accepted their hard lot fatalistically and concentrated on the education of their children—an obligation Jewish parents have always eagerly assumed.

Although many continued to practice their piety as well as they could, their uprootedness and new environment, at once mechanically modern and spiritually restricting, soon demoralized their orthodox orientation and exposed them to the mundane diversions of contemporary civilization. Thus, while a good many persisted in devoting their little leisure to holy lore, most of them, eager to keep some contact with relatives overseas and to learn the news of the world, began to limit their little reading to the emerging Yiddish newspapers. Somewhat later they also made up the audiences for the incipient Yiddish theater.

The first Yiddish periodical to be published in the United States, *The Post*, was started in 1870 by Z. Bernstein. At the time there were neither Hebrew type nor a Yiddish compositor, but Bernstein was able to import type, and H. Gersoni joined him as printer. The latter had apostatized to marry a German girl, but later returned to Judaism and left Germany for the United States in 1869. With few readers to support it, the newspaper was suspended after six months of effort. The next year Bernstein and J. Cohn issued *Hebrew News* in Yiddish, Hebrew, German, and English. Deliberately political in its aim, its life ceased after the election of that year. Another political sheet, *The Jewish Press*, was brought out by J. K. Buchner by means of lithography between 1870 and 1877, but came out mostly during campaign periods. This political support of certain Yiddish newspapers continued until recently.

K. Z. Sarasohn (1835–1905), who came to the United States in 1869 and was soon operating a printing shop, entered Yiddish journalism in 1872 with the New York *Yiddish Times*, which lasted five months. Two years later he started issuing the weekly *Yiddish Gazette*. With little capital of his own, he engaged several successive partners to keep the periodical going. In 1877 his printer left to bring out his own weekly, *Die Yiddish Folkzeitung*, but after struggling for three years he sold it to Sarasohn. Also in 1877 N. D. Etelson of Chicago launched *Isrealitische Presse*, which he moved to New York in 1880 and suspended four years later. These journalistic efforts, lacking adequate readership, were constantly in financial difficulties. Their contents were relatively meager and their Yiddish slipshod and usually Germanized. Their few stories and serials were of little worth.

Arrival in the 1880's of a relatively large number of Jews able to read Yiddish, and soon eager to do so, furthered the establishment of Yiddish journalism on a solid foundation. The *Tageblatt* (Daily News), issued on June 18, 1881, became the first Yiddish daily newspaper in the world. The time was still unfavorable, however, and after two months it was reduced to a weekly. Two years alter it was again tried as a daily, but after a few months was once more transformed into a weekly. Not till 1885 was its daily appearance made permanent. Orthodox in religion and didactic in aim, it preached at once greater piety and appreciation of America.

Among the early immigrants were a number of young radicals who had to leave Russia to avoid arrest and incarceration. These rebels, on the whole well-educated and religiously emancipated, were philosophically dedicated to world revolution. In their native homes they had embraced the doctrines of Marxism or Bakuninism and joined socialist and anarchist secret societies. In New York, forced to work in sweatshops, they concentrated their agitation against the prevailing capitalistic exploitation. Their audience was of necessity limited to their few fellow immigrants. Since most of the latter knew only Yiddish, more than one radical who did not know the language learned it in order to address them more effectively. Those who came by way of London, where they had been in contact with Jewish workingmen's associations already established there, began to form similar organizations in New York.

The New Times, started in 1886, was the first radical Yiddish weekly in the United States, edited by Abraham Cahan, among others. Unlike the *Tageblatt* it was written in a simple Yiddish and not the prevailing Germanized dialect. After four issues it had to suspend publication for lack of funds. In the same year the newly established *Yiddishe Folkszeitung* combined socialist and Zionist policies in the effort to attract a maximum readership. It encouraged new writers, among them Morris Rosenfeld, and serialized a translated version of Edward Bellamy's *Looking Backward*. After struggling for three years it had to cease publication. A new socialist periodical, *Die Arbeiter Zeitung* (Worker's Times), made its appearance in 1890, with Philip Krantz as editor; his salary of $7.00 a week is indicative of the financial precariousness of the venture.

In 1889 an anarchist periodical, *Der Emes* (The Truth), began to be issued. Highly idealistic and naively utopian, it asserted that it "will fight until slavery is abolished . . . fight against popes, rabbis, swindlers, laws, and chains." Antagonizing rather than attracting the average Jewish reader, it lasted only five months. During its brief existence it printed current verse, polemical articles, and translations of radical world literature. The following year the same group founded

Die Freie Arbeiter Shtimme (Free Worker's Voice), a weekly which after an insecure beginning became for many years, under S. Yanowsky's editorship, one of the better literary periodicals.

Approximately 70 Yiddish writers had their work printed in the various ephemeral periodicals of the 1880's. The first Yiddish book published in the United States was a volume of verse by J. Z. Sobel in 1877. In general, however, the few writers of books had to seek publication in Europe, where printing was easier and less costly. In this country Yiddish works were mostly serialized in a weekly or, later, a daily newspaper. Payment was of course minimal, except where a writer was employed as a regular contributor, an arrangement which was gradually made a general practice. Nearly all prominent Yiddish writers thus became salaried employees on the several dailies, which after 1900 became more literary in content than the best American newspapers.

One of the best-known writers of the period was Morris Winchevsky (1856–1932). Well-educated in his native Russia and in Germany, and a seasoned radical at 20, he went to London to avoid government hostility on the continent. There he became active in the socialist movement. Bitter and satirical in his verse and polemical writings, he began to write in Yiddish largely under the cognomen of "The Mad Philosopher." In 1884 he started the short-lived *The Polish Jew* and the next year *Der Arbeiter Freint* (The Workingman's Friend), a weekly which gained a relatively wide readership not only in England but also in the United States. His verses, which he had begun composing in 1887, were of genuine merit and reflected the influence of leading European poets. He also wrote numerous stories and did some translation. His reputation was high in 1894, when he migrated to New York. There he at once took a leading place in Jewish radical circles, published his work in both socialist and anarchist periodicals, and was fondly regarded as the "grandfather" of the Jewish socialist movement. A militant internationalist, he opposed Zionism and what he termed Jewish chauvinism. In his poetry he portrayed the exploited poor with sympathy and seriousness as well as with lyrical tenderness.

Young David Edelstadt (1866–1892) was an admirer of Winchevsky. Born in Kaluga, far from the Russian Pale, he grew up speaking Russian rather than Yiddish. A sensitive youth, well-read in romantic and radical poetry, he was a deeply tormented witness of the Kiev pogrom in 1881. No longer able to remain in the country he had loved as a child, the 16-year-old Edelstadt migrated to the United States. For three years he worked in a Cincinnati clothing factory making button holes. The Haymarket hangings of anarchists in Chicago shattered his equanimity almost as much as the pogrom in Kiev. To his agonized mind all government appeared tyrannical and ruthless. Having learned Yiddish from his fellow workers in the factory, he began to write passionate polemic verse in which he condemned organized government, exploiting capitalists, and the possessors of privilege. These poems, he explained, "were not born in a flower garden [but] in the dark world of slavery. They were written by a slave whose enthusiasm derived from the struggle against slavery." In one poem he wrote: "The ignorant slaves laughed: Crazy poet, stop your shouting. Why bother with freedom, with struggle, and with weapons? The rich are powerful, and the world is theirs." The workers he wrote about were lonely and miserable rather than class-conscious—expressing his own agonized spirit.

Coming to New York, he became one of the editors of *Der Emes*. He was also one of the founders and the first editor of *Die Freie Arbeiter Shtimme*. His poems gained immediate popularity among radical Jewish workers, and a number were sung by them as they labored in the sweatshops. At the height of his brief activity he was stricken with tuberculosis, then endemic among workers in the unsanitary sweatshops. He went to Denver to recuperate, but his lungs were already ravaged by the disease and he died at the age of 26.

On the day of Edelstadt's death, Joseph Bovshover (1872–

1915) wrote an elegy that was hailed in radical circles as a masterpiece. Bovshover had a sound Jewish training in his native Russia and knew Yiddish well when he reached this country in 1891. Like Edelstadt a poet of sharp protest, but more the dreamer than the polemicist, he wrote about abstract injustice and idealistic aspirations rather than specific inequity. His translations of *The Merchant of Venice* and part of *Faust* possessed remarkable felicity of expression. He also wrote critical essays on his favorite European and American poets, and a poem in English, "The Toilers," which added to his prominence. From the first, however, he suffered from unrelieved poverty which preyed on his sensitive mind. Unconventional and spirited, he began to show evidences of mental illness at 22, and four years later sank into a melancholy from which he never emerged.

Winchevsky, Rosenfeld, Edelstadt, and Bovshover were the popular poets of protest of the first generation of Jewish immigrants. To them might be added Eliakum Zunser, who had settled in the United States and whose verse retained its vogue during this period. There were also a much larger number of polemists, journalists, story and novel writers, and playwrights. The first popular producer of serialized fiction was M. Zeifert, who came to New York in 1886. His stories of intrigue and romance were on a level with Shomer's and successfully competed with the latter's later work. Shomer, arriving in the United States in 1889, wrote in addition to his widely read fiction a number of plays that thrilled and amused undiscriminating Yiddish audiences. Of the early journalists, D. H. Hermalin, G. Zelikovitch, and J. Paley stand out among the contributors to conservative newspapers. Philip Krantz, who began to write in Russian but whom Winchevsky persuaded to write in Yiddish, B. Feigenbaum, Leon Zolotarev, and J. A. Morison were among the writers on the radical press who acquired a relatively large following by 1900.

In the 1880's the Yiddish theater became an integral part of the emerging cultural activities of Jewish immigrants in New York and other large cities. Goldfaden's operettas, put on by Boris Tomashevsky (1866–1939), appealed to more and more of those who no longer could or would make the synagogue their center of concentration and who, after a week of toil, welcomed an evening of relaxation. In 1883 the ban on Yiddish productions in Russia soon brought Jacob Adler (1855–1926), David Kessler (1860–1920), and other established actors to New York. In need of plays that would entertain dramatically naive audiences, they availed themselves of the concoctions produced by Joseph Lateiner and Moshe Hurvitz, who soon became skillful in tailoring plays of sentiment but without literary quality. So popular had their comedies and melodramas become that neither Goldfaden nor Shomer was able to dislodge them from their near-monopoly.

In the early 1890's a few Yiddish actors began to experiment with plays of dramatic value. A decade of attendance and greater general sophistication improved the taste of many theatergoers, so that the Lateiner-Hurvitz vehicles, while retaining their superficial excitement, no longer fully satisfied them. At this juncture Jacob Gordin (1853–1909) appeared on the scene. He began his adult life as a writer in Russian, associating with the radicals who went to live with the people to help them. Attracted to the Evangelical Biblical Brotherhood, which limited its beliefs to the tenets of the Bible, he formed the Spiritual Brotherhood as a means of weaning Jews away from all dogma and having them abide by the ethics of the Torah. The pogroms of 1881 he blamed at first on the Jews because they had alienated the Russians by their peculiar orthodoxy and maintained that Jews must, like other peoples, become tillers of the soil. To practice what he preached he lived the ensuing three years as a peasant. Attracting no followers and beginning to be harassed by the government, he left for the United States in 1891. By that time he had a large family, and his need to provide for them was urgent.

Chance, with an assist from Philip Krantz, brought Gordin

to the Jewish theater, and before long he became its most fecund and prestigious playwright. Fully familiar with the dramatic literature of Europe and possessed of both a facile pen and a keen sense of dramaturgy, he wrote plays vastly superior to the current operettas and melodramas. Jacob Adler early perceived their appeal to the more sophisticated Jewish audiences. *The Jewish King Lear*, Gordin's first tragedy, modeled after Shakespeare but placed in a Jewish setting, brought into the open the increasingly troubling problem of the widening schism between medievally oriented parents and rapidly Americanized children. Its popularity was immediate, and it started a series of serious plays that in the course of three decades placed the Yiddish theater in New York on a level comparable to the best the American stage had to offer.

Among Gordin's better-known works were *Mirele Efros*, a female King Lear tragedy; *Sappho*, dealing with the place of the Jewish woman in her modern milieu; *Kreutzer Sonata*, a Tolstoyan adaptation; *God, Man, and Devil*, a combination of *Job* and *Faust* in a Jewish setting. These and other plays, while not noted for literary value, were skillful adaptations of classical works, well suited to Adler's histrionic talents, and possessing a seriousness, dramatic intensity, and sense of timeliness that placed them a cut above the average plays of most current theaters. There was, moreover, a dignity and firmness about Gordin that intimidated even the most conceited actors and compelled them to speak his simple Yiddish, and not the Germanized jargon they considered more elegant.

With the increase of newcomers to New York's East Side in the 1890's and especially during the next decade—nearly 2,000,000 in all by 1910—the Yiddish theater flourished. Tomashevsky, Adler, Kessler, Kenia Liptzin, Sigmund Mogulesco, Ludwig Satz, and Bertha Kalish were among the "stars," most of them lording it over a group of actors, and all performing in old and new plays to large and enthusiastic audiences in New York and other large cities. Goldfaden's operettas were in active repertory, and his new plays reaffirmed his popularity, although he himself received little financial return from his work and ended his life in neglect and bitterness. His last play, *The Son of My People*, based in great measure on George Eliot's *Daniel Deronda*, was first performed a few days before his death in 1909 and retained its wide appeal for many years; the return of the hero to Judaism and the Zionistic emphasis warmed the hearts of thousands of Jews who continued to think sentimentally of Israel.

Two other contributors to the Yiddish theater during this period gained a permanent niche in its history. Leon Kobrin (1873–1946) and Z. Libin (1872–1955) were both faithful admirers of Gordin. Having received a largely Russian education, Kobrin did not know Yiddish well and had no direct knowledge of Yiddish writings. He had only heard of "Jewish writers who wrote simple tales for servant girls and ignoramuses in the Yiddish Jargon. . . . About Mendele and Peretz I knew only a few translated things which I had read in *Voskhod*." He did, however, have a wide familiarity with Russian literature when he reached the United States in the early 1890's. Finding manual labor irksome and unremunerative, he learned Yiddish and began to write for the newspapers. Eager to please editors, he accepted their dictates and adapted his material to the level of his unsophisticated readers. He did the same in writing for the theater. Yet he never stooped to sentimental melodrama, and his Russian and French models helped him maintain a simple yet authentic literary standard. *Minna* (1899), his first play, written with Gordin's assistance, was followed by *Nature, Man, and Beast* (1900), a work of character delineation and moral probing. *Yankel Boila*, perhaps his most successful work, is based on a story written in 1898, and concerns a simple fisherman whose love for a Christian girl ends tragically, with its melodramatic action compensated by vivid characterization.

Libin (Israel Hurvitz) also began to write under Gordin's aegis. Less educated than Kobrin and for many years a worker in a sweatshop, he wrote of the life he knew with bold realism and sentimental sympathy. "The life of the Jewish workers in New York," he wrote, "is the life I know best. That is the life which flowed together with my own life. My muse was born in the dark sweatshop." Of his approximately 50 plays, most of them involving a tense family problem relieved by simulated comic effects, few are now remembered. Yet in their day a number were quite successful. *Broken Hearts* (1903) and several others had long runs. *Broken Hearts,* incidentally, was later filmed with Maurice Schwartz in the leading role.

B. Gorin (1868–1925), who came to the United States in 1894, wrote for the Yiddish stage with some success, as well as writing a number of stories and essays. His main contribution, however, was a two-volume history of the Jewish theater.

For nearly a half century after 1900 the Yiddish theater was held in high esteem by dramatic critics. Although part of it continued to offer insipid entertainment for those who wanted it, the more serious producers sooner or later put on the plays of such Yiddish writers of prominence as Sholom Aleichem, David Pinski, S. Anski, Sholem Asch, Peretz Hirschbein, and H. Leivick, most of them with unquestioned success. They also staged the dramas of Shakespeare, Tolstoy, Ibsen, Hauptmann, and other world-renowned playwrights. In 1918 Maurice Schwartz organized the Yiddish Art Theater with a company of fine actors, among them Jacob Ben-Ami and Paul Muni, and for more than two decades he maintained a high level of artistic production.

By the 1940's, however, signs of decline were fast appearing. Restrictive immigration laws in the 1920's had reduced Jewish newcomers to a few thousand annually. The old generation was dying out—including many of the actors—and younger Jews were becoming fully Americanized. These neither knew nor were interested in Yiddish and turned to the English-speaking stage for entertainment and employment. Thus while Broadway—and off-Broadway—was enriched by the inflow of Jewish playwrights, actors, and audiences, one after the other of the Yiddish theaters was forced to close its doors. In the 1960's only an amateur troupe still performs Yiddish plays on week-ends. In 1967 Ida Kaminska and her Yiddish group of actors from Poland came to Broadway and performed for eight weeks in *Mirele Efros* and *Mother Courage*.

After a decade of fumbling and furious effort, handicapped by idealistic confusion, financial insufficiency, and the unfamiliarity of a new environment, Jewish intellectuals in New York began to exert a strong influence upon their fellow immigrants. Most of the million or more that came to the United States in the 1900's were orthodox Jews from small towns, driven out by pogroms and desperate poverty. Many were as ignorant of modern conditions as their predecessors had been in the 1880's. In addition, however, there were among them a relatively large number of young radicals seething with resentment against autocracy and eager to enlist in the struggle for a better world. They readily joined the older intellectuals in a common effort to educate and organize the mass of Jewish workers. Their agitation led to the formation of permanent labor unions which struck again and again for better working conditions and higher wages. Socialists, anarchists, Zionists, and other political and cultural propagandists, they furthered the awakened social activities of tens of thousands of tailors and dressmakers and furriers, to whom victory was exhilarating and who eagerly followed their leaders with more ardor than understanding. They attended meetings and lectures, read Yiddish newspapers and magazines, and eventually made up the memberships of the most enlightened industrial unions in the United States and the backbone of the American liberal movement.

By 1890 only the conservative *Tageblatt* had firmly established itself as a daily newspaper. It favored religious orthodoxy and was condemnatory of the free-thinking radicals. In 1891 Abraham Cahan sought to attract the more intelligent readers to his *Arbeiter Zeitung* by printing the work of Peretz and other prominent Yiddish writers. In the same year *Die Zukunft* (The Future) was started as a socialist and literary monthly. After a precarious beginning it began to appear regularly, with Cahan as its energetic editor. When the socialists split ranks on theoretical grounds in 1897, the magazine was temporarily suspended, but was later reissued monthly and has been to the present the outstanding Yiddish magazine in the United States.

The faction breaking away from the Socialist Labor Party in 1897, headed by Daniel De Leon, started *Der Forverts* (The Forward) under Cahan's editorship. By this time the radicals had attracted a large enough readership to assure the firm establishment of the new daily. With a lapse during the years 1898–1903, Cahan remained its dominant editor almost to the end of his long life. He insisted that contributors use the simplest vocabulary and an artless style; he also encouraged inclusion of Englishisms current among the partly Americanized Jews. Yet he engaged such prominent writers as Winchevsky, Asch, Reisen, Kobrin, Libin, and numerous others to write stories, serials, and general articles; strangely enough, Cahan had a rather low opinion of Sholom Aleichem's writings. In time his daily, more than the other Yiddish newspapers, became not only a medium of Jewish and world news but also the daily guide and mentor of many thousands of immigrants in need of information, assistance, and encouragement. Its department entitled "Bintel Brief" (Packet of Letters) was for years the famous depository, real and simulated, of the questions, problems, woes, and perplexities affecting a people in the difficult process of reorientation to a life hitherto completely alien to them. Many readers followed its explanations and advice with guileless seriousness. At the height of its popularity, *Der Forverts* was the most widely read foreign-language newspaper in the United States.

In 1901 J. Sapirstein started *Der Morgen Journal* (The Morning Journal), edited by Peter Viernick, in competition with the afternoon *Tageblatt*. Orthodox in religion, Zionistic in attitude, and Republican in politics, it was widely read primarily for its early news coverage and want-ads. The newspaper also gained wide circulation because of its popular serials. One of them, *The Secrets of the Russian Czar's Court*, caused many of its readers to rise early in order to peruse the daily installment before going to work. Viernick also obtained such eminent critics as David Frishman and Dr. Eliashev and a number of fiction writers to contribute to its columns. Gradually, as the number of orthodox readers diminished, the newspaper absorbed the *Tageblatt*, its less vigorous competitor—only later still to be merged with *Der Tog*.

Also in 1901, Louis Miller left *Der Forverts* to launch *Die Warheit* (The Truth), with an editorial policy that avoided both the socialist stamp and orthodoxy. During election campaigns he supported Democratic candidates and was compensated by Tammany with paid advertisements. Miller stressed literary quality in all departments, and engaged such eminent writers as Zhitlovsky, N. Syrkin, B. Borukhov, and Sholom Aleichem. For a decade this daily appealed to a sizable number of the more cultivated Yiddish readers. In 1914, however, a new newspaper, *Der Tog* (The Day), edited by noted journalist Herman Bernstein, began to encroach on its circulation and soon absorbed it. With such additional contributors as Ossip Dymov, Yehoash, Abraham Koralnick, Joseph Opatoshu, Peretz Hirschbein, H. Leivick, S. Niger, A. Glantz-Leyeles, and B. Z. Goldberg, *Der Tog* soon became this country's most literary and highly regarded Yiddish newspaper, a position it retains to the present.

The last Yiddish daily of a permanent character, *Die Freiheit* (Freedom), was established in 1922 by the Jewish communists. Edited by M. Olgin, and after his death by P. Novick, it favored Soviet Russia and was critical of capitalistic exploitation, but also gave much space to literary and cultural material. Despite the anti-communist atmosphere during the 1950's, *Die Freiheit* has retained the loyalty of its basic readership.

It should be stressed that Yiddish newspapers differ markedly from the American press. The news of the day is the less important of its divisions, being overshadowed by material on current Jewish culture. Within its pages, and especially in its weekend editions, are found articles on science, politics, philosophy, and important current events, written by publicists and scholars of high repute; also poems, stories, humorous sketches, literary criticism, and essays in esthetics by leading Yiddish writers; also popular serials, prepared mostly by grubstreet journalists. This condition has served to minimize bookreading, which has in turn discouraged development of book publishing on a commercial basis. Yiddish writers, finding their income from books haphazard and scant, have been forced to earn their living by publishing in newspapers. In recent years, with Yiddish publishing houses in Europe no longer available, Yiddish writers were unable to get their books printed unless they were favored by an organization interested in Yiddish culture.

Of the early writers of note who contributed to newspapers, mention might be made of Kobrin, Libin, Z. Levin, and Zhitlovsky, as well as a number of the more eminent writers living in Europe. Kobrin's fiction conveyed more the spirit than the circumstances of his characters; more their colorfulness than their nuances. He was the first Yiddish writer to treat carnal passion naturally and openly, emulating his Russian and French mentors. With numerous radicals in the 1890's practicing "free love," he discussed passion in relation to one's duty, timidity, fear, and pride. One of the first to portray Jewish immigrant life on the East Side, he stressed its realistic and emotional aspects. Perhaps his best work, *Oreh the Beard*, first serialized in 1913 and reissued in a new edition in 1936 and retitled *The Golden Stream*, depicts a simple, energetic Jew who became rich as a participant in a real estate boom. Subjected to inner conflicts that differentiates him from common parvenus, he marries a young girl and ends in disaster. Kobrin's other fiction deals with the complexities of passion, life in Russia, and the effect of Americanization on the Jewish spirit. Although a sizable portion of his writing is too detailed and commonplace, part of it has the pulse and vividness of literature. Kobrin also did a considerable amount of translation, and his two volumes of reminiscence are rich in information and reflection.

Libin was much more limited in the range of his fiction, drawing mostly on his own circumscribed experiences. Many of his stories are concerned with Jewish workers treated in a warm, personal manner, underlining the differences in their circumstances and points of view from those of their parents in Eastern Europe. His genuine sympathy for them and his simple, realistic style were fully appreciated by his many readers. Lacking linguistic sensitivity, he marred much of his writing by the inclusion of Englished words and expressions —largely influenced by Cahan's dicta. Like Libin, Z. Levin wrote mostly about workers. His early stories, realistic and sympathetic, were generally more meritorious than those published in his later years.

Khaim Zhitlovsky * (1865–1943) came from a well-to-do and cultivated family in Vitebsk. Of a serious turn of mind, he early joined the revolutionary movement, and in 1882 went to distant Tula to work for the liberation of the Russian people from Czarist oppression. Manifestations of anti-Semitism aroused his interest in Jewish nationalism. Still considering himself a citizen of Russia rather than only a Jew, he regarded Zionism as utopian and preferred to work for establishment of the Jewish national entity within Russian borders. Kept by the leaders of his party from pursuing this project because of its separatist tendency, and disagreeing with his former classmate S. Anski and with S. Dubnow on the subjects of Jewish nationalism and Yiddish, he in time developed the thesis that the Jews were essentially a national unit and would remain so even if they abandoned Judaism; he also believed that Yiddish was their mother-tongue and therefore their national language. When he migrated to the United States and became a regular contributor to Yiddish periodicals, he discussed these ideas with a philosophic depth and stylistic felicity that made his articles and subsequently his books among the best polemic writings in Yiddish. His literary criticism was also of a high order. For years his popular lectures before interested audiences in the larger American cities, in a Yiddish that was at once simple, idiomatic, and explicit, gained him the admiration of many thousands.

Zhitlovsky was one of the most active participants in the 1908 Czernovitz Conference on Yiddish. Stimulated by Nathan

Birnbaum, an early Zionist who had become a strong exponent of Yiddish and had come to the United States to lecture on the subject, Zhitlovsky and several others joined him in issuing a world-wide call for a Jewish language conference. The meeting in Czernovitz was attended by Jewish writers and thinkers from various countries. Among the topics discussed was standardization of Yiddish grammar, spelling, and diction. The highly controversial subject of Yiddish as a national language was hotly debated and finally proclaimed under the skillful guidance of Zhitlovsky and Birnbaum, but its relation to Hebrew was left ambiguous. More effectively than any of his contemporaries, the handsome, bearded Zhitlovsky, a cosmopolitan in appearance and in his personal life, for years thereafter campaigned in his writing and on the platform for the literary excellence and national dignity of the Yiddish language.

CHAPTER SIX

MORRIS ROSENFELD

Sweatshop Poet

IN 1897 Professor Leo Wiener of Harvard University came upon a volume of Yiddish verse by Morris Rosenfeld. With the enthusiasm of a discoverer he proclaimed it as the work of a great poet. He wrote about it excitedly in *The Nation,* then the most respected critical weekly in the United States, and soon thereafter edited a prose translation of these poems under the title of *Songs of the Ghetto.** In the preface he stated that in their intense poignancy these poems of the sweatshop approach the vivid realism of Dante's *Inferno.* A number of prominent reviewers joined Professor Wiener in acclaiming Rosenfeld as one of the authentic poets of the time. Before long his verse became available in several European languages, and Yiddish assumed fresh respectability as a literary medium.

Rosenfeld's wide reputation arose more from interest in the exotic than from genuine critical discernment, and soon evaporated. For years thereafter Rosenfeld tried in vain to retain the favor of his non-Yiddish public; he even tried to write in English, but that only hastened the decline of his popularity.

His poetic gift was genuine but limited and ephemeral. His was the fierce, anguished cry of the sweatshop slave, the poetic plaint against the infernal conditions that were draining the life-blood of the wretched immigrant workers. When circumstances enabled him to leave the sweatshop and bask in the glamor of his new-found fame, his poetic potency underwent attenuation—a common phenomenon in literary history. Although he continued to sing against the enemies of freedom, of the poor, of the Jew, his voice became shrill rather than fierce. A verse here, a stanza there, recalled the lyric intensity of his first poems, but for the most part his passionate outbursts found clearer expression in his prose writings.

Yiddish critics, while at no time overrating his intrinsic merit as a poet, have been rather favorable in their estimate of his work. They deemed him of relatively minor importance compared with such poets as Peretz, Yehoash, and Leivick, but made clear that his historic significance was undeniable. He began to write when there was still no Yiddish verse except the ballads of popular bards. His poems were thus the first to possess artistic import and to be written according to the rules of versification. In the United States in particular he was for a time the leading poet produced by the Jewish immigrants, and his influence upon Yiddish writers who came after was evident enough to give him prestige despite the lesser merit of his later verses.

I was born on the twenty-third day of December, 1862, in the small town of Baksha, Poland. My grandfather, my father, all the members of my family, were fishermen. The little town was situated on a lovely spot between the forest and the sea. I was still a child when my parents were forced to move to Warsaw. I was sent to *kheder,* and there I studied the Talmud and a little of Polish and German. At the age of eighteen I married and went to Holland, where for six months I worked at diamond grinding. From there I went to England, and for three years I worked in the sweatshops of London. Afterward I sailed for America. It was in the dank, dark sweatshops of New York that I learned to sing of oppression, pain, and dreariness. During the day I worked; at night I wrote my poems. The workshop undermined my health, and I had to leave it. I turned to journalism, and for several years I wrote for the important American-Yiddish news-

papers. My circumstances became easier after the publication of
Songs of the Ghetto.

Rosenfeld's experience was in its essentials typical of most
Jews of his generation. Reared in the orthodox tradition, he
early felt the urge to emancipate himself from its dogmas.
The wretchedness of his Warsaw slum home only heightened
his memory of the beautiful natural setting in which he lived
until his ninth year—when his family was driven out by government restriction. Dire circumstances forced him to migrate
far from home, but his life in Amsterdam and London was no
improvement. Still young and full of hope, he did not let the
burden of family and poverty keep him from his awakened
muse. In London he circulated his verses among fellow
workers, and several songs became popular. Continuing to be
lashed by indigence, he migrated to New York in 1886.

In the 1880's the East Side of New York was still largely an
Irish neighborhood without economic grooves into which the
newcomer might readily enter. The Jewish immigrant underwent a grievous struggle to gain a bare livelihood. Having
crossed the Atlantic with visions of a land blessed with freedom and abundance, he soon found himself overwhelmed by
the oppressive sweatshop, his one source of employment,
where he often "sweated" as many as 15 hours a day.

Rosenfeld came to New York intent on saving enough money
to bring over his wife and children. To this end he worked
long hours and lived penuriously. With the break of dawn he
hurried to the foul and filthy factory, sometimes remaining
there overnight to be the first to get his "bundle" of work and
thus earn a few extra pennies. In the midst of unceasing din
and tumult he sat bent over a sewing machine or stood over
a hot iron hour after hour until late in the evening, stopping
at noon only long enough to consume a stale sandwich or
two. The angry frown of a driving foreman kept prodding
him on, and the axe of unemployment was ever over his head.
His earnings at the end of a week were pitifully small. Later,
when his family was with him and he hurried home weary
and worn, he usually found his children asleep and his wife

too fatigued to smile at his greeting. In silence he gulped some food and—when too tired to write—crawled into bed, bitter at the thought of the drudgery that awaited him in the morning.

He was naturally vain, of a quick, irascible temper, with a strong sense of justice, volatile of mood, and sharp of tongue. His secular schooling was rudimentary, but his reading knowledge of German and later of English enabled him to familiarize himself with a good part of the world's poetry. Even earlier he had memorized many of the Yiddish songs of Zunser, Goldfaden, and M. Gordon. The poetry of Heine stimulated him to persevere in his own efforts. Having learned the art of prosody, he began to write verses accordingly and recited them for the edification of his fellow workers. At first he wrote his lines down on the butcher paper in which he had wrapped his lunch. In the year of his arrival in New York he published in the *Yiddishe Folkzeitung*, his first poem, "The Year 1886," consisting of 13 eight-line stanzas of which one read: "The year 1886 is about to pass into eternity. Declare my people, declare it clearly, what you have been through during this time! What of use have the past years brought you? You're asleep, my people, you think it is night—arise quickly, do not get lost!" It is noteworthy that the poem appeared before Frug's Yiddish verse, and was therefore the first Yiddish poem written according to the rules of versification.

His best poems depicted his sweatshop experiences. The factory had become to him a living hell, a filthy dungeon: he was daily hating it more and more intensely, and it was not in his nature to accept torment meekly. Unlike most of the workers around him, who, inured to adversity and habituated to suffering, acquiesced in their exploitation with passive and inarticulate grumbling, he was outraged by the sordidness of the shop, and in sheer anger recorded his wretchedness. His song was an outburst of lyrical anguish, and his theme the story of his harrowed self. The poignancy and pathos of these poems were simply and effectively expressed.

"The Sweatshop" is a powerful indictment against the system in which the human element was ruthlessly disregarded. The confounding din of the machines and the threatening look of the foreman rob Rosenfeld of his ego and turn him into a productive machine. Its effective lyric plaint emerges even in rough prose translation:

> I work, and work, and work without end; I am busy and busy, and busy all the time. What for? And for whom? I know not, I ask not! How comes a machine to think at all? . . . The seconds, the minutes, the hours fly; the nights and days pass like swift sails;—I propel the machine as if seeking to overtake them: I hurry without avail, I hurry without end. . . .

Vaguely he remembers that the ticking of the clock was once the urge to reflection, but now every tick seems to echo only the employer's angry words. With the comparative quiet of noon the shop appears like a battlefield during a lull.

> I look at the battlefield in bitter anger, in terror, with a feeling of revenge, with a hellish pain. The clock, I now hear it aright, is calling: "An end to slavery, an end!" It vivifies my reason, my feelings, and shows how the hours fly; miserable I shall be so long as I am silent, lost—so long as I remain what I am. . . . The man that sleeps in me begins to waken—the slave that was awake in me goes to sleep. Now the right hour has come! An end to slavery, an end! But suddenly—the whistle, the boss—an alarm! I lose my reason, forget where I am; there is a tumult, a struggle, and oh, my ego is lost!—I know not, I care not, I am a machine. . . .

The mirage of a freer, happier life often lured him to the brink of despondency. How he grieved on waking from his daydreams only to find himself in the whirling toils of the sewing machine! His sensitive suffering is expressed in such poems as "The Pale Operator," "The Tear on the Iron," "The Shop and the Home," and "The Empty Spool." In the last poem, for instance, he compares himself to the spool—worthless and discarded: "My usefulness is now destroyed. . . . My life's thread is used up. It lies and rots in the garments of strangers."

"My Boy," which quickly became a popular folksong, tells of his deep love for his little son and how wretched he feels because he can seldom see him awake. Even a prose rendering gives evidence of its piercing pathos:

> I have a little boy, a fine fellow is he! When I see him, it seems to me the whole world is mine.
>
> Only rarely, rarely do I see him, my pretty little son, when he is awake; I find him always asleep, as I see him only at night.
>
> My work drives me out early and brings me home late; oh, my own flesh is a stranger to me! Oh, strange to me the glances of my child!
>
> I come home in anguish and shadowed in darkness—my pale wife tells me how nicely the child plays.
>
> How sweetly he talks, how brightly he asks: "O mama, good mama, when will my good, good papa come and bring me a penny?"
>
> I hear it, and I hasten: it must be, and it shall be! The father's love flares up: my child must see me!
>
> I stand by his bed, and see and listen, and hush! a dream moves his lips: "Oh, where is, where is papa?"
>
> I kiss the little eyes, they open: "Oh, child!" They see me, they see me, and soon they close again.
>
> "Here stands your papa, darling! Here is a penny for you!" A dream moves the little lips: "Oh, where is, where is papa!"
>
> I stand in pain and anguish and bitterness, and I think: when you awake some day, my child, you will find me no more! . . .

The death of this boy, full of promise, in 1905 caused Rosenfeld deep anguish and probably contributed to his paralytic stroke shortly thereafter.

Sometimes his pathetic plaint gave way to chagrin. Anger would well up in his heart and inflate his ego: he saw himself suddenly grown mighty, and uttered a leonine roar of defiance. In "The Lion" he declares:

> Why do you keep stuffing yourself with meat, and throw the bones to me? What do you think, am I a dog? A dog with communal teeth? . . . O shudder! for a lion am I! Play no tricks on me! For once I rise I'll tear you to bits. . . . Do not think me a

dunce because I appear meek; the day shall dawn, I'll break my cage, and dead you shall lie. . . .

Emboldened by his fancied strength, he even threatened to strike. In "I Strike" he exclaims: "An end to needle and shear! I am a tailor no longer! I'll work no more! I'll do no more cutting, I'll do no more sewing—may the whole business go hang!" Yet he soon loses courage and yields to gloom. In another poem he states: "Muse take back your fiddle. I have used it but little. Only my tears have sprinkled it occasionally."

These poems of the sweat shop are Rosenfeld's intense suffering translated into lyrical outcries—the most powerful of their kind in Yiddish literature. Peretz's and Reisen's poems on the theme of exploitation are more burnished, more objective, even more melodious, but Rosenfeld's are genuinely the direct expression of the worker * and possess the artless pathos of the folksong. Their fervent emotion compensates for their tendency to sentimentality, unrefined diction, and uneven meter.

This crystallized flow of lyric passion is reduced to a trickle in Rosenfeld's later verse, in which he is the propagandist seeking to imbue workers with a sense of class-consciousness. This poetry seems to have been written not with his heart's blood but with the crimson ink of the radical. The blemishes which were hardly noticeable in his successful lyrics appear bare and blatant in his verse of propaganda. It was as if, once his muse lost its freshness, he sought to depend upon the prosiness of rhetoric.

The truth is that, once his reputation became established, Rosenfeld began to believe that he was giving voice not so much to his own heartache as to the misery of the poor and oppressed. This belief he reiterated in a number of poems: "O, no golden tuning fork atunes my voice to song. No nod from on high can make my voice resound. The sigh of the slave, when fatigued, readily rouses my song, and my muse quickens eagerly for my poor brethren ("The Tear Millionaire"). "The worker's fate attunes my lyre. O, Heaven's daughter, many thanks for making *him* my life's song" ("The Old Song"). To a large extent he was right. In his most lyrical poems his own misery is transmuted into the mute emotional anguish of the exploited workers. His readers felt this, acclaimed him, and made a number of them their rallying cry of revolt. His later verse, however, lost its spontaneity and, consequently, its appeal.

The publication of *Songs of the Gehtto* brought Rosenfeld to the favorable attention of several wealthy German-American. Jews. For a time they made life easier for him, enabling him to leave the sweatshop. But their assistance was given as charity and not with the sympathetic understanding of the maecenas. When their efforts to make a candy storekeeper out of him proved futile—business repelling him as much as the factory—they lost interest in him.

Left to his own devices, Rosenfeld became a staff writer on *Der Forverts* and retained the position for some years, considering this a period of "pen slavery." Impulsive and irascible, thinking himself superior to the daily requirements of journalism, chafing at his neglect by the younger generation of writers, he finally quarrelled with Cahan, called him a "journalistic charlatan," and was dismissed with the statement that his "writing was not adequate in quality and quantity."

In his later years Rosenfeld suffered the fate of many minor lyricists whose poetic flame flares bright for a season and then only flickers. He himself ascribed his failure as a poet to the onerous demands of daily journalism. As before the shop, so now the press room became to him a loathsome prison—only worse, since he believed it subjugated his soul. This attitude he expressed in "Pen Slavery."

> I had thought that the shop was bad, and better the journalist's desk; now I am a pen slave—oh, what vicissitude!
> The pen which had served me, I now must serve—each drop of ink it uses wrings a tear from me.
> Once I clothed the world, arrayed it in robe and gown; now I am being clothed, while I leave the people naked. . . .

Who can realize my great sorrow? Deep in my heart I carry my woe and dare not mention it.

O, open again the shop to me! I will bear it patiently; O, drain my blood, you sweater, drain! I will complain but half.

I will work bitterly, work hard, yes, work without let; for I can let but my shears, the pen must remain my own!

Genuine as the complaint might be, the expression approaches bathos; since he had no intention of returning to the sweatshop, his outcry borders on bombast. Unable to admit it even in the privacy of his soul, he no longer had the emotional overflow which crystallizes into veritable poetry.

He was, however, deeply troubled. The decline of his popularity seared his vanity and irritated his irascible temper. He resorted to satire, especially against his disrespectful critics. Some were indeed mean and scurrilous in their denigration of his later verse, taunting him to return to his tailoring and patching. Lacking the dignity of silence, he retorted in kind, not hesitating in his anger to vilify them mercilessly. In one of his poems he admitted: "I am not of the sweet ones—I employ bitter weapons: I shout, I laugh, I mock, I curse. . . ." His sarcasm is most blunt in "The Patcher," in which he turns their taunt about his tailoring into a pun on *schneider* (tailor) and *schneiden* (to cut):

Tailor I am and will cut always more and more. Woe to him who must suffer from my sharp shears. They will cut you and pinch you and twitch you. Shudder, for I am about to begin tailoring!

Will my shears not cut well, my iron is red hot. I will press and I will burn, burn you to death. Will time cool my iron, my needle is handy too, and you will feel the prick to the very bone.

I am a "patcher," you are dunces—that is true! Things whole I cannot fix, scoundrels only do I fix. Therefore be mute in your mire, spreaders of deceit! For to cut you up, you scoundrels; I am good enough.

Despite his early radicalism, Rosenfeld devoted much of his writing to topics of Jewish interest. " 'Jew and worker' was always my motto." After leaving the sweatshop he reacted ardently to all phases of Jewish experience. Zionism stirred his enthusiasm; Judaism inspired or irritated him, being moved more by mood than by reason; anti-Semitism he fought with a torrent of anger and abuse. Here, as in his sweatshop poems, he reflected accurately, if not with the same lyricism, the attitude of the mass of Jews of his generation.

If these writings lacked his early poetic fire, they did achieve social importance. Perhaps more than any other writer of his time he strove to indoctrinate his fellow immigrants with a quasi-cosmopolitan culture. Writing in a language they appreciated, and presenting his ideas and views simply and vigorously, he exerted an influence quite apart from the intrinsic quality of his verse and prose. His attacks on dogma and superstition were highly effective. Although not averse to invoking the help of Jehovah in times of stress, he sarcastically exposed the incongruity of pious immigrants seeking to harmonize the medieval tenets of orthodoxy with the mundane conditions of their new environment. Usually terse and witty, he occasionally forced his derision to the brink of vulgarity. Thus in the portrayal of an old-fashioned *kheder* teacher he is unsparing in his caustic delineation: "A pious dunce, he is a stranger to soap, comb, grammar, and the Prophets. He need know no language but the Jargon spoken in Beggartown and Mudville! He must appear untidy, thin, pale, and be quick of temper."

If he despised the pietists who made a business of religion, he abominated the enemies of the Jews. Having been in his childhood exposed to the ignominy and invective of every drunken or disgruntled peasant near him, he grew up with an unabated hatred toward them. The massacres of 1881 left their searing imprint on his memory, and those of 1903–1905 sickened him acutely. He sang woefully: "I began to see red. Blood and fire filled the air about me. Blood rushed from my heart and from my head. . . ." Later, in the preface to a volume of articles on the calamity—having just partially recovered from a paralytic stroke—he wrote: "I am not exaggerating when I state that here in America I have lived through in spirit the entire havoc of those massacres. This havoc has made me so sick and weak that it positively was one of the chief causes of my present nervousness." Writing in acid prose, he returned again and again to the old queries:

Why do they kill us? What is our crime? Are we worse than other people? Have our babes sinned with the mother's milk? Do our daughters sin because of their innocence, our aged because of their gray hair, our women because of their love of family, our fathers because of their struggle for bread? Why do they murder us?

And the answer was the same each time: "Our blood is spilled because of a thousand sins, and the greatest sin is that we live."

In his pessimism he saw the Jews harassed and assaulted, driven from land to land by the lash of persecution, wandering like lepers in their isolation, without hope or comfort. In "A Goluth March" he sang:

With staff in hand, without home and without country, without ally and without friend, without future and without present; not tolerated but driven, elsewhere by day than at night. Always woe, woe, woe, always go, go, go, always step, step, step, while endurance holds out. . . . And thus, oh, year after year; and so, oh, generation after generation; hopeless, aimless, shrouded in dread and fear, we wander from desert to desert, out of misery into woe. Always march, march, march; always beg, beg, beg; always need, need, need; and no happiness even in death. . . .

Verse of this nature rises from the depth of sympathy, but in it the poet's voice is muted by that of the preacher. Here, as elsewhere, Rosenfeld wrote not so much with intuitive directness as with sentimentalized pathos.

When anti-Semitism activated the idea of Zionism, he responded with enthusiasm. The more he dreamt of a Jewish homeland in the ancient seat of Israel, of a Jewish nation spiritually rejuvenated, the more ardent was his fervor. In "Jerusalem" he sang: "It seems I hear familiar voices calling to me: 'Return home!' And deep in my heart begins to quiver a hope of revived happiness. It seems I see Carmel again, Sharon greeting me anew; the air smells and songs resound— my first May is returning. . . ." He felt himself called by God to announce His deliverance: "I shall bring back the old joy, and make an end to force; I shall come to break into a thousand pieces the gyves of the Diaspora."

His Zionistic ardor was intensified in 1900 when he attended the Fourth Zionist Congress in London. Contact with such leaders as Max Nordau, Israel Zangwill, and Theodor Herzl thrilled him to ecstasy. In the latter he saw the new Moses gathering the Jews from the farthest corners of the earth and bringing them triumphantly into the Land of Israel. Herzl's death four years later came as a deep shock, and he mourned his lost hero with passionate unrestraint: "O devoted leader! O Shaddai's pure flame! How you have left us, in the dark, to blunder!" The vision of Palestine inhabited by Jews at peace with themselves and the world remained to inspire and comfort him, and at every opportunity he expressed it glowingly and prophetically.

Next to Zion, Rosenfeld loved the United States, the country of Washington, Lincoln, and Whitman, about each of whom he wrote with deep admiration. In contrast to Russia this country was to him a haven for the persecuted, the home of liberty and equality, a great democracy of which he was a proud citizen. Yet he condemned the America of the sweatshop and the tenement. These two Americas were distinct and unassociated in his mind, so that he could without compunction glorify one and execrate the other.

Rosenfeld wrote a number of poems on love and nature. Those on love tend to be commonplace in conception and execution, depicting passion more as an emotion imagined than experienced. Having never loved as intensely as he had suffered, he tended to describe his feelings jejunely. His poems of nature are more genuinely lyrical. Thue he wrote: "Over me the golden rays, about me the green forest. Wherever I gaze, I see green flowering brightness. And in its midst music trilled and played, and in the midst of my soul I feel fresh happiness." The typical town dweller, he admired the beauties of the countryside without actually feeling at home there. His childhood memories of river and forest made him favor farm over city, but his many years in dank tenements had habituated him to the noise and asphalt of the busy streets, and he felt more at ease on crowded sidewalks than in the quiet of the field. When he did go to the country, and he did so often, he could not remain there long. As he wrote in "Man and Nature," "I left the streets, the wild confusion, the uproar; I sit amidst grass and trees, and hear the bird's song. A rare magic prevails, I breathe freely and I bless; and I am being drawn to a habitation—I long for sinful man. . . ." This attitude emerges even more strongly in "In the City and in the Field." No sooner was he in the deep forest than he began to feel himself in "a strange, unfamiliar world" and was seized by apprehension and fear. "I was with God and yet alone. It was quiet, holy, glorious, but dreary. I am a bird born in a cage; with wings—but not to fly, with love of the open fields and with fear for their freedom."

Rosenfeld's early lyrics were written at a time when Yiddish was developing from a Germanized Jargon into a literary language. In the United States the Yiddish spoken by immigrants from different parts of Eastern Europe was a veritable hodgepodge. His poems, possessing artistic appeal and written in a simple but idiomatic Yiddish, helped to give it in the United States somewhat of the dignity and grace achieved for it in Europe by Mendele, Sholom Aleichem, and Peretz. His ear for the Yiddish idiom was keen, and his use of East Side Americanisms minimal and in accord with the natural growth of the language. The popularity of his poems in the 1890's and his frequent recitals of them on the public platform after 1900 pioneered in setting a linguistic pattern for standard Yiddish in the United States. This achievement alone gave him an honored place in the history of Yiddish literature.

From a critical standpoint, however, he belongs to the class of one-volume poets. Had he not been the first to write commendable Yiddish verse in the United States, and had he not happened to compose his most striking poems early in his career and on a subject very close to the hearts of his readers, he would in all probability have suffered the oblivion reserved for many whose ambition is more laudable than their achievement. In his case time and theme united propitiously to give him the prestige of artistic importance undeserved by his later writings.

He himself was confident of his genuine poetic gift. "I sing —the singing is my end. In each song there is a feeling. I think not *what*, I think not *when*, but suddenly my heart gets aburning, gets a pull and a tug—sometimes of joy, sometimes of woe; that comes from the heart and not from the head, and the soul does not fool me." He also stated: "My song broke through like lava," which it undoubtedly did in the sweatshop poems. Subsequently the lava cooled off and his verse lost its fire. His persistent efforts to cling to the pinnacles of fame after his writing had begun to verge on the mediocre only intensified current criticism and neglect.

If his later verse lacks imaginative fineness, his prose writings were keen and gleaming. In his polemical articles and patriotic essays he wrote pungently and passionately—with a gusto reminiscent of William Hazlitt. Like Hazlitt he was an excellent hater, and what he hated he contemned with devastating satire; he was equally intense in praise of what he admired or cherished. He could not write complacently. Whether his subject-matter was the East Side, anti-Semitism, Zionism, or the United States, he expounded each with the zeal of emotional trenchancy. And if his prose of necessity suffers from the element of timeliness, so that much of it died with the day for which it was written, a good part abides within the covers of books or in the yellowed newspaper files awaiting inspection by the interested historian.

CHAPTER SEVEN

YEHOASH

The First Modern Yiddish Poet

EVEN MORE than Peretz, Yehoash (Solomon Bloomgarden) wrote with the tempo and temper of modern poetry. His mature verse compares favorably in essence and spirit with the best of contemporary poetry. From the first he strove to give his writing the breadth and quality of great art. A number of his poems express his philosophic latitude with sensitive fineness. In outlook he combined the passionate austerity of the ancient prophet with the sensuousness of the biblical Semite, and both were merged with the subtlety and freedom of the modern intellectual. He loved nature, and his spirit was most at peace in the vastness of solitude; yet human experience affected him intensely.

Although he never ceased experimenting, Yehoash most often expressed himself imagistically. He saw color and light, dawn and dusk, nuance of line and curve in their exact and exotic variegation. Sunlight and sunset, field and flower, ocean and forest, April and October and December—all of these he painted lavishly and lovingly. Sound and smell and touch, acutely keyed, entered recurrently into the symphony of his choice sense impressions.

Yehoash was essentially a poet's poet. An intellectual fervor pervaded much of his work: imaginative thought embodied in crystallized emotion. In this respect he was the antithesis of his contemporary, Abraham Reisen, who wrote with folk-loric artlessness. His writing is seldom simple and explicit; he never merely sang. Many of his best poems, though permeated with genuine feeling, are charged with subtle connotations not readily perceived on casual reading. Occasionally he wrote so pithily that in a stanza of four short lines he conveyed a complex concept. At times, however, his subtlety of mind affected his lyrical beauty with the obscurity of vagueness.

His versatility is noteworthy. In poetry he ranged from the lyric to the dramatic fragment, from ballad to subtle verse, from fable to songs of nature; in prose he wrote short stories, books of travel, philosophical epigrams, and polemical articles. He collaborated in the preparation of a dictionary of Hebrew and Aramaic words in Yiddish; he also translated various works into Yiddish, and his Yiddish rendering of the Old Testament—a work of more than 20 years' duration—is an epochal achievement.

Withal his personality was as remarkable as his writings. His erudition was catholic and deep; his lectures and conversation were delectable both to ear and mind. In person he was at once fascinating and aloof, pragmatic and positive, sagacious and simple. In his presence one sometimes felt that his writings were but fragments of an expansive and subtle intellect.

Yehoash was born in 1870 in a small town on the Russo-German border, of a father who was pious but already receptive to secular knowledge. He received intensive early training in Hebrew lore and attended the renowned Volozhin Yeshiva for a brief period. On his return home his elder sister taught him foreign languages, and he began reading works of world literature. At 18 he translated several of Byron's poems into Yiddish and wrote some verses of his own. When he submitted them to Peretz in 1890, the latter called him "our Byron" and included several in his *Yiddish Bibliotek*. This success pleased the youthful Yehoash but did not delude him; he knew the distance he must still travel before achieving poetic maturity. Yet he retained his admiration of Peretz to the end of his life. "Peretz," he later stated, "was the conscience of Yiddish literature. Every writer who took his work seriously, consciously or unconsciously felt Peretz's eye upon him. One felt that he must justify himself before him: 'What will Peretz say?'"

Tending to be hypercritical of his literary talent, and perhaps unwilling to be drafted into the Russian army, Yehoash rejected a literary career and migrated to New York in 1890. There he taught Hebrew, and worked at odd jobs and as a bookkeeper in a glass factory. He could not completely repress his muse, but wrote little during the 1890's, although encouraged by Professor Israel Davidson, with whom he had become friendly. In 1900 he contracted acute tuberculosis and was sent by his doctor to the Jewish Sanitarium in Denver, headed by Dr. Charles Spivack. For the next nine years he remained in Colorado, slowly regaining his health. Inspired by the awesomeness of the Rocky Mountains and the intensiveness of his spiritual solitude, he resumed his writing. In 1907 he published a volume of verse with a range and prosodic competence new to the still meager bulk of Yiddish poetry. With Spivack's collaboration he produced the dictionary previously mentioned, which was published in 1911. Concurrently Yehoash helped found the Jewish Consumptive Relief Society, which was very helpful to the many Jewish victims of tuberculosis in the 1900's.

In 1909, fairly well recovered, Yehoash returned to New York with his wife Flora, whom he had married in 1903, and their young daughter Evelyn. For the next few years he earned his living by writing for a Yiddish newspaper, much of it poems which he published in 1913 in a volume entitled *Through Mist and Sunshine*. In January, 1914, he left for Palestine and settled in Rehovoth. He studied Arabic and translated passages from the Koran, but his main aim was to saturate himself with the spirit of ancient Israel in order to devote the remainder of his life to a translation of the Old Testament and writing stories of the heroes and legends in Hebrew lore. He was thrilled to be living in Israel, but remained the scholarly realist in his researches. To Alexander Harkavi, the lexicographer, he wrote: "In general I derive great pleasure from being here. Here logic and questioning cease. The land of Israel is a miracle-land. You can hear the stalks of the new Jewish life bursting continually and new flowers are born here." In a letter dealing with the findings of scholarship he warned the erudite Davidson against making discovery of a minor linguistic point as important as a Napoleonic victory: "Beware of the library dust, as it is most dangerous and often secretly consumes the noblest flowers of the soul. . . . The book world and all studies of ologies and osophies have value only in their intrinsic relation with, and through their direct or indirect influence on, the healthy, fresh, and pulsating life."

The outbreak of World War I forced Yehoash to return to New York. He continued his work on the translation and wrote a considerable amount of verse. He completed a book of his travel experiences and reflections, which was serialized in *Der Tog* and later issued in two volumes in Yiddish—*To Rehovoth and Back*—and in a single abbreviated volume in English entitled *The Feet of the Messenger.** His feeling toward poetry remained highly sensitive. Although he knew he was not fully successful in reaching the lofty standard he had set for himself, he could not but be critical of efforts at versification by the new crop of Yiddish poets. To the artist Shlomo Witkovits he wrote in 1918:

> You know my recent feeling that current paintings and current poems lack "singingness" because modern man is in general no singer. Singability comes from simplicity, modesty, clarity, and the new contemporary man is neither simple nor modest nor clear. A few of the moderns, because they do not know the secret of singing, try to shout, scream, alarm, screech.

Yet he was very encouraging to real talent and told a young artist: "You have more than money, you have the urge to create and faith in your work, which are like all the wealth of Haroun-el-Rashid."

The more he wrote and experimented after his return to New York, the more sensitive and "singing" became his poetry. For a man in delicate health, who gave much of his time to his major work of translation, he was remarkably productive. His lyrics, fables, love songs, and nature poems appeared first, for the most part, in the newspaper which provided him with the means of livelihood, and then in several published volumes. During his last few years he became almost completely dedicated to his biblical research and translation. In 1923 he stated that neither leisure nor pleasure can any longer be for him: "Joy is no longer for me. I have only one interest, and that is to complete my work. Perhaps even more in the *completion* than in the work itself. And of work there is plenty. We are now working on 150 galleys. I work, Flora works, and I have harnessed others." It became in truth a race with death. To the very last day of his life he persisted in what became to him a holy obligation—purifying linguistic terms to give the exact nuance, adding comments of elucidation, making sure of the correctness of each letter in the proofreading. At his death in 1927 loose threads remained, but the translation and commentaries were complete. His wife took up the work and managed to live long enough to see it published.

Yehoash's poetic powers, after a brief youthful bloom, developed rather slowly, and his choicest lyrics were written after he was 40. From the first, however, his verses were noted for their newness and nervousness. In his bent for analysis and ratiocination he early mastered the prosody of verse, about which other Yiddish poets, young and unschooled, then knew almost nothing. He was fascinated by untried possibilities in matters of rhyme, rhythm, and meter. He maneuvered iambs and trochees, line lengths and stanzas with dazzling dexterity. This love of formal beauty, of verbal glitter, remained with him to the end. So sophisticated was his verse that although he was, next to Peretz, the oldest of the Yiddish poets in the early decades of this century, the rebellious "young" poets regarded him with respect and affection.

In his early career a keen curiosity prodded him to explore the inner recesses of the human soul. An ironic consciousness caused him constantly to psychologize over every impulse, never to be wholly engulfed by an emotional overflow, ever to keep himself in check in moments of grievous pain or happy rejoicing. In consequence his few early lyrics lacked emotional intensity and imaginative ardor. He emulated the satire of Byron, the beauty of Keats, the irony of Heine, and the fervency of Lermontov, but his critical consciousness perceived that he was wanting in possession of their poetic touchstone. For a decade after 1900 thereafter he wrote very little.

In the pure mountain air of Colorado his literary impulse reasserted itself. He wrote songs of love and nature, fables, legends, ballads; short stories, critical articles, philosophical aphorisms. He also did translations, and his Yiddish version of Longfellow's "Hiawatha" set a standard for future similar efforts. Yet little of this work possessed the beauty and depth of his later creations. In singing of the sublimeness of nature, the aphrodisiacal exultation of spring, the eternal charm and mystery of night, the aristocratic splendor of high mountains, his voice lacked natural sweetness and rarely reached the high notes.

This verse, however, not infrequently contained a metaphor of choice imagery, a thought of profound simplicity, a stanza of emotional loveliness. "Paganini," for instance, has grace and tempo; "The Unsung Song" and "How Songs Are Made" are two groups of lyrics of distinctive quality. His dramatic fragments were lofty in thought and firm of line.

Quite characteristic of his more successful verse is a cycle of 45 love lyrics, "Flowers and Thorns," in which the soul of the lover is depicted with aching irony. In these poems speaks not the naive swain or the sensualist, but the reflective yet passionate suitor. Love is examined in retrospection of emotion one felt but somehow feels no more; of "feelings, even the most beautiful, fading"; of the bruises of jealousy; of the pain one remembers keenly; of love as a mirage; of one's beloved's equal guile and innocence. The poems have the coldness of yesterday's fire, and are sung while "*cold reason reigns serene.*" A prose version of the final lyric intimates the spirit of the cycle:

It was a shot of light, a gleam of goldlike joy, compressing an eternity in one quick flash; fluttering forth and burning out, and never again returning.

And I have long remained aseeking: dreaming for days together, keeping wakes every night, and yearning always for that ambrosial moment.

It came and disappeared. Apart and alone we now are roaming, hither and thither through life's murkiness. Yet locked in our hearts lies the brief joy that so long you and I have awaited.

If this cycle is tinctured with irony and meditation, the love poems in *Through Mist and Sunshine* are permeated with sophisticated languor. They are more often the plaint of passionate decline than the gust of impetuous youth. Moreover, while the lover is real enough, and his tribulation genuine, his beloved never comes to life: she is a memory, tender and treacherous, an image, rare and fascinating, yet only a figure of white marble. In neither group of poems in this volume has Yehoash bared his inner heart; the love he depicts is woven not so much with the flaming strands of emotion as with the glistening threads of thought.

The poems in this book sound the first clear note of nature music in Yiddish literature. Yehoash writes with a free fancifulness. He jumps astride a spring cloud, braids sunbeams into golden tresses, pries into the secrets of the solemn forest, clothes with a soft white shroud the naked field harboring the wilted dreams of yesterday. "Twilight," the most ambitious poem in the book, is an achievement of almost pure melody and intuition. Each line sparkles with sprightliness; each image charms with its translucent loveliness; the divers rhythms merge one into the other, like curves of a graceful body, to embrace the golden quietude of a summer twilight. In all these poems Yehoash sings joyously, freely, yet aloofly. He neither distends his metaphors nor embellishes his rhymes, seeking only the simplicity of sheer loveliness. In "My Secret" he confesses:

> As much as I will sing for you, you will only get sparks. The flame—the flame remains in me, locked and hidden.
> As much as I will tell you, you will get only wave-sprays. The sea—the sea will remain my own possession. . . .
> As much as I will poetize, and my world describe, my secret —my secret none will share with me. . . .

Yehoash's sojourn in Palestine, brief as it was, greatly enriched his imaginative power and deepened his interest in the Jewish past. On his return he began to record in tranquility the spontaneous overflow of glowing emotion. *In the Weave,* I, II (1919, 1923) and later poems possess a beauty wrought consciously with the fine and firm feelings of the mature artist: a compressed flow of crystallized emotion, expressing multiple moods in subtle variegations—delicately impregnating words and images with their poetic values.

Yehoash was strongly influenced by English poetry both in outlook and form. Perhaps only Heine affected him more than Milton, Byron, and more recent poets. His later poetry in particular was written in the idiom of his own day, revealing his familiarity with the writings of contemporaries. Were his expressionistic verse composed in English it would have placed him among the leading imagist poets. Mention of several poems will indicate how accurately he sensed the spirit of modern verse. "Fifteen" picturesquely unites breasts, hips, eyes, lips, and voice—each drawn with short, sharp strokes and the whole emerging as a vivid sketch of a child-woman to whom the sun was about to reveal the secret of her sex. "Marjorie" presents a face of which three quarters are eyes—large eyes that question, laugh, mock, and sing a potpourri of the prairie and tall trees, of a thousand miles of cornfields, of a summer on the Mississippi, of deer in the mountains, and also of sky-scrapers, limousines, and white nights on Herald Square. In "Eyes" he delineates another concept of the modern girl: an oriental cabaret dancer—a painted, veiled, bewitching dance-sprite. The eyes of this embodiment of jazz—whose long, weary lashes are as parched grasses in the sun and in whose pupils are nests of sorrow—have been beautified by a hundred generations that sat on the ground in the night and wept for the return of God's favor. Youth, beauty, passion—Yehoash merges these three graces into a luminous image of living girlhood.

"Broadway" conveys imagistically the spirit of New York's limelight in the 1920's: "Night. Noise. Automobiles purr, street cars clang, horns blow, bells ring, fire engines screech: a cacophonous symphony. Feet. Armies of feet, feet of all kinds and colors. White throats, pieces of powdered skin, dark-painted brows, blond-bleached hair. Hats of all shapes and fashions. People. Men and women of all ages, stations, and climes, hastening to the night-hunt of Babel. Lights. Figures of fire overhead. Confusion." Composite Broadway comes to life in all its gaudiness and charm, its vulgarity and iridescence.

"Woolworth Building" sketches the one-time cathedral of business: "Twilight. The last of the day-madmen serpentive homeward; their eyes aglow, their faces—clay. Quiet creeps forth from its hiding place. Night falls like a dead wing on the messy knot of marble and concrete and steel. And over all buildings towers high and straight the cathedral of the gold-and-iron god." In like accumulation of imagery, at once compressed and suggestive, are described the subway, the cinema, the airplane, and other modern phenomena.

Color and sound, metaphor and rhythm and rhyme, poetically and imaginatively expressed, would not make Yehoash the distinctive poet he was were they not merely the means with which he gave voice to his centripetal view of life. The beauty of his verses attracts; their ideated depth affects the imagination. For what places Yehoash among eminent modern poets is that he possesses not only what characterizes contemporary artists—emotional restlessness—but also to a great degree the quality wanting in them—inner repose.

Because Yehoash was perhaps more at home in the great cultures of the world than other Yiddish writers of his time, many of his poems lack a particularly Jewish character. One can hardly think of Reisen, Asch, Hirschbein, or Leivick, for instance, as other than Jewish writers; even their work which suggests a foreign influence could not have been written by non-Jews. Yet a good portion of Yehoash's verse, if adequately translated, would speak in universal symbols familiar to the human intelligence.

In an equally significant portion of his writing, however, he is the inspired Jew delving deep into Jewish lore. He has taken for his treatment incidents from Jewish history and folklore, and dealt with them in a truly Jewish fashion. The ethical Hebrew note inheres in a number of his poems, which depict life not merely as a quest for beauty but primarily as the pursuit of truth. Life, he intimates, is not a free gift of the gods but the conditioned privilege of a just but stern Jehovah. "Psalms," * for example, is a paean to this Jehovah world (translated by I. Goldstick):

> Happy is the man whom Thou hast set apart
> For chastisement and then hast healed his heart.
> Happy is the man that saith: I trust
> And praise the hand that rolls my pride in dust.
> Happy is the man who saith: In burst
> Of anger I hated and I cursed.
> This curse upon me left a lasting stain,
> And rankling hatred proved my sorest bane,
> Until I drank my fill of galling woe,
> 'Twas then my heart was cleansed as pure as snow.

"Solomon's Ring" consists of a series of poems which retell a beautiful legend with moral overtones. King Solomon's infinite wisdom and knowledge are ascribed by tradition to a magic ring which he possessed as a favor of God. Yehoash transforms this legend into a love story of exotic charm and dramatic tenseness. After an introductory chant on the inconstancy of faith and the pathos of unrealization, the virtues of the ring are described, one of them being Solomon's control of Asmodeus and his demons.

At the behest of the young king a marvelous palace is completed for him overnight. As Solomon sees the structure rising higher and higher, his heart becomes prouder and prouder. Thereupon Asmodeus, his servitude rankling within him, comforts himself: "Sooner or later, proud Solomon, your ring will adorn my finger; and I shall rule from your throne and live in your palace and kiss to satiety the bodies of your beautiful wives."

The third poem in the series depicts Solomon's manner of living in his miraculous palace, wherein his thousand wives await his pleasure. All day he sits on his throne, with a thousand sages to his right and to his left a thousand demons, and judges with astute wisdom. With the coming of night he betakes himself to his palace, gives the proper sign and magic ring to Amina, his old governess and sole keeper of his secrets, and sings forth lustily to announce his arrival. He is answered in erotic song by the passionate voices of his awaiting wives, and abides with them through the night. Asmodeus, ever watchful, at last discovers what trust Solomon puts in Amina, and plans to steal the precious ring.

In the climactic poem the East Wind one day tells Solomon of Jerada, queen of an unapproachable isle and the most beautiful of women. Deeply excited by this news, he sees the bewitching image of the exotic queen everywhere and in everything. Yielding to his lust, he uses the ring to fit out an army of men and demons, and with them is carried on a magic carpet to the isolated and unapproachable island. There Solomon woos Jerada, promising to make her empress of his thousand queens. She consents on the condition that she be permitted to worship her personal god. Solomon agrees, whereupon the power of Jehovah leaves him. While he indulges in his passion, Asmodeus appears before Amina in the guise of her beloved king and takes the magic ring from her.

In the final poem Asmodeus rules in Solomon's stead. The

latter, full of sorrow and shame, bewails his fate in the back streets of Jerusalem.

Although an ethical purpose underlies all great tragedy, in "Solomon's Ring" it appears too obviously. Most probably Yehoash conceived Solomon as a tragic figure: a very handsome king, most wise, God's favorite, who becomes the victim of uncontrollable passion and ends his life in woe. Yet in the poems he appears as a lush, lust-drunk youth, forfeiting God's favor for Jerada's, and then wailing aloud when tricked by Asmodeus. Moral apart, however, the verses are delightful, rich in conception and highly imaginative in execution. The descriptions of the marvelous palace and Jerada's infinite beauty soar on the wing of verbal brilliance. In content the poems constitute a complete drama: each stanza advances the action to the inevitable catastrophe. The unrhymed trochaic tetrameters of the main theme are varied with like trimeters in the prologue and rhymed amphibrach trimeters in the two songs. The diction, highly musical, varies in tone with the changes in the action; the images are exquisite, and the metaphors and similes of oriental ornateness.

Yehoash's nature poetry reveals him in his musing and meditation, his aspiration and solitude: a poetical pantheist who sees not God over the universe but godliness in nature. He discovers it in the sky, the forest, the ocean, the mountains, the seasons. With an almost Rousseauistic confidence he approaches nature with pagan joy and simplicity. In poem after poem he sings mystically of the glory man derives from merging his puny being with the embracing and enhancing divinity of nature.

His moods in the presence of nature are diverse. Often he appears the lover anxious for the approaching tryst. It is not easy, he relates in "Summer Night," to await the hour when none talks or laughs or silently breaks the weaving of his thought. When at last alone he sits by the hour steeped in darkness and in himself. Night presses itself to him intimately and softly, listening with big eyes to what he thinks. The wind lies asleep somewhere in the mountains, and in the wooded valleys and over the hills the narrow brook keeps watch, chattering unceasingly with small pebbles. Suddenly night shudders, and someone begins to gather the stars—at first slowly and then more and more quickly. Out of the shadow creeps forth a gray, cool road, walking with itself over hill and across meadow. And big and white and solitary in the sky hangs the morning star.

In this and other poems Yehoash waited for night as for a well-beloved, and it came to caress his fancy and soothe his soul. Alone with himself and night, his imagination discerned a world in which everything is shrouded in mystery and beauty and love, in which he enjoyed silence, solitude, and serenity.

Grief sometimes gripped Yehoash's spirit. Always at the mercy of his own ravaged lungs, he tended to be keenly conscious of the distress affecting the world, of the sorrow that silenced the heart of man. Then life became dull, heavy; shadows thickened on all sides and the sky became overcast. Yet a defensive optimism caused him to shrink from the face of sorrow, from woes that wither the human spirit. His impulse was to withdraw from the presence of man, to turn away from human suffering to the light of the sun. In "Emergence" this mood is tersely stated: "I dried my last tear and vowed to myself: a new world, a new joy, and I—new-born. . . . A new joy, a new world, without groping and without questioning: the sun, the great sun rises; come, let us greet it."

He enlarged poetically upon nature's munificence, asserting that nothing in it is inherently evil, not even when it appears in a hostile guise; at all times it is the trusted keeper of man. In a group of poems entitled "On the Ocean," he describes the various moods of the great seas: a serene vastness reflecting a wildly enflamed sky; played upon by black grotesque shadows; suddenly seized by a surging storm. The last poem is a joyous hymn:

A great silent gift fell from the sky, a blessing descended like dew on my head. . . . A light appeared and illuminated my heart. Is my heart enlarged, or puny the cosmos? . . . Both ocean and sky I rocked within my breast; learning the secret of space and the stars. . . . Out of a large goblet I sipped a consecrated drink, and my heart swelled with happiness and joy and gratitude. . . .

A like attitude is seen in "Among Trees," a group of five short poems, of which the following is the prose substance of the first two:

Deep in the forest stands my tent and none shall find me. Late at night and early morn I hear the spring laugh, beneath the deep roots, to moss-covered trunks—out of darkly cold depths to the flaming sun. . . . The earth and the sky become allied; and I ally myself with both. . . .

Deep in the forest stands my tent and none shall find me. The wide, wide world recedes like a wave. . . . Daily I take deeper root, and daily my limbs become heavier with the sap of the forest. . . . Great stars are my auditors, green grasses my song. . . .

Dark cypresses told me: abide with us, no longer seek the chase. . . . Our drink and our food—rootsap and sunrays—we shall share with you. . . . You will not fly and you will not fall, you will rest and be healed. . . . A bee circled in the light and sang in my ear: Open is the gate to you, someone is expecting you, and you will meet him now. . . . Out of secret springs will he cleanse your soul afresh, and bring you new seeds. . . .

In these and similar poems Yehoash gives voice to his lyrical credo. At the core of his being was the repose of reflection, the life-love of solitude. Alone with himself he could hear the voice of night, see the beauty of heaven, feel the friendly serenity of the forest, and be free from the strife and vulgarity of man-made cities. He viewed life in all its relativity, and found most comfort in merging his small self with the larger self of nature. This puniness of man in relation to the universe, expressed not with the abject humbleness of the religious zealot but with the meek modesty of the seer, is the keynote of Yehoash's nature poetry.

Yehoash's prose was pliable, mellow; its aristocratic texture has a soft suppleness. At its best it approaches the precise perfection of Walter Pater's writing, but without its faint mustiness. While the emotional flow of his poetry was sometimes disturbed by ratiocination, his prose was strengthened by this intellectual proneness. For Yehoash was always a man of thought. His imaginative reason was keen, analytical, lofty; as soothing as a summer breeze and as incisive as conscience. This intellectual vigor, expressed with lyric overtones, made him one of the most artistic writers of Yiddish prose.

Of This World and the Other is a collection of short stories, sketches, legends, and "thought splinters." The stories describe romantically the enrichment of his childhood in Russia. Unlike Mendele or Reisen, he quarried his characters from his idyllic memory. Among them are the man of wealth who considers it his obligation to provide for the poor; the physically powerful Jew who is awed by feats of learning but understands only acts of strength; a naive shoemaker who confesses to an educated boy of 13 his lack of implicit faith in Jehovah; and the over-affectionate mother who desires to buy philacteries for her only son with uncontaminated money and proceeds to earn the needed sum by growing a vegetable patch. These artless people, delineated sentimentally, become quick with life because of the insight and humor with which they are conceived. Other stories, of a more general nature, also give evidence of his uncommon understanding of the human heart. Some, like "Hennesey," the tale of a dog, bubble with gentle humor; others, like "Story of a Painting," reveal an unfettered fancy. A number of *pensées* and maxims deal with mysticism, solitude, age, and genius, and are conceived not as platitudes of the moralist but with the wisdom of the sage.

To Rehoboth and Back is an informative and pleasing book of travel modeled after those by Goethe and Heine. He developed his theses with artistic ardor, strictly assaying each word and striving for spontaneity in each sentence. Like his mentors he was moved to song by the beauty of the Mediterranean, but also by the glory that was Palestine, so the narrative is studded with corruscant lyrics. He speaks here as the poet and the Jew: cosmopolitan in outlook, he always longed for "the land of milk and honey" in all its legendary grandeur. Great was his spiritual joy when his feet touched the land of David and the prophets. His experiences, observations, and reflections, from first to last, are described with humor and clarity in picturesque and pointed prose.

His translation of the Old Testament, strangely enough, was the first complete, scholarly, and authoritative rendering in Yiddish. Heretofore the Torah had been considered too sacred to be read in any other language than the hallowed Hebrew; only women, whose ignorance of the holy tongue was general, were sanctioned a partial translation in *Tzena-Urena*. The concatenation of religious liberalism and the emergence of a poet of Yehoash's stature and erudition made this undertaking possible.

He undertook it as a labor of enduring and absorbing love, ending only with his last breath. The impulse to attempt this tremendous task came to him as early as 1904, and in 1907 he began to realize "the dream of a lifetime." By 1910 he had completed translation of Isaiah, Job, Song of Songs, Ruth, and Ecclesiastes, but this work seemed to him imperfect and he destroyed it. With the passing years he achieved prodigious erudition in his determination to make the translation accurate to the minutest degree: without paraphrase, interpretation, or adumbration. He went to endless trouble to find in old tomes, folklore, and folk speech the idiomatic Yiddish words that rendered exactly the original Hebrew meaning. So eager was he to attain perfection that near the end of his life he told his sister: "To translate one sentence just as I would wish it gives me more pleasure than the writing of ten poems." In addition he compiled two volumes of scholarly annotation in which he astutely and with a wealth of erudition elucidates the obscure and confusing passages met with on almost every page of the Old Testament.

The translation is in itself a work of great art. It contains the spirit, poetry, color, and grandeur of the original, rendering the prose of the books of Moses, the loftiness of Isaiah, the eroticism of Song of Songs, the fervency of the Psalms with remarkable fidelity. The vocabulary and diction have enriched Yiddish enormously without resorting to solecisms or obsolete words. In a large sense his Yiddish has become the standard among those who now speak it, as the James Version had become that of English and Luther's translation that of modern German. This exceptional achievement alone will make his name endure as long as Yiddish itself.

CHAPTER EIGHT

DAVID PINSKI

A Dramatist of Disparate Qualities

UNTIL THE 1940's no other Yiddish writer had so much of his work translated into English and other languages as David Pinski. *The Treasure*, a comedy of oblique greed, was produced in German by Max Reinhardt in Berlin and in English by the New York Theater Guild, in addition to Yiddish presentations in New York, Warsaw, and other cities. This and others of his plays, as well as a number of stories, have gained him a prominent place in Yiddish literature exceeding his inherent merit as a writer.

Pinski was born in Russia in 1872 and received the usual religious training. In 1885, when his parents moved to Moscow, he experienced the secular awakening of other intellectually minded youths of his day. He began to write during his teens and went to Warsaw in 1892 to submit his first efforts to Peretz. Encouraged and admired, he remained with his mentor for several years, assisting him in his editorial enterprise.

One of the first Yiddish writers to become a socialist, Pinski persuaded Peretz to address a meeting of workers, and the latter was imprisoned for it soon after. Pinski's early stories treated the life of poor workers sympathetically and realistically. In 1899 he migrated to New York, and for the next half century was busy with his writing and his public career as a

Labor-Zionist and civic leader. In 1949 he left for Israel, where he made his home on Mount Carmel in Haifa and continued to write until his death in 1959.

In the process of artistic expression the inner censor—a component in which the writer's intellect and intuition are equally prominent—is the invaluable daemon. No matter how powerful, noble, and universal an original conception may be, it is in danger of becoming jejune, commonplace, and fatuous if expressed without the stern strictness of self-criticism. Pinski wrote a number of plays and novels without the full benefit of this essential inner guidance. He tended to regard all his work with the indulgence of a fond father, and ascribed to each creation more or less equal merit. Because the germinal idea of a drama or story seemed to him important, and because he labored over each with intent assiduity, he considered the finished product a work of literature. Yet, considered critically, a good part of his work falls short of this quality. As S. Niger commented on *The Family Tzvi*, one of Pinski's early plays:

> Reb Moshe Tzvi, the town preacher, is not a town preacher but a piece of pathos on two legs with a long beard—a piece of pathos that spoke with heart, with mind; but it is not the town preacher's but Pinski's heart, Pinski's mind. Even the language is Pinski's, not Reb Moshe Tzvi's.

This fault is basic in a number of his plays as well as his novels. Thus the fact that a drama has for its motif the death of a religion (*The Family Tzvi*, 1904), or the tragedy of motherhood (*Mother*, 1901), or the power of the beast in man (*Better Not to Be Born*, 1914), or the pathos of human cupidity (*The Last Reckoning*, 1918), is to him evidence of inherent literary quality; that these ideas become banal and without dramatic truth in the process of execution seemed not to have impinged upon his critical consciousness.

He regarded *The Family Tzvi* as one of his best creations. Taught as a child to believe in the tenets and dogmas of orthodox Judaism, and realizing in adolescence, with the shock of discovery, that his faith in Jehovah and formal Judaism was gone, he early conceived the idea of commemorating the event in tragic content. For more than a decade the thought lay dormant, but in 1903 the Kishinev pogrom gave him the impulse to visualize the savage hooligans as the murderers not only of Jews but of Judaism. In *The Family Tzvi* he has Reb Moshe, his pious protagonist, put all Jews to the same test of religious martyrdom which orthodox Jews had passed triumphantly in previous centuries. When his contemporaries consider such martyrdom as foolhardy fanaticism, Reb Moshe announces with his last gasp that Judaism is dead.

The death of religious faith in the heart of a people is indeed a fit subject for tragic treatment, yet *The Family Tzvi* impresses one as shrill melodrama. Because the present is not an age of religious martyrdom, Pinski's test cannot but appear fallacious. The contemporary Jew is not necessarily less a Jew for not adhering to the orthodoxy of his fathers. When Reb Moshe goes from group to group of Jews during the height of the pogrom, bombastically urging them to enlist in "the army of the Lord" in order to protect the holy scrolls in the synagogue from the unclean hands of the hooligans, he only makes a nuisance of himself. No emancipated Jew wants to risk his life to save a Torah.

When *The Family Tzvi* was first produced, its pogrom theme gave it popular impetus. As a drama, however, it is merely pretentious, without genuine motivation, and developed with the pseudo-logic of the propagandist rather than with the elements of pertinent probability employed by the dramatist.

A like disparity between theme and realization obtains in *Mother*. A handsome widow has devoted the best years of her life to the upbringing of her two children. When they grow up and no longer need her care, she yields to the wooing of a forebearing admirer. Her children, themselves about to marry, are shocked and chagrined that she should be unfaithful to their long-dead father, and refuse to see her again. After six years of painful separation the stricken mother begs them for a reconciliation, but so enduring is their anger that they reject her overtures, though aware of her fatal illness. Again the effect is that of poor melodrama. The behavior of the children is insufficiently motivated, and their extreme animosity to their mother cannot but appear improbable.

Similarly, in *Better Not to Be Born* Pinski seeks to demonstrate that man is never free from the impulses of the beast. An apparently normal young man, son of virtuous parents and betrothed to a girl he dearly loves, suddenly is seized with the beastly desire to rape a girl of 12. In his frenzy he stifles her. Why, he asks before shooting himself, should he pay with his life for a deed he had committed in a moment of madness? Pinski implies that he who is certain of not being tempted next may be the first to condemn the unfortunate young man. Presumably a psychological drama, the action lacks universal applicability. Although no man is altogether free from the impulse that overwhelmed the culprit in the play, only the extreme sex deviant would yield to the temptation. In the action his behavior is inadequately motivated even for the pervert.

The Last Reckoning has an ingenious theme. The dead mother of a flour merchant visits him in a dream and tells him that the flour from the current crop of grain will make people mad, and the flour from last year's crop will be the only antidote. Upon waking he tests both flours and finds them according to his dream. With the aid of the town's chief usurer, to whom he divulges the secret, he acquires all of last year's flour. Soon he becomes the richest man in the vicinity. After a time the "medicinal" flour is exhausted and before long, the cause of the plague being unknown to the people, insanity grips his townsmen. All this time the merchant has been infatuated with his neighbor's wife. When the husband becomes affected, the merchant offers her his riches for her love. Long critical of his crass behavior toward the plague-stricken, she repels him disdainfully, whereupon he hangs himself.

In the prologue Pinski declared that "riches alone make

none happy." To prove his thesis he resorts to trivial motivation, making the man who has the shrewdness to become master of a city fatuous enough to believe that his despised wealth would buy the love of a virtuous woman. And for him to commit suicide upon rejection is simply not in keeping with his character.

Although these four plays fail to achieve dramatic effectiveness, Pinski's ideas are commendable on the whole, and he could certainly write good dramatic dialogue. His fault lies in his failure to realize that he had not fully motivated the development of action and characters. Consequently his protagonists fail to acquire persuasive probability. In each of these dramas there are scenes of dramatic tenseness, but in their main action they do not impress with their artistic cogency.

Pinski's daemon is, happily, more alert in a number of his other works. The following six plays * reveal the able dramatist writing with the competence, if not always the mastery of the artist: *Professor Brenner* (1911), in which an elderly artist's Hamletian doubt of the love of his youthful betrothed is depicted with accelerating intensity; *The Dumb Messiah* (1911), a satiric study of the fleshpot attitude in the Jewish people; *Yenkel the Blacksmith* (1906), dealing with a spirited but successful struggle between prurience and prudence in the heart of a simple man; *Gabri and the Women* (1908), another study of sensuality expressing itself under uncommon circumstances; *Mary Magdalene* (1911), whose fascination no man can withstand until she meets her master in Jesus; and *Nina Norden and Her Lovers* (1915), in which a woman seeks to enrich men with the intensity of her love only to find herself their plaything. Each of these dramas is written more with intellectual dexterity than intuitive endowment. They make good material for the theater, but lack the insight of the first-rate dramatist.

Pinski's success as a playwright is evidenced in such plays as *Isaak Sheftel* (1899), *The Treasure* (1906),* and *King*

David and His Wives (1914).* The first is a tragedy of the thwarted creative mind. The protagonist belongs to the class of Jews which was gradually developing into the proletariat. He worked under very unfavorable conditions, his life spent in the midst of ignorance and squalor. Instead of bewailing his lamentable lot, rebelling against it, or seeking to forget it in drink, as others were doing, he concentrated his creative mind on mechanical inventions. Pathetically unequipped for the task, possessing neither technical training nor the necessary instruments, he persisted instinctively and stubbornly, and in time invented two small contrivances which proved of benefit to his employer but not to himself.

As the play opens, a new idea occupies Isaak's mind and dominates him so completely that he neglects his wife and children as well as his work. His inability to bring the new invention to a successful conclusion torments him cruelly. Meanwhile his family demands food, his employer threatens dismissal, and his acquaintances poke fun at his apparent eccentricity. The demands upon him and his own exactions finally prove too strong for his harassed brain. In a state of distraction he demolishes his unfinished as well as his completed machines, fills himself with liquor, and seeks escape in the deep forest. Freedom from anguish comes to him only when poison stops his aching and confused heart.

This drama was written in 1899, when workers were badly mistreated and their struggle for improved status was very close to Pinski's heart. He treats Isaak's problem with sympathetic understanding, so that his predicament appears real and poignant. One tends to forget that Isaak is regarded as a muddlehead by his wife and friends, that in his unrealized dreams he is only one of many; one envisages mostly the struggle of the creative spirit, an artless fledgling inventor caught in the talons of an unhappy fate; one does not even mind the contrived ending, despite its melodramatic impress, since it seems a logical solution to Isaak's entrapment.

The coincidence of Pinski writing *The Treasure* at the same time and with the same title as a comedy by Sholom Aleichem caused both some embarrassment, especially since both plays were to be serialized in the same newspaper. Even the content of both comedies had certain similarities. Both works, however, had great merit, and Pinski's had the wider vogue because it was better adapted to the Yiddish stage in New York. It also achieved considerable success on the non-Jewish stage, and Professor George P. Baker, then head of Harvard's famous drama course, pronounced it as one of the best comedies of the decade.

The Treasure is a boldly ironical portrayal of the state of mind of a poverty-ridden but fancy-fed community on the crest of acquisitive excitement. Here Pinski has indeed depicted Jewish life in a small Russian town with the insight and humor worthy of Sholom Aleichem. More than in any of his other plays his motivation and delineation of character are in keeping with his alert daemon.

Tillie, daughter of a poor gravedigger, possesses a delightful sprightliness and sense of humor. She quickly ingratiates herself in the hearts of her audience, which enjoys the gusto with which she plays a prank on the entire community. Her fantasy is given full rein. In the midst of dire poverty she dreams of the pleasures of luxury, and even dares to fancy herself as the Cinderella bride of a Rothschild. When her dull-witted brother accidentally digs up a handful of gold coins, her fancy enlarges the find into a treasure of great wealth. She shrewdly suggests the existence of such a cache to the townspeople. To obtain the secret of its whereabouts they seek to win her favor by every means at their command. Taking full advantage of her position, she orders expensive clothes and costly delicacies. Meantime, marriage brokers offer her the best available young men. In the end, when the populace realizes it has been duped, Tillie has the satisfaction of having lived like a princess while the agitation lasted.

In no other of his plays has Pinski written with such penetrating knowledge of human nature. Apart from creating a number of living characters, he has delineated mass psychology with particular verisimilitude. With the possible exception of the scene in which the half-wit furthers his sister's hoax with unexpected cunning, the action progresses with persuasive logic and high humor. We are shown a town of Jews, with emaciated bodies and fabulous fancies, so impoverished as always to be ready to follow the most ridiculous lure of sudden gain, pouncing on the possibility of hidden treasure and pursuing the hint frantically—until they realize at last what they should have known at the outset, that they were being duped by a waggish girl. The action, however, makes evident the pathos of their existence, the wretchedness of their economic plight, and the spiritual fortitude with which they encounter their unkind fate. The result is comedy of genuine humor.

Pinski's portrayal of amorousness has been most varied. There is hardly an impulse, nuance, grossness, or vagary of sexual feeling which he has not sought to analyze and describe. Yet he treats love more as a subject to be dissected and scrutinized than as an experience of man's basic emotional life. In his treatment of the amorous theme he is perhaps most successful in *King David and His Wives*. The play is composed of five episodes, each dealing with a particular emotional situation in the life of the passionate king. He appears first as the youthful conqueror of Goliath and timid lover of proud Micah; next as the leader of a band of outlaws, smitten with the beauty of Abigail and taking her to him; then as the lustful tyrant who sent the husband of charming Bathsheba to certain death so that she might become his; again as the elderly king, the sated husband of 18 wives and numerous concubines; and lastly as the decrepit old man, amorous to the end, warming his cold and shriveled body with the warmth of Abishag, the most beautiful maiden in the land.

As one episode follows the other, David's ardent character develops quickly and persuasively. He appears first as a meek and pious youth, not daring to accept the love of a haughty princess until fully worthy of it. As a mature man, fighting to gain a kingdom, his heart seethes with passion and he almost compromises his vows to Jehovah for the favor of a beautiful woman. In his next entrance on the stage he is the wanton autocrat. When the prophet Nathan urges him to keep faith with Jehovah's commandments, he is only annoyed. Is not woman the handiwork of God, and is she not made for man? His will is done and Bathsheba becomes his. There is a kind of grandeur in the very lustfulness of the man: David sins not because he is wicked but because his passion overwhelms virtue; so much so that Bathsheba, who at first scorns his overtures, ends by yielding willingly to the man who is obeyed by her husband with slavish fidelity. When the curtain rises again David's hair is already gray and his passionate nature has long passed the crest of human fulfilment. He is indeed a little weary, and his wives, now beldames, move him only mildly. He is the complete man still, but more the paterfamilias than the paramour. The last scene brings on the stage a shivering old man: age has laid its withering hand on the body of the great king, but not on his passionate heart. He is no sooner warmed by young Abishag than sensuality again agitates him, although all he can now do is keep her close to him—virginal, a temptation, a life stimulus.

It might seem odd that Pinski should have written plays of such disparate dramatic worth indicated in the foregoing pages, especially since they are often composed not so much with deep emotion as with conscious ideation. As already suggested, the explanation seems to lie in his defective daemon, which permitted him to assume that all his writing was of equal worth. The truism that a writer reveals himself more in the process of expression than in the originality or ingenuity of thought apparently meant little to him. The discrepancy, for instance, between *The Family Tzvi* and *The Treasure* was a matter of chance. Both plays are based on novel ideas and developed with like literary effort. One, the product of an idea dear to him, became mangled when mated with demented action; the other, conceived by the imagination in a happy moment and developed with mature and sympathetic humor, became a work of high dramatic quality. Similarly, the protagonists in *Better Not to Be Born* and *Isaak Sheftel* are alike seized by sudden frenzy. Yet in the first work a psychological truth is marred by having an apparently normal young man commit a hideous crime without any other provocation than the heat of a summer's day; Isaak's act of destruction is provoked by circumstances so dire and a temperament so brooding that his behavior seems almost inevitable.

A number of later plays—*Rabbi Akiba and Bar Kochba*, *Shlomo Molkhu and David Rubeni*, *Shabbati Zevi and Sarah* (issued in one volume in 1952), *Alexander and Diogenes* (1930), and *Saul*—while based on historical characters and conceived on a broad and philosophical scale, pursue the same emotional conflicts between virtue and temptation, ambition and personal contentment, and reveal the same strength of concept and imperfection of execution as some of his earlier dramas.

Although Pinski's reputation rests largely on his dramatic work, he wrote a good amount of fiction, both short stories and novels. To him belongs the distinction of having been the first Yiddish writer to treat the urban worker. Early acquainted with the hard lot of labor in Warsaw and a convert to socialism, he wrote about workingmen with fervent and sympathetic realism, attributing to them a groping awareness of their exploited condition which stimulated them to organize and fight for their human rights. Because his stories added a new facet to Yiddish literature, and because he treated the life of the poor with class-conscious perceptiveness, their literary worth was impressive. Yet his quick compassion caused him now and then to exaggerate the misery and sensibility of his characters. It was as if he attributed to them his own intellectual sensibilities, believing it his duty to depict them writhing in wretchedness. Stories like "A Tale About a Hungry Man," "Drabkin," and "Lost," though realistically conceived, become turgid and didactic in the telling.

Not so, however, a story like "In the Madhouse." Its theme is developed with commendable simplicity and restraint, and a subtle sense of humor intensifies its significance. The simple-minded son of a rich man, influenced by utopian idealism, comes to believe that so long as there are human beings suffering poverty he cannot partake of his father's wealth. He leaves his comfortable home and associates with the poor. Yet his new acquaintances regard him as a misguided simpleton. He does find solace and stimulation in the friendship of a young girl worker, and her sympathy encourages him to become a common laborer. One day his roommate, through whom he had found employment, is overcome by the torrid heat while at work. In his anxiety to help the stricken man he hurries to their employer to ask for an advance in order to obtain medical assistance. When the latter blandly rejects the request, the aroused samaritan throws a brick at the man's protuberant paunch. He is arrested and later confined in an insane asylum.

The story is told in the first person, and the young man cannot understand why he should be kept in a madhouse. Is he not capable of distinguishing between right and wrong? Was he not justified in leaving his father's house to earn his bread by the sweat of his brow? Was not the callous employer guilty of murder for permitting an honest worker to die for lack of medical help? Why, then, should he be immured with raving madmen? By means of such revealing irony the narrative shows him to be not a paranoiac but a guileless youth who sincerely believes in the brotherhood of man.

The tenor of "Reb Shlomo" is equally admirable. All his life Reb Shlomo was actively devoted to the welfare of his indigent townsmen. An orthodox Jew and learned in Hebrew lore, wise in the ways of practical affairs and giving freely of his time and wealth, he came to be one of the town's most respected elders. When two of his grandsons come from the country to live with him, he engages a tutor to instruct them in the elements of worldly knowledge—believing that one need not be less religious because of a secular education. During the hour of the lesson Reb Shlomo sometimes listens to the tutor's explanation of physical phenomena, and smiles skeptically at statements which seem to him preposterous. Yet the more he listens the more his interest is aroused, and in defense of his lifelong beliefs he tries to confound the young man with questions. The lucidity of the answers and the logic of the explanations so convince the old man that he also becomes a pupil. Hour after hour he and the tutor are closeted together, drinking tea and discussing the first principles of science and natural laws. Now persuaded that truth is not on the side of Genesis but on that of science, he feels it incumbent upon himself to introduce this knowledge in the town schools. But the parents, despite their respect for him, refuse to permit such sacrilege. Thwarted and hurt, he turns to the education of adult workers, but these tired and listless men also disappoint him, and his grief soon sends him to his grave.

In both stories the main characters are at odds with their environment, social misfits. Their mental obliqueness, however, is depicted as the naive idealism which agitated many a man during the 1890's. In presenting this form of altruism Pinski sought at once to emphasize its presence within the Jewish community and indicate its general misapprehension. In both narratives the clashes of opinion, naive attempts at orientation, and frantic defense of tradition are made the subdued but authentic background for subtly sketched characters.

The amorous theme is as prominent in Pinski's fiction as in his plays. In his early stories simple love pulsates with the tender emotions of fresh experience. In narratives like "Awakening" and "The Earth Spirit" the shy but ardent youth loves with adolescent innocence. In the first a studious youth of 17, his heart as chaste as a forest freshet, one day sees a cousin of his as he had never seen her before, and the shock of her beauty wakens in him a strange and irresistible emotion. Having never before even thought of girls, he dares not speak to her; but she perceives his love and rejoices therewith. The winsome tale is told in a simple style, and one knows that the artless emotion of the pair is real and natural.

"Johanan the High Priest," "Beruriah," and "The Temptation of Rabbi Akiba," three ancient legends dealing with temptation of the flesh and composed in Pinski's mature years, are written in a polished but quasi-biblical style and give the impression of having been more cogitated than felt. The legends no doubt attracted him because in one a High Priest lived a life of virtue and piety for 80 years and then, tempted by a prostitute, goes into the wilderness to die; in the second the most beautiful and chaste of women is tempted by her famous husband with the prolonged sole presence of his handsomest student, who is passionately in love with her, and after resisting the youth's advances for a month cuts her veins when she learns that her husband had arranged this temptation to test her fidelity; in the third, one of the most renowned of ancient rabbis, who regarded the flesh as sinful and practiced continence in the face of great temptation, one day is lured by one of Satan's minions to the point of carnality and weeps at his weakness. Each story is embellished with rhetorical brilliance, but because the impulse came not from the heart but from an intellectual endeavor to prove the infirmity of human flesh and the futility of resistance, the result is more artifice than art. Some of his later stories, based on similar forms of conflict, are likewise of uneven merit.

Pinski wrote three novels in his later years, all having their setting in the United States. *The House of Noah Eden* (1913) * is a family saga based on the thesis that life in America is antithetical to orthodoxy, and therefore deprives Jews of the very foundation of their spiritual existence. It appeared in English translation before it was published in Yiddish, and is on the whole a routine performance.

Arnold Levenberg * (originally entitled *The Torn Man*, 1920, in English, 1928) is set among the wealthy German-Jewish families in New York. Completely Americanized, successful in business and in the professions, these men and women are Jews in name only—and only because they are still excluded from the prominent Gentile clubs. Many are socially snobbish and personally debauched. The action centers on

Arnold's relations with several girls and his affair with the dissolute and brazenly ambitious Catherine—who attracts him physically but who also repels him by her vulgar surroundings and her obvious effort to trap him into marriage. One of his friends, a serious-minded woman doctor, introduces Arnold to several Russian-Jewish radicals and Zionists; their idealism appeals to him, but he is too habituated to his snobbish way of life to follow his impulse to get closer to them. The entire narrative is flawed with the speciousness of exaggeration. Most of the German Jews are drawn as caricatures; all the girls are beautiful; coincidences and accidents play an important part in the development of the action. Pinski's daemon was obviously in a state of suspense when this work was written.

Pinski was 78 years old when *When Roads Part* appeared in 1950. Placed in New York in 1931, when unemployment and poverty were agitating the radically inclined Jewish workers, the novel deals with a family in which the father has long been a member of the Socialist Labor Party, one son is an adherent of the Socialist Party and the other a Trotskyist, one daughter is an almost fanatic communist and the other a school teacher without intellectual interests. A young man of typical American-Jewish upbringing falls in love with the handsome communist, whom he meets by merest chance, and is ready to regard her views sympathetically to win her affection. Repressing her favorable emotional response, she in the end refuses to marry him and leaves for Soviet Russia to live in accord with her Marxian ideals. All through the novel there is much discussion about the nature of radicalism, the worker as a human being, and the conflicting views of the several socialist factions. One of the characters expresses the gist of Pinski's views when he declares:

> Where is there so much hate as among the socialist parties? Constant warfare, continuous jealousy, poison, rancor, cheap abuse. Instead of concentrating on common points and working together, they stress their differences and are ever knifing one another. Because they are driven by hate . . . the SLP against

the SP, the SP against the SLP, and both against the Communist Party. . . . Their hate has even penetrated the narrow circle of workers' families . . . made enemies between parents and children, brothers and sisters . . . all proletarians, all workers, torn one from the other, estranged . . . hate, hate, hate!

For all its realistic portrayal and cogent dialogue, the novel suffers from imperfect or exaggerated motivation. Actually very few radicals went to Russia for doctrinal reasons, and to make the main character do so detracts from psychological truth. This novel, indeed, illustrates the uneven nature of Pinski's entire work—in its depiction of human passion and intellectual and emotional conflict, in its authentic description, and in its imperfect expression of psychologically motivated themes. The moralist and the artist are equally active in his writing, and more often than he realized his daemon yielded to his overriding ethical nature—to the hurt of much of his literary productivity.

CHAPTER NINE

ABRAHAM REISEN

Poet of the Jewish Poor

LITHUANIA is a meager land. Marshy, deforested, badly cultivated for generations past, it yielded little to its relatively
large population during the 19th century. Periodic crop failures caused actual starvation, and many more aggressive inhabitants, the Jews in particular, migrated to the Ukraine and
elsewhere. Conditions were aggravated by large landowners
who appropriated the major share of the country's produce.
The stolid peasantry barely managed to have enough to eat;
the Jews who lived all around them, and of whom few were
producers, seldom had even that much. Forbidden to own
land and handicapped in other ways by a hostile government,
most Jews underwent an unceasing struggle against poverty
and privation. A few worked at essential crafts; many eked
out a precarious existence by trading; a number had neither
the mind nor the means even to trade. The bleak, murky
towns they inhabited reflected only too obviously their abject
circumstances.

Their grievous poverty and medievally orthodox orientation combined to sharpen their wits and make keen their
eagerness to seek compensation in the study of Hebrew lore.
Unlike their brethren in Poland and the Ukraine, however,
they rejected the spiritual exaltation of Hasidism, largely be-

cause of opposition to its tenets by the great Vilna Gaon, Elijah ben Solomon (1720–1797). The emotional exaltation of the Hasid appeared to their sober minds as fanatical frenzy. Instead, they devoted themselves to the fine exegesis of the Talmud, and a number became renowned Talmudic scholars.

Within the confines of synagogue or yeshiva, where learning was the criterion of intellectual aristocracy, they were audacious and adamant in disputing a point of erudition. Faced with dire reality in the marketplace, they tended to be cunningly meek. Their oppressive physical environment fostered a fatalistic acceptance of life on earth. With little hope of ever improving their material condition, they banked their faith on spiritual promises: if their brief life on earth was fraught with misery, they expected proper compensation in Paradise. In this dedication they observed the rigid and rigorous Judaic ritual and suffered malnutrition with passive equanimity.

Invaded by the industrial revolution during the second half of the 19th century, which brought in its wake an upsurge of religious and social reform, the Lithuanian Jews underwent the inevitable turmoil of emancipation from medieval orthodoxy. Worldly knowledge was increasingly welcomed with the timidity and eagerness of a new discovery. In the 1880's and later, youths by the thousands left the yeshivas and houses of study for the larger cities, where they might engage in secular schooling without parental censure. These young men, and not a few young women, quaffed their intellectual freedom with keen pleasure, but of necessity they lived precariously. Most were without a trade or profession, and at first they neither would nor could do menial work. In time, however, many either joined the proletariat or the professions, tutored or clerked, and lived frugally yet adventurously on the fringes of urban culture.

Abraham Reisen was such a young man. He was born in Kaidanov, near Minsk, in 1875. His father was an impecunious merchant in wheat and flax, already imbued with the spirit of the *Haskolah* movement, and even wrote Hebrew and Yiddish verse on occasion. He saw to it that his children received traditional schooling in Hebrew lore, but also had them study a little Russian and German. Abraham was a bright youth, and at 14 considered himself intellectually mature enough to tutor in order to contribute to the family's meager income. His reading at this time was wide and eclectic, and he soon wrote verses and stories emulating the authors who appealed to him. In 1890, at the age of 15, he was bold enough to send specimens of his writing to Peretz, and when one of his poems was included in the 1891 edition of *The Yiddish Bibliotek*, he was ecstatic in his happiness. His youth and natural bent made him the first Yiddish poet to sing without the self-consciousness of the reformer: he wrote to give voice to his feelings, often wistfully sad, in a Yiddish at once idiomatic and lyrical.

At the age of 18 Reisen suffered a severe emotional wrench in the death of his mother. That same winter he went to Minsk to live, and was often without food and shelter. He met others who were interested in Yiddish literature and also lived precariously by occasional tutoring. Continuing to write and occasionally be published, he soon became known to Jewish readers, and some of his songs achieved relatively wide circulation. At the age of 21 he was drafted into the army, and for four years experienced the hard and harassing life of the Russian soldier—mitigated somewhat after he had managed to join the regimental band.

Once free again, he soon gravitated to Warsaw, then the most active center of Yiddish culture. He was welcomed by Peretz, Dinesohn, and others of the elder writers. He also became intimate with youthful aspirants like himself, in particular with H.D. Nomberg and Sholem Asch, with whom he shared shelter, food, and ideas. The early 1900's were a generally exciting period for these writers. Paid little or nothing for their published pieces, earning a little by means of editing and tutoring, they dreamt dreams of literary grandeur and partook enthusiastically in the social and nationalistic turmoil that then agitated Jewish groups and factions. Reisen was not naturally a reformer, but he sympathized with the aims of socialism and wrote verses and stories on the subject of social amelioration. In one of his poems he stated: "I gave an oath not to wish for good fortune or joy, but to devote my life to human loneliness and need."

In 1902 he brought out a 48-page volume of his poems entitled *Current Songs*. It was well received, and he drew great joy from noting the orders from booksellers in various cities. His work was also soon published in New York, and Abraham Cahan praised it highly in *Der Forverts*. After a brief sojourn in Vienna, Reisen went in 1904 to Cracow to edit *The Yiddish Word*, in which he proclaimed Yiddish as the national language of the Jews, thus arousing much heated discussion among Yiddish and Hebrew proponents. In 1908 he was an active participant in the Czernovitz Conference, and subsequently joined Peretz, Asch, and Nomberg in a tour of a number of cities to advocate the national position of Yiddish. Later that year he visited the United States, but returned to Cracow early in 1909, where he soon brought out a literary weekly. The next year he gave public readings in the larger cities of Europe and later visited the United States again, editing *The New Land* for several months. All this time his stories and poems appeared frequently in Yiddish periodicals in Europe and the United States, and some of his work was issued in English translation.

After the outbreak of World War I Reisen settled in New York, and contributed regularly to Yiddish newspapers and magazines. Volumes of his poems and stories were published from time to time. For many years a gallant bachelor, he married, became a sentimentally devoted husband, and adored his only daughter. He was also proud of his sister Sarah, a gifted writer and translator, and of his scholarly younger brother Zalmon, whose four-volume *Lexicon*, now in a new and enlarged edition prepared by others, is still the chief reference work on Yiddish writers. In later years he intensified his interest in young Yiddish writers and reviewed their work with indulgent commendation. By the time he died in 1953 his name had long become enshrined in the history of Yiddish literature.

In appearance, manner, attitude, and interest, Reisen gave the impression of the composite village intellectual. Though a seasoned cosmopolite, he remained outwardly the typical European Jew. The mental outlook and naive shrewdness of his Lithuanian brethren characterized him to the end of his life. He was goodnatured, friendly, always ready to give himself to worthy causes and to uphold the rights of others. All the while, of course, he continued to be the genuine poet, endowed with a truly sensitive intuition, so that he perceived perspicaciously what appears blurred or opaque to the rational mind. He rode on the crest of emotional experience with the same natural ease with which he scraped the trough of artless humility. In song and story he gave artistic expression to the aspects of Jewish life of which he was an integral part.

The themes characteristic of Reisen's lyrics and stories are poverty, love, longing, and sympathy, and all are expressed with a simplicity that often conceals depth of feeling and thought. Some of his verse, set to music, has assumed the popularity of folksongs familiar to nearly all who understand Yiddish.

Reisen's poetry has conscious artlessness. When he first began to write, verse meant to him rhymed couplets. The keen emotions of adolescence overflowed into tender lyrics. Later, reading and the incitement of Peretz taught him the technique of versification. Prosody, however, was to him a necessary means rather than a stimulus to experimentation, as it was to Peretz and Yehoash; he was mostly concerned with what he wanted to say, not with how to say it. When he wrote of Jewish life in its penurious nakedness his very soul sang in wistful sympathy. His clear, gentle reflections, impressionable melancholy, ironic sentiment, social radicalism, pensive yearning, and feeling of precariousness were all expressed with lyric and artless spontaneity. He lingered unobtrusively along the lanes of pure emotion, and wrote modestly yet sensitively in the presence of nature, love, and human vicissitude. Sometimes sorrow affected him unto tears, or love lifted him into blissful ecstasy; his melancholy plaint reverberated in both alike. Even when on the wing of sheer gladness he seldom burst forth in emotional unrestraint.

At its best his poetic voice is soft and still and unpretentious. Even when aroused and rebellious he sang in a muted key. His lyrical response to the cross-currents of Jewish life was natural and immediate, with the sympathy and directness of the true bard. The scope of his verse is thus more inclusive and intensive than that of his prose, although both are suffused with nostalgic yearning and a fondness for things that were but are no more. Memories of his childhood experiences, of the religious life in which he grew up, and of the pity and devotion of the older generation of Lithuanian Jews he described with love, longing, and lenity; the behavior of the Jews in their American milieu aroused only his critical irony. Although he also tended to philosophize, his verses always possessed more beauty than deep reflection. To the end of his life he wrote with a simplicity of form and a salutary sadness that made him the most appreciated of Yiddish lyricists.

Lyric verse rarely lends itself to translation at once accurate and poetic, especially if the mold into which it is to be transmuted is as alien to the original as English is to Yiddish. This was true of Peretz's and Yehoash's poetry, and is even more true of Reisen's. The following prose renderings of several specimen lyrics will convey at least a modicum of Reisen's attitude and sensibilities. In "How Come I" he gives voice to the confined and oppressive conditions of the Russian Jews: "How come I to beauty? How, my child? The way to the fields

—through Gentiles and dogs. . . . The street is so poor and drear; at each door—a heap of refuse. . . ." "My Songs" tells that although he wrote his verses in black ink, he finds on reading them that he has used his heart's blood; the more he reads them the more red they seem, and the longer he writes the paler and deader he feels. Many of his love songs are tinctured with the wistful sentiment found in "Healing," in which he tells his beloved to kiss his gray hair to make it turn black again; to kiss the anguish and doubt away from his eyes, so he may again be good and devout; to kiss the venom from his tongue in the hope that he may again be foolish and young.

As a socialist sympathizer he wrote much against Russia's autocratic government. "In Our Land" conveys concisely his revulsion to its oppressiveness. The first and fourth stanzas read: "In our land, dear friend, life is dead and ugly; the one free songbird one hears only at hangings. . . . In our land, dear friend, it is a favor—you know what? Instead of hanging one is killed by bullets. . . ." The pogroms in the 1900's deeply angered him, yet he lacked the prophetic chagrin of Bialik or the emotional clamor of other poets; his was the repressed weeping of the meek—blaming not the killers but the government which spurred them on.

> The wind struck my hut and scattered it to pieces; soon I heard the roll of thunder—and many souls were struck down.
>
> How can I be angry with wind and thunder, how do they know what they are doing? . . . But my anger is aflame—how could it have happened when the sun shone so brightly?
>
> The wind and the thunder, O, forgive them, they were merely blind forces; but how could the sun shine so brightly, and peacefully, and permit the sin?

Reisen's philosophical mood is evidenced in "World Sorrow":

> I walked in the quiet field, driven far from sorrow, till I stood still, having heard the world's sorrow.
>
> It was quiet, but I heard someone walking quietly, and the atmosphere became full of sounds, and the entire earth sorrowed quietly.

And it became night, with the moon high—I know not how or whence, but on the sky it stood shivering and, seemingly, sorrowing.

And what the whole world experienced, and suffered through the ages, quietly passed through me, full of sound and flutter.

One of his most popular songs, "Ma-Kamashmalon" (What Is the Meaning of This) is the pathetic plaint of a Talmudic student who devotes his waking hours to Hebrew lore and knows not where he will eat his next meal or obtain new garments that he badly needs.

What is the rain saying to me, what message is it bringing? It beats against the window pane with the sound of melancholy tears. Soon winter will be coming, with its mud and slush, its cold and dreariness, and I have neither coat nor boots to wear.

What is the clock saying to me, what message is it bringing, with its wizened old face, as it ticks in my ears? It's a wound up instrument, without life or will power, and knows not why it ticks and strikes the hour.

What does the candle tell me, what is the message it brings, with its tallow dripping till it is all gone? So I too will flicker and pass out quietly in the east corner.

What can my life tell me, what is the message it brings, as my youth fades away and grows beyond my years? I eat dry crusts and drink tears and my heart grows numb with hopelessness, destroying my will to live while waiting for the hereafter.

The pathos and pensiveness of this lyric, beautifully rendered in the original, particularly quickened the sympathy of the many Jews who had themselves experienced the dreary existence of the Talmudic student, who "ate days"—each day with a different family—and slept on a hard synagogue bench, devoting the years of their adolescence and young manhood to intense study. Set to music, it soon became one of the most popular songs in the repertoire of professional vocalists, and was sung wistfully in many homes.

In his prose writings Reisen is more the humorist. His smile, however, is quiet, ironic, saturated with pathos, motivated by repressed poignancy. Many of his stories treat poverty with exceptional fidelity and pensiveness. Other Yiddish writers have depicted it with either pity or satire; Reisen delineated it realistically, without moral overtones. To him it was part of the life he knew, and he accepted it with complacent, if plaintive, matter-of-factness. Yet he felt keenly the suffering it caused, and portrayed its victims with warm sympathy. He emphasized not incident but one's reaction to it; the manner in which he revealed how men and women were being intimidated by poverty into humble, docile, dispirited creatures constitutes the essence of his art.

"Flax," typical of numerous similar stories, and no doubt based on the memory of his own father, tells of Zalmon, a young learned Jew, trading first in wheat and then in flax, and in the end being ruined by monopolistic brokers much shrewder than he. He is drawn with sharp strokes. A scholar and naive, he buys wheat according to quotations in *Hamelitz*, the Hebrew weekly. Because he is the sole reader of this learned periodical in the entire town, he considers himself superior to his fellow traders. Paying no attention to the actual fluctuations in price, he soon loses half of his capital. He then turns to flax.

> He could not reconcile himself to the idea of doing business like other traders. If he could not trade according to the quotations in *Hamelitz*, a means of enhancing him in the eyes of his colleagues, he must deal with a product superior to all other products and for which one must have some special aptitude. . . . Since Zalmon became a trader he was attracted to flax. Flax is fair to the eye, refined, and requires much good judgment. And Zalmon believed he was specially fitted to deal in flax.

In time flax becomes to Zalmon not merely a means of gaining a livelihood but an obsession—somewhat as the stock exchange was to Menachem Mendel. He putters with the bundles of flax as a miser with his hoard, and soon loses count of his debts. Years pass. The business is to him a game: how to outwit the rich merchant. Inwardly he knows he cannot do it, that he has neither the shrewdness nor the capital with which to compete, yet he cannot let go of the accumulated flax at the necessary loss. When his creditors begin to insist on payment, and one warns him that his flax might catch fire, something snaps in his brain.

> He went into the barn as usual, with the intention of sorting out anew the precious bundles of flax. This time he sorted them with special tenderness. The most beautiful bundles, known as crown flax, he took in his arms, played with their long, blond locks and caressed their bound heads. . . . Then he lit a cigarette. . . . The faces of all his creditors passed one after the other before his mind's eye, and the face of the rich merchant lingered longest —the face that wanted to cheat him out of his crown flax!

He drops the lit match and leaves the barn. When he sees upon his hurried return how the voluntary firemen are pouring buckets of water upon the flaming flax, he is seized with genuine anguish; then the sight of several of his most urgent creditors suddenly strikes him as so amusing that has to repress the impulse to laugh.

Zalmon is drawn with ironic insight. Learned but inept in business, he buys unwisely and is too proud to sell at a loss. His act of incendiarism is the suicidal impulsion of a despondent failure; he would rather lose everything than let the rich merchant gain at his expense. Ordinarily one would become impatient with such a ne'er-do-well, yet as the story develops Zalmon rouses the reader's sympathy. He is shown as a person of sterling spiritual honesty, lofty of view, capable of deep feeling; a man unfitted by his erudition for the competitive shrewdness of the marketplace, but worthy of an environment of a higher order. The lambent humor with which he is described humanizes and deepens his lifelikeness. One smiles at his gullibility, his pride of scholarship, his business misadventures, but the smile comes from sympathetic understanding. He appears very much like Menachem Mendel, only more pathetically individualized, lacking the latter's universalized vigor and gusto.

Zalmon's act of rebellion places him above many of Reisen's

other characters. The docility of some is extreme, but not because they are without conceit or pride; on the contrary, in the struggle against dire circumstances a mock hauteur crushes their very souls. "A Pinch of Snuff," "The Loan," and "The Last Hope" exemplify such characters. In the first story, Gronem is a very timid Hebrew teacher whose dependence upon the good will of his townsmen for his pitiful existence in time squeezes him dry of his natural self-esteem. He feels at once timorous and lowly.

> He would have given half of his life to speak but one word with the town's richest man. It would have rejuvenated him. He dared not attempt it, however. The man's appearance, his height, his paunch intimidated him; he was frightened by the clear full face, by the severe stare. He wondered at the butcher's boldness, who was not afraid to stand near the rich man, and sometimes even to engage him in conversation. He thought: One must have the strength of a butcher to dare do this; I cannot.

One day Gronem decides to ask the rich merchant to let him teach his grandchild—a decision made only after prolonged effort. He begins to prepare himself for the task: he memorizes the exact words he is going to say and rehearses them again and again. One morning in the synagogue the time seems opportune. To lessen his self-consciousness he takes a pinch of snuff. Approaching the rich man, he bids him "good morning" in all boldness and is about to deliver his request when he sneezes straight into the man's face. Humiliation and failure follow. The incident has the elements of a bathetic anecdote, yet so deftly does Reisen prepare the reader for the dénouement that the result puts into relief the creation of a fine character. Gronem is overwhelmed by his feeling of inferiority, yet struggles to retain a semblance of self-respect. He fills his nose with snuff as another would a stiff drink—to bolster his miniscule courage. When this act causes his undoing, the derisive laughter that would normally follow becomes metamorphosed into soft sympathy.

In "The Loan" Khaim, a wheat broker, is badly in need of money with which to do business at the annual fair. His friends cannot lend him any, as the approaching event has similarly affected them. His only hope is a wealthy neighbor who is a lumber dealer and not concerned with the fair. He dreads being refused, however, until necessity finally compels him to approach the man. He finds him at tea, and is invited to join him at the table. Khaim is anxious to act not the poor man in need of help, but a businessman requiring a temporary favor. When asked how he is faring, he boasts of doing well. Although he is aware of exaggerating, he cannot control his tongue. When asked, "Don't you sometimes find yourself a little pinched?" he replies proudly, "God be praised, I am never lacking in money." Even as he is saying this his conscience torments him and he is frightened at his own words: "What am I saying? Woe is me! How am I now to ask for a loan?" And he leaves without making the request. Here again one laughs at his mock-pride, but not derisively; his pathos is not unfamiliar.

The same subject is treated somewhat similarly in "The Last Hope." Here the poor man believes that his rich neighbor, with whom he grew up in friendship, will lend him what money he may ask for, only he is too proud to ask for any. The very thought that his friend may feel obliged to help him keeps him from making the request when in need. His reluctance soon becomes a last hope which he cherishes dearly. He feels comforted to think that by having this wealthy friend he need never despair. Time and again poverty presses him hard, but he suffers patiently in order not to resort to his last hope. Finally adversity drives him to his friend for help, but as he slowly approaches his neighbor's house he walks like a man doomed.

In other stories Reisen's characters exist on the lowest scale of human ambition. "The Three Notes" deals with this kind of aspiration. Khaim is an unobtrusive youth who always keeps himself in the background. His employer tolerates him but cannot depend on him. Even in the army, where all recruits are presumably on an equal footing, he is made to feel insignificant. Then comes an event of great importance to him. Because of his full thick lips he is chosen to play a horn in the regimental band. After a year's practice he has not quite mastered his few notes. When the senior hornist is discharged, Khaim is asked to play a three-note solo in one of the marches. The thought of being a solo player makes him very happy; he now feels himself an individual in his own right. But for a moment his joy becomes a mirage. The junior horner, a Russian, aware of Khaim's timidity, tells him he intends to accompany him during the three-note period. Khaim becomes panicky. Not realizing that the bandmaster would not permit a solo turned into a duet, he obtains the junior's promise not to join him by agreeing to keep his horn in good polish.

The timidity, even abasement, of a number of Reisen's creations evokes pity. They appear as frail, sensitive souls made humble by their intensely penurious existence, growing up with a consciousness of being nonentities. Their inferiority appears in their exaggerated awe of material abundance. The pathos they call forth is quickened by the realization that, because they tend to regard as wealthy anyone above their indigent circumstances, some are reduced to acting the fool, others the braggart, and still others the sycophant. This kind of human lowliness Reisen describes with the sympathy of intimate knowledge. His poor differ from those depicted by other Yiddish writers in their realistically meek acceptance of fate. They behave as if they live on sufferance, and suffer the more in consequence. And because Reisen has treated them artistically, they emerge quick with the breath of life.

In his stories of city life, young men and women are also for the most part "three-note-solo" types. Though they appear active and alert, they are incapable of genuine enthusiasm. They are almost always too hungry for bread and affection to give their minds to other things. They are aware of the ideas and ideals agitating their environment, but only peripherally.

His private tutors, of which there are a number, have few or no pupils, are always but a step from starvation, and are ragged and inadequately housed. One of them loses the bot-

toms of his shoes while on his way to his only lesson and becomes frightened when his footsteps make no echo. Another,
hungry and without money, enters a restaurant he has fre-
quented on occasion in the hope of finding someone who will
buy him a meal. He finds none, but the waitress mentions such
tempting dishes that he cannot refuse her—and then has to
wait until late in the evening when an acquaintance appears
to pay his bill. Still another is in possession of a counterfeit
coin, but cannot cheat a little girl clerk who waits on him, and
so remains hungry. For a long time it was the ambition of a
somewhat less indigent young man to have in his room a couch
in addition to a bed. One day he succeeds in renting a room
with both articles of furniture. He boasts of this to a less
fortunate friend, who lacks even a bed, and soon feels impelled
to invite him to use the couch, thereby depriving himself of
the long-wanted luxury.

When in possession of a few coins these young men are
happy and carefree. The spirit of discontent is absent in them;
the impulse to rebel against a society that keeps them in a
state of penury seldom possesses them. They are timid and
meek souls, living only in the present and interested mostly in
their docile selves. They live in a world apart, hardly aware
of the revolution with its assassinations and hangings con-
vulsing their environment. Reisen, essentially one of them,
portrayed them with broad and tender humor. He saw them
as Talmudic students catapulted into an alien milieu. No
longer quibbling about moot points of Hebrew lore, they daydream about knowledge in general without benefit of academic training. Their pitiful economic condition does not
trouble them too much, as it differs little from the life they
had led in yeshivas and houses of study in their native towns.

In "A Summer Coat," a monologue, a young man has only
his summer coat to wear during a hard winter, and is very
self-conscious about it. The stare of passers-by makes him very
uncomfortable and drives him to morbid acerbity:

Did you ever wear a summer coat in the winter time? No? You
put on a winter coat at the first sign of frost, hey? Oh, you shiver

with cold, you frozen souls! On your account are shattered my heart, my life, my youth, my hopes, my happiness. . . . On your account! For if you were not so fearful of the cold, and did not befur yourselves with warm coats, I would not have to become sick. For I became sick not from cold but from shame— I was ashamed. . . .

He continues to argue that one can easily become inured to cold, that warm clothes are not essential even in the coldest weather, that one should not be laughed at for wearing light clothing. His argument makes him eloquent:

I swear to you in all seriousness that I have not the least fear of the cold. On the contrary, I like the cold: the cold embraces me and caresses me and kisses me. . . . What have people against me? Why do they look at me so? Do they pity me? I do not need their pity; I am better off than they. I laugh at their clothes! I carry fire in my heart and am warm! . . . Things are somehow not right. What is wrong I do not know myself. I am a fool. One who is wise, especially one who is strong, would spit at these little men with their puny minds and say, "I am above you, I am above cold!"

This young man differs from those in other stories only in being sick; his sickness combined with poverty causes him to speak querulously in an effort to mollify his injured vanity— his reasoning made obliquely sophisticated by his Talmudic training. Such as he were found in every city during the last years of the 19th century and even later, but he is not representative of the dominant Jewish youth who fought for their people and for a better world at the risk of incarceration and exile.

Unsatisfied love ranks next to poverty in Reisen's city stories. Here again the reason is to be found in his own life, he having been a bachelor until his middle forties and markedly, if mildly, nympholeptic. The sight of an attractive woman excited his pliant and impulsive heart to ecstasy; in her presence he often acted as if charmed, and he was not too selective in his choices. Thus he was in a state of infatuation as often as he made the acquaintance of a pretty girl. When his attentions were met with rebuff his heart ached sorely and he expressed his pain in tender, wistful lyrics and humorously pathetic prose.

Most of these stories are about young men who long for love and are unrequited. Their poverty keeps them from conjugality. Seeking to satisfy their yearning for feminine affection, they flirt at every opportunity. Although the girls they meet are not averse to a flirtation with young intellectuals, they are seldom imprudent enough to go further; instead they marry men able to provide for them. When these young men occasionally patronize a prostitute, their sentimental souls suffer to think that their gratification requires a business transaction. Thus they fluctuate between unrealized longing for love and the depressing reality of the brothel. Even when love does favor them, it usually appears disguised and sad, as if ashamed of itself.

In one of these stories a young man enjoys the affection of a girl until a workingman wins her away from him by offering her an engagement ring. Another sits down near a young woman on a park bench in the hope of making her acquaintance; he does, only to find her a practical prostitute. Still another is interested only in the exceptional woman; when he at last meets one to his liking, he finds later that she has given him an illegible address. Yet another engages a prostitute to be with him for a day in the country, only to find her more interested in grass and flowers than in his caresses. In one story a girl comes to a young man of her own free will, but he is too shy and she leaves chagrined.

"Iron" is perhaps the most popular of this group of stories. A young man becomes infatuated with a girl clerk in a hardware store and buys some article almost daily in order to look into her cold but luminous eyes. To avoid the sentimental tinge of direct narration, Reisen relates the story as reminiscence; to keep the reader from laughing at the narrator, Reisen has him laugh at himself first. He begins:

Do not expect anything unusual. It is a foolish story, or better— no story at all. It happened five years ago. I was then five and twenty, twice in love and both times foolishly disappointed. But again I wanted to be loved and to be fooled, and I sought love in the long streets of the large city. . . . I knew, of course, that love cannot be found when sought. The other two affairs came unexpectedly and went as suddenly as they had come. But one does not stop to reason when the heart yearns; one seeks. . . .

One day he saw two large, black, but very cold eyes of a girl who stood at the door of a hardware store. They fascinated him and he approached. The girl asked him coldly what he wanted. He ached to tell her how her eyes had attracted him, but instead he bought a hammer. He came again almost every day and each time bought another piece of hardware. The girl appeared as aloof and cold as the iron articles she sold him; her indifference only fascinated him all the more. One evening he came to speak his heart to her.

> The girl stood as if of cast iron; only her two black eyes were alive and were observing me quietly and shrewdly.
> "What do you want?"
> "I need a lock."
> "This I can give you."
> "Please," I cried almost tearfully, "you have such wonderful eyes . . . and if something other than a lock. . . ."
> She looked at me coldly and asked:
> "Do you wish a large lock or a small one?"

Thus ended his visits, and he concludes his monologue: "The whole world then appeared to me as hard and cold and dry as iron. And even today I retain a strong interest in iron. . . ."

Here, as in most stories, the young man is meek and shy. He feels the urge to love but has only the bashfulness and not the boldness of the lover. His sense of inferiority makes him feel unworthy, and his advances are more of the beggar than the beau. Within him expands a tender, aching emotion but, knowing his inability to express it persuasively, he lets it die with a pensive sigh. In this story the articles of iron, the cold eyes of the girl, and the oppressive atmosphere of the store contribute to the feeling of frigidity, indifference, death—the death of a wistful emotion. Similar incidents and emotions are described with almost equal persuasiveness in numerous other stories, with characters who, whether they suffer or savor, appeal to the reader with singular similitude.

Reisen came to New York to live when he was one year short of 40. His view of the world was becoming somewhat less subjective. He began to observe life with greater detachment, to express his reflective experience more impersonally. Contributing regularly to a Yiddish newspaper, he was paid well enough to end his previously precarious existence. This and a satisfying marriage weakened his interest in the two subjects which had hitherto most occupied him.

He soon discovered that a few years' residence in the United States resulted in a marked spiritual slackening in the life of the immigrant Jews. No longer in the grip of dire poverty—indeed, enjoying luxuries unknown to them in Europe—they were paying dearly for their fleshpots. They had to work hard, and the strenuous hours in the shop and store sapped their vitality more readily than their previous indigence. He saw them bereft of their former sensitivity, their Sabbatic sedateness, their faith in God. Saddened by this apparent vicissitude, he began to write about them critically; not forcefully, like Opatoshu and others, but with meek melancholy. In his verse he became sentimental. He visualized tired shop girls as princesses in bondage, their employers as heartless exploiters, and the wealthy as vulgar parvenus. His stories, while continuing to deal mostly with workers and artists, became less tender. He also resorted to reminiscence. In the afterglow, his youthful impressions became enhanced in the telling. He now perceived life in the small Lithuanian town in idealized and idyllic terms. Yet these stories no longer possessed the patricular intimacy and naturalness of his earlier work.

The sketches having their setting in America tend to skim along the surface. "The Businessman" depicts a Jew who takes advantage of his slight linguistic knowledge by suiting his business to a neighborhood where he can put to use his meager foreign vocabulary. In "Men" a group of intellectuals prefer the company of an ignorant but pretty girl to their well-educated hostess. In "Estranged" a man, naturally friendly, feels guilty toward his neighbor because he alone is able to send his wife to the country for the summer. "Mother Goes to the Library" tells of a girl of 12 who thinks of herself as American because she goes to school and visits the library, and is ashamed of her mother who does neither—only to respect her when the older woman learns that she can borrow Yiddish books from the library and does so.

Reisen found poverty in America even in the hectic 1920's. He wrote about the uncertainty of employment, meager earnings, the physically detrimental effect of the shop and factory. "Automobile" tells of a girl who learns the craft of drapery only to find no work during an unusually long "slack" season. Seeing a dentist's advertisement for a receptionist, she goes after the position on foot, as she has no money for carfare. On the way she accepts a ride from a friendly chauffeur. When she reaches her destination, the dentist happens to see her leave the automobile and refuses to employ her in the belief that she must be a wealthy girl.

In "The First Photograph" Zelda, a girl of 18, was very much annoyed by the unevenness of the large house mirror, an article of furniture not often found in the home of a small-town Jew in Lithuania. "She wanted to know the truth whether or not she was beautiful, but the mirror would not disclose the truth. Zelda could only see that she had black eyes and black hair, but of the appearance of her face she could get no idea for she knew that the mirror was false." So she decided to be photographed, and after much pleading her father permitted her to do so. "Only then did she realize who she was. Until then she did not know herself. She was beautiful. And what goodness was in her face! With such a face one need no longer remain at home and await a bridegroom. . . . The world was open to her. . . . America!" After some time in New York she grew accustomed to a number of things that at first seemed strange or ridiculous. She managed to find "steady" work, roomed with a "missus," and went to the "movies." But again she became apprehensive of her mirror. True, she now had one of good quality, but could not see in it the face shown in her first photograph. As she no longer had the original with her, she decided to be photographed again. "But in America photographers are peculiar. Instead of dimples they show wrinkles, and in the place of geniality they reveal anger and seriousness." Six months later she was once more photographed, this time in an expensive studio, but the result was equally unsatisfactory. "It was truly exasperating. These pictures too were unlike the first, those she had taken in her native town. It seemed that in this country photographers were bunglers. . . ." Thus indirectly and ironically Reisen describes the effect of long hours in an unsanitary clothing factory.

Reisen thought some of the newly adopted habits and customs of the Jewish immigrants were either vulgar or grotesque. Sometimes he described them ironically, sometimes satirically. The desire to emulate one another and to conform to a common standard is dealt with in "A Greenhorn Destroys a Temple." The several Jewish residents of a rural town wish to appear as respectable as their Christian neighbors, so they build a temple and conduct religious services in the reformed manner. One day an immigrant Jew settles among them and begins to attend the temple. He prays in the loud chant of the orthodox custom. The older members try to have him give up the old-fashioned form of prayer, but he persists in his loud chant. Gradually his form of worship affects the others and they revert to the orthodox chanting of their fathers.

It is only seldom that the old ways prevail in Reisen's stories. In most instances the more prosperous Americanized Jew is the stronger. "New Employers" concerns an elderly rabbi engaged by an Americanized congregation upon his arrival in this country. His first sermon, with which he wishes to impress the members, is a failure. His learned allusions and Hebrew phrases are over their heads. When the president suggests that he confine himself to racy comments, the rabbi's first impulse is to resign. All his adult life he has been accustomed to advise, and he would not now be advised—and so stupidly. A true Reisen character, however, he soon acquiesces in this humiliation—assuaging his outraged dignity with the thought that his family is dependent upon him, that since his new flock is ignorant of Hebrew lore it is better to preach to it popularly and teach it something. Deep within him, however, he knows he is degrading himself.

"The Guest" presents another aspect of this inevitable evanescence of spiritual values. A young girl comes from war- and pogrom-ridden Russia to an older sister in New York. She brings with her the ingenuous enthusiasm for books, socialism, and kindred subjects which had exhilarated the older sister at a like age. What tender and precious memories stir within the older girl's consciousness! She eagerly questions the newcomer about the life that once was her life but is hers no more. She dotes on the least detail, the merest remark, and relives the lofty dreams which the intervening years had long dissipated. Soon the newness and sentiment begin to evaporate, and the younger sister also joins the ranks of shop workers.

In "The Revolutionary" this nostalgic reminiscence is lost in crass grossness. An elderly Jew managed to escape from Soviet Russia because of his belief in the sacredness of private property, and is telling his story to a group of listeners in a cafe.

> "Where do you find yourself here?" he was asked.
>
> "Ha, ha, ha," he laughed bitterly. "I live with a son . . . another revolutionary. . . ."
>
> "Did he come together with you?" he was again asked.
>
> "No," the old man answered with a smile. "He is here about fifteen years. He belongs to the period of the Czar. . . . He ran away from Nicholas and I from Trotsky. . . . You understand?"
>
> Just then there entered a man of about forty, with the appearance of an Americanized *allrightnick*. He looked about until he

espied the old man. Coming over to him he asked in a somewhat displeased tone,

"Father, what are you doing here?"

In the conversation that follows the old man tries to prove to his son that his cause was more worthy than the one once advocated by the younger man. "After all, it is not the same. I fought for something respectable, for property. . . . And what did you fight for?" The son, who is now quite wealthy and who has long abandoned all radical sentiment, smiles and admits: "Yes, father, your fight is just. . . . I admit it." Reisen implies that this one-time revolutionist is too engrossed in business to regret his idealistic decline. Yet here as elsewhere he is not really critical of those who have discarded their ideals. Unlike other Yiddish writers, he is more interested in the personality of his characters than in social or religious reform.

When he wrote about poverty and unrequited love he put something of himself in every story; each narrative originated in a feeling or sentiment in his own experience and was developed lovingly, with irony but with tender sympathy. This is not the case in his later work. In America he tended to become irritated by much of what he saw and heard, and this irritation crept into his poems and stories—especially as they seldom dealt with his own direct experiences. Like so many essentially sentimental writers, he could not quite adjust himself to his American milieu, to the exchange of leisure and dreams for hustle and material comfort. Remaining fundamentally European in orientation, he tended to recoil from the grossness of *allrightnicks*. In writing about Jewish life in the United States he could not employ the lyric simplicity and gentle humor that enhanced his earlier work. As if aware of this condition, he turned to reminiscence, and the three volumes which followed his life up to 1910 are written with the beauty and gentleness of his best efforts.

The brevity of some of Reisen's sketches often gives them an anecdotal character. Even in the least of them, however, he is the gifted storyteller. From the first word to the last he is in unerring control of the pattern he is designing. His stories, like finely carved cameos, are skillfully etched, with a maximum of verbal economy. He knows exactly the effect he is seeking, and usually achieves it with simple directness. His style appears short of breath, without the brilliance of imagery or prodigality of metaphor, but it truly expresses his natural restraint. Its clarity is like the ring of a silver bell; and, as in his lyrics, the limitations of his vocabulary fit well the narrowness of his thematic scope. Character and incident sometimes act one on the other to bring about a contrived dénouement, giving incident the guise of accident; occasionally the limits of probability are stretched for effect. Yet these artistic shortcomings are rarely obvious. Even the repetition of themes in his early work impresses one as variations, more the result of fertility than of fatigue.

Within his limitations Reisen has created a surprisingly large number of living characters. Famished Jews, hungry dreamers, painted prostitutes, meek lovers, fatigued shop girls, vulgar parvenus, Bohemians of all ages and postures—all gain reality in his pages with the simple magic of an apt phrase or a few strokes of characterization. Rarely are they drawn in full color, for his medium does not aim at full-fledged portraiture; but they always think and act truly, making themselves humanly convincing. One reason for this is that he dwells not on poverty but on the psychological effects of it on his characters; another reason is the gentleness of his ironic humor. Reisen thought always in terms of human values. Knowing them to be relative, he tended to smile as he saw circumstances distending and distorting them; his smile turned to soft sympathy as he realized that men often accept these values not as they are but as they appear to be. His heart was attuned with keen fineness to human suffering, and its cords vibrated with compassion at the first evidence of pain. His humor was therefore consciously tempered to avoid exaggeration and to convey lifelike behavior.

A writer is usually esteemed in accordance with the world

he has envisioned and encompassed. Reisen's world is penurious, circumscribed, and lowly. His people are mostly humble, hardly aware of noble visions and lofty aspirations. Their outlook on life is narrowly subjective, passively meek; even their indigence concerns them only quiescently, and only in so far as hunger makes them aware of it; the impulse to rebel against a system which treats them so unfairly and cruelly seldom agitates their minds. Even in his New York stories, where hunger no longer prevails, the same timid Jews are in one way or another overwhelmed by their new environment. They become involved not with problems of dominant intellectual and social import—as a number do in real life—but with matters of a commonplace or idiosyncratic nature. Many of them arouse sympathy, but not intimate identification, as do characters more deeply conceived. Yet lowly in attitude as Reisen's world undeniably is, he has perceived it concretely and constructed it artistically—thereby making himself truly the poet of the poor.

CHAPTER TEN

SHOLEM ASCH

Novelist of Lyric Intensity

SHOLEM ASCH was the first Yiddish writer to gain worldwide renown. Born in 1880 in the small town of Kutno, Poland, he devoted his childhood years to study of Jewish lore. "The Bible was the first book that I ever held in my hand. From it my father taught me the alphabet. It was my textbook and my book of boyish joy, my grammar and my storybook, my geography and my history book." The youngest of ten children, son of a pious and prosperous Hasid who dealt in sheep and other animals, with one group of brothers sturdy traders and another group steeped in learning, young Sholom was bright and zealous enough to give promise of rabbinical stature. In his sixteenth year, however, he came upon some secular books and was soon questioning what he had heretofore taken for granted. He studied German from Moses Mendelssohn's translation of the Psalms, was caught at it and admonished, so at 17 he decided to leave Kutno to tutor in a nearby village. There he also became a letter writer for the illiterate, and his need to express their feelings of love and longing taught him the secrets of the human heart. Meantime he read the work of Heine, Tolstoy, Hauptmann, and others which came his way.

Moved by the yearning to write, he composed some

sketches in Hebrew. When he learned of Peretz and had read some of his stories, he journeyed to Warsaw to show the great man his own attempts. Peretz encouraged him but suggested that he write in Yiddish. Asch did so, and "Moshele," his first story, appeared in *Der Yud* toward the end of 1900. Asch now settled in Warsaw and devoted himself to writing. His first collection of Hebrew stories was published in 1902, and a volume of Yiddish stories came out a year later. During these early years he earned very little and often suffered hunger in company with two other literary aspirants, Abraham Reisen and H.D. Nomberg, with whom he had become intimate. According to Niger, Asch "lived in dark and dank holes and came in contact with human need." Peretz helped these neophytes when he could, and managed to free Asch from military service.

A handsome youth, of an intensive nature and confident of his own future greatness, he soon won the attention of the highly attractive Mathilda Shapiro, daughter of a Hebrew teacher and poet, and they were married in 1903. The next year he serialized the first of his longer works, *A Town*, in *Der Freint*; the book was brought out in 1905.

A Town immediately placed Asch in the front rank of Yiddish writers. It is in essence a long prose poem. Saturated from early childhood with the passionate piety of a Hasidic environment permeated with the wholesomeness and earthiness of nature, pastoral in its simplicity, and almost primitive in its lusty animality—Asch described this medieval milieu with the ecstasy of first love. In contrast to the sordid and squalid life in the Warsaw ghetto, where he then lived, the simple Hasidim of his childhood memory appeared in his imagination as an idyllic folk: firmly founded in the revered faith of their fathers, inured to their static social customs and economic practices, endowed with the carnal robustness of their peasant neighbors, yet childlike in their placid innocence. In this story they therefore appear quite unlike the Jews met with in the Polish towns of the late 19th century and described by Linetsky, Spector, Dinesohn, and Peretz;

Dr. Eliashev stated critically that "Asch's *shtetl* is a town inhabited by children with beards and earlocks." Indeed, they emanated from a nostalgic self-love that visualized these Jews in Asch's own romantic image. In depicting them as pulsating with pristine potency he also revealed a love of nature as novel to his Yiddish readers as his romanticized townsmen. He was the first Yiddish writer to portray the out-of-doors with pagan exuberance, to luxuriate in the description of sensuous beauty for its own sake.

Asch soon began to experiment with the dramatic form. In 1904 his two-act play, originally named *The Return* and later retitled *Downstream*, was produced in Polish in Cracow. It dealt with the skepticism which began to gnaw at the minds of young Talmudic students in the 1870's. David is exceptionally bright and his father-in-law, a learned rabbi, expects much of him. But the dogmatism of the yeshiva soon palls on the youth's spirit and he begins to feel chained to the tomes in which he is presumed to find the source of life. He therefore breaks away, leaving wife and child for the freedom and "sunshine" of the city. To his wife he says in parting: "Understand, the people here are dead, wintry: born in winter, living in winter, and dying in winter . . . extending one long winter from generation to generation. . . . Spring has awakened in me: I feel that life wakens in me: I want to go out into the world. . . . I want a 'God' for my child, a 'Torah'—to create a 'God.'"

David loses himself in the city, and drifts from ideal to ideal, without faith in the old and not strong enough to embrace the new. After some years he returns to his long-neglected family. When asked by his father-in-law how he had fared, he replies: "One can believe only once in him who is believed! I went out into the world, crumpled my soul and scattered the pieces; each piece bore a different name. . . ."

Here Asch propounded the self-evident truth that once one is infected with doubt, faith is doomed—even where there is nothing to replace it. Yet the drama is wanting in conviction, having been developed more by means of rhetoric than action.

Moreover, David is hardly representative of the emancipated intellectuals of his generation. Most of them were no weaklings; having broken the gyves of orthodoxy, they found faith in Zionism, radicalism, scholarship, or mammon.

This futile faith-seeking is imputed with more truth to the succeeding generation. In *The Messiah Period* (1906) and *The Inheritors* (1913) Asch posed the problems besetting Russian Jews in the 1900's. In the first, Khonon, an octogenarian patriarch, calls together his more or less emancipated children for a final meeting before leaving for Palestine. Three generations are brought face to face: the grandparents, solidly entrenched in their piety and enjoying spiritual serenity; their bourgeois children, steeped in the present and motivated by their economic and social interests; and their grandchildren, struggling in a spiritual morass and grasping at the straws of assimilation, Zionism, or socialism. Only one pious and poor son joins the trek to the Holy Land; the others either cling to their fleshpots or flounder in intellectual confusion.

In *The Inheritors* the same three generations are posed more realistically. A wealthy banker, priding himself on his tolerant rationalism, finds himself despised by his own children as too materialistic. His oldest son leaves him to devote his life to Jewish affairs, and his beloved daughter is kept from apostasy only by the sagacity of her pious grandfather. When her father does not object to her accepting Christianity in order to marry a Polish count, the grandfather tells him:

> How can I be silent when I see my light growing dim, my child making nothing of all that I and my parents have saved with their blood? Should I say nothing when I see the pit into which I and everyone coming after me are falling into, as in a black hell? Do you call this tolerance?

And his granddaughter confesses:

> They gave me everything, except one thing—faith. A God they did not give me . . . that which every person needs for his daily existence—a faith, love of God, love toward people. . . . I am no philosopher, I am not interested in whether or not there is a

God, I need faith . . . in a dark hour, I should have someone
to pray to, someone to appeal to for help. . . .

In both plays Asch is at pains to demonstrate the spiritual
bankruptcy of the middle generation, and to point out how
the youth are desperately seeking to forge a new religion. His
characters, however, are mostly without dramatic vitality.
Both dramas are weak polemics leavened with incidents of
poetic charm. *The Messiah Period* was produced not only in
Yiddish but also in Polish and Russian versions—the latter
with the famous actress Komisarzhevskaya—making Asch favorably known in both countries.

In 1907 Asch completed *The God of Vengeance* * and
arranged to read the drama in Peretz's home before a group
of Jewish writers and intellectuals. The reaction was not
favorable. Peretz advised him to "burn it." Asch was not persuaded. He next read it to Max Reinhardt, who understood
Yiddish, and the enterprising producer liked it well enough
to have it translated into German and staged in his famous
Berlin theater. Although the play was withdrawn after 18
performances, it aroused much discussion, spread Asch's fame
over Western Europe, and was produced in other large cities.
When it was staged in New York in 1923, it was stopped by
the police as immoral. Soon after, Asch himself refused to
permit further performances.

The theme of the play is essentially spurious drama. The
action concerns Yekel Shabshevitz's attempt to strike a bargain with God to preserve his daughter Rivkele's moral purity.
The absurdity of Yekel's behavior is immediately obvious.
Asch might legitimately have pitted him against a vengeful
Jehovah who visits the sins of the parents upon their offspring
if he had conceived Yekel as one who, while himself a hardened sinner, took every possible precaution to preserve his
daughter's innocence. The Yekel we actually see is the sordid
yet superstitious owner of a brothel who invokes God's help in
his desire to keep Rivkele from following the evil ways of her
parents. It is his notion that Jehovah can be bribed by place-

ment of a parchment-inscribed Torah in his home above the brothel. When the offering is of no avail and Rivkele yields to temptation, Yekel rants hysterically against God's vengefulness.

Yekel fails to become a tragic figure because he is the creation of Asch the moralist. In life Yekel, eager to protect his only daughter from the influence of the brothel, would either have abandoned the bawdyhouse altogether and given her a respectable home, or sent her away to some distant place where she would remain unaffected by his immoral activities. If, after he had done either of these two things, Rivkele nevertheless took the path trodden by her mother, Yekel's frustration would have assumed a tragic aspect. Asch, however, compels him to keep Rivkele in his apartment over the brothel, within easy reach of temptation, and to seek her protection by the presence of a holy scroll. When he learns of Rivkele's enticement, he is made to bluster bombastically:

> I know, you are a great God! You are indeed our God—I, Yekel Shabshevitz, have sinned (beats his breast with his fists). . . . My sins. . . . Show a miracle, bring down a fire and consume me—even as I stand here! Cleave the earth and let it swallow me. . . . But preserve my child . . . bring her back as pure, as innocent as she was. . . . I know . . . all is possible to you. . . . Show a miracle. . . . You are indeed a great God. . . . If not—you are no God! I tell you, I Yekel Shabshevitz, that you are no God. . . . You are vengeful, even as a human being.

This ranting, under the circumstances, sounds hollow and sentimental, as if spoken not by a man in deep anguish but by a character in a brash melodrama. That the play achieved a certain notoriety was due largely to the novelty of the setting and to its moral overtones. Also in its favor are the vigorous and vivacious brothel scenes and the poetic tenderness of the lesbian affection between Manka and Rivkele. Less cogent, if superficially effective, is the symbolic emphasis on the disparity between weakness of the flesh in the brothel and the presumed spiritual striving in the apartment above it.

In 1908 Asch projected the same conflict between carnal

lust and spiritual dedication in the drama *Shabbati Zevi.* Here the erotic impulse is described with oriental cadence, and sexual exultation is made the cause of tragic disaster. After prolonged fasting and prayer, Shabbati, the 17th century Turkish Jew, feels himself called as the long-awaited Messiah. He proclaims his divine mission and is ready to perform the symbolic marriage ceremony with the Torah. Thousands of Jews, grievously persecuted and yearning for deliverance, revere him as God's anointed. Unknown to him, an impassioned Polish Jewess named Sarah is simultaneously insisting that she is his fated helpmate. By the time she reaches him in Cairo her following exceeds his. Shabbati welcomes her but asserts that he is already pledged to the Torah. Sarah, however, insists that she is his God-ordained wife. Persuaded by her strong hold on the people and moved by her passion, he agrees to the marriage—only to lose God's favor and suffer dire ignominy. A poetic drama, it was never performed.

In the same year Asch exposed himself to severe criticism when he publicly sided with the father who refused to have his dead boy circumcised in order that he might be buried in a Jewish cemetery. Writing in *Courier Warshavsky*, an anti-Semitic daily, he condemned the "barbaric Jewish circumcision ritual." Orthodox Jews considered the attack sacrilegious —impugning the most holy covenant of Judaism—and chastised him accordingly. Peretz, while considering Asch's censure of circumcision drastic and inopportune, came to his defense by stating: "If one wishes to stop the mouth of an artist with dirty rags, we must declare: 'Dirty people, hands off!'" Nevertheless, not a few Jews looked askance at a Yiddish writer who created so objectionable a character as Yekel for the world stage and was ready to abandon the ancient rite of circumcision.

By now a regular contributor to the Warsaw *Haint* (Today) and the New York *Forverts*, Asch earned enough to indulge his restless nature. He traveled to Palestine in the spirit of a pilgrimage and later incorporated his impressions in reportage and fiction. In 1908 he also attended the conference on Yiddish at Czernovitz, spoke in favor of Yiddish, and joined Peretz in the subsequent lecture tour on the subject. The next year he visited the United States, making use of his observations and experiences in *The Landsman*, an unsuccessful play, and a number of stories.

The year 1913 was a fecund one for Sholom Asch—he published *Wealthy Reb Shlome, The Inheritors, Jephthah's Daughter, Mary*, and *The Road to Oneself*. The first is a poetic idyl. Returning to the scene of his childhood, he made it symbolic of Jewish life within the static orthodoxy of the Russian-Polish Pale of Settlement. The dedication expressed his sentiment:

> To my father, the complete Jew and the whole man; to him, whose life is a light before me like a bright star in a misty night, whom I see but cannot reach—to him I bestow this work. Father, if I cannot emulate you in my life, I want to do it in my dream.

Wealthy Reb Shlome is a more mature and variegated portrayal than *A Town*. In neither story is action of much consequence, but in the later work character becomes a more positive factor. Reb Shlome, patterned after the elder Asch, is imbued with the glow of romantic reality. From the moment he enters the narrative on his return home for the Sabbath, until he celebrates the betrothal of his son to the daughter of his favored rabbi, Reb Shlome lives by virtue of his positive personality. His genuine benevolence, intense piety, warm sympathy, and repeated triumphs over his "evil thoughts"— these traits combine to give him the rich humanity of a biblical patriarch. Winsomely animated also is his young wife Khanele. Marrying at 18 a widower thrice her age and father of seven children in order to obtain a comfortable home, she soon learns to love her husband with the warm chasteness of her simple heart. Like all pious Jewesses she seeks to please God and Reb Shlome by managing the large establishment in the manner of the original mistress. By the time her first child is born toward the end of the narrative, she has ingratiated herself as much to the reader as to her indulgent husband.

Milieu, rather than character, assumes first importance in this work. The market square, the synagogue, Reb Shlome's open house, the Vistula River, the soil and its products, Jews and peasants, all play their poetic parts in this idyllic symphony. Each day has its own significance, every season its special character. The peace of soul and spiritual beauty with which Jews welcome their beloved Sabbath are intimated in the following brief excerpt:

> The Sabbath came at a peaceful gait. The dark night spread over the sky like a black silk shawl spangled with stars. The village was enveloped in somber shadows, all stores were closed, lit Sabbath candles peered from many windows. Jews were already returning from the synagogue. Reb Shlome was with his son-in-law, his sons, his servants, and a group of impecunious guests. He walked leisurely, with Sabbath steps, stroked his thick black beard, spreading it over his starched white shirt and his black silk gabardine, and his Jewish spirit was very evident in him. He looked at the poor village Gentiles who idled about in the streets and pitied them with all his heart.

As the Sabbath is welcomed, so are the market days. Once or twice weekly farmers from the outlying countryside arrive with wagon loads of produce, the Jewish merchants and traders come with manufactured articles and cash, and both groups barter and bargain until dusk. Not infrequently a Jew tries to take advantage of a lout, or a farmer gets drunk with his new-gotten money, and the result is a free-for-all. Peasants enter the fray, and embattled traders fight back with courageous zeal. Heads are hurt and noses are bloodied. Presently a Jew like Reb Shlome joins with some elder peasants to arrange a truce; the culprits are chastised and the erstwhile adversaries toast one another with vodka and agree that one God rules over Jews and Gentiles.

Asch depicted these village scenes with romantic gusto. Drawing upon authentic memories of his early youth, he invested the narrative with epical breadth and beauty. He endowed his rustics with pristine appeal, and the magic of his glowing prose transformed their homely environment into an idealized community. Unlike Mendele's acrid realism, Weissenberg's dry naturalism, and Reisen's ironic pathos, Asch's idyllic sensuousness impregnated Jewish life with the simple charm of the pastoral.

Jephthah's Daughter is a poetic drama set in the days when men lived in caves and the gods stalked the earth in human guise. The region inhabited by Jephthah is in the domain of Moloch, to whom belongs every firstborn. The Hebrew chieftain refuses to acknowledge Moloch's supremacy or give him his eldest child, and the action concerns the god's triumph over the bellicose eccentric. Jephthah's daughter is lured to her doom by Moloch's rays, and she goes to the pyre willingly, believing that she belongs to him. Although this anthropological interpretation of the Biblical story results in feeble drama, it provides Asch with the opportunity to interpret poetically the sexual and superstitious characteristics of primitive man.

Mary, and its sequel, *The Road to Oneself*, treat the Russian revolutionary movement during the 1900's. Ten years earlier Asch and Reisen had discussed Peretz's suggestion that they write a novel. Asch was ready: "That's right. Another story, another sketch, another poem, but we must have a novel. With short stories and poems alone one doesn't achieve greatness." His initial efforts lacked fictional mastery. He depicted Jewish youths in the first enthusiasm of political rebellion, in the reign of terror by the anti-Semitic Black Hundred, and in their Saninistic escapism soon after. Shedding their orthodox upbringing and aflame with idealistic zeal, these youths eagerly and recklessly identified themselves with the movement to overthrow Czaristic oppression. They naively assumed that success would automatically liberate the Jews. Willingly they sacrificed their immediate careers and endangered their freedom and even their lives. The 1905 constitution, granted by the Czar under duress and at once drenched in Jewish blood, was a cruel mockery that struck these youthful idealists a mortal blow. Long thereafter pessimism gnawed at their vitals, and to deaden the pain they yielded to the moral lassitude aptly described in Artzibashev's *Sanin*.

Asch's treatment of this theme emerged as loosely constructed *tendenz* fiction. Village life and carnal beauty he described with lyric tenderness; social strife and political revolt he treated cerebrally rather than with imaginative insight. Mary, Kowalsky, Mischa, Rahel, and lesser characters are quick with life in their personal relations, but when exploited as social symbols tend to become nebulous and indistinct.

To the same period belong *One Faith*, *The League of the Weak*, and *Prestige*, all dramatic attempts in a minor key. The first is straight melodrama on the theme of intermarriage, with love triumphing over religious prejudice. The other two plays are obviously influenced by Asch's Russian contemporaries. In one a rejected husband drinks himself to sleep and dreams of uniting all the weak and poor and degraded into a league headed by himself and the woman whose husband is his wife's paramour. Fantastic, yet in part poignant, the play lacks the adroitness and motivation of Andreyev's model. *Prestige* possesses the semblance but not the dramatic delicacy of *The Cherry Orchard*.

In 1914, with Europe engulfed in war, Asch decided to make his home in the United States, and became an American citizen. As the leading contributor to the *Forverts* and other periodicals and recipient of royalties from plays, he earned enough not only to live in comfort with his family but also to indulge his penchant for collecting works of art and Jewish rare books and artifacts. The first major work he completed in the United States, serialized in the *Forverts* and *Haint* before it was issued in book form in 1916 and later successfully dramatized and produced, was *Mottke the Thief*.* Here Asch contrasts the simple and static life of the Jewish poor in a Polish village with the gaudy and grimy sordidness of the Warsaw slum. The first half is written with inspired gusto, the character of the youthful Mottke drawn with Rabelaisian strokes. Red Zlatke, Blind Layb, Blind Pearl, Burek the trick dog, the acrobat troupe, and numerous others are delineated with realistic clarity. The strong elemental attachment between Mottke and his harassed mother is etched with rare tenderness and insight.

The life of the poor is portrayed almost epically. In their midst the youthful Mottke is evoked with gargantuan vividness. Born in abject poverty, he is no sooner able to creep than he manages to steal the food belonging to a little girl nearby. Dire need and parental neglect force him to depend upon his instinct for guidance. He has no moral scruples, no squeamishness of conscience; to him life is a scramble for food and shelter—a matter of overcoming opposition, of getting something for nothing. He lives like a stray puppy, only with greater cunning and insistence. He is beaten at will by his father, his teacher, his master, the town constable. When resistance is futile, he accepts punishment without a whimper; but he bides his time, forgets nothing, and avenges himself upon his enemies the first chance he gets. At the age of 13 he has reached maturity and decides to leave the town which has treated him so shabbily. Meeting with a trouple of vagabond vaudevillians, he is befriended by them. His strength, endurance, and gameness in time win him the affection of Marie the rope dancer and the jealousy of Kanarik the pander. How he adapts himself to his new environment, arranges to kill Kanarik and elope with Marie to Warsaw are told with the sweep and spirit of the Teutonic epic.

In the Polish metropolis Mottke appears to have acquired Kanarik's personality along with his passport. His elementally normal and therefore appealing traits become lost in the crass and conceited behavior of the successful pimp. One day, however, he is strongly attracted to a virtuous girl and suddenly converted. His subsequent action reminds one of Yekel. Chastity now appeals to him as the greatest good, and he woos the demure Khanele with maudlin sentimentality. To make himself worthy of her he disposes of his "girls," breaks with his shady companions, and engages in honest work. Yet the metamorphosis lacks conviction; it is simply incredible that this unscrupulous thief and cunning criminal could become a simple and simpering swain merely in reaction to the allure of a virgin. Even less likely is his reckless credence in those whom he has every reason to suspect; when his gullibility leads to his arrest, one cannot believe that he and Kanarik's murderer are the same person.

Asch's fertile and quick imagination could not but be stimulated by the teeming life of New York's East Side. He was especially affected by the pathetic attempts of Jewish immigrants to adapt themselves to American ways and practices. His sympathy notwithstanding, he tended to be repelled by the crass and vulgar factors in their new mode of life. In the decade he sojourned in the United States, and later, he wrote about them in a number of long and short narratives.

Uncle Moses * (1918) makes painfully clear that in their attempts to gain a footing in their new and alien environment, many Jewish immigrants unavoidably relinquished or deliberately discarded the traditions and faith of their fathers. "Uncle" Moses is already a prosperous manufacturer of clothing when persecution in his native Polish village forces many of its Jewish inhabitants to seek asylum in the United States. Moses welcomes his hapless townsmen with the readiness of a magnanimous provider: all are given work in his sweatshop, and all their affairs are conducted with his advice and assistance. When Mascha, the pretty child of one of them, attracts his fancy, he decides to marry her at the earliest opportunity. The girl grows up to despise him, but is forced to marry him nevertheless. His doting passion, especially after he becomes a father, gradually attenuates his former enterprise and mastery, and he ends by losing control of his business.

The novel begs comparison with *Wealthy Reb Shlome*. In both stories the people have a similar rustic origin, and interest in each is centered in the potent leader of the communal group. In writing about the Jews in their native patriarchal setting, where they were ready to defend their faith with their very lives and endured the week for the serene pleasure of the Sabbath, Asch tended to wax idyllic and give his words the glow of lyric gusto. In describing the drab and dreary existence in their sweatshop environment of the same Jews—to whom the bliss of the Sabbath has become a troubled memory, whose religious orthodoxy was being devitalized by the vulgarities of a leveling freedom, and whose weary minds were of necessity concentrating on the economics of the factory—he could only write with the bluntness of uninspired irony. Moreover, serializing the story in a popular newspaper, he found it necessary to concoct a palatable plot, so that while many pages contain cogent writing, the narrative ends melodramatically.

The persecutions and pogroms in Eastern Europe during and immediately following World War I, causing death and destruction in scores of Jewish towns, profoundly perturbed Sholom Asch. With characteristic fervor he helped gather funds for relief of the victims and excoriated their oppressors in newspaper articles. In his effort to comfort his people he turned his mind to these and earlier calamities, and wrote about them to exalt the spiritual faith and perseverance of the victims.

The first of these works was *A String of Pearls* (1916). The setting of the drama is the Russian war zone. A troop of soldiers enter a Polish village, and the commanding officer orders the Jewish inhabitants first to provision his company and then to evacuate the town in 12 hours. Aged Reb Melekh, the most prominent Jew and a genuine patriarch, accepts the harsh order with a dignity befitting his firm faith in God. Even when the officer, instigated by a scoundrelly Pole, commands Reb Melekh to deliver his beautiful daughter to him forthwith, the old Jew remains unshaken in his belief that the ways of God are not for man to question. However, he tells his daughter to don the clothes of her saintly grandmother and to put on the latter's pearl necklace with the secreted poniard, which she is to use as a last resort. It is his hope that the garb of an old woman will detract from her appeal to the officer. The ruse works only too well: when the orderly comes to fetch her, he finds a gray-haired and wrinkled-faced old woman!

To this injection of the miraculous is added a final symbolic scene in which Reb Melekh reveals himself as the Messiah and the officer appears as his eternal antagonist Titus. The evicted Jews are wandering in a wilderness, but the ram's horn is heard and Reb. Melekh proclaims an end to war and the beginning of an abiding Sabbath. The mixture of the real and the allegorical, expressed rhetorically and at the expense of artistic truth, resulted in a work of good intention but spurious drama.

Of greater literary import is *The Sanctification of the Name* * (1919), which delineates Jewish life in Poland during the bloody massacres perpetrated by Bogdan Khmelnitski and his kossaks in the decade following 1648. The Jews were then, even more than in 1918–1919, on the brink of annihilation. Asch wished to indicate that, as before, the undying faith of the Jews would keep them from extinction. The early pages of the narrative are devoted to the innkeeper Mendel who manages, as the only Jew in the vicinity, to live in peace with his Ukrainian and Polish neighbors, but who misses his fellow Jews and exerts himself, in time successfully, to develop a Jewish community with a synagogue of its own. The Jews live precariously as middlemen between the Ukrainian kossak peasants and the Polish nobles, warding off as best they can the threats of the one and the insults of the other. Emphasis is then laid on the Jewish town in distress, and not so much on Jews in danger as on Jews combatting danger. When the kossaks rebel and begin to attack the Jews, the latter flee at the urging of their rabbi, are betrayed by the Poles, and are finally trapped and massacred when they refuse to accept the offered cross.

Asch's compassionate brooding gives the tragic tale the poignant quality of imaginative truth. He makes clear, through the mouth of the rabbi, that every Jew has the obligation to save his life when endangered, as it belongs not to him but to God; only the highest motives justify the final sacrifice. Mendel, the chief character, is earthy enough to die a martyr, but not a pure martyr; his daughter-in-law Deborah is a pure martyr because, to save her honor, she persuades her kossak captor to shoot her on the pretense that no bullet could hurt her!

In the 1920's Asch sojourned in Europe, going first to Poland. The dramatization of *Mottke* proved highly popular in Warsaw and other cities. Equally successful was the dramatic version of *The Sanctification of the Name*. During this period he serialized and later published three novels dealing with Jewish life in the United States.

The Mother * (1925) is a loosely told story. The first half concerns the vicissitudes of a Jewish family as it leaves its native Poland and strives to establish a footing in New York's strange and squalid East Side; the remainder concentrates on Jewish Bohemian life, particularly Bucholtz's struggle for artistic recognition. The novel is thus dichotomous and without inner interrelation. Nor are the main characters fully realized. Soreh Rivke lacks the robust earthiness of Asch's other mothers despite the wonders she achieves with her "magic pots"; by stressing her instinctive motherliness rather than her unique personality he tends to attenuate her essential appeal. Even more negative is her daughter Deborah, to whom Asch also ascribes the "secret mission" of motherhood, and whose self-sacrifice—giving up the unborn child fathered by Bucholtz in order to mother him, only to yield him to Miss Foster to assure his happiness—is hardly credible. And the towering, uncouth Bucholtz, to whom sculpting is as natural and vital as breathing, often acts too much the boorish clown to arouse one's sympathy. What saves the novel from mediocrity is the realistic insight which quickens the chapters dealing with the provocations and tribulations of the immigrant family in the effort to get established in its new home.

In *Electric Chair* (*Judge Not—* * in English, 1926) Max

Stone, a successful banker, meets by chance in a hotel with an old Kentucky colonel (an Iowa realtor in the English edition) and his beautiful mistress, who have come to New York on a spree. The woman's ingratiating charm attracts him and he soon yields to her overt advances. During the night the old man discovers the couple in Stone's room and accidentally dies in the scuffle that ensues. The banker is arrested on the charge of murder and subsequently sentenced to die in the electric chair. His lawyers and friends, aware of his wife's unfaithfulness and eager to make use of it in an appeal for a new trial, are not permitted by him to do so. Sojourn in prison has changed the aggressive and sensual banker into a resigned and forbearing stoic. For the first time taking stock of his past life, he comes to realize the futility of his prosperous enterprise and the essential justice of the verdict brought in by a callow jury. With his wife refusing to help him, life has lost its allure, and he spends his last days seeking clemency for his fellow convicts and cogitating the inexorable nature of the eternal verities.

Although the narrative is developed with literary skill and the ironic exposition of conventional justice is, in small compass, as effective as in Dreiser's *An American Tragedy*, the story as a whole suffers from the fallacy of Stone's inadequately motivated conversion—as little warranted by the facts of human conduct as the change of character in Yekel and Mottke. Rich and influential, in the prime of life, about to attain the pinnacle of financial success, he is hardly the man to permit a chance circumstance to send him to the electric chair. Nor is he likely to succumb to remorse so completely as to choose death rather than expose the infidelity of a wife he has long ceased to love.

The protagonist of *Khaim Ledere's Return* * (1927), having reached the age of 60, decides to retire from his flourishing shirt factory in order to return to the things of the spirit which he had abandoned in youth for the lure of riches and security. He soon discovers, however, that his early ideals have slipped from him beyond recovery. Reflection reveals to him the mockery of his career: for years on end his thoughts have been so monopolized by shirts and the profits from making more and more shirts that he is no longer fit for anything else. "What hurt him most of all was to see that the life led in his own home now seemed strange and offensive to him. . . . That worried him, taunted him, tortured him." His increasingly morbid attempts to recapture the past only alienate his family and increase the torment of his futile existence. In the end he decides to give up his wealth, flee from his philistine environment, and seek the bliss of obscurity as a worker in a distant factory.

In this short novel Asch is at his best as a delineator of Jewish life in America. Unlike *Electric Chair*, this book offers adequate and persuasive motivation for Lederer's behavior. Asch's incisive analysis of the impelling drive for economic security, which had turned Lederer into a money-making machine, appears cogent and credible. Equally acute is the satirical portrayal of Lederer's children, who are so steeped in the conventionality of bourgeois respectability that they are not even aware of their father's awakened ideal of "the common good." Yet the book is primarily the study of a state of mind of a man chained to the habits of a lifetime and struggling in vain for release. Although both Stone and Lederer come to regard the emptiness and falseness of their lives, only the latter has the fortitude to make amends; ironically, one passively and the other actively end in futility.

To these three novels may be added *God's Prisoners* (1933), a sensitive study of eccentric love. After living for nearly 20 years with a man she disdains, Emily Brown breaks away from him and her grown daughter and goes to France to live her own life. On the Riviera she meets Frank Melbourne, and the two are immediately attracted to each other. Although Frank is ten years her junior, they become inseparable, yet Emily cannot consummate her overpowering desire for him. Her "cursedly loyal nature" keeps her back, and "the smell of a strange male" in him frightens her. Terribly distressed, she confesses to him her unshakable ties to the past. "Aren't we like prisoners," she asks pathetically, "forged with unbreakable chains to our time and our inescapable environment? . . ." After months of self-torture and even an attempt at suicide, she decides to return home and leaves before Frank can dissuade her.

If this love story emerges pathetically real, it is by virtue of the deep tenderness which lifts it out of the commonplace. A lyrical poem of love, its singular aspect gives it an aura surpassing external actuality. Knowing Emily's austere and moral Jewish upbringing, one can well sympathize with her emotional inability to deny a conduct which her intellect is eager to abandon. She can no more overcome "the smell of a strange male" in Frank than she could help falling in love with him. Nor is one surprised that Frank accepts her recoil with complete understanding. He also comes of Puritanical stock and has reached his 28th year without meeting a woman worthy of his affection. Emily has unlocked his heart and revealed to him a new and delightful existence. His deep attachment enables him to perceive the mystical ties which inhibit her: he accepts her rebuff as if she were his dear mother as well as his unresponsive lover. He does not misconstrue the note Emily leaves for him: ". . . I am not only your beloved; I am your mother who gave you birth. For that reason I am leaving you—because I am afraid I might weaken and kill our love. . . ."

In its broad scope and complex treatment, *Three Cities* * (1929–1931) is definitely a work of major importance. It was translated into numerous languages and on the whole very favorably received. In the United States and England it was the first of Asch's books, in English translation, to become a "best seller." The novel depicts the three significant aspects of the Russian drama which ended in the triumph of the Bolshevik leaders. "Petersburg" deals with the commercial and industrial expansion in Russia at the turn of the century, with energetic Jews striving to stimulate this economic development and thereby obtain the wealth to give them personal security and individual recognition. "Warsaw" presents a sympathetic account of the social unrest and political turmoil just prior to World War I, especially as they affected the poor Polish Jews harassed by venal officials and constrained by economic restrictions. "Moscow" provides a liberal's analysis of the social forces released by the 1917 revolution and the acute conflict between individuals who seek to retain personal integrity and party discipline, which demands blind loyalty.

Asch is here as much the social historian as the imaginative novelist. He exposes the corruption and ineptitude of government officials, the stupid extravagances of the entrenched rich, the squalor and rancor of the oppressed poor, and the fanatic zeal of the revolutionists—all the elements of national decay and dissatisfaction which, aggravated by disastrous war, hastened the downfall of the Romanov empire. Simultaneously he poses the part played by the Jews in this epic drama, centering the action in their midst. In the first part he concentrates on the rich, enterprising Jews who gained their wealth by exploiting the practically virgin resources of the land; who live ostentatiously, yet must curry the favor of anti-Semitic officials; who pose as urbane liberals and yet are ready to defend their haute-bourgeois perquisites with their lives. Finding them essentially distasteful, he drew them with the flatness of routine sketches; even Gabriel Mirkin, the most sympathetic, lacks depth and variegation. "Warsaw" portrays the poor Jews herded together in the dank and dilapidated slums, harassed during the day and hounded at night, forced to live in a continuous state of semi-starvation. Here Asch is at his fictional best, as nothing moves him so deeply as the suffering of the poor and rejected. In concentrating on the Hurvitz family and its satellites—fervid Jews who cram their minds with intellectual fare, guide the less sophisticated to a new outlook on life, conspire against Czarist oppression, and dream of a new and better world—he quivers with the excitement of artistic intensity. Both groups meet in "Moscow" during the early days of Bolshevik triumph. Their roles are now reversed—and so are Asch's sympathies. The former outcasts, now in control and vindictive, evoke in him anger and aversion. He is indignant at the bullies and fanatics who take advantage of chaotic conditions and sneer at the scrupulous as weaklings and renegades.

Zachary Mirkin, about whom the entire narrative revolves and who bridges the gulf between the antagonistic groups, emerges as a pale and passive protagonist. He belongs more to the negatively speculative milieu of the 19th century Russian novel than to the dynamic turbulence of a major revolution. The only son of a rich industrialist, hypersensitive and sentimental, he reaches manhood burdened with a mother fixation; he becomes engaged to an attractive girl chiefly because of his attachment to her handsome mother. Unable to cope with the perverse situation, he flees from home and betrothed and seeks to begin life anew in the obscurity of a Warsaw slum. Befriended by Mrs. Hurvitz, whom he had met by chance when she visited Petersburg, he is mothered by her to his heart's content. When he learns that his betrothed married his father, he refuses the latter's help and suffers the same privation as his poor neighbors. Now more certain of himself, he becomes engaged to Mrs. Hurvitz's elder daughter and joins the revolutionary underground. October, 1917, finds him in Moscow fighting with Bolshevik workers for control of the city. He is, however, troubled by the lack of scruples and needless cruelty on the part of his companions. When his father's sincere efforts to serve the new government do not save him from being condemned as a bourgeois, and his own endeavors to extricate him are met with snubs and sneers, he flees to Warsaw, which has become the capital of a rejuvenated Poland.

In a novel of profound social crisis the main character must possess the dynamic inner drive which enables him either to ride the crest of the forces unharnessed by the cataclysm or to stand up against his explosive environment and be destroyed by it. Zachary, however, is a weak and worried young man, neither accepting nor fighting the life about him. Self-centered and lonely, if well-meaning, he complains to Mrs.

Hurvitz: "I've nobody, nobody in the whole world. I'm so wretched." Incapable of positive action, he broods and talks. When he tries to merge his lot with that of the poor, his passivity makes him only a shadow of a shadow; having neither the means to help nor the strength to lead, he clings to Mrs. Hurvitz and bemoans his sad plight. One need only call to mind Gorki's Clim Samghin, also a passive but decidedly positive participant in the Russian revolutionary movement, to see how much more alive he is than Zachary.

The War Goes On * (1937) is in a sense a sequel, following *Three Cities* chronologically and pursuing the story of social upheaval from the savage civil strife on the Russian border in 1918 to the economic and spiritual collapse in Germany five years later. The early chapters add little to development of the main theme, and Aron Yudkewitch's undue prominence deprives Hans Bodenheimer of his rightful place as chief protagonist; moreover, the portraits of several prominent characters emerge flat and flaccid. Yet the book towers as a work of historical fiction. It depicts with notable clarity and acuteness the suffering, pathos, chaos, and most of all the unmitigated despair which spawned the Nazi rulers of Germany. Again and again the narrative flares forth with the passion of the proud Jew; over the whole hovers the artist's wistful and compassionate insight into human vicissitude.

Foremost among the lesser characters is Aron Yudkewitch, the extraordinarily clever *luftmensch* who escapes from the Bolsheviks, settles in Germany, and rapidly forces his way to control of the large Bodenheimer bank. Yet his fabulous wealth, which he loses in the inflation, is as ashes in his mouth because his wife despises him for his impotence, and because Asch never lets him forget that his life is a fraud and a mockery.

Yudkewitch is the interloper, the disdained insect feeding upon a diseased body until quashed. More central are the Bodenheimers, the von Stickers, and the Spinners—all representative of the German tragedy. Max Bodenheimer, dignified head of a Jewish banking family, and his brothers Heinrich and Adolf—one an advocate of Nordic superiority and the other dedicated to art—typify the cultivated Jews of Germany. Hans, Max's only son, is the most pathetic and best drawn of the family. Baptized as a child to be spared the ignominy of Jewishness, he suffers most of all for his non-"aryan" origin.

The tragedy of the German is given equal significance. When the elder von Sticker, a Goethe scholar and anti-Semite, learns that his daughter is in love with the converted son of his Jewish banker, he drives her out of the house. His son, brutalized by the war and subsequent chaos, becomes a Nazi gangster and later kills his sister when she refuses to abort the child of her Jewish-born lover. Albert Spinner, an honest worker and loyal Social Democrat, is forced by prolonged undernourishment to lend a willing ear to Nazi promises.

Asch is at his keenest in describing the pathos of a haughty people made desperate by defeat. He makes painfully clear the terrible postwar conditions which forced the truculent and recalcitrant Germans to nurse delusions of grandeur, to make the small Jewish minority their needed scapegoat—to fall like overripe fruit into the lap of "Death's Prophet." Simultaneously he dissects and exposes the crooked roots of hatred of which the Jews become the outraged victims. His objective and perspicacious treatment makes the indictment all the more crushing.

More than any other Yiddish writer, Asch was subjected to carping criticism from the early years of his successful career. Some was deserved, but more than once it was unfair and instigated by envy. Asch was egotistical, impulsive, inconsiderate, and avid for praise. Shlomo Rosenberg, long his secretary and editor as well as a writer in his own right, wrote: "He loved to feel that he is being noted, that people see him, talk about him. . . . Asch had . . . a weakness for titles, the rich, and . . . Gentiles." When still a young man he was honored in Odessa by such eminent men as Mendele and Bialik, but because they praised him as a Yiddish writer, he interrupted to exclaim: "I am not a Yiddish artist, I am a universal artist." In the habit of tearing up the written pages that did not please him, he remarked one day, "What I discard, other Yiddish writers would have made into entire books." His critics never forgot his alleged malignment of the Jews in *God of Vengeance*, his outburst against circumcision, or his manifestation of conceit.

In 1926, when Pilsudski turned Poland into a dictatorship and the lot of the Jews worsened, Asch praised him fulsomely as a "noble knight" in a letter that outraged a good many of his readers. Six years later, when the government awarded him the order of Polonia Restituta, making him the first Yiddish writer to be so honored by any government, Rosenberg wrote that "Asch longed for the medal as a child longs for a pretty shiny toy," intimating that if Asch had not encouraged its receipt it would most likely not have been offered. When Asch appeared to hesitate about its acceptance, sensing Jewish resentment, a number of his friends pointed out that rejection would make the semi-fascist government even more anti-Semitic. The Jewish PEN club in Warsaw importuned him not to decline the award, but David Pinski, then president of the Jewish PEN club in New York, cabled to urge rejection. Asch followed the advice of his friends in Poland, and for a while proudly wore the rosette in his lapel. In 1936, however, when Jewish persecution in Poland was intensified, Asch returned the medal to the Polish ambassador in France.

Personal peccadilloes notwithstanding, Asch felt a deep attachment to his fellow Jews and suffered acutely at the upsurge of anti-Semitism in Europe. In 1935, for instance, he interrupted his writing of *The War Goes On* to go to the United States on a tour, collecting money for Jewish victims. He also did what only he could do so well: write a book steeped in the Jewish spirit in order to give courage and comfort to his harassed fellow Jews. In an interview in 1934, at the time *Salvation* was about to appear, he stated:

> Just as the Ukrainian pogroms in 1918–1919 created in me the desire to write a work like *The Sanctification of the Name* ° of Khmelnitski's time and to portray the ennoblement of the earlier

Jewish martyrdom, so the current sad conditions have driven me to write this new work. The dastardly attacks of the pseudo-scientists in Germany and the so-called German culture not only on the living Jews but on the Jewish spirit, the Jewish morals and ethics, aroused in me the urge to describe a martyrdom not only of the living Jews but also of the Jewish spirit as it was incorporated in Jewish life. . . . I believe and am certain that in a godless, discouraged, desperate time in which we live it is good to give such a book in which faith is mirrored. This should stimulate and inspire the younger generation as much as I was stimulated and inspired to write it.

Jewish piety, whole-souled adoration of Jehovah, and devout observance of the 613 precepts had from childhood fascinated Asch's romantic imagination, and he tended to write about it with the ardent tenderness of lyric love. Composing *Salvation* as an antidote to Hitlerism, he stressed the moral beauty of Jewish piety, as if urging his readers to "seek the ideal, the noble, and the beautiful in our historic past." His protagonist, Jekhiel, born in an atmosphere of intense Hasidic spirituality in the early 19th century, cleaves to God from infancy. From childhood "his heart was barred against all that was complicated or distorted." When his boyish mind fails to grasp the intricacies of the Talmud and his pious father frowns upon him, he suffers agony. Forced to leave school at the age of ten in order to assist his sick mother, he is overcome by a feeling of doom. One day a strange old man assures him that the Psalms are as acceptable to God as the most intricate tome, and advises him to recite them at every opportunity. The boy does so with such devotion and enthusiasm that he soon attracts the favorable attention of his elders. Almost as strong as his attachment to Jehovah is his quickened sympathy for all living things, having "a gift of entering into the feelings of others and completely identifying himself with them." He is always ready to give the little that is his to those who have less, and often shares his bread with the village fool and the stray beggar.

In time his saintliness becomes apparent to the simple folk of the town, and they begin to crowd about him daily to join in the recital of Psalms and seek his advice and assistance. Once, to obtain a draft horse for a poor peddler, Jekhiel assures a wealthy dealer that for the good deed of giving the horse God will make his barren wife fertile within a year. Realizing at once that he has pledged God's name presumptuously, he is deeply distressed. When his own young wife dies soon after while in labor, he takes it as a sign of God's anger and in expiation assumes the ordeal of a wandering beggar. After months of severe self-chastisement he is located by an admirer and told that the horse dealer's wife has given birth to a girl and that the townspeople revere him more than ever. At the man's insistence Jekhiel returns to assume his destined role of teacher and adviser. Eighteen years later the horse dealer's daughter falls in love with a Christian youth and enters a nunnery to be baptized. All attempts to prevent her apostasy fail, and the Poles are ready to celebrate their great victory over the Jews when the conscience-stricken girl throws herself from an upper window to her death; the Jews recognize in her desperate act the efficacy of Jekhiel's prayer.

The lyric beauty of the prose imbues the narrative with artistic authenticity. Asch's delineation of the piety and mystical aspirations of ordinary Jews is as vivid and veracious as if he were describing his own inmost emotions. Their pathetic and at times pathological behavior assumes inherent reality in their sincere yearning for spiritual beatitude. Their implicit faith is set off throughout against the poverty and earthiness of their daily lives. Their supreme representative is Jekhiel, who believes that not erudition but faith leads to salvation, that the love of God ennobles man's spirit. He naturally cleaves to God with all his soul. He believes that man is a chip of God: a soul sojourning on earth but longing to rejoin his Maker. Hunger and suffering in others so wring his heart that soon the magic of his words gives bread to the hungry and comfort to the sick. Asch, confronted by Nazi brutality, concluded the book with the pious hope that "each generation will see its own righteous man. For is it not written that the righteous man is the cornerstone of the world?"

Another visit to Palestine, primarily to gather material and saturate himself with its atmosphere for his next major work, led Asch to write the brief novel, *The Song of the Valley* ° (1938), dealing with the efforts of young pioneers to redeem the inert and swampy plains of Israel. The song of the kha-lutzim—the Hebrew cry "Long live Israel!" chanted repeat-edly with increasing intensity—resounds through this idyllic narrative. Shortly after World War I a group of young Jews from Eastern Europe, of diverse origin and dissimilar educa-tion but united in the glowing zeal to rejuvenate the land of their forefathers, undertake to reclaim the infested swamp-land on the outskirts of Nazareth. City-bred, inexperienced, without adequate shelter or necessary tools, these dedicated pioneers experience many disastrous hardships. The native Arabs scoff at their insane persistence; insects, malaria, and rain torment their bodies and sap their strength. But their in-domitable will to succeed in time overcomes all obstacles and brings the promise of a permanent settlement.

Writing the book in painful awareness of Hitler's intensified ruthlessness, Asch tended to exalt the courage and heroism of the Zionistic youths. Ready to risk their lives for the success of the colony, they meet each hardship with a song and undertake onerous tasks with fanatical enthusiasm. The vision of a thriving Jewish Palestine is ever before them, and how they seek to realize their dream is developed with idyllic simplicity.

When Asch was seven he was attacked by Christian boys who accused him of having killed Christ. Fearing a beating and damage to his new coat, he admitted the charge. He had then never heard of Christ, but later learned about him "through fear and terror, through blood and fire." In maturity, reflection made him perceive Jesus not as the cause of nearly two millennia of grievous Jewish persecution, but as one of the greatest Jewish saints whose martyrdom had been made a sword against the Jews by their enemies. "Jesus Christ, to me," he wrote, "is the outstanding personality of all time, all history, both as the Son of God and the Son of Man."

Profoundly Jewish in spirit and outlook, Asch was nevertheless early attracted to the personalities and fervor of the founders of Christianity. As early as 1909, shortly after his first visit to Palestine, he envisioned and described Mary's journey from Bethlehem to Jerusalem with a reverence predicting his later pious treatment of Jesus and the Apostles. At that time, as later, he expressed his perturbation that Jews and Christians, both going to Palestine on pilgrimages, should "travel to *two* Gods." Nor did he see why they should read "the same Psalms in two languages to two Gods." It was his sincere hope that both would one day cease to say: "Each one has his own God, we—ours, they—theirs." Twenty years later, again writing about Palestine, he admitted: "I must confess that I became infected with the Jesus legend while in Jerusalem (I hope my pious readers won't stone me because of this)."

The barbaric attacks on the Jews in the 1930's caused Asch great agony and led him to profound soul-searching. Emotional and intuitive, intent on defending the Jews from Christian calumny, he persuaded himself that by retelling the story of Jesus he would expose the enemies of the Jews as defilers of Christianity as conceived by its founders. To strengthen his thesis he determined to follow the New Testament and accept the miracles and mysticism without question. By depicting Jesus as a pious Jew, he hoped to demonstrate the falseness of the anti-Jewish position taken by later followers of Christ.

Asch, more than most writers, tended to become completely absorbed in his characters. He acted them out, lived their lives, and loved them as he did himself. Having done this with Mendel and Jekhiel, both idealized pious Jews, he now proceeded to identify himself with Jesus. In his imagination Jesus and Jekhiel were both God-lovers, only Jesus was to him also the Son of God. "*Salvation*," Niger pointed out, "is actually nothing else but an introduction to *The Nazarene;* *The Nazarene* is first of all the realization, the completion and crowning of *Salvation*."

To add fictional credence to his narrative, Asch employed indirect means of portrayal. Jesus's story is told in turn by the anti-Semitic Pan Vladomsky, in a former existence Cornelius, the efficient and worldly governor of Jerusalem under Pilate; in the secretly discovered gospel of Judas owned by Vladomsky; and by the young Polish Jew who in a previous incarnation had been Jokhanan, a contemporary of Cornelius and sympathetic witness of the self-proclaimed Messiah's last tragic days in Jerusalem. The composite portrait differs in no essential particular from the New Testament version, except that his Jewishness is stressed and he emerges artistically full-bodied against the background of spiritual turmoil and anxious aspiration. Jesus's comings and goings, preaching and healing, exhorting and denouncing, from his early soul-searching in the wilderness to his final crucifixion and burial, are enlarged upon with the fervor of faith and great evocative beauty.

The book combines the soundness of scholarship with intuitive art. The oriental pomp and pretense within the court of the High Priest, little Salomé's dance before Herod and her bloody reward, the jostle and bustle within the Temple courts at festival time, the squalor and misery of the Jerusalem poor, the pious earthiness of Jewish peasants, the intellectual probing and mystical yearning of the erudite seekers after the Messiah—these and other aspects of Palestinian life are described with lively authenticity and in picturesque detail. With equal sympathy are depicted the scores of men and women who crowd the pages of the narrative. Cornelius, Pilate, Rabbi Nicodemon and his pupil Jokhanan, Mary Magdelene, Simon, Judas, and the other Disciples, are all subjects for Asch's great skill at portraiture. Jesus himself appears as an extremely sensitive youth who feels so acutely the craving of his oppressed people for the advent of the Messiah that he in time believes himself called by God as their redeemer. As his mother tells Judas, "he sought the justice of God among men and found it not. And I perceived that with each injustice he loses the blood of his heart." When he returns from the wilderness he is ready for his holy mission. He begins to preach, succor the sick, and perform miracles. Disciples cleave to him and spread his fame.

Various learned Jews, yearning for the Messiah, seek for a sign from the new rabbi; not receiving it, they refuse to follow him. The eminent Rabbi Nicodemon sympathizes with Jesus's preaching but concludes that "the Rabbi's doctrine is good and great for those that are born without spirit, or for such as would deny the spirit. But we are born in the spirit and of the covenant which God made with Abraham—how shall *we* be born again without denying the spirit?" For the Jews, groaning under Rome's heel and seeking salvation, the advent of the true Messiah was still in the offing.

When Jesus finally reveals himself to his Disciples and proceeds to Jerusalem to exhort the populace, he openly courts apprehension and execution as a rebel and blasphemer. Asch indicates emphatically that guilt lies with Pilate and not with the Jews, for even the High Priest fears this strange and enigmatic rabbi and does not molest him until forced by the Roman's imperative command. As stated by Jokhanan during the crucifixion:

> We had thought that now, now, the measure of his suffering had been filled, now the salvation was at hand, now he would lift his head, and his enemies would be utterly destroyed. Our hunger had filled our hearts: let it happen now! Let God's name be glorified! God's name must be glorified! But the moment had passed, the miracle had not burst upon us. There only stood before us a tormented and beaten Jew, and at his side his hangman, Pilate.

Asch's Jesus appears as a righteous Jewish man following in the path of the prophets before him and bringing faith to its ultimate goal—making him blood-brother to the saintly Jekhiel. One hardly thinks of him as anathema to the pious Jews he so closely resembles. It was this uncritical, even misconstrued conception, coming at the height of the fiendish Nazi persecution, that shocked many of his erstwhile admirers and brought abuse and obloquy on Asch's head.

The first to react inimically was Abraham Cahan, the able but gross-grained editor of *Der Forverts*. He had long been critical of some of Asch's writing. Years earlier, after the third installment of *The Sanctification of the Name*, he called the work trash and urged Asch "to write a *Mottke the Thief* and not such Bove stories." It was only at the urging of his associates that he relented. On seeing the first part of *The Nazarene* in 1938, he strongly exhorted Asch to stop writing it. Refusing to serialize it, he broke with Asch and thus lost his most distinguished contributor. About the same time the editor of the Warsaw *Haint* regretfully informed Asch that he dared not serialize the book for fear that the Polish censor would consider it blasphemous and suppress the daily. Consequently *The Nazarene* did not appear in the original Yiddish until 1943.

Cahan and Khaim Lieberman led the attack, excoriating Asch for his presumed adherence to Christianity. Lieberman, speaking without warrant, asserted: "The Jewish public was shocked and scandalized as by no other literary event before or since. It was a sword plunged into the very vitals of the people." He called *The Nazarene* "an obvious missionary tract . . . a deadly crime against the Jewish people." However difficult it is for Jews to be objective about Jesus and Christianity—associated as they are with a millennium and more of persecution and martyrdom—a number of Yiddish writers came to Asch's defense. Niger, the leading critic, wrote about the book as "Asch's highest achievement." To the end of his life, however, Asch was stigmatized by a portion of Jews as an apologist of Christianity.

Asch defended himself in interviews, articles, and *In What I Believe* * (1941). He insisted he was a devoted Jew, dedicated to the welfare of his people. As an artist, however, he maintained his right to express himself according to his ability and conscience.

In everything that I have done, everything that I wrote in the book, in the interviews that I gave, I have aimed at one thing: to help the Jews in their present dire circumstances. Never before have the Jews been so isolated in the world. They have no defenders, and are surrounded by enemies. My only aim was to create friends for them. I do not take back one word that I have written in *The Nazarene* or said in interviews.

On another occasion he defended his uncritical adherence to the Gospels.

I have the utmost reverence for the authors of the New Testament. As a Jew, I believe with all my heart that many chapters and parables were written in the holy spirit. . . . Jesus did not come to tear asunder the society he lived in; on the contrary, he came to strengthen, to secure, and to extend it. Jesus was not a Christian; he was a Jew.

He repeated that his aim was to demonstrate the Jewishness of the followers of Jesus and the deplorable discrepancy between his ethics and the subsequent practices of the Established Church. It was Asch's endeavor, he asserted, to build "a bridge that shall rest on the twin pillars of love of God and love of Man." He further hoped "to create a family feeling between us and the Christian world in order to awake in the latter a feeling of protest against the evils perpetrated against the Jewish people and against the individual Jew because he is a Jew." Admitting that the record of Christian civilization "is stained with blood, and of that blood not a little came from the veins of my forefathers," he felt nevertheless that the book's "spirit was drawn from the sources which feed my soul." He therefore stated that as a true follower of Jesus "my Christian brother has his equal share in the God of Israel." He concluded: "The one ambition in my life is to acquire for the Jews the full credit for their contribution of the Jewish spirit to the world's treasure of faith, culture, civilization."

Undeterred by criticism, however much he resented it, Asch continued to probe into the nature of Christianity. He steeped himself in research, reading many old tomes and recent studies before writing *The Apostle* (1943). The book on Jesus had stressed the Jewishness of his ethics and outlook; in the story of Paul he makes evident the gradual emergence of the Apostle's anti-Jewish attitude and exhortation. Again adhering faithfully to the New Testament in all essentials, he describes the process of Paul's conversion from aggressive persecutor of the followers of Jesus to zealous and hysterical missionary intent on winning the entire world to a Christianity of his own making. The long narrative provides a detailed and imaginative account of the Jewish, Hellenic-Roman, and pagan cultures which form the background for Paul's intensive activities.

Paul is depicted as an inspired fanatic. Peace of soul was not his. From early youth his turbulent spirit demanded conviction, compliance, and conformity. A student of the renowned Rabbi Gamaliel, the wise and gentle Pharisee, he is not satisfied, like his mentor, with mere disapproval of dissidents; he feels the need to hound them without let. For a time he is their most aggressive persecutor. His inner perturbation sometimes brings on an epileptic seizure, and he is so seized on his way to Damascus in search of new Christians—when he sees a vision of Jesus and is converted.

A newcomer to the sect, he cannot acquiesce in the policies and preaching of the leading Apostles. Having been chosen by Jesus the Messiah, he is not content to bring his gospel only to his fellow Jews. Disregarding the firm disapproval of Simon (Peter) and the censure of James, Jesus's pious brother, Paul proceeds to preach the message of Christ to all who will listen. In every town he enters he first seeks out the synagogue and exhorts the Jews in it. When most of them reject his message, he turns to the pagans. Although Jesus had appeared to him, according to Asch, as a Jewish rabbi in prayer shawl and philacteries, Paul depicts him to his auditors as the Son of God who assumed human form and suffered crucifixion to save mankind from original sin. He preaches not fear but love of God, and assures everyone that Christ brought the world a new faith. To attract converts he gradually sanctions abrogation of circumcision, *kashruth,* and finally the laws of Moses. "The Torah," he asserts, "made man sinful," and Jesus "was releasing man from his bondage to sin."

News of his missionary zeal and deviation from Judaism strongly perturbs the Apostles in Jerusalem, who continue to consider themselves Jews and Disciples of Jesus. Simon, to whom Jesus "had entrusted the care of the flock, bidding him to guard it against all evil from without and from within," meets Paul in Antioch and speaks plainly to him:

> "Brother Paul," he said, "what hast thou done? Our Messiah sent us forth to plant his good vine in the garden of God, but thou tearest out the tree of Israel, in which all of us are rooted. The Messiah sent us forth to be a light to gentiles, but thou takest the light and with it settest fire to the House of Israel. . . . The Messiah is the fulfilment of the promises made to our forefathers, the fulfilment and hope of Israel: without Israel there is no Messiah!"

Paul, restraining his anger, disagrees and tells Simon that he received his mission from the Messiah himself.

> I say there cannot be one God for the Jews and another for the gentiles: there is but one God. Likewise there cannot be a Messiah for the Jews and a Messiah for the gentiles: there is but one Messiah. Thus there cannot be a congregation of Jews and a congregation of gentiles: there can be only one congregation.

When the Jews persist in rejecting his gospel, which to their minds shakes the very foundation of Judaism, Paul begins to attack them as ferociously as he had previously attacked the first Christians. As the dynamic and zealous "missionary to the gentiles," he suffers recurrent physical distress but perseveres in his self-assigned task: establishing churches in every city he visits and exhorting his followers in letters written with passionate zeal and dwelling on the promise of salvation.

At the end of the long narrative, immediately following the martyrdom in Rome of both Peter and Paul, Asch added, presumably with unintended irony, a prayerful coda in the manner of the pious Jewish writers of religious tomes:

I thank Thee and praise Thee, Lord of the world, that Thou hast given me the strength to withstand all temptations and overcome all obstacles, those of my own making and those made by others, and to complete the two works, *The Nazarene* and *The Apostle,* which are one work; so that I might set forth in them the merit of Israel, whom Thou hast elected to bring the light of the faith to the nations of the world, for Thy glory and out of Thy love of mankind.

The Apostle has not appeared in a Yiddish edition. Some Jews who read the English translation could not help reading into it the source of anti-Jewish prejudice that pervaded the minds of most Christians over the ensuing centuries. They reacted plaintively or violently, according to their nature. With the gas ovens in Auschwitz and other concentration camps going full blast, no sensitive Jew could react with equanimity to Paul's fanatical tirades against his fellow Jews. Asch himself, before actually writing the book and identifying himself in his imagination with the Apostle, recoiled from the results of Paul's missionary zeal. In an article entitled "The Guilty Ones" in *The Atlantic Monthly* of December, 1940, he wrote:

> That same bubbling passion with which Paul pursued Jesus's followers up to Damascus was carried over by him after Damascus to his own compatriots. He infected all those around him with a sectarian passion for his faith; Paul sacrificed everything for his faith—not only his health and his life, but also his great love for his own people.

Having written about Paul with his usual artistic empathy, he could not believe that the book was anti-Jewish in character. The accusation of apostasy hurled at him by his detractors horrified him. He defended himself with the not altogether pertinent analogy that he was no more pro-Christian than Rembrandt was pro-Jewish in his paintings of rabbis, or Michelangelo in his statues of Moses and David, or Thomas Mann in his *Joseph* series.

> It is absolutely false that I preach Christianity to the Jews. Some ascribe to me things that are alien to me. I do not preach Christianity. For me it is the stuff of our lives. Did I in enhancing

artistically the religious striving of the Jews in *Salvation* preach Hasidism? Did I urge Jews to visit rabbis and believe in saints?

In *One Destiny: An Epistle to the Christians* * (1945) he eloquently presents his view on the relations between Jews and Christians over the many centuries, and concludes that, despite the persecution and blood-letting, the two faiths are inextricably interrelated and depend one on the other. He restates his belief that Judaism was enlarged by the advent of Jesus and that Jews must share the goodness of Jesus's ethics even as the Christians must accept the God of Israel.

> I consider my Christian brothers as the spiritual children of Abraham, Isaac, and Jacob, entitled together with me to our birthright from God. . . . Notwithstanding the heritage of blood and fire which passionate enmity has brought between them, they are two parts of a single whole, two poles of the world which are always drawn to each other, and no deliverance, no peace, and no salvation can come until the two halves are joined together and become one part of God. . . . That is my credo.

Having stated his position, he reviews the "disease" of modern anti-Semitism in Germany and describes, by way of contrast, the heroic martyrdom of the Jews in the Warsaw ghetto. He further asserts that "the whole German people—man, woman and child—is infected with the leprous plague, the disease of bestiality and blood lust," and concludes that "the guilt is carried, the accessory guilt if not the full one, by the whole Christian world." He blames the Church for having "invented the role of a Judas and an Ahasuerus for Israel" and for "becoming the chastising rod for the Jewish people." He ends with the statement: "It is my profound belief that only the Jewish-Christian idea contains in itself the possibility of salvation for our tortured world."

Four years after *One Destiny* he completed *Mary* * (1949), the third of the Christological novels. The simplest and least important of the three, it portrays the mother of Jesus with loving piety and pastoral artlessness. Again Asch follows closely the account in the Gospels, adding only imaginative details that enhance her image and infuse her being with the essence of reality. A distant daughter of the House of David, Miriam yearns so ardently and earnestly to be the chosen mother of the expected Messiah that God hears her prayer and causes her to conceive immaculately. Thereafter she dedicates herself to her first-born. A good wife to Joseph and a devoted mother to the other children, she watches over Jesus, in boyhood and maturity, with surpassing love and reverence. When Nazarene townsmen become suspicious of the youth's strange behavior, and members of his own family urge him to conform, Miriam defends him with inner understanding and firm steadfastness. Later, when Jesus begins his preaching and Miriam perceives intuitively the terrible yet glorious end, her mother's heart cries out against the inevitable event, but her pious spirit accepts God's judgment as the foreordained fulfilment of Jesus's heavenly mission.

In the last decade of his life, Asch, *Mary* excepted, returned to his Jewish setting. *East River* * (1946) and *A Passage in the Night* * (1954) concern Jews in the United States who are already well established and Americanized. In the first he poses the problem of antagonism among peoples, nations, and religions, and suggests that amicable relations are possible among them. The question of intermarriage is treated sympathetically, and he implies that not religion but character is basic to human amity. The novel lacks the freshness and lyricism of his earlier work, although it is more deftly conceived. In the second story Grossman, the protagonist, had in his youth stolen a wallet from a Polish peasant, and its content enabled him to start his climb to considerable wealth. In his old age he becomes eager to find the Pole and compensate him generously. In both narratives three generations are contrasted and their interrelationships described in detail. Both works are in a minor key, but evidence the literary dexterity of the mature novelist: the characterization is firm and the motivation lyrical and persuasive.

The Burning Bush * (1946) is a collection of short stories
dealing with Nazi atrocities. In one a Jew is hanged because
he would not desecrate the Sabbath. "A Child Leads the Way"
tells of 93 girls in an orphanage, aged 12 to 18, being led by
the youngest in committing suicide to escape falling into the
lascivious hands of Nazi soldiers. "Christ in the Ghetto" concerns a group of Jews driven by Nazis into a Polish church
and ordered to profane a painting of Jesus. When their rabbi
refuses, he is shot. Thereupon Jesus steps out of the painting,
dons the rabbi's garments, and walks out of the church to pay
condolence calls on the bereaved Jews. In still another story
the female supervisor of the woman's division at Buchenwald
has a pair of earrings made and ingeniously set with the eyes
of a little Jewish girl.

Asch followed *Mary* with *Moses* * (1951). Here, as in the
Christological volumes, he adheres to the religious sources,
adding legendary and mythological as well as anthropological
embellishments to provide a psychologically sympathetic portrait of Moses as a revolutionary and prophet. Like Jesus, he
emerges as through a misted glass mystically: a noble human
being, a seeker of truth and justice, but no Son of God. In the
grandeur of the epic panorama, Asch first shows the enslaved
Israelites suffering harsh exploitation and yet too intimidated
to dream of liberation. When Moses, the adopted princeling,
in a rebellious spirit slays the Egyptian guard, the Israelites
force him to flee to the wilderness to save themselves from
further punishment. Years later, when Moses returns with
God's message of redemption, these same Israelites manifest
little faith and less courage, and it is only the miraculous
plagues that persuade them of Jehovah's might and Moses's
mission. Once in the wilderness, they grumble when inconvenienced, sigh nostalgically for the Egyptian fleshpots, and
are ready to turn to idols like the golden calf. Their slavish
spirit lacks the vision and animus of free men, and their trans-
gressions against God doom them to die in the desert.

For 40 years Moses looks after them as their dedicated

leader, attending to their needs, grieving for their deplorable destiny, and inspiring their free-born offspring with a love of Jehovah and a faith worthy of the Promised Land. To the very end on Pisgah Heights he serves his people with selfless devotion and inexhaustible sympathy. Asch dwells lovingly on his human qualities and spiritual afflatus, ennobling him as the founder of Judaism and Jehovah's exalted prophet.

For his next book Asch chose Deutero-Isaiah, the humble prophet who sang God's word because he could not silence the voice within him. Isaiah in *The Prophet* * (1955), like Jekhiel in *Salvation*, is from boyhood possessed by consuming love of God. The Babylonian exile preys on his youthful mind. So eager is he, dwelling with his parents in the outskirts of Jerusalem, for the return of his people and restoration of the Temple that he soon begins to hear God's voice in his heart, and is impelled by an irrepressible urge to journey to Babylon to preach the word of God to the exiled Jews. His message is a song of love and hope, proclaiming God's mercy and the advent of Judea's restoration. The pious poor welcome him, and a few prominent exiles are impressed with his spirituality. But the wealthy and worldly Jews, who have become more materially powerful than they had ever been in Jerusalem, denounce him as a troublemaker and false prophet and urge his stoning. One of them exclaims:

> Who said that we want to return to Judah and Jerusalem? What have we to hope for there? . . . Our people sit here on the most fruitful part of Babylonia, eat of the fat of the land. . . . We have spread our commerce over the whole of Babylonia. . . . If God loves us and is concerned about us, let him leave us here. He did us a great favor when he sent Nebuchadnezer to free us from the narrowness of Judea, which Moses had pressed us in.

Isaiah, sick and starved, suffers grievously at the hands of his rich and powerful tormentors. Yet he persists in his inspired preaching and prophesying, and his life is saved by the poor who believe in him, particularly by Zerubabel, destined to lead the exiles back. When Cyrus does permit the return of the Jews, as the prophet had predicted, but in the name of Bel-Merodach and not of Jehovah, Isaiah is distressed unto death; in his agony he sees in a vision, shown him by the elder prophet, the "man of sorrows" whose "name was with God in heaven before He created the world." Before he breathes his last he tells Zerubabel, whom he assigns as leader of the exiles: "Not for your sake alone do you return to Judah. You go back to Judah for the sake of the salvation of all the nations." This intimation of the advent of Jesus, as well as of Israel's place in the world, is in keeping with Asch's continued belief that the salvation of mankind lies in the recognition of Judeo-Christian concord.

Despite criticism and ostracism on the part of his Jewish critics, Asch remained a deeply rooted Jew dedicated to writing about and loving his people with passionate intensity. When he settled in Israel in 1955 he felt hurt by snubs and rejoiced in signs of recognition and respect. He was deeply moved when the Jewish writers decided to welcome him publicly. As for his critics, he told a young friend: "I won't live that long, but you will when all these will feel sorry that they have caused me so much suffering without cause."

He began to write the story of Jacob and Rachel, but after completing a half dozen chapters his interest turned to Abraham and Sarah, and he decided to combine the two stories. In January, 1957, he suffered a mild stroke, which temporarily interrupted his writing. In need of an operation, he went with his wife to London that June. There he died suddenly soon after.

Sholom Asch possessed a lyric flow and an emotional intensity that suffused his best writing with poetic beauty. He was no formal stylist and no master of verbal refinement. When his early work was criticized for its sometimes faulty Yiddish, he replied: "My standard is my mother, long may she live. Each word she uses is to me pure and holy Yiddish." He excelled, however, in the expression of simple sensuous feeling. He wrote of nature and human emotion with loving ebullience. When in love with his characters he became lyrical and his prose sang. Endowed with deep emotion, he often wept when depicting suffering and laughed when telling something amusing. When delineating the earthy behavior of pious Hasidim or the wretched existence of the city poor, his ardent sympathy flowed fresh and pure.

In his early work he was not fully at his artistic ease when dealing with the social and intellectual complexities of urban life; in *Three Cities,* however, he achieved the breadth and depth and color of a major novel. He attained his fictional eminence in his religious writings. His pious rustics—Mendel, Jekhiel, and even more Jesus, Paul, Moses, and Isaiah—emerge refulgent with the halo of fervid faith, loving God with all their heart. If his reverential treatment of Christianity raised acrimonious controversy among Jewish readers, and if his credulous and uncritical acceptance of mythical miracles seem naive if not preposterous to sophisticates, his work as a whole nevertheless has the literary quality of the major novelists of the 20th century.

CHAPTER ELEVEN

PERETZ HIRSCHBEIN

Dramatist, Novelist, World Traveler

A CONTEMPORARY of Abraham Reisen and Sholem Asch, Peretz Hirschbein differed markedly from both in personality and artistic expression. Unlike Reisen he was an esthete, a mystic, yet a man of the world; unlike Asch he was at his best as a writer of dramatic idyls, while his novels had none of Asch's lyric intensity.

He was born in November, 1880, in the house adjacent to his father's mill, some two miles from a village in Lithuania. The mill was situated on a fast-flowing and sweet-smelling stream, surrounded by low undulating hills and fragrant green meadows. A silent solitude hovered about the place, making it easy for an imaginative child to fancy it a trysting place of sinister spirits. Its haunting loneliness and pristine beauty impressed themselves on the mind of the gentle and reticent Peretz. Of a roving disposition, shy but inquisitive, he took boyish delight in exploration of his surroundings. He roamed the fields and swam in the stream, studied bird calls and insect buzzings, examined the variegated wild flowers and manifold trees, and timidly envisioned fancied fairies. In his eagerness to learn the ways of nature he familiarized himself with the folklore and superstitions which enriched the talk of young and old within his hearing.

The youngest son and of delicate health during his early years, Peretz remained under his mother's tender and solicitous care longer than most Jewish boys of that time. He was tutored at home, mostly by his old grandfather, from whom he learned many religious and lay songs, grouped according to "color." At the age of seven he began to attend a town *kheder,* fearfully walking the distance by himself. His quick mind and zeal for knowledge encouraged his parents to hope that he might become a rabbi—the dearest ambition of pious Jews for a gifted son. With this in mind they permitted him, when he reached his thirteenth year, to leave home for the houses of study in the larger nearby towns. For five years he lived the hard, indigent life of the yeshiva student—eating meals at a different table each day of the week, sleeping on the bare bench he occupied while at study, and poring assiduously over books of Hebrew lore.

He was not long in learning from an itinerant bookseller about the availability of current books in Yiddish. Somewhat later, like many other yeshiva students, he began to study German and Russian in the necessary clandestine manner, and gradually emancipated himself from the dogma and doctrine of orthodox Judaism. In 1898 he went to Wilno, then a center of Jewish culture. Continuing the life of the yeshiva student in order to obtain free meals and lodging, he soon made the acquaintance of minor Jewish writers and showed them the Hebrew verses he had been writing since he was 15. To earn some money he began to teach Hebrew to a group of girls. He also became interested in the intellectual ferment of the time and listened sympathetically to the endless discussions and serious rivalries between Zionists and Bundists (socialists).

His emotional life took a tragic turn when his cousin Shayndel suddenly died of poisoning. They had been idyllically in love for several years, and wrote to each other in the naive but heartfelt terms of the Song of Songs. He was the more timid of the two, but his affection for her brightened his lonely nights in the house of study; a part of him died with her.

Years later he wrote: "Sadness, sadness without limit encased my whole life. Sadness inwardly, sadness outwardly."

He began to read widely of world literature, and was particularly influenced by contemporary playwrights. He considered the dramatic form the medium best suited to depicting human emotions. Subsequently he wrote: "Drama, it seems to me, was a form superior to the novel, which dwells in detail on one or more persons. The process of description and narration is clumsy compared with the sharpness of dialogue. . . . It is more natural to hear the hero speak and uncover the tragic or comic in his life."

Thus conditioned, it was normal for him to turn to writing plays. A chance encounter with a very young and pathetic prostitute gave him the stimulus to write *Miriam* (1904), a drama in which a poor orphaned girl is seduced by a wealthy philanderer and driven in desperation to a brothel. In the final act the moralizing is shrill. Years later, in Buenos Aires, Hirschbein saw it produced in Yiddish (entitled *Downhill*), and wrote that "it caused hysterical weeping among the prostitutes who then filled the theater. Possibly more than one 'Miriam' recognized herself in the play." This work, as well as *Driftwood* and *The Intellectual*, which followed, were comparatively naive in conception and sentimental in treatment.

In 1904 Hirschbein made his way to Warsaw, where he soon met Peretz, read his plays to him, and received the hoped-for praise and an offer of tutoring if he wished to remain in Warsaw. Through Peretz he came to know Bialik, Dinesohn, and other Jewish writers. Bialik was then editing a Hebrew journal and offered to print *Miriam* in it, but Hirschbein, having heard that it was Bialik's habit to edit manuscripts drastically, decided not to let him have it. Sensitive and easily depressed, he found Warsaw uncongenial and returned to Wilno.

He next wrote *The Carcass* (1905), a work of improved merit but still not free from the defects of the literary novice. Cellar-poverty again dominated the setting, but character began to emerge into individualized creation. Mendel, brought up brutally by a besotted father and early set to skinning dead horses, grows into a stupid and slovenly lout, never free of the stench of carcasses. When he becomes infatuated with Reisel, his stepsister, a gay and michievous girl, he lacks the sense to improve his personal appearance. When she scorns his courtship and recoils from his very presence, he becomes violent and raves about avenging himself; finding his father in a drunken stupor, he chokes him. The action lacks conviction: a moron who does not know enough to deodorize himself before wooing Reisel is made sensitive enough to stress the goodness of his heart. Yet faulty as the motivation appears, the play is pregnant with dramatic potential.

Where Life Passes (1905) is another drama of the poor: "young lives, in deep and dark and dirty cellars, whose love of life withers without protest." *Lonely People* (1906), a one-act play written under Gorki's influence, again deals with inhabitants of a cellar home, people who live in close quarters and yet are strangers, each for himself and to himself. *'Twixt Day and Night* (1906), his first play in Yiddish, is a dramatic poem reminiscent of Maeterlinck's symbolism but without the latter's artistic firmness. A sudden inundation washes away the house of a blind old shipwright, and he and his young granddaughter find shelter on a nearby knoll. The weather is raw and the wind merciless; during the night the old man freezes to death but the girl is saved by the warmth of a strange young man. At dawn the stranger crosses the river and disappears. The girl's longing for him soon causes her to throw herself into the river. A vague mystery pervades the action: the old man and the girl talk as if alone in the world, and the stranger comes out of nowhere and vanishes into nowhere.

In 1907 Hirschbein again went to Warsaw to visit Peretz. From there he traveled to Berlin, where he sojourned for several months and wrote *The Earth*, a dramatic étude. A girl, having graduated from *gymnasium*, returns home, abandons her urban habits and outlook, turns to nature, and falls in love with a man of the soil. Angered by the tubercular people who come to her father's forest for recuperation, she persuades her lover to set fire to the trees and thus drive the city people away. Reuben Brainin, the distinguished Hebrew writer whom Hirschbein visited in Berlin and who had dubbed the earlier plays "cellar dramas," considered the symbolism in this work sick and anarchic. Later that year Hirschbein returned to Wilno, where he wrote *In the Dark*, in which poverty squeezes a young girl dry of the zest of life she prizes so highly. To her blind grandmother she declaims:

> I went to the factory and withered there. All about me the faces were yellowish, greenish, and silent: faces withering in silence. And I was also silent. And within me something was rent and made me sad. Oh, how sad! It was like a candle flickering and going out. And when human beings flicker and go out—bend and fall to the ground—one becomes frightened. I became frightened. Granny! Granny! Did I do wrong in running away from fire, so as not to melt away like a candle? . . . Tell me, granny, don't you feel while in this cellar that the whole building rests on you, on your head, pressing down upon your skull and brain together? . . .

Unable to shake loose from the withering grip of poverty, the girl ends her suffering by suicide.

Throughout his twenties Hirschbein seethed with literary ambition. Without notable originality or talent but intimately familiar with the grinding effect of unrelieved poverty, anxious to emulate the writers he admired most, and genuinely affected by the revolutionary turmoil of the 1900's, he chose to write about the dreary cellar life of the pauperized workers. His dramatic gift still fledgeless and frail, he tended to make poverty the protagonist. Consequently, none of the characters in his early realistic plays possess the life of artistic creations. Equally weak are the symbolism and mystic milieu of his poetic études, since they lack both clarity of expression and coherent action.

Toward the end of 1907 Hirschbein went to Petersburg to supervise publication of a Russian edition of his plays. There he wrote *The Contract*, a folkloric play on the mystic theme which S. Ansky ten years later developed into the highly popular drama, *Between Two Worlds: The Dybbuk*. Hirschbein conceived it poetically and rather sketchily, emphasizing the passivity of Jewish girls in pious homes. Khanele's secret betrothed becomes very ill and dies without releasing her from her pledge to marry him. Meantime her parents arrange for her marriage to another, but the spirit of the dead youth hovers over her and finally forces her to fulfil her troth as her life ebbs away. The scenes exude superstitious fear, and all the characters succumb to its spell.

Early in 1908 Hirschbein went to Odessa, where he renewed his friendship with Bialik and met Mendele and other Jewish writers. Encouraged by Bialik, he organized a group of actors for the purpose of producing plays of high merit. For the next two years he directed, managed, and acted in a repertoire of the best available Yiddish plays, including several of his own. Censorship gave the group a good deal of trouble in some cities, but everywhere it was greeted by enthusiastic audiences. By the summer of 1910, however, Hirschbein realized that he had written nothing for more than two years and decided to let the company continue without him. Although among the actors were such fine performers as Jacob Ben-Ami (Shirin), who later contributed notably to the Yiddish Art Theater in New York, the troupe found itself at a loss without Hirschbein and soon disbanded.

Hirschbein's restless nature kept him moving from city to city of Eastern Europe. In 1911 he came to New York, where he saw some of his plays produced by an amateur group led by Yoel Entin, a perceptive critic. Having a difficult time financially, he spent a season as a farm hand in the Catskill region. All the while, however, he wrote plays and had some of them published, among them *Eva* (1910), *From Road to Road* (1911), and *The Last One* (1911). These works were comparatively mediocre, for Hirschbein was still groping for suitable themes. Instead of concentrating on the life he knew best, as he was soon to do, he wrote relatively ineptly about artists deprived by time of zest and power; about the Jew who resolves to leave no heir to his unfortunate racial heritage; about the man who, at 48, discovers the secret of life in making toys. In these philosophical problem plays he was merely emulating feebly the work of more gifted contemporaries.

In *The Last One,* for example, Yekhiel, the only son of a very pious rabbi, resolves not to have any child of his undergo the suffering to which he was destined, believing that a Jew lives like a lamb among wild beasts. To his wife he declares:

A people lives for thousands of years and its greatness consists in the ability to relate and enumerate the many times it has had to undergo burning, the many times it has had to suffer the rack. As if we were most fortunate in being able to recount our sorrows without end. . . . But what is suffering for? To what purpose? If the Jew needs to reach nations and lead them to the right road —then let him realize through his own suffering that *suffering must be eradicated and destroyed!* Destroyed must first be he whose fate it is to suffer throughout life! . . . Those who have acquired the bitter secret of life *should be the last ones on this earth and life should end with their life.* . . . You shall not bear a child under your heart on my account, because I do not want to be a *father* and do not want *to bring children* into the world.

His drastic decision wrecks the lives of his pious parents and drives his wife to insanity.

Hirschbein's protest against the fatalistic meekness with which Jews accept their suffering is in itself a theme worthy of development. In selecting a zealot like Yekhiel as his protagonist, however, he tended to vitiate the validity of his theme. Yekhiel's insistence on race suicide as the only solution to Jewish persecution is the nihilistic notion of a paranoiac. Moreover, stressing not his spiritual resolve but the agony he causes his wife and parents, Hirschbein blurs the motivation of the play.

In January, 1912, he completed *The Haunted Inn,* the first of his notable folk dramas. This was followed by *A Child of the World,* a symbolic play depicting the double life of contemporary civilization, and *A Wayside Nook.* The next year he returned to Europe. There he published *My Book,* a small volume consisting of thought splinters and emotional moods, expressed in poetic prose. Steeped in the spirit of nature, his sketches of the seasons, of human feelings and aspirations, and of wistful dreams appear fanciful and sentimental.

Early in 1914 he went to Argentina to work on land acquired by Baron de Hirsch for Jewish settlement. When war broke out in Europe he took a boat bound for New York. On the high seas the ship was sunk by the Germans and Hirschbein was among the passengers transshipped to the United States. In New York he became a regular contributor to *Der Tog*, which had been started earlier that year, and serialized his travel experiences, later published as *From Distant Lands*. His *The Prophet Elijah* and other one-act plays also appeared in *Die Zukunft*. Commissioned by the newspaper to attend the World Exposition in San Francisco, he visited a number of cities and sites on the way, and his sensitive travel descriptions were incorporated in *Travels in America* (1918).

Heretofore Hirschbein had been the intrinsically pastoral poet seeking to emulate the urbane naturalism and mystic symbolism of his prominent contemporaries. Largely self-taught, eager to break new ground in the terrain of Yiddish literature, abashedly affected by the pervasive literary trends of the day, he concentrated on currently realistic or symbolic themes. His theatrical interlude of two years, a period in which he did no writing but kept close to the pulse of Jewish audiences and Jewish life, served to release him from essentially foreign influences and turn his attention to the rustic milieu of his childhood. Forsaking the turmoil of the city and its intellectual vagaries for the idyllic earthiness of the pristine village, he hit upon a theme congenial to his innate talent.

During the next several years he wrote his best plays. His people became alive and appealing in proportion to their intimacy with nature. They aired no philosophical problems, suffered from no forced sophistry, and kept close to human probability. Among his characters in several preliminary efforts were the strong-willed grandfather who, unable to dominate his spirited granddaughter, retaliates by disinheriting her; the girl who finds it difficult to stifle her love for the betrothed of her dearest friend; the mother who coddles her daughter excessively; the aged couple amused by the idyllic affection between their merry servants; and the scholarly youth torn between affection for his cousin and his genuine love of learning. In these sketchy efforts the villagers quickly come to life and the action develops naturally and persuasively.

The Haunted Inn * was the first of a series of dramas about Jews living on farms and in hamlets in Lithuania. Very few of them have more than a superficial knowledge of Jewish lore. In contact with the soil and farm animals rather than with the town synagogue and holy tomes, they wax strong physically but remain spiritually benighted—although their piety is sincere and ardent. Having, in a sense, straightened their backs, they acquire the characteristics of the earthy peasant. The settings for these plays are a wayside nook, a small hamlet, an inn at the crossroads, a little truck farm, a mill on a flowing stream. These Jews love the land and rejoice in the wholesome sim-plicity of nature—not with the sensitivity of the poet but with the quiet tenacity of the rustic. All work hard and accept their lot with firm faith. Physically sturdy, impetuous, superstitious, stubborn, and pious, they are governed more by impulses than reason.

Hirschbein lacked the genius to create characters in depth. Many are varied impersonations of one actor—himself; others are stereotypes, reappearing in play after play. Thus all young men are boisterous, headstrong, free sons of nature; their fathers, burdened with work and ambitions for their children, are stubborn and aggressive; their grandfathers, in the eve of life, are ripe with nestorian wisdom, love of peace, and homely friendliness. The girls are like their brothers, only more mis-chievous; their mothers work hard, worry over their children, and envy their neighbors.

If these characters lack dramatic depth, the atmosphere in which they exist possesses the stamp of authenticity. In almost every play this effect is achieved by an imperceptible aggrega-tion of intimate detail deftly interwoven with the action, for Hirschbein was intimately familiar with the environment, habits, and idiosyncrasies of his characters. Significantly, most of these plays bear such atmospheric titles as *The Haunted Inn*, *A Wayside Nook*, and *Green Fields*.

When *The Haunted Inn* was produced in English on Broadway nearly a half-century ago, poorly translated and ineptly staged, its exotic theme could not but seem bizarre and grim. Yet the drama possesses merit. A subtly superstitious atmosphere pervades and dominates the action, with the haunted inn the prevailing force. There evil spirits are said to hold their trysts and sprees, and their insinuating influence upon the people of the vicinity becomes evident as the play progresses. Bendet, a headstrong, willful man, is chagrined when he suspects Itsik, his daughter's lover, of having stolen one of his horses. In his anger he marries her to the son of a neighbor. At the wedding Itsick takes advantage of the general excitement and runs off with the bride. Since that same day the unused inn, said to be haunted, had been razed to make room for the newlyweds' home, the mishaps that occur are ascribed to the vengefulness of the evil spirits. To assuage them, the inn is rebuilt. But Bendet, sorely troubled and considering himself victimized, becomes distraught and burns down the rebuilt inn as well as his own house.

What perplexed Broadway audiences appears quite natural to one familiar with the prevailing superstition of these Lithuanian villagers. They believe in Satan and his cohorts of evil spirits as implicitly as they believe in Jehovah and his good angels. To Satan they attribute the evil that befalls them, even as they regard their joys as the gifts of God. Bendet, inwardly feeling guilty toward Itsik, fears the antagonized evil spirits. The untoward incidents convince him that they are seeking his ruination, and his mind gives way out of sheer terror. In this atmosphere of superstition, pristine life and human pathos emerge vivid and real.

A Wayside Nook has a similar setting but with a simpler situation. Two families have long lived as neighbors, the head of one being a miller and the other a gravedigger. Both men have been friends from childhood and look with favor upon the growing affection between their children. When a wealthy stranger comes to woo the gravedigger's daughter, the serene atmosphere is disturbed. The intruder tempts the gravedigger by offering to build him a mill in exchange for his consent. The latter, anxious to quit the cemetery for a more dignified task, eagerly accepts. His neighbor and friend naturally resents the prospective competition, insisting that there is hardly enough work for one mill. Neither will listen to reason and in the resulting feud the lovers are separated. At that juncture the gravedigger's father asserts his parental authority in behalf of peace. The play ends with the old friendship restored and the marriage of the enamored pair.

The action scintillates with humor. Despite the mounting tension during the fight at the close of the third act, it is quite apparent that the spirit of comedy will prevail. The characters, though not individualized, are well drawn. With the exception of the disturbing intruder, everyone talks and acts with natural simplicity. Their petty jealousies and affected animosities, their stubborn and naive behavior endear them to the audience. The atmosphere in which they are placed is pervasively bucolic: genial, simple, and charming.

The Blacksmith's Daughters and *A Life for a Life*, both written after Hirschbein's return to New York late in 1914, vary only slightly from the other rustic plays. In the first, two journeymen blacksmiths woo the twin daughters of their employer, though neither is quite certain on which his heart is set. Both pairs are shuffled until the right combination is achieved. The situation is genial and idyllic, well adapted to the comedian's art. In the second play a man of affairs offers his wealth and in the end his life for the sake of his heir, bowing with superstitious faith to the inevitability of the ancient Mosaic law.

The idyllic spirit is also evident in the one-act plays Hirschbein wrote during this period. If his longer works sometimes become tenuous and diluted, his briefer ones are comparatively meaty and solid. In *The Prophet Elijah*, *The Storm*, and *Raisins and Almonds* the folkloric themes are aptly expressed. The first deals with an old but agreeable anecdote about the man whose greed deprives him of his erstwhile Midas touch, and is developed with accelerated tempo and mild humor. The second sketch depicts the ecstatic joyousness of rustic Jews on a night of celebration. *Raisins and Almonds* possesses a fine blend of character and atmosphere. Freydele, age 14, assumes the burden of housekeeping when her mother dies suddenly. She tries to nurse her sick little brother and comfort her bereaved father. A fairylike old woman peddler visits her, presses beautiful finery upon her, and helps to find her a handsome suitor. Freydele is etched with tender strokes: her pathetic situation, naive earnestness, natural goodness, and childlike innocence combine to give her the warmth of quick life. In a sense the action is pure make-believe, but to her wistful mind it attains a reality deeper than surface truth.

Establishment of the Yiddish Art Theater in 1918 led to Hirschbein's popularity as a playwright. Previously his works had been produced by professionals in Europe, without much success, or by amateur groups interested in presenting dramas of artistic merit. For years his admirers in New York sought in vain to attract the attention of prominent Yiddish actors to his plays. When David Kessler was persuaded to read *The Blacksmith's Daughters* in 1915, he considered it too "literary" for the theater. Maurice Schwartz and Jacob Ben-Ami—the latter formerly with the Hirschbein Troupe—were confident of the popular appeal of these plays and eager to stage them in their new theater. Schwartz's financial partner, however, wanted him to begin with "a sure thing," and insisted that it be *Man and His Shadow,* by the popular playwright Z. Libin. To the producer's chagrin, but the secret delight of the more serious actors, the play proved a failure.

Schwartz was now able to produce *A Wayside Nook.* Intelligently directed and excellently acted, it became an immediate and noteworthy success. New York Jews, nostalgic for the bucolic milieu of their native towns, were charmed by the authentic presentation of Jewish life in an idyllic setting. Early in 1919 the company played in *The Blacksmith's Daughters* with equal enthusiasm and similar success. Also popular were the next two plays—*Green Fields* and *The Haunted Inn*—staged during the same season. All four works became part of the theater's repertoire. Other Hirschbein dramas produced by Schwartz—*A Life for a Life* and *Spirits Know Why*—without the rustic setting and idyllic atmosphere of the earlier plays, failed to appeal to the theater's clientele. Nor did Bertha Kalish, the prominent actress, have any better luck with *A Child of the World*.

While lecturing to Jewish audiences in cities over the North American continent, Hirschbein met Esther Shumiatcher, a young and attractive Yiddish poet, in Calgary, Canada. Emotionally frozen for two decades, ever since the tragic death of his beloved Shayndel, he now found himself strongly drawn to this girl. After a brief courtship they were married and made their home in New York. Restless as ever, always eager to see new places and meet new people, Hirschbein in 1921 set out with his wife on a two-year peregrination to Australia and South Africa. In 1924 they embarked on a tour of the world which lasted five years. They sojourned several months in India and made friends with Mohandas Gandhi and Rabindranath Tagore; traveled from country to country in Asia, meeting local Jews, noting the life of the natives, and enjoying the sight of indigenous works of art; and lived for nearly a year with the Jews who came to Crimea in 1927 to farm the land and form Jewish agricultural settlements. All through his travels Hirschbein recorded his impressions and reflections in serialized chapters in *Der Tog* which he later published in several volumes. His freshness of approach and the poetic charm of his prose made a noteworthy contribution of travelogues to Yiddish literature.

In 1916 Hirschbein wrote *Green Fields*—according to David Pinski it was composed in his house within eight days—the first of a trilogy in which Levi Isaak is the protagonist. His most ambitious dramatic work, it concerns the spiritual struggle of a rabbi who lacks the confidence and compulsion of the religious leader. In *Green Fields* the characters are similar to those of the other bucolic plays, only the fathers are less headstrong, the mothers more assertive, and the girls more mischievous. Into their workaday midst comes the demure Levi Isaak, a youthful itinerary student, and his deep, devout nature impresses itself very positively upon the small settlement. He becomes the teacher of the younger children, and his lofty mien and pious reticence lift the parents onto a higher spiritual plane. All revere him as one belonging to a superior species. The action of the play revolves around the ambition of two mothers to acquire Levi Isaak as a son-in-law and the manner in which Tzineh wins him as her betrothed. As in the earlier rustic dramas, the situation is portrayed idyllically and the dialogue is genuinely humorous.

Two Towns, the second play, presents the same characters after an interval of 20 years. Levi Isaak is now a renowned rabbi, and the leaders of neighboring towns are anxious to obtain him as their spiritual leader. Finally accepting an attractive offer, he causes a feud between the two communities— much to his regret. Fighting ensues, even an attempt at incendiarism, and angry taunts are flung at the rabbi himself. Distressed at being the cause of such enmity among his zealous followers, Levi Isaak is ready to give up the rabbinate and assume the life of a sequestered scholar. At that juncture the happy suggestion is made that his competent son Khaim be appointed to the office he was vacating, thus ending the feud.

The action in *Levi Isaak,* the final drama, concerns the proposed but unconsummated betrothal of Khaim to his cousin Dvoreh. Although the setting is the same as in *Green Fields,* the attitude of the characters is quite different. Also altered are the circumstances of the action. The old order is obviously crumbling, the ancient customs rapidly deteriorating. The rising generation is impatiently seeking to demolish what remains of the old. This disruption becomes pathetically apparent at the family reunion occasioned by the prospective engagement between Khaim and Dvoreh. The latter, influenced by modern ideas, refuses to marry without love. Her attitude appears preposterous to all but Levi Isaak; none but he appreciates her rejection of a brilliant young rabbi. He speaks to her sympathetically and defends her before the others; happy as he would be to have her as daughter-in-law, he respects the dictates of her heart. Khaim thereupon indignantly refuses to further the suit. The resulting gloom is intensified when Levi Isaak announces his decision to resign his rabbinate for the spiritual seclusion of his country home.

Dvoreh and Khaim are drawn realistically: the first, having partaken of worldly knowledge, refuses to adhere to the orthodoxy of her parents; Khaim, possessed of practical sense and aware of his own importance, accepts the rabbinate with the seriousness of the true leader. Levi Isaak is portrayed most vividly. He enters *Green Fields* as a meek and pious youth, his mind yearning for spiritual loftiness. His sojourn on the farm wakens in him a love of nature, and his resolve to avoid temptations of the flesh fails in the presence of Tzineh. For 20 years he flows with the current, becoming a highly respected rabbi and father of two children. Yet the more the routine duties of the rabbinate pall on him and he feels himself unfit for the leadership thrust upon him. Unlike his tougher-minded son he longs for the seclusion of his study, for the idyllic existence on the farm. Visiting his father-in-law and rejoicing in his beloved fields, he gains the strength of will to give up the town and its social squabbles.

In the later plays Levi Isaak loses the clear simplicity and warm personality that made him so attractive in *Green Fields*. As leader of his flock he appears intellectually flaccid. His virtues are feminine, his sympathies and yearnings sentimental; reason guides him only weakly, and like Tzineh and Dvoreh he heeds too readily the heart's innuendoes: "Where there is a heart there is everything; only the heart always leans to the right." Inured to study, he prefers to muse in solitude; chosen a leader in Israel, he confesses himself incapable of leadership —reminding one of Moshe, the "weakest link" in Peretz's *Golden Chain*. In many respects a self-portrait of Hirschbein, Levi Isaak was given by Ben-Ami the semblance and mannerisms of his creator when he played the role in *Green Fields*.

Spirits Know Why (1922) and *The Mouse with the Bell* (1924) are two quite distinct studies in mystic symbolism. The first play is a poetic delineation of folkloric superstition. Wolf, a young and moody forester, while walking one morning along the river edge, hears a girl's voice call his name from among the tall rushes. The voice tells him she is Ritele, who died a sinner at 18 and was turned into a rush. As if entranced, he heeds her plea and puts a ring over the rush. Immediately he hears girlish laughter, and a moment later Ritele stands before him in the flesh. He feels himself possessed. His affection for Rivkeh is attenuated, but he proceeds to become her fiancé. Ritele tells him she is in fact his wife, and his marriage to Rivkeh will really be the celebration of their own wedding; when Rivkeh bears him a child, he is assured by Ritele that she and not Rivkeh is the mother. In his confusion he appears bereft of sanity, and Rivkeh is frightened away from him. To rid himself of his bewitched state he flagellates himself in emulation of an ascetic of his acquaintance. The latter, endowed with occult powers and aware of Wolf's distress, instructs him in the divorce procedure with Ritele. This done, the possessed youth regains his former normal status.

The action is charged with a rich blend of cabalistic folklore. More than in Hirschbein's other works, the superstitious atmosphere is developed with poetic intensity. The quixotic speculations of the cabalists have in time evolved a highly fanciful code of action between man and the supernatural. Pious Jews assume that Satan is ever intent on causing them to sin, and that they are protected from him, as if by a magic circle, so long as they keep to the prescribed ritualistic obligations. They believe that the souls of dead sinners are damned to enter lower animals and inanimate objects, and for anyone to heed their piteous or fiendish appeals is to court calamity. Amulets and charms are worn to prevent such temptations. Wolf's act of pity toward Ritele exposed him to dire punishment, and only the ascetic's intervention in his behalf saves him from fatal consequences.

In one sense the play is a pathetic fairy tale, but in a deeper sense it is an attempt to treat dramatically a mystic aspect of Jewish folklore. Supernatural acts are presented against a realistic background to intimate the poetic quality of Jewish superstition. The fanciful is grafted on the real without sophisticated implications. As in other similar works, atmosphere dominates; stress is laid not on the development of character but on the superstitious piety of orthodox Jews.

The Mouse with the Bell, a dramatic poem, reflects certain similar characteristics. A supernatural incident is the basis in each, and in both the individuals are motivated by superstitious impulses. Here semblances cease. Written in free verse, expressionistic in form, with the setting in an American steel foundry and only one Jewish character, the work is obviously an effort on Hirschbein's part to strike out in a new direction. In its expressiveness one may detect certain similarities to the plays of Eugene O'Neil and Ernst Toller. Gad, the Jewish foundry worker, is thrown into a mass of molten metal by an anti-Semitic fellow worker. To the amazement and consternation of the men discussing the dreadful act, Gad emerges from the furnace apparently alive and ennobled in mien. Their first impulse is to flee in terror; then, struck by the miraculous manifestation, they acclaim the saintliness of the despised Jew. Thompson, the braggart owner of the foundry, and Tom, the one worker who had been friendly with Gad, speak to the apparition and are answered with their own last words. The agitation accelerates and chaos prevails. Thompson, madly defying the supernatural, sets fire to the building—to the mounting terror of the employees.

Consisting of one long scene, the work attains a spectral mood. Incident follows incident with quickened tempo. The darkness pierced by tapering tongues of flame, byplays not pertinent to the main action but charged with symbolic intent, speeches made more to elucidate subconscious thought than to further thematic development, and the mass psychology in a moment of madness—all signify an endeavor to create an atmosphere of fantastic eeriness. Yet the weird is not truly achieved; one feels all the while that the action has no basis in probability. Without the artlessness of folkloric background the supernatural appears merely simulated. To bring about the mystically symbolic resurrection in an American factory is a daring conception, but its poetic validity is weakened by its obviousness as a *tour de force*.

In 1932 Hirschbein completed *Years of Childhood*, his recollection of the first 18 years of his life. From a literary standpoint the book is unquestionably his best work. More vividly and veraciously than in his major plays, in these pages he portrays the life of rustic Jews among whom he grew up. His father's mill, the river on which it was situated, the fields and meadows on either side of it, the effect of the different seasons on the people—these and other aspects are described with remarkable tenderness and lyrical eloquence. With even deeper love he depicts his centenarian grandfather, who taught him songs according to a color scheme of his own devising; his taciturn father, already elderly, who hoped to see his youngest son grow up to be a rabbi; his affectionate and fearful mother, whose strong love gave her profound instinctive wisdom. His own childhood feelings, thoughts, and moods, altering and deepening with the years, are delineated with appealing sensitiveness. We see him develop from a weak and timid child into a curious, experimental, playful country lad, and then become a studious and serious youth of 13 who is nevertheless loath to forsake his beloved countryside for the confinement and privation of the house of study. He unfolds simply and artlessly how he discovered the world of books proscribed by the pious, and how eagerly and joyously he perused volume after volume. When he was 14 his father one day found him absorbed in a book of Yiddish songs by Eliakum Zunser. "Father looked into the book with curiosity. It was hard for him to understand that with the same letters with which the holy tomes were written one should also inscribe such songs." He also tells how he began to compose his own verses at 15; how he gradually came to learn of the world outside of his pristine environment; about the ripening of love between himself and his cousin Shayndel, and the shattering effect of her sudden death upon his adolescent emotions.

These memoirs are continued in *In the Process of Life*, which concerns his experiences up to 1910 and which appeared as a book in the year of his death, 1948. Less nostalgic and without the poetic quality of the earlier volume, this work provides a clear account of his years of development as a writer. Without means or profession, without guidance or stimulation, but with an indomitable will to succeed as a dramatist, he readily suffered privation—earning a mere pittance as a tutor—read current books by prominent writers, sought out kindred spirits, found his way to Peretz and Bialik, experimented with writing in various genres, first in Hebrew and later in Yiddish, founded the theatrical group that bore his name, and played before audiences throughout the Russian Pale. All the while he was deeply interested, without committing himself to any ideology, in the intellectual, revolutionary, and nationalistic philosophies agitating his social environment. Above all else he stressed his dedication to the artistic life and his yearning to achieve distinction as a Yiddish writer.

The ten months Hirschbein sojourned in Crimea left a deep impress upon his imagination. Soon after his return to the United States in 1929 he recorded his experiences and reflections in a volume of stories and essays. The projected settlement of Jews in Crimea farm communities and later in Birobidjan, debated intensively within and outside of Russia, long stimulated his thoughts. Having a deep love of nature, he was eager to see Jews, after many centuries of forced exclusion from the land, become tillers of the soil and eat bread made from grain which they themselves had grown. The result of his cogitation was a long two-volume novel, serialized in 1932 and published in 1935, in which he gave fictional expression to the effort of Jewish settlement in Crimea and the problems and difficulties confronting some of the pioneering settlers.

Jewish families of towns which had suffered from pogroms during the civil war following the October, 1917, revolution volunteered to farm land in Crimea. They formed a number of colonies, grew wheat and vegetables, milked cows, and sought tenaciously to live the life of peasants. *Red Fields* concentrates on one such settlement. Among the leading settlers are Bereh Kowalski, a young blacksmith and zealous communist who heads the group and seeks to establish it as a communist cooperative; Lana Brezer, dynamic daughter of a former wealthy merchant, whose mother was brutally murdered in a pogrom and who has dedicated herself to the soil and communism; and Joseph Ratner, a tailor's son and former student who now wants to become a farmer and work for a Jewish homeland under the aegis of Soviet Russia. These and others work day and night to build homes for themselves and assure the success of the experiment.

Bereh, the physically strong blacksmith, and Lana, the delicate yet dedicated girl, vie with each other to be the first in the settlement to complete a dwelling for their respective families. Lana wins out by a day, much to everyone's admiration. The two are strongly attracted to each other, but each has strong reservations. Bereh, the zealous communist, considers it improper to love the daughter of an expropriated bourgeois who is still not above suspicion; Lana, aware of his constraint and not without a feeling of guilt because of her middle-class upbringing, nevertheless resents his deprecation of her avowal of communism. Consequently their emotions fluctuate between affection and antagonism.

He resents it that each time he means well and wants to discuss with Lana the great achievements of the revolution, his feelings interfere—feelings that belong to a dying world, to the Brezer world, and destroy his good thoughts. . . . Each time he gets near Lana, an estrangement sets in. The nearer he comes to her, the further she jumps away from him. Contrariwise, when she tries to get near to him, he jumps away a thousand miles. . . .

His mind becomes confused; his emotions darken. Often it makes him hot all over, and again he shudders with cold.

Joseph Ratner, endowed with some of Hirschbein's characteristics, is neither dedicated communist nor zealous Zionist. He wants to see a solution to the millennium-old Jewish problem and is ready to accept Crimea as a homeland for his people. Wiser and more clear-visioned than Bereh or Lana, he is friendly with both and often serves as a stimulus for them to express pent-up emotions and thoughts. Bereh at first suspects him of communist deviation, but accepts his friendship after long observation and discussion. Lana likes him and uses him as a foil against Bereh, but neither feels the surge of love toward one another. In the latter part of the book the three partake in protracted discussion of the problems confronting the settlement, Soviet Russia, and Jewish nationalism.

When the announcement is made that Soviet Russia has allotted Birobidjan as a Jewish autonomy, Ratner feels impelled to go there. With him go Bereh and Simkeh Kretchmer, a girl of proletarian origin who loves him and whom he finds congenial. Lana remains in the settlement and finds comfort and affection in Benie, a son of the land who accepts communism as a way of life but is not governed by doctrinal restrictions or intellectual confusion.

In this novel we have a different Hirschbein, as much the social historian as the novelist. Jews in relation to the Soviet government and their settlement in Crimean farmland are discussed with full knowledge of the situation and with sympathetic insight. As a novelist he is less successful. His main characters lose themselves in what becomes an artificially contrived emotional struggle with pride and prejudice. Bereh and Lana are forced to remain to the end in an unresolvable conflict. Moreover, Bereh's doctrinal rigidity detracts from his human appeal, and Lana is so idealized as a paragon of prodigious energy and dedication that one tends to question her reality.

If the leading characters fall short as fictional creations, some of the less important ones are drawn more acutely.

Ratner, Lana's father and sister, Bereh's parents, Simkeh, Benie, and others are individualized portraits of Jews striving to adjust themselves to the profound changes forced upon them by a social revolution. Even better artistically are the sections describing life on the land from season to season. Here one seems to see the wheat grow, the winter storm piling up the snow to the housetops, the golden sun warming the cold earth for spring plowing. This description of nature plus the sensitive historical aspects give the book its minor distinction.

Babylon, serialized for over three years in *Der Tog* and issued in revised form in 1942 as a three-decker novel totaling 1400 pages, has a similar historical emphasis but a much broader scope—incorporating a half-century of Jewish life in the United States. The story is largely about the family of Isroel Lurie, a hardware merchant who migrated to this country in 1883 with his six sons and one daughter—his wife having died on shipboard and been buried at sea. The Luries are a typical Jewish family from the Ukraine, semi-emancipated from traditional orthodoxy, moderately educated, deeply interested in world affairs and Jewish problems. The older children are devoted to socialism or Jewish nationalism, and two of them consider the journey to America as a station stop on the way to Palestine.

In Castle Garden they are befriended by Label Halfon, a recent immigrant who has become a contractor for a shirt manufacturer and is looking for newcomers to work in his sweatshop. The father and two sons accept his offer of employment. Another son refuses to be "buried" in a factory and becomes a peddler of notions; a fourth works as a laborer but hopes to find a place on a farm; a fifth becomes a cigarmaker, and the last prefers to look for jobs that yield a "quick dollar." The girl remains at home to keep house for the men. Sweatshop labor is onerous and oppressive, causing the Luries to feel trapped in an alien and hostile land. Kreyndel, the 16-year-old girl, exerts herself to the utmost to make life toler-

able in the dingy tenement, and when Label begins to court
her she does not repel him for fear that he might make things
harder for her father and brothers.

Eventually these immigrants find their various places in the
scheme of life on the East Side. The elder Lurie becomes
rejuvenated when he falls in love with a girl worker, but their
marriage breaks up the family. Kreyndel goes to work in a
shop other than Label's in order not to be beholden to him.
Within a year the new Mrs. Lurie dies in childbirth, and
Lurie becomes so broken in spirit that life ceases to maintain
its hold on him and he dies not long after. His oldest son,
Nathan, who had come to this country imbued with the ideal
of socialism, finds work in a sweatshop intolerable and gradually becomes a labor leader involved in union organization
and periodic strikes. Shlome, the cigarmaker, is not long in
contracting tuberculosis and dies at an early age. Hillel does
find work as a farm laborer and dreams of a community of
Jewish farmers—only to end as a farmer catering to summer
boarders.

Daniel, the peddler, suffers beatings and abuse, but continues to prosper and becomes owner of a department store.
His dream of becoming a pioneer in Palestine evaporates
early, but he salves his conscience by retaining his interest in
Zionism and contributing large sums to its activity. While still
a newcomer he meets a young Irishwoman, the common-law
wife of a drunkard, and the two are immediately strongly
attracted to each other. After much effort he buys her release
from her husband. Her love for Daniel makes her fond of
Jews, and she readily accepts his religion and has her name
changed to Lillian-Ruth. She becomes the most pious member
of the Lurie family and her home is made the center for
celebrating Jewish holidays and other events.

Osher, a middle son, finds an easy, if illegitimate way of
making money, causing the family to cast him out in disgust.
In Chicago he becomes a successful racketeer, but again and
again he is sentimentally drawn to his brothers and sister,

although only Zachary, the youngest and most tolerant, will see him.

Zachary enters the sweatshop at 16, nursing neither ideals nor illusions. He goes to night school and persists at his studies until he graduates from a medical school. Like Ratner in *Red Fields*, he appears as Hirschbein's alter ego and manifests a wisdom and sympathy that endear him to all with whom he comes in contact. He continues to maintain his office on the East Side despite his increasing professional prominence, and serves the poor of the neighborhood with tireless devotion. Although he was in his youth attracted to Lillian-Ruth's sister, he knew that he would not be at ease with a Catholic-oriented wife and broke away. Some years later he becomes strongly interested in a young patient of his, Emma Berger, whose betrothed had been killed in a pogrom shortly before her migration to this country; Emma responds warmly, but in the end Zachary persuades himself that she is not the help-meet he wants. When he is a bachelor of 50, the 20-year-old daughter of one of his patients strikes fire in his heart and she loves him in return, so their marriage proves highly congenial.

Kreyndel, later Caroline Stone, remains a central character. For several years she holds Label Halfon off and prefers to earn her living as a factory worker. A cigarmaker in the same shop as her brother Shlome arouses her interest because of his poetic vision and intellectual depth, but he too is a victim of tuberculosis. His friend, a hunchback philosopher, also attracts her, but he too dies young. During her last visit to his bedside he tells her: "It doesn't pay to destroy one's life in the struggle with poverty. If you can free yourself from it, do so. You can gain joy from doing good deeds." She knows he is intimating that she should marry Label, now Leonard Stone and an increasingly wealthy clothing manufacturer. Following this advice she lives a loveless life, exerting her influence upon him in favor of his employees and using his money to help those in need.

The second generation of Luries and Stones, native born and mostly professionally trained, is shown to manifest the effect of Americanization upon the Jewish community. Daniel's two sons grow up at loggerheads to each other: the older, influenced by his mother's Irish family, is ashamed of his Jewish origin, marries a Catholic girl, becomes converted, and ends as a judge, like his father-in-law; the younger son takes after his father and feels deeply Jewish. Hillel's two sons also differ in their outlook on life: the older dislikes the farm, becomes a lawyer, and glibly favors assimilation; the other graduates as a doctor, is strongly influenced by his uncle Zachary, feels drawn to the farm, and marries an American girl who acquires a deep sympathy for the ideal of Jewishness. The Stone children are shallow participants in the process of assimilation.

The long narrative deals with all important facets of Jewish life and includes dozens of additional characters. Hirschbein has in effect provided a fictional overlay on a survey of a half-century of American Jewish experience. The story element, for all its widespread canvas and complex structure, gives little of the creative insight into human behavior expected of a major novel. Instead, one gains the impression of a prairie flatness: the characters move along the surface, wisely and humanely or foolishly and meanly, without penetrating into the fresh sluices of profound emotion. They are credible in being typical, but few attain lifelike individuality. As Hirschbein comments in one place: "It happens and happens and it seems as if nothing happens and yet a lot happens."

The characters represent clearly and cogently the social and spiritual metamorphoses of the first and second generations of East European Jews in America. They illustrate the decline of orthodoxy among the pious and of idealism among the emancipated; the manner in which absorption in work dominates the rich and poor alike. One of the newer immigrants exclaims: "It is a crime the way the millions of Jews live here. A crime that Jewish history will never forgive. Work and eat, work and wallow in one's spiritual filth . . . this is what we're doing." Hirschbein dwells at length on the effect of intermarriage and the relation between Jew and Christian, and most of all on the problem of Jewishness as a way of life and what remains of it among the American-born generation. His earlier poetic mood and mystical lyricism, which happily grace his best rustic plays, are here replaced by the considered wisdom of the fictional essayist.

In 1940 Hirschbein moved with his wife and six-year-old son to Los Angeles. There he completed the revision of *Babylon*, wrote the second volume of memoirs, and began a new novel, *On Strange Roads*, which was serialized in 1947. In 1945, however, he, who had always prided himself on his superb physical strength and believed he would live to at least 80, became invalided and suffered acutely until his death in 1948.

If on the whole Hirschbein's writings failed of literary greatness, they do fill an obvious lacuna in Yiddish literature. His portrayal of Jewish life in Lithuanian "wayside nooks" is unique; equally distinctive are his several books of travel. Immanently a mystic, his mysticism is not of religious ecstasy but of poetic folklore: earthy, naive, and whimsical. The superstitious beliefs with which he grew up lay in the front of his subconscious imagination and became sublimated in his best work. He tapped the sources of Jewish folklore and dramatized them vividly and poetically. This natural charm is absent from his later realistic fiction. Only in his nostalgic reminiscence was he able to achieve the poetic magic of idyllic prose.

Hirschbein developed a pure but passive style, truly reflecting his personality. Fastidious in his use of words, striving for rhythmic order, he restricted their meaning to pale exactness. Rich in his idiomatic expression, unerring in his folk speech, he achieved a diction at once poetic and plain, labored and lucid, dignified and unadorned. His place in Yiddish literature, measured by the solid part of his work, is therefore sizable and secure.

CHAPTER TWELVE

THE EFFLORESCENCE
OF YIDDISH IN AMERICA

DRIVEN from their native homes by pogroms and aggravated poverty, nearly a million and a half East European Jews migrated to the United States during the years 1901–1914. They ranged culturally from Hasidic pietists to conscious atheists, from bare literates in Hebrew to university graduates. Unlike the immigrants of the 1880's, they found in their new home a fully settled Yiddish culture to lean upon: several solidly established daily newspapers, weekly and monthly magazines, a flourishing theater, and a variety of social, economic, and religious organizations. Equally advantageous were the improved work opportunities: the sweatshops were then giving way to relatively sanitary and well-lit factories, wages and working conditions were being considerably improved as a result of persevering efforts of the existing unions, and opportunities for employment in other than needle trades were more abundant. It was therefore easier for them to find their economic groove and orient themselves toward the available cultural facilities.

Most of these immigrants came from medievally entrenched towns. With little or no knowledge of the modern non-Jewish world, they were at first dazed and dazzled by the radically different American milieu. Once their confusion subsided, however, most of them readily acclimated themselves to their new environment. They read one of the Yiddish dailies, attended the theater and even lectures, joined unions and social and religious organizations—which in turn greatly accelerated the cultural activities of the Yiddish-speaking Jewry. The four leading Yiddish newspapers of the 1900's—*Tageblatt, Forverts, Jewish Morgen Journal*, and *Warheit*—gained considerably in circulation as well as in quality, and became the most influential factors in shaping the cultural development of their readers.

Der Forverts, for instance, printed stories, poems, serialized novels, and critical essays by some of the leading Yiddish writers, including Peretz, Asch, Reisen, and H.D. Nomberg, as well as the writings of its regular staff. Abraham Cahan developed in 1904 the highly popular *Bintel Brief*, and soon after "The Gallery of Vanished Husbands." The first, as earlier indicated, consisted of letters that, according to Cahan, "bared the wounds of the soul"—and editorial responses that were both sympathetic and morally correct. The other feature contained detailed descriptions and photographs of men who had deserted their families—a fairly common occurrence during the years of social adjustment. The editor of this weekly column cooperated with the National Desertion Bureau, a division of Jewish Social Service maintained to help abandoned wives and their children. These features and the sentimental serials, even more than the literary contributions, served to make *Der Forverts* the most widely read Yiddish newspaper in the world, with a circulation of over 200,000 at the peak of its popularity.

With the number of Yiddish writers in America increasing markedly at the turn of the century, one or another of the newspapers engaged as regular contributors those who met with popular approval. A good many had little literary ability but a journalistic flair prized by newspaper editors. Typical among the storytellers in this group was M. J. Adershlager (1881–1940). Born in Galicia, where he received the usual *kheder* training, he turned at an early age to barbering when his father's death made him the family's chief provider. In 1899 he migrated to New York. In 1905 a letter about his union written to *Der Forverts* brought him to Cahan's attention, and his stories and sketches began to appear regularly in that newspaper. Of a trite yet titillating content, these pieces evidenced a realistic irony which appealed to many readers. His first collection, *Weltelekh* (Petty Worlds), appeared in 1910, with an introduction by Morris Rosenfeld. *Greenberg's Daughters,* his only play, was produced in 1927. A posthumous collection of his stories was issued in 1941, with an introduction by Abraham Cahan.

Among the more notable of the newer writers were H. Roisenblatt, Abraham Liessin, L. Shapiro, and Joseph Rolnick. Roisenblatt (1878–1956) came to this country in 1891. Though only 13 years old, his imagination was already aglow with memories and emotions of his native Ukrainian landscape. In time he became fully Americanized, yet his spirit remained grounded in his Jewish roots. He wrote many poems of American content, but his best lyrics sang of his childhood in Europe. Of modest aspirations and realistic self-evaluation, he wrote ironically, softly, with somewhat muted feeling; if few of his many poems attained lyrical eminence, they seldom veered from the essence of poetic expression. Some of his best verses, unfolding his sage views of the universe and his love of nature, were written in his seventies. For some years a resident of New York and Detroit, he long made his home in Los Angeles.

Liessin (1872–1938) was born Abraham Walt, of a distinguished family of rabbis. Steeped in yeshiva study during his most impressionable years, he entered adolescence kindled by the flame of social revolt. Ready to die "a martyr to the faith" as well as "a hero in battle," he expounded his views with passionate zeal and gained numerous followers. His fiery agitation soon made life too risky for him in Russia, and in 1897 he migrated to New York, where he associated himself with the Jewish socialists. He joined the staff of *Der Forverts* and contributed articles on topics of the day as well as poems of social content. In 1913 he became editor of *Die Zukunft* and during the next 25 years, despite Cahan's later antagonism and obstruction, made it the leading literary and liberal monthly in Yiddish. His personal life was clouded with tragedy: his wife died in 1912, leaving him with a daughter crippled with paralysis. To the end of his life in 1938 he devoted himself to her care; although he accepted the grievous burden devotedly, it increasingly weighted his spirit.

He began to write poems in early youth, inspired by passionate visions of social justice and the heroic lives of martyred Jews. His talent, according to B. Rivkin, was "grounded in an awareness of a feeling that burned in him with an unquenchable fire—his eternal-Jewish emotion." Being both a firm socialist and a deeply felt Jew, Liessin was not at one with either the socialists or the nationalists. Shortly after his arrival in New York he wrote: "I wander about like a stranger without any aim in the world, without striving, and I have none for whom to die and none for whom to live." He immersed himself in political work, writing eloquently of the sweatshop and its victims, but knew he was performing a social duty without the authenticity of an inner outcry. Dissatisfied, after 1904 he ceased writing verse for a number of years. Eventually he found emotional release in the Jewish past; he turned to the sages and martyrs of previous centuries and sang of their wisdom and dedication. "From Worms, Mainz, Speyer, through Prague and Lublin and Odessa, one fire extended itself, one miracle repeated itself." The tragic events in Eastern Europe during World War I and immediately after, the failure of ideals in Russia after the revolution, deeply affected him. He began to write philosophically, not abstrusely or mystically, but in the belief that suffering must lead to spiritual enlightenment if it was not to be futile and worthless; he regarded suffering as such as a Christian doctrine, a denial of life, and Jews never denied life. "For the greatest triumph," he sang, "is the triumph of the spirit which conquers the body and performs great miracles."

When L. Shapiro (1878–1948) came to New York in 1906

he was already a prominent young writer. Somewhat earlier
he had begun to write pogrom stories characterized by controlled anger and epic strength. "The Cross," "The Kiss,"
"Silence," and other brief narratives were powerful in their
tragic effectiveness and tense verbal economy. In "The Kiss"
a hooligan permits a Jew to live but forces him to kiss his foot,
whereupon the Jew bites a toe with all his might and does not
let go until both die in the scuffle. In another tale a young
Russian with an axe corners an old Jew and splits his skull
with one blow. A Jewish youth sees the murder and fires his
revolver at the hooligan, but misses. Running after him, he
finds the Russian cowering in a yard, but instead of killing
him he shoots himself.

In New York Shapiro at first wrote about immigrant Jews
settling in the Bronx section of the metropolis, workers and
petty merchants in the process of adapting themselves to their
new environment. Soon his writing almost stopped, since he
was neither interested in his new milieu nor able to delve
further into the painful recesses of his consciousness. Years
later he wrote: "The real source of my early writings were
stubbornness and stoicism, in a deeper sense—*to strengthen
the heart.* However, having written 'The Cross,' I said to myself: 'Enough, no more pogroms! I can no longer live with
pogroms in my heart'. . . ." Instead of writing, he turned his
attention to experiments with color film. Disappointment
caused him to seek forgetfulness in alcohol. Not till 1931 did
he write enough to fill a volume. *New Yorkish* contains a
mature combination of lyrical prose and satiric humor etched
with artistic acuteness. Then he again lapsed into literary
silence, having in the meantime made his home in Los Angeles. His final published work, *The Writer Goes to School*
(1944), was made up of a medley of essays, reminiscences,
reviews, and critical reflections. It was writing at a high level,
though it failed to meet his exacting hope of achievement.

Rolnick (1879–1955), spending his childhood beside his
father's isolated mill, absorbed its somber aspect of moody
loneliness, so that in many a poem he recalled its winter

dreariness rather than its summer brightness. Restive and depressed, he migrated to New York in 1899, but after two years left for England. Finding London no improvement on New York, he returned to Russia. In 1907, however, he again went to the United States, this time for the rest of his life. He always worked hard for his living, first in a factory and later in a newspaper proofroom. He began to write as a youth of 17 and in 1901 *Der Forverts* printed one of his poems; but he was unwilling to adapt himself to the newspaper's required social rhetoric and for several years did no writing. Yet the "sickness" of versifying never quite left him. "When I was not writing I felt dumb and desperate and considered myself a worm unworthy of the earth on which I found myself. I felt as one of the lowest beings in the world."

Rolnick had the acuity to perceive the dramatic as well as the pathetic aspects of commonplace events, to discover the universal in isolated and casual experiences. Obsessed by loneliness, he wrote mostly about himself with wistful sadness, yet with generic implications. Although he sang of suffering and woe, of hunger and death, he also praised love and yearning. In a characteristic poem he stated: "I am not rich. I have one garment for home and synagogue and travel. I go with it to trade on market days and to pray to God on holidays. The dust of summer falls on it, the dirt of autumn days, the filth of the gutter—and no soap can wash away the spots. . . ." In his later work he was less plaintive, manifesting a broader perspective. In "A Window to the South" his verse is freer, more lyrical, and expressive of his peace with the world. In a series of poems on the Persian poet Hafiz he gives voice to melodic allegory and metaphysical pessimism.

A dedicated individualist, a confirmed worrier, a singer of solitude and loneliness, for years angry at the world and himself, he was not a "joiner," and never became fully associated with the rebellious contemporaries with whom he was in general sympathy. "In the whole world," he asserted, "there are only two: I—who speak, and the other—who understands."

Among the immigrants in the 1900's were a number of youths who had followed the common path of childhood study in Hebrew lore and adolescent absorption in the literature of the world. In the Ukraine, Lithuania, Poland, and Galicia they had dreamt of enriching Yiddish writing with their own contributions in emulation of contemporary masterpieces. Reuben Eisland, one of them, later stated: "Only the non-Jewish writers which we then read satisfied us; from the Russian, the German, the Polish, and the French we moderns read and learned."

When social vicissitudes drove them to the United States, these youthful poets and storytellers were bursting with literary energy and zeal, bent on bringing forth the art and dreams and visions which for centuries past had been repressed in the cramped life of the ghetto. They longed to do what writers the world over were doing: mine the golden ore of folk life and give it the beauty and sparkle of esthetic expression. Determined to root themselves in the American soil, they yearned to portray the moods, feelings, aims, joys, and woes of their fellow Jewish immigrants. Repelled by the prevailing rhetoric and didacticism of established Yiddish writers, who aimed primarily to educate and guide the Jewish workers, they concentrated on artistic form and literary sophistication. As one of them later pointed out, they turned away from the prosy socialist verses preferred by *Der Forverts*, from Yehoash's and Liessin's Hebraic poetry, and sought to emulate the contemporary gentile esthetes whom they admired. Eisland remarked years later:

> When we came, Yiddish literature was in service to ideas and movements, social and national. The poets were highly respected, but their poetry, like every servant, was disdained. We proclaimed its liberation and its right to independence. We maintained that poetry must not be bound to ideas, as it exists for its own sake. . . . The new trend in Yiddish poetry is toward life, toward the daily life of the individual, with his sorrows and his joys, and all his experiences. That is why the modern poet seeks first of all to be true to himself. That is why he concerns himself

so little with world woes and national suffering, with lofty ideas and social problems. Because he knows that first of all and stronger than anything he is interested in his own self and in the thousand small events that surround him.

The need to sustain themselves sent these youths to shops, factories, and various handicrafts. In their little leisure they wrote about their dreams and doctrines. When they sought to have their stories and poems published in newspapers, then as later the prime source of publication in Yiddish, they were confronted with what seemed an insulting indifference. Occasionally some of their writing was accepted by an editor, and Sh. Yanovsky of *Die Freie Arbeiter Shtimme* opened his columns to many of them, but most of their work remained in manuscript.

As happened in other countries and on earlier occasions, the literary newcomers became rebellious and aggressive. On free evenings they gravitated to an inexpensive cafeteria, where they drank tea and read and discussed their latest compositions. Their first definite action, in 1907, was to form *Die Yunge* (The Young Ones), composed of the more enterprising writers intent on bringing their work into print. Lack of funds limited the first issue of their initial anthology, *Yugend* (Youth), to 24 pages. Some of the older writers met it with mockery and abuse, accusing these youngsters of pretense and perversity. Ignoring, even defying this carping criticism, leaders of this first "school" in Yiddish literature published *Literatur* (1910) in two successive issues extending to 144 pages each, and two years later began to bring out *Schriften* (Writings) in hefty volumes which extended, with lapses, to 1926. In 1914 the "Neo-realists" of the group, headed by Joseph Opatoshu, dissociated themselves from the "abstract romanticists" and issued their own anthology, *Die Neie Haym* (The New Home), a volume in excess of 300 pages, devoted primarily to writing of an American content. The next year Eisland and others took over *Literatur und Leben* (Literature and Life) and brought out five issues. In 1916 David Ignatov also edited *In and Out of the World*.

Together and separately the *Yunge* succeeded in moderniz-
ing and enlivening Yiddish literature, extending their influence wherever Yiddish was being written and read. Their
freshness of view and esthetic emphasis gave Yiddish writing
a new and vigorous impulse and direction. Striving for psychological insight and artistic nuance, they dug into old Yiddish tomes and enriched their diction with largely forgotten
words and idioms—an achievement of particular value in a
land where Yiddish had no roots.

In the course of time, however, some of these young
rebels grew to be "literary allrightnicks." B. Rivkin commented on this point: "They poetized the same idyls: town
idyls, Jewish idyls, love idyls, evening idyls—as if nothing
had changed." Meantime the tragedy of Jewish suffering
during and immediately after World War I had brought an
end to idyls. Moreover, as the *Yunge* as a group declined in
impetus and influence, there begun a gradual falling away of
those who had the talent and the impulse to stand alone and
produce works in the mainstream of Yiddish literature. Even
earlier, several younger writers had veered away to start
a new group, termed the *Neo-Yunge*, but after a few years
they too broke up and went their individual ways.

David Ignatov (1885–1954) was the dynamic leader of the
Yunge. Born in the Ukraine of Hasidic ancestry and strongly
impregnated with Hasidic lore in his early years, he became a
political rebel in adolescence, and went to Kiev at the age
of 18, where he was soon arrested and imprisoned. Migrating
to New York in 1906, he became a factory worker. When his
first literary efforts were rejected by several editors, he led
other youthful aspirants into the formation of *Die Yunge*. He
edited their initial anthology, *Yugend*, in which appeared his
first published story, as well as later anthologies sponsored by
the group with the cooperation of various associates. His
domineering behavior led to a split in 1914, but his energetic
efforts in behalf of young writers was recognized even by his

opponents. More than anyone else he fought for their rights in the face of an almost closed system of publication. He rejected the implication that those who failed to become regular contributors to Yiddish newspapers were *ipso facto* unsuccessful. In the anthologies he edited he included poems and stories rejected by established periodicals, thus encouraging many of the aspiring writers. Stressing art for art's sake, he made the compilations attractive in appearance as well as theoretically pleasing to his esthetic colleagues.

If Ignatov distinguished himself as a literary leader and dedicated editor, his achievement as a writer is less notable— largely because his ability could not always match his vaulting ambition. At once an exponent of pure esthetics, deeply Jewish in spirit, and a man of the world, his effort to unite all three factors in his fiction resulted, more often than not, in excessive rhetoric. Endowed with a fine sense for language and vivid descriptive power, he tended to write nervously, even pretentiously, thus reflecting his own ebullient personality.

To him, a Hasid at heart, "reality is a wonderful dream and the dream a mystic reality." Two of his works, *The Hidden Light* (1918) and *Wonder Stories of Old Prague* (1920), were written in the Hasidic tradition: mystically, romantically, sentimentally. In *The Golden Boy* (1921) he symbolized light as the glorious brightness of the Sabbath, the radiant essence of the universe—a haunting vision of the elect. In his realistic fiction, especially *In the Cauldron* (1918) and *On Distant Roads* (3 volumes, 1932), he himself is obviously the protagonist. In the first he is a writer and literary leader who wants to see factory workers farm the land; in the second, a highly ambitious and much too involved vista of Jewish life in America, he is a socialist labor leader who believes in God and is buffeted by both radicals and the orthodox. In both novels he is primarily concerned with the ideal of social salvation. Only in a story like "Phoebe" (1918) is he at his best, delineating the character of a flirt with mastery and insight. In 1939 he published *To a New World*, a biblical tragedy; another drama on a biblical theme, *Gideon*, appeared in 1953, a year before he died.

Mani Leib (Brahinsky, 1884–1953) came to the United States in 1905 and worked for many years in a shoe factory. Like Ignatov a revolutionary in Russia, of a theoretical bent and emotional temperament, he wrote lyrics within the framework of the doctrine he had evolved for the *Yunge*. Boldly imaginative, without reticence, consciously Bohemian, he wrote of his most intimate experiences and reactions with the outcry of a tortured soul. Having sung folksongs with his mother from infancy, he injected their rhythm and melody into much of his verse, so that a number of his poems, according to B. Rivkin, read like "folk songs that became folk tales," and therefore had immediate appeal to children. Although his poetry was one long exposition of himself, it combined national and social content with folk legends. A man of many moods, he sensed tragedy and mystery everywhere. In "Quieter, Quieter," a poem about the Messiah, he ends pathetically: "If we are fooled, and we are mocked, and we waited in vain the whole long night, we shall in our anguish bow down to the hard floor, and we shall be quiet, quieter and quieter." Whether he wrote of Elijah, the poor, or the city, he employed a diction at once sensitive, precise, and evocative. Concentrating on his insistence that verbal art is the instrument of self-enrichment in literature, he attained a mastery of lyric nuance and beauty. Many of his poems appeared posthumously, as did the article in which he summarized his life and work:

> An immigrant, bringing with me native landscapes, ideals of socialism and humanity, nebulous artistic impressions of German romanticists and French symbolists, of Russian writers from Pushkin to Blok, and thrust into a sweatshop and poverty, with little time to write, what could I do? But the little I did do is my own, achieved by myself.

Zisha Landau (1889–1937), youngest of the original *Yunge*, was the most colorful of the group. Born of a distinguished rabbinical family, early imbued with the spirit of Hasidism, he came to New York in 1906 a romantic rebel. Handsome, extroverted, impetuous, a brilliant conversationalist, he quickly established his eminence among the *Yunge*. Working as a house painter to earn his living, he devoted his free time to poetry. Influenced by Heine and later European poets, he extolled art for art's sake. Mani Leib wrote to him: "You came, Zisha, and said: 'Yiddish poetry must begin with us as purely artistic song.'" Landau wrote romantically of longing, moodiness, and depression; a modern troubadour, he was playful, ironic, and sensuous; yet much as he shunned rhetoric, he could not avoid thinking rhetorically. Later he admitted that his early verse was of little worth.

Having in time outgrown his theatrical cleverness, he began to write poems of social and spiritual content. A number were in the form of prayers, and one of his best was a song about the founder of Hasidism. Yet in his continued effort to appear contradictory he wrote with more sophistication than originality or deep feeling. "Contradictions," he admitted, "are the logic of my soul, my need, my habit." Thus he was critical of women and socialism largely to be different. His puppet plays under the general title of *Nothing Really Happened* were satirical to a point of banality. Yet a good part of his poetry contained exceptional verbal sensitivity and evocative imagery.

Reuben Eisland (1884–1955), also a prominent protagonist of the *Yunge*, came to this country in 1903 and was one of the first to expound the doctrine of esthetics as opposed to the prevailing emphasis on social content. A worker like the others but neither as dynamic as Ignatov nor as boisterous as Landau, he was more imagist than lyricist in his poetry. Much of his verse dealt with the daily life about him: the poor and drab existence of the factory worker. He also wrote about important literary personalities, centering his attention on what seemed to him the essential trait. His great emotional experience concerned his love for Anna Margolin, the poet whose life was as adventurous as it was unfortunate, and which he described with deep feeling in his valuable reminiscences. It stimulated him at the age of 35 to write love lyrics of emotional depth and beauty. Later, suffering from a weak heart, he made his home in Florida.

I. J. Schwartz, another conspicuous member of the *Yunge*, was born in 1885 and came to the United States in 1906. He evidenced the strong influence of the Hebraic poetry of Yehuda Halevi and Kh. N. Bialik—one of whose poems he had successfully translated while still in Russia—in his Yiddish verse. He possessed the healthy peacefulness of nature at rest, and even his poems of America were imbued with the Sabbath spirit. Dissatisfied with life as a worker on the East Side and longing for more intimate association with the land of his adoption, he settled in Lexington, Kentucky. Familiarizing himself with the poetry of Walt Whitman and recent American poets, he began to write about life in his new home. *Kentucky* (1925) is a volume of verse about Negroes, Southerners, and Jews, written with strong sensuousness, fresh observation, and sympathetic insight. Equally significant was his briefer poem, "George Washington," a study of an easygoing, simple-minded Negro controlled by his instincts who emerges an alive and attractive personality. Other of his American verse extols the prairie and the land. In the mid-1920's he returned to New York, published translations of *Julius Caesar* and *Hamlet*, wrote again on Jewish themes in an American setting, and composed "Childhood Years," a long autobiographical poem. *The Golden Epoch in Spain* contains translations from the Hebrew writings of Yehuda Halevi, Solomon Ibn Gabirol, and other medieval Spanish Jews. Never careful with his diction and prosody, his verse had a poverty of language and imagery that gave it the effect of prosiness.

Isaak Raboy (1882–1944) grew up in Bessarabia, and his childhood closeness to the soil colored his outlook and interest. He arrived in New York in 1904 and had his first stories published two years later, sketches of his native land in all its natural beauty. The least bohemian of the *Yunge*, he worked in a hat factory and wrote evenings. The urge to live close to the soil did not leave him, however, and he decided to attend the Jewish Agricultural School in Woodbine, New Jersey, supported by Baron de Hirsh. Two years later he left for the Middle West, worked on farms, and took root in rural America. His first novel, *Mr. Goldenbarg* (1913), depicts farm life in the Dakotas, a setting new to Yiddish literature. Its protagonist loves to farm, obtains a homestead section of land, and to the surprise and envy of his unfriendly Christian neighbors not only fully develops his 160 virgin acres but becomes the most efficient and successful farmer for miles around. Having no son of his own, he is very anxious for his one Jewish farm hand to marry his daughter and inherit his land. Isaak, however, depicted in Raboy's image, longs to settle in Palestine and leaves Mr. Goldenbarg a lonely and disappointed man. Raboy's second novel, *Seaside* (1918), deals with Jewish farm life in Connecticut. One of his best works, *A Jew Came to America* (1926), delineates realistically immigrant efforts at adjustment in the tenements of Delancy Street. *Bessarabian Jews* (1928) and *Nine Brothers* (1936) treat nostalgically yet somewhat dully Jewish rural life in his native land. In the latter autobiographical novel he has Isaak (himself) come to America, attend an agricultural school, and go west to domesticate wild horses. In *The Jewish Cowboy* (1942) another Isaak goes to North Dakota, works as a cowboy, and makes good despite the antagonism of those around him. In all these books Raboy writes simply, even baldy, yet with an intimacy that frequently verges on the lyrical. He creates his main characters out of his fantasy and gives them the impress of his own personality, so that American and Bessarabian farmers are hardly differentiated, yet his portrayal of horses is tender and truly affectionate. In the 1920's Raboy joined the communist *Freiheit* and broke politically with most of his earlier friends.

A.M. Dillon (1883–1934) arrived in New York in 1904 and was an early member of the *Yunge*. His verses appeared in the second volume of *Literatur*, and later he published much of his work in *Die Zukunft*. Of a pessimistic turn of mind, he was romantic enough to court poetically a Brooklyn Dulcinea and extol the feminine ideal. He occasionally attacked his alleged detractors, although he was not unaware of his shortcomings. In one poem he wrote: "I fool myself. I transform thorns into flowers and carry the thorns about the world, and now my fingers are bloodied red." His best verses are of death, as if with his death he wished to hurt the world inimical to him. In a cycle of 18 poems he describes his disgust with life and his decision to sell his soul to Satan in order to taste of worldly pleasures. His later work, however, reveals a more positive attitude toward life.

B. Lapin (1889–1952) was of a more optimistic temperament, although fear and apprehension characterize a number of his poems. Brought to Argentina as a child of six, only to be returned to Russia four years later, he came by himself to the United States in 1909. Already a published poet by then, he joined the *Yunge* and contributed to the refinement of Yiddish prosody and verbal assonance. In 1913 he went to Argentina but returned four years later. Much of his verse has an ethical base and concerns the common life of Jewish workers, who are treated more with a sense of wonder than of pathos. His religious poems are noted for their metaphysical and mystical groping. His translations from English poetry are particularly distinguished, and those of Shakespeare's sonnets, on which he labored nearly eight years, are impressive for their sensitive accuracy and lilting subtlety. In a volume appearing shortly before his death, *The Full Pitcher* (1950), he manifests a mastery of new words and original rhymes as well as a humane view of life.

Although Moshe Leib Halpern (1886–1932) associated for a time with the *Yunge*, he was personally too eccentric to adhere to any group. Born in Galicia, he went to Vienna as a boy of 12 to study painting and remained there for ten years. In the interim he familiarized himself with modern German literature and was particularly influenced by

Nietzsche's writings. Coming to New York in 1908, he worked at various tasks to earn a living—and often had hardly that. "In dingy saloons," he wrote, "I live my nights, a heavy grayness fills my days." While still in Vienna he had begun to write in German, but association with Jewish writers turned him to Yiddish. In New York the bitterness and coarseness characterizing his verse did not help his literary career. He went to Montreal in 1912 to assist in editing a weekly, but soon returned when it failed. His feeling of uprootedness deeply disturbed him and he complained that he was "everywhere a stranger, struggling worriedly like my brother Don Quixote with his wind mills." This sense of alienism he best articulated in the poem "In a Strange Place," published in the 1913 issue of *Schriften*. Averse to the bombast and didacticism of the older poets and repelled by the emphasis of the *Yunge* on verbal dexterity and esthetic form, he rebelled against both in verses at once coarse and lyrical. In poem after poem he bemoaned his fate, and none of his outwardly droll fooling or mocking negation concealed his inner hurt and suffering, his anger and despair. "Much as I struggle with myself to see only what is pure and beautiful," he exclaimed, "I see only what is as repulsive as a piece of rotten carcass, which waits in the sun to become food for worms, flies, and mice." Nor would he make peace with life. "In the Golden Land" began: "Would you believe me, mother, that everything here is turned to gold, that gold is made of blood and iron, of blood and iron day and night?"

In 1917 he wrote to Raisele Baron, his future wife: "You know, often it seems to me I will lose my mind from pondering and suffering. What do I want? There is a world full of people—many of them live better than I. How do they comfort themselves? Are their shoulders so broad that they can carry the burden of life and not feel it?" He did not lose his mind, but acted the mountebank in public and wept in the loneliness of silence. *In New York* (1919), which contains some of his best poems, is at once lyrical and sardonic, gentle and coarse; now "raging as the waves of the ocean" and now sitting with head lowered in his isolation, he gave voice to the strangeness and suffering that made up his life.

> The restiveness of a wolf, the peace of a bear, the wildness cries in me; boredom listens to it—I am not what I think I am, I am not what I want to be. I am a magician, and the plaything of magic. I am a puzzle that struggles by itself, fleeter than the wind but bound to a stone.

In 1921 he joined the *Freiheit* and was made much of by the communists, but in 1924 he resigned, unable to conform to the constraints of proletarian dogma. In that year he published his best-known book, *The Golden Peacock*, a collection of poems displaying new forms, new rhythms, new attitudes; but it is also sharp and prickly with mockery and repressed anger. Some of the lines are obviously permeated with painful intensity and are a powerful indictment of human hypocrisy and cruelty. He deliberately appeared the opposite of what he really was: sardonic when in earnest, coarse when gentle, brazen when shy. Like his father before him he clowned and acted the buffoon to conceal his suffering and sadness. His last eight years were a period of illness, pain, and neglect. B. Rivkin stated: "Moshe Leib was starved physically and spiritually, and thus we lost him." In his search for bread he sojourned in Detroit, Cleveland, and Los Angeles. Sickness and indigence dogged him everywhere, and he returned to New York "as a bird shot down in the field grass, whatever is ill and dying weeps in me; my life is a wound, unseen, a wound within the world."

All his adulthood he struggled to reach the peak at the risk of falling to death. Aware of his own poetic prowess, impelled to prophesy, he would not yield to reality, as the weak do, and in his attempt to climb over obstacles he kept stumbling, to his grievous hurt. "Has the eagle large wings? I have broad strong hands. Does life consist of struggle and love? I have blood that shouts and burns." In "My Will" he told how he packed his poems into his old coat and hung it out of his window, and when asked about it replied: "These are my years that became mildewed between the old wisdom-stink of my wonderful book case." He died of a heart attack at the age of 46, and two of his volumes appeared posthumously. Mostly lyric in tone and gentle in content, the poems cry for peace and recognition. In "Momento Mori" he asked: "If Moshe Leib would vow in tears that death drew him as one is drawn on a lonely evening to the window of his dearly beloved—would anyone believe Moshe Leib?"

Isaak Reis, better known as Moshe Nadir (1885–1943), also came from Galicia and similarly resorted to clowning, the better to aim his barbs at the smug and submissive behavior of his fellows, although late in life he became overly satirical. He arrived in New York in 1898 and attended American schools. In 1902 he published his first verses under his own name. When the *Yunge* rebelled against the literary establishment, he associated with them as a matter of course. He edited humorous journals and contributed to *Der Kibitzer* and *Der Groiser Kunds*, popular comic weeklies. Wit, humor, and satire were meat and bread to him and he began to write under the pseudonym of Moishe Nadir, which signified: "Here you are, simpleton." In 1915 he published *Wild Roses*, an irreverent, moody, gently caustic collection of his early verses. About that time he became a regular contributor to *Der Tog*, and his popularity increased from year to year. A highly dexterous verbal juggler, making ingenious use of his Galician Yiddish dialect, he manipulated words and their combinations to achieve his incisive humor. He created his "genial idiot" and similar characters to bring to his readers truths he dared not convey in serious prose. In 1921 he changed to the *Freiheit* to be with his friend Halpern, but his commitment to communism was sentimental and lyrical. He wrote plays and did a good deal of translation. In 1939 he left the *Freiheit* in protest against the Stalin-Hitler pact. By this time he was obsessed by a deep fear of death, which came to him in 1943. It might be said of him that a vulgarly comic overlay hid a genuine sensitivity in much of his writing. In splintering himself into several character segments, he only weakened his authentic talent. Soft and sentimental, he avoided the bother of discipline. His word-play and whimsey overshadowed his spiritual seriousness. Yet while his work lacks wholeness, individual poems and prose sketches stand up with the best.

By the end of World War I the more successful of the *Yunge* were employed by newspapers or organizations, and their writings were finding permanence in bound volumes. Time, while revealing their weaknesses and limitations, impelled these rebels of a decade earlier to protect their vested literary claims against younger and critical competitors. Eisland wrote retrospectively in 1944:

> The *Yunge* sought to avoid themes of which it was easy to become rhetorical and declamatory. . . . This led the *Yunge* to psychological insights and variegated nuances. It also led them to dark corners. Every poet who is in the least self-critical knows his weaknesses before anyone else. There are times, however, when he ignores them. The remedy was brought by the Introspectivists. The leaders of this school, as we before them, perceived our weaknesses and did not hesitate to expose them.

These rebels, maintaining that the world exists only to the extent that it is reflected in us, contended that the esthetic emphasis and rigid prosody of the *Yunge* was stifling the creative impulse and producing little more than literary chaff. The chief exponents of this subjectively idealistic assumption were Glantz-Leyeles, Glatstein, and Minkov. Calling themselves *Insichisten* or Introspectivists, they in 1920 published *In Sich Anthology*. Disdaining the constraints of rhyme and rhythm, and consciously avoiding national and social subjects, they declared: "We Introspectivists believe that free verse is best suited to the individuality of rhythm and therefore, and for no other reason, we prefer it to other forms of verse." They were of course embracing the current tendencies in American and European poetry, just as the *Yunge* had been influenced by earlier literary fashions.

The most articulate and aggressive Introspectivist was

Aaron Glantz-Leyeles (1889–1966). Born and educated in Lodz, Poland, he went to London in 1905, where he remained until he settled in New York in 1912. A socialist-territorialist from adolescence, he devoted himself to advancement of Jewish education and culture. He began to publish his poems in 1909. When *Der Tog* was founded in 1914 he became a member of its staff and remained a regular contributor to the end of his life, using his own name for his prose and Leyeles for his verse. A man of varied interests, strong convictions, and impetuous enthusiasms, he wrote on cultural, literary, and political topics in a prose that effervesced with verbal vividness and ideational zeal.

In *Labyrinth* (1918) and subsequent poems he manifested the tenets he had evolved in his Introspectivist credo:

1. Employ simple language, always exact and not merely decorative words.
2. Create new rhythms, as an expression of new moods; introduce free verse, but not as the only method of writing poetry.
3. Permit absolute freedom of thematic selection.
4. Present images . . . create clear and definite poetic concentration—the quintessence of poetry.

He further elaborated:

Each poem must be a discovery and a work of creation. . . . New forms are the expression of new content. . . . Is Homer old? And the Bible? And Dante? And Shakespeare? And Goethe? Yes—they are old. Moreover, for me they are no longer literature. Their value is great—the value of monuments.

Later he retreated from this extreme posiiton. At the time his assertions aroused much debate and discussion among Yiddish writers, but in the end it was generally admitted that Glantz-Leyeles and his associates had helped free poetry from the constraints imposed upon it by the *Yunge*.

Leyeles experimented with rhymes, rhythms, meters, and forms. Ingenious and imaginative, he composed triolets, ballads, villanelles, chansons, sonnets, and études. Words and images crowded his consciousness, and he had to curb his impulses to keep from losing control of the poem in progress. "As far as I'm concerned, I say it clearly and directly that when I write I must deliberately repress the surge of words and rhymes that come to my pen, to my paper. . . . More, I do not strain in the least. I could write in even more complex forms if I would yield to temptation."

Like a number of other Yiddish writers, Leyeles had great admiration for the American democratic spirit. He loved not only the stone-and-steel maelstrom of New York but the broad valleys and high mountains of the country's continental expanse. In many earlier poems and in *America and I* (1963) he sang of his adopted land with affection and gratitude.

> Only in the land America, of all the Jewish tribes, did my people eat bread in security, rest in their own beds, lived, worked, and built in freedom. . . . Here I have dreamt my boldest dreams, here I have best understood the Jewish spirit as well as the man in me with his breadth and restrictions.

Intense Jew that he was, Leyeles was inspired by visions of the messianic ideal. In *Osher Lemlen* and especially in *Shlomo Molkhu* he dramatized the conflict between the dream of redemption and unyielding reality. Basing his tragedy on the historic Shlomo Molkhu, born a Christian of Marrano parents in Portugal and a favorite at court until he became a Jew in the belief that he was the God-inspired Messiah, Leyeles developed the theme of redempiton with poetic pathos and fictional exuberance. Moved now by his irresistible mission, Shlomo disregards the realistic caution of David Rubeni, a more pragmatic self-styled savior, and of the cowed Jews of Rome, and boldly proclaims his mission to the pope and the emperor—and goes to his doom a confident visionary prophet. Each of the ten scenes sparkles more with crackling rhetoric than lustrous poetry, but the work as a whole possesses the elements of dramatic distinction.

His poetry was honored when *A Jew at Sea* (1946) won the Lamed Prize and when he received, in 1965, the Leivick Award for Literature and an honorary degree from the Hebrew Union College in Cincinnati.

The Hasidic spirit is more deeply ingrained in Jacob Glatstein, born in Lublin in 1896, than perhaps any other contemporary Yiddish writer. He came to New York in 1914 and attended New York University Law School. Association with his classmate N. B. Minkov turned his attention to Yiddish and in 1919 he published his early poems. In that year he joined Leyeles and Minkov in proclaiming the Introspectivist credo. His first volume, *Jacob Glatstein* (1921), stimulated interest in that the few poems presented him as a person of intellect with latent sensitivity to Yiddish and Jewishness.

During succeeding years he published a number of other volumes of poetry as well as works of fiction and literary criticism. Since 1926 he has been a staff member of *Der Morgen Journal* and *Der Tog* and active on *Der Yiddisher Kempfer* and civic and literary undertakings. From the first it was readily obvious that his literary gifts were of superior merit. His mastery of diction and prosody, expressed in a pure, musical Yiddish, quickly placed him among the leading contemporary writers. His first four volumes, written in free verse, were noted for their lyrical lilt, occasional satire, and affectionate regard for Jewish themes. In *Credo* (1929), for instance, he is cynical, if occasionally lacking in clarity; yet "Shinny Mike" is, in L. Shapiro's phrase, an "etching in bronze." In other poems he is more the painter and sculptor than the singer, although he is always lyrical.

In 1938 he visited his native city of Lublin and was deeply shaken by the hatred toward Jews in that part of Europe, which he felt hovering over them with the oppressive ominousness of impending catastrophe. In his prose triology— *When Yash Traveled* (1938), *When Yash Arrived* (1940) (*Homecoming at Twilight*, in English, 1962), and *Emil and Carl* (1942)—he related his depressing experiences and reflections, weaving into its pages fictional speculations of Hasidic thought and affirmation that highlighted his own foreboding while stressing the unique faith of pious Jews in their certainty of survival. In the third volume he deals directly with Nazi persecution and brutishness. He also wrote a highly pessimistic poem, "Good Night, World," in which he expressed his deep disgust with a civilization that permitted Nazi genocide. With a cry of despair but also of disdain he exclaims: "Good night, broad world, big stinking world, not you but I shut fast the gate. . . . I go back to my old quarters, away from Wagner's idolatrous music to the pious melody. I embrace you, my grubby Jewish life. The joy of returning weeps within me."

The holocaust in Europe preyed upon his consciousness and gnawed at his conscience. Almost without being aware of it, he returned to conventional rhyme and meter in poems that seared the mind. In "Millions Dead" he exclaimed: "When the earth will be plowed and sowed, it will yield pitch-black bread; the wheat and corn will ever smell with millions dead. . . . Mark not that they died for us, for we are sentenced to live for them, so that their death shall flow in our veins in order that the world may shudder." His thoughts also turned nostalgically to his martyred father and the latter's way of life. In "The Sabbath" he wrote: "Once in my youth I compared a violated Sabbath of mine as a common weekday to my father's Sabbath made holy by observance. . . . Even then it became clear to me that my Sabbath passed like a short Friday, while my father's Sabbath extended to a year of mine." And thinking of his youth in Lublin and the people he knew there, he declared: "Folk of my good father, on alien Polish soil. How much goodness you have taught me from my earliest school days!"

All his affection for his fellow Jews, and especially for the Hasidim, he concentrated in his love of Yiddish. In *The Joy of the Yiddish Word* (1961) he sings of the tragedy of his generation and of his pride in Israel. These lyrics relate communal experiences and sorrows; they become ecstatic when they concern Yiddish: "How can I be false to you? You are not merely my mother-tongue, the speech of my cradle, but the seal on all of my thought." And in what Eliezer Greenberg calls his Song of Songs, he exults: "O let me approach to the joy of the Yiddish word. . . . Let me not for one moment forget the Yiddish word."

On the occasion of his seventieth birthday Glatstein was honored with the Leivick Award for Literature, no doubt for what Greenberg summarized as "a magic combination of meditative intellectuality and glowing emotion."

The third of the original Introspectivists, N.B. Minkov (1893–1958), was born in Warsaw and came to the United States in 1914. Although he later graduated from New York University Law School, he earned his modest living as lecturer and teacher, giving courses in literature both in Yiddish and English. He was also managing editor of *Die Zukunft*, and edited *Foundation* in the 1930's, in which he included his studies of classic Yiddish writers, later issued in book form. His first Yiddish poems were printed in 1918. Influenced by American imagists as well as European contemporaries, he permeated his verse with the flavor of intellectualized emotion. Primarily a philosophical poet, a nay sayer, and deeply ethical, he ever searched for order, but his abstract images and thoughts did not always emerge clearly enough. In one of his poems he states: "You wrote that clarity is the essence. This thought perturbs me—at times hatefully—because our time is drunk with insanity and betrayal, because our sweetest dream is affianced to a shudder." His later studies of Elia Levita and Glückel of Hameln, *Six Yiddish Critics* (1954), and *Pioneers of Yiddish Poetry in America* (1956) are acutely interpretive volumes of literary criticism.

The foregoing survey dealt with the most prominent of the Yiddish writers who had come to America prior to World War I—Joseph Opatoshu and H. Leivick excepted. Scores of others were of course contributing to enrichment of the literature during the 20th century. Among them were members of the several "schools" as well as those who belonged to none. In addition there were a goodly number of literary critics and publicists who have added considerably to the range and richness of Yiddish writing. The following discussion includes some of the additional well-known poets and storytellers.

A. Almi (Sheps, 1892–1963) was born in Warsaw and had his first poem printed in 1907. For some time he was a staff member of *Der Moment*, in which he published humorous essays and stories of folklore. In America, where he arrived in 1912, he worked on *Die Tageblatt, Der Keneder Adler* (The Canadian Eagle), and other newspapers. His several volumes of verse are inclined to satire and humor. His study, *Chinese Philosophy and Poetry* (1923), was a novel addition to Yiddish literature. Equally important are his polemical literary criticism and memoirs. Of an unhappy disposition, he ended his life by suicide.

A. Allquit (1896–1963) came to the United States in 1914 and became a tailor. In 1926 he joined the staff of *Der Morgen Journal*. Earlier he had associated himself with the Intro- spectivists and wrote expressionistic verse and stories. None were collected in book form.

Ephriam Auerbach, born in Bessarabia in 1892, began to write in Russian in 1908 but turned to Yiddish a year later. He sojourned in Warsaw in 1911 and then went to Palestine to join a kibbutz. In 1915 he came to America. An active Zionist, he taught in Jewish schools and contributed to various periodicals. His first volume, *Caravans* (1918), was a collec- tion of poems about Israel. *The Red Thread* (1927) contains notable lyrics on social and national themes. *Clear Is the Old Spring* (1940), devoted to verse on the nature of eternal Jewishness, was awarded the first Lamed Prize. *Jacob's Tents* (1953) treats national Jewish life, *White City* (1954) con- cerns life and activity in Tel Aviv, and *The Steppe Is Awake* (1962) returns nostalgically to the land of his birth.

M. Bassin (1889–1963) was drafted into the Russian army in 1907. Caught agitating his fellow soldiers with his radical views, he managed to escape and came to the United States. Of a literary turn of mind, he wrote poems and articles for various newspapers and magazines including popular verses for children. He is best remembered for his editions of *500 Years of Yiddish Poetry* (2 volumes, 1917) and *American Yiddish Poetry* (1940).

B. J. Bialostotsky (1893–1962), born in Kovno, began to publish his poems in 1909. Two years later he migrated to the United States, where he taught in Jewish schools. In 1922 he joined the staff of *Der Forverts*. Addicted to constant inner perturbation, he evoked in his several volumes of poetry the turbulence of seething lava. Z. Weinper stated that Bialostotsky's poems have a tune "not melodic, which enters the heart, but one that boils, seethes, seizes, calls, and gives no peace." Bialostotsky, describing himself as "short and thin and pointed," intimated: "It is possible that if I were the son of normal people, I might not have become a writer. The longing for the normal, healthy life made me impatient, and it was this restlessness which made me seek an outlet through writing." None of this restiveness, however, is evident in his comprehensive and competent volume of literary criticism.

Menakhem Boraisho (Goldberg, 1888–1949) came of a literary family and began to write under his given name. In 1905 he went to Warsaw to show his poems to Peretz and, with his encouragement, printed his first verses in 1907. He wrote for *Haint* (Today), the Warsaw daily, until he was drafted into the Russian army. Migrating to the United States in 1914, he became a journalist and contributed to several periodicals. *A Ring in the Chain* (1916) and *Sand* (1920) contain poems of distinction. *Zavel Riemer* (1923), published under his final pseudonym, is an epic poem free of his early sentimentalism. Zavel, a poor, shy, gifted worker, buys a violin with his small savings and teaches himself to play well and to compose songs of love and longing that soon become popular among the youth of the town. He himself remains too timid to mix socially until a wealthy student on vacation cajoles him into visiting his wealthy home with the promise that his sister will give him lessons in languages. The effect of this association on him and his family and the unhappy outcome are told with lyric felicity and sympathetic realism. In 1926 Boraisho joined *Die Freiheit*, but left it in 1929 when it condoned the Arab attack on the Jews, and worked on several short-lived weeklies. In 1933 he was employed by the American Jewish Congress and remained with it for 14 years. His most important work during this period was *The Walker* (1943), which summarized his life of suffering in Noah Markan's wanderings. A work of 500 pages, it seeks to ascertain the essence of Jewishness, to discover the center underlying the diverse elements in Jewish history. Lyrical yet reflective, the sense of the poem flows from fear to faith. In all his mature writing Boraisho scrupulously avoided the easy way, shunned verbal conventions, and ever sought new words and novel rhythms—at times to his own hurt.

Barukh Glazman (1893–1945) studied in a yeshiva before he came to the United States in 1911, where he worked as a house painter and went to school evenings. He enrolled at Ohio State University and graduated in 1918. For a time he wrote in both English and Yiddish, then limited himself primarily to Yiddish, in which he had begun to write in 1913. In 1924 he went to Russia, then to Poland, and sojourned there until 1930. During this period he published his work in both Europe and America. *Lands and Lives* (2 volumes, 1935) depicts a Jewish family from its Russian origins to its establishment on American soil. In all his writing he manifested a realism that reflected the influence of the newer fiction in other languages. One of the most Americanized of Yiddish writers, he delineated mainly uprooted and upset Jews on both sides of the Atlantic.

Isroel Goichberg was born in 1894 and came to the United States in 1913. He studied engineering at the State University of Iowa but did not practice it; instead he became a teacher of Yiddish. He began to write in 1914, and his verses for children and adults appeared in a number of periodicals. Like so many other Yiddish poets in America, he wrote much about the city: its manifold sounds, variegated sights, swiftness of pace, magical skyscrapers, and human turmoil. *Songs of Our Generation* (1925) is a work of translation from the Russian. *Good Morn-*

ing (1928) and *Verticals* (1935) are poems for children which have attained considerable acclaim. In 1946 he published *Nemerov*, poems steeped in the Jewish tragedy in Europe. For many years he has edited a juvenile journal used widely in Jewish classrooms. He has also continued to translate Russian poetry.

Khaim Grade, born in 1910, spent his youthful years in yeshiva study. When he began to write Yiddish verse in 1932, his superior poetic talent became readily apparent. As a leading member of the "Young Wilno" group, his work was published in Yiddish journals the world over. Niger commented: "Khaim Grade's poems are ecstatic nature hymns. He humanizes nature. . . . He loves to portray it in its turbulent and stormy state." Grade's first volume appeared in 1936; a number of others followed. His authentic poetic voice is especially evident in *A Mother's Will* (1949), which was awarded the Bimko Prize the following year.

During World War II he found refuge in Soviet Russia. With the coming of peace he sojourned in Paris and helped organize the surviving Yiddish writers seeking to make their home in France. In 1948 he came to New York and has since written lengthy poems, fiction, and his memoirs. He also edited a one-volume edition of Yoneh Rosenfeld's writings. His volume of short stories, *Mother's Sabbath* (1955), received the Lamed Prize. Of particular interest is the first story, "My Quarrel with Hersh Rasseyner," which is essentially a philosophical-religious dialogue between the author, who is religiously enlightened, and his fellow yeshiva student, an intense *Mussar* fanatic, on the nature of Judaism and its relation to the holocaust. Its charged emotional current stings the reader with its agonized analysis of the two poles of human thought.

Eliezer Greenberg was born in 1896 and grew up in Lipkan, Bessarabia, for which he has yearned nostalgically long after leaving it. He came to Boston, where he worked in a leather factory. In 1920–1921 he studied at the University of Michigan for a year. Having begun to write verses shortly after his arrival in Boston, and eager to familiarize himself with the theory and art of versification, he delved into the works of eminent world poets and critics. He moved to New York in 1927, where he published *Streets and Avenues* (1928), *From Everywhere* (1934), *Fisher Village* (1938), *The Long Night* (1946), *Night Dialogue* (1953), and *Eternal Thirst* (1968)—all having a quiet lyricism, a warm sentiment, refined reflection, and, particularly in the later volumes, an increased mastery of rhythm and prosody. Whether he writes of his beloved Lipkan ("Who knows if I shall again set foot on your soil, O Bessarabia my home. Though I now live in a rich land and fat, I fondly recall your huts of clay"), or of the dreams and visions of Leonardo, or of human loneliness and longing, he imbues his lyrics with a sincere softness of sentiment. He has also written brief but acute studies, enriched by his wide familiarity with the field of literary criticism, of the work of M. L. Halpern, H. Leivick, and Jacob Glatstein. In addition he has co-edited with Irving Howe the English edition of *A Treasury of Yiddish Stories* (1954), with an excellent summary analysis of Yiddish writing.

Abraham Lutsky (Zuker, 1894–1957) had his early literary efforts, begun in 1908, rejected by editors. Arriving in New York in 1914, he peddled notions for several years before he became a teacher in a Jewish school. In 1917 his first poem appeared in the conservative *Tageblatt*. Later *Der Forverts* printed one of his poems each Saturday. The *Yunge* could not quite categorize his mock-simple verses and considered him an imitator of Reisen—until Reisen himself praised Lutsky's originality. A soldier in World War I, he on his return again had difficulty getting published. "The young poets considered my verses prior to the war too old and those after it as too new. They maintained that I do not write as one should." In 1921 he began to act out his poems before audiences, and his improvisations made him quite popular; "A Wedding," "A Valse," "At the Rabbi's Table," and "A Pot of Beans" gave wide range to his lively histrionic talent. For many years *Der Tog* printed his verses regularly. Extraordinarily skillful in manipulation of words, he injected humor into his lilting lines, but with a mockery that hid an underlying wistful pathos. These poems were published in several volumes: *Sad and Jolly* (1927), *In the Beginning* (1932), *Portraits* (1945), and *All That Is Good* (1958). M. Ravitch characterized him well: "One of the most original Yiddish poets. His writing has a kind of poetic pantheism. Everything in his poems is alive, speaks and sings, everything is not only made alive but also humanized."

Itzik Manger is also a word magician, but a more subtle artist. Born in Rumania in 1901, he published his poems in New York long before he settled there in 1951. For a time a tailor's apprentice, in 1918 he began to write verses in Yiddish and soon published them in various periodicals. *Stars on the Roof* (1929), his first volume, placed him among the prominent younger writers. *Lantern in the Wind* (1933) added to his fame as a balladist with a humorous turn of phrase but a serious undertone. He wrote many lyrics on Biblical characters and events—most of them charged with playful whimsey. *The Book of Paradise* * (1939), a droll prose fantasy about life in heaven depicted as very similar to that on earth, was issued in 1965 in an English translation. Manger was living in Paris when it fell to the Nazis, but managed to escape to London, where he was befriended by several English writers. *Clouds over the Roof* (1943) was a collection of recent poems. On his arrival in New York *Song and Ballade* (1951) was brought out in honor of his fiftieth birthday and received the Lamed Award. His latest work, *Intimate Persons and Other Writings* (1961), a collection of his critical essays, was published in celebration of his sixtieth birthday.

Manger sings as a natural lyricist, and his poems combine pathos with soft satire with remarkable felicity. A highly personal poet, he manifests the the flow and spontaneity of the folksinger, but with the purity of tone and musicality of sophisticated prosody. Typical of his poems of woe blended with mystic irony is "The Ballad of Petlura."

> Under little Jacob's crib lies slain the golden kid—it is the hour of blood and demons.

From the church midnight sounds tremble—the twelfth hour hanged itself, and Petlura stands at the window.

"What does he want, the evil Haidemak, with the curved sword, with the sharp axe? What does he want of us?"

"He came from far away, and wants a shovel and no more—your dead father to bury."

"—Black birds of night, why did you bring Petlura here with his bloody hands, with his sinister eyes?"

—He stands and begs with a sad gaze. "Give me a rope, a piece of rope—a pull, and my throat is pulled."

"Let him go where the wind goes, where night becomes scabby dogs—so let him become:

"And every night, in the hour of blood, in the hour of our melancholy mood, let him burn with our tears."

Fanciful humor prevails in his numerous Biblical poems. The first two quatrains of "Abraham and Sarah are perhaps typical:

"Avremel, when will we have a child? We are both already old. Normally a woman of my years is in her eighteenth pregnancy."

Father Abraham smiles and is silent as he slowly emits smoke from his pipe. "Be trusting, my wife; if He above wishes, even a broom can shoot."

His wistfulness is evident in "For Years I Have Wandered," in which he tells of his long homelessness and of his feeling when visiting Israel:

For years I have wandered as a stranger, now I ride to wander at home, with one pair of shoes, one shirt to wear, a stick in hand —how can I be without it?

I shall not kiss your dust like that great poet, although my heart is full of song and tears. How can I kiss your dust? I am your dust. And who, I ask you, kisses himself?

A distinguished poet, Manger has the special gift of fusing lyrical pathos with ironic playfulness—a rare combination in Yiddish verse.

Leib Miller, born in 1889, came to this country in 1906 and

worked in various cities in an effort to establish himself economically, finally settling in New York. The tragic Triangle fire in 1911, in which many working girls were trapped and burned to death, stimulated him to write a moving elegy. After its publication he associated himself with the *Yunge*, although he continued to write poems of social content. These verses appeared in *In God's World* (1919). He also wrote poems for children. For a time he edited a weekly in Chicago, then joined the staff of *Die Freiheit* and published poems of a radical content. In addition to translating numerous American poems he brought out *Here Is My Home* (1939), in which he stressed his attachment to America and expressed an engaging optimism toward people and life. "Let sing who will of death, fear, and misfortune, and who must may doubt, deny, and negate; I—I sing of life. Life is dear to me and mine, and I see now the bright aspect of the future." In the 1940's he wrote much about the tragedy in Europe.

Sh. Miller (1895–1958) came to the United States in 1912, worked at manual tasks, and studied bookkeeping evenings. While employed in the latter capacity he began to write fiction during his leisure time and published stories in various magazines. He also did much translating for *Die Freie Arbeiter Shtimme*. In 1922 he moved to California, where he associated with L. Shapiro and other Jewish writers. His novel, *Red and Black* (1945), won the Lamed Prize. His fiction is notable for its psychological insight, realistic frankness, and reflective calm. Despite a chronic illness during the last eight years of his life, he continued to write to the end.

Kadia Molodowsky, born in 1894, is the most distinguished of the numerous women poets. Sensitive, sympathetic, deeply affected by the poverty around her, she wrote poems expressing her emotional reaction to her environment. Her first volume, *Heshvon* (Autumn) *Nights* (1927), was praised for its poetic maturity. Her later work continued to sing of the moody lives of the poor. Many of her poems for children are tenderly beautiful, none of them mythical in content. The adult poems of her later years are imaginative, pictorial, and metaphysical.

In one poem a young scholar tells a girl: "The dream is wiser, knows more and knows better, and sees far away." In 1935 she came to this country and continued her writing, not only poems but fiction. Her three novels, imbued with nostalgic wistfulness, are *From Lublin to New York* (1942), *Grandparents and Grandchildren* (1944), and *On One's own Soil* (1957). The brutal slaughter of Jews during World War II, which included many of her family and friends, seriously affected her health. During these years of grief she wrote elegies of dolorous lament. In one she pleads with God to select another people for sacrifice—the Jews have suffered enough from being the chosen children. Her latest volume, *Light from the Thornbush* (1965), which subtly integrates fantasy with reality and in which the longest poem is a paean to the building of Israel, received the Kovner Award. In 1943 she founded *Seviva* (Environment), a quarterly devoted to literature and criticism, but had to stop it when her health broke down. In 1960 she resumed its publication and has included in its issues a number of her sensitively conceived stories.

Aaron Nissenson (1898–1964), the son of a miller, migrated to this country in 1911 and attended American schools until he graduated as a pharmacist. More interested in writing, however, he joined the staff of *Der Morgen Journal* and remained on it for 30 years. Having begun to write at the age of 13, he became a member of the *Neo-Yunge*. His several volumes of verse exalt faith and hope, and are kindled by the firm flame of thought. His drama based on the life of Eugene V. Debs, *The Way to Man*, seeks to probe the depths of human existence.

Melekh Ravitch, born in Galicia in 1893, began to write at the age of 16. His first volume, *At the Entrance* (1912), was favorably received. Having gone to live in Vienna in 1913, he served in the Austrian army during World War I. In 1921 he came to Warsaw, became active in literary circles, and was one of the editors of *Literarishe Bletter* (Literary Leaves), a highly respected and influential periodical. Among his own writings was a perceptive study of Spinoza. He has lived in various parts of the world, and everywhere he was active as a writer. In 1934 he settled in America and continued to publish poems and critical prose. His affection for his new home is expressed in a poem on the Statue of Liberty: "Your torch is turned toward New York, but your light shines in all parts of the world. You are blessed and cursed, respected and hated, earnestly and in jest; and I—I simply love and believe, because curses and hate are wind, mere dust." His two volumes of memoirs from 1893 to 1921 appeared in 1964.

I.A. Rontch was born in 1899 and came to New York in 1913. For several years he worked at manual labor, but the urge to write was strong and he managed to get his first verses printed in *Der Groiser Kunds* at the age of 16. In 1918 he went to Chicago, where he taught in a Jewish school and wrote poems and articles for local Yiddish periodicals. His volume of verse, *Winds* (1923), was favorably reviewed by Ben Hecht in the *Chicago Daily News*. The following year Rontch returned to New York, where he continued to busy himself with his writing and editing.

Yoneh Rosenfeld (1880–1944) was very young when orphaned, and suffered extreme poverty and harsh beatings throughout his early apprenticeship to a turner. He worked at carpentry for a decade before he began in 1905 to devote himself to writing. Three years earlier he had shown his first story to Peretz and was encouraged to continue. "Competitors," which concerns a warped ne'er-do-well who attends to the house work while his wife earns the family's meager living by selling edibles in a market stall, and who cannot accept his young daughter's attempts to compete with him in looking after the house, made Rosenfeld widely and favorably known. His novel, *In the Quiet* (1912), deals with the life of poor and oppressed workers. His tendency to explore the pathologic recesses of the mind caused him to delve into abnormal human behavior. In 1921 he went to New York and became a contributor to *Der Forverts* as well as other periodicals. His stories continued to delineate with psychological acuteness characters who acted irrationally and futilely, and many dwelt on the subjects of fear, death, eroticism, and insanity. Yet out of the dark depths of human behavior he groped for the clarity of life, for a logic out of illogical circumstances. His autobiographical novel, *All Alone* (1940), vividly describes his early suffering and apprenticeship. Other of his books are *Between Day and Night, In the Shadow of Death, Women, At the Border*, and *He and They*. His creative fantasy enriched his analysis of character, but his later writings suffer from oversimplification, verbosity, and a tendency to vulgarity, especially in his numerous sketches of girls in the process of becoming women. He died of cancer after a protracted illness of eight years.

J. I. Segal (1896–1954) experienced a traumatic wrench at the age of 13 when he was accused of stealing and brutally beaten by the police. In 1911 he came to Montreal and worked as a tailor. Later he taught in a Jewish school. In 1923 he went to New York but returned five years later. Although he had begun to write in Hebrew in 1916, he very soon turned to Yiddish and participated in the anthologies published by the *Yunge*. His *Of My World* (1918) contained poems of deep feeling and universality. He was on the staff of *Der Keneder Adler* for many years. In common with other Yiddish writers who were torn from their native homes and thrust into the American maelstrom, he wrote many poems on the subject of loneliness. "In the whole city I have nobody. All my childhood and adolescence I was attached to nobody and nothing. I know some people, meet them in the street, stop and chat a while, and the words neither near me to them nor them to me." *Poems and Praise* (1945) was awarded the Lamed Prize. Leivick wrote of him: "Segal, more than others, has woven his love of the Jews with the love of life and love of Yiddish; because the three were discriminated against, insulted and abused, he has lifted them to the greatest height, to the purest substance."

Joel Slonim (1884–1944) was brought to this country at the age of two and educated in American schools. Although he began to write in English, his father influenced him to turn to

Yiddish. In 1906 he became a staff member of *Die Warheit* and continued on *Der Tog* when that newspaper absorbed the older one. In 1908 he began to associate with the *Yunge* and was one of the editors of *Literatur*. An able journalist, he wrote widely on English and American literature. His verse is noted for its modern idiom and imagery.

I. I. Trunk (1887–1961) was born near Warsaw of a rabbinical and wealthy family. In Lodz, where he spent his boyhood, he studied Hebrew lore and secular subjects with private tutors. He traveled widely, and lived in Palestine in 1913–1914. Through his father he came to know Peretz and was influenced by him to turn from Hebrew to Yiddish. Early interested in the radical movement, he described it in his initial fiction. He also wrote poems, essays, and criticism. The years of World War I he sojourned in Switzerland, then settled in Lodz in 1919. Six years later he moved to Warsaw, where he was active in cultural affairs and headed the P.E.N. Club in the 1930's. At the outbreak of World War II he left Poland and traveled eastward, finally landing in the United States in 1941, where he remained for the rest of his life.

Of a philosophical turn of mind and highly endowed as a literary critic, Trunk produced some of the most penetrating Yiddish works in each of these fields. Among them are *Of Nature* (1914), *Dorian Grey* (1923), *Idealism and Naturalism in Yiddish Literature* (1927), *Near and Far* (1936), *Sholom Aleichem* (1937), *Tevieh the Dairyman* (1939), and *Poland* (1946–1953), a work in seven volumes providing "a portrait of my life in the frame of and in relation to the portrait of Jewish life in Poland," which received the Lamed Award. Trunk also published *Leaves in the Wind* (1944), "poems in old age," and a number of novels and stories, among them *Fig Trees and Other Stories* (1922), *Josephus Flavius of Jerusalem and Other Stories* (1930), *Wise Men of Khelm* (1951), *The Happiest Jew in the World* (1955), the story of Herschel Ostropoler, a folkloric wit, and *Messiah Storm* (1961), concerning Sabbati Zevi.

Trunk's analysis of *Dorian Grey* is the most acute study of a non-Jewish work in Yiddish. He also excels in his highly perceptive interpretation of Sholom Aleichem's writings, and his *magnum opus* on Poland is a monument to his impressive scholarship and perspicacity. In a sense a follower of and successor to Peretz and Sholom Aleichem, he succeeded in integrating the qualities of both in his own work.

Zisha Weinper (1893–1957), of Ukrainian-Hasidic background, went to Warsaw in 1910, where he published his first poems. In 1913 he migrated to New York, worked as a house painter, and later taught in a Jewish school. His literary interests remained paramount with him and he took a leading part in the activities of the *Neo-Yunge*. "In the winter of 1914," he wrote later, "we were still boys, a group of boys from different countries and of different perspectives, but with one dream, one will. At the cafeteria tables we met, came to know one another, and partook in the development of Yiddish literature." His poems were included in various anthologies. Eventually he brought out several volumes of verse as well as a fine critical work on Yiddish writers. His early poems were fresh and lyrical, with the impress of the esthete; later his verse became more narrative in form and consciously social in theme. His Ukrainian and Hasidic influence was apparent in a number of his poems, and his love of American landscape gave his verse an optimistic quality. *At the Grand Canyon* (1947) is one of the best descriptions of American scenic grandeur in Yiddish. A founder of *Yikuf*, an organization furthering Jewish culture, he remained one of its devoted leaders to the day of his death.

Aaron Zeitlin was born in 1898 the eldest son of the distinguished Hebrew scholar and writer, Hillel Zeitlin. In 1914 he published his first Yiddish poem—having written in Hebrew even earlier. Six years later his younger brother and he traveled to Palestine and remained there for more than a year. Subsequently he wrote poems, essays, critical reviews, and a major work on Lord Byron. His novel, *Shadows on the Snow* (1922), was highly praised, and his play about Jacob Frank was well received. He came to the United States at the outbreak of World War II and has since been writing for *Der*

Tog. His collected poems in three volumes and his prose writing have been awarded nine literary prizes.

No single chapter can treat adequately the rich and variegated Yiddish literature produced in America during the 20th century. Scores of writers have regretfully been omitted, among them some no doubt as gifted as those included, on the perhaps fallible assumption that they have merely enriched but not advanced the literature. Particularly in the early decades, Yiddish writing flourished with remarkable zest and creativity. Scores of books published annually were only a small part of the material printed in numerous newspapers and magazines. Even more important was the relatively high quality of much of the poetry, fiction, and criticism—assuming, as one must, that much of what is printed in any literature is written for the day and forgotten by night. Of significance is that most of the writers came to America in the flush of youth, an intrinsic part of the mass migration, deeply grounded in Jewish tradition, and naturally expressed the hopes and woes, the joys and sorrows of their people with almost folkloric informality and directness. In one form or another they gave voice to the common restlessness, loneliness, stubborn will to survive and prosper, deep grief for their massacred brethren during and immediately after World War I, and the excruciating awareness of millions of their kin dying in the Nazi crematoria. Khaim Grade spoke for all when he pointed out: "It was not a third of our people who were murdered, but rather that a third was cut out of the flesh and soul of every Jew who survived." Equally meaningful is the warm affection and admiration with which many of these writers described their new American home and the beauty and grandeur of its broad extent. Although not much of this writing has appeared in English so far, and its poetry offers formidable hurdles to translators, enough is becoming available to give non-Yiddish readers a sampling of its literary wealth and specific Jewish insights and way of life. Regretfully it must be added that many of these writers are now dead or nearing the end of their creativity, and very few new ones have come to replace them.

CHAPTER THIRTEEN

JOSEPH OPATOSHU

A Novelist of Imaginative Gusto

Two STRAINS in Opatoshu's ancestry competed for dominance: centuries of dedicated intellectuality on his father's side and the rustic vigor and vitality that characterized his mother's family. These influences contended and yet combined in molding his concept of Jewishness. Much as he enjoyed the dynamism of physical prowess, he early became proud of the ethos and passion for righteousness which he accepted as the essence of his Jewish inheritance.

Opatoshu came of an old rabbinic family, with pious scholars gracing each generation back to the 16th century in Germany. Born in November, 1886, in his maternal grandfather's forest home, he roamed the woods in his early childhood and familiarized himself with the coarse, active life of Jewish foresters as well as the tough, thieving ways of peripheral rustics. Very early he was taken in hand by his scholarly and mildly enlightened father and taught Hebrew lore. Thus, by the time he was ten years old and sent to a Russian school in nearby Mlave, he was both impressed by the physical exploits of horse thieves and shady characters who inhabited the forest area and awed by his father's erudition and spiritual earnestness.

While at school and through adolescence he was artlessly proud of his native Poland. In his late teens, however, he real-

ized that most Poles were pervasively anti-Semitic and unworthy of his allegiance. He was then studying engineering,
but the longing to write began to dominate him—an ambition
stimulated by the fact that his father and elder brother were
both doing some writing. When lack of funds forced him, after
a year's stay, to return from Nancy, France, where he attended
a technical school, he wrote the first version of his story, "On
the Other Side of the Bridge." He composed it in Yiddish because he knew it better than Hebrew and because it was the
language his characters spoke. Like so many other beginners,
he managed to show it to Peretz in Warsaw and, although
surprised to have the great writer address him in Russian was
pleased with his encouragement.

At the time, while glorying in his Jewishness and yearning
to enhance it, he was highly critical of what he considered the
decadent condition of Hasidism. He was also emotionally attuned to socialist ideas and incensed against government oppression. With his father already in New York, he decided to
join him early in 1907. He was eager to take root in American
soil and write about Jews in their new home, which he regarded as the new center of the Jewish diaspora. Years later
he wrote:

> Here, in New York, I went through all the gates of hell. I am not
> one of those who thought that in coming to the United States
> they were bringing only the body, leaving the soul in Poland.
> I burned my bridges behind me. I came to settle down, to be-
> come a pioneer, like the Pilgrims of three centuries ago. And I
> did. No more Kotsk [center of Hasidism], no more family pride.
> It was necessary to be like the horse thieves, the *hoi polloi*.
> I began to work in a shoe factory, cut soles 8–9 hours a day until
> my palms became like soles. Later I sewed shirts in a shop,
> delivered newspapers.

During this period of manual labor, especially as a newspaper deliverer, he met a number of underworld characters
whom he later depicted with vivid verisimilitude. For a time
he taught in a Hebrew school and studied civil engineering
evenings at Cooper Union Institute. All the while he lived in

a dingy tenement crowded with various kinds of immigrant Jews, and these too became fecund material for many of his early stories.

In 1910 he published a revised version of "On the Other Side of the Bridge" in *Literatur*—having become an active member of *Die Yunge*. Two years later his short novel, *A Romance of a Horse Thief*, was included in the first volume of *Schriften*. Both works are set in Poland and suffused with nostalgic tenderness. The environs of the forest village in which he grew up, viewed from the bleak prospect of his tenement window, possessed a pristine quality; in contrast to the semi-gangsters and hoodlums he met daily on Goerck Street, the horse thieves and gypsies of his native milieu assumed a dashing glamor. Zanvel and Wolf are depicted as hearty brigands, robust and romantic lovers. Other of his characters are also strong and impulsive, without education or intellectual interests, engaged in material pursuits and devoted to physical pleasures. For all their appealing simple traits, however, they remain social pariahs in the community, branded by the rogue's badge of shame.

In his stories of New York slum Jews, about whom he wrote next, Opatoshu could not keep his pen from the acid of satire. In "Morris and His Son Philip," included in the second volume of *Schriften*, in *Out of the New York Ghetto*, appearing in *Die Neie Haym*, and in numerous brief stories he wrote with a feeling of both attraction and repulsion. Proud of the Hebraic ethos, eager for enhancement of Jewish culture, he was keenly disturbed by the moral chaos of his East Side environment. He perceived these immigrant Jews as bereft of the social and religious props which had supported their parents' morality and succumbing to the crassness of the slum gutters; living in a spiritual jungle and affected by the strength of the fist and the power of the dollar. Simultaneously he was fascinated by their physical force and their uninhibited sensual indulgence.

Sholom Aleichem read these stories shortly after his arrival in New York and wrote encouragingly to Opatoshu: "Write about Jews in America, describe the life of the New York ghetto, that is your genre. . . . You will enrich our literature with a new chapter." He and others sensed that while the action in these stories suffered from fortuitous and melodramatic development, their artistic merit inhered in the array of picturesque characters against a realistic setting. Sam, Mrs. Rich, her father, Pauly, Mr. Pollack, Alec, Jake—these and others are depicted with imaginative gusto. Their grossness, lechery, and animalistic cunning are enhanced by their intense physical vitality; their coarse impulses and carnal infatuations remain memorable.

Opatoshu considered it an indignity to have to teach Hebrew prayers to boys who would much rather play baseball, a resentment he expressed in *Hebrew*, his next long work. Here he deplores the spiritual debasement of reputable Jewish immigrants. He presents parents who are too preoccupied or negligent to care for the cultural integrity of their children; trustees of schools and synagogues by virtue of their financial success, vulgarizing these institutions by their philistine arrogance; academic intellectuals groveling before insolent employers in their need to earn a living. Green, one of them, reflecting Opatoshu's own attitude, "could not understand how people can live in so circumscribed a world in which jealousy prevails, in which each one considers himself the greatest, in which everything is petty and small—petty perceptions, petty ambitions, petty honors."

With the establishment of *Der Tog* in 1914 Opatoshu was engaged as a regular contributor and remained on the staff until his death 40 years later. He moved from his drab tenement to the open spaces of the Bronx and soon assumed the responsibilities of married life. The need to contribute a story or article each week sent him to the highways and byways of his American environment for material. In the process his sarcasm became less scathing, yielding to irony and sympathetic insight. Most of his sketches, some anecdotal in nature, dealt with people working hard for their sustenance in the face of conditions which oppressed, thwarted, and vulgarized. He wrote frequently of the struggles of class against class, race against race, in their various complex manifestations. Many of these works are notable for their incisive etchings of men and women who remain essentially unaltered despite the assaults of time and circumstance.

The iniquity of racial and religious prejudice quickened Opatoshu's indignation. Having suffered from it in Poland, he reacted the more forcefully when encountering it in the United States. In a number of stories he depicted the clash between Jew and gentile, white and black, Catholic and Protestant. *Race* (1923) is a collection of some of these sketches, "Lynching" being the longest and best. It describes the murder by burning of a young Georgia Negro with simple, stark power. Accused of rape by a hysterical girl, the daughter of a man who had raped the boy's young sister, the victim is tracked down and punished by his white tormentors not out of angry justice but sadistic cruelty. Gossip and agitation foment fanatical excitement within the town, and the lynching is turned into a savage orgy.

> McClure was inflamed, intoxicated with happiness. He threw off his coat, began to beat himself on the chest, jigged about and shouted in a hoarse voice. A number joined him; an elderly butcher embraced him. The two kissed, threw themselves on the ground, rolling their heated bodies in the grass. The crowd became wild with excitement. They hugged and shouted—as if suddenly freed of something alien, something which had hung like a chain about their feet. It was as if their pagan spirit had awakened after lying dormant for two millennia, was avenging itself for the emaciated bodies and flagellated backs, was eager to throw off generations of restraint.

For all his determination to burn his bridges behind him, Opatoshu kept reverting to the Jewish milieu in which he grew up. He conceived the idea of writing a historical novel—the first in Yiddish literature—that would embrace the sweep and spirit of Jewish life in Poland during the deterioration of Hasidism. Years later he pointed out:

> We have almost no historical novels because we Jews, as a world folk, have not yet any written history. . . . Both Graetz and Dubnow wrote the history of the Jewish Sabbath, of the Jewish holiday. The six weekdays they omitted. Both historians have ennobled *the book,* the spirit, and have overlooked *the body.* . . . Where the historian stops, the artist begins.

Never inclined to overestimate his powers, he hesitated to begin the work evolving in his mind. To test himself, he decided to experiment with a briefer narrative having the same historic setting and some of the characters he hoped to include in his major novel. The result was *Alone,* started in 1914, serialized in *Die Zukunft* in 1918, and published the following year. It is primarily the story of Sarah, the only child of Mordecai, the wealthy and respected forest overseer. Motherless at a very early age, raised in the isolation of her sequestered home, she eagerly absorbs the folk tales and legends of a friendly peasantry, fills her mind with Polish love stories, and longs for romance and excitement. When her father arranges her engagement to a learned and sensitive youth whose timidity and modesty diminish the masculine appeal she has come to expect of her betrothed, she acquiesces in the matter without complaint but also without complacence. When she subsequently meets a student on vacation, she responds to his ardent wooing. Unable, however, to disappoint her moody father, she goes through with the marriage. Later, already a mother, she rebels at her loveless existence and elopes with a dashing gallant.

While relatively hackneyed and immature as a work of fiction, *Alone* is rich in vivid and intimate descriptions of forest life, folk tales and religious lore that add flavor to the historic setting, and masterful portrayal of character. One feels the throbbing reality of Sarah despite the haziness of her romantic behavior. Baruch, her abashed husband, is drawn with tender sympathy, so that his awkwardness and diffidence only add to the appealing pathos of his being. And the silent, resigned Mordecai, while a minor figure and shadowy in his appearances, possesses an ominousness that begs for elaboration.

A year after he had begun writing *Alone*, Opatoshu turned to his major work, *In Polish Woods*.* Completing it four years later, he had it published in 1921. It was at once hailed as a work of ficitonal excellence and became a relative "best-seller" in the United States as well as in Poland, where it sold over 15,000 coipes within two years. Translations in several languages followed. A sequel, *1863*, appeared in 1926 and was received with nearly equal favor.

In these two volumes Opatoshu is the artist steeped in Jewish and European history. He delineates graphically a people in time of spiritual flux: Hasidism at the beginning of its disintegration, the *Haskola* movement in its early stages, and the factious and futile struggle for Polish independence culminating in the abortive insurrection of 1863. The narrative begins with a magnificent reconstruction of Jewish rural life in Poland during the first half of the 19th century: Jews living close to the soil, strong of body, salutary of spirit, generous, vivacious, and ardent Hasidim. Abraham, whose son Mordecai is the protagonist of the work, is the wealthy manager of a large forest area; his honesty and magnanimity have made him beloved by both Jews and gentiles. He is a high-spirited Jew, proud of his origin and station, steadfast and pious, yet capable of innocent levity. No less attractively portrayed are his wife Dvorele, his housekeeper Braine, and the village folk living off the forest and the motherly Vistula River. Mordecai emerges very much in the image of his father, a dreamy and thoughtful youth shuddering at the sight of blood, yet capable of butchering a hen in the spirit of experimentation. Tender and wistful, he is at the age of 16 secretly infatuated with the daughter of one of his father's employees and is sent off to Kotsk, the seat of the renowned Rabbi Mendele, in the company of his teacher Reb Itche.

The remainder of the first volume deals in detail with the slow journey to Kotsk—the people Mordecai and Reb Itche meet, their various experiences in traveling from place to place. In the process Reb Itche emerges as a humble saint within a Hasidism in the process of decay. When the pair reach Rabbi Mendele's large court they learn that the eminent Hasidic leader has long been living in self-imposed seclusion and refuses to show himself to his clamoring followers.

Rabbi Mendele realized that Hasidism was degenerating, losing its content, its substance; that the rabbi's "chair" was becoming a matter of inheritance. He saw that the true essence of Hasidism was disappearing: that Hasidim were assuming a materialistic attitude, failing to understand the spirit of Baal Shem Tov's teaching and interpreting it from a purely Mosaic standpoint. . . . Rabbi Mendele was therefore in deep anguish, and for seven years he was absorbed in study, devoting much of the time to *cabala*, to spiritual probing. When he began to feel himself qualified to elevate Baal Shem Tov's teaching to a higher eminence, to give definite meaning to Polish Hasidism—he perceived that he was not being understood, that the people were smug enough to forego any meaning, that only of few may it be said: "Man does not live by bread alone." . . . And it was difficult to believe that this man, who was the essence of sympathy, who had befriended the sinner above the saint—that this man should indeed isolate himself, come to hate people, and to tender them nothing but curses.

How differently Opatoshu and Sholem Asch conceive the same subject is evidenced in their treatment of Rabbi Mendele. The first to depict him in Yiddish literature, Opatoshu presents him at odds with himself, full of doubt and even despair, angry and bitter. To his followers he exclaims: "Oxen, what do you want of me? Go be burned! Why are you pestering me? I'm no rabbi!" Asch, on the contrary, depicts him in *Salvation* as at odds with his followers rather than with himself, confident, clear-minded, spiritually exalted. To his followers he declares: "Cows, I am a rabbi of Hasidim who want to do things. Give me 50 Hasidim who are of my mind and we could do something; not a herd of cows who only want to feed. I am no cowherd, I am a rabbi!"

Historically, Opatoshu's portrayal of the rabbi is more realistic. He himself stated: "In 'Kotsk' I wanted to show the decline of Hasidism, a decline which comes from inner fatigue, inner depths. . . . Anyone who delves into the decline of Hasidism must see that I could not convey any other 'Kotsk.' If my 'Kotsk' were merely embittered, not despondent, it would be a lie."

Despite Rabbi Mendele's hostility, his court remains crowded with Hasidic followers seeking not so much spiritual salvation as sublimation of daily cares. Most picturesque among the fresh arrivals is the demented Isroel, a religious ascetic who excoriates Rabbi Mendele for the depraved behavior of his own family and agitates for ordainment of Reb Itche as the true rabbi; the latter is the rabbi's most intimate disciple, dedicated to comforting the afflicted and composing the irascible. The rabbi's middle-aged son Dovidel, a *malade imaginaire*, and son-in-law Doniel, a cabalistic sensualist, exemplify the actual debasement of Hasidic spirit.

Witnessing an orgy of religious debauchery in Doniel's quarters, Mordecai is disgusted and distraught. He begins to frequent the home of Joseph Shtral, an exemplary intellectual. Wealthy, erudite in both Jewish lore and worldly knowledge, a correspondent with important scholars in other lands, for 15 years at work on a Hebrew translation of Goethe's *Faust*, Shtral is withal a genial and sympathetic personality. Under his guidance Mordecai soon acquires the perspective of the cultivated European, and although he remains a Jew always, he becomes critical of Hasidism. In Shtral's home he meets Philip Kahane and Count Komarovsky, leaders of the Polish revolt, and is drawn into political agitation.

The Polish insurrection of 1863 is described from its inception among the more restive nobles and clergy to its final fiasco in the disastrous rout of the rebel army. Kahane is depicted as the guiding spirit of the movement: a dreamy, impassioned Jew dominating and directing the destiny of a proud and capricious Poland.

At first glance his figure appeared comical. The lively Kahane, with black curls, was almost obscured by the tall, blond Poles.

When he began to speak, however, his fair auditors forgot that they were listening to a puny Jew. They envisaged a prophet who hurled the lightning and thunder, moved huge boulders and mountains; who disseminated an aching restiveness which spread over the fields and forests of Poland, announcing that the hour was at hand. And youths left their schools and books and peasants their plows and families, and assembled in the woods.

Kahane is proud of being a Jew, and his fervent agitation for liberation of Poland is in part actuated by the belief that a freed Poland meant an emancipated Jewry. Yet as the time for the revolt approaches he perceives that but few Polish nobles have entered the struggle unselfishly, that the peasants are too embittered against their landlords to join forces with them, that there is friction and jealousy between the revolutionists abroad and the leaders in Poland, and that the movement is doomed to collapse at the first impact with the Czar's kossaks.

Mordecai's association with the rebels makes it obvious to him that ultimate failure is inevitable, but like Kahane he continues to aid them in any way he can. Idealist that he is, he casts his lot with the peasants, and wanders among them with prophetic zeal.

The unrest among the peasants against the landlords was growing, and soon spread over Poland. . . . The leaders were arrested. They blamed an ill-clad young man, who moved from village to village agitating the peasantry. Everybody saw the young man, repeated his speeches, yet none knew who he was, what his name was, where he came from, and where he resided. He was sought in each village in vain. . . . The landlords were certain the agitator was a Jew, but the peasants swore by the cross that he was a pious Catholic—he kneeled and prayed to each holy image—and the old men among them were of the belief that he belonged to the devil.

When government spies at last track him down, Mordecai borrows money and flees to Paris. There the ubiquitous Kahane introduces him to the Polish patriots, and for two years he lives among rebels and dreamers, studying the past in the hope of discerning the future. He meets the envious Michael Bakunin, the visionary Moses Hess; he makes a study of Diego Pieres, the Portuguese Marrano who, as Shlomo Molkhu, aspired to become a messiah and was burned by the Inquisition as a heretic. When the call for recruits reaches Mordecai, he enlists as a matter of duty; the vanity and prejudice of the Polish leaders notwithstanding, he is eager for Poland's liberation. On reaching camp he witnesses the petty intrigues at headquarters, Kahane's last desperate endeavors to cajole the conceited officers and cheer the grumbling recruits, and the final rout of the rebellion.

All through the narrative Opatoshu repeatedly stresses the prejudice that reared a wall between Jews and Poles. With psychological sensitivity he exposes secret impulses, uncovers layers of emotional conflict, and dissects the varieties of hypocrisy. His large and variegated canvas encompassed a Poland in·which Jews and Poles lived in close proximity and yet kept deliberately apart, were strongly dependent on one another economically and joined in hatred of their Russian oppressor, and yet remained wholly incompatible socially and spiritually.

In this two-volume novel he manifested not only an acute sense of history but also uncommon intellectual subtlety. He has recreated imaginatively the world of Hasidism with its mystical, superstitious, and degenerate manifestations. Equipped with broad erudition and a realistic view of the social forces operating in the 19th century, he has successfully created a fictional world at once authentic and significant. Interested more in people than in plot, he delighted in delineating the essential nature of his numerous characters, so that most of them emerge vivid, vital, and individualized, abiding in the reader's imagination.

In *The Dancer* (1929), Opatoshu has examined the agonized persistence of a disintegrating Hasidism transported to the United States early in the 20th century. The characters are the children and grandchildren of Rabbi Mendele's followers in the process of adjustment to their new home. With a realism that cuts to the quick, Opatoshu depicts a group of elderly Hasidim occupying a tenement on Goerck Street and as oblivious of the gangsters on the corner as of the politicians in City Hall. Although forced to earn their bitter bread as best they can, they are pathetically determined to save their souls at all cost. Yet their endeavors to establish their withered and worn Hasidism in "godless America" are doomed. Rabbi Shabsi and Reb Avremel, shabby replicas of Rabbi Mendele and Reb Itche, strive persistently, each in his own way, to bring God's spirit to their unreceptive fellow Jews. Reb Avremel, who is goodness personified, attracts followers by his very meekness; Rabbi Shabsi, like Rabbi Mendele a descendant of the strict Rabbi Shammai, scorns to traffic with servile or skeptical minds and seeks the isolation of a New Jersey retreat. His cave is soon discovered, and many simulated Hasidim flock to it, drinking lemonade and supplicating blessings. Seeking frantically to escape his tormentors, starved and confused, he meets death under the wheels of a speeding train.

With equal perspicacity are portrayed the sons and daughters of these Hasidic Jews. Many of them, bereft of spiritual propensity, have adapted easily to the current ways of American life: they become businessmen, grow stout and prosperous, indulge their gross appetites, and partake in ostentatious philanthropy. Yet not a few are unable to live for themselves alone. While not perplexed by the religious doubts of their fathers' generation, they are stimulated by a zeal for salvation —not of their souls but of society. They become radicals, social workers, groping intellectuals; some devote themselves to study for study's sake, others yearn for love and yet fear it, and most are earnestly in search of the essence of human existence. Shlome, Reb Avremel's son, an idealistic radical, speaks for all of them:

> Ninety-nine percent of the people work for their appetites. Nothing matters to them but their appetites. If not for their appetites, men would cease to exploit their fellow men. My father, Reb Avremel, yours, and other such Jews have rid themselves of their appetites—subdued them! This, you see, is an

achievement, a high achievement. And I have great respect for such Jews. I regard each of them as a high-priest who has been attending the holy of holies for thousands of years and is certain he is heedful of God's word—when within the holy of holies everything has long been dead! The priests must be reappareled in garments more suited to the 20th century, and within the holy of holies we must install new tablets—the tablets of the man who works.

Over this group of pharisees and dreamers hovers Regina, the redheaded dancer who is the embodiment of physical loveliness. A creature of impulse, completely self-centered, thoroughly amoral, she cunningly coils her charm about the hearts of various young men. None can withstand her beauty and willfulness. The simple, materially successful Wolf, the wealthy and aggressive Abe, the intensive, tubercular medical student, the timid and timorous Pinchos—all become victims of her irresistible allure. She uses each of them without scruple or compunction, getting what she wants like a spoiled child. The weakness of *The Dancer* lies in its faulty conception. It is not so much an organic novel as a group of related sketches. What makes the book a work of literary merit are the qualities inherent in all of Opatoshu's writings: vivid characterization, intellectual acumen, and dynamic action. His men and women quickly achieve reality—as alive in their spiritual striving as in the indulgence of their appetites, as animated in their pathetic frustrations as in their infelicitous love affairs.

In 1933 Opatoshu issued a slender volume containing two novelettes of Jewish life in the 16th century. He had been delving for years into Jewish history, combing old tomes in Hebrew and Yiddish for descriptions of Jewish daily life in medieval towns. The more he learned the more convinced he became that Jews in previous centuries, while undergoing harsh persecution and massacres, did not lead the drab and dismal ghetto existence described by Graetz and Dubnow. "We," he asserted, "like others, led a full life and had contacts with the outside world. . . . So I decided that even in the Middle Ages Jews were not locked in their ghettos, as the historians wrote, and their life was not as shabby and murky as indicated in histories."

The longer story, "A Day in Regensburg," concerns an important wedding within the ghetto. As was the custom on such occasions, beggars are the first to arrive, and they come in wagonloads from nearby cities and towns. Local minstrels vie with those imported from Prague in entertaining the numerous guests. Jew Street, the main thoroughfare, becomes alive with laughter and merrymaking. The inn is filled with a gay crowd whiling the time away before the ceremony, and a rich merchant flirts drunkenly with a Prague dancer until pounced upon by his outraged wife. The marriage ceremony itself, performed with much pomp and formality, is graced by the young duke and his lively retinue. There is a great deal of eating, hilarity, even horseplay; much music and singing and dancing, but also the Jewish wail of the harp, reminding all of their long exile.

The shorter piece, "Elia Bokhur," consists of three sketches, each presenting a different aspect of the popular bard and scholar, author of *The Bovo Bukh* and *Paris and Vienna* as well as a Hebrew grammar for gentiles: he inveighs against a scribbler who had plagiarized one of his poems; he discusses with a wealthy and intelligent matron the proposed contents of a prayerbook for her betrothed daughter; and he appears as the trusted secretary and teacher of Hebrew to Cardinal Egidio da Viterbo, a prominent young Renaissance scholar.

Opatoshu wrote a number of other, briefer stories of historic Jewish life, ranging in time from the early centuries to the 19th century and in content from minor incidents to important episodes. One of the best is "Worms," in which the historic Glückel von Hameln learns of Shabbati Zevi's betrayal and opens the barrels of food which had long remained in readiness for the hegira to Palestine—only to find them swarming with worms.

All these stories, while told with fictional grace and realistic gusto, are in a sense linguistic exercises. Their vocabulary is ingeniously limited to the Yiddish spoken during the life of the characters; Opatoshu, having carefully culled words from contemporary sources, refrained from using any that came into popular speech subsequently. He was thus a literary innovator as well as the first to give a fictional mold to the Renaissance centuries in Jewish history.

Ever the experimenter, researcher, keen observer, and most of all the imaginative artist, Opatoshu wrote hundreds of sketches, most of them about Jewish life in Poland and the United States. With the skill of the trained writer and the sympathetic insight of the acute student of character, he roamed the gamut of human experiences and plucked incidents pregnant with emotional vitality. Often he presented a contrived episode more revealing than actual reality. In all of the sketches the basic element is a struggle of forces. Each story is developed with the utmost verbal economy: without lengthy description or extensive background, but with the direct impact of concise narration. His characters, usually drawn with few strokes, emerge vivid and real in the very struggle which enfolds them.

Opatoshu is not merely the psychological realist but also the serious and sensitive Jew. The events taking place during his adult years, mostly tragic but occasionally controversial, became themes for many of his stories. The havoc caused by World War I in Jewish towns in Eastern Europe affected him deeply, and he depicted the tragic effects of forced evacuations and massacres in sketches included in *About the Ruins* (1925). Having learned from his mother that "of Mlave, dear child, not a token is left," he described the expulsion with controlled anger, yet irrepressible grief. He stressed the pathos of refugees from the war area, the brutality of soldier hordes during the civil war years along the Russian border, and the suffering from economic pauperization and open anti-Semitism.

Not all of these are solemn with effects of adversity. Some are written with a humor that conceals a clawing rancor. In one a rabbi clings to his synagogue after all the congregation has fled, praying and preaching to empty pews, until he is at last forced to alleviate his family's hunger by pawning a silver chalice. In another a Polonized Jew seeks to place his son in a German school because in the Polish school the boy is attending he is being driven by anti-Semitic classmates into willful Jewishness. A third tells of a wealthy American Pole who returns to his native town and devotes his wealth to anti-Jewish agitation. A fourth concerns poor boy-peddlers in search of Americans because of their easy generosity. A fifth tells of a religious procession on Holy Wednesday in which a stuffed Judas dummy, dressed like a Hasid, is thrown from the church spire and sunk in the river. On the way the caricatured Judas asks Jesus, "Why are you silent?" "What shall I say?" he is answered.

> "You ask, Jesus? You who were sacrificed for the sins of mankind? What have you done to people? Look at this excited mob, seeking a live Jew as a sacrifice, and when none is available I, your brother, was stuffed as children stuff a doll to still the animal in them. But why are you weeping, Jesus?"

Opatoshu visited Poland in 1922 to gather material for some of the stories. Revisiting it on his return from Palestine in 1934, he was even more depressed by the strained antagonism between Pole and Jew. Nor could he fail to feel the effects of Nazi anti-Semitism in Central Europe. These impressions and observations he expressed artistically in a number of stories, most of them evidencing a reflective attitude weighted with Jewish woe.

The Nazi genocide against Jews agonized Opatoshu's spirit. In his imagination he experienced the grief of the concentration camp and the martyrdom of the crematorium. From his safe distance in New York he could only write about the tragedy with fortitude and indignation, stressing Jewish courage and giving intimations of Jewish hope. A number of these tales are included in *When Poland Fell* (1943). The initial sketch is about a Jew like himself on a German train going to the Polish border. The car he is in is crowded but he feels isolated and depressed. The door opens and a man shouts: "If there is a

German Jew in the car, he should give his seat to an Aryan!"
A quick repetition of the order grates on his ear and causes an
inner trembling.

> I wanted to cry out so that the heavens should hear me, but my
> lips were pressed together like millstones. I felt miserable and
> strongly envied our forefathers, *whole Jews*, who accepted the
> evils of the gentile world as one accepts dark natural forces, a
> storm, a thunderclap, or even a mad dog. Such an attitude
> placed our forefathers miles above the evils and saved them
> from extinction. And I asked myself: What strength have we,
> *modern Jews*, to withstand the present-day evils?

Many of the stories concern the blind hatred of Poles toward
Jews, although several tell of Poles who shielded Jews from
the Germans at the risk of their own lives. Some describe the
heroism, daring, and courage shown by Jews in the face of
Nazi bestiality. In one a Jew is hiding in a garret, loaded pistol
in hand, when three German soldiers come up after him,
cursing at the trouble he is giving them. As they approach he
shoots each one so fast that they have no chance to fire back.
He is then ready to put a bullet into his mouth the moment
others come after him. "When none showed up . . . a feeling
of security possessed him that . . . *a Jew can also shoot a
German.*" In another story, a 12-year-old boy, questioned by
Nazi officers, pulls out a hand grenade from inside his bosom
and kills them along with himself. A third tells of another
Jewish boy knowingly taking a group of German officers on a
mined raft across the Dnieper, and all losing their lives in the
explosion. In a fourth, the father of a Jewish partisan leader is
vengefully hanged and left dangling for two weeks. One night
the son and a friend steal up to the gibbet, kill the guard before
he has a chance to cry out, put him in the old man's place,
and take the latter's body away for burial.

In the title story, set in New York, a millionaire manufacturer of lamp shades and a Yiddish journalist cousin of his,
equally distressed by news of the destruction of their native
town in Poland, feel the urge to visit Reb Itche on the lower
East Side. Long alienated from the Hasidism of Reb Itche,

they now yearn for the comfort of his faith. In their talk with the pious Hasid they touch upon the nature of Jewishness and ask him to define its meaning. He replies in a Hasidic manner:

> What is the meaning of Jewishness? Jewishness is what Irving Trives, the king of lamp shades, after living for 25 years without faith, has suddenly felt an inner burning. . . . Such burnings we have always had. Polish Jews continue to feel the Kotsk fire.

And he concludes that Jews will not be destroyed by Hitler. "We will emerge from the world catastrophe badly beaten, but yet strengthened, true Jews of faith."

In a later collection, *Jewish Legends* (1951), Opatoshu included a number of additional stories about German atrocities. These concern not so much the victims as the Jews who escaped the martyrdom and returned at the war's end to find their native towns with not a Jew left. Again and again he intimates that the Nazi nightmare has driven all types of Jews closer to an identification with their fellow Jews. In a number of other stories, in this volume and elsewhere, he also turns to Jewish life of the past and reiterates the stress Jews have always laid on study as man's highest attainment. Typical is the attitude of a barely literate rustic who has grown rich—modeled after Opatoshu's maternal grandfather—who wants his only daughter to marry a scholar. To his rabbi he confides:

> God has blessed me with everything good, even though I'm an ordinary man and can just about read the book of prayer. He has also blessed me with a fine daughter, called Nantche, a bright child. So, holy rabbi, I would like a scholar as a son-in-law. I'll support him all his days so that he may devote himself to his studies.

Hitler's German victory in 1933, ominously forecasting an intensification of Jewish harassment, profoundly agitated Jews in other parts of the world. Sholem Asch, then residing in France, and Opatoshu in New York, both men of vision and ardent Jews, felt impelled to offer sympathy and encouragement to their distressed readers by finding in past calamities the hope of survival and continuity. Both went to Palestine in 1934 to seek inspiration for their self-imposed task; to familiarize themselves with the lie of the land and become saturated with the spirit of the ancient Jewish homeland. Asch, the romantic and impassioned storyteller, while writing as a by-product *The Song of the Valley*, a paean to the dedicated *halutzim*, studied the places and monuments associated with the life of Jesus, convinced that by retelling His life and thought he would awaken a feeling of friendliness among present-day Christians toward their Jewish neighbors. Opatoshu, the realistic and rational novelist, certain that the Jews would find comfort in the heroism of the early martyrs, chose for his theme the uprising in 132 A.D. of the Jewish remnant in Palestine against the mighty legions of the Roman Empire, spearheaded by the renowned Rabbi Akiba and led by the doughty soldier Bar Kokhba. For years, however, work on the book languished, held back by aggravating news from Europe. Only after the defeat of the Nazis was he able to concentrate on the novel, completing the first volume in 1948 and the second shortly before his sudden death in 1954.

In an essay on the background of his writing, appearing in *Die Goldene Keyt* at the time of his death, he stated:

> In *Rabbi Akiba* * [volume one of *The Last Uprising*] I gave the static life of the Jews and, most important, the Jewish outlook on life, the Jewish world outlook, the clash between Judaism and vulgar Hellenism, the conflict between Jews and the first Jew-Christians. In the second volume, *Bar Kokhba,* I dealt with the dynamic life of the period, the war with Rome. In both I have endeavored to give plausible rationalization to the old human fortuities. Whether I succeeded or not I do not know. The fortuities, however, occupy as important a place as the economic and social elements.

The novel is notable for its sustained literary mastery. Opatoshu was not content merely to sing Judea's praises or indulge in sensuous verbalization. Intent on intimating that calamity lay not in defeat but in the fear to fight back, he sought to demonstrate that resistance was in itself an act of salvation. To this end he selected for treatment the period after destruction of the Second Temple, when the Jews remaining in Palestine were dispirited and constrained, neither reconciled to their hapless subjugation nor hopeful of ever regaining their national independence. In chapter after chapter and in burnished and purified prose he describes the daily life of these Jews prior to the uprising. He introduces the reader to aristocrats, patriots, assimilationists; to the inns with their lusty and lively patrons; to the farmers and villagers and manual workers; to the urbanized inhabitants of Jericho and Caesaria; to the quavering and assertive new Christians. Everywhere he depicts the sounds and smells and sights affecting the lives of these people; their individual speech and thoughts, attitudes and reactions, yearnings and ideals—and fears; the conditions and incidents which aggravate peasant and landlord alike and which lead finally to the insurrection in the face of tremendous odds.

Emergence of the heroic Rabbi Akiba as their spiritual leader serves to revive confidence even among the timid and discouraged. Unlike other eminent scholars, he refuses to acquiesce in Roman rule and secretly begins to build up a resistance movement which eventually leads to the uprising under Bar Kokhba. The rabbi, introduced at the height of his fame, is drawn with the insight and incisiveness of imaginative sympathy. His profound wisdom, innate simplicity, tireless energy, and love of the people, revealed gradually by word and deed, combine to authenticate his heroic stature.

As worldly as he is erudite, Rabbi Akiba knows that the success of an uprising against Rome depends on the sinews of war and on a trained army under skilled generalship—in addition to the grace of God. The first he accumulates covertly with the eager and ingenius aid of scores of dedicated patriots. His search for a military leader brings him to an estranged scion of the House of David who was at the time head of a Roman legion in Carthage. On their first meeting the perceptive sage is overjoyed to find in this trained soldier the modesty and mettle of a messiah.

Bar Kokhba describes the speedy and intensive preparations of the secret army and the actual engagement of the powerful Roman legions. The early skirmishes, having the advantage of surprise and initiative, are phenomenally successful. Bar Kokhba's inspired strategy and the dedicated combativeness of the Jewish rebels combine to outwit and outfight the bewildered enemy troops. An entire legion, marching from Egypt toward Jerusalem, is ambushed in the desert and annihilated; the cohort in the walled Judean capital is tricked and destroyed. The Jews in Jerusalem exalt the victor and clamor for the crowning of Bar Kokhba as their king—an action Rabbi Akiba deeply deplores but dares not oppose.

Adulation goes to Bar Kokhba's head. He demands the prerogatives and perquisites of royalty as his due, and begins to act with the arrogance of the impetuous ruler rather than the innate modesty of God's messiah. Rabbi Akiba is grievously disappointed, fearing the consequences, but is loath to criticize him in the midst of war. Gradually, as the fighting becomes a test of endurance, it appears obvious to the distressed sage that Bar Kokhba has lost God's favor and that it is only a matter of time before the besieging Roman legions overrun and crush the trapped Jewish defenders. Bar Kokhba soon senses his predicament, yet he is unwilling to consult with his advisers. For months on end he holds the enemy at bay, warding off attacks with bold ingenuity. When defeat is at last imminent, he deliberately joins the fighting and is slain.

For some time before the collapse, Bar Kokhba's erstwhile admirers realize that he is not their true deliverer; they perceive, moreover, that they have erred in conceiving of the messiah in the singular. In the words of one of them, they conclude that "where there are Jews, there is the messiah." They therefore comfort themselves with the thought that in their defeat they have "lost a battle, no more." On this hopeful note the novel ends.

In this poignant chronicle Opatoshu has combined historic events with artistic invention to give the stamp of reality not only to the actual fighting but also to the gamut of simple and complex activities of the Jews at that time. Rabbi Akiba, Bar Kokhba, and other prominent characters pulsate with the quickness of life—their ideals, ambitions, vanities, jealousies, and heroism merging to give them unique individuality. Equally admirable are the finely wrought Yiddish diction and evocative Hebrew aphorisms and precepts that enhance the narrative. Whether *The Last Uprising* or *In Polish Woods* is Opatoshu's *magnum opus,* there is not doubt as to the excellence of both works.

CHAPTER FOURTEEN

H. LEIVICK

Poet of Pain and Pathos

H. LEIVICK (a name he assumed because his real name, Leivick Halper, was being confused with that of M. L. Halpern) was born in December, 1888, in a small town near Minsk, the eldest of nine children. His father, a redhaired *kahan* and a proud scholar, was reduced to teaching poor girls how to read and write love letters in Yiddish—an occupation which kept him perpetually impoverished and humiliated. The thought that his young wife had to bake and sell bread and bagels to help eke out their wretched livelihood only exacerbated his natural irascibility. This poverty and sense of stigma deeply impressed themselves on little Leivick's mind. Not until he reached manhood did he appreciate and sympathize with his father's choleric state of mind, but his compassion for his mother, as he watched her night after night kneading dough, tortured him to tears from early childhood.

An acutely sensitive boy, endowed with a highly inflated fantasy, Leivick was early inhibited by his father's irascibility —intimidated by his "flaming beard . . . eyes like swords, sharpened for murder." Naturally introverted, he feared to speak up and resorted to silence. Later he wrote in a poem:

> Even as a boy, when all children were at play, I already considered myself grown-up. I lived by myself, aloof from others,

as if I had something to conceal. Even then I saw how people suffer in silence, and I took their silence into myself and imagined that in the far, far distance something great and wonderful will come out of this suffering.

No doubt aware of his responsibility for this muteness, his father nevertheless tormented him with the epithet, "Fool!" This expletive burned itself into Leivick's consciousness: "My irascible father is long dead, but his outcry lives in me." He referred to it over and over in his verse, yet later realized his father's inhibited love for him—so common among fathers of an earlier generation—and imagined being told by him: "Feel on your hand my caress, carry on your mouth my kisses which I wanted to give and should have given you and forever felt too embarrassed to give."

If young Leivick was not loquacious, he evidenced a keenness of mind, so his father believed him capable of becoming a rabbi. In his fifth year the boy began going to *kheder,* and made great strides in his studies. Two years later he experienced a series of traumas. One morning he saw his little sister of four accidentally scald herself to death: "a young, live body scorched, twisted, haphazardly, thoughtlessly." The cruelty of the child's fate long tormented him. That same day in deep winter, he was passing a church on his way to *kheder* when suddenly a tall Pole tore off his cap, knocked him down, and shouted: "*Zhid,* when you pass our church you must doff your hat, *zhid!*" This early taste of anti-Semitism pervaded his memory. In school that morning he studied the story of Isaak's sacrifice with deep apprehension and burst into tears at the end. When asked by his rabbi why he was crying, Leivick exclaimed: "But suppose the angel was a minute late!" The assurance that an angel was never late did not satisfy him: in his imagination he saw Isaak slain by his own father! On his way home he passed a Polish palace and was curious to see for himself if the rumor that the noble's demented son was chained in his room was really true. As he approached one of the windows he saw a giant of a man standing disheveled and wild-eyed. Feeling sorry for him and wishing to make him laugh, he stuck his tongue out and pressed it against the iron bar. It became frozen to the metal, and when he finally managed to tear it loose it bled copiously. Years later he wrote: "These four experiences in one day lay a permanent stamp on my entire life and became the susurrus of all my later poems and plays."

In his tenth year he began a five-year period of study in yeshivas, of eating "days" where he could obtain them and sleeping mostly on the bench where he studied. Although he often went hungry, he luxuriated in the absorption of holy lore and legend. Late in the evening he took advantage of the opportunity to learn Hebrew grammar and diction with a volunteer teacher. The latter also loaned him Hebrew works that in time undermined his piety. Three years later he went to a yeshiva in Minsk, where he gained his first inkling of the world outside of religious tomes. In 1902 Hirsch Leckert, a journeyman shoemaker, tried to assassinate the governor to avenge his brutality to radicals, and the brave worker's stoic behavior during his hanging impressed Leivick deeply. He also learned about the *Bund*, the Jewish socialist organization, and became interested in the revolutionary movement. Expelled from the yeshiva for reading Mapu's *Love of Zion*, a Hebrew novel of enlightenment, he decided to give up the idea of becoming a rabbi.

The 15-year-old Leivick now experienced another traumatic incident. No longer pious and loath to dissemble, he refused to join his father and other *kahanim* in blessing the congregation of Jews on Rosh Hashana. This rejection of his *kahanite* prerogative greatly aggravated his father. In the process of scolding his firstborn he took hold of some of Leivick's Hebrew writings, tore them and threw them into the fire, and said: "For this you gave up your *kahanite* privilege?" Deeply hurt, but refusing to recant, Leivick began to earn his own living as a private teacher to the children of a backwoods Jew. In the two years that he remained in the country he read widely and wrote not a little—crude poetic efforts.

Back in Minsk in 1905, Leivick joined the Bund and devoted

himself to radical activities. He was soon arrested, badly beaten, but released as a minor. The next year he was again arrested and kept for two years in jail awaiting trial. When his case came up, he refused to be defended. Idealistic, romantically heroic, he told the judge: "I will not deny or conceal anything. I am a member of the Jewish party *Bund* and I'll do everything I can to overthrow the Czarist autocracy, the bloody hangmen together with you." He was quickly silenced and sentenced to four years of hard labor followed by permanent exile in Siberia. These years in a Moscow prison were a period of frequent inhuman beatings and deep suffering.

> The prison was for me a fundamental school. I absorbed the special human pain and anguish, depression and exaltation. I saw hangings in the prison yard. We knew that in a certain hour a comrade would be brought to the gallows. The entire prison fluttered: a human being was to hang for his beliefs. . . . I witnessed the depth of human suffering, but I saw not only the suffering of the victim but also his ecstasy.

In an autobiographical volume, *In the Czar's Prison* (1959), he gives a graphically poignant account of his incarceration—an experience that seared his imagination and haunted him day and night for the remainder of his life. Associating with criminal as well as political prisoners, whose torment under almost unbearable conditions brought out beastly as well as noble impulses, he learned the extremes of human behavior and reacted with comprehending compassion.

Having early felt the impulse to write, he composed some verses while in prison and managed to send them to a friend who had migrated to New York. One of these poems was printed in 1907. Most important of his writings in prison was the dramatic poem, *The Messiah in Chains*, which he completed in 1908. For all his youthful agnosticism and radicalism, in this work he gave expression to a source of Jewish lore and legend which had become deeply imbedded in his imagination. Another contemporary poem, "A Soul in Hell or Job the Second," described a spirit in revolt—a youth who rebels against God and strives to become his own master—grieving to see the suffering of his people and impatient for their salvation. Largely autobiographical, the poem is composed of the elements of folklore, poverty, social satire, inner struggle, and the messiah complex—components which were to dominate much of his mature work.

At the completion of his four year sentence in 1912, he was led on a six-month trek to the frozen vastness of Siberia, 2000 miles from the nearest railroad. There he managed to live through the winter by teaching several Jewish children of exiles. He also wrote a drama, *There Where Freedom*, which explores the deeper psychological aspects of human conflict. David, exiled to Siberia, is voluntarily accompanied by his wife Rachel. There they meet Koitman, another exile, and the native-born Lena. Although Koitman loves Lena, he fears to yield to his emotion because it might destroy his hard-won inner freedom. Meantime David, while painting Lena's portrait, falls in love with her and realizes that he had never really loved Rachel. This development drives both Koitman and Rachel to the verge of suicide, and all four end in profound misery. Immature in motivation and dramatic dialogue, the work forecasts the approach and treatment evident in his later writing.

His friend in New York, with whom he had kept in touch, arranged to send him a sum of money with which to make his escape and reach the United States. This Leivick succeeded in doing, arriving in New York in 1913. He became a paperhanger, but soon went to Philadelphia to learn the trade of cutting children's garments. There he published some poems in a local weekly. Not satisfied with his prospects, he returned to New York in 1915 and resumed work as a paperhanger. Evenings he devoted to writing poems, mostly about his prison life. A romantic visionary as well as an intensive pessimist, he sang dreamily, wistfully, yet plaintively of suffering and death. In 1918 his friend B. Charney Vladeck helped him with the cost of printing his first volume, *Behind the Lock*. The initial poem, "Fallen Snow," which Leivick liked best and which had appeared in *Die Zukunft* in 1914, set the tone:

Somewhere far, somewhere far, lies the forbidden land; silver-blue the mountains, not yet stepped on by anyone; somewhere deep, somewhere deep, kneaded in the land, treasures wait for us, covered-over, treasures wait.

Somewhere far, somewhere far, a prisoner lies alone, and over his head the light of the sinking sun is dying; somewhere some-one wobbles in the deep snow and finds no way to the forbidden land.

In poem after poem he relates his pain, fears, dreams, and visions. It was as if his imagination were wholly engrossed in his feelings and perceptions while in prison. "It seems I'll always remain chained, never perceive a sunset; suddenly night comes and seizes me like a wolf his prey, tramples me, bloodies me, rolls me in the dust." Pain, blood, death were his recurrent topics, white snow covering the blood underneath. When he occasionally removes the snow, the blood is still warm. He was asked irascibly: "Why do you torture us with blood?" And his poems, he complains, were trampled upon in anger.

My poems—they cried out, as is the habit of pain, and remained lying on the earth, but no longer covered with snow. Forever a writer, my truth is still in that in the blood of whipped bodies lies my own whipped self. . . . Perhaps I'll again cover them when I'll have new snow. . . .

The woeful years 1914–1920 turned Leivick from his agon-ized personal memories to the immediately tragic suffering of the Jews in Eastern Europe, which galvanized his thoughts of salvation and stirred his vision of the legendary golem as a mythical redeemer. The Golem,* published in 1920, was at once recognized as a masterly work of the poetic imagination. In 1925 it was performed by the Habima troupe in Moscow, and many years later was produced in English both as a drama and as an opera.

The dream of a messiah had early occupied Leivick's fantasy. It took concrete form after the pogroms in the early 1900's, when it seemed that salvation by a messiah was the only solution to Jewish persecution. All through his years in prison he struggled with the problem—his revolutionary ardor warring more and more feebly against the vision of redemption ingrained in him during childhood. *The Messiah in Chains,* his first dramatic rendering, became in effect the introduction to the two major dramas Leivick was to write.

Following known legend and improvising his own myth to give cogency to the narrative, Leivick tells how, on the third day after the destruction of Jerusalem by Titus, angels went to the wilderness to forge a chain with which to bind the young messiah. "Out of pain of Jerusalem's destruction in fire and smoke, he was born to be for Israel an eternal dream and for the world a prophecy of peace."

Azriel, one of the angels, rebels against God's punishment of Israel and insists that "one death of a child is enough to keep all worlds in fear, to overflow the cup of tears"—according to legend the messiah must wait until the cup is filled. He tells the other angels that he cannot remain in heaven while people on earth are suffering. "Although we all know that it is the will of God, every grain of sand is crying out: Why? Why?" He adds that the messiah must not be chained, that "the world can't wait, the destruction is too great." When he begins to strike at the chain, lightning burns off his wings and a voice calls out that he is doomed to the end of time. Satan now appears and states that it is his mission to be guardian of the messiah. Elijah then brings in the sleeping messiah and weeps as the chain is forged on the youthful redeemer. He counsels the awakened youth to be patient, for the world is still too sinful to warrant his coming. The messiah thereupon exclaims: "People of Israel, do not keep quiet, do not wait, call me as I do—call me; come, break my chains, come, liberate me." Satan, however, prevents it.

This youthful work gives evidence of the imagination, rebelliousness, and beauty which were to characterize Leivick's later poetic dramas. Azriel speaks for him as the rebel against tradition and conformity, the visionary who risks his own doom in the effort to redeem suffering humanity, the prophet who

chides his fellow angels "who love only themselves and Paradise." Elijah, complying with God's command, nevertheless
weeps for the chained messiah and tells him: "I'll go over the
earth and tell all the people that you are here; and all will
bless themselves in your name."

Leivick continued to ponder the messianic dream, com-
mingling it with both his prison pains and the agony of Jews
in the pogrom-ridden areas. In 1917 he began to write *The
Golem*. Long attracted to the legend, he conceived of the
golem as the precursor of the messiah, the son of Joseph who
is to serve as the temporary redeemer at a critical juncture
and use force as necessary, which the real messiah—the son
of David—must not employ. Following the legend, Leivick
has Rabbi Levi of Prague mold the golem out of clay, breathe
into him the breath of life, and endow him with supernatural
powers. It should be stressed that Rabbi Levi, unlike other
mystical experimenters with creation of life, resorts to this
cabalism not for personal gratification but to save his fellow
Jews from grave danger—and only because the time is not
yet ripe for the advent of the real messiah. Thus he informs
the golem of his powers:

> Through suffering and tears I have supplicated God to give you
> miraculous powers: you should be able to see that which none
> can see, and hear all that none can hear; to feel with your tread
> nine ells deep; fire shall have no access to your body, and deep
> water shall not drown you; and your nose shall smell the odors
> of the farthest winds; and when necessary your body shall be-
> come diaphanous as rays, as air, and change form at will—you
> shall be *seeing, unseen*. . . .

Early in the poem Tadeusch, the evil Christian spirit, approaches Rabbi Levi just as he is about to instil life into the
golem and is shocked by what he sees in the sage's eyes. "How
does murder come to a rabbi? In my life I have seen many
faces of Jews in prison and on the stakes of the holy court,
eyes of all description, but I have not seen Jewish eyes that
look upon me with such murder, angry hate, as yours—they

look like the eyes of a wild golem." So in truth they are, for in the process the rabbi's eyes assumed the aspect with which he was to endow the golem.

The golem is no sooner alive than he becomes subject to human feelings and impulses. He serves the rabbi unwillingly, and only on command. When he sees Dvorele, the rabbi's granddaughter, he is immediately attracted to her and resents being snubbed by her. His mission begins when Tadeusch and a monk place two flasks of blood, extracted from a slaughtered Christian child, deep under the synagogue in order to provoke a massacre with the blood accusation. The rabbi is aware of this dastardly deed and empowers the golem to penetrate the magically secured hiding place and remove the flasks of blood. Tadeusch exerts himself to keep the golem out, but fails.

In the meantime Rabbi Levi learns that Elijah and the messiah, aware of the peril to the Jews, cannot remain in the wilderness, and are approaching as beggars to the place of the fiendish plot. Fearful of the risk they are taking by appearing before their time, he forces himself to drive them away, indicating that the golem is their surrogate and therefore empowered to use force.

His assigned mission performed, the golem feels restive and wretched. He doesn't want to be subservient to the rabbi, and yearns to live like a human being and love Dvorele. In a moment of distress he takes up his axe—the symbol of force—and runs amuck splitting the heads of Jews. Rabbi Levi hurries to him and subdues the golem with his gaze. Shocked by the havoc the golem has caused, he cries out: "Did I bring you here to be like other people? . . ." And he laments: "On my head falls the blood, on my head. He came to rescue—and now he himself spills blood. . . . I sought to avoid blood—and let blood flow. . . ." He then forces the golem to lie down in the garret of the synagogue and become inanimate clay again.

The poem is rich in symbolism, allusions, and mystical and legendary intimations—sometimes nebulous, sometimes murky, but always deeply and imaginatively felt. In certain respects the golem represents the Russian revolution, which Leivick feared as much as he admired. In the golem is also symbolized the idea that whatever is alive seeks freedom and independence. He further represents the symbol of resistance as opposed to the age-old Jewish nonresistance in time of danger, which so nonplussed the Jew-hating Tadeusch. In addition to its poetic imagery and symbolism, its minor *walpurgisnacht* and the Jesuslike Tanhum, the work is suffused with an authentic sense of suffering, which according to legend must precede messianic salvation. Leivick stated: "I wrote *The Golem* out of my own direct jail experience. If I had not been in prison, if I had not *lain* stretched out on a stone floor in an ever-dark cell, and if I had not seen others lie similarly, I am not sure I would have written *The Golem.*. Certainly I would not have written as I did." S. Niger, who has made the most thorough study of Leivick's writings, declared:

> Not always do depth and insight combine in *The Golem.* This defect notwithstanding, the impression remains that according to its scope, its basic problem, its deep and broad breath of fearful worlds, the extraordinary dramatism of the main figures and the superb lyricism of many specific passages, it must be considered as the highest achievement in Yiddish poetry.

About the time Leivick completed the work, he showed signs of tuberculosis and had to be treated in a sanitarium in the mountains, where he remained until 1922. He did not, however, stop writing and composed numerous poems about the pogroms in Europe as well as prose plays about Jewish life in the United States. All the while he continued to ponder the problem of messianic salvation, and in 1932 finished *The Salvation Comedy—The Golem Dreams.*

In the interim Leivick's golem has undergone considerable transformation. After four centuries of inanimation, though passively yearning for the life of a messiah, he awakens in the garret of the Prague synagogue as Yosel, the very image of the authentic messiah, Hanina ben David. He has not forgotten his former existence as the golem, and when he sees Dvorele, a descendant of Rabbi Levi, he is reminded of the Dvorele he had once desired. When asked who he is, he says: "He who dreams." Yearning for the messiah, he goes to the wilderness to release him from his chains. They declare their affection for each other, and Yosel tells Hanina that he is now needed not only in Prague but in the entire world; that "wars, hunger, final outcries, final hopes, and ben Joseph in danger—" "That is the evidence," Hanina cries out. "That is it—quick, come."

Legend has it that when the evil Gog and Magog will rule the world, ben Joseph, as the precursor of the real messiah, will come to destroy them. He will himself then thirst for power, and this will bring ben David and world redemption. Along with these protagonists are Armilus, "the prophet of the eternal now," who is faithful to none and fearful of none, for he symbolizes inevitability. With him is the executioner with the axe, who does the bidding of each ruler in turn—a mere instrument in the hands of those in power.

Magog overthrows Gog and is in turn defeated by ben Joseph. Eager to perpetuate his power yet aware of his relation to Hanina ben David, ben Joseph is ready to follow the ordained course of events. But his wife Lilith hates Hanina and goads her husband into becoming a usurper—encouraged by Armilus, who tells him enigmatically, "Whatever is, has to be." Hanina now approaches. Elijah, blind but able to go about as he wishes, urges him in vain to return to the wilderness. "I can't go back. I am no longer the solitary coddled one of the wilderness. . . . I want to be with the people, and that which awaits me—let it come. And that which I must bring—I shall bring through will and testing and not through chance, as once in Prague." He thus becomes a revolutionary, and does not turn back when Elijah warns him that he will not be greeted with joy, that he will be jailed and tortured, that man is still evil, and that even Yosel will betray him. "Salvation is more important than the savior," Hanina declares. "My fate should also be no more than fate."

So it happens. Hanina is beaten by the mob which hails ben Joseph; he is accused of always preaching restraint and pain. Elijah tries to save him from arrest, but both, together with

Yosel, who now regrets having momentarily turned from the messiah, are imprisoned on ben Joseph's orders. When tortured, Hanina does not even emit a sigh. Ben Joseph urges him to abdicate, but is told that his mission is already at an end. Ben Joseph then begs to be saved—admitting that all he wanted was happiness. Hanina tells him that a savior need not be happy, only the people. "You want *too much* and therefore you have betrayed your mission."

Meantime the people reject ben Joseph and hail ben David. Armilus, as always, prophesying what is and denouncing what was, tells ben David that he must execute ben Joseph or be killed by him, that as long as ben Joseph is alive fear will prevail. Ben David is given the axe and told it is inevitable. "First was the axe, and as it was in the beginning so it must be at the end." Hanina ben David then states that if ben Joseph has to be killed, he himself must do it. Elijah, whose tongue ben Joseph had cut out, approaches and motions that he must do it—indicating that salvation does not come about peacefully. Ben David kills ben Joseph and weeps that he should have blood on his hands—for he fully accepts the responsibility. For a day and a night he mourns, locked in his cell. Then he emerges and tells Yosel to take his place as the messiah. "You are I—only more plain, more whole. . . . You are I—only jollier and stronger and healthier. The people will see in you one of their own." Turning to Dvorele, who has followed him devotedly from the beginning, he tells her he deserves no pity and asks the executioner to do his duty.

Yosel, now acclaimed as the messiah, tells the assembled people: "Listen again and again to the story of love that became blood, the story of blood that became wine." And the people respond: "Wine of salvation, wine of salvation, it goes into the blood."

The Salvation Comedy does not measure up to the poetic fervor of *The Golem*. It is a mature work architectonically, the characters are drawn with imagination and insight, and the complex symbolism is clearly intimated, but poetically the work seldom rises to the ardor and intensity of the earlier drama. For all that, it is a major achievement and completes Leivick's artistic near-monopoly of the messiah theme in Yiddish literature. His view of human salvation is well expressed in the foreword: "Each one of us is responsible for everything and for the deeds done in the world; each is a partner and shares in the guilt, even when it seems to him that he is standing apart and does not partake in the deeds of the world, and each must pay for his responsibility. Each one."

Of the numerous poems included in *In No Man's Land* (1923), the pogrom poems "He," "The Sick Room," "The Stable," and "The Wolf" are among the longest and most weighted with the symbolism characteristic of Leivick's agonized fantasy. The first is largely a monologue by Jesus on visiting the poet in time of a pogrom. Leivick regarded Jesus sympathetically: "The Nazarene himself, as a man of suffering, attracted me. I saw in him simply the prisoner. . . . I am excessively pained by the figure of Jesus Christ. He is to me the expression of all who find salvation through pain." In this poem Jesus is such a figure. He decries the falseness of his position and is distressed by the behavior of his followers. He is also deeply troubled by his mother who, "when she saw me dying, tortured, kissed me with hot lustful lips, as if she were my bride and not my mother." Ever since then He has been tormented by the impulse to slay her: "The world is now filled with pogroms, with butchery and the law of murder—why should I be an exception? Why should I not fulfill the law of murder as others do?" "The Sick Room" is a fantasy about a king lying ill in bed and giving voice to his dreams and fancies. The four walls of the room and furniture within it express their reactions to the patient. Here the symbolism is stressed to the point of fogginess and is saved only by its lyric intensity.

"The Stable" is headed by an excerpt from a letter: "Our cold synagogue was turned by the Germans into a stable—they kept the horses there." In verses charged with pain Leivick describes the coming of the soldiers, their brutality toward the town's inhabitants, and their defiling of the synagogue. A family of brothers with their wives and children find a hiding place deep in the forest. The older ones accept their plight fatalistically, but not the youngest. "Consumed in the brothers' eyes is the last spark of anger; but one of them—the youngest in years—still caresses the flame of fever, of longing for the home in the village, of longing for deliverance of himself and all his brothers." Unable to contain himself, he runs off to the village to see what is happening. On a hill overlooking the ruined homes, hidden by merciful night, he sees visions of symbolic gladness. "With his heart full of song and his mind full of dreams, the younger brother left the hill and ran back to his elder brothers in the forest to tell them what his eyes had seen, and what his ears had heard on the hill," only to find them with their throats cut—in sheer despair of deliverance. This summary gives but a faint notion of the poem's beauty and pathos; while the symbolism which colors it is sometimes recondite, the poet's grief at the desecration of life and home throbs with the freshness of suffering.

Even more gruesome is "The Wolf," a chronicle of stark fantasy. A rabbi regains consciousness on the third day of a pogrom to find himself the only survivor. His memory gone, he cannot even recall his daily prayers. He beats himself in his anguish and seeks shelter in a nearby wood, where he is suddenly turned into a wolf.

In time Jews who had survived pogroms elsewhere come to settle in the deserted town and soon rebuild the ruined synagogue. One day they see an old Jew, in a rabbi's torn garb, hurrying to the synagogue. There he shouts angrily: "Who asked you to rebuild the ruins? What is ruined should remain ruined. And who asked you to become my inheritors? Bring an axe and a knife and do me justice, do me justice, I beg you." And he howls like a wolf and weeps like a Jew, and slinks back to the wood. Thereafter, night after night, a howling is heard from midnight to dawn, causing great fright among the Jews. On Yom Kippur afternoon the ghostly wolf suddenly breaks into the assembly of Jews in the synagogue, jumps upon the cantor and begins choking him. A worshipper seizes a desk and strikes the wolf over the head, breaking its skull. What the Jews then see is not a wolf but the rabbi. Dying, he whispers comfortingly, "Now I feel good, very good – Jews, do not weep."

The scores of briefer lyrics in the book evidence Leivick's new interest in free verse as well as his concern for the polished expression of diction, rhythm, metaphor, and imagery. They are poignant, dream-ridden, at times murky of meaning, yet haunting in their lyric intensity and impassioned pathos.

In the 1920's Leivick turned to the theater in the hope of earning enough from playwriting to give up paperhanging. Although the first of his plays was highly popular, the others either failed or were not even produced. He was no man to truckle to the vulgar stage, and the theses he propounded were not only inadequately motivated but too painfully idealistic to have wide appeal.

Rags (1921) was produced by Maurice Schwartz of the Yiddish Art Theater and had a long and successful run. Abraham Cahan was so favorably disposed toward it that he not only reviewed it at length and enthusiastically but also serialized it in *Der Forverts*—an exceptional instance that went far to assure the play's popularity. Theatrically the best of his dramas, *Rags* deals with the tragedy of the individual thrust into a world alien to him. Mordecai Maze, in his native Russia a dignified scholar and a man of substance, cannot adapt himself to his crass American milieu and resists its influences with all the strength of his character. Forced to become a rag picker to earn a meager subsistence, he refuses to join the other old men in striking for an extra dollar a week—to him a feeble and futile gesture against their sorry fate. Nor is he understood by his wife and children, who in their eagerness to conform ignore his sense of dignity and decency. His firmness and integrity, preserved by a feeling of resignation, separate him from Leivick's other nonconformists by the genuine tragedy of his condition. In the grip of circumstances he cannot control, he remains grieved but determined, bearing his adverse fate without flinching and retaining his faith in God.

Different (1922) and *The Impoverished Kingdom* (1923), both produced by the Yiddish Art Theater without success, fail to develop protagonists of dramatic stature. In the first the main character, having fought in the war "to make the world safe for democracy," expects on his return to find life different from what it was when he left. Sorely disappointed, he rebels against bourgeois smugness, behaves quixotically, and seems like a sick soul fighting phantoms. In the other, Melekh wants to be king of his circle of friends and business associates. Stronger and more brutal than his competitors, he prevails against their mediocrity. His lack of happiness, however, tends to humanize him—especially when he comes up against a son who insists on being different from him. In neither play is the motivation strong or persuasive enough to endow the protagonists with sympathetic credibility.

Bankrupt (1924) and *The Shop* (1926) are concerned largely with radicals in a capitalistic environment. In the first Urie Don, a socialist and Siberian exile, hopes to find the United States a land of ideal freedom. Quickly disillusioned, he remains disoriented and depressed. Unable to adjust to the materialistic attitude of the labor leaders, he is forced to accept the offer of his wife's wealthy uncle to set him up in business. The routine of storekeeping soon palls on him and he listlessly lets himself go bankrupt. Worried into a state of neurosis, he refuses to meet creditors, makes vague intimations of self-destruction, and generates misery in himself and those close to him. In *The Shop* Minna represents political socialism, Lipman—ethical socialism, Wolf—the radical become boss, Gould—his aggressive and ruthless partner, and Barkan—the crafty designer ready to demean himself for material gain. In the action stress is laid on the disparity between human ideals and industrial reality, yet incident follows incident without well-motivated psychological verity. One gets the impression that Leivick wrote these plays without the insight and intensity that enhance his poetic dramas.

Hirsch Leckert (1927), produced in several parts of the world, is a romantic treatment of a hero of Leivick's adolescence. In prison awaiting execution, Hirsch is visited by a rabbi and told that the governor whom he had wounded would commute his hanging to imprisonment if he would reveal the names of his associates. The illiterate but idealistic shoemaker scorns the very thought of becoming an informer. He still burns with indignation at the governor's brutal behavior toward radicals and feels proud to be dying for the cause of freedom. In verse that sings and shouts and takes wing, Leivick glorifies the idealistic individual in opposition to a brutal bureaucracy.

The last of these plays, *Chains* (1929), was staged by Schwartz and also played in Poland and Tel Aviv. Set in prison, the action generates social conflict and political rivalry. Levine is an orthodox Bolshevik who insists that political change will alter man; Joseph, though also a Marxist, believes that man must change first before he can transform society. Neither yields in their frequent discussions. Donie, a new youthful prisoner, enters as a disciple of Levine but in the end is converted to Joseph's view. When an officer, as a means of punishment, orders the sixth in line to be shot, Levine takes that place and dies a hero. Here, too, Leivick's intent falls short of dramatic achievement; neither protagonist comes alive. Bogged by his dichotomous evaluation of Russian Bolshevism, which in 1925 he had observed wistfully at first hand, four years later he favored Joseph's human position without completely rejecting Levine's revolutionary ethic.

Leivick had a compulsion to write, ending a day's work as a paperhanger with a long evening at his desk. His mind seethed with ideas, impulses, emotions of anger and affection. These thoughts and feelings he expressed in poems, short or long, which served to give him a modicum of relief from the agitation of his driven conscience. In many verses he continued to give lyrical voice to visions arrogating his imagination, to the theme of death which never fully left him. In the foreword to *The Salvation Comedy* he stated: "I do not seek destruction but, on the contrary, I seek with all my strength to perceive in the world, in human history, the law of pure conscience, the meaning of destroyed lives." This seeking, emphasized over and over in numerous poems and plays, was to him an endless and vain yearning—as ineffectual as his effort to discard his "prison coat." In the process he produced verses of inspired beauty, not always unambiguous of meaning but often brilliant in their prophetic passion.

Pertinent is the series, "Poems to a Distant Friend," written in the late 1920's. These verses about his life in America are moody, reflective, sad, stating with painful honesty his difficulty of orientation. In one he writes: "There is a song which is sung without words, with a closed mouth lowered to the earth; to be understood, to be heard I am not always fated." In "Love": "The truth of the word I apprehend as the truth of death. I see them always paired—they accompany me with much love." In other poems he voices similar sentiments: "To tell the whole truth, I am surprised at myself, and how could I plant you in my heart—the granite stone. And how could I suddenly spread out like a deep-rooted tree, when I carry seven deaths within me and the dumbness of a clay golem?" "I live at the brink of an abyss with a coldness of view, from the first day I landed in this country sated with happiness. . . . I tell you again plain and open: I feel cold and alien in this land, and may my present verses be for the Yankee as prickly as sand." "I wish fate had made me able to lie at the feet of the world, so that all may see, and all may believe, that hate is love, and poison is sweet. And death is—life, and earth is— fire, and the body is wavy and flows as light; for everything in the world wants to be kissed, as a face." These excerpts intimate his ambivalent feeling toward his adopted land, despite his frequent expressions of love for it.

In 1932 Leivick's tuberculosis worsened and he became a patient in the Denver Sanitarium. There he remained three years, a period not only of physical recuperation but also great literary productivity. He spent another year in the sanitarium of the Workmen's Circle in Liberty, New York. A number of his verses naturally were stimulated by his experience as a patient. The first poem begins: "Open up, gate, approach, doorstep—I come to you again, roomlet, cell. My body—fire, my head—snow; and on my shoulders a sack of outcries." Yet his room was hardly a prison cell and his outcries were controlled—soothed by Colorado's natural beauty and grandeur. The poem ends: "I lay at your feet my sack of outcries, land of Colorado of fire and snow." During this period his poems became quieter, clearer, more reconciled. "Mendel the Fool," for instance, was a lilting, simple, yet insightful poem about a dull-witted watercarrier of his childhood whom he had reason to remember because his father had often compared him to Mendel.

A longer and more important poem is "The Ballad of Denver Sanitarium." Reflecting a healthy and sympathetic attitude toward the hospital and its patients—"one thread of blood binds us all, white wisdom rests on all our lips"—he continued: "I do not fear my own death—I fear the death of my neighbor." This thought governs the ballad, essentially the pathetic story of Nathan Newman, who entered the sanitarium at the age of 16 and remained there until his death 15 years later. A sensible youth, eager to live but ready to die, he clings to life and appreciates Leivick's interest in him. When at death's door, he writes to his betrothed not to visit him and to forget him, for he is already pledged to death. He offers Leivick a trinket as a memento—only to retain it in the hope of living another day. The ballad of this youth surges with deep feeling: not woefully, yet wistfully, and in quatrains that sing and sigh with verbal felicity.

In addition to many poems Leivick wrote *Sodom, The Sacrifice, The Poet Became Blind,* and *Abelard and Heloise,* truly a prolific output in a time of recuperation.

Sodom is a dramatic retelling of the destruction of this wicked city. The three angels approach it to do the will of God, but the third, like Azriel in *The Messiah in Chains,* rebels against this arbitrary punishment of men. "My heart is full of anguish and tears, of outcries and compassion, of insult and revolt. I remain here on earth. . . . Men suffer, and I want to suffer with them." Like Abraham he hopes to find ten virtuous men and thus prevent the city's destruction, but his effort is in vain. Sodom, depicted too obviously like Nazi Germany, is dedicated to evil. King Bre forbids the poor to weep or cry out when overburdened. He commands his followers: "Hate the weak unto destruction. Do not fear to kill or shed blood." Strangers are despised and maltreated. Only Lot's older daughter defies these inhuman laws, and Lot weakly resists them. Consequently destruction becomes inevitable. The fine sentiments of the third angel notwithstanding, the acid of antipathy sears the action and gives it an aspect of subjective exaggeration.

The Sacrifice (1933) is of a much higher artistic order. The dedication reads: "To the memory of all who lost their lives innocently as a sacrifice on any altar, whether a group of stones, a hole in a jail, a bed in a hospital, or even the stoop of a house." Abraham, commanded by God to sacrifice Isaak, is emotionally shattered but obedient. Satan, here more ironical than evil, approaches him baitingly, telling him that not he but Abraham's own heart tempts him and urges him not to slay Isaak; Satan assures the distressed patriarch of his pity for the living, of feeling the quaking pain of the least living thing. Abraham, however, ignores him and proceeds to carry out God's command. Sarah, unaware of the dread mission but conscience-troubled about her bad behavior toward Hagar and Ishmael, fears that the latter may harm Isaak in the wilderness, but Abraham reassures her. When, on reaching Mt. Moriah, Isaak is told of his fate, he cannot understand it. "But why should *I* be the sacrifice? Why did not God ask me if I want to be it?" Abraham explains that God "needs not to ask anyone," but Isaak counters: "But you—why did *you* not ask me if I want to die?" All Abraham can say to that is that it is "God's will."

When a voice from on high saves Isaak and the sheep is

discovered and sacrificed in his stead, both father and son are emotionally spent and fall asleep. Ishmael comes upon the comatose pair. His fife awakens Isaak, now gray and aged, and he keeps Ishmael from his impulse to slay Abraham. Ishmael comments bitterly: "He made himself the chosen one, keeps blessing the future generations which will issue from him . . . and to achieve these blessings he is ready to commit crimes against those near to him." Shortly after he leaves, Abraham wakens and Isaak, telling him he is now "fire and knife," forces Abraham to undergo his own ordeal. When Abraham asks for pity, Isaak exclaims: "Silence! You saw my death throes and merely simulated pity, and I don't simulate." Then, when he is satisfied that his father has experienced his own mortal anguish, he tells him: "That which I needed, I have already achieved. I don't need your death. On the contrary—live. *Now live!*" And to God he declares: "This will be my pact, God, with you and the world. And this shall be a reminder to all who will raise a hand against a living being; a sign for all generations that none may raise a hand against a living being."

This is Leivick speaking. From the time, as a boy of seven, he first learned about Isaak's plight, he could not reconcile it with his concept of God's goodness.The more he thought about it the more firmly he believed that life was too precious to be destroyed—not only human life but all life. He therefore concluded that it was even wrong to slay the sheep in Isaak's stead. When, as a boy of 11, he took the part of the sheep in a yeshiva performance of *Isaak's Sacrifice*, the beet juice spilled over his sheep skin had a terrible effect upon him. In the drama he stresses this preciousness of life. Because he believed that Abraham had. no right to agree to sacrifice Isaak under any circumstances, he subjects him to the same ordeal which had turned his 13-year-old son into a grayhaired man. Leivick, indeed, rejects "a sacrifice on the altar of ideals no less than a sacrifice of fate." The drama, giving expression to a point of view he maintained tenaciously, and to resulting emotions of sublime grandeur, is replete with felicitous phrasing of ideas, images, and feelings.

The Poet Became Blind (1934) was dedicated to Morris Rosenfeld and is based in part on the poet's life—alluding to the general lack of appreciation of poets. The one in the play, lonely, dejected, despairing, pretends blindness as a means of arousing interest in himself—and it works! All kinds of people express their pity and regard, but he now drives them away. Later, unable to attend the celebration of his 25 years as a poet because of illness, he is cheered by a chorus coming to his home to sing his songs. In paying homage to Rosenfeld's memory Leivick had himself in mind, and his pride and sense of dignity engendered a restraint which made the play a work of relatively minor import.

In the same year Leivick completed *Abelard and Heloise*, a poetic drama of intense emotion and lyrical fineness. As in more than one other instance, he preceded the major work with a series of individual poems on the immortal pair. In one Abelard hears Heloise: "It is I in truth, I—your sister, I—your mother, I—your dream, all together. . . ." The play begins with Abelard, elderly and in dire pain from beatings for heresy, refusing to submit to Father Gregory, the head of the monastery. The latter taunts him with having found and read Heloise's letters. "So bless the hand which out of pain deserves to offer you such love. Here I see what she writes to you: such repressed outcries, so much woe, such stubborn patience, such devotion, such responsibility for your fate; and each word is blood." Gregory then informs Abelard that 15 years previously it was he who had castrated him because of his own love for Heloise.

Heloise, disguised as a dumb monk, visits Abelard in his cell, and the two reiterate their devotion to each other. She calls him husband and intimates that she has inflicted upon herself the punishment meted out to him. He tells her of his childhood dreams, of his vision and love of her, and expresses the hope that both be saved from their common betrayer. Later, with the help of a friendly monk, the pair meet in a nearby wood. In embracing her he feels the chain around her body, and she tells him she feels easier having the chain on her, since it makes her partner to his suffering. "The world has wildly and coarsely tortured your body—so my body must be equally tortured. And if the executioner spared me, you'll forgive me—although I cannot forgive myself—so I sought out a long chain and wound it around my body. . . ."

Abelard speaks with Leivick's own distaste of bodily lust, his own struggle between physical desire and spiritual loftiness. And he has ennobled the ideal of human devotion in paeans of praise that flare into fiery lyrics. The love burning in Heloise and Abelard—both physically worn with prolonged torture—is a pure flame fed by emotion purged of all grossness and sensuality. Wholly romantic in concept, it is elegized in verse that sings and soars.

In 1936 Leivick was well enough to return to New York. Employment on *Der Tog* enabled him at last to give up paperhanging. That December he was chosen to represent Yiddish writers at the P.E.N. conference in Buenos Aires. Since it was a time of aggressive fascism and Jewish persecution in Europe, he took this opportunity to lash out against all who actively or passively condoned these political and religious abuses. Maintaining that by their silence they "paint its [fascist] face with lying words," he elaborated:

> The conscience of contemporary literature is sick, dying. . . . Genuine art does not tolerate mobism, pride of power, discrimination. We respect and value deeply the great artistic achievements of the European literatures; we do not respect and do not value them if they assume privileges which have no relation to art, and value even less the snobbism which certain literatures show to those of smaller nations, and we despise the strains of racial hatred, bloodthirstiness, and sadistic enmity which wound the face of contemporary world literature.

Turning to the subject of Yiddish literature he declared: "The main problem of our literature in the 20th century is to find the synthesis of the national with the universal Jew and world —that is the basic drama of our life and literature." His earnestness and forthrightness were truly impressive and gave many of the delegates their first inkling of the significance of the writings in Yiddish.

In 1937 he attended the conference of the Jewish World Congress in Paris, where he expounded the importance of Yiddish in Jewish life. He also visited Palestine and parts of Europe. The upsurge of Nazi hatred caused him to cry out in Joblike prayers. In a series of 20 poems, "Hitler Night Motives," he records his reactions to and reflections on Nazi brutality. One begins: "I could never understand where lies the true sense, that the strong hands of the torturer should *always* find a sacrificial body." "Poems On the Yellow Patch" propound the thought that he as a Jew should also wear one—and proudly. In another poem he declared: "Each day brings us full cups of poison, horrible news of death and destruction; my dream of being good like a lamb evaporates, as do my poems with their quiet, silenced lines."

On his return to New York Leivick wrote *Who's Who* (1938), a drama about a Jewish victim of a pogrom who vainly sought to escape the ordeal of being a Jew. Alexander Schelling's wife was raped and his infant daughter crippled by Petlura's hooligans in 1919. He flees with them to Germany, becomes a teacher of mathematics, and passes as a non-Jew in his effort to escape further persecution. When Hitler comes on the scene and a friend urges Schelling to acknowledge his Jewishness as a matter of self-respect, he asks: "Return to what? Where? Jewish life means Jewish suffering; without suffering Jewish life has no meaning. But suffering must have a meaning. He who suffers must know *why* he is suffering. But you and I—where is the meaning for us? Misfortune—that is all I see in Jewish suffering. Misfortune and soul-searing." He forbids his son to associate with Jews and seeks to prevent *Who's Who* from mentioning his Jewish origin. When his son learns this he feels too proud to "hide the truth of their life." In the end Schelling, after acute soul-searching, decides to acknowledge his Jewishness.

In treating a problem which grievously afflicted many Jews in Germany and elsewhere in the late 1930's, Leivick conceived it intellectually rather than intuitively; for all his sympathy with their plight he could not repress a feeling of contempt for the self-seeking denial of their Jewishness. Schelling emerges with a diminution of dignity—and a vivid awareness of personal failure. Years later Leivick told an interviewer:

> I led all the heroes in my plays into the depth of suffering and sought together with them how to rise out of this depth—cleansed. Man is sentenced to sorrow and enters into its depths, is tossed about. But he must remain master of himself, not yield to his suffering, save himself from his suffering, save himself from the dictates of chance.

Schelling is in the end neither cleansed nor saved.

During World War II Leivick could not drive from his mind the thought that he was safe in New York while millions of fellow Jews were being tortured and burned to death. His earlier keen sense of suffering became an open, festering wound again. In poem after poem he expressed his feelings of woe, guilt, and death. *In Treblinka I Never Was* (1945), in which they appear, is dedicated to his sister and brothers who had lost their lives in crematoria. "In Treblinka I never was, nor in Maedaneck, but I stand at their entrance, on their doorstep. . . . I stand and wait, great world, on your command: 'Jew head, into the gas chamber!' " Like Isaak he feels guilty to have escaped "the fire of Treblinka. . . . From Mt. Moriah to Maedaneck is not more than an Isaak step." Again: "I envy more the martyr than the hero. My father also loved them more, and so my grandfather and great-grandfather. They were more attracted to the victims on the gallows than to the heroes on the barricades."

His imagination scans the millennia, as if seeking comfort in past persecutions, and covers his grief with the gleam of irony. "The Ballad of the Wilderness" is a long dream fantasy on the 3000-year trek which the Jews have been making in the wilderness from Egypt to Treblinka. In folksong form are woven the experiences of the Israelites led by Moses, among whom he saw his parents and his rabbi as well as himself; the yellow patch flowers on the arms of these Jewish wanderers as they die, are reborn, and die again—and all is told in cadenced lines of repressed anguish. In a series, "In the Garret the Roof Complains," are songs about the holocaust to be sung by street singers: "Our people are being murdered, and the world ignores it, and the whole world remains dumb to the pain of our outcries. Let us break every door, let us knock down every wall, let everyone's heart freeze in the grip of German hands." In the elegy on the Warsaw ghetto he reminds his readers that the desperate Jews there exclaimed in their uprising: "*Gewald*, Jews, do not despair!"—a call that became "the Eleventh Commandment"—and concludes: "The Germans silenced everything in Warsaw, but not these few small words."

In "A Letter from My Father, May His Soul Rest in Peace," he is told by his father that after lying 30 years in his grave his spirit became restive and decided to visit the town again— only to find it in ruins. "So woe is me, what shall I say, my devoted son—and ask me why did I compose these rhymes? Perhaps only to report, perhaps only for that—that your brothers like heroes died as martyrs." In a letter to his long-dead mother Leivick apologizes for being already older than she was, but that life is as Isaiah foretold: "The earth yields our people red honey, sticky, sweet-tasting honey. Nations surround it with kindness and love and throw entire suns before its feet. On all trees hang Stars of David, and in all fields lie holy scrolls, and in these scrolls man, wife, and child in all forms lie in sweet sleep."

With the war ended, he advises no vindictiveness: "We curse you, murderers, we rejoice in your defeat; we curse you even more because you have poisoned our hearts with curses." And in a series of 14 sonnets, "Cycle of Summation," he states: "I know, now is not the time for sonnets, now is the time for cannon and tanks; man is dark and his spirit is sick, there is none whom to reach, whom to beg. Yet my heart sings thanks —that under mountains of hangman's decrees there still quivers the dream of true poets: man will be bright as God's thoughts."

During these years of agony Leivick also wrote *The Miracle of the Ghetto* (1944) and *Rabbi Mair of Rothenburg* (1945). In the first Rabbi Isaak helps prepare for the armed resistance of the Warsaw Jews. The cry, "*Gewald*, Jews, do not despair!" is the tocsin to revolt. His disciple Isroel, returning from Lublin where his family was exterminated, feels that guns are not enough—he wants a miracle. "I ask you, rabbi, can you do just what the murderers are doing—slay children, break heads and bones, rape mothers? For if you can, then you must do with them as they do with us, become as animal-like as they, burn, torture, and enjoy it as they enjoy it. . . . Can you do this, rabbi?" Advancing the motto of "Let not the weak denigrate their weakness," he fasts and prays for a miracle. The rabbi wins him over to his view, however, and he becomes one of the boldest defenders. And at the end Rabbi Isaak declares that the Warsaw uprising was part of Israel's eternal resistance to evil.

Rabbi Mair of Rothenburg treats the same theme of resistance to evil as it manifested itself in an earlier time of woe. Ahasuerus, the Wandering Jew, visiting Dachau, tells Doniel, one of the victims: "Where Jews are, there am I." When Doniel states that he thought him only a legend, he is told: "And what Jew is less than a legend? Even you are legend, and so is your neighbor." He is informed that it is necessary to endure prison when evil seeks domination, for a Jew is more durable than prison. Doniel is then led into Mainz of 1286, where a massacre had just occurred.

The duke of Hohenberg orders Rabbi Mair, the most renowned scholar of his generation, to bring him 50,000 marks as a tax upon the Jews of his dukedom. The rabbi refuses, though aware of the danger to himself. Nor does he make any effort to escape. "Why flee?" he says to his friends. "Why? A Jew does not flee from his fate." Imprisoned, he forbids the Jews to offer more than the normal ransom for a prisoner. "Not for myself, but for the honor of Israel have I lifted my weak arm against the wicked one to show him at least once that he cannot carry out each of his evil intents. . . . There is a limit

374

which none must exceed, none!" For, he maintains, if in our fear we acquiesce in our punishment, "we are lost. . . . Oh, then our freedom is even darker, worse than prison, and this is just what these wicked ones, from the highest to the least, want. They want to kill our souls even more than our bodies."

After seven years of incarceration and torture the rabbi is visited by the duke to ascertain the reason for his stubbornness; the duke asks the aged sage what gives him this power of resistance. "My power," is the reply, "consists in being powerless." Angered and thwarted, the duke orders him tortured to death. Rabbi Mair accepts his fate calmly but urges his relatives to flee without delay, knowing the duke's vindictiveness. When questioned about this apparent contradiction, he replies: "There is absolutely no need and no virtue that *all* Jews should be martyred—for then Israel would perish! You should know, my children, that martyrdom is a virtue only when it strengthens Israel." And he forbids his friends to ransom even his dead body.

In April, 1946, Leivick, with two other representatives of the Jewish World Congress, visited D.P. camps in the American sector in Bavaria as guests of UNRRA. In camp after camp they read their work or sang—one was a singer—before gathered survivors, listened to their tales of horror and heroism, and offered them words of comfort and courage. What impressed Leivick most was the fervent eagerness of these harrowed Jews to get away from Europe and reach Palestine. He found many tormented by a sense of strong guilt of having remained alive when those dearest to them died in crematoria. Again and again he was told: "I am the only one of my family to survive"—and the anguish in their eyes tormented him long after. "Against even the least of the victims I feel weak, powerless, puny." His volume, *With the Saved Remnant* (1947), contains a day-to-day account of what he saw and heard and felt—and it is painful reading.

The Wedding in Fernwald (1949) derives from these camp experiences. It depicts symbolically and mystically the celebration of a wedding among the survivors. Abraham, a young merchant, is taken by the Nazis to Dachau to work, while his wife Sarah and son Isaak are sent to the crematorium. Alive in 1945, Abraham feels culpable, yet also resentful: "Not I am the guilty one! . . . Not I am the coward, but you! I tell it to you openly, Creator of the world!" He meets another Sarah, whose husband had perished, on the way to Fernwald, and the two are called by God to rebuild the house of Israel. Elijah as an aged survivor encourages the union. "It is well that Jews are still able to believe and wait, it is well that Jews do not despair out of loneliness and abandonment." Abraham is deeply troubled by the spirits of his dead wife and son and faints before the marriage ceremony at the vision of the first Sarah resisting his new marriage. But Elijah commands her to leave and she thereupon begs Abraham's forgiveness. The messiah also appears, and the intimation is made that he is no longer waiting for mankind's readiness but came in response to new life in the presence of millions dead. For Elijah tells him that "the living Jews are more to be pitied than those dead." For all of Leivick's good intention, the work is relatively weak—the mystic symbolism verges on bathos and blurs the thematic portrayal of fresh hope and new life. He was still too imbued with the poignancy of the subject to treat it with the required esthetic objectivity.

In 1953 Leivick completed another of his important poetic dramas, *In the Days of Job*. All through his conscious life he was painfully plagued not only by Isaak's sacrifice but by God's permission to heap havoc on Job. These two "testings" are here combined in one action, accepting a rabbinical supposition that Job and Isaak were contemporaries. The drama is mystical, imaginative, philosophical in concept and form. Satan, who always taunts Isaak with the sacrifice, now asks how he can go about "peacefully, prayerfully, dreamily," when a victim of another sacrifice is at death's door. He disappears immediately in a burst of laughter, leaving Isaak wondering painfully if he must worry about every unfortunate. All the while Satan is perturbed by Job's continued silence when so

sorely afflicted. After seven days of extreme anguish Job does
cry out, and Satan is jubilant. "When he curses, he will blaspheme. He will." But Job curses only himself, not God. Yet
the mere fact of the outcries displeases God and makes Job,
unlike Abraham and Isaak, unworthy of becoming one of the
chosen.

"Job's lament tears my heart," Isaak tells himself, and he
goes to seek out the sufferer. He speaks to him about his own
sacrifice and wonders if the present affliction is not another
test. "Test?" Job cries out. "To test one who is without sin or
crime? Even that comfort is no comfort to me. If I'm to suffer,
I must know clearly why. For you were bound by a father's
hand, and me—the hand of God."

Job's agonized shouting is heard far away and attracts many
cripples and beggars who seek him out in the hope of being
helped along with him. One of his comforters says: "His voice
has stopped the entire order of the universe. . . . Animals
begin to talk like men, even sheep open their mouths; even
the dead, they say, arise and question." Indeed a sheep approaches Isaak and asks: "And to cut *my* throat is permitted?"
It reminds Isaak that he was pleased to have the sheep's throat
cut instead of his; and why did Isaak place it on the altar?
The sheep ends its harangue by putting Abraham and Isaak
in a class with Cain.

Job, having refused to blaspheme God in his moment of
deepest anguish, foils Satan and passes the test satisfactorily.
God then tells Satan: "I permit you to go about freely among
men, to enter the depth of their hearts, even as I permit man
to go his ways, do as he wishes, have the ability to recognize
you within him, and have the capacity to liberate himself from
you." Overnight Job is miraculously cured of all his afflictions
—much to the distress of the cripples, who did not share his
miracle.

Although this drama, seeking to sense the meaning and
suffering of the postwar world, treats legends and symbols
with Leivick's involved fantasy, it is primarily a work of imaginative poetry. Satan is much more prominent than in the

Biblical account, and is the constant critic of God's ways toward men. Isaak, unable to free himself from his traumatic experience, remains distraught and perplexed. For all his brave virtuousness, Job emerges less heroic than in the Biblical portrayal. He does not cry out until he himself is afflicted, and he makes no effort to seek justice from God for others. The drama as a whole achieves distinction not so much by originality of treatment or depth of philosophical insight as by the emotional intensity of its poetic art.

In his last two collections of poems Leivick again wrote verses of snow, but they no longer repelled him—as his earlier ones had—although the pain and woe which they hid never actually left him. In *A Leaf on the Apple Tree* (1955), a cycle of poems, "The Fire," continues his poignant recollections of the concentration camps, and the lyrics breathe with pain and verbal beauty. Nor is he forgetful of Isaak's sacrifice and the substitution of the sheep. In "My First Boyish Vision" he tells: "At first I begged God for mercy to Isaak, then my heart turned to the sheep." "In the Forbidden Land" voices his tragic view of the world: "Humankind hangs on a hair, dew-thin, between forest animal howls and Isaiahlike prophecy." In one of a series of sonnets he records his feeling on seeing again the grave of Nathan Newman in Colorado. His visit to Israel in 1950 resulted in a number of poems bright with imagery and charged with pathos. The tragic fate of Yiddish writers in Soviet Russia evoked "Brothers of Woe," a lament for their persecution: "Markish and Bergelson, my brothers of woe, where is the darkness which swallowed you? Jail? Siberia? Or a cage in the Ukraine?—payment for the odes which you have sung. . . ." In addition he wrote a number of fine nature lyrics.

Songs to Eternity (1959), containing his last poems, is distinguished by its sensitive nature lyrics. It was as if, in the evening of his long literary career, he permitted himself the pleasure of singing for its own sake. Moon, stars, ocean, grass, trees, mountains—these and other elements soothed his senses

with their healing serenity, and he wrote about them sensu-
ously, gratefully, lovingly. Yet he could not wholly block out
of his consciousness the persistent memories of his youth,
recollections which continued to plague and provoke his
imagination and poetic impulse. Among the poems are several
about his father, whom he feared and admired. Isaak again
appears in "Prayer to God": "Once He kept the knife from
falling on a throat, the stretched Isaak throat, and since
Moriah it became an anointed brand on a Jew for ever after."
In another prayer Leivick himself speaks: "I am sad, God,
after the passing of years. . . . I stand at the door and plead
—what do I plead? And what need have I to plead? I am sick
of being a poet—free me from the group of poets." Nor can he
forget the holocaust: "The generation in the wilderness of
today's world has a face—unrecognizable: in its pupils burn
gas chambers, its lips—crooked up to the neck, its forehead
bloody with Cain's brand, and a spotty glow shines on its
cheeks and cries with a strange cry: whence comes my help?
Whence?" These and other poems, serene or sad, are sung
with a lyricism adorned with sensitive imagery.

In 1957 Leivick went to Israel for the third time to address
a conference of scholars in Jerusalem. He spoke out in favor
of Yiddish as the language of the intimate folk spirit. The next
day he became ill and was hospitalized for a month. Not long
after his return to the United States the Hebrew Union College awarded him an honorary degree in literature.

Late in 1958 a paralytic stroke laid him helpless and speech-
less, although it was apparent that his mind remained unaffected. After four years in this condition his heart gave way
in December, 1962.

H. Leivick was not only a highly gifted poet but a sensitive
spirit cruelly bruised in his formative years. In his maturity he
used his gift and his pain in passionately poetic outcries
against the vicissitudes of human destiny. Despite his early
rejection of orthodox piety, he remained a Jew in a deeply
spiritual sense; because in his lifetime Jews suffered cruelly,

he protested with the passion of a prophet. His friend Opatoshu pointed out: "One must not approach Leivick as one
would a poet who had conceived a book and executed it well.
One must approach here a soul, a wounded soul, that has
experienced everything."

Steeped in Jewish lore, acutely idealistic ethically, a poet
embracing legend, myth, and fantasy as essential realities,
quickly angered by injustice and evil, Leivick often "fevered
with ecstasy and strong emotion." He could never forgive God
for the Isaak sacrifice, and maintained that nothing justified
the destruction of life; nor did he see any virtue in the temptation of Job. Distressed by Jewish persecution in Europe, he
yearned for salvation with such emotional intensity that he
added to the myth of the messiah by hastening legendary
redemption before the appointed time. In expressing these
ideas and hopes he often became exalted and inspired—if not
always direct and explicit. "I do not deny," he admitted, "that
in writing a poem I often feel as if I'm praying, that the poem
itself is a prayer." Dov Sfard, an eminent critic and writer,
elaborated:

> In the whole range of his poetry and drama Leivick never sang
> like the bird in the forest, but he ever sought to bind together the
> fateful problems of our existence. The inner bloody relationship
> to these problems gave his words weight and responsibility. One
> heeded Leivick's words even though they at times lost themselves
> in the misty spheres of messiah-mystic moods.

Essentially and primarily a poet, he wrote his major works
in drama form to stress their innate conflict. Those which
remained conceptually poetic became vehicles of high esthetic
quality—their passionate inspiration preserving the mood of
loftiness even when the motivation tended to murkiness and
the action limped on its legendary legs. This was not the case,
however, with his prose plays, which had to depend on realistic situations or resorted to mystical legends and myths without providing them with either dramatic logic or the veil of
poetic emotion.

Leivick's eminence was recognized early; indeed, his work
has been discussed and evaluated at greater length and with
deeper seriousness than that of any other Yiddish writer.
Relatively little of his writing, with the exception of *The
Golem*, has appeared in translation, owing largely to the difficulty of rendering his poetic imagery and legendary allusions
in another language.

CHAPTER FIFTEEN

YIDDISH

IN THE SOVIET UNION

THE FIRST two decades of the current century were a cruelly destructive period for the Russian Jews. The Czarist government persecuted them harshly and callously, instigating pogroms and depriving them of human rights. Soon after the outbreak of World War I Jews were banished from their homes in the fighting zones, and suffered devastation and death. With the revolution in 1917 came turbulence and trouble along with release and hope. The ensuing civil war made them the scapegoats of the reactionary malcontents: they were slaughtered by the thousands.

During these years Yiddish literature in Russia was also undergoing a radical transition. The classic writers died one after another, and a number of their talented successors were migrating to more hospitable countries. New ones were emerging, but few possessed the promise of artistic maturity. Moreover, after 1914 all Yiddish publishing was stopped by government order, so that only those few writers who had access to periodicals and publishers abroad were able to bring out even part of their work. Some of the younger ones were of course drafted into the army and had no time for writing.

This situation was changed radically by the revolution,

which made Jews full citizens and abolished all restrictions aimed at them. Yiddish was proclaimed the "Jewish mother tongue," and periodicals in Yiddish and Hebrew, along with anthologies and books, were soon being published in all Jewish centers. The vast majority of young Jews, no longer bound by traditional piety, embraced the revolution with dedicated enthusiasm; a number of them burst into song and became its troubadours, acclaiming its political and social grandeur.

When the Bolshevik government was attacked by counterrevolutionary armies, Jewish youths eagerly enlisted in its defense. The dastardly pogroms perpetrated by the hooligans under Denikin's and Petlura's leadership only intensified their fervor in combatting the enemies of Bolshevism. Among their many casualties were the young poets Beinush Shteyman and Osher Schwartzman and the storyteller Isroel Wakser, who had joined the Jewish self-defense of the town in which he was a teacher and was killed during a pogrom. Shortly before that he had written to his father: "O, when your son feels bad and bitter unto death, when the sky is dark and the earth enveloped in black, he takes his pen and writes, and writes, and writes until the sky clears, the earth brightens, and the heart becomes light. . . ."

Shteyman had written three poetic plays of much promise on the messianic theme by the time he was 22 years old. In 1919 he went to Kiev, did defense work during the civil war, and was killed in a pogrom. His drama, *Messiah Ben Joseph*, was produced in New York during the 1920's.

The most talented of the three was Schwartzman (1889–1919). His 60-odd poems, many published posthumously, had the fresh feel of the scented Ukrainian woods in which he grew up. His buoyant outlook on life is expressed in a poem written in 1911: "Even as a child, long ago, I once went out of the house and in the open steppes I heard the silk sounds; the laughing day rang like steel, God's whole world was joyous." His love lyrics sing with genuine pathos: "And when our love will die, we shall mourn it quietly, as an only child which death carried away. And separated, our hearts long will yearn;

and long both of us will remember it gratefully." A moody soldier in the Russian army from 1911 to 1917, he was wounded in 1915 and earned two George Crosses. The revolution liberated him spiritually. Enlisting in the Red Army, he urged his friends to do likewise. One of his last poems was a call to arms:

> Black mother—night is torn with woe: the enemy at the gate!
> Out of the depths of the heart a wild outcry emerges: the enemy at the gate!
> Quick upon horse, steel the hand, now it's the sword—the bayonet—the flag: the enemy at the gate!

The brutal havoc of the civil war deeply affected the Jewish writers, who wrote about it for years thereafter with passionate anger, among them Dovid Bergelson, David Hofshteyn, Leyb Kvitko, Moshe Kulbak, Aron Kishnirov, and Peretz Markish. The latter, in a series of poems on the pogroms, expressed a common anguish:

> Away! I stink, insects crawl over me! You're looking for your parents here? You're looking for your friend? They are here! They are here! But they too stink! Away! . . .
> A heap of dirty linen—from bottom to the top! Here, whatever you wish, mad wind, scratch it and take! Across stands the church, like a skunk over a heap of choked chickens. . . .

The triumph of the Red Army assured the rule of the Bolshevik leaders over the vast area of Czarist Russia—minus some of the western border areas. Anti-Semitism was made a crime, and for the first time in their long history Russian Jews were the equal of their compatriots. It mattered little to most of them that in 1919 Hebrew was officially condemned for allegedly favoring "clerical and Zionist organizations"; that Judaism was, like other religions, declared to be opiumlike in its baleful effect. Being neither religious nor adherents of Hebrew, but rather dedicated supporters of the ideals of social revolution, the majority of Jews eagerly accepted official policy and acted accordingly. The younger ones scorned the trading occupations forced upon their fathers, the devotion to the synagogue and Hebrew lore, and became workers, farmers, and students.

Numerous new Yiddish writers joined those already established in giving passionate voice to the communist precepts of Marx and Lenin, but many also set forth their mournful recollections. Much of their verse and fiction lacked polish and mature form, but sparkled with the brightness of optimism or crackled with anger against the enemies of revolution. Their work appeared freely in periodicals they themselves established—such as *Eigens* (One's Own), *Der Shtrom* (The Current), *Der Shtern* (The Star), and *Roite Welt* (Red World) —and in books brought out by their own organizations. During the 1920's, the three Yiddish publishing houses issued more books than were published in the rest of the world. Jewish scientific institutes were formed in Kiev, Kharkov, and Moscow, with about 100 research scholars working in the Kiev academy alone. Yiddish schools flourished in every Jewish center, with around 160,000 Jewish students attending them in 1930. Yiddish theaters were also started in the larger cities, producing many distinguished plays under the guidance and stimulation of A. Granovsky and Shlome Mikhoels.

Jewish political and cultural leaders were naturally grateful for these opportunities and responded with enthusiasm for the ideals of communism. More self-conscious than the Russians— more self-analytical and driven by a feeling of inferiority—a number of Jewish critics and bureaucrats considered any deviation from proletarian orthodoxy bordering on treason. They were quick to chastise Yiddish writers who failed in the slightest degree to adhere to the official line of political ideology. Editors of periodicals insisted on conformity and urged "self-criticism" upon their contributors. Pessimism, for instance, was declared a bourgeois neurosis, and nostalgic accounts of the destroyed *shtetl* life was frowned upon as political regression. Writers were urged to build a *crib* for the new life and a *coffin* for the old. In 1926 I. Kipnis was accused of "Jewish petty-bourgeoisism" because he wrote about "the idyllic attractiveness" of the Jewish town instead of depicting it so as "to disgust the reader with the town's Friday." Everything, indeed, had to be "socialist in content and realistic in form." Praise for party leaders was strongly encouraged, resulting in considerable bombast and rhetoric.

This condition, however, did not deter several important writers, who had left Russia shortly after the revolution, from returning to the Soviet Union "to serve the revolution." Emotionally and culturally attached to their native land, they felt ill at ease and without needed ties in a Germany hectically gravitating to Hitlerism. Thus Der Nister, Kvitko, Hofshteyn, Markish, and Kulbak returned by 1926, and Bergelson some years later.

A dominant censor of Yiddish writing during the 1920's and later, Moshe Litvakov (1875–1937) was largely responsible for its strict conformity. A yeshiva student until 17, he subsequently concentrated on the study of secular subjects. From 1902 to 1905 he was absorbed in philosophy at the Sorbonne in Paris. Active in politics since 1895, and for a time interested in the Poale (labor) Zion movement, he returned to Russia in 1905 and became a zealous participant in revolutionary agitation. For a time he worked on the staff of an influential Kiev newspaper. After the revolution he headed the Jewish writers' section and in 1919 edited an anthology of Yiddish writing. An energetic member of the Communist party, he sought to "Octoberize" (Bolshevize) the work of Yiddish writers. In 1921 he went to Moscow and three years later became editor of *Emes* (Truth), the most influential Yiddish newspaper. Rigorously anti-religious, he was severely critical of any account that treated religious life in the least sympathetically; an opponent of Hebrew, he attacked Hofshteyn for signing a petition in its favor and had him expelled from the Yiddish writers section; a strong Yiddishist, he encouraged the spread of the language and was active in the development of the Yiddish Kamer Theater.

For all his rigid censorship and orthodox communism, he

was a keen and discerning literary critic; many of his reviews and essays revealed clearly and effectively the weak and strong elements in a work of literature. His aggressive castigations, however, were strongly resented by a number of writers, and in 1931 they accused him of "national Menshevism." He struck back, but also admitted some "errors." Thereafter his leadership zigzagged until 1937, when he was arrested in the Trotskyist purge as "an enemy of the people" and died in prison.

Literary control was nevertheless mild until 1929, when the organization of writers became rigorously political in its ideology. In 1934 the Union of Soviet Writers was formed to take control of all literary groupings. The effect of this increased supervision on Yiddish writing was a considerable reduction in its publication. While 326 writers published one or more books during the decade 1926–1935, the number of books issued annually shrank considerably immediately thereafter. With the coming of the purges in the 1930's, Yiddish writers were victimized along with others. In 1934 "a nest of Jewish-nationalist group" (those friendly to Poale Zion) was uncovered in Minsk, involving several writers. Those found guilty of "chauvinism" were sentenced to ten years in prison, while those accused of "terrorism" were executed. The closing of the Kiev Scientific Institute marked the beginning of liquidation of Jewish culture in the Soviet Union. Among Yiddish writers, in addition to Litvakov, arrested and exiled or killed were several of notable merit: Isroel Tzinberg, Moshe Kulbak, Max Erik, and Izi Kharik.

Tzinberg, born in 1873, studied chemical engineering in Karlsruhe, obtained his doctorate in Basel, and from 1898 to the end of his life worked in the Putilov factory in Leningrad. An eminent scientist, he devoted his leisure time to study of Jewish culture. He wrote frequently for *Voskhod*, the Russian-language newspaper concerned with Jewish life, and in 1918 published a history of Jewish periodicals in Russia. Three years later he began his research for the monumental *History of Literature Among Jews,* a work of vast erudition extending from early times to the late 19th century. The entire work comprises ten large volumes, some of which appeared posthumously in the United States. In the late 1930's he became a victim of the Stalin purge.

Max Erik (Z. Merkin, 1898–1937) was another eminent literary historian to die as one of Stalin's victims. He attended *kheder* until the age of 12, and at one time studied with the poet Bialik. In 1918 he graduated from a Polish gymnasium and published his first critical essay. During the civil war years of 1919–1921 he served as an officer in the Polish army. Later he taught in Wilno Jewish schools and took an effective part in the city's cultural activities. Pursuing a broad historical study of Yiddish literature, he went to England and France in search of old manuscripts. His completed work, *History of Yiddish Literature to the Haskala Movement* (1928) was generally regarded as a work of notable scholarship. In 1929 he went to the Soviet Union and lived in Minsk and Kiev, where he headed the Scientific Institute. Thereafter, as a convinced communist, he was very critical of Yiddish writers in other countries who did not conform to Marxist standards, calling Sholem Asch, for instance, "a degraded troubadour of fascism." Nevertheless his next major work, *Studies in the History of Enlightenment* (1934), was a critical contribution of solid merit. In April, 1936, he was falsely implicated by apprehended Polish spies, arrested, and executed the following year.

Moshe Kulbak (1896–1940) received his Hebrew training in a yeshiva and became a teacher in Kovno in 1914. Two years later he published his first poem. In 1920 he went to Berlin, where he had difficulty earning a living. "There are weeks," he wrote, "when I have no faith in myself, perhaps because I am not productive." He did complete a drama, *Yakov Frank,* published in *Die Zukunft* in 1923. That year he returned to Wilno and taught in a Jewish gymnasium. His *Messiah Ben Ephraim* (1924), a poetic novel, combined the traditional with the fantastic in expressionistic form. Bold and original in concept, it is written with concentrated clarity. A poor miller, left only with his cow, goes about the woods, fasts and prays, and is mystically followed by his cow. In his prayers he exclaims:

> Why is one so tortured, God? Wherever I stand, I am too much, and wherever I go, I carry with me the smell of darkness. I envy the bird, who is better off than we, and the clay, which is best off; what shall I do with my hand, which is superfluous, and with my heart, which is superfluous?

In 1926 Kulbak published *Monday*, a novel of revolution with an underlying messianic implication; also *Bunie and Berieh on the Road*, a long poem which appeared in *Die Zukunft*, about two Jewish soldiers in the civil war who became quixotic robbers in retaliation for their grievous poverty. Half clowns, half heroes, they symbolize the recklessness and revenge of social revolution. The work abounds in lyric passages:

> Land and sky become mixed, sounds, field and air, knit together; a swallow on a telegraph pole is somewhere dotted in smoke and wiped off. It is a dream. Real is only the piece of road one walks on. . . . He wept, and unexpectedly a white fiddle emerged, out of pieces of light it played a wild song, cold and dumb—and Bunie and Berieh heard it and Comrade Bik apprehended it. . . . And Bunie said: "Listen, you fool, listen to the end of dire human suffering—a leopard will sleep alongside a cow and a child will play with both; there will be peace, and knives will rust in their sheaths."

It was of this poem that S. Niger said: "He does not destroy the daily realities, he does not even cover them with a magic veil; he gives them to us with their entire rawness, their naked freshness . . . but suddenly we see in the reflection of the water the sky and stars and the furthest worlds."

Motivated by idealistic ardor, Kulbak in 1926 decided to go to Soviet Russia "to serve the Revolution." Too much the individualist to subject himself to the proletarian harness, too much the poet to submit to political restrictions, he continued to write verses and stories in accord with his artistic impulses. In one poem about the saintly poor he wrote: "I am a Jew, Shmuel Itzi the chimney sweep, I lie deep in the chimney of the world and cry out; I have suffered silently and can suffer no more, although I'll suffer more anyway. . . ." In another poem he describes glowingly his 16 uncles and their work in the forest and on the farm, and about the love of one of them for Anastasia, a peasant woman. He speaks of his love of his native tongue: "I saw Yiddish words, like small fires, like sparks from dark ore. I felt Yiddish words, like pure doves, like pure doves, doves cooing in the heart."

His most important work, *Zemelnianer* (1931–1935), is a two-volume novel of genuine humor depicting the older generation of Jews in conflict with their revolutionary children, their reluctance and difficulty in adjusting to Soviet life. There are no heroes in the story, only ordinary men and women caught in the turmoil and perturbation of social orientation. Thus an elderly woman, forced to overcome her lifelong illiteracy, cannot keep her mind on lessons and dreads the daily arrival of her young tutor. One day, fully dressed and ready to go out on an errand, she is told that the tutor is approaching. She jumps into bed with her shoes on, covers herself, and pretends illness. Again, when one of the younger members of the family proudly installs electricity in the house, one of his uncles persists in ignoring the bright light and continues to read by lamplight. The book was not received without criticism for making the characters humorous rather than ridiculous and for not "organizing his material on a proletarian basis."

In *The Disner Childe Harold* (1931), a long poem, Kulbak relates his sojourn in Germany a decade earlier and describes the speculation, extravagance, hectic behavior, jailed radicals, and rising hatred that spawned Hitlerism. He had found it a country "in which every worker is a Marxist and every merchant is a Kantian. . . . It is the dying of a distant tumult, it is the death, which is sweet.—Expressionism strides on red feet, Dada—with its trousers down." And of himself within it: "I am strangely sick, as the century, and yet I once in wonderment sprang away from father's doorstep! Bravery, youthful noise and daring, a little Blok, a little Schopenhauer, cabala, Peretz and Spinoza, and uprooted, and sad, sad, sad."

Boitre, Murderer (1936), a play, has its setting in the early 19th century, when Jewish towns were still governed more or less autonomously by wealthy merchants. Boitre, a poor orphan who was subjected to cruel abuse and later forcefully recruited into the army, escapes and takes revenge on his wealthy tormentors by becoming a Robin Hood type of robber with his hideaway in a nearby wood. In love with the daughter of the leading citizen, he stops her wedding to another and takes her to his hiding place in the forest. The outraged father succeeds in enlisting a police posse to seek Boitre out, and in the commotion both lovers are killed. The play proved highly popular when produced in Moscow and other cities. When a high official saw it, he criticized it for having too many beggars and beards and not enough workers. Soon after Kulbak was arrested for "ideological deviation" in connection with another play—*Benjamin Magidov* (1937), a comedy about a Jewish radical worker who did secret partisan work during the Polish occupation—and exiled to Siberia, where he is said to have died in 1940. He was rehabilitated in 1956.

Izi Kharik (1898–1937) began to work at the age of 12. The revolution in 1917 was to him the unfolding of a new and wonderful world. He became a member of the Bolshevik party and joined the Red Army. A highly gifted lyricist, he began to publish his poems in 1920. *Shudder* (1922) and several other volumes attest to his natural purity of poetic expression. In 1924 he went to Moscow for additional study, and four years later he settled in Minsk.

Deeply Jewish in orientation, though a sincere communist in his ideology, he drew his poetic inspiration from traditional sources. In a series of lyrics entitled "Townlet" he wrote:

Townlet, townlet, silent and worried, to the last roof neglected and alone. . . . At times, on the highest building your dry

weeping reaches me. . . . I have myself helped to destroy them
and to send them up in smoke. . . . Now I hear the shudder of
the stars, as I'm drawn and carried upward.

In another poem he longs to dress his townlet "in steel and
stone." And he continues: "I bend my young head and am
silent, and my heart can find no peace; townlet, my withered
branch, again you want to blossom; I go about like a quiet
guest and am silent."

He sang of his shoemaking father and envied his singing at
work. Self-conscious of his, at times, harsh criticism of traditional Jewish life, he stated in "Bread": "On empty and weary
streets my stiff footsteps pass. . . . Today a town full of Jews
called me: 'Anti-Semite!' All of them, in wrinkles and rags,
pointed to me with their hands: 'This one—we know him, him
and his parents, he became estranged from us'. . . ." They
want to tell him how hard their lot has become, but he sees
them only as "dead beards," and tells them to go to the soil or
else!

New Earth (1925) contains his famous poem, "Minsk Mud,"
which was praised "as a new achievement in our October
literature." The next year he wrote a poem on his feeling the
oncoming of death.

Oh, my life, my restless friend, I shall long not separate from you
—and I shall certainly live long and perhaps longer even than my
grandfather. And if a bullet will strike me silently, it will certainly not take me. Today I have felt death and am ashamed of
myself. . . .

Body and Soul (1928) is a work of singular merit. Equally
lyrical is *On a Strange Wedding* (1936), which portrays his
grandfather, the *badkhen*, who had to amuse the wedding
guests with happy, spontaneous rhymes to earn his living.
A simple folk type, poetically conceived and lovingly delineated, he is evolved with verses that trill and thrill.

His political sincerity notwithstanding, Kharik began to be
accused of lack of zeal in expounding proletarian ideology. In

1935 he was investigated by the N.K.V.D., the secret police, in connection with an alleged Zionist plot. Cleared this time, he was arrested in 1937 and accused of Trotskyist influence—despite the fact that the year before he had published a poem highly critical of the deposed leader. In prison he was tortured, forced to "confess," and killed. His books were removed from all libraries, but in the middle 1950's he was rehabilitated and again included in the Soviet encyclopedias. A volume of his poems, in Russian translation, was published in 1958.

The status of Yiddish writing continued to deteriorate throughout the late 1930's. The number of books published diminished from year to year, periodicals were either stopped or handicapped in various ways, scientific research in Yiddish culture was progressively restricted, and Jewish schools were closed at every opportunity. Interest in Jewish affairs came to be regarded as a source of political deviation. Yiddish writers felt that their freedom, if not their lives, hung on a word. They began to conform without regard to how much their work was crippled in the process. Markish, for instance, modified the title of his famous poem on the civil war pogroms from "Heap" to "Requiem" and altered various passages—to the hurt of its life and spirit; the same occurred with Hofshteyn's "Spring." Bergelson revised each new edition of his novels and stories. Although Soviet leaders had assigned Birobidjan in Siberia as a national home for Russian Jews, they preferred to see them assimilated and submerged within the Russian populace. It is significant that not a few Jews sympathized with this attitude: what need had Jews of a separate entity in a land in which all men had equal rights?

Many thousands of Jews did make the long trek to Birobidjan and strove zealously and painfully to develop the wilderness into a land which would provide a rewarding life. Most Jews, however, preferred to remain in their native regions, where the climate was temperate and they were not forced to become farmers and laborers. Nor did all who went to Birobidjan remain, finding the effort too onerous for their town-bred bodies. Several Yiddish writers, among them Bergelson, were sent there to write encouragingly of the life and prospects in Birobidjan, but their reportage, glowingly optimistic, failed to attract more than a few thousand.

The outbreak of World War II, preceded by the Stalin-Hitler pact, was a shattering experience for most Yiddish writers. Aware of the devastation in Poland, they soon learned that criticism of Nazi atrocities was considered by Soviet leaders to be synonymous with partiality to the capitalist countries at war with Germany. These authors had to hide what they could not keep from writing about their anguish, or disguise their outraged feelings in murky symbolism. Halkin described the dreadful situation: "And this is the fate of all of us: If only you live, you must show a trick—throw a rope across the chasm and walk on it as if on an iron bridge."

The situation changed radically overnight with the German attack on the Soviet Union. Restrictions against Jewish emphasis were lifted and Jewish cultural leaders were encouraged to appeal to Jews abroad for help. The Jewish Anti-Fascist Committee was formed in 1941 to expedite contact with Jewish organizations in countries at war with Germany. In 1943 Shlome Michoels, the leading Jewish actor, and Itsik Fefer, a popular poet and a colonel in the Red Army, were sent to the United States and England to solicit help and encourage good will.

Yiddish writers responded to the war with genuine enthusiasm. At last they felt free to express their anguish about the destroyed Jewish communities in Poland—but they soon discovered that they were not expected to stress the horrors already experienced by Russian Jews in the wake of the rapid German advance. The intimation was made that all Russians suffered from Nazi atrocities; moreover, nothing was to be said about the Ukrainian anti-Semitism which had flared up on the arrival of the Germans. Practiced conformists by now, Yiddish writers concentrated on the war effort. Over 60 of

394

them enlisted in the armed forces, and nearly 30 died on the battlefront. All Jews, indeed, were combatting the enemy not only at the front—which contained some 700,000 of them—but as partisans in the woods outside many towns, thousands of them dying heroically in the process. They were in truth stirred by a double patriotism: allegiance to the Soviet Union was strengthened by hatred of Hitlerism.

Yiddish writers depicted the agonies of Jews caught in the Nazi net across the border, and stressed the danger certain Ukrainians and Russians underwent in their efforts to protect Jews within Russia. They also hailed the heroic spirit of the fighting men on the front. After 1943, when the Moscow siege was lifted, writers found it advisable to criticize one another's work to make sure they were following the approved "line." Occasionally, when one of them transgressed the line in the heat of emotion, he would be reproved accordingly. This happened when Hofshteyn pointed out the Ukrainian hatred of Jews and ended with the Hebrew phrase, "For learning issues from Zion." He was severely chastised for this lapse. The next time he read his poems publicly, his verses were faultless ideologically but flat in spirit. Privately, however, he read other poems about the tragedy in the Ukraine that throbbed with lyric anguish, and these he called "double-entry bookkeeping."

An instance of this caution occurred in 1943, when Michoels and Fefer were in London. Having met the poet Itzik Manger and having been offered an inscribed copy of his new book, *Clouds Over the Roof*, they thanked him but suggested that he omit the inscription—Manger being unacceptable politically. In 1944 Abraham Sutzkever, a poet then in Moscow, submitted an article on underground museums to Bergelson, an editor of *Einigkeit* (Unity). He also sent the same article, in Russian, to *Literature and Art*. The latter magazine printed the piece without change. On the day the article appeared Sutzkever happened to meet Bergelson and was told that various editorial excisions had to be made in the Yiddish version. When informed that none was made by the Russian editor, Bergelson was visibly upset. "It must appear in Yiddish just as it is in Russian," he explained, and hurried off to restore the emendations.

Anti-Semitism became generally evident in 1944, when the Nazi armies were being driven back. Fefer, the most patriotic of Jewish writers, was accused of cooperating with socialists and Zionists while in New York. Only 14 Yiddish books were published in 1945 and 19 in 1946, but the number increased to 60 in 1948. Yet the spirit of reaction was on the rise. Zhdanov's speech in September, 1946, against liberalism in literature placed it in a Sodomite bed and helped liquidate all Yiddish activity two years later. Ilya Ehrenburg, who often, chameleonlike, reflected official policy, made a giant step in Jewish subversion. In a speech in 1946 he asked: "Jews are spread over many lands. They speak different languages and live in different cultures. What ties them together? . . . The thirst for truth and freedom unites all Jews." Two years later, however, he wrote that Jews in one country have no relation with Jews in other countries; that "Soviet Jews no longer want Yiddish, so that the government need not support Yiddish literature against their will." The falseness of this assertion was evident in the current issues of *Einigkeit*, which contained the work of numerous writers and was being read widely.

On November 20, 1948, on the pretense that Jews were seeking a grant of autonomy in Crimea, all Jewish institutions and organizations were dissolved—except the Michoels theater, which was not closed until the following year, probably in deference to Michoels' murder in Minsk early in 1948. The Anti-Fascist Committee was accused of being "a nest of folk-traitors" and disbanded. At a meeting on the matter, called by the Russian Writers Union, Kushnirov, one of the most respected Yiddish poets, whose son was killed in the war and who had himself, although in his fifties, excelled on the battle-front, was called upon to denigrate Yiddish literature in justi-fication of its abolishment. On reaching the platform he was struck dumb; his lips moved spasmodically, but no voice came. Elie Gordon, a truckling Jewish communist, replaced him and did what was expected of him. Mass arrests followed. When Nister was not among the first to be apprehended, he felt aggravated to remain at large when his colleagues were in prison. All were accused of "criminal nationalism" and "association with enemies."

Not a word of their fate or whereabouts was made known. All inquiries from outside the country were ignored or parried. For years Russian Jews dared not be seen with a Yiddish book in their possession. Not until eight years later did any definite news reach the outside world in an article in the Warsaw *Folkshtimme*, a communist newspaper—24 Yiddish writers were shot on August 12, 1952.

It is still not definitely known how many Jewish writers and cultural leaders were arrested in 1948–1949, and how many died in prison or were shot. At the time there were several hundred published writers. Since the revolution they had produced a literature of solid significance. The proletarian gloss they put on, either out of communist dedication or simulated homage, detracted little from the inherent merit of much of their fiction and poetry. Their tragedy arose from the fact that most of them remained intuitive Jews despite their devotion to communism, and the Kremlin leaders tended to associate Jewishness with Zionism.

Within the scope of this chapter, only a few of the better-known writers can be dealt with. Shmuel Persov (1889–1952), a relatively minor writer, came of a very poor family and began to work at an early age. In 1906 he migrated to the United States and published his first story three years later. At the outbreak of the revolution he returned to Russia and devoted himself to writing stories about communist and factory life. *Shards* (1922) is a novel dealing with the effect of the revolution on the people who made it. He subsequently published much fiction of this nature. During World War II he wrote about partisan activities, and *Your Name Is People* and other stories are based on actual cases of daring and heroism. He was arrested in 1948 and shot in 1952.

Moshe Brodersohn (1890–1956) was born in Moscow, but his family, expelled from the city during his infancy, settled in Lodz, where he grew up. He published his first poems in 1913 and several volumes of verse subsequently. Bold, boisterous, experimental, he became active in the little theater movement and established himself as playwright, actor, and producer. He was particularly skillful in originating neologisms in his writing, and combined folklike language with modern themes in his plays. *Resurrection* includes many mythical and legendary world figures. *A Little Wedding* is also composed of mystical elements—with Ahasuerus as a *badkhen,* Columbine seeking to entice him, and Harlequin acting the clown. Very few of his plays, while attractive on the stage, were published. Having settled in the Soviet Union in 1939, when Hitler invaded Poland, he became an active participant in the Yiddish theater. His play, *Holiday Eve,* was successfully produced in Moscow in 1947. Arrested the following year, he remained in prison until released in 1955. Shortly thereafter he died of a heart attack.

S. N. Godiner (1892–1942) was born near Minsk, but moved with his family to Warsaw in 1908. He joined the revolutionary movement early, worked in a factory, and studied in his free time. Having the urge to write, he showed his first efforts to Peretz and was encouraged to continue. In 1912 he was drafted into the Russian army, and was wounded in World War I. He joined the Communist party soon after the revolution and studied in the Moscow Literary Institute. He published his first story in 1921 and became one of the prominent Yiddish prose writers. Sojourning in Birobidjan during two different periods, where he was active in cultural affairs, he wrote many stories and did much translation. He is best known for his two-volume novel, *The Man with the Gun* (1928–1933), a dramatic story of the civil war period. During World War II he became a partisan and was killed.

Ezra Fininberg (1899–1946) was a prominent poet, translator, and editor. Among his published works are *Land and Love* (1922), a volume of verse, *Gallop* (1926), a novel, and a play, *Young Ones* (1927). During World War II, having enlisted at the age of 42, he was seriously wounded. He wrote numerous poems about his experiences at the front. In one he exclaimed: "To the west I cry: O, my people, where are you? —None answers. Only the wilderness answers: No Jewish sound, no Jewish breath, millions—buried, millions—under ground."

M. Alberton (1900–1947) studied until 14. After the revolution he enrolled in a school of engineering. In 1926 he began to publish stories about factory life and coal miners, introducing Jewish workers in heavy industries into Yiddish literature. Going to Birobidjan in 1928, he wrote about its various activities at considerable length, describing certain Jews' dissatisfaction with the place with much humor. He stressed the opportunities of the region and indicated that only those Jews who lacked the ability or the will to become farmers were critical of it.

Another writer who settled in Birobidjan was M. J. Goldstein (1900–1943). In 1923 he had migrated to Argentina, where he worked and wrote stories about life in his new home. In 1932 he left for Birobidjan. There he published *Birobidjan on the Amur* (1934), a novel of considerable merit. When the Germans invaded the Soviet Union he joined the Red Army and was killed two years later.

David Hofshteyn (1889–1952) was born in a village near Kiev, where he went in 1907 to study in a gymnasium. Devoted to the revolution, he published his first poem about it in 1917. A collection of his verse, *Along the Way*, appeared two years later. A stanza in "City," one of the poems, is typical:

City! You called me from afar with the whirring of wires! I always saw you from the hilltop! You drew me from a distance with your brightness and glitter—you lured and captivated me! The peace of my village room you have destroyed with the whistle of trains, broken and splintered with the quiver of rails. . . . On high forever hung and forever continued the restlessness of your bewitched sounds—city! You have captivated me!

In another poem, "Conscience," he wrote: "Conscience! I know, it is said you are a dog, a dog that has broken away from your chain."

Quickly becoming a leader in Jewish cultural affairs during the early years of the revolution, he protested against the suppression of Hebrew, which he knew well and had loved from childhood, and was severely criticized by writers who had made themselves apologists for government policy. In 1924 he went to Germany, and a year later to Palestine, where he published some Hebrew poems. He also had his play, *Saul the Last King of Israel*, printed in *Die Zukunft*. In 1926 he returned to Kiev to look after his two young sons—Shammai and Hillel—whose mother had died. To be reinstated in the writers' organization, he published a recantation in *Emes* and joined other writers in a declaration that all nationalistic remains must be rooted out of Jewish writing. Inwardly, however, he could not tear the love of Hebrew out of his consciousness, and in a 1927 poem about his childhood states: "A quiet hour of rest in a green corner not far from the city of Kiev, so what if once a small boy had studied a bit of Job?"

As a leader of the Jewish section of the Ukrainian Writers Union he was critical of symbolic writing, especially that of Nister. Yet he was again in trouble in 1930 on account of his friend Kvitko, and was criticized for "petty-bourgeois nationalism." Supporting himself by doing translations, he produced Yiddish versions of *The Merchant of Venice* and Ibsen's *A Doll's House*. On his fiftieth birthday in 1939 he was honored by the government. In 1941 he was prominent in the formation of the Anti-Fascist Committee and wrote numerous poems about the war. Three years later, with the Nazis in retreat, he stated in "At My Window": "I stand at my bright window. . . . The insolent, cursed murderers wanted to drive me away from beloved homey places. . . . They with their curses shamefully destroyed themselves—I stand at my bright window and say to the world: 'Good morning!' "

At the end of the war he stated: "Soviet Russia saved our Jews and some of those near us: Poland, Lithuania, Galicia, Letland, Estonia. The ruins are terrible, and the greatest sacrifices were ours." In 1946 the government awarded him a medal "for heroism" during the war. Two years later, in a moment of poetic euphoria, he sang: "I stand on the doorstep of the future—its nearness I feel all around. As fruit from endless fields, our love now ripens." Shortly thereafter he was arrested; the shock and grief deranged his mind, and he died in a prison for the insane.

Leyb Kvitko (1893–1952) was one of the most popular children's poets in Soviet Russia. Orphaned in early childhood, he lived with a grandmother and was apprenticed to a tailor at the age of 10. He began to write in his teens, but did not publish any of his verses until 1917, when the revolution brought him to Kiev and he was befriended by Bergelson and Hofshteyn. In *Steps* (1920), his first volume, he favored darkness and the recondite, no doubt influenced by Nister; it pleased him to be "a groom of night." In 1921 he went first to Kovno and then to Berlin and Hamburg. On his return to Kiev in 1925 he interested himself in Jewish cultural activities. Although he was much more poet than politician, he earnestly tried to serve the state, but could not repress his Jewishness when Jews were involved.

Kvitko's poems for children became highly popular not only in Yiddish but in numerous translations. He also brought out successful versions of poems from other languages. Playful, rhythmic, folklike, emotional, his verses had a warm vividness that appealed greatly to youngsters of all ages. Poems like "Piglet," "Oh, When I Grow Up," "The Violin," and the long narrative *Liam and Patrick* (1930) were translated into numerous languages and dialects and recited by millions of children. "A Letter to Voroshilov" was made part of most elementary textbooks in Russian and other languages.

Kvitko wrote many poems for adults—paeans to the forest and other aspects of nature, plaints about illness, attacks, and suffering. His devotion to Russia and communism he expressed with deep feeling and even ecstasy, but also with bland humor. In "Russian Death," for instance, he wrote: "Russian death is deadest of all, Russian pain is most painful of all. Does the world's wound fester? How is its heart now? Ask a little child, ask a Jewish child."

In 1930 he was accused of being a "rightist." *Liam and Patrick* was found faulty in "socialist realism," and he was expelled from the writers' group. He went to work in a tractor factory, demonstrated his zeal to excel, and was honored by the government. He was thereupon reinstated as a writer, and *Liam and Patrick* appeared in "improved" editions in 1932 and 1938. A collection of his poetry to 1927 was issued in 1933. He moved to Moscow in 1936 and three years later was awarded the "Red Workers Flag" in recognition of his zeal with pen and hand. The war in 1941 intensified his patriotism as well as his Jewish consciousness. "This is the first time in the dispersion of the Jewish people," he wrote, "when it became possible for them to organize openly and en masse in a struggle against the destroyers."

It was natural for him to sing of the joy of life, the beauty of nature, and the triumph of righteousness. His was a simple mind, but with a heart overflowing with love and goodness. By 1948 around 7,500,000 copies of his books in various languages had been sold. In that year a collection of his children's poems in Russian was printed in an edition of 75,000 copies. Several months later he was arrested, and shot in 1952. Subsequently he was rehabilitated and his poems again became available in Russian and other languages, but not in Yiddish.

Aron Kushnirov (1891–1949) was born in a town near Kiev. He began to write verses in his teens and served in the army during World War I. The excitement and idealism of the revolution inspired him poetically. He joined the Red Army and fought during the civil war, but found time to write enough verse for a volume, *Walls* (1921), with a generous introduction by Hofshteyn. In a poem dedicated to the latter, Kushnirov wrote:

> I'll not hang my harp on trees—for all winds to start her sounds. . . . I do not own, even in a dream, a land of honey and milk. In my soul a little mouse is scraping—father's or grandfather's tune, but the door of my own Sabbath the week has sealed with a star.

"Autumn" is a nostalgic poem, with keen remembrance of massacres, ending with the comforting thought of a new home. The first stanzas read:

> Every man has a nest for longing in his heart. No man is protected against recollection. Perhaps because late autumn is severe and beautiful, perhaps because late autumn puts out the last gold—I have today recalled my home, which I shall never go to again.
>
> O, my gray home on a strange street, where sky dripped with rest on the dust of alleys—all grindstones of love and hate have sharpened a knife for you!

In the 1920's he achieved a prominent place among Yiddish writers with *Children of the People* (1928) and the play, *Hirsch Leckert* (1929). His mind was attuned to the spirit of social revolution and he rejoiced in being part of the rising proletarian world. To Itsik Fefer he wrote in 1930: "The poem is worth only zero unless it is completely fulfilled: full of powder inside and on the outside the mail of steel. . . . We need no jewelers now, we need metalists! We must harness our poems in ordinary weekdays, to trot in the tempo of our great epoch." And in poem after poem he sang of the pride of his generation in seeing the rebirth of the world. When he was not writing his own verse, he was editing suitable anthologies and translating from other languages. In 1940 he published another play, *An Ordinary Man*.

In his fiftieth year he enlisted to fight the Germans and

distinguished himself in the fighting. He fought all the more fiercely because of his grief for his son who was killed on the front and for the slaughtered Jews in occupied areas. In 1944 he wrote to a friend of his anguish about "the eternal Jewish tragedy," for he was aware by then that not only Germans but also Ukrainians and others were manifesting their hatred of Jews. Even in Moscow, where he lived after the fighting ended, he felt keenly the restrictions placed upon Jewish cultural activity. To another friend he confided that he and other writers were working on historic national themes, "but only for themselves." When asked why, he explained: "The inmost longing to free creativity is so great with a number of Russian-Jewish writers that they seek an outlet in the darkness of the writer's secret chamber."

For publication he prepared a volume of poems, *War* (1946), *Selected Poems* (1947), and additional war poems, *Father-Commander* (1948)—a body of work distinguished for its pathos and sensitivity. When the Stalinist purge forced him, the most prestigious of Yiddish writers, to act the informer at a public meeting, the shock paralyzed his vocal cords. Completely shattered, he died soon after.

Peretz Markish (1895–1952), born in Volhynia, received a traditional Hebrew training and went to Berditchev at the age of 11 to sing in a synagogue choir for three years. Thereafter he worked at various tasks until drafted into the army during World War I, where he was wounded. In Kiev shortly after the outbreak of the revolution, he became friends with Hofshteyn, Kvitko, and other Yiddish writers. His verses, which he had been writing for several years, appeared in a volume, *Steps* (1919), and were judged crude but impetuous, with a flair that reflected his flamboyant personality. In 1921 he went to Warsaw, where he associated with *Die Khaliastra*, the newer writers who stressed modern literary forms and tendencies. Subsequently he visited Paris, London, and Tel Aviv.

Highly attractive physically—his resemblance to Byron was noted by many—with an ebullient temperament, steeped in

Jewish sentiment yet strongly stimulated by revolutionary idealism, Markish freely reflected his complex personality and immediate emotions in his verses. While in Warsaw he was exposed to heated explications of impressionism, futurism, dadaism, and other current fashions in literature. He could not but be influenced by these rebellious voices. All the while he wrote with passion and power about the revolution, the civil war, and the massacres. His poem, *The Heap* (1922)— dedicated: "To you, slaughtered in a 'heap' in Horodovitch, a town at the Dnieper—Kadish!"—is a painful outcry against the pogroms perpetrated during the civil war; other of his verses expressed his enthusiasm for revolution and freedom: "A victor is not he who puts a bridle on another but he, who bridled, breaks the bridle." Some of his poems, written while he was in Paris, were imbued with nostalgic sentiment. In one about a letter from his father: "The letter is yellow as the worn face of my mother, the lines are like deep wrinkles in my father's brow; 'for God's sake, child, be careful of the ocean, one hears such terrible news!'" And he adds that the "good simple words come with blessing and with joy, as simple and dear guests."

In 1926 Markish returned to Russia, eager to take his place in a communist society. He believed that the ideal of social revolution was the noblest aim of mankind, and that the blemishes appearing on the Russian surface were but superficial and temporary defects. He at once found himself actively involved in cultural affairs, and wrote with enthusiasm about the prospects of the proletarian state and critically about the old, traditional life in which he grew up. He was not long, however, in finding himself at odds with Litvakov's rigid interpretation of communist policy. When attacked in 1928 for the "political error" of partaking in periodicals inimical to Soviet Russia, he had to apologize publicly. A story of his was next criticized for evidencing "a crippling ideology." Litvakov also rebuked him for tending to a "national apologetic" in *The March of Generations* (1929) and added that the characters "are bound ideologically with national limitation. . . . The heroes are almost all Jews." To which Markish countered: "To a Russian novel . . . which has only Russian revolutionaries no one seems to object."

This novel indeed depicts great social events, stressing the psychological differences among Jews, Russians, and Ukrainians during World War I. The pious Jews are drawn in darkest shades, with the town leaders made wicked and the average townsman stupid. The revolutionaries are painted with bright colors, but flatly. War, revolution, and pogroms destroy the traditional Jewish town along with the old generation symbolized in Mendel Milner; his son Ezra, representing revolutionary youth and the Red Army, is shown breaking fresh ground and starting a new life. It was obvious that, heeding Litvakov's earlier rebuke, Markish was paying his "tax" to "Prolet Cult"—to the detriment of his quality as a writer.

His long poem, *Brothers* (1929), concerns Ezriel and Shlome Ber, sons of a poor tailor, who dedicate their lives to the revolution. It is a song of insurgence and war, impetuous and exciting. Dynamic yet lyrical, it stresses folk tunes and broad humor. Every chapter has its own rhythm and verse lengths, with the diction hospitable to provincialisms and localisms. Again the wealthy Jews appear materialistic and harsh, while the workers are treated with praise and exclamations; most alive, however, are the ordinary Jews, whose humorous portrayal is expressionistic and fresh. Although the work is uneven in treatment and poetic sensitivity, the reigning critics were concerned not with its qualitative lapses but with its political content, and accused Markish of Zionistic tendencies, of serving "the reactionary ideology of the Jewish bourgeoisie." A similar complaint was made against *Pasted Watch Dials*, a contemporary collection of poems.

Markish was too impetuous and impassioned a poet to be harnessed to a rigid ideology. He replied to his critics in kind and continued to write as he felt: in praise of Soviet society, critical of traditional Jewish life, and mingling the pathetic with the heroic. Everything was on a large scale, expansive and intensive, whether his topic was the city, rebellion, or love.

All his work aimed in the same direction: the building of socialism. Moved to modify some early poems which had been criticized, he justified his action metaphorically: a poet is like a tree, which renews its leaves annually.

In *One After Another* (1934), a novel later adapted to the screen, the individual and the collective are woven harmoniously together. Nathan Becker, the protagonist, is a bricklayer who had lived 30 years in the United States and then returned to Russia "to lay bricks for socialism." In the ensuing events Russian and American work methods and political perspectives are compared and contrasted. This and earlier works gained Markish wide popularity and in 1939 he became the only Yiddish writer to receive the highly coveted Lenin Award.

Brooding over the Nazi atrocities in Poland in 1940, Markish wrote a series of 40 poems, only a few of which appeared in Russia, entitled *The Jewish Dancer*, a lyrically tragic plaint on the suffering of Jews through the ages, permeated with historic and philosophical associations and concepts. Addressing himself to the Jewish girl dancer he tells her:

> The yellow patch should not weigh heavily on you. Be not ashamed, homeless one, with hair loosened. Go straight, as have your grandfather and father; the old roads will recognize you. The crossroads will recognize you, my beloved, on which, with head proudly bent, went Akiba against the darkness, and his furthest descendants—hardened, as steel. . . . Generations of suffering dance out of you. . . . You must dance the generations-old shame, you must dance the generations-old pain. . . . There is no sword which has not been sharpened against you, there is no sword which will not break against you. . . .

Markish achieved full expression of his great poetic gift during World War II. His deep sorrow for the slaughtered Jews combined with an intensified patriotism to broaden the scope of his lyricism and deepen his intellectual perceptions, so that he depicted events in their full grandeur. *For the People and Homeland* (1943) sings of ravaged cities and their anguished inhabitants in verses intended to hearten the nation in its dark hour. *War* (1948), a very long poetical work, became the apotheosis of his life's many literary efforts. Ironically, some anti-German passages were deleted by the censor. He was at this time not only a dedicated communist but a Jew grieved to the depth of his being by the holocaust. In the poem, "The Jewish Army Man," he combines two emotions in a passionate lyric:

> I know: you kissed the gun that day, which placed on scales the life of the people, and with each shot, as with a thunderous bell, you blessed the land that gave it to you.
>
> You have made a solemn declaration with fire and blood through uprise and pain—you! The Jew! The Citizen! The Soldier! You! The Jew! The Red Army Man! . . .
>
> Over butchered communities, over scattered poverty, centuries roll over like hoops. Jewish soldiers, do not part with your gun even as your grandfather did not part with the book. . . .

At times his Jewish sorrow becomes dominant. In an unfinished novel, *In the Steps of Generations*, when the statement was made that the Nazis were destroying many nations, an old Jew exclaims: "It's a lie! False! They destroy Jews! Of other peoples they want to make slaves and of us they make soap! And the world looks on. . . ." He adds that nations usually mark past events by their connection to wars, but Jews associate past occurrences with massacres. This work was later published outside of the Soviet Union, but was issued in Moscow in 1966—in a Russian translation.

Even while in Caucasia for a rest in 1947, he was unable to close his mind to the horror of the Jewish slaughter. In a series of poems on the sea and other scenes of nature, he wrote: "My killed in Volhynia, my butchered in Podolia—the fields are green again, and bread once more grows in the valleys. My beheaded thousand years of Bessarabia and Poland—the dawn again rises over the mountain, on the mountains the sky is still naked."

When the order to arrest Yiddish writers was given, Markish was not spared, and in 1952 he was executed with the others. Five years later he was restored to good standing and a collection of his poems, translated by 42 different poets and with an introduction by Boris Lavreniev, appeared on the occasion. Lavreniev ended his laudatory discussion of Markish's career by stating:

> Markish was at the height of his mighty talent, and he would certainly have created additional noble works, but his life was cut down in the middle. He fell a victim of enemies, innocently sullied. The enemies of the fatherland have physically destroyed this great poet, but they have not killed his song.

Shmuel Halkin (1897–1960) was an innately elegiac and tranquil poet, although his verses, expressing current experiences and events, were charged with inner conflicts and deep feeling. With remarkable verbal economy he created a mood in a few lines. For a time unable to decide whether he wanted most to paint or to write, he began to publish poems at the outbreak of the revolution and brought out his first volume in 1919. Toward the end of his life he stated that his first poem, "Father's Lips," already contained the basic motives of his later verse: "The painful transition from the spirit of holiday to that of the weekday and the striving to heighten the week to a holiday." While in Moscow in the early 1920's he considered going to Palestine, but decided to remain with communism. Yet he was not, like some other Yiddish writers, blind to the blemishes marring proletarian society. In a poem entitled "Russia" he complained: "Russia! Were it not for my strong faith in you, I would now talk differently. I would perhaps have said: 'You have betrayed us; you have beguiled us, young gypsies.'" And he ended by stating: "We go in harness and die of your kisses." It is no wonder that his volume, *Woe and Courage* (1929), was harshly criticized as giving expression to "the voice of an excited petty bourgeois."

Many of his poems were written in a nostalgic spirit. "All that my child eyes have seen, absorbed, hidden a thousandfold deep, now appears like a bright rainbow, and rises like an old, sunken ship." This is the final quatrain on his father: "He remained a clear, silvery oldster, a white birch in winter dawn, and the wish is to laugh to tears and say: how good that such as he I now own." In a poem addressed to Yiddish writers in the United States he avowed defensively: "Fortunate brothers in distant lands—I would not exchange my fate with yours." In another poem on Sholom Aleichem he declared: "I call him again, for who can feel as he when Adam sees himself naked again?" He also wrote about the great philosophers and poets of the world with reverence and modesty.

When chastized for petty-bourgeois tendencies, he had no choice but to plead forgiveness. In a poem dedicated to Kharik, "I Belong to You," he admitted that some of his verses were "subjective in their expression of circumscribed nationalism." He did his best to conform and to assert his social responsibility in *Contact* (1935), a volume of poems free from political taint. Avoiding controversial topics, he wrote *Bar Kokhba* and *Shulamith,* plays that had successful performances in various Yiddish theaters. In 1939 this effort was rewarded with a formal honor by the government.

Germany's attack on Soviet Russia released Halkin's pent-up emotions and enabled him to pour out his agony and anger on the common enemy. In poem after poem he expressed his pain, hope, and vengeance. Typical is "Deep Trenches, Red Clay," an anguished elegy on the martyred:

> Deep trenches—red clay. Once I had a home. Spring—orchards blossomed, autumn-time birds passed by, winter—snow would fall. Now blossom only wind and woe.
>
> My home had a catastrophe—door and gate are open to the murderers, to the skinners, those that kill young children, those that hang old men, those that spare no one. . . .
>
> Year after year has passed—full are those trenches, and redder the clay. That clay is now my home: there lie my brothers, those torn limb from limb, the butchered in the house, those shot at the trench.

His final works—*The Songbird* (1943), a play performed but not published, *Earth Ways* (1945), and *The Tree of Life*

(1948), are of notable distinction. Arrested along with the other Yiddish writers, he became sick and remained in a prison hospital for a year and a half. In 1954 he returned from Siberian exile, one of the few survivors. He was honored officially in 1958 and died two years later. In 1966 *Sovietish Heymland* printed one of his characteristic lyrics:

> My glass is transparent and clean—through it you see the whole world: who weeps and who laughs. But when one side of it is covered with silver paint, worth a penny or a little more—the entire earth disappears from view, and from the clean glass becomes a mirror; and no matter how clean the mirror, you see in it only yourself.

Itsik Kipnis, born in 1896, became a storyteller in the tradition of Sholom Aleichem. More interested in the inner and enduring aspects of life than in current political ideology, he wrote with a sense of humor that annoyed proletarian-oriented critics. In addition to numerous short stories he published *Months and Days* (1926), a novel which achieved considerable popularity. In it Isaak-Leyb, a simple-minded worker, loves Buzi deeply and devotes himself to his personal happiness rather than to the revolution flaring all around him. When the enemy threatens, however, he enlists in the Red Army despite the fact that he has just become a father. The narrative treats love and politics with lyric simplicity and broad humor, conveying clearly the life of a hardworking family before and during the revolution. Among Kipnis' later writings were numerous popular stories for children.

In 1944 Kipnis was the first writer to tell about the Babi Yar slaughter in the outskirts of Kiev. Three years later he caused an outburst of anti-Jewish sentiment in reaction to his article expressing a wish that Jews spoke Yiddish, and ending with the statement: "It would be proper for all Jews who now parade on Berlin streets with the assured strides of victors to wear on their breasts, next to their Soviet medals, a handsome little Shield of David." The editors of *Einigkeit*, alert to the

danger, severely reprimanded him for not realizing "that So-
viet-Jewish soldiers did not fight for David of the Old Testament and for his ideals, but for their Soviet way of life, for the
Soviet government, for their Soviet fatherland." The Ukrainian
Writers Union expelled him. A year later he was among the
arrested and imprisoned. Fortuitously, he was not among those
shot in 1952 and was liberated shortly after Stalin's death. He
now lives near Kiev.

Itsik Fefer (1900–1952), born near Kiev, became a printer's
apprentice at the age of 12. In 1919 he joined the Communist
party and the Red Army, fought against the Denikin forces,
and was imprisoned for six weeks by the enemy. Already composing verses, he published his first poems in 1919. He was
soon editing anthologies, writing critical essays, and lecturing.
His volume, *Splinters* (1922), contained a foreword by Hofshteyn stating: "In this book there are motives which have
never before appeared in Yiddish poetry."

For all his youth, Fefer quickly became an aggressively influential member of the Kiev Yiddish writers. A class-conscious
radical, he was critical of symbolic writing and demanded
"plain, but firm and secure steps" from his fellow writers. He
loved Yiddish and praised it highly: "Yiddish smells with ripe
earth, Yiddish smells with stiff sword, Yiddish is a language
like other languages, not homeless on the road. . . . Yiddish
has both ash and fire, and that is why it is dear to us." Unlike
other Yiddish writers, he seemed devoid of nostalgic sentiment
and did not concern himself with any distinctive Jewish problem. He firmly believed that communism had made Jewish
separatism unnecessary, and united Jew and Russian in a common bond.

Fefer was a highly productive poet. *About Myself and
Others Like Me* (1924), *Found Sparks* (1928), and subsequent
volumes gave him an eminent position as a writer and strengthened his leadership of the Kiev group. When critics in the late
1920's found Trotskyist tendencies in some of his poems, he
became deeply distressed and hastened to make amends. Con-

sciously political, he stressed his proletarian loyalty. The following two excerpts, the first written in 1926 and the second from a poem addressed to Kushnirov in 1930, are typical:

> The hungry ruins lie like orphans, of everyone forgotten and neglected. I love words that are naked, I love poems that are plain. Do I have the right to sit here and sing songs, do I have the right to sing on paper? My brothers sing with axe and hammer, and axe and hammer wait for me.

> We must with sharp political poems drive away the lyrical mumble. . . . We build the poem, as one builds a house, as the Party builds its theses! . . . We need to freshen with the poison of the pamphlet, stab with the sword of satire! And to the brothers who tickle the rhyme we warn with mischievous strophes: poetic east—to battle! to the factory! to the barn! to the newspaper!

Politics notwithstanding, his poems were lyric in form and mood and epic in content. Niger aptly characterized them: "I. Fefer's lyricism is so natural, and so soft, that even the loudest and noisiest Red Army steps become stilled in him, become *ordinary* human steps."

In extenuation of his almost sycophantic homage to Stalin, it should be pointed out that, at the time he wrote, Stalin was the admired leader and Fefer was undoubtedly sincere when he stated in a poem: "Streams will ever flow, fields will ever be green; Stalin's name, like the sun, will ever shine on the world. He is deeper than the oceans, he is higher than the mountains, there is not another on this round earth."

It was in this spirit of adulation that Fefer wrote "A Wedding in Birobidjan." Believing that Birobidjan was the happy solution to the age-old Jewish problem, he was not concerned that the place was not suitable for settlement by a people inured to a temperate climate and with no farming experience, so that most Jews soon regarded Birobidjan as a Siberian exile to be shunned. It was enough that Soviet leaders decreed that Jews should develop this unoccupied wilderness for him to accept the news with gratitude and praise. A gifted poet, he described the wedding with symbolic merriment. Light and lyrical in style, the poem rejoices that life is being rooted in this new homeland by Jews from all parts of the Pale and that they are enriching "our Stalin earth."

During World War II Fefer was active in both the army and the Jewish Anti-Fascist Committee. He became deeply perturbed by discrimination against Jews by the government, and even more by the anti-Semitism of the Ukrainians in the occupied areas. Later, when the towns and cities were liberated by the Red Army, he saw hundreds of complaints from Jews who had been mistreated. As a leader of the Committee to which these complaints were sent, he once remarked: "Jewish woes come to us from all sides like rising rivers. The Committee can't dry these woes. The woes will drown the Committee." Yet he kept these plaints to himself when he and Michoels went to the United States and England to solicit help and sympathy.

In his poems, however, his troubled Jewish spirit became painfully apparent. His famous poem, "I am a Jew," surveys the highlights of Jewish history and stresses the bravery, heroism, and rebelliousness of the people, each stanza ending with the refrain, "I am a Jew." The first and final stanzas indicate his admiration for Jewish endurance as well as his persistent devotion to Stalin and the Soviet Union:

> The wine of generations of endurance has strengthened me in my wandering. The angry sword of pain and sadness has not destroyed my possessions—my folk, my faith, and my flowering, it has not chained my freedom. From under the sword I shouted: "I am a Jew!"
>
> I am a Jew who has drunk from Stalin's magic cup of happiness. Whoever wants to let Moscow sink, to turn the earth backward—to him I say: No! To him I shout: Down! I go with the eastern peoples, the Russians are my brothers—and I am a Jew!

The more he learned about the Jewish devastation in the border areas the deeper became his anguish, and he expressed it pathetically in *Shadows of the Warsaw Ghetto* (1945), a long chronicle of the beastly brutalities and heroic resistance.

"Each line," N. Meisel wrote, "is saturated with the blood of the murdered, with the fierce outcries of the raped and tortured, with the clarion call of the martyred resisters." And Fefer truly said: "The proud shadows of the Warsaw ghetto—they live in us with woe and pain."

Now grievously aware of the growing antipathy toward Jews on the part of Stalin, he strove to keep his fellow writers from making statements open to "nationalistic" interpretation. He deliberately continued to voice his loyalty to Stalin and to criticize Zionism as favorable to capitalism. Yet his Jewishness asserted itself in 1946 when he, in effect, wrote his own epitaph:

> Each man has a dream which lives with him, sometimes as a warm friend, sometimes as a cool neighbor. One dream, one great dream accompanies me, lives in me, as my heart and my song: when I shall alone remain in the bare earth, when the Jewish cemetery will take in my bones, let the passerby, noticing my grave, seeing the grass which rises from my source, say to the living wind: He was a man and served his people.

His comedy, *To Health,* written after the war, was performed in several theaters, as was *Times Change.* He was working on a novel in verse, *King Solomon's Inheritors,* and his last collection of poems appeared in 1948—when he was among the first to be arrested, and later among the executed in 1952. Subsequently he was rehabilitated and a volume of his selected verse appeared in Yiddish.

Der Nister (Pinhas Kahanowitch, 1884–1950) was *sui generis* among the Yiddish writers in the Soviet Union. Born in Berditchev, he was early influenced by his older brother, who had become a Braslaver Hasid, and was until adulthood steeped in the study of Hebrew and cabalistic literature. To avoid the draft he lived under an assumed name and earned his bread as a teacher of Hebrew. Unlike other young writers of his day, who saw only the ugly and musty side of Hasidism, he approached it sympathetically and appreciated the simple goodness and pure piety of the dedicated devout. This attitude he manifested in his first volume, *Thoughts and Motives* (1907). His next two books, *Higher than the Earth* (1910) and *Song and Prayer* (1912), concerned themselves with cabalistic themes and mystical attitudes. He sought to dig even deeper than Peretz, and more subjectively, into the sources of pietistic treasure, and wrote about it in the spirit of Nahman Braslaver: symbolically, secretively, concealingly. It was thus that he came upon his pseudonym, Der Nister, the Hebrew for concealer.

He came to Kiev in 1908, a gentle, modest, reticent young man, rather mysterious in behavior, obviously groping, searching for the hidden path to spiritual essence, sometimes losing himself in the byways of his own labyrinth, now and then emerging into a world completely unrelated to the one around him. In 1910 he went to visit Peretz and was elated by the older man's encouragement, yet he refused to remain in Warsaw because he felt the city was too large for him.

During World War I he exempted himself from the army by doing war work. When the revolution overthrew the Czarist government, he was one of very few Yiddish writers to remain apolitical. In 1918 he published *Tales in Verse,* stories charged with mystical groping. Finding himself out of tune with the revolutionary exhilaration around him, he in 1921 left for Berlin, where he issued a new collection of his visionary fantasies. Neither was life in Germany to his liking, and he returned to the Soviet Union in 1926, settling in Kharkov. Unchanged in attitude, unwilling to become harnessed to political agitation, although acquiescing in the tenets of the revolution, he lived in relative seclusion and penury, without the perquisites reserved for accepted writers.

Orderly and punctual of habit, reticent and taciturn, though eager to see people and observe them closely, he worked steadily at his desk, revising and polishing his sentences as if he were performing a holy task. He lived with his characters and suffered with them. In some of his stories he would begin realistically, only to have his protagonists become drunk or fall asleep and be subject to fantastic visions or symbolical allegories. In one of his best-known stories, an elderly scholar becomes mystically enamored of a circus rider and recalls a prophecy that "he will be poor and without ability, and will earn his living from a basket of mockery which he will carry attached to himself . . ."; that he himself will act as a circus rider. The entire narrative is thus woven out of dreams and visions which he relates to his daughter. Most writers, while finding his stories irrelevant to the temper of the revolution, respected his moral integrity and persistence. It was easier for them to praise his stories for children, which were written with folklike simplicity, with an allegorical yet winsome content.

In 1929 he managed to publish *Of My Possessions*, a volume of mercurial fantasies, replete with magic and mystery and an underlying arcane symbolism. Critics demanding "socialist realism" derided the work as reactionary, thereby depriving him of his stipend as a creative writer. To support himself and his small family he now had no choice but to resort to reportage and write more realistically. This was for him a very complicated process, as he indicated in a letter to his brother in 1934: "I, as is known to you, have always been a symbolist. To change from symbolism to realism for one like myself, who had labored strenuously to perfect his method and manner of writing, is very hard. This is no question of technique. One must be born to it. It means turning one's soul inside out. . . ." The first result of this transmutation was *Capital Cities* (1934), a series of relatively realistic descriptions of the socialist changes in Kharkov, Leningrad, and Moscow.

Even earlier Nister had begun to write *The Mashber Family* (1939, 1948), his chief work. Set in his native Berditchev of the 1870's, when it was still a commercially busy and teeming city, he depicts the rich and variegated life of the Jews with extraordinary vividness and insight. His general theme is social: the boorishness of the rich, the suffering and soundness of the poor, and the deep, simple faith of the Braslaver Hasidim.

His canvas is broad, rich, colorful. The major characters are portrayed with striking suggestiveness and sympathetic understanding; life spurts from them even though they become overshadowed by the veil of mysticism.

To give the novel the required "socialist realism" for purposes of publication, Nister wrote an introduction in which he makes clear that his particular subject matter cannot well be narrated without a description of medieval mysticism:

> I have done it, however, for the sake of historical awareness, to acquaint the young generation with the extraordinary distance which we have traveled during a relatively short time, which separates our reality from that one. . . . Depicting these characters, already completed physically and spiritually, I have tried not to "fight" them but to let them go, quietly and slowly, to their distinct fate, to their last historically necessary way—to perdition. . . . The main purpose of my work was not to put an end to the old generation sunk up to its neck in medieval ways of life, but to show those secret powers, which lay deep in the "third estate" [the Jewish slum] and which were so tragically destroyed under the weight of life's yoke.

The novel teems with numerous characters but concerns primarily the brothers Luzi and Moshe Mashber and Sruli Gol, a thoroughly unconventional young Hasid and lout who becomes Luzi's disciple and protector. In the first part of the narrative, Moshe is the wealthy merchant and banker, doing business on a grand scale, living lavishly, arrogant as befits a moneyed man, but pious and respectful of his older brother Luzi, who disdains worldly goods and devotes himself solely to his spiritual salvation. In this Luzi follows their father who, in seeking absolution for his father's sin of having been a follower of Shabbati Zevi, had died young from fasting and self-abnegation. After visiting the courts of various Hasidic rabbis, Luzi gravitated to the dwindling group of Braslaver disciples. Now firm in his faith, he changes from reticence and seclusion to an attitude of embracing friendliness. He settles in Berditchev, "N" in the novel, and associates with the small sect of Braslaver followers, the poorest and most despised Jews in the city.

Although he is on good terms with his brother and often visits him, Luzi prefers the bare table of the poor Braslavers to the rich food in Moshe's home.

Sruli Gol is an enigmatic character, careless in appearance, intimate with none, brazen in behavior, bold in action, uncurbed in his cursing, ready to intimidate the richest men in town if necessary for his mysterious purposes. In general he favors the poor at the expense of men of wealth. Highly articulate, ready to shout his anger at those he dislikes or who cross him in any way, he shows no outward love even to those he favors. He would attend the wedding of a poor couple "to make them happy," and he enters the homes of the rich uninvited and behaves as one of their intimates.

When one of Moshe's clerks becomes seriously ill and his mother comes to Moshe's home for help and is refused, Sruli, who happens to be present, commands Moshe to give the needed assistance. Angered at such brazenness, Moshe orders Sruli out of his house. Whereupon Luzi, who had sat quietly up to that moment, tells his brother to ask Sruli's pardon. All the angrier, Moshe tells Luzi that he too can leave. This the two ejected men do without delay.

Sruli had sometime back inherited a large bequest from a grandfather, but had made little use of it for himself. Like a fairy godmother he now provides the clerk's family with every possible assistance without revealing the source. He does the same for other poor families that seem worthy to him. From that day he makes Luzi his confidant, provides him with his meager needs, and watches over him with devoted solicitude.

At this juncture in the narrative Nister gives a masterly description of the behavior of Polish nobles and squires at the annual fair: their orgies and gambling proclivities, their financial decline, and their haughty behavior toward the Jews who finance them with loans and the purchase of chattels. The year being one of economic austerity, Moshe is unable to collect the large loans made to Polish squires and cannot meet payments due to his clients. When this becomes known, he is driven to bankruptcy and prison by the callousness of his fellow bankers.

The events leading up to this financial and personal deterioration are related in vivid detail and with psychological acuteness. Without stating it, Nister implies that Moshe's arrogance toward Sruli and Luzi cursed him with Job's afflictions. A daughter sickens and dies, he himself—forsaken by his associates—is imprisoned for debt, his wife becomes stricken with paralysis, and both die shortly after he is released from prison. Moshe loses his arrogance in the process, achieves genuine meekness, becomes reconciled with Luzi, and dies purified of common dross. This gradual transformation is narrated with such insight and felicity that one accepts it as a matter of course. This is the more remarkable in view of Nister's old-fashioned personal intrusions, so common in 19th-century fiction.

When he could not publish the second volume in Russia, Nister managed to send it to the United States, where it was brought out in 1948. The dedication to his daughter, who had died of starvation during the siege of Leningrad, reads: "May thy father's broken heart be a monument on your lost grave, may this book be dedicated to your eternal memory—your father, the author."

The narrative proceeds with Mikhel, a poor teacher, a Braslaver Hasid and Luzi's friend, struggling with his religious doubts until he finally rejects his traditional piety. When this becomes known, his pupils are withdrawn by outraged parents and he and his family become destitute. Sruli secretly comes to their assistance, but in his anger at the respectable community becomes drunk and is robbed and abused. When Mikhel dies of a stroke and the city fathers refuse to give his body proper burial, Sruli creates a scene and succeeds in having his way by paying the required fee. Again and again he acts like a *deus ex machina* in seeing justice done and succoring the poor. He is most solicitous about Luzi's well-being, knowing that the conventional community looks askance at Luzi's consorting with the poor and dejected. Luzi has reached the spiritual condition which tolerates all human behavior and befriends all who have need of his word of comfort. No longer to be countenanced by the city fathers, a plan is made to drive him out of the city. But Sruli learns of the plot and manages to leave with Luzi in safety some hours before the planned expulsion. The peculiar personal relationship between the Nazarite Luzi and the irrepressible and loutish Sruli is made a beautiful manifestation of man's inner goodness and insight.

The long narrative provides a richly vivid panorama of traditional Jewish life and lore. With a wealth of intimate detail and illuminating description it expounds hoary customs and conventional piety as well as the various ways in which Jews carried on their businesses and trades. The mystical modesty and humble self-abasement of the destitute Braslaver Hasidim are depicted with singular and fascinating simplicity—Nister being the only one in the Soviet Union to have written about them with such sympathetic understanding. Of the dozens of characters in the book, nearly all come alive with a few deft strokes, as may be seen from the description of Itsikel, a cemetery official, who is very homely: "Not so much his body as his bit of a face, shrunken like a dried fig, with a few hairs on it and with two narrow eyes like slits, and with the voice of a newborn kitten." And if Luzi dominates with his saintly passivity, Moshe with his arrogance turned to sorrowful acquiescence by repentance, and Sruli with his mysterious and boisterous behavior, the story as a whole centers in the absorbing and unforgettable portrayal of traditional Jewish life in the 1870's.

During World War II Nister, like other Yiddish writers, could only write about the catastrophe in Nazi-occupied Poland. These stories were published in New York in 1957. One of the longest and best of these narratives, "The Grandfather and the Grandson," tells of an old and very pious rabbi who ate little and prayed much, and of his grandson Itsik, the only remaining member of the family, who became a radical and atheist when he grew up. When the Nazis enter the town on Yom Kipper, the rabbi advises his parishioners to remain at prayer. With the aid of an informer, Itsik is the first to be arrested. Soon the rabbi and those at prayer are driven to the town square, where grandfather and grandson are ordered to spit at each other. They refuse and shout defiance in unison as they are led to the scaffold to be hanged. Other narratives have a similar intent and impact. Flora, for instance, the daughter of a highly respected and conscientious doctor who commits suicide in a Nazi prison, is plucky enough to outwit the German officers and become a successful partisan.

In 1947 Nister was sent to Birobidjan on a journalistic mission. He wrote with enthusiasm about his warm reception and the active life of the Jewish inhabitants. On his return he was delighted to learn that the first volume of *The Mashber Family* was being brought out in Hebrew. Very early in 1949 he was arrested. By then a sick man, he was operated on in a prison hospital and died in 1950.

In January, 1964, *Sovietish Heymland* published Nister's last novel, *Of the Fifth Year*, on which he had worked on and off for nearly a decade. It concerns Label, an only son brought up by a hard-headed and domineering mother to be the pride of her life. When he is 17 she begins to ask matchmakers to find him a bride worthy of her wealth and position. Label, however, in possession of her own drive and determination, is caught up in the political turmoil agitating Russia in 1905, and in his association with underground radicals meets Millie "with the young light deer feet," and both love each other at first sight. His mother learns of it and insists that he give up his friends and do her bidding. When he refuses and leaves home, her anger and frustration are extreme. In her fury she informs the police and the group is arrested. Soon conscious-stricken and partly deranged from rankling aggravation, the mother hangs herself. At about the same time the abortive 1905 constitution is announced, political prisoners are released, and Label and Millie are reunited in freedom.

It is quite conceivable that another writer would have confined the narrative within the limits of a short story. Nister, however, did not write concisely. His interest here was not so much in the action as in the background, motivation, and individuality of his characters. Indeed, the most significant fact about this book is its realistic style. Even in *The Mashber Family* he had not yet freed himself from the allegorical mysticism and fantasy which characterizes his earlier writing. In *Of the Fifth Year* he achieved the directness and psychological perception of the fictional realist. Writing with the old-fashioned leisure of 19th-century prose masters, he adds word to word and phrase to phrase with sculptural concreteness in building up the vivid uniqueness of his characters. In his description of the political turmoil of 1905 he is graphic, factual, and suggestive: police oppression, economic exploitation, and underground revolutionary agitation are shown in clear and comprehensive focus. At the same time he writes about idyllic young love with poetic beauty and remarkable freshness.

For 11 years no Yiddish periodicals or books were printed in the Soviet Union, nor did any Jew presumably dare to be seen with a Yiddish work in his possession. Some time after Stalin's death in 1953, one after another of the executed writers were quietly rehabilitated by the Writers Union, and the few who survived were liberated. In 1959 four Yiddish books were published in Moscow: a volume each of the three classic masters—Mendele, Sholom Aleichem and Peretz—and an anthology on the occasion of Birobidjan's twenty-fifth anniversary. Not many more have appeared since.

In 1961 *Sovietish Heymland* (Soviet Homeland) was started in Yiddish, first as a bimonthly and more recently as a monthly. Edited by Aron Vergelis, it contains fiction, poetry, and criticism of notable quality—although everything of current vintage breathes with euphoric optimism, a well-being that becomes cloying. Although the writers, around 100 in all, are in their forties and fifties and surely aware of the situation before and now, the work they publish in the magazine deals mostly with successes and achievements of their Jewish characters. To the credit of the monthly are the poems and stories of the martyred writers as well as critical and reminiscent essays about them.

Of the older writers now being published in Soviet Russia, Elya Schectman and Noteh Luria are most representative. The first, born in the Ukraine in 1908, published his first novel in 1930 and two additional ones during the next decade. He served in the armed forces during World War II and apparently escaped apprehension in 1948. In 1962 *Sovietish Heymland* printed his novel *Erev* * (On the Eve), and it has since been published first in Russian and recently in Yiddish. An English edition was published in New York in 1967. Dealing with Jewish life at the turn of the century, it depicts Jewish persecution by anti-Semitic officials and the prevalence of pogroms. The sturdy Boyar family centers in the narrative, beginning with Avrom, who returns wounded from the Russo-Japanese War to find his sister killed in a pogrom and he himself falsely accused of revolutionary activity, and ending with his father, who would not save his own converted daughter from exile even though he suffers torment in the process. The thwarted affection of Eva for her cousin Doniel is vividly depicted. Exceptionally well portrayed is Aunt Liba, who understands much and says little.

Noteh Luria, born in 1905, first became favorably known for *The Steppe Calls* (1932, 1948), a two-volume work on Jews farming the land and acclimating themselves to peasant life. Folklike in his psychological treatment of these Jews, Luria presents Elke Rudner as a free-thinking person who brings light to the people and liberates many from traditional limitations. Perhaps an even greater literary achievement is Sheftel Kobiletz, who begins as a simple peasant but in time develops into a devoted and successful Soviet worker. He and Elke love each other, but fate drives them apart. *Heaven and Earth* (1965), printed in *Sovietish Heymland*, continues the story of the two protagonists. Sheftel, having fought in the war, has become a leader in a cooperative and is married and the father of four children. He learns by chance of Elke's whereabouts nearby, visits her, and learns that she too has been married, is the mother of a little girl, and works to support herself in the absence of her husband, who is in prison on an allegedly false charge. Their renewed relationship and life in the cooperative are described in firm, clear prose and with robust optimism. Luria was among the arrested in 1948, but survived the ordeal, and now lives in Odessa.

Aron Vergelis, born in 1918, grew up in Birobidjan. A parachutist during World War II, he was wounded several times. He began to write lyrics in his teens and published his first volume, *At the Spring*, in 1940, and *Birobidjan Generation* in 1948. He has edited the work of several older Yiddish writers in Russian translation. As editor of *Sovietish Heymland* he has become spokesman of the living Yiddish writers and has made several trips abroad to visit Jewish centers. He is not optimistic about the revival of Yiddish in the Soviet Union. "The Jews," was his official explanation, "have less of a yearning for Jewish culture than they had in the 1920's and 1930's and therefore one cannot artificially expand, without rhyme or reason, the scope of cultural work in Yiddish." This is probably true in the light of what has happened in the past two decades, but it is also obvious that interest in Yiddish or Jewish culture is decidedly not encouraged by the official in the Kremlin.

CHAPTER SIXTEEN

DOVID BERGELSON

Novelist of Psychological Refinement

DOVID BERGELSON was born near Kiev in 1884. His father, already elderly, was a Hasid, well versed in Hebrew religious tradition, a wealthy merchant in lumber and wheat. The most prominent citizen in town, he frequently entertained neighboring businessmen and pious scholars. Dovid, a precocious child, readily absorbed the talk at his father's table as well as the personal peculiarities of the participants. At the age of four he began going to *kheder*, and for the next decade studied Hebrew books on Judaism. In 1901, with both his parents dead, he went to Kiev to live with a much older brother. By that time he was already reading Russian and Hebrew books and felt quite at home in his new and comparatively enlightened environment. He had also been practicing writing for several years and was giving much of his time to a novel in Hebrew—which was never published—undeterred by the awareness that his older brothers and sisters ridiculed his literary ambition.

After preliminary efforts at Yiddish composition, Bergelson completed "The Deaf One" in 1906 and *About the Depot* two years later. None of his early attempts to see his work in print were successful; editors either rejected his stories or did not even trouble to acknowledge them. When he sent a manuscript to Peretz, he received no reply. Encouraged, however, by friends who were also fledgling writers, Bergelson went to Warsaw, then a center of Yiddish publishing, and arranged for publication of *About the Depot* by assuming part of the cost. The brief narrative, issued in 1909, was generally acclaimed as a fresh and vivid portrayal of Jewish middlemen and a positive addition to the burgeoning Yiddish literature. A first review stated: "It has a mood, a feeling—and it is difficult to grasp its origin, its magic." Another critic hailed Bergelson as "an artist of both wisdom and talent, with a style of his own, with his own view of the world." All were surprised to learn that the author was in his twenties, as the story gave the impression of long familiarity with habits and attitudes of Jewish merchants and *luftmenschen* and of seasoned insight and understanding.

In this story the depot is the center of activity for neighboring businessmen, brokers, agents, porters, and hangers-on. Among them are men of shrewdness and enterprise as well as futile ne'er-do-wells, the serious and the wits, the smug rich and the anxious and ingratiating poor. For a little while after the train arrives there is a great deal of bustle and excitement; when the train leaves, life about the depot lapses into its trivial drabness. The narrative is concentrated on Rubinshteyn, an intelligent and well-educated young man who has no head for business and is frustrated at every turn. Although aware of his incompetence and his inability to stand up against shrewd and aggressive competitors, he feels impelled to make a show of business activity. In time he loses the capital with which he started. His personal life is no more satisfying. His first wife, who was beautiful and whom he loved deeply, died shortly after their marriage; his second wife is homely, sickly, and clumsy, and he soon leaves her and lives in a peasant's house near the depot. He is daily aggravated by failure and the mockery of unsympathetic observers. Angered one day by one of these men, he slaps him, is sued, and has to spend a fortnight in prison. When released, he resumes his listless, daydreaming, hate-ridden existence.

About the Depot is an impressionistic prose narrative. It depicts Jewish life in the small town neither romantically, as did Sholom Asch, nor naturalistically in the manner of S. Weissenberg, but with a sensitivity of mood and an incisiveness of feeling. Shortly after the book's appearance Bergelson explained his method of writing in a letter to S. Niger:

> This is how I write: First is born the mood of the story together with the main character (the latter almost always not quite clearly) and so affects the soul that it becomes almost unbearable. . . . With the mood comes a strange yearning for that unique aspect of the world which brings in the protagonist and the mood. My entire aim thereafter is to express this mood together with the life and events which occur around it and (if one might say it) in it.

What he succeeded in doing was to infuse the dreariness of their environment into the characters he depicted; the atmosphere of repression, fear, and weariness prevailing in Russia during the 1900's weighted the pages of this and later stories —yet was brightened by a style of acute sensitivity and verbal scintillation.

"The Deaf One," a long short story which he later successfully dramatized under the title *The Bread Mill*, reveals Bergelson's strong sympathy for the poor and oppressed. A deaf mill-hand, uneducated and not very bright, is painfully sensitive of his lack of hearing. Broadboned and middle-aged, with a scarred, strained face, he is anxious to know what the other workers are saying but is ashamed to expose his deafness by asking. When spoken to, he makes believe he hears and replies noncommittally. He falls from a height when a rope breaks and is laid up. His daughter, who works as a servant in the miller's house, visits him and her hard weeping troubles him, since he knows that she has been annoyed by the miller's wanton son. Soon after she commits suicide and he is called to the scene.

> Someone pulled his sleeve and showed him the ceiling. He looks: a rope hangs there from a hook. He now understands that she had hanged herself and he wants to ask, "Why?" but doesn't ask.

He takes a look at the old Jewess who stands at the head of the corpse, her face in pain, hunched, her toothless mouth open, her head thrown back with eyes closed and face awry. She wept presumably with a heart-rending voice, but he is deaf and doesn't hear. He also makes a wry face, also tries to cry, but can't.

Bereaved and distraught, unable to sleep, eager to avenge himself on the greedy miller and his worthless son, he becomes almost deranged. When he sees a cow outside his window, he assumes it to be the miller's and cuts off its tail with an axe —only to learn the next morning that the cow belonged to a poor dairywoman. Written in the wake of the abortive revolution of 1905 and amid widespread restlessness, the story stresses the abuse and exploitation of the poor by the callous rich, but intimates that the workers are developing a spirit of rebellion—even though in the futile and stuttering manner of the deaf one.

The End of Everything (1913) was Bergelson's first major novel. It was serialized in Wilno's *Die Yiddishe Welt* (The Jewish World) and was highly lauded on publication. Sensitively impressionistic in treatment, acutely psychological in character analysis, almost Chekhovian in mood, the narrative stresses the disintegration of Gdaliah Hurvitz, a wealthy and learned Jew, the rise of the gross and aggressive businessmen, and the pathetic chaos of generations in transition. Most of all, however, it concentrates on the fate of the intelligent, well-educated, and handsome Mirel Hurvitz, who cannot adjust herself to a world governed by coarseness and cupidity. The only daughter of refined and respectable parents in the grip of financial decline, she suffers from frozen feelings which make her behavior pathetically foggy.

Her impulses and moods hasten her disintegration. She breaks her engagement to a youth deeply in love with her but continues to interest herself in the affairs of his family; she permits a lame student to accompany her on long walks and yet treats him shabbily; she has a high regard for her father but cannot get along with her conventional and silently accusing mother. Sometimes she wonders what makes her behave the way she does. "She smiles and is silent, as if on purpose. . . . Someone might think she has much to say and keeps quiet because she is too wise." She does not know what she wants, what is troubling her, but is keenly aware that "her life sinks in dullness."

After much hesitation she agrees to marry the son of a rich man in order to bolster her father's financial precariousness, for she cannot see him depressed by it. "His sad appearance shattered her. Always she had believed that he, her father, is strong and can do everything, in order to be proud and not let herself down. And now she saw him for the first time helpless and with the mien of a lost bankrupt." At the celebration of her betrothal, repelled by her fiancé and his half-drunk father, she leaves them and locks herself in her room. Eager to break the engagement yet unable to let her father down, she is moody and restless. "It seemed to her that she did not live like other people, that she was always alone, on the outside of life, in *tohu-vohu*, and wanders as if lost from childhood in an evanescent, confused dream, which has no beginning and no end."

Marriage does not alleviate her sadness and boredom. The prospect of the same shallow banalities day after day frightens her. Anxious for some form of release, she thinks of suicide. Rejecting her husband's advances one night, she wakes the next morning feeling "something heavy and repulsive weighting her spirit, just as if her heart were dipped in something filthy. And outside a cloudy sky showed a new dreary Sunday and spread its sole boring thought: a new week . . . a dreary week . . . an empty week."

A visit home only intensifies her depression. On her return a divorce is agreed upon and she insists on going through an abortion. Alone and miserable, she feels "as if someone stood bent over her head, choking her, reminding her: 'You have destroyed your life . . . and it is lost, forever lost.'" She goes away, and no one knows where.

Mirel Hurvitz is the first girl in Yiddish literature to behave not like a traditional Jewess but like a unique individual at once emancipated and fettered to subconscious ties of the past. Her sense of refinement and intellectual sensitivity, sharpened by generations of pious and learned ancestors, kept her from acquiescing in the coarseness and shallowness of her contemporaries. No man pleased her completely—so few matched her qualities or stirred her emotions—and her behavior toward her husband, who is good and well-intentioned, if foolish, is at once cruel and unmerited. Yet she is unquestionably a great fictional creation. Bergelson reveals the inner goodness of her being, her deep maladjustment, her futile striving to rise out of the emotional morass in which she found herself. Like her father, she has neither the will nor the strength to make amends and permits herself to drift to perdition. Her moodiness and misery are depicted with keen sympathy and psychological insight. In her failure to adjust is reflected the dispirited and doleful attitude of the Jewish youth in Russia after the failure of the 1905 revolution. Bergelson was not unaware of the novel's literary excellence: "The book is *Jewish*," he wrote to Niger. "I love it and it seems to me *to have a soul*. At the end one may become reflective, but one can also take the Book of Psalms and pray for the souls of both Gdaliah and Mirel."

In *A Coarsened City* (1914), Bergelson provides another aspect of the social satire that characterized his first decade as a writer. Heretofore he had depicted his own intimate environment; now he dealt objectively with people as he observed them with the perspicuity of the novelist. Burman, a student who did not complete his course, is appointed government rabbi in a neglected, sleepy border town. He is soon affected by the lazy and languid atmosphere. "He sat in his bachelor quarters. There everything was dirty and gray: gray the walls and the balcony, gray the pile of dusty legal tomes, which looked upon him so sadly—as if they wished to lead him in the right direction and say critically: 'Burman, you're going around idle, Burman. . . . You'll have a bad end.' "

The grandson of a man of wealth, recently deceased, comes

from another town to claim his inheritance. Unlike his grandfather, he refuses to give the charity expected of him, and behaves in other ways to antagonize the people. He is refused the office of collector of the meat tax, held by his grandfather, and in the ensuing quarrel the butchers beat him up and he dies. Other aspects of the town are equally coarse and common: marriages are mercenary events; women indulge in sordid affairs; businessmen try to get the best of one another. Burman becomes resigned: "The world is mud, as I am a Jew." Even the few educated men and women lack sensitivity and refinement; the general dullness prevails. Thus the narrative becomes a stinging satire on the lack of idealism and decency in certain sections of the burgeoning bourgeoisie of prewar Russia.

World War I depressed Bergelson and inhibited his literary activity. In 1933 he recalled:

During the war I wrote almost nothing for a variety of reasons: the war oppressed me, and it seemed as if belles lettres had become superfluous. There was also no possibility of publication, as the Czarist government had stopped all Yiddish printing. I was not even in the mood to complete the things I had already begun. This general crisis made me feel that with *Departure* I would write my last book, that I had no more to say, no more to write.

The revolution of 1917 revived his spirit and his literary activity. He became one of the founders of the Kiev League for Culture. He also participated in the editing of *The Yiddish Almanac*, in which "The Deaf One" appeared, and in anthologies which included the writings of both established and new authors. The civil war and the resulting pogroms caused him much grief—he lost an unpublished novel in the pogrom that occurred where he then lived. A visit to Moscow in 1920 did not quiet his perturbation and he left for Berlin a year later. There he and Nister tried to edit a periodical. At that time he arranged to contribute stories to the New York *Forverts* and the Warsaw *Folkszeitung*.

For several years he was subject to intellectual dichotomy. As an idealist and skeptic he was both repelled by the social injustices of capitalism and equivocal about the promises of Bolshevism. In 1926 he persuaded himself that the Soviet Union was the only place in which Yiddish literature could develop into full efflorescence. He left *Der Forverts* and began to write for the communist *Freiheit*. He also started to edit the short-lived pro-Russian monthly, *In Shpan* (In Harness), and urged Yiddish writers the world over to "orient themselves toward Moscow," asserting that the only hope of Jewry was "the emerging Jewish center in the Soviet Union." On a visit to Moscow he accepted co-editorship of *Emes* (Truth), declaring himself a Soviet writer and in favor of the dictatorship of the proletariat. He continued to live abroad, however, and late in 1928 came to the United States, where he remained for six months. Neither America nor Western Europe gave him the peace of mind he craved, and he came to believe that only in Russia could he function naturally as a writer—drawing on the rooted Jewish environment of his characters. With the capitalist world in a state of economic collapse and Europe in the darkening shadow of fascism, he decided in 1933 to return to his native land. In the interim he had written and published several volumes of fiction.

Departure, begun in 1913 and published in 1921, is like *The End of Everything* a work of lyrical and moody wistfulness. It, too, depicts the decline of the traditional Jewish way of life and the resulting restiveness of the younger generation. The style is again at once incisive and tentative, so that the atmosphere of doubt prevails throughout the action. Sated and dull philistines mingle with lonely and unhappy intellectuals in a world undergoing painful transition.

The story begins with Melekh's death in Rakutne, presumably by suicide. His friend Khaim Moshe comes to town to ascertain its cause. Melekh had been a revolutionary, had served two years in prison, and had come to Rakutne to open a drug store. The townspeople are naturally very inquisitive; whatever occurs to one is soon known to all. Thus when Ethel, a student, shuts herself up in her room and remains silent for two months, everyone speculates as to the cause. This curiosity is increased when it is learned that Melekh had visited her and that the next day she broke her seclusion and silence and called upon Melekh in his drug store.

There is the town's rich merchant, Ezriel Pozner:

> He had the velvety face of a respectably genteel priest and had the habit of testing the health of his lungs with a gentle cough. Once he had weak lungs—a long time ago. Now they are fully covered with yellow eggnogs and with eggs. And his face is the same—it smelled with yellow-egg cake, with butter cookies, and with sweat.

His daughter Eva is a handsome, enigmatic girl thoroughly bored: "When you add the new part to the old town there are about 9000 persons in Rakutne," she said, "yet thus far it has not produced a single interesting individual." She was also supposed to have had an affair with Melekh, and letters by her were found in his possession. Yet none in the town wish to talk about Melekh's death or about those with whom he had associated. Khaim Moshe finds few clues. The young people he meets are dissatisfied yet yearn for nothing definite; they either run away from love or find it beyond their reach. Nothing really happens throughout the narrative; Melekh's suicide is not resolved, and none of the characters emerge clearly defined. The end is inconclusive, yet with obvious intimations. As one remarks: "Everything has cloth on the outside and lining on the inside, and there is something in between," and that something is left for the reader to discern.

Storm Days (1928) is a collection of stories about the revolution and the civil war. The chaotic conditions of the period are described graphically and in detail. Soldiers abandon the front, and on their way home rob and beat up Jews to get what they want. There are no officers to discipline them, and none feels responsible; each man is for himself, and everything is haphazard and disorderly. When Petlura's hooligans arrive, they make merry by shooting up towns and raping women.

Anti-Petlurists then take over, but to them Jews are bourgeois enemies to be treated accordingly.

In "Behind the Burning Town" an ugly young man cannot keep from lusting after a girl despite the danger from approaching anti-communists. In "On the 101st Mile" the presence of a Red Army youth stationed at a telephone post dominates the behavior of a group of Jews who sympathize with neither side. "Among Emigrants" tells of a highly disturbed youth who comes to Berlin to assassinate the leader in a pogrom and ends in suicide. "A Strong Ending" is a particularly well-told story about a young communist writer who, as he describes caustically the sinfulness of an attractive young neighbor, becomes so enamored of her that he gives the narrative an unexpected ending. "Ruins" tells how two young sons of a wealthy family impoverished by the revolution take up farming, much to their parents' dismay. These and other tales are written in a minor key, with relative objectivity and literary finesse.

Divine Justice, completed in 1925 and published five years later, has its setting in a border village during the civil war period. Although in Bolshevik control, conditions remain fluid and anti-communists as well as smugglers are actively seeking to destroy the Red Army unit. All groups are depicted through the eyes of several characters. Filipov, the Bolshevik leader, represents the rigid morality of the revolution. He suffers from festering boils and is overworked, but he persists in carrying out his assignment without flinching. He seeks to outsmart the smugglers—most of them poor Jews bribed by rich ones to do their dirty work—and to suppress the Social Revolutionaries and anti-communist bandits. Since he lacks an adequate contingent, he is accused by his associates of being too proud to ask for help—although he had already requested it and been refused. In the struggle that ensues, Filipov is killed and is avenged by the aroused workers of the vicinity.

Bergelson treats the communists sympathetically, yet realistically. All characters are delineated with intuitive understanding as human beings moved primarily by motives of idealism or survival. Their life in the thick of civil war—hectic, hard, dangerous, zigzagging—is described vividly, imaginatively, and effectively.

Two volumes of short stories followed: *Out of the World and In It* (1929) and *Air Current* (1930). Varied in content and setting as well as in point of view, the stories present a host of characters in telling situations. "Sisters," for instance, is about a serious-minded girl of 28, about to take her medical examination. She misses one of her texts and finds it in possession of her much younger sister, and in it a love note arranging for a date. She scolds the adolescent for taking up with strange men and decides to meet the lover and warn him to leave her sister alone. She finds him to be a painter, an attractive fellow, and as he gets closer to her and embraces her, she begins to feel guilty toward her younger sister. In "Enemies" two brothers, neighbors and wealthy merchants before the revolution, had quarrelled and remained enemies for 29 years. When the daughter of one of them is to be married, the father calls out to the brother next door: "Come to the wedding, come I say. . . . We quarrelled when we were still merchants. . . . Now a merchant is dirt. . . ."

Air Current contains mostly stories about the civil war and its immediate aftermath. In "A Story about the Rich" ten wealthy Jews are arrested by the Red Guard for not paying the assessed tax. Unwilling to part with their possessions, they face the threat of being shot. When their fellow townsmen learn of this danger they seek to save the lives of the prisoners by contributing what they have of value to make up the fines. An old sick mother of a poor worker who had been mistreated by one of the prisoners also makes her contribution and says of him: "He was of course a murderer against my Itzi. In the middle of winter he threw him out of his mill. But to be shot? . . . Here, I brought you my silver cup." Later the Jews learn that the threat to shoot was only a means of getting valuables, and the ten are released that evening—much to the chagrin of Itzi, who is now minus his one silver cup.

"Rebirth" tells of a very conscientious young doctor who

had volunteered in World War I and was wounded. When the civil war started, he enlisted in the Red Army and sent his wife and child to her parents. During a pogrom his wife was refused shelter by a Polish doctor with whom the husband had been friends, and she and her child were killed. When the doctor learns of the fate of his family he cannot continue to treat the same kind of Ukrainians who had murdered his dear ones and obtains leave to go home. On the way he thinks only of shooting the Polish doctor. When he is about to carry out his act of revenge, the sight of the crawling Pole begging for mercy gives him a feeling of ugliness. " 'Here,' he said and put the revolver back in his pocket. 'I give you alms—your stinking little life. . . . Not out of pity, but because I'd feel ugly to shoot you, so keep it.' " Soon after he meets the leader of the Jewish self-defense and is told that when his men used up their bullets, none would take any of them into shelter for fear of reprisal; although Red Army soldiers are no angels, he has no choice but to join the party. The doctor finds himself similarly placed and rejoins his regiment.

In "Citizen Wolie Brenner" old Brenner, very proud of his communist daughters, becomes angry when his former employer, who had lost status under communism, proposes a marriage between his bourgeois grandson and one of Brenner's daughters. The former employer cannot understand Brenner's indignation. "After all," he says, "you were once in my employ." "If you don't understand," the old man shouts back, "it's even worse. I am no longer your 'employee.' You don't have any employees any more. . . . And I tell you, if you still think of me as an 'employee' then, then . . . get out!"

One of the best civil war stories, "Hershel Toker," concerns a young Jew caught by White Guard officers at the border. He is considered a Bolshevik spy and incarcerated in a ward filled with sufferers from spotted typhus. He is questioned repeatedly about his companion, a girl, who had succeeded in escaping, and is not believed when he maintains that he does not know anything about her. Much to the annoyance of his interrogator he becomes infected with typhus. In his delirium he is happy with the successful escape of his companion and with reminiscence of his friends. He feels vaguely that someone is helping him but cannot tell who. When he is dying the orderly, a secret Bolshevik sympathizer, covers him with a large red flag—to the consternation of the officers.

Penek (1932), the first volume of *At the Dnieper*, is a quasi-autobiographical novel about a boy very much like himself both in character and milieu. Born into a wealthy and highly prestigious family, he is an unwanted child of elderly parents, with a considerable gap between him and the next sibling. Precocious, mischievous, sensitive, early aware of the inequalities between rich and poor and intuitively partial to the underdog, he is driven to the side of the humble by the overt hostility of his mother and the older children. Only his father, Mikhel Levin, a learned, pious, and successful merchant, treats him with kindness, but he is often away on business and has little time for the boy. The mother, a commonplace and coddled woman, had not wanted another child and feels resentment toward her youngest. As soon as he is able to walk he is left mostly to the care of the kitchen servants. Penek retaliates by being contrary and troublesome. Only seven years old, but already quite aware of the intricacies and inequalities of life, he finds the companionship he craves in the hovels of the town's poor. They appeal to him as being much more interesting than his own family. Restive, intellectually alert, he wants to see and know everything, and soon familiarizes himself with the affairs of and gossip about almost every family in town.

Unlike his mother, who becomes panicky at the least feeling of pain, his father is of a stoical nature and does not yield to minor ailments. Years before, when he needed an eye operation, he refused to take ether. "I don't need a sleeping drug. I mean—I'll think a little and won't feel the pain." Now his illness is serious and persistent, and this draws Penek closer to him. Anything out of the ordinary, like illness or death, gives the boy much to think about.

Always eager to do the poor a favor, he no sooner hears his oldest sister Sheyndel say that the floors need painting than he hurries over to the town painter, who is penniless and badly in need of work, and brings him to the house. But Sheyndel has a city painter in mind and tells the man she has nothing for him. At this point the ailing father intervenes and tells her to let the painter do the job. Stubborn, she settles by giving him only two of the lesser floors.

Mikhel Levin is portrayed sympathetically, though not without the warts of his wealth. The town's leading citizen, he is shown to be good-natured, modest, and generous. His boyhood friend Yeshiah, a poor but scholarly person, does not hesitate to contradict and criticize him, but every Thursday he is given three rubles "for the Sabbath." Once in a while, when on a trip, Levin forgets to arrange for the stipend. Yeshiah on such occasions says nothing but thinks: "Of course, forgot. . . . How else?—a rich man!" And on reflection he has the satisfaction of concluding that no matter how learned and pious a rich man may be, he remains a pig. And in fact Levin forgets his friend in his will.

The house servants are friendly to Penek, and he spends much time with them. They protect him and see that his mischief and misbehavior remain unknown to the family. Yet when the cook sees him steal food to give to a poor friend, she remarks to her assistant: "Do you see or not? . . . Now he's still all right, with a heart, since he's only ten years old. . . . But let him grow up and he'll be as wormy as the others in the house."

Penek is not long in learning the mystery of procreation and his father's part in it. "Penek felt: he suddenly lost all respect for his father. It means that his father is a common, ordinary man. . . . One would have thought that he was an angel. . . . He was annoyed with all the pious Jews who make believe they're angels." He begins to wonder who is a truthful person, and if piety is a cover for lust. He notes another aspect of adult hypocrisy when a smooth-tongued fellow begins to court the assistant cook, for it is obvious to him that the man is only after her hard-accumulated dowry. When this happens, Penek feels sad.

Penek is most at home in the slum. He loves to see people happy and tries to help them in every way he can. Not eager to study, he nevertheless goes through the routine because he knows his poor teacher depends on the tuition for his lessons. But if he neglects Hebrew lore, he makes sure to learn everything about the people of the town—about their children, their wives, their worries—all of whom he knows as he knows himself—"one could even ask him in his sleep and he will say at once how each one feels in his heart and thinks in his head."

The elder Levin is a long time dying, and the poor of the town comment: "A poor man dies quietly, but when a rich man dies the heavens split." Three doctors are called from the nearby city, but they can do nothing for him and he suffers intense pain until he dies. Meantime the ailing and crippled poor gather before the house, hoping that the doctors might help them, but Sheyndel refuses to send the doctors out to them and Penek feels that "this won't be forgiven."

At the Dnieper: Young Years (1940) continues the narrative of the Levin family, again with emphasis on Penek, but broadened to include the social and political agitation of the 1900's. The older Levin's children are coarser and less able than their father, without his piety or generosity, each one interested only in getting as much as possible out of the family inheritance. They move to Kiev, where the older sons unsuccessfully seek to pursue their business enterprise and their mother devotes herself to arranging marriages for the older children. Penek continues to be neglected and disdained, much to his indifference, as he becomes interested in the growing revolutionary movement and makes his initial attempts at authorship. He finds new friends and revives old acquaintances from his native town, especially with Manya, a girl who has attracted him from boyhood.

In this volume Bergelson writes more consciously from a communist standpoint. He is acidulous concerning the attitude of wealthy Jews toward anti-Semitism, as may be seen from his description of one of them, a rich jeweler active in civic affairs:

> He is blondish, corpulent, with the delicate, modest face of a person who is confident that he does only good. His feet are thickish, as those of a sea captain who is seldom on land; his lips are full, feminine, very naked, bright red, as if frequently kissing the good friends he has all over the world—good friends among Jews, among Christians, good friends without end and without number.

He gains friends among the important officials by gifts of costly jewelry and exploits these connections in his efforts to mitigate the agitation against Jews—to his own enhanced prestige as a man of influence and good will.

Penek enters casually but more and more fully into the activities of the revolutionists. He makes friends with poor workers in crowded tenements, learns about Lenin and the split in the Socialist party in 1903. That year the Kishinev pogrom deeply depresses him. Disgusted and distressed by this show of gentile brutality, he is forced to reflect on the history of the Jews:

> A deep shame lay on him like a heavy burden, as if upon him alone were attached all the badges of shame which he recalled in Jewish history. For over 17 centuries none can tolerate him, Penek. He is persecuted, his behavior and origin mocked at, he is ever being driven. No plague but is tried out on him, no hatred and abuse that are not used against him. "Penek" he is only to friends; in the world at large his name is "Zhid" [sheeny]. . . . Under the weight of that shame he that morning wrote: "Twenty centuries of Jewish oppression have today burdened me."

His grief makes him chagrined with the petty complacency of his family. He wonders whether it is physical or spiritual failure on his part to have reached his eighteenth year in the midst of anti-Semitism and not to have been aware of it. He decides to leave home and goes to the slum, where he sees frightened Jews beaten by drunken peasants.

Fear of a widespread pogrom becomes aggravated when

the body of a little Christian girl is found under the house of a Jew. Three Jews are at once arrested, and priests begin preaching revenge. Wealthy, public-spirited Jews feel an obligation to defend the prisoners, to expose the hoax of blood accusation, but their intent and actions concern only the immediate incident and not the underlying factors bringing it about. When conditions worsen, many of them close their homes and leave for foreign parts.

Penek's first story, with its setting in slum tenements, is published and praised by a prestigious critic. Instead of elation, however, he feels as if he has suddenly lost his youthful self and experiences a sense of guilt. He takes a more active part in the work of the revolutionists and becomes antipathetic to the Jewish nationalists who place the interests of the Jews above those of the nation as a whole. Yet when he and Manya visit the home of a prominent Jew and learn of the imminence of a planned pogrom, he "suddenly felt most strongly the endless repetition of centuries and the agedness of the Jews—how many times during the centuries people in Jewish homes have sat as they were now sitting, worried and waiting for it to begin. . . ."

The next morning, when a radical demonstration was to be repressed by the police with a pogrom, a member of the Jewish self-defense hands Penek a package of guns and knives for distribution. Penek cannot help reflecting: "Bennie Gurland's quick mind can think only of Jews who suffer from pogroms. All other world events do not concern him." The thought that both Zionists and socialists seek to use him makes him feel dishonest and troubled. At a mass meeting in a synagogue he helps the revolutionists scatter propaganda leaflets and is arrested along with many others. The end of the volume indicates that Bergelson had no doubt planned to continue the narrative, but nothing further is known to have been written.

From a fictional standpoint the first volume is undoubtedly a major novel. Life in a Jewish town is depicted with exceptional vividness—mirroring the penurious and pernicious condition of the mass of the people and the slow death of the petty-bourgeois merchant class. Many of the characters are trenchantly alive, and Penek is portrayed with notable creativity and keen insight. In the second volume, which in addition to further sensitive delineation of Penek and others also dwells at length on the politics of the time as well as on the problem of anti-Semitism, Bergelson occasionally writes with the prejudice of the propagandist. The narrative as a whole, however, sparkles and soars with overriding fictional excellence. As Niger has pointed out, the propaganda passages become like driftwood on a floating expanse of intense creativity.

Bergelson returned to Russia convinced that the future of Jewish life would develop best under the benign aegis of communism. Niger describes this optimism: "The new Bergelson is new in the sense that he wants to persuade us and himself that his dissatisfaction with the world is a class feeling, that there are no ugly and fine individuals, only ugly and fine social classes; he is new in the sense that he strives to become an optimist, a believer."

Bergelson was in this euphoric state of mind when, shortly after his return, he was asked to visit Birobidjan and write about it. After observing the place and the people for two months he published *Birobidjan* (1934), a highly favorable account of how the newcomers were developing their Jewish region and becoming healthy and satisfied human beings in the process. He deals harshly with the few malingerers and skeptics, especially in the person of Yudel Lifshits, who is delineated as a destroyer rather than a builder. Of the devoted and determined pioneers, former indigent workers or *luftmenschen*, he wrote with idyllic praise: how two of them, for instance, strike out in the primeval forest to establish a place of settlement, chop down trees, build huts, dig wells, and develop homesteads. Of one he writes: "His face is lit, his gaze is lit—in Shimke's eyes candles are burning. For the first time in his life Shimke experiences the taste of good fortune, of real luck." The hardships these pioneers encounter are not minimized. Of the stinging insects that infest the forest and make life miserable he states: "They rise like clouds out of each dank place and attack—not like flies but like dogs who are curious to taste human flesh and human blood." The keynote of the narrative is stated by Mendel Saks, one of the prominent pioneers, in a speech celebrating the completion of a hamlet: "We, the hardworking poor, were never short of hard times. . . . Of those hard times we gained nothing, really nothing; now, from several hard months with the Soviet government we have a settlement in the forest . . . that's what we have!" Underneath this thin layer of sugarcoating Bergelson has written a work of creative fiction, with beautiful descriptions of pristine nature and a number of characters who are artistically realized in the course of the story.

During the ensuing 15 years Bergelson exerted himself, eagerly yet tragically, to be a loyal communist, to find acceptance and approbation in the eyes of both his fellow writers and government censors. He craved affection, and now and then demeaned himself to gain it—at great cost to his conscience and self-respect. He began to decry religion, to criticize deviation from official policy, to praise the pursuit of communism, and to chastise such "bourgeois" writers as Sholem Asch and Bialik. In the spirit of will-to-believe he spoke and wrote about himself as if his return to Russia had rejuvenated him and brought him a long-desired exaltation. To Opatoshu he wrote in 1935: "Here I feel happy and free and young and needed and appreciated, full of energy to work, happy about myself, about Markish's rise during the past two years, and about the surge of our Soviet-Yiddish literature." He became interested in getting his novels and stories published in Russian translation and began to speak of likely Jewish assimilation in the Soviet Union without the tragic overtones a Yiddish writer would normally employ. When no government honors came to him in the late 1930's, he was deeply aggravated and suspected malice and false innuendo on the part of envious writers.

The tragic destruction of Jews in the Nazi-occupied areas grieved Bergelson as much as it did all Jewish writers, but he dared not express his distress in his writing. When Germany invaded the Soviet Union and the government relaxed its censorship, he actively partook in the formation of the Jewish Anti-Fascist Committee and became one of the editors of *Einigkeit*. He wrote a play that year, *We Want to Live*, which was later performed in the United States, Argentina, Rumania, and in a Hebrew version in Tel Aviv. A number of his stories appeared in various periodicals and were collected in a book.

Prince Reuveni, a drama of the well-intentioned impostor who sought to ameliorate the lot of the Jews in the 16th century, which Bergelson completed in 1946 and which was published in New York and produced in Moscow and Warsaw, reveals his entwined Jewishness and communism. Reuveni is presented as a Bolshevik leader who seeks to save the Jews from Christian oppression not by prayer but by fighting. He cunningly acts his role as distant prince to gain his ends, and almost fools the Pope and some cardinals—only to be discovered and killed. In fighting back he discards his princely robe, dons the rags of a Jew, and calls his fellow Jews to battle. Wounded unto death, he is told that Portugal will deal fairly with his group if it will submit. "Tell the Portuguese," he replies, "'the people will die, but will not submit—that's the kind of people it is.'" And to his good friend Shabsi the clown he says: "Don't worry about me. I taught the people how to fight—that is a lot, Shabsi, a lot." So it is, and so it became in present-day Israel, but that was not the lesson of the sages or the practice of the Jews through the centuries of persecution.

For all his efforts to conform and demonstrate his loyalty to the Stalin regime, Bergelson was arrested early in 1949 and executed in August, 1952. Some years later his name was exonerated and in the next issue of the Russian *Short Literary Encyclopedia* the sketch about him reappeared with the following addendum: "He was repressed illegally. Rehabilitated after his death." Some of his work was reissued in Russian translation, and a 762-page volume of his selected writings in Yiddish was published in 1961.

Two posthumous volumes of his stories appeared abroad: *New Stories* (1949) in Buenos Aires, and *Two Worlds* (1953) in New York. Most of these stories are first-rate and treat incidents and events related to the holocaust. "Between Mountains" is about three German soldiers who, lost in the Caucasian mountains, come upon a young Jewish native, whose father had been tortured to death by the Nazis, and force him to direct them to the main highway. Despite their threats he keeps leading them astray and deeper into the mountains. When their food begins to run low one of the soldiers attempts to hide some of it, which leads to quarreling and results in one being killed, a second escaping, and the third, wounded, left to die by the liberated Jewish youth. Each of the four characters is vividly delineated; their thoughts and individual differences emerge in sharp and memorable outline.

In "The Witness" an old Jew, shabbily attired and obviously very perturbed, arrives in a town at the end of World War II to be "a witness"—he being the only survivor in his village. "The Jew's darkened face reminded one of a charred piece of wood saved from the flames of a fire. He gave one the feeling, it seems, of the smoke of charred bones. . . . He can just about walk, so weakened is everything in him that is still alive." He meets a girl who is also a lone survivor and insists on dictating his experiences to her. He speaks in Yiddish and she writes his words down in Russian. When she asks him if her translation is accurate, he replies: "You ask my opinion? What can I tell you? . . . the suffering was in Yiddish. . . ." When he tells her of a very beautiful girl whom the Nazis had made a Jewish artist paint in the nude before sending her to the gas chamber, he cannot control his tears. Asked why he wept, he explains that it is because the Nazis had burned such beauty. Later he faints out of sheer weakness and is thought dying, but he revives, realizes what has happened, and says:

"How can I die? . . . I am a witness!" Here Bergelson intimates his deep Jewishness, permitted him only when writing
about the Nazis. The pathos of the incident is the more poig-
ant because it is written with the controlled delicacy of sentiment and in a prose of pure radiance.

"Chapters of a Longer Work" is set in prewar Soviet Russia.
Professor Kalmans of the University of Chicago, an expert in
agriculture, is visiting Russia on his sabbatical in order to see
his native town again and to be of help in any way he can. At
51 he is still a bachelor, having early been disappointed in
love. In Moscow he learns that Eva, the girl whom he had
once loved, is now a widow and living in Birobidjan. He goes
there, is quite pleased with the progress being made by Jewish
settlers, and gives them advice on how to plan a commune of
5000 people, to which they react skeptically. "From all this
the professor realized that these people have their own plans
and their own ways of life—ordinary people." Then he meets
Eva and is again thrilled at the sight of her.

> He could not now express his thoughts. No doubt they related to
> this: life had favored him and had brought him here to Eva. And
> here he sits near her and repeatedly observes her fire-red ear lobe
> with such a thought in his dead heart and with such pleasure—
> that she is in her 41st year exactly as he had known her, a nice
> one!

Bergelson was perhaps the most refined master of Yiddish
prose. His diction was delicately polished, and both vibrant
and lyrical. He described every nuance of thought and feeling with melodic exactness and suggestive overtones. There
is a tantalizing tentativeness about his writing, giving his
style the aura of deftness and promise: an unuttered perception seen between the lines and enjoyed as an intimacy
between author and reader. He achieved this style by deep
cultivation of his native gift—by remaining a prisoner at his
desk. As he once said: "I rise in the morning and immediately
begin to work. I sit down at my desk like a bitter pauper, but
after laboring honestly until evening I rise from my written

447

pages with a feeling of a bit of a rich man." Often, however, he tore up a day's work when he thought it did not convey what he had wished to express.

A novelist is of course judged by his ability to create living characters. In this respect Bergelson excels. Mirel and Penek are only the most successful of the numerous men and women who throb with fictional reality in the unfolding of his stories. Impressionistic, psychologically analytical, richly intuitive, he probed human motives and emotions to their inner recesses, bringing forth human beings palpitating with feeling and bursting with life. Even in his later years, when he felt impelled to demonstrate his communist orthodoxy, he seldom strayed from genuine dedication to his art. For no matter how wobbly he sometimes behaved personally—and his yearning for affection and approval occasionally made him say and do things he inwardly regretted—he was a dedicated writer once he sat down at his desk and put pen to paper.

CHAPTER SEVENTEEN

I. J. SINGER

Novelist of Satirical Pessimism

IN THE early decades of the 20th century, Yiddish literature flourished not only in the Soviet Union and the United States but also in all of Eastern Europe, particularly in Poland. Of the scores of writers who have made their mark in this area, Israel Joshua Singer is best known to American readers. Since he, like other creative artists, naturally built on the foundation laid by his predecessors, a brief survey of a few of them not discussed previously will suggest some of the implicit sources which had influence on him.

S. Ansky (S. Z. Rapoport, 1863–1920) began to write in Hebrew, soon turned to Yiddish, and then to Russian. He resumed writing in Yiddish after 1900 and published a number of volumes of fiction and folklore. His poem "The Oath" became the theme song of Jewish radicals, and his satiric poem, "Asmodai," is, according to Noah Prilutsky, a contemporary critic, "a veritable encyclopedia of Jewish folk demonology, grouped in a series of plastic portraits." A folklorist of prominence, Ansky is best known for his dramatic legend, *Between Two Worlds: The Dybbuk*,* which he wrote in Yiddish and Russian and which became world famous after it was first produced in 1920. The work deals with the supernatural love between Khonon and Leah, whose marriage was arranged by their fathers before they were born. Subsequently Leah's father repudiates the compact. The youthful Khonon, having become a mystic cabalist, dies of grief and his spirit enters Leah and will not leave her. To exorcise the dybbuk, her father resorts to the help of rabbinical powers. The action of the drama evolves as a problem of unrequited love and poetic justice, laying open the profound psychological phenomenon of dual personality and its supersititious treatment by Hasidic rabbis. For all its melodramatic essence, the play possesses deep emotional tension and was for a time highly popular.

H. D. Nomberg (1876-1927), a sober intellectual and for a time a close friend of Sholem Asch and Abraham Reisen, was the first conscious esthete in Yiddish literature. In much of his writing he portrayed the intellectual, the dreamer, the artist— to whom life meant relatively little and who felt isolated and apart from the people around them. His analytical studies of the poor were both realistic in content and burnished with verbal beauty, but they were few in number and practically ceased after 1908. Some of his verses had a haunting quality and reflected the moods and dreams of yeshiva students. The final two decades of his life were devoted to journalism and civic leadership. He traveled widely and his reportage was featured in various newspapers.

I. M. Weissenberg (1881-1937) was a contrary figure in both character and point of view. A factory worker, he wrote grimly and naturalistically about his immediate milieu. His first stories appeared in 1904 and described the life of Jewish workers with an almost brutal intensity. His major work, *The Town* (1909), was in marked contrast to Sholem Asch's story of the same title, stressing the prevailing medievalism of the people with realistic earthiness. The workers of this town, having learned that strikes in Warsaw had greatly improved wages and working conditions, begin to agitate for similar benefits. Their primitive radicalism and direct action, instigated by timid and inexperienced leaders, fail miserably when the police move in. Written in a hard, sharp style, the narrative is too discursive to attain artistic objectivity. Dr. Eliashev commented: "Weissenberg had woven his picture of the town with the thread of socialism that was penetrating its inhabitants. The conflict after a pogrom is between the radical carpenter who demanded self-protection with arms and the rabbi who urged praying with Psalms." His later work deteriorated considerably, and after 1918 he turned into a mystic.

Oizer Warshavsky, born in 1898, carried naturalism to a point of no return. His most important work, *The Smugglers* (1920), brings the Jewish town to the brink of moral collapse. It is written without sentiment and with *galgenhumor* about a group of people degraded and demoralized by the exigencies of war and persecution. Degeneracy prevails, with smugglers, thieves, prostitutes, and whiskey-makers as the main characters. Its naturalism is candid, pessimistic, and cynical—mocking and destroying every sign of goodness and virtue, and stressing the inner worthlessness of the protagonists. The one exception is Mendel, a smuggler who, having been nursed by a prostitute during a serious illness, falls in love with her. This part of the story is marked by lyrical beauty and is in striking contrast to the novel as a whole.

Zalman Schneor (1887–1959) came under Peretz's personal tutelage at the age of 16 and was later befriended by David Frishman, the critic. He wrote a good amount of prose and poetry in both Hebrew and Yiddish. Some of his verses have been set to music and have become popular folksongs. His best-known work, *Noah Pandre*,* a two-volume novel, was published in an English translation in 1936. Much of his writing concerns his native Shklov and its various inhabitants, with emphasis on their physical powers and eroticism. Some of his later fiction has appeared only as newspaper serials. An extensive traveler—he lived in Western Europe during 1906–1913 and was imprisoned in Germany as an alien during World War I—he achieved a cosmopolitan point of view, and the locale of a good deal of his writing is in New York and other parts of the world. One of his last major works was *Philistines*, a long poem about the holocaust and its terrible aftermath.

Born in 1893 in a rabbinical home, I. J. Singer grew up steeped in Hebrew lore and Hasidic tradition. Until the age of 17 he had not only to study abstruse religious tomes but to observe the ritualistic piety expected of a rabbi's son. When his father urged him to prepare for rabbinical service, he rebelled. He had by then become aware of the world outside of his father's court, having surreptitiously familiarized himself with books, ideas, and activities considered sinful by his father. He started to slough off the obligations and restrictions imposed on him from infancy. He began to dress in clothes worn by emancipated youths; he cut off his earlocks and started to shave; he read voraciously books in Hebrew and Yiddish, and soon in Russian and Polish—building up a cultural reservoir based on these writings. His mild-mannered and ineffectual father grieved to see his eldest son abandon traditional orthodoxy, but took no action against him. At 18 Singer, living in a Warsaw slum, worked at various tasks and studied in his free time. For a while he made efforts to become a painter, then decided he wanted to be a writer.

His first stories had their setting in the Hasidic milieu of his childhood, and several were published in *Dos Yiddish Wort* (The Jewish Word). In 1917, idealistically attracted by the promise of the Russian revolution, he went to live in Kiev. There his stories appeared in journals and anthologies. He also wrote two plays—*Earth Woes* and *Three*—impressionistic dramas which he soon preferred to forget, and "Pearls" (1919). His more than three years in Bolshevik Russia sufficed to disillusion him with the promises of communism. In 1921 he returned to Warsaw.

Pearls and Other Stories appeared in 1922 and was praised by critics. The featured story gives an impressionistic sketch of Moritz Shpielrein, an elderly man "without lungs" and bedridden much of the time. A jeweler, pawnbroker, and landlord, he is quite wealthy but stingy and lives alone with the aid of a boy servant. The story concentrates on his daily routine, the house he owns and the various people living in it, and is highlighted by a jewel auction at which Shpielrein buys a costly pearl necklace. At once vividly told and charged with lifelike reality, the story is persuasive in its portrayal of people. The other stories, while less significant, are noted for the mood each creates in its specific setting. In the same year he completed *Earth Pain,* a minor symbolic drama of the revolutionary period evidencing his disillusionment with Bolshevism.

Abraham Cahan, visiting Eastern Europe in 1922, came upon the volume and was highly impressed with the literary quality of "Pearls." He obtained it for reprinting in *Der Forverts* and engaged Singer as a regular contributor as well as correspondent. Now an established author with a relatively sizable and secure income, he took an active part in Warsaw's Jewish cultural affairs, and became an editor of *Literature and Life* as well as a member of the radical and modernistic group of writers known as *Die Khaliastre* (The Gang).

On Strange Soil (1925) was Singer's second collection of stories. The title narrative is set in the civil war. A troop of soldiers enter a Jewish town, and its inhabitants fear a pogrom. They hide as best they can and pass the long hours of the night in prayer and dread. The next morning they learn that Red soldiers had been trapped by Whites and a number killed. Several Jews approach the fresh mass grave and say Kaddish on the assumption that among the buried may have been Jews.

Soldiers camp near another Jewish town in "During Warm Days." The military doctor, a Jew, comes to the market square in full uniform, buys what he needs on credit, flirts with the girls, treats the ill without charge, and makes himself highly regarded—only to leave in the fall without paying his bills. "Blood," based on an incident in Singer's childhood, tells of a boy born to a Jewish innkeeper who grows up dull-witted and physically strong "like a gentile." He behaves like a peasant boy, and no amount of beating and chastisement have any effect. In late adolescence he is lured into marriage and apostasy by a competing woman innkeeper considerably older than he. Later she tries to instigate him to kill his parents in order to inherit their inn. Confused and dully irritated by her nagging, he kills her instead. These and other stories are told with realistic clarity and in impressionistic prose, but with the obvious minor flaws of as yet unperfected literary skill.

In the middle 1920's Singer was asked by Cahan to visit the Soviet Union and report on his impressions of Jewish life under Bolshevism. Inimically minded but a keen observer, he indicated in his articles that in the seven years since he had been in Moscow conditions had become less strict, largely influenced by NEP circumstances, with a good deal of extravagance by a few and with many beggars in the streets. What troubled him particularly were evidences of anti-Semitism and its effect on many Jews. Thus on visiting a secluded midnight celebration of "Lubavishe" Hasidim he was surprised to find among them engineers, students, and other enlightened men who had become pious *after* the revolution.

Singer inspected Jewish farm colonies, where he found the older generation acquiescing in the new regime and the youths definitely enthusiastic. He was impressed by the skill of some of the farmers and talked with others who hated collectives or planned to migrate to Israel. Everywhere he came upon homeless drifters, orphaned youths who existed by begging and stealing. He also wrote with considerable concern about the loose marital practices, and in particular about the numerous mixed marriages. Finally, although Yiddish was generally flourishing, he noted that government officials looked with suspicion on Yiddishism. These observations, which only confirmed his anti-communism, he published in a volume entitled *The New Russia* (1927).

In the same year appeared *Steel and Iron,** a novel on the war, revolution, and civil strife, based largely on his own experiences as a worker in Warsaw. Benjamin Lerner, after nine months on the war front, deserts and comes home to his uncle, with whom he had been living before he was drafted. In love with his cousin Gnendel, and happy with her favorable response, he learns that his uncle is planning to have her marry a rich man in order to gain materially from the relationship. In a quarrel on this account, Benjamin is forced to leave the house. Penniless and without friends, fearful of arrest as a deserter, he reaches Warsaw and walks the streets during the day and sleeps where he can at night.

When the Germans occupy Warsaw, Benjamin obtains work as a laborer on a bridge project. He hates the bullying and brutal German officers as well as the coarse and anti-Semitic Poles, and has a hard time with both. Nor is he happy with the pious Jews working with him, although he tries to help them perceive their wretched precariousness. He becomes friends with a Polish radical who seeks to enlighten the Polish workers to the same end. Another of his new friends is the hospital doctor who treated him when ill, an idealistic revolutionary and Siberian exile who had joined the Russian army and was captured by the Germans.

The agitation among the workers is effective, and on New Year's morning they rebel. In the fighting that ensues, Benjamin and his Polish friend escape. Stopped that night by a German guard, they kill him and find shelter with local peasants. Later Benjamin returns to Warsaw. A fugitive with a prize of 1000 marks for his capture, he is fearful of meeting anyone who might recognize him. Chance favors him when he comes upon Gnendel, who had quarreled with her father and is working as a nurse in the typhus ward of a hospital, and he makes his home with her.

Meeting again by chance with a wealthy philanthropist whom he had visited while in the army, Benjamin and Gnendel are sent by him to work with Jewish refugees in a nearby town. They find the latter filthy, scabby, sick, and suspicious of any effort to make them help themselves. When Gnendel recoils from contact with them, Benjamin advises her to work out of duty, not pity. He himself manages to make the men work the land, repair a mill, and do other chores for their own comfort. News of the revolution coincides with a deadly epidemic among the children. Benjamin and

Gnendel do their utmost to nurse the sick and stop the contagion in the face of obstruction by panicky parents. Benjamin himself is infected with typhus but recovers. Their benefactor goes to Russia as the Germans take control of the camp. When Benjamin refuses to do their bidding, he is arrested on charges of treason. After weeks in prison he escapes through a sewer and finds his way to Russia. Gnendel, however, remains and is abused by the Germans.

Not yet master of the art of the novel, Singer has made the action replete with melodramatic material. Its kaleidoscopic character clutters it with incidents and gives the impression of a mosaic of stories and types. Consequently, it lacks clarity and conviction. Nor are the main characters developed into fully lifelike human beings. Indeed, Singer gives evidence of having scattered his obvious literary talent in various directions instead of focusing it into a crystallized unity. The novel, nevertheless, provides a realistic flow of robust prose and provocative action.

Idealistically disillusioned and inwardly apprehensive, Singer was acutely sensitive to criticsm. Ever since he had become one of Cahan's retainers he was deprecated and impugned by fellow writers: communists considered him a turncoat because of his critical attitude toward the Soviet Union; others, living precariously, tended to be jealous of his secure financial position as a *Forverts* contributor; critics considered his fiction of interest but lacking in deep insight and artistic empathy. Not unaware of the weakness of some of his stories, he decided late in 1927 to stop writing fiction. He also withdrew from active participation in cultural affairs. To a friend he admitted his discouragement as a writer. Perhaps N. Meisel exaggerated when he wrote: "We continued to meet daily, and it was painful and regretful to see the self-torture of this erstwhile life-loving, joyous Singer," but the fact remains that he was experiencing an inner crisis and that for nearly five years published no fiction.

In 1931 Singer visited with Cahan in Berlin, and the energetic editor importuned him to resume writing fiction. Friends of Singer have stated that he was then actually hard at work on *Yoshe Kalb,* based on an actual incident. At any rate, the following year the manuscript was sent to Cahan and it appeared serially both in *Der Forverts* and in the Warsaw *Haint* (Today). In 1933 it appeared in an English translation entitled *The Sinner.* The novel was also dramatized by Maurice Schwartz and produced successfully in New York and other cities.

The action begins in the 1870's, when Hasidism was still entrenched and secure. Rabbi Melekh, already in his sixties and with a large Hasidic following, is eager to marry off his youngest daughter, Serkele, a buxom and bovine girl of 14, in order that he might be free to take a fourth wife. His choice is Nahum, a rabbi's son, a gentle and scholarly youth of 14. Brought to his prospective father-in-law to be questioned concerning his erudition, he is upset by the coarseness of the rabbinical court in contrast to that presided over by his father. Although he has no wish to be married, he lacks the will to assert himself.

Nahum feels no affection for his wife, who seems to him a common, dull girl, without physical appeal. He knows, however, that it is sinful to entertain such thoughts and tries to submerge his discontent in concentrated study.

Rabbi Melekh now arranges to marry Malkeh, an orphaned girl of 18 brought up by relatives, self-willed and unrestrained. She rebels against marrying a man old enough to be her grandfather, but is forced to consent. Yet she balks: she refuses to have her hair cut *before* the wedding, as is the local custom, nor does she permit the rabbi to do his duty on the night of the ceremony. His subsequent effort to bribe her with the jewels of his dead wives fails to lessen the dull misery of her existence. Then she meets Nahum.

Both immediately became confused, frightened; one wanted to avoid the other, to say something, but neither had a word to utter. Suddenly their eyes met. Two pair of black, burning, animated eyes lit upon each other, scorched one another, twinkled with at-homeness, joy, and became fixed, as if hypnotized.

Thereafter Malkeh thinks of Nahum with inner pleasure. "Together with the fire of a man he also awakened in her a mother love, as to a child. . . . She wanted to caress him, press him to her breast, curl his locks with her fingers, and offer herself, give her entire life." Nahum is similarly affected and cannot keep his mind on his studies. "He was seized by a powerful yearning, a longing that drew his nerves like strings. Malkeh appeared before him so sharp, so clear, as if she really stood before him. He hugs her, kisses her, stretches his hands to her, but when he finds nothing before him, he awakens from his revery." Feeling guilty of the sin of lust, he suffers acutely, but no amount of self-torture can keep his mind from dwelling on her. And Malkeh tempts him at every opportunity—much as he seeks to avoid seeing her.

When Nahum's mother sends a messenger to bring Nahum to her for the winter, Malkeh feels miserable. "Her days were long and senseless, days full of sadness and emptiness. Very long and endless were the nights, the long winter nights. . . . She lay awake, not closing her eyes even for a minute. She bit the pillow, wept, wept from strong longing and desire to be with him who was now so far."

Nahum returns in the spring, appearing handsomer than ever, and Malkeh loves him even more intensely, but he deliberately avoids her. In a surge of desperation she sets fire to one of the buildings in the rabbi's court. In the commotion she sees Nahum and leads him to the solitude of the woods, where their bodies join. He leaves her obsessed by extreme guilt. Nine months later Malkeh dies giving birth to a dead child. That night Nahum disappears.

For years he wanders like a beggar. Then he remains in a town, where he sits in the rear of a synagogue and recites Psalms. Acting the simpleton, he is called Yoshe Kalb (calf) and made fun of, but he pays no attention. The beadle has him attend to the chores of the place and gives him a place to sleep in his hovel. There he is bothered by the beadle's moronic daughter, and although he repels her advances he feels miserable. When a plague fatally affects a number of children and their ignorant and superstitious parents assume that some great sin was the cause of the affliction, their suspicion is confirmed on discovery that the beadle's daughter is pregnant —she having lain with some thievish youths in the cemetery. The beadle assumes that Yoshe is the culprit and brings him to the rabbi for judgment. Questioned, he refuses to answer; asked who he is, he replies: "I am a stone." He is thereupon made to marry the girl on the cemetery grounds—a procedure believed likely to pacify God's anger. But on the night of the wedding Nahum disappears.

After the absence of 15 years Nahum returns to the aged Rabbi Melekh and identifies himself. He refuses to explain his disappearance, and when pressed merely says, "I had to." He resumes his life with Serkele but keeps very much to himself, so that the court Hasidim soon begin to think of him as a saintly scholar.

Not long after his return a man from the town where Nahum was known as Yoshe recognizes him and accuses him of having deserted the beadle's daughter. Rabbi Melekh dismisses the charge, but the man persists, brings the beadle and his daughter as witnesses, and finally arranges for a court of 70 rabbis to sit in judgment upon the accused. Again Nahum remains silent. The octogenarian Rabbi Melekh insists that Nahum is not Yoshe and dies in the excitement. At the end of the trial Nahum again disappears, presumably to do additional penance.

Yoshe Kalb is a work of fictional fascination. It plumbs the human depths of Hasidic life: its rich, colorful piety along with its supernatural and superstitious practices, not to mention its commercial hypocrisy. Yet Singer does not treat it with the sympathy and insight of Der Nister or with the romantic tolerance of Peretz and Sholem Asch. Instead he tends to be critical and caustic—not with the artistic objectivity of Opatoshu but with a kind of personal animosity. Stressing the gross and gullible aspects of the Hasidic court as well as its materialistic activities, he fails to intimate the genuine spiritual fervor germane to Hasidism. Niger has pointed out:

> Unintentionally I. J. Singer has omitted or, more truly, failed to see and feel and paint to the end the *spiritual ecstasy* possessed by Hasidism and Hasidim. He excelled in making clear and lifelike the Hasidic elements of *this* world, but left in the shade that which pertains to the *other* world, that which is real to the truly religious person.

Singer tends to romanticize the irrepressible passion that draws Malkeh and Nahum together, yet he writes more sympathetically of the sex impulses of the moronic girl than of Nahum's emotional struggles. And while Nahum's years of abject expiation are understandable in a man of deep piety living in a time of prevailing orthodoxy, his refusal to explain himself at a cost of committing another grievous sin—an act of bigamy and desertion—and his further refusal to offer the slightest explanation to the 70 rabbis become more the behavior of a deluded mystic than of a pious sinner. This conception of a protagonist cannot but weaken an otherwise powerful love story and a fascinating account of Hasidic life of a century ago.

Singer's financial and relatively critical success with *Yoshe Kalb*, and his increasing sense of alienation in Warsaw, inclined him favorably to Cahan's urging to migrate to New York. In the midst of his preparation to depart, his firstborn, Jacob, a bright and handsome boy of 12 and much loved by Singer, became sick and died. Loath as the deeply bereaved father was to leave the place where his son was buried, he was also eager to get away from the seat of his tragedy and arrived in New York with his wife and younger son in 1933. Unable to forget his grievous personal loss and retaining his pessimistic view of society, he nevertheless strove to establish himself culturally in his new environment and to concentrate on his writing.

The Brothers Ashkenazi * (1936), the first novel he wrote in the United States, became his major literary achievement. First serialized in *Der Forverts*, it was quickly translated into English and several other languages and was everywhere hailed as an epic masterpiece. It brought him fresh popularity and large royalties, but did not lessen his inner gloom.

The long novel depicts the rise of Lodz from an insignificant village at the end of the 18th century to its leading position in Poland as a center of textile production, from its gradual domination by Jewish entrepreneurs to its ravagement by war, revolution, and Polish anti-Semitism. The development of the city parallels the upsurge of the Ashkenazi family, soon dominated by the twin brothers, Simkha Meyer and Yakov Bunim, later known as Max and Jacob. They differed from birth: Simkha, older by several minutes, was puny and homely and later manifested keen business shrewdness; Yakov was big and handsome, easygoing and prodigal, but with inordinate luck. As they grew up Simkha resented his brother's popularity, and his own desire to play with boys was repressed by "something hard and obstinate, something which isn't himself, won't let him budge."

Their father, Abraham Hirsh, a pious Hasid but a keen merchant, takes a prominent position in the industrial development of the city, yet he does not let his mundane affairs interfere with his Jewishness, his journeys to his favorite rabbi. He knows that "one mustn't expect decency and gratitude in business. Only money counted, and if money ceased to count, it was only to give way to something worse." A man of wisdom and affability, in time he persuades the proud Heinz Huntze, who had become the leading Lodz industrialist, to combine forces with Goetzke, his hated but energetic competitor. His reward is the firm's selling agency, a highly lucrative post.

The increasingly ambitious Simkha, in his late adolescence a prodigy in the Talmud, disregards his father's wish for him to become a rabbi and determines to excel in business. Jealous of his brother's easy way with girls, he manages to marry Dinah, Yakov's beloved, by impressing her father with his intellectual acumen. Somewhat later he lends his large cash dowry to his financially hard-pressed father-in-law and soon gains control of the latter's factory. Now launched on his business career, he "had Napoleonic visions."

His financial success notwithstanding, he cannot forgive his brother's "stupid, incredible luck" when Pearl Eisen, granddaughter of the wealthiest Jew in Warsaw, falls in love with him. Aware, however, that Yakov will now be a rich man, he cultivates his friendship. He is the more aggravated because of the failure of his own marriage. "With all his contempt for women, partly instilled in him, partly the result of his own character, Simkha Meyer could not bear Dinah's coldness. He could not bear, to be more exact, that a person should escape him, defying his mastery."

In his eagerness to increase his profits from the factory he reduces the meager wages of his weavers, making them desperate in their steeped poverty. Instigated by Tevieh, a radical worker, and Nissan, whose father had taught both him and Simkha and who had become a socialist agitator, the men go out on strike. Soon reduced to starvation, nagged by their lamenting wives, and deprived of their leadership by imprisonment instigated by Simkha, the weavers humbly acquiesce in the acceptance of lower wages.

Simkha's financial horizon continues to expand. When he learns that the spendthrift sons of old Huntze are anxious to buy a title from the Czar but are refused the money by their imperious father, he approaches them with an offer to lend the desired amount on notes which he believes will one day lead to control of the Huntze factories. When old Huntze dies Simkha obtains his coveted reward: the agency long operated by his father. Jacob, in Warsaw, learning what happened, comes to Lodz and gives Simkha a thrashing. Their father, hearing that Simkha, now calling himself Max, has shaved off his beard and abandoned his observance of Jewish ritual, considers him an apostate and an outcast. This does not impress the rapacious Max, but his brother's continued good fortune aggravates him; without any effort on his part Jacob is given the sales agency of M. Flederbaum, the wealthiest Jewish industrialist in Lodz, and by acting on a tip from the governor at a Flederbaum party he profits hugely from a realty transaction.

Tevieh and Nissan return from prison and resume their agitation of the oppressed weavers. Numerous disturbances and strikes lead to a pogrom in the workers' slum. Nissan is again arrested and imprisoned, only to return several years later and this time manages to get the Huntze gentile workers to strike. All through the 1900's Lodz is shaken by revolutionary agitation, assassinations, arrests and shootings, spying, and betrayals.

Jacob is too flirtatious and nonchalant for the jealous Pearl and they arrange a divorce. Not long after he marries Max's daughter Gertrude, who forces herself upon him despite their differences in age, and thus prevents a probable union between him and her mother. For Dinah too has been recently divorced by Max—he being tempted by the wealth of an elderly, homely widow. He uses her money to acquire a majority of the Huntze stock and has the gratification of living in the Huntze palace, although happiness continues to elude him.

During World War I the Germans occupy Lodz and their commander takes over the Huntze palace. Max, having gone to Russia on business before hostilities began, remains there and establishes a weaving factory in Petrograd. When the revolution begins, he is perplexed by ensuing events. "He began to perceive a tremendous force in those Russian yokels, those gross, unclean, lumpy slaves who filled the factories and who could not even sign their names—a force to be reckoned with, lest it break loose and destroy everything." Wary of their demands in his own factory, he again meets his old antagonist Nissan and knows better than to try to win him over to his side against the workers. Before long he is stripped of everything and feels fortunate to have escaped alive.

Nissan, too, feels the axe of the revolution which he had struggled so long and hard to bring about. Elected to the

Constituent Assembly and looking forward to an idealistic future, he feels "broken, humiliated, astounded" when ruthlessly driven away from the Assembly's meeting place by the Red Guard.

> For this he had waited all his life, for the hour when a free Russia would send to the capital the representatives of its will. For this he had struggled, for this borne imprisonment, exile, and loneliness. . . . He crawled wearily into his tiny room, threw himself on his narrow bed, buried his head in the pillow, and sobbed for the great triumph which he had lived to salute and which he was not permitted to share.

In his grief and disappointment he is very much the radical ascetic, even as his scholarly father was the religious ascetic.

Now that all his labor, enterprise, and wealth are completely forfeited, Max suddenly realizes how foolish he has been. Without being fully aware of it, he resumes his former religious habits. Anxious to return to Lodz, now a part of Poland, to his wife and what remains of his factory there, he yields to the wiles of a government informer and is clapped into prison, where he becomes a complete wreck. When Jacob comes to Petrograd in search of him and manages to obtain his release, he is shocked by Max's filthy appearance and physical and mental debility. When Jacob tells him that Dinah and Gertrude have sent him a package of food, "a faint tinge of color crept into Max Ashkenazi's yellow face, and he drooped his eyes. For the first time in his life he felt the sensation of shame."

At the Polish border an obstreperous young officer abuses the brothers and orders them to shout "To hell with all Yids!" Max does so, but the outraged Jacob slaps the bully's face and is shot dead. Bereaved, Max reflects that his brother had the pride of gentiles, that he was unlike their forefathers who "despised the gentile inwardly and refused to take to heart his so-called insults. . . . In these hours of bitterness it was wrong to throw one's life away; one tried to soothe the rage of the murderer; one did not provoke him."

In taking over the land ruled by their ancestors, the Poles were seized with "an insane blood-lust. . . . A furious wave of anti-Semitism was passing through Poland, and the Lemberg pogrom had been the signal for a series of murderous assaults on Jews." On returning to Lodz, Max finds the Jewish section burned and pillaged, and many of its inhabitants tortured and murdered. Determined to assert his legal rights, he fights in the courts until he succeeds in ousting the Polish nobleman from the Huntze palace. When Polish bankers refuse to extend him the needed credit to re-establish his factory, he goes to England and obtains the latest weaving machinery. Soon his factory again becomes the most efficient in Poland. A fatal heart attack ends the saga of his life.

In the breadth of its scope and its richness of human life and economic and political events, the novel is indubitably a work of major importance. Extending over three generations, delineating the rise of industrialism in Eastern Europe, describing graphically the effects of war, revolution, and pogroms on the people involved, depicting the development of labor unrest and bloody strikes, and most of all, concentrating on the portrayal of numerous significant characters, Singer has in this novel achieved a literary height that brought him within reach of the world's great novelists. While not without minor flaws of organization and outlook—he still stressed human idiosyncrasies and instinctive brutality, although they are no longer naked and unrelieved, and his prejudices remain self-evident—and while some of the actions of his major characters are open to question and the emphasis on their chief traits limits their portraiture to profiles, the narrative as a whole is written with great clarity and animation.

Spring * (1937) is a collection of several long stories. In "Willie" Wolf Rubin is from early boyhood more interested in horses than study, much to his pious father's aggravation. When Wolf is discharged from the army and finds that his father has sold the farm and is living in town, he becomes disgruntled and goes to the United States. Failing to find suitable work in New York, he becomes a hired man on a Catskill farm. In time he and the farmer's daughter marry and inherit the farm. Years later, learning about the pogroms in the wake of World War I, he feels conscience-stricken not to have been in closer touch with his parents and arranges to have them come to him. His pious father soon complains about the lack of Jewishness in the home, although the daughter-in-law had sought to please him by converting to Judaism and observing *Kashruth*. Bored and longing for the company of congenial Jews, the father is happy to find the town druggist a former yeshiva student and is pleased to associate with him. Soon he meets other cronies—mostly fathers of Americanized children who are in the country for the summer. On Rosh Hashana he is proud to conduct the service for the Jews of the vicinity. All the while Wolf, or Willie, estranged from his father's pious ways, finds himself ill at ease to see his farm turned into a Jewish center.

"Spring" is about Leyb Hersh, a buyer of horses and cows, who feels a great longing to get to his wife and children for Passover but is held up by heavy rains. Unable to sleep because of aggravation, he decides, against the advice of farmers, to cross the still frozen Vistula River with a pack on his back and leading a young bull on a rope. On the ice the bull refuses to budge, and in the effort to move him the ice breaks and both are drowned.

Quite a different story is told in "Parents' Graves." An Americanized watchmaker, a bachelor of 40, having accumulated $3000 in savings, decides to visit his native town and erect a headstone on the graves of his parents. Taken for a rich American by the poor townsmen, he acts the part and is soon besieged by matchmakers. One of the girls attracts him and he marries her. Having spent half of his savings, he returns with his wife to Brooklyn and installs her in a modest flat. Now pregnant and skimping like all poor housewives, she feels cheated.

In these and other stories Singer is relatively relaxed and

permits himself the pleasure of mild humor and good-natured tolerance. He writes with obvious ease, with notable clarity and compactness, and draws his characters with sharp and precise strokes. He was not particularly proud of this material, written to meet his contractual obligations to *Der Forverts*, but it obviously possesses the skill of the seasoned storyteller.

Morbidly disappointed in the Soviet Union ever since he left it in 1921, he wrote about it caustically and cynically. Heretofore he had dwelt on it only briefly and incidentally, as in *Brothers Ashkenazi*; but in *Comrade Nahman* * (*East of Eden* in English, 1938) he made it his major subject. Nahman, born to very poor parents, has every children's disease during his infancy. When he is five years old his mother dies in childbirth. His father being away all week in petty trading with peasants and the woman he soon marries being indifferent to the boy's needs, Nahman lives haphazardly. When he is old enough to study independently, he obtains his meals from charitable townsmen—much to his increasing shame.

His older sister Sheyndel, having become a maid at the age of 12, goes to Warsaw four years later to improve her lot. There she is impregnated by a soldier who promises to marry her—only to leave her soon after. She keeps the child, brings her family to Warsaw, and becomes its main provider. Nahman is apprenticed to a baker, but when he is ready to begin earning a baker's wages three years later, Warsaw is occupied by the Germans and he is left jobless. In a soup kitchen for the indigent unemployed he meets a girl who invites him to a meeting of radicals. Attracted to each other, they attend other meetings. Nahman is persuaded that socialism is the only solution to the ills of the world. Attending a May Day celebration, he is arrested and deported to Germany as a laborer. At the end of the war he returns to Warsaw, joins the Polish army, and is wounded. Polish brutality and arrogance, especially toward Jews, intensify his revolutionary ardor. He be-

comes a devoted disciple of Daniel, a pragmatic and pretentious socialist agitator, favoring his leadership over a sincere
and seasoned labor leader.

Now a dedicated socialist, he is sorely disappointed in his
common-law wife, the girl who had introduced him to radicalism, when she becomes pregnant and wants him to legalize
their union. He urges her to have an abortion, maintaining
that radicals must not become enmeshed in family responsibilities, but she has by this time lost interest in radicalism and
wants him to devote himself to her welfare. He ignores her
pleas and intensifies his revolutionary activities. It is difficult
for him to understand the bickering, jealousies, and divisive-
ness within the radical movement. To his simple mind it is
self-evident that all must work toward the same end: the overthrow of capitalism and its oppressive governments. But his
attitude is met with snickering and scorn by the more sophisticated comrades.

The head of the police, needing a hostage to exchange for a
Pole arrested by the Bolsheviks, arrests Daniel and Nahman.
The latter is tortured brutally when he refuses to incriminate
Daniel and is later sentenced to nine years at hard labor.
Daniel, however, is exchanged for the Pole, accepted by the
Russians as a revolutionary hero, and given a substantial post
in one of the government agencies.

On his release from prison, Nahman is broken in health,
alienated from home, and ignored by the radicals. Knowing
that Daniel has become an important functionary in Moscow,
he longs to go to him. To his dismay he fails to obtain a visa
—Daniel, the local party, and the Russian embassy ignore his
pleas. Certain there must be some misunderstanding which
will be cleared up once he reaches Daniel, he steals across the
border. There he is nabbed by Red guards and accused of
spying. After two months in jail, he is sent to Moscow for
identification by Daniel. In his spacious office the hypocritical
bureaucrat tells Nahman that he should have remained in
Poland and worked for its liberation, but relents sufficiently to
arrange for him to become a worker in a bakery and a party

member. Laboring long hours and living in crowded barracks, Nahman contents himself with the thought that these hardships are only temporary. At the October celebration he is among the political refugees. "For the first time in his life he felt true happiness, a happiness worthy of all his suffering and pain."

Red tape frustrates his efforts to obtain visas for his wife and child. His wife, however, manages to get the visas and reaches Nahman. With the aid of a little money she brings with her she acquires a room and some furniture—which Nahman had failed to receive through legal channels. Even so, life is onerous and deplorable. Nahman's uprightness is taken advantage of by all types of bureaucrats. Although both husband and wife work full time, they do not earn enough for their basic needs.

When Nahman defends an elderly worker accused of drunkenness on the job, he is judged a rebel and expelled from the party. On complaining to Daniel, he is told he was defending a "wrecker." Nahman reminds him that he himself had taught him to defend workers, but is informed: "You're a communist and should not think but carry out orders. Your stand among the workers against the party is counter-revolutionary!"

Having accidentally burned some bread, he is arrested as a wrecker and Polish spy. His wife pleads with Daniel, but he refuses to intercede. The questioning in prison is prolonged, repetitious, and accusatory, all aimed at extracting a confession. When he refuses to yield, his wife is brought to see him, and her pleading causes him to weep and sign the document. No promises made to him are kept, and he is expelled from the country. At the border he sees a dying horse in the woods. "Nahman felt a strong closeness to the expiring creature and patted its skin out of pity. In the dying horse, overworked and overbeaten, he saw himself, his own life."

The novel contains some poignant and perturbing descriptions of poverty and slum life in Poland and Russia. Some of the characters are sharply delineated and lifelike, and the manifestations of radicalism among oppressed workers, as well as the attitudes and activities of certain of their leaders, are depicted with the cogency of intimate knowledge. The book as a whole, however, suffers from subjective exaggeration. Although charlatans like Daniel are no rarity in real life, his unrelieved villainy and the absence of honest counterparts detract from his fictional credibility. Even harder to believe is Nahman's excessive naiveté. Simple as he is, he is no simpleton, and his behavior in the Soviet Union is gullible beyond plausibility. Moreover, assuming that the arraignment of communist life in Moscow has validity, it suffers from emphasis on evil aspects and complete omission of the spark of idealism which was surely a part of it. Certainly not all officials in the Soviet Union were as corrupt and degenerate as they are presented in the narrative. One has the impression that Singer was seeking to expel the traumatic bitterness out of his system, and produced a novel streaked with bias and hyperbole.

The upsurge of Hitlerism affected Singer as much as it did other Yiddish writers. In *The Carnovsky Family* * (1943) he dramatized the plight of enlightened German Jews, who have been making every effort to emulate their Christian neighbors and live ethically and culturally on a high plane, only to be coerced and crushed by Nazi brutality; also the tragedy of those born of mixed marriages and considering themselves more German than Jewish—only to be equally derided and rejected.

David Carnovsky, inheriting his family's traits of brilliance and arrogance, early rejects the traditional piety of his Lithuanian parents and embraces the Judaic reforms expounded by Moses Mendelssohn. Soon after his marriage he decides to migrate to Berlin, where he hopes to live like a cultivated European. He prospers, makes friends with enlightened German Jews, and when he becomes father of a son he names him Moshe Georg in order that he might be a Jew among Jews and a German among Germans.

Georg, the only name he uses, is puzzled when his Christian

playmates call him a Jew and a Christ-killer. He wants to be liked by the boys in school and makes up to them. He plays pranks, spends money freely, and avoids his lessons—much to the aggravation of his parents. At the age of 15 he suddenly begins to concentrate on his studies, and upon graduation from gymnasium enrolls in the philosophy division of the university, not in the commerce school advised by his father.

His life takes another turn when he meets Doctor Landau, one of his father's tenants, and his daughter Elsa. This doctor is one of those rare practitioners who are completely devoted to healing the sick. Most of his patients are poor Germans and he treats them without regard to the fee they can offer. Soon attracted to Elsa, a medical student, Georg decides to take up medicine. They see each other frequently, both at the university and at her home, but Elsa remains aloof, though friendly. When he receives his diploma shortly before the start of World War I and is drafted into the medical corps, Elsa accompanies him to the place of mobilization and spends the night with him.

After the war Elsa becomes dedicated to socialist activity and is elected to the Reichstag. She refuses to marry Georg and devotes herself to the amelioration of the German workers. Chance brings Georg into Dr. Halevi's famous clinic and he soon becomes the latter's favorite assistant. He begins going out with Theresa, one of the nurses, much to the objection of his father—to whom time and conditions have revealed the flaws in Mendelssohn's reforms. On his way home from one such altercation with Georg he happens to pass the statue of the Jewish philosopher. "Rabbi Moses," he says, "our children are leaving us. Their way leads to apostasy."

David Carnovsky indeed grieves to see his son so thoroughly Germanized, for he is painfully aware of the anti-Jewish attitude of postwar Germans and fears it. He now feels as if he is of the last generation of Jews. Seeking solace from his friend Ephraim Walder, an elderly bibliophile and scholar, he is told: "Life is a mischief-maker, Reb Carnovsky, it likes to play jokes. Jews wanted to be Jews at home and human beings outside. So life changed the matter—we are gentiles at home and Jews outside."

Georg marries Theresa despite the objection of his parents and the hostility of her brother Hugo, a Hitler admirer. Theresa, however, wins the favor of the Carnovskys by behaving like a Jewess, and Georg circumcises his firstborn, named Joachim Yegor, despite his personal objection to the rite; Hugo, however, remains inimical. Meantime Georg gains prominence as a gynecologist and becomes head of the Halevi clinic when Dr. Halevi suffers a mild stroke.

German intellectuals at first scoff at the antics of the Nazi rowdies, but sooner or later most of them acquiesce in their brutalities, and some even begin to extol them. One of these is characterized by Georg: "Such a man can be dangerous and brutal. He belongs to the predestined hysterics, who suffer both from megalomania and a persecution complex. In time of revolution they are most dangerous." Yet many German Jews refuse to admit that the Nazis have them in mind when they fulminate against Jews. Their reasoning is:

True, they belong to the Jewish group, but only formally. Otherwise they have no connection with Jewishness. They are rooted in German life, in the culture of the country. They have contributed much to the country. Most of the younger ones were also in the war and have distinguished themselves. If anything should happen, it will be to the real Jews of the city, to the national Jews who adhere to the Hebraic culture, some of whom dream even of migrating to Asia and other such things.

Once the Nazis become powerful, they begin to abuse and beat up all Jews. Elsa, still in the Reichstag and fearless in her criticism, is shouted down and derided even by workers she had long defended. Georg and Landau are ordered to refrain from treating German patients. When Georg visits his father in a spirit of reconciliation, he is told: "Be strong, my son, as I am, as all older Jews are—we are used to it for generations and we endure it, like Jews."

The relationship is quite different between Georg and his son, who is also suffering from being a Jew without having any feeling of being one. The only Jew at his school, he is isolated, abused, and scorned. Blaming his father for his plight, he hates him and all he stands for. When he is made an example of Semitic biology by his sadistic teacher and forced to stand naked before his jeering classmates, his mortification makes him sick. But instead of detesting his tormentors he despises himself for being a part Jew.

The Carnovsky family migrates to the United States, along with many other Jews of their acquaintance, and go through the onerous process of orientation and establishment. Georg, having difficulty learning English and failing to pass what seems to him an unfair medical examination, has to resort to peddling notions. His father, now elderly and grown pious, becomes a beadle in a synagogue and is pleased to mingle with his fellow Jews. Only Yegor refuses to adjust to his new environment. He dislikes the boys of the neighborhood and the atmosphere in the school, and insists everywhere that he is not a Jew and has not run away from the Nazis. Pathologically miserable, he is coarse and boorish to those who seek to help him.

Learning about Yorkville, he leaves home and poses as a Nazi sympathizer. A German intelligence official engages him to spy on German Jews, but he dislikes mingling with them and is let go. He starts out on a spree with a brutish boy and two girls, but soon tires of them. Penniless and desperate, he goes to the home of the German official to ask for help. Offered support in return for a homosexual relationship, Yegor seizes a gun and kills the official. He then returns home and shoots himself at the entrance.

The Carnovsky Family has a broad canvas, a vital theme, many truthful, even towering passages, and a host of realized characters. Yet the action borders on the obvious and banal, and the protagonists lack the distinction of uniqueness. The Carnovsky males do not behave with the naturalness of inner logic but are manipulated by the author to accord with his thesis. All three—David, Georg, and Yegor—run away from themselves, each in his own way, but each as if subject to the pull of specific strings. And although the tragedy of each one is real and increasingly poignant, they are maneuvered to demonstrate that to discard traditional piety is to risk losing all Jewishness. Some of the lesser characters, however, do possess a life of their own. Elsa may be a strange girl by conventional standards, but she knows what she wants, suffers for her beliefs, and continues her social activity in her American home. Her father and Ephraim Walder, while typical of their kind, likewise live in accord with their convictions and remain true to themselves to the end. Several others are equally well drawn and readily come to life.

Singer was at this time at the height of his popularity. The dramatizations of his novels were successful beyond anyone's expectation, and their editions in English and other languages elicited favorable reviews and attracted a good many readers. Yet he remained fundamentally at war with himself. As his close friend Aaron Zeitlin indicated: "The outward conditions of his life were good. To the world he appeared as a man satisfied with his achievement. Yet the illusion of the 'broad world' had long since vanished from the mind of the wise Singer, and only an inner bitterness replaced it." The idols of modern man—and of the modern Jew—no longer appealed to him, and he knew there was no return to the traditional life of his childhood. Yet he longed to recall the dogmas and beliefs of his rabbinical father, in which he now saw a wholesomeness unperceived by him in his rebellious youth. These "truthful happenings" he described lovingly and at length in a volume which, like all his writings, was first serialized in *Der Forverts*, and later published posthumously under the title of *Of a World That Is No More* (1946).

In this work Singer reminisced nostalgically about his father's and grandfather's pious ways and benign spirits, impregnating the pages with a glowing appreciation of the traditions and folklore he had derided in his early fiction. With rich sentiment and salutary humor he described his early youth at study, at play, and in his father's study. His parents were not a congenial couple: his father was a pious, gentle, erudite optimist, suffering poverty because he would not learn Russian as required of legally accepted rabbis; his mother, on the contrary, was intellectually keen, practical, worrisome, pessimistic, and a poor cook. As rabbi of an unimportant village, the only post open to him, his father had to deal with all kinds of legal and religious matters, and the people who came with their complaints and contentions made themselves at home in the kitchen while waiting to be heard. His father was also in the habit of inviting the lowliest beggars, unwanted by others in the synagogue, to his Sabbath table, so that his wife had to eat in the kitchen. To alleviate their dire poverty, she would spend summers with her more affluent father, thus enabling her husband to accumulate a little money for their winter needs.

In writing about his childhood Singer intimates the early symptoms of the creative mood. As a boy he was little interested in the exegesis of the Talmud—moot problems of *kashruth*, commerce, and other topics alien to a ten-year-old boy who longed for horses and the out of doors. He swallowed these teachings as one does "bitter medicine," hurriedly and unwillingly. But human behavior fascinated him. He was extremely curious and keenly observant of everything that took place in his father's study—the various people who came to demand justice or merely to complain about their wretched lives.

> An enormous curiosity about people and their activities burned within me from earliest childhood. What I saw in one person I could not find in a thousand books. I could not satisfy my life-thirst in books and ran from them to the soil and plants and cows and birds and people, especially ordinary people, who live a full life.

The stories Singer wrote in the early 1940's were collected in a volume and published in 1949. "About the Black Sea" concerns Pinhas Fradkin who, at the age of 18, is stimulated by Yehuda Halevi's poetry to go to Palestine. But World

War I had started and he is drafted for the duration. Released after the revolution, he cannnot find a boat in Odessa going to the Holy Land. While there he learns that his entire family was murdered in a pogrom. Eager to avenge the crime, he persuades the commander of the Red soldiers in Odessa to let him lead a company to his native village and wipe out the counter-revolutionary hooligans. Given the soldiers, he achieves his mission with determination and dispatch. When asked what he is planning to do next, he replies: "I will go on a ship eastward . . . to farm a piece of land in a kibbutz."

"Doctor Georgie" is the story of the youngest son of a poor junkman. Unwilling to study medicine, as his father wants, he enrolls in an engineering school because he is handy with tools and machinery. He drops out of school when he meets a girl he likes and marries her, much to the displeasure of her wealthy father. To earn a living he opens a "hospital" for "sick" cars, which he "doctors" well. More interested in mechanics than in making money, however, he charges little for his services and remains poor—to the distress of his wife, who remembers that she could have married a real doctor and lived in comfort.

In "Sender Pragner" a philandering restaurant owner decides to marry the daughter of the town's late ritual slaughterer at the urging of his rabbi. On the day of the wedding he wishes to atone for his sins by feeding the poor of the vicinity. At the ceremony the bride's relatives, pious and proud Jews, look down their noses at the groom, considering him beneath their dignified level. That night he discovers to his chagrin that his bride is no virgin, as the rabbi has assured him. Thereafter he ignores his wife, resumes his dissolute life, and behaves recklessly until he dies of a stroke.

"In the Mountains" relates how Sholom Melnick, a house painter affected with lead poisoning, buys a neglected farm in the Catskills in order to live a more healthful life. His wife Betty, having expected him to open a candy store, where she could help and be with people, refuses to be "buried" on the farm. His son, however, wants to go with him and leaves high school to do so. Betty and her young daughter remain in the city for the winter, and there is talk of a divorce. In the spring her sisters and their wealthy husbands suggest that the farm be made a summer boarding house. This appeals to her, and she soon turns the place into a successful vacation center—to the displeasure of her husband and son. The following spring Betty engages a brash and flirtatious waiter, who makes up to her and soon runs the enterprise. He begins talking about going to Florida for the winter, and Betty is tempted to join him. At this juncture the son steps in and drives the waiter away. His mother, impressed and intimidated by his manliness, becomes reconciled to the farm.

In "A Fated Thing" Fishel, a simpleton, deals with pig's hair all week and smells evilly. Every Friday he attends the synagogue service, and the beadle has difficulty finding someone to take him home for the Sabbath. Eating little all week because of his strict adherence to *kashruth*, he consumes food lustily when in a Jewish home. On Passover Eve a flood keeps him from reaching town in time to clean up and none will take him home. Thereupon the rabbi invites him and later promises to find him a wife. Mischievous young tailors lure Fishel to their shop to meet a prospective bride, a youth in disguise, causing him to weep with shame. Not long after that, the two young brothers who had instigated the prank become seriously ill. When ordinary medication fails them, the suggestion is made that they are being punished for insulting an innocent man, and it is necessary for Fishel to forgive them before they can get well. Fishel, however, refuses to come to their bedside. Finally the beadle hits upon the idea of having the widowed mother of the sick youths marry Fishel. This pleases him and he readily forgives his grown stepsons.

These and other stories in the collection are told with literary skill, wry humor, and a firm grasp of human essentials. They add little, however, to Singer's stature as a writer.

As the war intensified in 1943, and the Hitlerian genocide in Eastern Europe accelerated, Singer's restlessness increased.

More than ever before he was impressed by the littleness of man in a world of evil and brute force. He considered leaving the United States, of forsaking the diaspora and making his home in ancient Israel. Suddenly all his worries, dreams, and plans came to naught when he suffered a fatal heart attack at the age of 50.

CHAPTER EIGHTEEN

I. BASHEVIS SINGER

Novelist of Hasidic Gothicism

ELEVEN YEARS younger than his brother Israel Joshua, Isaak Bashevis Singer grew up in Warsaw, where his father had moved from the small town in which Israel Joshua had spent his childhood years. The family lived in a ghetto tenement, inhabited by all kinds of poor people, while the elder Singer earned a meager and precarious living as a local rabbi. Like his older brother, Isaak Bashevis devoted his childhood to study of the Talmud and various other religious tomes, and during his few free hours lived the life of a carefree boy with his playmates. At home he observed all the obligations and restrictions incumbent upon the pious Hasid—as was expected of him by his rabbinical father. Also, like his older brother, he was extremely curious about the ways and thoughts and emotional quirks of people, and listened intently to the questions and problems propounded in his father's study—the gamut of human woes and experiences in miniature; and like Israel Joshua he recorded the exotic, peculiar, and amusing incidents in a discursive but telling memoir, *In My Father's Court* * (1966).

Born in 1904, Isaak Bashevis Singer grew up with little of his brother's insurgence and social idealism, and therefore never experienced the latter's bitter disillusionment. More cynical than romantic, and with a firmer grasp of the postwar world of the 1920's, he proceeded surefootedly toward his lifework as a writer by training as a journalist. He made no effort to enter the mainstream of literary fashion, but wrote about what he knew best—the Hasidic aspects of Jewish life. At a time when Yiddish literature had reached maturity and was concerned with the grievous events of the day rather than the pious medievalism of the past, young Singer devoted his first major work to the spectacular and psychotic aspects of 17th-century Jewish life—and not as certain other writers, with a view to extolling the faith in survival but, on the contrary, to expose and satirize the psychopathic messianism of the time.

Satan in Goray * (1935, in English 1955) has its setting in a Jewish town in Poland shortly after the terrible massacres perpetrated by kossaks under Bogdan Khmelnitski in 1648–1649. The town was practically devastated, and many of the Jews killed or maimed. But once the kossaks left, the survivors exerted themselves to rebuild their homes and businesses. The elderly Rabbi Beinush, having escaped death, ruled them rigorously by virtue of his great prestige and commanding personality. He had no use for his two mature sons, one a gourmet and an incompetent and the other a dandy and a mystic, and felt lonely and isolated, with no obvious successor.

The tragically haphazard condition of the Jews stimulated fantastic messianic hopes. Fantasies of once reasonable men ran riot; neurotics dreamt of or envisaged the appearance of the promised messiah; and wandering beggars, eager for bigger alms, brought news of messianic expectations in different parts of the Jewish diaspora. Rabbi Beinush was sharply critical of these mystical assumptions and far-fetched rumors—he believed that the recent massacres were God's punishment for serious sins—and more than one of these gossip-mongers left town hurriedly after an interview with the old rabbi. Despite his efforts to quash false expectations, news of messianic deliverance kept spreading. False and deluded messengers excited the people with joyous reports of the oncoming restoration of Israel. Hysterical believers in the forthcoming redemption fought with skeptics who refused to partake in the emotional orgy which, nevertheless, kept spreading like an irresistible tide.

In every country new prophets arise. Simple people, even virgins and Nazarites, fall to the earth and shout that Shabbati Zevi was anointed by the Creator of the world to redeem the chosen of the sons of Israel. Sinners who have hitherto denied God and scorned Him, are now repenting with bitter tears, putting on coarse sacks and wandering from city to city to suffer for their sins and to arouse the populace. Apostates of prominence discard their wealth and fall to the feet of rabbis to be accepted into the faith again. Jerusalem was already building and establishing itself in all its glory. In a number of towns people ceased to die. . . .

Into this setting Singer has placed the protagonists of the novel. Rekhele grew up motherless and absorbed the medieval legends and fantasies told her by elderly women. One Yom Kippur eve, while still a child, and just after the burial of her grandmother, she was alone in the house and became so obsessed by fear that she fell sick and was left emotionally impaired. Reaching maturity as a sickly, neurotic, and friendless maiden, though quite pretty, she is generally assumed to be a lost soul.

Itche Mathis, an ascetic and mystical book peddler, comes to town to preach the advent of Shabbati Zevi and readily gains numerous followers. When he meets Rekhele, she tells him that she is a victim like Jephthah's daughter and no man will marry her. She attracts him and he informs her that he is her destined husband. Although Rabbi Beinush learns that the man is an imposter, he fails to stop the marriage—and dies in the effort—which is attended by the town's mystics and enthusiasts. Itche Mathis, however, enigmatically fails to assert his rights as a husband.

Soon after the event Reb Gdaliah arrives. His extrovert zeal puts Itche Mathis in the background and he establishes himself as the vicar of the expected messiah. With the aid of a kerchief which has the name of Shabbati Zevi sewed on it, he begins to perform miraculous cures and makes himself the town's leader. Handsome and exuberant, he appeals to many women, but is most attracted to Rekhele. When she comes to tell him of a vision she had, he extols her prophetic powers and has her repeat her perception of the messiah to the Jews assembled in the synagogue. He then sends Itche Mathis as a messenger of good tidings to other towns and takes Rekhele to live with him. Gradually all moral restraint is eased, and men and women act without their normal modesty or moderation —much to the aggravation of the few level-headed skeptics.

A severe drought that summer causes much hardship, but Gdaliah assures the people that there is no cause for worry; a cloud will lower itself before Rosh Hashana and carry all Jews to Israel. Consequently none does any business and none makes any preparation for the winter. When nothing happens and Itche Mathis returns in rags to announce Shabbati Zevi's conversion to Mohammedanism, Gdaliah insists that this was only a feint on the messiah's part and that he will soon return from Heaven and deliver the Jews. He forces Itche Mathis to divorce Rekhele and marries her without waiting the prescribed three months. By now, however, more and more of the people have roused themselves from their hypnotic nightmare and Gdaliah's influence is on the wane. When Rekhele begins to have hallucinations and fears that Satan has impregnated her—a dybbuk has entered into her and has been abusing the pious—Gdaliah is beaten and bound as an evil magician. The narrative ends with Rekhele's death and Gdaliah's escape and apostasy.

Intentionally or not, Singer in this book employs his obvious literary talent not to soar spiritually or depict the tragic situation sympathetically, but to destroy illusions and satirize the potency of faith. He presents the epoch of Shabbati Zevi in its extreme superstitious grotesqueness: its depression of reason and exaltation of unreality, its asceticism and eroticism. He hardly dwells on the pathos which led to the madness but stresses instead the childishness, even foolishness, which this madness revealed. His cynicism is all the more devastating because it is barbed with the sharp-edged refinement of fictional art. His preoccupation with hysterical and knavish characters to the near exclusion of sane ones—he kills Rabbi Beinush early in the narrative—gives the book an aspect of negativism which tends to weaken its undoubted literary merits. As a novel, moreover, it does not hold together, consisting mostly of a number of decorative scenes. As I. I. Trunk has validly pointed out, it is "a Jewish Gothic palace, very beautifully built, but without doors and without exits." Verbally beautiful it is, with the diction carefully chosen to match the Yiddish of the time and highly polished. Compared to the fiction of his Yiddish contemporaries, *Satan in Goray* is, in the expression of his admirer Aaron Zeitlin, "*a noble anachronism.*"

In 1935 Singer was brought by his brother to the United States. He wrote on a free-lance basis, publishing stories and articles in *Der Forverts* and other periodicals; he also did some translating. In 1943 he became a regular contributor to *Der Forverts*, and nearly all of his writings under his own name and under pseudonyms have first appeared in that newspaper. Publishing only short stories, he remained relatively obscure until 1950, when his second major work, *The Family Moskat*,* was first serialized and then issued in both Yiddish and English with notable success, capped by the Louis Lamed prize. The dedication to his late brother is significant: "To me he was not only the older brother, but a spiritual father and master as well."

Old Meshulam Moskat is a typical business leader: rich, generous, enterprising, domineering, not erudite but well informed and a respecter of learning, pious but no fanatic. Like other men of his kind in Yiddish fiction, he is burdened with incompetent sons and commonplace daughters: "I've got seven, and in everyone of them there is a worm gnawing." Thus he is forced to depend on his bailiff for assistance in the management of his various affairs. At the age of 80 he marries precipitously for the third time while vacationing in Karlsbad and brings his new wife and her daughter Adele to Warsaw.

He knows very soon after that he has acted foolishly but decides to make the best of it. His children and their spouses —nervous wrecks, gluttons, and lechers—are perturbed by this unexpected threat to their inheritance, but are unable to protest. Despite his age, Meshulam dominates their lives and those of their children, supporting them financially and arranging their affairs as he sees fit.

Into the family's orbit enters Asa Heshel Bannet, 19 years old, scion of a long line of rabbis, and a prodigy in the Talmud. He has decided not to be a rabbi and has come to Warsaw to obtain a worldly education. Chance brings him to the attention of Abram Shapiro, Meshulam's philandering, intelligent son-in-law, who is given to quick enthusiasms. He arranges for his niece Hadassah, a young student, to give Asa lessons in Polish and Russian. The two are soon attracted to each other, and Hadassah refuses to become engaged to Fishel, a pious and able youth whom Meshulam has chosen as her husband. Abram encourages her, maintaining that Jewish parents are fools to presume their educated daughters would marry yeshiva students: "The damn fools. First they send their daughters to decent, modern schools and then they expect them to forget everything they've learned and suddenly become old-fashioned, orthodox, meek Jewish housewives. From the 20th century straight back to the middle ages."

There is a lot of quarreling and sparring among various members of the family, revealing tensions and cleavages despite their basic community of interest. They also exemplify the moral looseness among emancipated Jews in the 1900's. Abram is most conspicuous in this respect, and his wife tires of his promiscuity and returns to her father's house. The youngest of Meshulam's daughters decides in middle age to divorce her husband and marry her father's bailiff, after forcing him to divorce his wife.

To avoid coercion, Hadassah arranges to elope with Asa. They plan to study in Switzerland, but at the border Hadassah is caught by a guard and jailed. A fortnight later she is returned by the police, bedraggled and depressed, unaware of what has happened to Asa. While in this state of dejection, and failing to hear from Asa, she acquiesces in the marriage to Fishel.

Asa, in the meantime, having eluded the border guards, goes to Switzerland. His efforts to communicate directly with Hadassah having elicited no response, he writes to Adele for information. Long fond of him, she immediately goes to him, tells him of Hadassah's marriage, and persuades him to become her husband. Continuing to be deeply in love with Hadassah, he remains cool to Adele and refuses to be supported by her while at the university. Some time later he receives a letter from Hadassah in which she relates her capture, her resentment on not hearing from him, and her forced marriage. He replies at once to avow his strong and abiding love for her. When Adele discovers their continuing correspondence, Asa admits his indifference to her. "She had known the very day she dragged him to the canopy, that he loved Hadassah and not her. She herself had called their marriage an experiment—two people living together without love. He could show her these words in her own handwriting." Soon after that they return to Poland and live more or less apart. Adele's mother seeks out Hadassah and abuses her for taking away her daughter's husband—thereby, in effect, throwing the two lovers together in ecstatic affection.

Meshulam having died in the interim—and robbed by his bailiff Koppel of a large sum of money hidden in a safe—and World War I having caused great hardship everywhere, the tightly connected Moskat family breaks up and disintegrates. The middle-aged children remain impotent, are unable to maintain their assumed dignity and easy living, and gradually decline into futile old age. Only Leah, the youngest, marries Koppel, far below her social station, and the pair make their home in the United States. Most of the Moskat grandchildren live in "hatred and bitterness," and a mixed marriage by one of them leads only to tragedy.

Adele becomes pregnant and gives birth to a son. Asa, drafted into the army, is a poor soldier. He returns from

Russia in 1917, is maltreated by a Polish lieutenant on his way home, and witnesses the poignant events of the civil war. Pessimistic and dispirited, he refuses to have any more children and leaves Adele. Hadassah has in the meantime divorced Fishel, and she and Asa live together and subsequently marry when Adele agrees to a divorce after much bickering and bargaining.

Asa is again disturbed on learning that he is once more to become a father. While in this dismal mood he quarrels with Hadassah and wants to run away from everything. "This whole marriage business is not for me," he ponders, and cries out: "I hate God, I hate Him and His creation. How can one love a dead God, a paper God?" Yet he soon realizes his predicament: "It seems that I cannot live without a God; doubt has made me sick."

His earnings as a teacher hardly cover his numerous obligations and he remains moody and edgy. Frequently returning to his beloved Spinoza and to Malthus, he reflects: "I have been an outsider all my life." While in this state of spiritual misery he drifts into an affair with another woman, and Hadassah leaves him. By this time Hitlerian war clouds darken over Europe and Hadassah is killed by a Nazi bomb when Poland is invaded. Everyone who can leaves Warsaw, but Asa refuses to depart while members of his family remain.

Covering a half century of Jewish life in Poland during the break-up of its traditional piety and its grievous persecution, the novel depicts its various aspects with masterly familiarity and a firm grasp of essentials. The range in personalities—and a number are vividly portrayed—is from the extremely pious Hasid to the complete skeptic, from the wealthy businessman to the hapless poor, from the philosophical rationalist to the self-indulgent sophist; in events it covers the traditional town in the process of disintegration and destruction as a result of intellectual emancipation followed by war and massacre, the city ghetto in all its poverty, grime, bustle, intellectual ferment, and individual aspiration, overwhelmed by social cataclysm and world chaos. With magical literary power, Singer brings alive a host of human beings struggling and suffering in a world they never made, loving and hating, believeing and doubting, dreaming and planning and quashed as they play their miniscule parts in the arena of human existence. In the process one overlooks the partial artifice of plot and the actions of certain characters which accord less with their inner logic than with the author's particular purposes. To give one instance, Asa is made not to remember Hadassah's correct address, so that she remains unaware of his escape—which leads to her marriage to Fishel and Asa's to Adele. These and other flaws of construction do not, however, detract from the major significance of the novel as a work of fiction: it is an intensely conceived narrative pulsating with human life and revealing the inner emotional recesses of the individuals involved.

Singer is not only a fine novelist but also a master of the short story. In his first collection, published in 1957, the title story, "Gimpel the Fool," * has similarities to Peretz's "Bontche," but with Singerian differences. An orphan, extremely naive, innocent, and meek, Gimpel believes what he is told and is regularly fooled and exploited. The girl he marries is already pregnant and treats him shabbily. She continues to cohabit with other men and has a total of six bastards, but he shows no anger or resentment, and readily forgives her when she confesses shortly before she dies. Then, tempted by the devil, he avenges himself on the world by pouring urine into the dough of the bread he is about to bake. Yet immediately thereafter he is conscience-stricken and begins to atone for his misdeed by becoming a wandering penitent.

"The Gentleman from Cracow" is a satire on greed in a context peculiar to Singer. A doctor comes to a starving village and supplies it with bread. He also deliberately loses money in cards with some of the townsmen. When marriage is proposed to him, he arranges for all eligible girls to come to a ball so that he might make his choice of a bride. When all

are present, he announces himself as the richest man in the
world, sent by the king of the ten lost tribes to help the village,
and ready to give each girl a large dowry if she chooses a husband that evening. Couples are united by lot, and Hodel the
ragpicker's daughter is the lucky winner of the doctor. In
the midst of the general hilarity both the doctor and Hodel
reveal their devilish identity. By that time a fire is consuming
the town, and the rabbi has a hard time calling people to
come to their senses and repent.

"The Wife Killer" concerns a rich miser who has driven
three wives to their death in order to inherit their wealth.
His fourth wife, however, is a wicked slut and a match for
him. In time she forces him to assign all his assets to her and
to make his home in a poorhouse. When she comes to him to
demand a divorce, she collapses and dies, so that he regains
his wealth and lives alone to the end of his life.

"The Little Shoemakers" tells of a family of shoemakers in
which the eldest male of each generation remains in town
and the others go elsewhere. Though the oldest son, Gimpel
decides to migrate to America. There he prospers and brings
over all his brothers. Together they develop a large shoemaking business. When their mother dies they persuade their
father to join them. Unable to remain idle though old, he
resumes his custom-fitted shoemaking and is so successful at
it that his wealthy sons soon make it their avocation.

"From the Diary of One Not Born" is another characteristic
story. An imp takes pleasure in playing pranks on people.
He causes an impoverished man who has begged 500 gulden
from his wealthy brother-in-law to drop the bill in the fire;
he poses as a young man eager to marry an old maid only
to denounce her as a whore after the wedding, so that she
drowns herself out of shame. These misdeeds are told with a
relish of devilish humor.

In "The Old Man" a Jew of 90, surviving his son and
family after World War I epidemics, lives alone as best he
can. Then he decides to visit his rabbi in Austria and goes
through many hardships to reach him. He is welcomed,

treated well, and married to a deaf and dumb woman of 40. Nine months later she bears him a son.

"The Unseen" is the story of a rich and pampered couple whose loyal servant dies and is replaced by one sent by the devil, an impudent and imperious young woman. When the wife goes to visit a dying sister in a nearby town, the servant arouses the husband's lust—only to refuse his desire until he promises to divorce his wife and marry her. The wife is upset but soon remarries. A year later the first husband returns a beggar, having been robbed and deserted by his devilish spouse. His first wife takes him into an empty house on the premises and supplies him with his needs. When she dies he cannot mourn her at the funeral because he is no longer related to her.

These and other stories in the volume are written with sprightliness and skill, but with a mischievousness bordering on antipathy. Fully aware of human weaknesses and the ease with which most men are tempted, Singer seems to enjoy depicting and disclosing their individual foibles. For all his rare insight and masterly description, he tends to yield the quality of sympathy to the temptation of clever disparagement.

The Magician of Lublin * (1960) is the piquant story of Yasha Mazur, an ingeniously clever acrobat, magician, and lock picker. The loving husband of Esther, a good and devoted wife, he is also the paramour of Magda, his acrobatic assistant, and Zeftel, a lively grass widow; in addition he courts highborn Emilia, a professor's attractive widow. A man of 40, at the height of his "hidden powers," an agnostic and inclined to reflection, he enjoys his various involvements.

After a visit home for a holiday, he leaves for Warsaw, where Emilia lives and where he is billed to perform a novel new act. He is worried about his promise to divorce Esther and convert to Christianity in order to marry Emilia—a procedure which requires a large sum of money, as he feels it necessary to provide for Esther. His conscience troubles him, and he tells himself that in his lust after women he is like a drunkard who hates alcohol—"that his worst enemy was ennui. To escape it he had committed all his follies."

On an impulse he decides to rob a rich Polish miser he had been told about, but in his nervousness fails to pick the lock of the chest and has to flee, hurting an ankle in doing so. Refusing to see a doctor before keeping his appointment with Emilia, and quarreling with Magda, who resents his neglect of her, he confesses to Emilia what he had tried to do and leaves her. On returning to his rooms he finds Magda hanging from the ceiling. Too perturbed to remain and suffering from his hurt ankle, he thinks of visiting Zeftel—only to find her in bed with another man. He becomes sensible of "the humiliation of one who realizes that despite all his wisdom and experience, he has remained a fool."

Although hitherto an agnostic, he now turns penitent. Returning home, he builds near his house a brick cell with one small window and no door, and remains in it in constant prayer and reflection. Esther attends to his few needs. Temptation and desire continue to plague him, but he fights them with prayer and Psalms. In time his condition becomes widely known, and Jews begin to come to him as if he were a saintly rabbi. Several years later Emilia learns of his whereabout and isolation from a report in a newspaper, and writes him a long letter full of affection, admiration, and self-reproach.

Much more limited in scope and conception than *The Moskat Family* and less intensive and meaningful than *Satan in Goray*, this novel has a lustiness and psychological overtones that keep it from becoming mere picaresque fiction. Yasha is not a conventional philanderer and rogue; even when he commits wrongs he suffers from pangs of conscience and wishes he had not become so involved. Moreover, he has the moral courage to admit his misdeeds and to atone for them with a self-punishment reserved for the ascetic and saint. That his singular behavior, which would normally seem queer, appears plausible is due to Singer's powers of exposition and characterization. Yasha in particular, but also the others in the novel, are portrayed realistically, without affection or sympathy, but also without manipulation and artfulness. One has the feeling, indeed, that Singer enjoys depicting the Yashas of the world more than the Asas.

In 1961 Singer published another volume of stories, *The Spinoza of Market Street*,* both in Yiddish and in English, a procedure that became standard. In the title story Dr. Nahum Fishelson, son of a rabbi, had studied philosophy abroad and majored in the ethics of Spinoza. On returning to Warsaw he is made librarian of a synagogue and is generally respected as a scholar. Modeling himself after Spinoza, he prefers the freedom of bachelorhood and fails to see eye to eye with the rabbi of the synagogue, so he soon loses his job and has to live very modestly on a small pension given him by the Jewish community in Berlin. He devotes most of his time to Spinoza's *Ethics* with a view to writing about it. The outbreak of war in 1914 stops his pension and he nearly starves until an old-maid neighbor takes pity on him and brings him some food. Before long he agrees to marry her and responds to her caresses. Then, aware of his misconduct, he murmurs: "Divine Spinoza, forgive me. I have become a fool."

"The Black Wedding" is a tale of evil spirits. Hindele, orphaned by her rabbinical parents who had feared the work of devils, agrees to marry a widower with five children. A hysteric and superstitious, she fears that her bridegroom is a demon, as are the wedding guests, and considers herself undergoing "a black wedding." Following a conventional precept, she does nothing voluntarily in order not to yield to Satan. Later, when she becomes pregnant, she assumes she will bear a demon and worries so grievously that she dies in childbirth.

"The Shadow of a Crib" also has mystical content. A young doctor, an admirer of Schopenhauer, settles in a Polish town. The daughter of an older doctor resents his presence as inimical to her father and will have no contact with him. Only long after her father's death does she consent to go to a party to which the doctor is invited. When introduced, she impulsively kisses his hand. Late that night she attempts suicide. The doctor, unable to sleep and seeing a light in the window of the town rabbi, takes a stroll and comes upon her in time to save her life. They become engaged, but the doctor regrets becoming involved in marriage and leaves town. Thereupon the girl enters a convent. Years later the new rabbi and others begin to see the image of the doctor, whom they did not even know, staring at them in the night. The story ends with the statement: "Heaven and earth conspire that everything which has been, be rooted out and reduced to dust. Only the dreamers, who dream while awake, call back the shadows of the past and braid from unspun threads unspun nets."

"The Beggar Said So" is the story of a Nicholas I soldier who comes to a town and says that a beggar had told him it needed a chimney sweep. He is informed it is not so, but is permitted to carry water. One night he dreams the poorhouse is on fire and rushes out—to see it actually burning. He helps to put out the fire, and on inspection it is found that the chimney sweep had neglected to clean the chimney. The job is then given to the old soldier. Soon after he comes upon the beggar who had led him to the town and realizes that it was God's work. He takes good care of the beggar, has a scroll made in his name when he dies, and he and his wife arrange to be buried near him.

In "The Man Who Came Back" an honest and respectable Jew dies, but the weeping and clamor of his wife bring him back to life. The recovered man then acts as if another and inferior soul had entered his body. He begins to cheat, is dissolute, and soon forces his wife to divorce him. He leaves her penniless and marries an unscrupulous woman who is not long in robbing him of his money and having him jailed. His first wife takes pity on him and obtains his release, but he continues to misbehave and is shot by kossaks for thievery.

"The Destruction of Kreshev" tells how Satan arranges a

marriage between a nice girl and yeshiva scholar who is a disciple of Shabbati Zevi. The couple indulge in lewd acts, which he instigates. To compound his dissoluteness he urges her to have intercourse with a handsome coachman, and explains by cabalistic casuistry that in an earlier incarnation they had been lovers. Then the husband confesses the adultery to the rabbi and the synagogue elders. Their judgment is that the three culprits be paraded through the town in disgrace, that the husband divorce his wife, but that she not marry the coachman. The next morning the wife is found hanging from a rope, and the husband thereupon goes into exile to do penance.

These and other stories in the collection are similar in character and quality to the previous group. They are very well told, and the moral in them is implicit—Satan and his minions are again shown to succeed in tempting man and causing him to falter and fall. Singer effectively employs traditional Jewish legends and superstitions to demonstrate man's littleness and weakness, doing it with sardonic humor and a mastery of the genre.

The Slave * (1962), like *Satan in Goray*, has its setting in 17th-century Poland shortly after the devastating massacres of 1648–1649. Jacob, the protagonist, married at the age of 12 to a sourish little girl of 10 and during the ensuing dozen years becoming the father of three children and eligible for the rabbinate, is captured by brigands during the massacres and sold to a farmer in a remote mountain village; his wife and children are killed without his being aware of it. For the next four years he works as a cowherd and does so well that his owner admires his ability and keeps him from being harmed by nearby cowherds, who fear his strange ways and want to get rid of him.

Wanda, the farmer's daughter, widowed young from a drunken lout, comes to love Jacob and wants to cohabit with him, but he has no knowledge of his wife's fate and controls his growing desire for her. One evening they are caught in the barn during a rainstorm. Overcome with passion, he has Wanda immerse herself in an adjacent stream according to the Jewish ritual before lying with her. She is ready to become a Jewess and marry him, but he tells her that Polish law punishes such conversion with death.

About that time, Jews from his town learn of his slavery from a strolling player and come to ransom him on a day when Wanda is out of town. When he learns of the death of his wife and children, his passion for Wanda compels him to return secretly and take her with him to a strange town. There Wanda, now named Sarah, acts deaf and dumb in order not to reveal her gentile origin, and Jacob teaches her nightly the Yiddish tongue and the ritual practiced by a pious Jewess. He earns a living as a teacher.

When the local squire Politski becomes displeased with his Jewish overseer and comes drunkenly to abuse all Jews, including Jacob, Wanda forgets herself and speaks up in his defense. This is taken as a miracle, and Politski makes Jacob his administrator. Loath to become a public figure, Jacob nevertheless manages the estate honestly and efficiently, gaining the respect of his employer.

Wanda is now regarded as a blessed woman, and Jews come to her as if to a saintly person. All through her pregnancy Jacob fears that the pain of parturition will make her scream and reveal her identity, but Wanda insists she will control herself. When her suffering becomes unbearable, she screams and speaks Polish to the women attending her—who assume it is a dybbuk speaking in Wanda. News of her speaking Polish spreads, and Politski comes to question her. When he learns the truth he cautions Jacob to escape before he is caught by the priests and killed.

Wanda gives birth to a boy and dies. The rabbi forbids having the child circumcised, since according to Jewish law it belongs to the mother. Jacob now sees that "his acts, in a perverse way, were an offense to the government, the community, and to God." He recites Psalms and confesses to the synagogue assembly, feeling like "a branch torn from the trunk." Arrested, he escapes, prays at Wanda's grave, and enters the empty house of study for meditation:

> Suddenly, as Jacob stood there, he knew exactly what he must become: an ascetic who eats no meat, drinks no wine, does not sleep in a bed. He must atone for his sins. In winter he would immerse himself in cold baths, in summer lie on thorns and thistles; the sun would burn him, the flies and mosquitoes bite him. For the rest of his life and until his last breath, he must repent and ask forgiveness of God and of Sarah's sacred soul. Perhaps then he would not have to linger too long in this most imperfect of worlds.

He goes to the woman who is nursing his infant son, whom he named Benjamin, as Jacob of old, and goes with him to his destined habitation—Israel.

Twenty years later Jacob returns to the town where Wanda is buried. He had lived all this time by hard labor, like a Nazarite and penitent. Benjamin turned out to be a prodigy and has become a lecturer in a yeshiva and the son-in-law of a rabbi. While in town Jacob becomes ill and dies. Digging a grave for him, the digger comes upon Wanda's body, well preserved in the dry sand, which seems a miracle to those present, and both bodies are buried together.

For all its melodramatic content, the novel is an intense and passionate love story in a setting of medieval Jewish life. Jacob and Wanda are perhaps the most appealing characters created by Singer; their simple, pure hearts and keen suffering give them an engaging and palpitating reality. Equally attractive is the primitive background: the pagan peasants on the mountainside, living close to nature and unrestrained in their fears and brutishness; the medieval town steeped in piety and superstition, ridden by fear of the Polish squire and his constables; and the passions, jealousies, and greed generated by human beings in close association. All of this folklore, exotic atmosphere, and genuine emotion is depicted with an intimate knowledge and artistic sensuousness that combine to give the book major status as a work of fiction.

Short Friday * (1964) is Singer's third volume of short stories, and in content and effect they are again similar to the earlier collections. Many deal with witches, demons, and evil spirits—all titillating human beings to sin and forbidden pleasures. In "Teibele and Her Demon" a wag has his way with a grass widow by posing as a demon. In "Big and Little" a short-bodied husband, mocked by many, goes to the city and engages a giant as his assistant. He deeds his wealth to him, much to the objection of his wife; but when he dies she readily marries the giant. "Blood" relates how an elderly merchant permits his young wife to take over his business. She soon lusts after a gay ritual slaughterer and they commit adultery. To have him nearer to her she adds a meat market to her activities. More and more wanton, she persuades him to let her do the butchering—a grievous sin among orthodox Jews. On discovery, the man escapes, but the woman, aided by her peasant servants, drives away the avenging Jews. Thereupon she apostatizes and lives alone until one night, while acting as a werewolf, she is killed. "Alone" is the story of a married Jew who comes to Miami on business and stays in a deserted hotel, where he experiences a hurricane and the temptation of a hunchbacked female clerk—embroidered with talk of witches.

Other stories, while more or less bizarre and odd, have a relatively natural setting. "Yentl the Yeshiva Boy" concerns a girl who wants to study like a man. Highly endowed mentally, she goes to a strange city in male attire and enrolls in a yeshiva. Her student partner, somewhat older, has just been rejected by the father of his betrothed, who has learned there has been a suicide in the youth's family. The father finds Yentl more to his liking and has her marry his naive daughter. Meantime the rejected student marries a girl who turns out to be a shrew. Yentl and he, visiting another town during a holiday period, discuss their affairs, and Yentl confides to him her sex and her determination not to return but to send her wife divorce papers. Her fellow student then divorces his wife and marries his first betrothed. "A Wedding in Brownsville" is about a prominent doctor, originally from Poland, attend-

ing a wedding to please the *landsleit* of his native town. In the
crowd he sees a woman he had loved as a youth and who was
supposed to have perished in a Nazi camp—and feels as if he
were seeing a ghost. "I Place My Reliance on No Man" tells
of a rabbi who cannot abide the gossip and jealousies to which
his parishioners expose him and decides to become a laborer
in order to live his own life. The title story concerns a botchy
tailor but good and pious man and his devoted and faithful
wife who love each other idyllically. One Friday night they
become asphyxiated—only to wake up and talk about their
death.

In all these stories Singer exploits the taboos, legends, and
superstitions in Jewish folklore, and weaves his narratives out
of the beliefs, fears, and abnormalities of the characters he
delineates. His remarkable talent as a writer of exotic tales
and Hasidic life imbues the volume with a literary charm
that tends to favor it with a significance greater than it really
has.

In the fall of 1967 Singer published *The Manor*,* which he
had written some years earlier, the first of two volumes in
which he provides an epic account of life in Poland during the
last third of the 19th century. The ignoble rout of the Polish
rebels in 1863 causes many of them to be deprived of their
estates and exiled to Siberia. When this happens to Count
Yampolsky, and his manor is awarded to a high Russian official
in St. Petersburg, it is leased by Calman Jacobi, a local innkeeper. Calman has the good sense to let the count's family
remain in the manor house, but he gradually makes efficient
use of the land and prospers. A pious Jew, not scholarly but
devoted to learning and to his rabbi, he acts generously to the
poor and does not let his increasing wealth modify his simple
behavior. When his older daughters reach marriageable age,
he selects rabbinical students for sons-in-law and provides
them with liberal dowries.

When the Count is pardoned after several years in exile, he
returns with a Russian mistress, whom he keeps in town. A
spendthrift and indolent, he makes no effort to improve his

low material condition. His daughter Helena becomes friends with Calman's daughter Miriam, who admires Polish literature and disdains the Hasidic piety of her parents. Lucian, the Count's son, returns home from his hiding place in Warsaw, and he and Miriam fall in love and elope to Paris. There Lucian becomes disgruntled with the more realistic Polish exiles and takes to drink. Without means, arrogant and restive, he mistreats Miriam, who bears him a son and is forced to work as a humble laundress.

When Calman's wife dies and his youngest daughter marries, he is left alone. Having never had a sexually satisfactory life, he is eager to remarry and is attracted to Clara, the daughter of a competitor. He knows she is not pious and not a proper match for him, but she strongly appeals to him and he yields to his aroused sexual urge. As he feared, she is not only very extravagant, but behaves wantonly and alienates his children. In time she bears him a son who turns out to have a savage and uncontrollable disposition. Calman is very unhappy, but every time he decides to break with Clara she wins him over with a little flirting. While on a visit to Warsaw she meets Zipkin, a student who attracts her, and she employs him for the summer as tutor for her son. They become lovers, and on discovery Calman drives Zipkin out of the house and determines to leave Clara and again lead "the life of a Jew."

Jonathan, husband of Calman's youngest daughter, is a highly erudite young scholar and the favorite of his rabbinical grandfather. On the latter's death his disciples insist that he be replaced by his grandson and not by one of his sons, and Jonathan yields despite his preference for the solitude of the study. He performs his duties as rabbi with becoming modesty and humility, to the satisfaction of his followers and to Calman's great pleasure.

Ezriel, an older son-in-law, gives up his Talmudic study and goes to Warsaw to prepare for a medical course. There he meets Wallenberg, a very wealthy industrialist, an apostate who continues to interest himself in Jewish affairs and is very

generous to those in need. In his house Ezriel learns about
Miriam and Lucian, whom Wallenberg has helped to return
to Warsaw. Their wretched existence, aggravated by Lucian's
unscrupulous and criminal behavior, troubles Ezriel, and he
does what little he can to mitigate his sister-in-law's misery.
Later, now a doctor of nervous diseases and tired of his commonplace wife, he becomes infatuated with an apostatized
Jewess and begins to lead a double life—much to his mental
distress.

Meantime Calman cannot control his desire for Clara and
returns to her. Yet his conscience does not permit him to forget her lechery and continued misconduct, and he divorces
her. Still moved strongly by lust at 65, he refrains from remarriage and concentrates on his prayers and piety. Clara,
now alone, seeks out Zipkin and induces him to divorce the
girl he had recently married and become her husband.

This incomplete outline does not do justice to the richly
colored and comprehensive canvas of the narrative. As in his
earlier novels, Singer deals at length and significantly with the
events and salient thoughts and ideas of the time in which his
characters live and function. Moreover, the protagonists have
a much more complicated and tangled existence than is here
indicated. Love and lust, piety and enlightenment, serene and
stormy cohabitation, the problem of Jewishness in a gentile
environment, and the miserable individual decline of haughty
and romantic Poles after 1863—all of these aspects are treated
in vivid detail and with artistic zest. As in his other works,
Singer here also tends to overstress the traits and egocentrici-
ties of his characters, giving their personalities a somewhat
uneven reality; nor is any protagonist endowed with the imaginative universality of great fictional art. Yet the narrative as a
whole has real magnificence.

Singer has recently entered the juvenile field with *Zlateh
the Goat,** a story for young children which has proved quite
popular. *Mazel and Shlimazel* * and *The Fearsome Inn* * were
published in the fall of 1967 and are equally attractive and
appealing to the imaginative child.

CHAPTER NINETEEN

YIDDISH IN ISRAEL

As STATED previously, Yiddish was the speech of East European Jews from the time of their settlement there in the late
Middle Ages, and was developed by them into a modern
literary language during the second half of the 19th century.
The pogroms and activated anti-Semitism of the early 1880's
started an exodus of these Jews to nearly every part of the
inhabited earth. For years it was a mere trickle, with most
migrants going to the United States, but some settled in Western Europe and a few went to Canada, South Africa, and
South America. A handful of dedicated Zionists departed for
Palestine (hereafter referred to as Israel). After the widespread massacres of 1905, the exodus rose to a tidal wave,
adding up to millions, and remained an outpouring in the
1920's. It ceased catastrophically after 1939 when around six
million Jews were trapped and incinerated in the Nazi crematoria—only to resume as a pathetic outflow of the few thousand
harrowed survivors.

Wherever these Jews gained a foothold, they were quick to
establish their religious and cultural institutions. Not knowing
the language of the land and unfamiliar with the social pat-
terns of their native neighbors, at first they clung of necessity
to their own intellectual and artistic resources. Where they
were concentrated in sizable numbers they started their own
newspapers and periodicals and imported or printed the avail-

able Yiddish books. In time each center had its own group of Yiddish writers who kept in close contact with colleagues in other parts of the world. The United States apart—its Yiddish activities having already been dealt with—major cities in Western Europe, Canada, Mexico, Argentina, and South Africa had their Yiddish writers adding their work to the mainstream of Yiddish literature. After World War II, with many Yiddish writers in Eastern Europe killed and Jewish presses stopped or destroyed, Jewish communities in other parts of the world printed and promoted books written by the survivors. This effort was made in the face of declining interest in Yiddish on the part of Jews who have become more or less assimilated into the cultures of their adopted lands.

In recent decades Israel has developed an active Yiddish publication program. This was a marked departure from conditions prevailing before 1950. The first Zionists who settled there in the 1880's and later were ardent Hebraists, and took pains to keep Yiddish from becoming the prevailing language of the Jewish community. This definite antagonism persisted until after the formation of Israel and the enactment of Hebrew as its official language. It is of interest that in 1931 Hebrew University in Jerusalem, greatly in need of support, refused the financial offer of a prominent American Jew for establishment of a chair in Yiddish. The *sabris*, or native born, were particularly inimical to the mother tongue of their parents.

This hostility became muted and largely dissipated as more and more martyrs from concentration camps arrived in Israel, most of them knowing little or no Hebrew and forced to communicate in Yiddish. Simultaneously, many writers who reached Israel from Poland and adjacent areas asserted their right to employ the language in which they were best able to express themselves. Sympathy with their harrowing ordeal under the Nazis favored them. President Khaim Weitzmann stated that "Hebrew is . . . the holy tongue, but Yiddish is . . . the martyr's tongue." His successor, President Isaak ben Zevi, also declared: "The strength to build Israel did not come from heaven. It came here from the diaspora. . . . Hitler had burned the Yiddish speech. Stalin liquidated it. . . . This created an attitude to Yiddish as to a holy tongue."

Although early Yiddish writers in Israel were ignored or disdained, so that some were completely discouraged, the more presistent had sufficiently established themselves by 1934 to issue a newspaper and form the Yiddish Writers Union in 1941. This early group was greatly strengthened by the larger number who reached Israel in the late 1940's. A scholar like Professor Dov Sdan, who holds the chair in Yiddish at Hebrew University, which was accepted from an American donor in 1951, has greatly stimulated a tolerance for Yiddish by the excellence of his linguistic and literary research. Born in Galicia in 1902 of a long line of learned forebears, he went to Israel in 1925. Highly erudite, endowed with a photographic memory, he has done much journalistic and critical writing as well as translations from several languages. It is his credo that the Jews must have "a pluralistic literature, a literature created through various orientations and powers." To Jacob Pat he declared:

One requires a total literature: Haskolah, Hasidism, Enlightenment. The preacher's sermon is literature, as is that of the Mussar [Moralizer]. All of this is one great source for our literature to draw upon. In Hasidism there is a sea of literature: stories, parables, legends. So are all other sources. The current writer must draw upon all.

Foundation by Abraham Sutzkever and others in 1949 of *Die Goldene Keyt* (The Golden Chain), which quickly became the leading literary periodical in Yiddish, brought the language to a highly respected level. Of equal advantage was formation of the Peretz Verlag, which brings out Yiddish books of good quality. Israel also has a widely read Yiddish daily newspaper, and evenings of Yiddish readings and discussions are held in various cities and communities.

Among early writers who made Israel their home, Khaim Nahman Bialik was pre-eminent. Born in 1873, he had a very difficult childhood after his seventh year, when his father died and he had to live with a dour grandfather. Very bright, he studied in the Volozhin Yeshiva, which permitted an interest in mundane subjects. About that time he came under the influence of Ahad Ha'am (A. Ginsburg, 1856–1927), a leading Zionist and Hebrew writer, and turned to Hebrew as his medium of literary expression. A poet of strong feeling and intense imagination, Bialik made his words and images into sharp knives that cut to the marrow. Dr. Eliashev has written of him: "He is the first of our poets to discern and develop the poetic form for the mightiest feelings of our tortured spirit. . . . Bialik's poetry is the highest lyric, which expresses *objectively* not only the subjective suffering but the suffering and sources of an entire people." Generally acknowledged as the greatest Hebrew poet in modern times, Bialik also wrote in Yiddish. His best-known poem, "The City of Murder," is a dirge on the Kishinev pogrom of 1903 written with naked and natural indignation and with the moral fury of an outraged prophet. He also wrote numerous simple lyrics which read like folksongs. In 1924 he migrated to Israel and lived there until his death ten years later.

Among the largely Yiddish writers to settle in Israel in the early years of this century were Z. Brokhes, Moshe Stavsky, and Yakov Shtol. Brokhes, born in 1886, went to Israel in 1903, where he became a worker. Beginning to write in 1907, he published a number of stories and essays. In 1914 he left for Paris to study, but the war caused him to leave for Argentina, and later the United States. He returned to Israel in 1918, the year in which his first volume appeared. In later years he issued other of his writings in book form.

Stavsky (1883–1964), the first husband of Anna Margolin, with whom he went to Israel in 1911, developed a successful dairy business and wrote fiction in his leisure hours. In his view it was folly to depend upon one's writing for a livelihood: "Better to skin a carcass in the market than to depend on literature for bread." Much of his fiction was about household animals and Arab life. After 1930 he wrote only in Hebrew.

Shtol (Simkha Eisen, 1897–1959) went to Israel in 1912. He served in the British army in both world wars. One of the first Yiddish writers in Israel and intimately familiar with the land and people, he wrote about both with deep love. His *A Wedding in Kastra* (1931) is a romantically original creation, describing with sympathetic sensitivity the moods of the natives and newcomers, their traditions and tendencies. His depiction of Arab life is poetically empathic.

At least a dozen Yiddish writers from Eastern Europe went to live in Israel during the 1920's despite the known antipathy to the language. Z. Onoikhi (Z. I. Aronson, 1878–1947), whose father was a rabbi and head of a yeshiva, had a strictly orthodox upbringing but became emancipated in late adolescence, took up general studies, and joined the radical movement. He began to write in Hebrew, but turned to Yiddish in 1905. His stories and monologues, collected in a volume entitled *Between Heaven and Earth* (1909), stressed the various psychological conflicts of enlightened intellectuals in an atmosphere of orthodoxy and oppression. He visited Israel in 1910–1911, left Russia for South America in 1923, and settled in Israel a year later. A number of his stories treat Hasidic life. After he became a tax collector in Tel Aviv he practically stopped writing.

M. T. Barr (Berman, 1889–1954) was born in Warsaw and remained in Poland until 1925, when he migrated to Israel. For a decade he worked in various kibbutzim, then returned to Poland as a Zionist representative. In 1939 he escaped from the Nazis and landed in Mexico. He did not return to Israel until 1953. His numerous stories and poems as well as articles are mostly on Zionist themes.

I. D. Berkowitch (1885–1967) was best known as Sholom Aleichem's son-in-law and translator of his writings into Hebrew, but he was also highly regarded as a writer of stories and plays in both Yiddish and Hebrew. He began his literary career as one of the editors of *Die Neie Welt* (The New World) in 1910. Four years later he came with the Sholom Aleichem family to New York and remained there until 1928, when he settled in Israel. He was an active writer of stories and essays to the end of his long life, and his multi-volume memoirs are a distinctive contribution to the history of Jewish life and literature.

Arya Shamri, born in Poland in 1907, went to Israel in 1929. Publishing his first verses in 1937, he evidenced a maturity of poetic expression. Bold and optimistic in attitude, he gave voice to the dedicated determination of the people to develop the land. Thus, in "In the Gate of Days," he exclaims: "Enough the waiting on the doorstep with prayer, tearful, and not heard. See. Wolves in the clouds! Is it perhaps too late?" "A Star in the Field" presents broad pictures and ideas, emotions and moods, arising out of concrete situations and actual experiences. His motto in much of his poetry is: "Always the dream will move the heart." "In Such a Night I Shall Not Die" tells at length about the power of dreams and the reality of hopes: "Only a human child am I, who goes from dust to dust and sees on the way the distant stars, yet with the daring of my suffering I say the hard word: In such a night I shall not die."

Chronologically Uri Zvi Greenberg belongs to this group. One of the great Jewish poets of this century, he was born in Galicia in 1894, the son of a rabbi. After receiving a strict religious education, he became an uncompromising rebel. Drafted into the army during World War I, he served until 1918. While in Lemberg he witnessed the massacre and was traumatically affected by it. Already a writer, he went to Warsaw in 1920 and joined *Die Khaliastra,* termed by some "a group of reckless bums" but actually composed of young poets and storytellers rebelling against stultifying conventionality and voicing their insurgence in expressionistic form. In 1924 he went to Israel, where he became a leading revisionist of Zionism. Seven years later he returned to Poland to edit *Die Welt* (The World) for revisionist labor unions. In 1935 he went back to Israel and has remained there ever since.

From the very first Greenberg's verses evinced a Jeremian

pessimism combined with Isaian indignation. Very early he
exclaimed: "I stand against the rock of Jewish misfortune and
strike at it with the hammer of song." His first two volumes,
In the Rush of Time (1919) and *Twilight Gold* (1921), contained numerous religious poems charged with "holy" sentiment and termed by him his "heart's song of songs."

In *Mephisto* (1922), however, holiness is turned into di-
abolism. Unable to conceive of the world without a guiding
force, and having rebelled against God, he assumes that
Mephistopheles is in control: with the world sodden in suffering and bitterness, pain and shame, "there must be *someone*—
other than God—who resides in the blue and breathes of evil."
This someone was Mephisto: "And Mephisto always conquers!
If you doubt, you doubt forever! You let the grapes in the
vineyard burst, the wine leaks into the grass, and you go seeking oases in the Sahara." Temptation and allure assail human
beings in every walk of life, and Mephisto boasts of being the
tempter in everything and everywhere: "Well, the world is the
world; but day turns to night—and then Mephisto is master.
And millions of men become wild and hate. And the stone of
grandfather Cain is still hot. And what further? People fruc-
tify, people run; it is all nonsense; and all hearts shudder in
lust: gold and blood. . . ."

Shortly after settling in Israel, Greenberg stopped writing
in Yiddish. In Hebrew he extolled the Halutzim who were
dedicating themselves to building up ancient Israel. In a characteristic poem, "The Thirteenth Tribe," the first stanza reads:

> Don't ask our blood, it might tell you: it's old. . . . It is quite a
> distance between Abraham and today's Halutz! (Old blood, it
> trembled in Christian coldness of fear.) Ask our hand, the hard-
> working hand—it will surely tell you as with a map with signs:
> our development and our spread over fields and swamps and
> sand wilderness—over the high-risen stony curse—from the flat-
> lands to the heights of Galilee.

After 1956 he resumed writing in Yiddish, which had become to him "the language of martyrs." In numerous poems he
depicted the terrible ordeal of the Jews under the Nazis. To

Jacob Pat he said: "Before my eyes lie dead Jews, Jewish
martyrs, great Jews. How can I sing of birds? I had a family.
I had a city. Where are they? All were killed. I live and they
are dead! What happened to me, to you, is deep inside of us.
My Jews were killed. I was killed. . . ." And his poetic outcries were a dirge bewailing the millions dead in Jeremian
lamentation and a call to anger and rebirth.

Another prominent poet who came to Israel in the same year
as Greenberg was Yosef Papiernikov, born in 1897 and deeply
devoted to Yiddish. Son of one of the early "Lovers of Zion,"
he grew up imbued with a yearning to live in the "Land of
Israel." In Warsaw after 1918, he joined the Poale Zion party.
On arriving in Israel in 1924, he worked hard to earn a bare
living, but his love of the land made him sing with joy and
enthusiasm—but also with a clear perception of things as they
are. At one time he stated: "I knew that in my new land, in
my new home, no milk and honey would flow from the walls,
but I did not know that bread would cost dear only to those
who raked fire with bare hands. . . ." Yet he gloried in the
blood and fire with which Israelis have had to build the land.
"When I shall cease singing about you—it will be that a poet
has died, who had through you—spoken to God." *In the Sunny
Land* (1927) and *Red on Black* (1929) give poetic voice to
his joy in and hope for Israel. His enthusiasm is evidenced in
the brief poem, "What My Father":

What my father, lover of Zion, dreamt into his silver-white hair—
I have realized without a dream, in actuality; without Zion—
longing, without Zion—pain. I have lived to eat the fruit of my
own planting: the fruit of sweat and blood, on my own soil,
which my brothers have delivered—with the sharpness of the
plow and sword.

This paean to Israel he sang again and again. In "On the
Way to Jerusalem" the first stanza reads: "In the hills of Jerusalem, where the roads hide and scatter like snakes—I, riding,
saw you, mother—mother earth." Similarly, "In Blood and in
Fire" extols the work of the Halutzim:

In blood and in fire we build our homes, in blood and in fire—
lay bricks and steps, and grow and rise upon them in the blue
skies which lie aflame on the roofs, on the towers, and on the
heads.

In blood and in fire we march against everything, in blood and
in fire—to lead the plow in the field, and throw, as bridges, paved
scattered roads, and feel in achievement—the axis of the world.

Papiernikov has been the staunchest Yiddishist in Israel.
In his resentment against those who belittled his mother
tongue he has refused offers of editors of Hebrew periodicals,
preferring to remain isolated and poor. "For more than 30
years," he told Pat in the 1950's, "I've lived in poverty, loneliness, and love of the land, and almost alone I wrote songs to
Israel in Yiddish." And he added:

> The new land did not receive me together with my child, the
> Yiddish poem. And it let me remain outside. As one impover-
> ished at a wealthy man's celebration, I am in my own land, where
> after decades I've not yet become a part of it. I remain as out-
> sider with my abashed poem: my Yiddish song of love, praise,
> and thanks.

The 1930's brought several more Yiddish writers into Israel.
Abraham Lev, born in Wilno in 1911, came to work in a kibbutz. He tilled the land and rejoiced in nature. His poems sing
of the soil and of his physical exertion in its cultivation, and
of the fragrance of growing plants. Quiet and modest in expression, he writes with rustic solidity and idyllic lyricism.
"Of course I'm tired, weary in my walk . . . but through the
years my Yiddish song always accompanied me." In "How
Good" he praises the simple life of the kibbutz: "The effort
here is healthy and fresh as the clear, joyous spring. The joint
table smells with the blessing of sweat and stable. . . . Who
works in the garden, in the kitchen, who works in the large
orchard: alone—how small the 'I,' together—how great the
miracle." And of himself he intimates in "The Peasant-Poet":
"Solid is the earth on which the peasant-poet works, and al-

though the body is tired and weary—yet his song and his speech are filled with the light and joy that is in him."

Samson Meltzer, born in Galicia in 1909, studied Hebrew for many years and graduated from a teachers' seminary. He began early to write in Hebrew and Yiddish, but when he went to Israel in 1933 composed his lyrics mostly in Yiddish because he felt a greater intimacy with his mother tongue. He earned his living as a builder, painter, and teacher, and was also connected with the Hebrew newspaper *Davar* (The Word) for many years, for which he translated numerous poems from the Yiddish. In his own verses he dwelt largely on reminiscences of his youth. He also wrote popular stories for children. His novel *On Grandfather's Fields*, which depicts an old Jew who clings to the soil in the face of loneliness and fatiguing exertion, also provides a realistic description of Jews and gentiles living together in rural friendliness.

Yoel Mastboim (1884–1957) was born in Poland and became a house painter at the age of 15. He joined the revolutionary movement in 1904 and suffered imprisonment. His early literary efforts were not liked by Peretz, but others found them promising. His first collection of stories, *Of the Red Life*, appeared in 1912. He lived in London between 1919 and 1922, where he was active in literary affairs and published two additional volumes. He had brought out five more books by the time he reached Israel in 1933. There he continued his literary activity, and among his published works are *My Stormy Years* (1950), a Hebrew account of his youth, and *The Power of the Soil* (1951), a novel describing the daily toil and Sabbath spirit of newcomers in Israel and the orthodox Jews in Jerusalem. As a writer he tended to be careless of style and uncontrolled of form, yet musical and picturesque in his prose diction.

Malkeh Locker, wife of Berl Locker, the Zionist leader, was born in Galicia in 1887 and grew up steeped in Hasidic piety. Yet she early became intimately familiar with European literature and was an enthusiastic admirer of Jean Arthur Rambeau, whose biography she published in 1950. She went to

Israel in 1937, but left the next year with her husband for London, where he held an important Jewish office, and did not return until 1948. She wrote about Israel with mystically symbolic affection. In a poem on Jerusalem she declared: "I seek in your memory the song of the world that existed before the Flood and what will be—the song of recognition, the song of love." Among her published volumes are *World and Man* (1931), *Thou* (1932), *Cities* (1940), and her diary, *The World Is Without a Keeper* (1947).

Moshe Gross-Zimmerman was born in Galicia in 1891 of a Hasidic family. In his late teens he began to write articles on politics and literature. In Israel, where he settled in 1937, he published fiction and criticism. A characteristic story, "The Grandfather," is a mildly humorous account of an elderly Jew who lost his wealth in 1939, went to Israel, and found satisfaction in making his living as a watchman. *Jews Among Jews* (1956) is a work of literary criticism noted for its Heinesque ésprit and his caustic view of Peretz's writing.

The European cataclysm of the early 1940's, in which millions of Jews suffered martyrdom, made Israel the logical and unique asylum for the surviving thousands who could no longer remain in the land of their birth. Overcoming extreme difficulties and endangering their lives in leaky and overloaded tubs, many defied British antagonism in order to steal into the land of their ancient forefathers. Among them were a number of Yiddish writers. After the establishment of Israel in 1948, many more entered the land, and most of them persisted in the use of Yiddish until they succeeded in gaining for it the position and prestige it now enjoys.

Foremost among the present protagonists of Yiddish is Abraham Sutzkever, who entered Israel illegally in 1947. Born in Smargon in 1913 of a rabbinic family, he was taken as an infant by his father to Siberia to escape the ravages of war. There he lived until 1920, when his father died and the family returned to Smargon and then settled in Wilno. Young Sutzkever early manifested an interest in writing, first in Hebrew and then in Yiddish. In 1932 he went to Warsaw, where he published his first poems. During the next few years he wrote a notable group of poems about the Siberia of his childhood. He was caught in the Nazi net in 1941 but succeeded in escaping and found shelter with partisans in a nearby forest. Owing to enthusiasm for his poem "Kol Nidre," which he managed to send to Jewish writers in Moscow, a Russian plane brought him to that city, where he was warmly welcomed.

In 1946 he was flown to Nuremberg to be a witness against the Nazi crime of genocide in Polish concentration camps. In Israel he served as a correspondent in the war for independence in 1948. The following year, with the uneasy armistice arranged, he started *Die Goldene Keyt* together with Abraham Levinson and Eliezer Pines, and the financial backing of Joseph Shprintzak, secretary of Histadruth, the Israeli labor organization. All the while—before and since—he wrote much verse as well as magazine articles.

Sutzkever is a poet of effervescent emotion and social depth. His verses on Siberia established him as a lyricist of nature and master of the picturesque phrase. His series of 28 poems entitled "Ecstasy" give tender expression to his sensibility of longing, desire, and beauty. In the early 1940's he wrote poems almost daily in which he described the agony of the Wilno ghetto and the haphazard hardships of partisans in the forest. Thus, while in a wood near Wilno in December, 1941, he wrote:

At a warm hill of horse dung I warm, warm my icy hands. I warm my hands and thereby resent: until now I have apprehended, recognized, the greatness of smallness. It can happen that the warm breath of a hill of dung can produce a poem of noble beauty.

"Kol Nidre," written in February, 1943, is a long poem of anguish about a father of five sons who finds his eldest in the concentration camp of his own imprisonment—a wounded Red Army soldier betrayed as a Jew. When ordered by the sadistic Nazi officer to cut his son's tongue out, he plunges the knife into the heart of the youth, the last of his living sons.

A different kind of poem is "A Little Flower," written in May, 1943:

My neighbor paid seven lashes for bringing a little flower through the gate. How dear to him is now the blue spring—the little flower with the eye of gold! My neighbor carries the memory without regret: the spring breathes in his skin—he wishes it so. . . .

In his dejection at that time Sutzkever wondered if he were the last poet in Europe—"singing for the dead, singing for the crows." In the midst of his misery in hiding he thinks of his father's death and writes in "To Thirty Years":

My father's heart, when he was thirty, broke one evening while playing Rabbi Levi Itzkhak's tune on his violin. The violin on his shoulder trembled like a child, and its speech—a bright magnet—attracted the wide world in the shadowy farm, while I, a seven-year-old dreamer, wound about my father's knees.

Secret City, written in 1945–1947 and published in 1952, is a long verse narrative about a group of Jews who have escaped from the Nazis "in the abyss of canals" (sewers) and live there as best they can by appointing duties to each and by depending upon friendly gentile partisans to provide them with food. When a child needs milk, one of the men steals into the nearby village and procures a goat from a peasant. An unhappy youth, unable to satisfy the hunger of the sick girl he loves, commits suicide, and on a board over his grave this epitaph is written: "His life was torture, death—heaven's relief."

The group experiences other dire events: members sicken and die; a Lithuanian informer, losing his way in the tortuous canals, is not killed but sent on to perish in the distant sewers; a child is born and somehow survives; a man cheats by not contributing to the common food fund money he had swallowed when searched by the Nazis and then rescued from his feces—only to be driven away by his conscience the next day; a tubercular girl is taken into a convent as a Christian; a pious Jew insists on returning to the abandoned synagogue in the

city to pray on Yom Kippur. The Nazis at last discover the
hiding place and begin to attack it, but are frightened away
by the coming of the Red Army. Once freed, the refugees go
their separate ways. These and other episodes are related with
poetic fervor and sympathy, and with an implicit epic indignation at the beastliness of man and a warm admiration for
the nobility suffering brings out in some of its victims.

In 1947, having spoken with dignity and effectiveness on the
witness stand, he wrote "Before the Nuremberg Tribunal":

> They say that I demand justice for the millions. That the hour
> will forever remain—only the millions are *gone*—so what kind of
> justice can I demand?
>
> I should be a Shylock a thousand times over to cut out the
> evil on earth. My people! You will still forge such a sword, if
> God is too weak to demand this portion.

Spiritual Soil (1961) treats poetically the emergence of
Israel as a nation. "On the Sea" describes refugees seeking to
reach port and what happens to them on the way. "Sabras
Bloom" tells about the expiration of the British Mandate and
the diplomatic and terroristic events leading up to independence. "A Dream of a Goldsmith" depicts Israel in the throes of
war with the Arabs. "Epilogue" is dedicated to the occupation
of the Negev and the commemoration of the sixth anniversary
of the Warsaw uprising. Here, too, Sutzkever writes epically
and emphatically about experiences which have ignited his
imagination and inspired his enthusiasm.

In his 20 years in Israel he has written much incisive prose
and several volumes of poetry not only about the life around
him but also about his experiences in Poland and Russia. He
sings with an overtone of chagrin, for instance, about the
Polish mistreatment of Jews: "If I were now, after my sacrifice,
not born anew with the land, where every stone is my grandfather—bread would not sate me, water would not quench my
palate. . . ." And as late as 1966 he writes of Germany: "Don't
tell me about good Germans. . . . I have seen how good Germans murdered unconscionably and simultaneously performed

on a silver flute. And play football with a Jewish child. May its spilt blood forever and ever penetrate their thick skulls."

As a poet Sutzkever has achieved a prominent place in Yiddish literature not so much by his exceptional sensitivity or depth of imagination as by his epic breadth and his giving passionate voice to the tragic events of his time. If his poetry is sometimes more rhetorical than purely lyrical, it is nevertheless imbued with a sympathy and sensibility that give it the stamp of lyrical authenticity. And as spokesman for Yiddish in Israel he has no peer. As he told Pat: "I am more and more certain that in our time, after the destruction in Eastern Europe, Yiddish can nowhere be as free as here. This mysterious land reveals itself to the Yiddish word. Yiddish in Israel flows like the Jordan."

The number of Yiddish writers who have reached Israel since 1947 is too great to permit comment on each one, but a brief discussion of several will suggest their general range and character.

Rivkah Bassman was born in Lithuania in 1925 and graduated from a gymnasium. Trapped in the Wilno ghetto in 1941, she was fortunate enough to survive the ordeal of imprisonment in concentration camps. She went to Israel in 1947 and has since published numerous poems. "Birth of a Song," "In the Field," and "Generations Look" are perhaps most suggestive of her lyric gift. To quote from the first: "When a song is born, a little star is lost, and in its empty place sparkles, lights up a pure word. Over seven distant countries I have gathered words. And I placed them in the sky over the great, great world." The second poem expresses the loneliness of the early pioneers in the kibbutz: "Let us go and cry out! Mama! Lonely and lonelier are we: Mama! . . . Why do we feel a yearning when we come to the field and our steps weep?" The third is very brief: "Generations look silently into my windows. When the sun disappears—my little room is gray—they flutter like doves." Her latest publications are *Doves at the Wall* (1959) and *Leaves along the Way* (1967), both works of solid merit.

Abraham Rintzler, born in Bukovina in 1923, also reached Israel in 1947. He has become an acknowledged poet, and his "Credo" voices the uncertainty and danger felt by Halutzim over the years. "And where will this way lead? And are we truly the first newborn, or still the thousand-year ones? And from which corner will the reflection of the enemy's knife glisten? Will we with our bit of belief, our meager effort, further have the strength to nurse eternity?"

Moshe Yungman, born in Poland in 1922, managed to find asylum in Soviet Russia during World War II. He arrived in Israel in 1947 and became a teacher. Some of his verses have a bucolic wholesomeness, but his awareness of the enmity surrounding Israel is expressed in a number of poems with patriotic fervor. "Ode to a Cow" is an artless and grateful acknowledgment of the cow's goodness to man. In "Bees" he wishes his poems would hum like bees and attain their honey. "My Hands" reveals the common fear: "My hands, my hands, mine white from prayer—I'll extend them today like two spears against the enemy; I'll spread them wide, shut like gates—to hide my land from eyes that lurk. . . ."

Abraham Karpinowitch, born in Wilno in 1913, spent two years in Cyprus before he was able to enter Israel in 1948. Like other writers, he has taken his material from early observations in Poland as well as experiences in his new environment. "The Black Leyke" is about a brothel in Wilno. A journalist has exposed it by using Leyke as his source of information—she having told him her life story. Sometime later, while hunted by the police for his radicalism, he becomes sick and seeks shelter with Leyke. She nurses him back to health at a considerable cost to herself. When he leaves she cannot resume her harlotry and becomes an honest worker. In "Do Not Forget" a Jewish soldier in 1948, fresh from Cyprus, captures an Arab soldier and does not know what to do with him, but finally kills him. In other stories Karpinowitch describes newcomers whose morality and honesty are at an ebb but who feel the urge to begin a new and better life.

Yakov Friedman, born in Galicia in 1910, entered Israel in 1948. His poems are characterized by simple lyricism and

Hasidic piety. Some depict uniquely the various times of day from the standpoint of a highly imaginative boy. Other poems of childhood dwell on the mysteries of nature and the complexities of mind. In "Night," the first stanza reads: "When my mother turns off the light in the room, darkness climbs like an animal into my bed. I feel its heavy body, alive, with flesh and limbs, as it reaches its paws out to caress and stroke me. The silence breathes like a living clock and billows mysteriously far, far. . . ." In "A Shepherd's Prayer" he says in part:

> Be good to me, God, I do not ask for much: I want to feel your love resting on my roof.
> And at the doorstep of my house, when I open the door, let the sun and the rain speak of you.
> And let a spring and a field and a herd of cattle tell me "good morning" every day.
> As I come in my linen garment with my wooden fife toward the Jordan.

Similar faith but greater piety is expressed in "Moshe-Leyb the Nister," which tells about a shoemaker who is full of pity for every living creature:

> "What is my guilt, dear God, when my heart cries with compassion. . . . I ask no questions, I only pray—accept my prayer, o Creator: I want to partake of the suffering of a spider, of the suffering even of a moth. And when a pigeon is destroyed, let my blood flow with hers. And when an ant is crushed somewhere, let my flesh suffer with it." Thus speaks Moshe-Leyb the shoemaker to God, and the mountain waters burst in song: Praised be the dear Name who gave priority to man.

Although Mendel Man left Israel in 1961 and has resided in Paris since then, his association with Israel remains close. He was born in Poland in 1916 and studied painting before he turned to writing, and published his first literary efforts in 1938. A year later he fled to the Soviet Union and was drafted into the Red Army. At the end of the war he returned to Lodz, and his volume, *The Stillness Calls* (1945), was the first Yiddish book to be brought out in postwar Poland. He entered

Israel in 1948 and many of his stories deal with life in his new environment. In 1954 he became secretarial editor of *Die Goldene Keyt*, and most of his fiction was first printed in that periodical. *By the Vistula River* (1958) has for its protagonist an energetic and dynamic youth who flees from Poland during the war and organizes the local defense against the enemy. The life and attitudes of Russian peasants are described with realistic clarity. This novel precedes an engaging autobiographical trilogy of the war period, which goes back to his early life in the 1920's, and deals with his friends and enemies at school, the rising fear among Jews in the face of aggressive anti-Semitism, and the events leading up to the holocaust.

Man's Israeli stories in *Awakened Soil* (1953) are less dramatic but more picturesque. Of significance is the narrative of how an abandoned Arab village is settled by refugees from both concentration camps and Arab countries. It tells sensitively and sympathetically how they appropriate the mean huts and begin to farm the fields; how they overcome the antagonistic attitude existing between the two groups and establish a viable social life. The discouragement of certain individuals and their painful adjustments are treated with understanding and compassion. Here, as in his other writings, Man manifests a painterly view of nature and a bold conception of his characters.

Yeshayahu Shpiegel, born in Poland in 1906, went to Israel in 1951. A writer of simple yet sensitively symbolic fiction, he has depicted at length and painfully the martyrdom of the Jews during World War II. As he summed it up: "In each dewdrop I see my mother's tear. In each flutter of the wind —my father's prayer. And I myself—I carry in my heart the blessing and the curse of all, all times." One of his popular stories, "The Bridge," symbolizes the merger of destruction and resurgence. Jews from various parts of the world are at work on the building of a bridge; the one from Poland finds the heat unbearable, but he persists with his last bit of strength —until he is struck by an enemy bullet.

Shpiegel dedicated his latest novel, *Stairs to the Sky*

(1966), to his only daughter Eva, who perished in the ghetto during the war. No doubt autobiographical, it is written from the point of view of a naive but sensitive boy and describes what he sees and hears and how he reacts to the people close to him and to the events he witnesses. Thus he is puzzled when his mother is away and he hears that she is sick and that his new little sister is dead; he is equally perplexed when his father puts up a mill in the house and says: "Blessed be God in Heaven! From the mill we'll surely have bread." When he is taken to his grandparents temporarily and hears his scholarly grandfather talk, he cannot make any sense out of his words:

> These strange, peculiar words put me in a misty, heavy darkness, where it is always night. None of the grown-ups around me made any effort to tear the black veil which hung about these unintelligible words and events. It always seemed to me that the world of grown-ups is a world of all black and obscure signs which they, the grown-ups, have devised only for themselves, in order to live in their own groove, which is full of magic—and then they die mysteriously.

A great deal of action takes place in his family: love-making among the younger members; an aunt is hunted by police for suspected radicalism, but they arrest her sister by mistake and thus enable her to escape across the border; his father is arrested for his involvement with the aunt; his mother becomes ill from aggravation—these and other incidents, taking place in a Russian town in the 1900's, are described from the standpoint of an ingenuous boy, but with clear implications of the poverty and persecution experienced by Jews under the Czar.

A. M. Fuchs, born in 1890, for many years the Austria correspondent for *Der Forverts*, is a gifted storyteller who came to Israel in 1951. Although most of his writing was naturally done in Europe, he now has a number of stories about Israel. Many of his fine, realistic stories have their setting in his native Galicia and in Russia. Typical of them is "Difficult Days," a story of civil war in Russia shortly after the revolution. A young Bolshevik in the Petlura area risks his life by agitating

young men to form partisan groups against the "Whites."
To his worried parents he explains that he is doing what
former Jews have done: striving for justice in the world. When
he is danger of arrest by Petlura hooligans, his hostess assures
them that he is her son and not the agitator they are seeking.
In "The Day" Fuchs describes life in Israel, especially as it
manifests itself in the farmlands, stressing the picturesque
ways of animals and plants and farmers; the description of
sunrise over the hills achieves poetic beauty. In 1961 a collection of his stories, *The Night and the Day*, was published in
New York.

Yekhiel Hofer, born in Poland in 1906, reached Israel in
1951. He has written notable verse, fiction, and literary criticism. Since coming to Israel he has published several novels,
many poems, and a provocative volume of criticism, *With
Others and With Oneself* (1964). A representative story, "The
Death of Reb Tankhum," depicts an elderly Hasid who is
separated from his wife. He grieves at the lack of piety in his
own children as well as in those of others, but is most distressed to see his estranged wife, who would not divorce him,
doing better in business than he does.

Binem Heller was born in Poland in 1908. Becoming a communist in his adolescence, he had to flee to avoid arrest. He
returned to Warsaw in 1947 and was active in the Jewish
Writers Club. A writer since 1930, he published much verse
and numerous essays—collecting them in several volumes. By
the time he arrived in Israel in 1956 he had become disillusioned with communism and expressed his contrition in a
pathetic lyrical outcry: "Oh, How My Life Was Broken!"

In writing of his early youth he expressed a nostalgic guilt
toward his pious parents and toward his people: "And perhaps
part of the guilt falls on me—because I too was silent? Fear
had numbed and confused me and I did not oppose the lie."
He has also dwelt on the holocaust and on Israel's insecurity,
intimating that although he was no longer in Europe he continued to feel enmeshed in "the dark shadow of the demon";
that in Israel "I am between desert and ocean—a place of

safety in a narrow pass—a wall of water and a wall of fire must
save my life from hate." Singing of the destruction in Europe
with bursts of pain and anger, he intimates a resignation saturated with woe. "Now I must rinse with silence the last trace
of false belonging. As long as I'll remember a sound it will be
difficult to believe in myself." Yet he takes comfort in the feeling that "the new song will come. . . . In the garden of my
Yiddish speech ripens the fullness of small flowers." In much
of his verse there is the lyric magic of natural song, even as
there is a keen-cutting edge to his critical essays. In his latest
volume of poems, *Generation and Endurance* (1967), his
poetic vein flows rich and pure.

Of significance to the survival of Yiddish literary activity is
the adherence to it of some of the younger writers in Israel.
One of these is Rokhel Fishman, who was born in the United
States in 1935 and settled in Israel in 1954. Writing lyrical free
verse, she exudes a deep love for both Yiddish and Israel. Her
nature poetry expresses her personal feeling for the land:

> The moon rises in the east. Heavy with itself, with sin. Orange
> red, it tears itself over trees. The higher—the yellower. And in
> an hour, pale and white, it will deny everything.
> Do not ask her where she lay all day. She rises in the evening
> and the entire horizon is aflame with her.

The second stanza of "In the Beginning" is also characteristic of her imaginative flair: "When the sun looses its tresses
and the black hair spreads over the cushion—night appears.
Only we know its rosy ear which moves out of the coverlet—it
is the dawn, the new beginning." "Sabbath" eloquently intimates her emotional lyricism:

> Only now, when I lie in the shade, cool and covered with
> shadows, my eye dares, and my palate dares, to take the suns of
> the week, all suns of the week, and with cool Sabbath hands
> imprison them in a drop, all suns in a drop. O, how hot, o, how
> red.
> I dip my pen in the deep drop—and it flows. Sun-song flows,
> flows with hope, only it burns, it burns, it burns. When a song is
> written with sun, it does not mean that it is good. But one thing

is certain, certain: the sun will enter the blood, a steam will rise from the lines, and their breath—hot. Who will put them to his heart will feel the sun with sweat. I dip my pen in the red drop and will—burn your fingers with all the suns of the week.

O, the full sun week.

Israel is now the home of scores of Yiddish writers. Their union in Tel Aviv has around 130 members, and among them are young Yiddish poets and storytellers who belong to "Young Israel" and have definite literary promise. The writings of many appear not only in *Die Goldene Keyt* but in Yiddish periodicals in other parts of the world. Their work is also being brought to the favorable attention of Israeli readers unfamiliar with Yiddish, and a substantial volume in Hebrew translation was brought out in 1966. M. Halomesh, a writer and secretary of the Yiddish Authors Union stated recently in a report of a trip to Europe and the Americas: "In no other country in the world does Yiddish throb with so much life as in Israel. Not only is a live and juicy Yiddish spoken there in various dialects but it is also read widely, and Yiddish books and periodicals are published there." Indeed, more books in Yiddish are now being issued in Israel than in the United States. With the roots of Yiddish as a language and literature obviously, and perhaps inevitably, drying up in the diaspora, its chance of survival as a living linguistic expression of the Jews depends on its likely pullulation in Israel. And of that only time can tell.

YIDDISH WRITINGS

IN ENGLISH TRANSLATION

Anski, S., *Between Two Worlds: The Dybbuk*, New York, 1926.

Asch, Sholem, *America*, New York, 1918; *The Apostle*, New York, 1943; *The Burning Bush*, New York, 1946; *Children of Abraham*, New York, 1942; *East River*, New York, 1946; *From Many Countries, Collected Short Stories*, London, 1958; *The God of Vengeance*, Boston, 1916; *In the Beginning*, New York, 1925; *Kiddush Ha-Shem* (Sanctification of the Name), Philadelphia, 1926; *Mary*, New York, 1949; *Moses*, New York, 1951; *The Mother*, New York, 1930; *Mottke the Thief*, New York, 1935; *The Nazarene*, New York, 1939; *One Destiny*, New York, 1945; *A Passage in the Night*, New York, 1953; *The Prophet*, New York, 1955; *Shabbati Zevi*, Philadelphia, 1930; *Salvation*, New York, 1934; *Song of the Valley*, New York, 1938; *Tale of My People*, New York, 1948; *Three Cities*, New York, 1933; *Three Novels: Uncle Moses, Khaim Lederer's Return, Judge Not—*, New York, 1938; *The War Goes On*, New York, 1937; *What I Believe*, New York, 1941.

Ausubel, Nathan and Marynn (eds.), *A Treasury of Jewish Poetry from Biblical Times to the Present*, New York, 1957.

Basic Facts About Yiddish, New York, 1946.

Bellow, Saul (ed.), *Great Jewish Short Stories*, New York, 1963.

Bergner, Herz, *Light and Shadow*, New York, 1963.

Block, Etta, *One Act Plays from the Yiddish*, New York, 1925.

Bryks, Rakhmiel, *A Cat in the Ghetto*, New York, 1959.

Chanukoff, Lou, *Submarine Z-1*, New York, 1960.

Cooperman, Jehiel B. and Sarah H. (eds.), *America in Yiddish Poetry*, New York, 1967.

Dawidowicz, Lucy S. (ed.), *The Golden Tradition*, New York, 1967.

Frank, Helena, *Yiddish Tales*, Philadelphia, 1912.

Glatstein, Jacob, *Homecoming at Twilight*, New York, 1962.

Goldberg, Isaak, *Six Plays of the Yiddish Theater*, first series, Boston, 1916; second series, Boston, 1918.

Goldberg, Itche, *Yiddish Stories for Young People*, New York, 1966.

Goodman, Henry, *The New Country*, Stories from the Yiddish about Life in America, New York, 1961.

Grade, Khaim, *The Well*, Philadelphia, 1967.

Grafstein, Melekh (ed.), *Melekh Grafstein's Sholom Aleichem's Panorama*, London, Ont., 1948.

Greenberg, Khaim, *The Inner Eye*, Vol. 2, ed. by Shlomo Katz, New York, 1964.

Ha'am, Ahad, *Selected Essays*, Cleveland, 1962.

Hirshbein, Peretz, *The Haunted Inn*, Boston, 1921.

Horowitz, Nathan, *Sabbath and Other Tales*, London, 1926.

Howe, Irving, and E. Greenberg, *A Treasury of Yiddish Stories*, New York, 1954.

Imber, S. J., *Modern Yiddish Poetry: An Anthology*, New York, 1927.

Katz, Meinke, *Land of Manna*, Chicago, 1965.

Kobrin, Leon, *A Lithuanian Village*, New York, 1920.

Kreitman, Morris, *Jewish Short Stories of Today*, London, 1929.

Leftwitch, Joseph, *The Golden Peacock*, new edition, New York, 1961; *Yisroel*, London, 1933.

Leivick, H., *The Golem (Poet Lore)*, Boston, 1928.

Levin, S., *The Arena*, New York, 1932; *Childhood in Exile*, New York, 1929; *Youth in Revolt*, New York, 1930.

Liptzin, Samuel, *In Spite of Tears*, New York, 1946.

Lowenthal, Marvin (ed. and trans.), *Memoirs of Glückel of Hameln*, New York, 1932.

Man, Mendel, *At the Gates of Moscow*, New York, 1946.

Manger, Itzik, *The Book of Paradise*, New York, 1965.

Mendele, Mokher Sforim, *Fishke the Lame*, New York, 1960; *The Nag*, New York, 1954; *The Parasite*, New York, 1956; *The*

Travels and Adventures of Benjamin the Third, New York, 1949.

Opatoshu, Joseph, *The Polish Woods,* Philadelphia, 1938; *The Story of Rabbi Akiba,* Philadelphia, 1952.

Peretz, I. L., *As Once we Were,* Selections, Los Angeles, 1951; *Bontche the Silent and Other Stories,* London, 1927; *The Book of Fire,* New York, 1960; *In This World and the Next,* Selected Writings, New York, 1958; *My Memoirs,* New York, 1964; *Stories and Pictures,* Philadelphia, 1906; *Stories from Peretz,* ed. by Sol Liptzin, New York, 1964; *The Three Canopies,* New York, 1948; *Three Gifts and Other Stories,* New York, 1964.

Pinski, David, *Arnold Levenberg,* New York, 1938; *Cripples,* New York, 1932; *Dollars,* New York, 1932; *Forgotten Souls,* New York, 1932; *Generations of Noah Edon,* New York, 1931; *King David and His Wives,* New York, 1923; *Temptations, A Book of Short Stories,* New York, 1919; *Ten Plays,* New York, 1920; *Three Plays,* New York, 1918; *The Treasure,* New York, 1915; *To Each One His Own God,* New York, 1912.

Reisen, Abraham, *A Game,* Boston, 1919.

Roback, A.A., *Curiosities of Yiddish Literature,* Boston, 1933.

Rosenfeld, Morris, *Songs of the Ghetto,* Boston, 1898; *Songs of Labor and Other Poems,* Boston, 1914.

Schectman, Elya, *Erev* (On the Eve), New York, 1967.

Schneor, Zalman, *Noah Pandre,* London, 1936.

Schwartz, Leo W., *The Jewish Caravan,* rev. ed., New York, 1965.

Sholom Aleichem, *Adventures of Motel the Cantor's Son,* New York, 1953; *The Bewitched Tailor,* Moscow, 1958; *The Great Fair, Scenes from My Childhood,* New York, 1955; *Inside Kaserilevke,* New York, 1955; *The Old Country,* New York, 1946; *Selected Stories,* ed. by Alfred Kazin, New York, 1956; *Stempenyu,* London, 1913; *Stories and Satires,* New York, 1959; *Tevieh and His Daughters* (play by Arnold Pearl), New York, 1958; *Tevieh's Daughters,* New York, 1949; *The Wandering Star,* New York, 1952.

Singer, I. Bashevis, *The Family Moskat,* New York, 1950; *The Fearsome Inn,* New York, 1967; *Gimpel the Fool,* New York, 1951; *In My Father's Court,* New York, 1966; *The Magician of Lublin,* New York, 1960; *The Manor,* Vol. 1, New York, 1967; *Mazel and Shlimazel,* New York, 1967; *Satan in Goray,*

New York, 1955; *Short Friday and Other Stories*, New York, 1964; *The Slave*, New York, 1962; *The Spinoza of Market Street*, New York, 1961; *Zlateh the Goat*, New York, 1967.

Singer, I. J., *Blood Harvest* (*Steel and Iron*), Boston, 1935; *Brothers Ashkenazi*, New York, 1936; *East of Eden*, New York, 1939; *The Family Carnovsky*, New York, 1943; *The Sinner*, New York, 1933; *Spring and Other Stories*, New York, 1937.

Sinkin, Menashe, *Through the Eye of a Needle*, New York, 1955.

Soltes, Mordecai, *The Yiddish Press, An Americanizing Agency*, Philadelphia, 1925.

Spector, Mordecai, *The Three Worthies of Brebendefka*, New York, 1905.

Weinper, Zisha, *At the Rich Man's Gate*, New York, 1935.

White, Bessie, *Nine One Act Plays from the Yiddish*, Boston, 1932.

Yehoash, *Feet of the Messenger*, Philadelphia, 1923; *Poems*, London, Ont., 1952.

Zhitlovsky, Khaim, *The Future of Our Youth in This Country*, Pittsburgh, 1935.

Zunser, Eliakum, *Selected Songs*, New York, 1928.

BIBLIOGRAPHY

OF SOURCE MATERIALS

MY RESEARCH has been more extensive than is here indicated, as I have listed only the critical and historical items which have been of use to me—and none of the works discussed in the text itself. Nearly all of them are in Yiddish. I hereby acknowledge my indebtedness to these writers.

Almanac of Yiddish Writers in Israel, Tel Aviv, 1962.

Almi, A., "Sholem Asch—A Resumé," *Unser Weg*, n.d.

Berkowitch, I.D. (ed.), *The Sholom Aleichem Book*, New York, 1926, 1938.

Bialostotsky, B.J., *Dream and Reality*, New York, 1956.

Bickel, Shlomo, *Writers of My Generation*, 2 vols., New York, 1958, Tel Aviv, 1965.

Bickel, S. (ed.), *Pinkus, Research in Yiddish Literature and Press*, New York, 1965.

Bickel, S., and L. Lehrer (eds.), *The Book of Samuel Niger*, New York, 1958.

Briansky, Sh., *D. Bergelson in the Mirror of Criticism, 1909–1932*, Kiev, 1934.

Bronshteyn, Y., *Of One's Own House*, essays, Tel Aviv, 1963; *"Secret City" by Abraham Sutzkever*, Mexico City, 1952; *Strengthened Positions*, Moscow, 1934.

Cahan, Abraham, *Sholem Asch's New Way*, New York, 1941.
Domankiewicz, L. (ed.), *Sholom Aleichem Anthology for His 100th Birthday*, Paris, 1959; *Words and Values*, Tel Aviv, 1965.
Dubnow, Simon, *From "Jargon" to Yiddish*, Wilno, 1929.
Dunetz, B., *About Writers and Their Works*, Minsk, 1933.
Elbogen, I., *A Century of Jewish Life*, Philadelphia, 1944.
Eliashev, I. (Baal Makhshoves), *Selected Works*, New York, 1953.
Epstein, Melekh, *Profiles of Eleven*, Detroit, 1965.
Erik, Max, *see* Z. Merkin.
Finkel, Uri, *Sholom Aleichem*, Warsaw, 1959.
Freilich, I., *Joseph Opatoshu's Creativity*, New York, 1951.
Gaster, M., *Yiddish Literature in the Middle Ages* (chapter), London, 1927.
Glatstein, Jacob, *Sum and Substance*, New York, 1956.
Goldberg, B. Z., *The Jews in the Soviet Union*, Tel Aviv, 1965.
Gore, Norman C., *Tzeena U-Reenah*, New York, 1965.
Gotlieb, J., *H. Leivick, His Poems and Plays*, Kovno, 1939.
Green, Ber, *Yiddish Writers in America*, New York, 1963.
Greenberg, E. *Central Motifs and Motivations in H. Leivick's Works*, New York, 1951; *Jacob Glatstein's "The Joy of the Yiddish Word,"* New York, 1964; *Moshe Leyb Halpern in the Frame of His Generation*, New York, 1942.
Grobard, B., "Personalities and Characters in Our Literature," *Zammelbikher*, No. 6, 1945.
Hofer, Yekhiel, "Dovid Bergelson," *Die Goldene Keyt*, No. 25, 1956.
Iceland, R., *Of Our Spring*, Miami Beach, 1954.
Ignatov, D., "P. Hirschbein ('The Man Who Isn't Here')," *Turnover Leaves*, 1957.
Insikh Antology, New York, 1920.
Katz, M., *The Moshe Katz Book*, New York, 1963.
Kobler, F. (ed.), *Letters of Jews Through the Ages*, London, 1952.
Lexicon of the New Yiddish Literature, prepared and published by the Congress for Jewish Culture (with additional volumes in preparation), 6 vols., New York, 1956–1965.
Lichtenstein, Isaak, "Meetings with Sholem Asch," *Die Goldene Keyt*, No. 29, 1957.
Lieberman, Khaim, *The Christianity of Sholem Asch*, New York, 1953.
Lifschitz, E., *Morris Rosenfeld's Letters*, Buenos Aires, 1955.
Liptzin, Sol, *The Flowering of Yiddish Literature*, New York, 1963.

Die Litarische Welt, 1912 and later.

Lis, Abraham, *Home and Endurance*, Tel Aviv, 1960.

Lowenthal, Marvin, *A World Passed By*, New York, 1933.

Mark, Yudel, "Yiddish Literature," in *The Jews*, ed. by L. Finkelstein, New York, 1949.

Marmor, K., *The Birth of Yiddish Literature in America*, New York, 1944.

Meisel, N., *Backgrounds and Perspectives*, Tel Aviv, 1962; *Dovid Bergelson*, New York, 1940; "Dovid Bergelson, Der Nister, Peretz Markish," *Zammelbikher*, No. 6, New York, 1945; *Isaak Leyb Peretz and His Generation of Writers*, New York, 1951; *Jewish Creative Activity and Yiddish Writers in the Soviet Union*, New York, 1959; *Joseph Opatoshu, His Life and Work*, Warsaw, 1937; *Letters and Speeches of I. L. Peretz*, New York, 1944; *On Our Culture Front*, Warsaw, 1936; *On Sholom Aleichem*, Warsaw, 1959; *Precursors and Followers*, New York, 1946; *Recollections of Mendele*, Warsaw, n.d.; *To the Centenary of Morris Rosenfeld*, New York, 1962.

The Mendele Book, ed. by N. Meisel, New York, 1959.

Merkin, Z., *History of Yiddish Literature From the Oldest Times to the Enlightenment*, Warsaw, 1928; *On the Old Yiddish Romance and Novel*, Warsaw, 1926; *Sholem Asch, 1900–1931*, Minsk, 1931; *Studies in the History of Enlightenment*, Minsk, 1934.

Merkin, Z., and A. Rosenzweig, *Jewish Literature in the 19th Century*, Kiev, 1935.

Minkoff, N.B., "David Pinski," *Die Goldene Keyt*, No. 12, 1952.

A Mirror on a Stone, An Anthology of Yiddish Writings in the Soviet Union, ed. by Kh. Shmeruk and others, Tel Aviv, 1964.

Nathanson, W., *H. Leivick, The Poet of Advent and Awakening*, Chicago, 1936; "H. Leivick's *In the Days of Job*," *Die Goldene Keyt*, No. 21, 1955.

Neiman, V., *Struggle: David Ignatov as Writer and Fighter*, New York, 1937.

Niger, Samuel, *About Yiddish Writers*, Warsaw, 1922; "The Dramatic Works of David Pinski," *Die Zukunft*, July 1922; "From God to the Devil (U. Z. Greenberg)," *Der Tog*, June 10, 1923; *H. Leivick, 1888–1948*, Toronto, 1951; *I. L. Peretz*, Buenos Aires, 1952; *Mendele Mokher Sforim*, Chicago, 1936; "One Epoch—Two Novels," *Die Zukunft*, April 1935; *Sholom Aleichem*, New York, 1928; *Sholem Asch: His Life and Work*, New

York, 1960; "Singer's *Brothers Ashkenazi*," *Die Zukunft*, Dec. 1936; "Singer's *Yoshe Kalb*," *Die Zukunft*, Feb. 1933; *Story-tellers and Novelists*, New York, 1946; *Studies in the History of Yiddish Literature*, New York, 1959; *Yiddish Writers in Soviet Russia*, New York, 1958.

Opatoshu, Joseph, "H. Leivick," *Jewish Culture*, Jan. 1939; "My Way of Writing," *Die Goldene Keyt*, No. 20, 1954.

Panner, Isaak, *Sholem Asch in His Last Home*, Tel Aviv, 1958.

Pat, Jacob, *Chats with Writers in Israel*, New York, 1960; "A Talk with Leivick," *Die Goldene Keyt*, No. 19, 1954.

Pomerantz, Alexander, *The Soviet Martyrs*, Buenos Aires, 1962.

Rabinowitch, Wolf, *My Brother Sholom Aleichem*, Kiev, 1939.

Raisin, Jacob S., *The Haskolah Movement in Russia*, Philadelphia, 1913.

Rapoport, I., *Seeds in the Wind*, Buenos Aires, 1961; *Sholem Asch's Literary Victories and Defeats*, Melbourne, 1953.

Reisen, Zalmen, *From Mendelssohn to Mendele*, anthology, Warsaw, 1923; *Lexicon of Yiddish Literature*, Wilno, 1926–1930.

Rivkin, B., *Basic Tendencies of Yiddish Literature in America*, New York, 1948; *H. Leivick, Poems and Dramatic Works*, Buenos Aires, 1955; *Jewish Poets in America*, New York, 1947; *Joseph Opatoshu*, Toronto, 1948; *Our Novelists*, New York, 1951.

Roback, A. A., *Peretz, Psychologist of Literature*, Cambridge, Mass., 1935; *Story of Yiddish Literature*, New York, 1940.

Rontch, I. A., *America in Yiddish Literature*, New York, 1945.

Rosenberg, Shlomo, *Face to Face with Sholem Asch*, Miami, 1958.

Salit, L., *Messiah Visions in Leivick's Dramatic Poems*, Munich, 1947.

Samuel, Maurice, *Prince of the Ghetto* (Peretz), New York, 1948; *The World of Sholom Aleichem*, New York, 1943.

Schweid, Mark, *Console My People: The Life of I. L. Peretz*, New York, 1955.

Seviva, currently edited by Kadia Molodovsky, various issues.

Sfard, Dovid, *Writers and Books*, Lodz, 1949.

Shamri, Aryeh (ed.), *Roots* (An Anthology of Yiddish Writers in Israel), Tel Aviv, 1966.

Shatsky, J., *Anthology in Honor of 250th Anniversary of the Jewish Press*, New York, 1937.

Shriften, 1912–1913.

Shternberg, Yankev, "The Great Prose Master," *Sovietish Heymland*, July–August 1964.

Shtieff, Nahum, *The Older Yiddish Literature*, Kiev, 1929.

Simon, S., H. *Leivick's Childhood*, Wilno, 1938; H. *Leivick's Golem*, New York, 1927.

Sovietish Heymland, 1961–1967.

Steinberg, Noah, *Young America*, New York, 1917.

Tabachnick, A., *Poets and Poetry*, New York, 1965.

Trunk, I. I., *Idealism and Naturalism in Yiddish Literature*, Warsaw, 1927; *Tevieh and Menachem Mendel as Expressions of Eternal Jewish Fate*, New York, 1944; *Yiddish Prose in Poland Between Two World Wars*, Buenos Aires, 1949.

Tzinberg, Isroel, *The History of Jewish Literature*, 9 vols, Wilno, 1930–New York, 1966.

Vergelis, A. (ed.), *Thus We Live*, Moscow, 1964.

Weinper, Zisha, *Jewish Writers*, 2 vols., New York, 1933, 1936.

Weinreich, Max, *For Max Weinreich on His 70th Birthday*, New York, 1965; *Tableaux of Yiddish Literary History*, Wilno, 1928.

Weinreich, Uriel (ed.), *The Field of Yiddish*, New York, 1954; The Hague, 1965.

West, Benjamin, *Struggles of a Generation—The Jews Under Soviet Rule*, Tel Aviv, 1959.

Wiener, Leo, *History of Yiddish Literature in the Nineteenth Century*, New York, 1899.

Wiener, M., *Concerning Sholom Aleichem's Humor*, Moscow, 1941; *Our Relations to the Literary Inheritance of Mendele*, Moscow, 1935.

Wiernick, Peter, *History of the Jews in America*, Philadelphia, 1931.

Yanasowitch, I., *With the Yiddish Writers in Russia*, Buenos Aires, 1959.

YIVO Bletter, various issues, and especially the Peretz issue, Vol. XXVII, No. 1, Fall 1946.

Zammelbikher, ed. by J. Opatoshu and H. Leivick, several annual volumes,

Zhitlowsky, Khaim, *Vision and Thought*, New York, 1951.

INDEX

(Articles are omitted from titles)